# Social Knowledge Creation
# in the Humanities

NEW TECHNOLOGIES IN MEDIEVAL AND
RENAISSANCE STUDIES 8

SERIES EDITORS William R. Bowen and Raymond G. Siemens

# Social Knowledge Creation in the Humanities: Volume 2

*Edited by*
Aaron Mauro, Brock University

## Iter Press
NEW YORK | TORONTO

2022

978-1-64959-008-4 (paper)
978-1-64959-009-1 (pdf)
978-1-64959-084-8 (epub)

Library of Congress Cataloguing-in-Publication Data

Names: Mauro, Aaron, editor.

Title: Social knowledge creation in the humanities. Volume 2 / edited by Aaron Mauro.

Description: Toronto, Ontario : Iter Press, 2022. | Series: New technologies in medieval and renaissance studies ; 8 | Includes bibliographical references. | Summary: "Social media has transformed the ways new knowledge is understood to be created, validated, and reviewed in every academic field of study. In the humanities, Social Knowledge Creation has helped define how social media platforms and other collaborative spaces have shaped humanistic critique in the 21st century"-- Provided by publisher.

Identifiers: LCCN 2019029150 (print) | LCCN 2019029151 (ebook) | ISBN 9781649590084 (v. 2 ; paperback) | ISBN 9781649590091 (v. 2 ; ebook)

Subjects: LCSH: Social media. | Knowledge, Sociology of. | Critical pedagogy.

Classification: LCC HM742 .S62814 2022 (print) | LCC HM742 (ebook) | DDC 302.23/1--dc23

LC record available at https://lccn.loc.gov/2019029150

LC ebook record available at https://lccn.loc.gov/2019029151

Cover Illustration

Yuen, Lysander. Simply Books, Municipal Library, Prague, Czechia. Digital image. Unsplash. Web. 9 Oct. 2019 <https://unsplash.com/photos/wk833OrQLJE>.

# Contents

# The Influence of Social Media on the Humanities

Aaron Mauro

Brock University

We live in an attention economy. Corporations, governments, and individuals of all kinds are vying for our views, impressions, and engagements. Where once print, radio, and television were largely responsible for the mass manufacturing of societal consensus and political consent, social media now increasingly drives consumer habits and political opinions through direct and targeted messaging. The friendly face of this new media landscape is an online pseudo-celebrity we now call an *influencer*. Those whose followings are large enough are able to leverage real political power and real wealth for sponsored posts thinly veiled as authentic content. Often, an influencer's day job is to sell products and present a desirable life online for all to see, but they are also able to sway followers by tying the image of a desirable life to a political opinion. Of course, there is a secondary economy at work as well. The flow of social data represents a raw resource for marketers, governments, and other political actors to mine and refine in order to persuade, cajole, or influence individual actions en masse. In an effort to naturalize this reality, Google CFO Ruth Porat claimed during the 2019 World Economic Forum in Davos, Switzerland, that "data is more like sunlight than oil ... It is like sunshine, we keep using it and it keeps regenerating" (Ghosh and Kanter 2019). In a twisted twenty-first-century form of greenwashing, data collection is naturalized in an attempt to place it outside the reach of legal oversight or regulation.

None of this is new to anyone living online today, nor would the growing influence of mass media have been new to anyone in much of the twentieth century. However, this is not as natural a phenomenon as Google would have us believe. Ownership of, use of, and access to personal information and new knowledge will be a social, political, and cultural fault line in the coming decades.[1] Where once the copyright of cultural objects such as Mickey Mouse or

---

[1] In the sweep of social media posts and 24-hour news cycles, I am reminded of Dr. Jonas Salk, inventor of the polio vaccine. In a televised interview in 1955, Edward R. Murrow asked him who held the patent on the vaccine. Salk responded, "Well, the people, I would say. There is no patent." He then added: "Could you patent the sun?" For Salk and other scientists at that time, new knowledge was not proprietary but in fact owned by the people. See Haberman 2016.

ISBN 978-1-64959-008-4 (paper) ISBN 978-1-64959-009-1 (pdf) ISBN 978-1-64959-084-8 (epub)
*New Technologies in Medieval and Renaissance Studies* 8 (2022) 1–23

Ronald McDonald represented the real wealth of mass media generators, we will now swing our attention to the ownership of our own digital identities. Privacy will become the most valuable commodity for those living a connected life online. Social media means everyone is a knowledge worker, and most of us work for free. The social realities of the Web are political and legal regimes that have been designed and implemented with intent and purpose. While the media landscape of today functions similarly to twentieth-century precedents, the speed and ease of these platforms represents a qualitative difference from previous periods.

Within this context, I want to suggest that this economy of attention, influence, and data gathering represents a *critical structure* within the process of how we make new ideas—how we innovate and reshape our world—and how we communicate them. Within these pages, we are beginning to see the form of how such an economy influences research and teaching. *Social Knowledge Creation* represents a distinct moment of reflection within the humanities to imagine how social media, as well as broader social networks made available by digital technology, work to shape how we make, critique, and disseminate new knowledge. The scope and scale of the situation is immense, and I surmise that we are in the midst of a generation-long attempt to reflect on these relatively new social systems. The creation of scholarly research will require many other volumes to address the myriad ways in which social media has influenced every corner of our lives, both online and offline. In support of this goal, this volume has had the opportunity to publish a revised bibliography in Part 3 to help frame the scholarly precedents that will guide this work.[2] Academics and cultural critics alike will need to draw on the lessons of past media contexts to grapple with this fast-moving environment—after all, the wider effects on everything from child development and socialization to economic productivity and political engagement will continue to be studied for years to come. So, in the context of this volume, let's take a moment to reflect on the current state of social media with regard to humanities-based research and teaching as a means of framing this anthology. If social media is shaping how scholars and academics create new knowledge, there must also be a broader social, political, and cultural valence from which we can extrapolate affordances and effects of social media on scholarship.

---

[2] The bibliography is reprinted with permission of *KULA: Knowledge Creation, Dissemination, and Preservation Studies*. Our lightly edited version of the KULA bibliography overlaps in scope with what was published in *Social Knowledge Creation in the Humanities: Volume 1* and, accordingly, repeats some entries. For further details on the history of the Bibliography, see pp. 251–52 of this volume.

Discussions of education and pedagogy are a common thread in these essays. This collection, as an extension of the first volume, seeks to define the scope and direction of our use and critique of social media in the era of, as Shoshana Zuboff has so presciently defined it, "surveillance capitalism."[3] While the first volume of *Social Knowledge Creation* (Arbuckle, Mauro, and Powell 2017) was concerned with framing the field by organizing the literature on social media in the bibliography found in Part 3, the present volume is taking steps to define the modalities and edges of critique of social knowledge creation. There are consistent themes relating to generosity, community, and collaboration, as well as justice and equality, within this economy. There is a shared sensibility facing our systems of education as the bedrock of societal cohesion, and the role of the university in educating citizens to participate in our democracies. Our systems of knowledge creation and sharing are rapidly being augmented by informal social networks that trade in opinion, critique, and increasingly radical viewpoints, expert or otherwise.

The work of Bruno Latour seems to represent one of the most useful and important starting points for understanding the relationship between social media and knowledge creation. Latour's *Reassembling the Social* (2005) defines Actor Network Theory (ANT) as a sociology of objects working in complex, ever-shifting relationships. However, the word "object" is important here, because objects are not just individual people. Latour understood that our relationships are mediated by systems, technologies, and ideas that influence our behaviour in ways that would make any ardent individualist feel uncomfortable. Beyond some vague sense of social constructionism, ANT promises a way in which we can understand ourselves and our relations in a network. The challenge for many disciplines in the academy is to understand how the ideas we produce are influenced by their place within this network, since ideas in ANT have agency insofar as any object or node in a network is able to influence other nodes. We may be entering a new period in which Harold Bloom's *The Anxiety of Influence* (1997) offers a new way to describe our influences beyond just literary authors. By including AI agents, memes, crowds, and platforms, social knowledge creation represents a theoretical frame well suited to understanding the way research and teaching is influenced by social networks of all kinds. After all, the creation of knowledge has always been dependent on social networks seeking consensus and authority. In *Pasteur: Guerre et paix des microbes* (1984), translated as *The Pasteurization of France* (1988), Latour shows

---

[3] Zuboff first articulated surveillance capitalism in her essay "Big Other: Surveillance Capitalism and the Prospects of an Information Civilization" (Zuboff 2015), and later in a monograph, *The Age of Surveillance Capitalism* (Zuboff 2019).

that Louis Pasteur was not just factually correct about microbial life and infection, but that the reality of microbial life constituted both a scientific and a social construction working in tandem. Latour describes how Pasteur was able to marshal a whole host of actors to validate and authorize the idea in order for *a fact to become true.*

The humanities trades in facts as well, but scholarly consensus regarding interpretive acts also requires a political acumen not often associated with scientific discovery in the public imagination of knowledge creation. Even with so much optimism in the digital humanities sphere regarding the use of social media, it is well to be aware of broader societal cynicism about these technologies and methods, and to offer a reality check as a sort of protective inoculation for academic researchers invested in them. How do we choose which articles are published, for example? The simple answer is peer review, of which there are many versions and systems: double blind, single blind, and open peer review all offer a means for granting authority from the crowd, albeit a select crowd of scholars who are in turn authorized by other scholars. Latour's approach to this system of knowledge making would also ask who chooses the peer reviewers. How are they chosen, and what political currents reinforce ideas as true or as a foregone conclusion? How are ideas reinforced or destroyed in the classroom or through editorial review? Is there a discoverability issue that ignores some authors through passive omission? Or, as human readers, is there a limit to how much we can read? Are there simply limits to our human cognitive bandwidth? Are we really only able to give attention to the most popular authors? How do we trade in authority, either by editing a book or by following someone on Twitter? We might say that "someone is on my radar" as a means of casually drawing lines or "edges" of authority in our network, just as we might say that "someone is off my radar" as a casual dismissal of another person's accrued authority. How do these systems validate, authorize, and disseminate ideas that may or may not be any good? What works of genius are lost? Are we at risk of perpetuating a "winner takes all" scenario, as in music, television, film, software, or game development? Without any assumption regarding the relative wisdom of the crowd or social networks, how do these economies of scale influence or shape our attention to certain ideas, certain models of education, or certain students? Where and how does privilege move, if such a system does indeed privilege certain points of view? These questions are only an opening gambit for a much larger set of questions facing the humanities in the age of social media.

Any time we stop to examine our privilege, an almost pro forma behaviour for most academics, we confront the reality of being so close to our object of study that we lose sight of it. We invariably fail to understand our position of privilege precisely because of the perspectives and opinions that are not present in our network because of our privilege. Twitter, for instance, marks hierarchies of influence explicitly. Those who are followed on Twitter and those who follow say a lot about one's relative status as an academic author. While these systems are explicitly hierarchical, the fact that they "say a lot" masks the implicit and unsaid nature of just what these hierarchies actually mean in an academic context. Again, these implicit systems of authority granting are not new, but we must attend to the latent forces of knowledge production and the shadowy power they produce as they become manifest.

I suspect that there are many competing histories for the rise and dominance of social media in the past decade, and I would like to suggest that academic systems are not immune to our current political climate of rising extremism and divisiveness. Political caricatures of left and right held fast since the French Revolution are now unrecognizable by the standards used even just a few years ago. Basic binaries of social cohesion and public debate are quickly becoming unreliable, which in some cases is cause for celebration but in other cases is deeply troubling. The basic binaries I'd like to follow here, because they are so germane to the project of knowledge creation, are simply fact and fiction, truth and lies, and reality and artifice. Anyone living within the orbit of American politics since the 2016 presidential election will hear the urgency in this line of inquiry: Kellyanne Conway's "alternative facts" (Bradner 2017) and Rudy Giuliani's "truth isn't truth" (Moore 2018) are a harsh reminder that facts matter.[4] So, where did this system capable of putting facts into question emerge? In a world in which the political elite have embraced a tenuous relationship to facts, it is perhaps no surprise that the fact-checking site Politifact (https://www.politifact.com/) won a Pulitzer Prize in 2009. There were certainly antecedents to this situation in the political and economic realm that led to this state of affairs in the United States, including growing dissatisfaction with the country's two-party system and increasing pressure on employment from globalization and automation. However, the denuding of reality and artifice that allows for an open culture of lies to support blind political tribalism began much earlier.

---

[4] This introduction was written in February of 2019, well before the rise of Qanon conspiracies, the "stop the steal" protests including the attack on the Capitol of January 6th, 2021. Please see my book *Hacking in the Humanities* (Bloomsbury, 2022) for a more thorough treatment of these trends.

In one such narrative, we could return to November 2007, when the Writers Guild of America (WGA) went on strike. This labour conflict represented some 12,000 workers seeking a greater share of corporate broadcasting profits. The WGA had previously gone on strike in 1988, with an attendant loss of nearly 10 per cent of overall viewership; at that time, there was not yet an alternative media to absorb the displaced audience. The 2007 strike was a much different matter. It occurred at a moment in which we saw the levelling of the content creator's influence and the radical democratization of content creation platforms—and, coincidentally, the release of the first iPhone. This strike resulted in the cancellation or postponement of many fictional programs from the largest content-producing corporations in the U.S. (Handel 2011)—and, more significantly, in the rise of "reality television," which presented "reality" as something effectively "produced," and by a real producer. "Reality" had become entertainment.

Pop culture reporters such as Leigh Blickley (2018) have speculated about the impacts of the 2007 strike—the larger shift to alternative content production and the rise of new media platforms within traditional media and communications industries. Where once narrative fiction offered some level of separation between the real world and entertainment, quasi-fictional narratives now crossed into the "real world." Today, it is not uncommon to see news personalities performing their roles as journalists in fictional film or television scenarios. Whether the relationship is causal or part of a larger tidal shift in the makeup of mass media, there is at least some connection between the rise of reality television and the rise of a former reality television star becoming the president of the United States in 2017, using showman-like tactics and publicity stunts. With a president content to play executive producer as well as commander-in-chief, Politifact had found its niche tracking and recording an endless stream of questionable utterances.

The 2007 WGA strike did not just change television forever: it appeared to usher in the ascendance of social media platforms such as Myspace, Twitter, and Facebook. Although it is difficult to imagine now, Myspace was the world's largest social media site from 2005 to 2009. The rise of social media platforms virtualized the water cooler conversation and created digital spaces for social cohesion and community to emerge irrespective of geography or interpersonal proximity. The result was a rapidly growing and increasingly mediated sense of belonging. While our collective identities have been radically redrawn by these networks, however, we have looked less often at how these systems have shaped how and why knowledge is made. We have redefined the methods and means by which we authorize opinion and recognize certain voices. Retweets and likes now stand as an objective measure of collective validation of opinion, with or without citation, support, or adequate research. A well-curated social media feed may now stand in place of traditional university credentials or a lauded publishing record. Where once authority was granted by accredited degree-granting institutions, social media now serves as an authorizing agent that can lend validity and impact to influential opinions.

In many ways, social media platforms have enabled underserved and under-represented groups within the university to find voice and footing, to speak truth to power. After all, the hearts and minds that matter most in this distributed, socially mediated global commons are the hearts and minds that lead to broad support with analytics data to support those actions. However, just as socially progressive voices can be heard on social media, so too can fringe opinions promoting discrimination and hate. Many in positions of privilege within the university and college community may bemoan David Shaw's (2017) "rise of stupid" on social media, but it is our own self-satisfied, self-righteous opinions that led to the shock of the 2016 U.S. election. Eli Pariser's (2011) concept of the "filter bubble" has also helped prefigure the political division of the U.S., with groups of voters consuming siloed "diets" of news through social media alone. It comes as little surprise that a president who is highly engaged on social media would be so adept at masking real policy decisions in the veneer of sensationalism, bullying, partial truths, and outright lies. But how can so many follow an individual so invested in obvious falsehoods? Here we have the great connecting thread that links the animating spirit of our age: facts matter little when belief feels so good.

So, where does this leave academic culture and the practice of scholarship? Digital humanities has been bullish about social media for many years, represented by journals such as *Digital Humanities Quarterly* and the reflective *Journal of Digital Humanities*; *Kairos*, too, has published several articles on teaching rhetoric with social media. Melissa Terras's (2012) "The Impact of Social Media on the Dissemination of Research" is an honest reminder about why social media matters in academia and beyond. Mobilizing research is hard but valuable work, and Terras is a role model to be followed. She describes in plain terms how blogging and posting her research on social media has increased her readership dramatically and boosted her citations. She summarizes her experience this way:

> The final point to make is that people don't just follow me or read my blog to download my research papers. This has only been part of what I do online—I have more than 2,000 followers on twitter

now and it has taken me over three years of regular engagement—
hanging out and chatting, pointing to interesting stuff, repointing
to interesting stuff, asking questions, answering questions, getting
stroppy, sending supportive comments, etc.—to build up an
"audience" (I'd actually call a lot of you friends!). If all I was doing
was pumping out links to my published stuff, would you still be
reading this? Would you have read this? Would you keep reading?
(Terras 2012, n.p.)

There is a seemingly simple logic here. If you have something interesting to
say, people will read it. If they read it, they will cite it. Even the introduction to
the previous volume of *Social Knowledge Creation* claimed that "[c]entral to any
discussion of social media and social knowledge is an understanding of how
profoundly normal such activity is now taken to be by the public" (Arbuckle,
Mauro, and Powell 2017, 10). There is an inevitability to the power of social
media to influence. Even Terras, who has used it so effectively, explains, "I
suspect this little experiment only worked as I already had a 'digital presence,'
whatever that may mean. All the numbers, the statistics. Those clicks were
made by real people" (Terras 2012, n.p.). The meaning of a "digital presence"
is precisely where the study of social knowledge creation resides. From this
perspective, social knowledge creation represents a digital ontology of online
life in which individual identities are constructed to support opinion. In some
ways, Terras describes a solution to the current crisis in scholarly publishing.
Her influence comes first and foremost from the high quality of her scholarship, and her work gains a broader hearing from her productive use of social
media. A well-curated digital presence is merely an extension of effective
scholarly communication in the twenty-first century.

Social media offers the promise of hearing marginalized voices, which will inevitably release voices and opinions less concerned with compassion, care, and
goodwill. There are questions that emerge directly from such a divided view of
our society. Where once our society was stitched together with narrative, we
now have a socially networked mesh of opinion. In the tradition of Benedict
Anderson's *Imagined Communities* (1983), national media once served to define
the identity of many millions of people separated by distances of space, time,
class, race, and gender. We were capable of sympathizing with our neighbour
because of the stories we shared. In exchange, society agreed to allow a dis-
proportionate amount of power to be placed in large media companies and
those who worked for them. This process has always occurred in a multimedia
environment, whether the tool to tell these stories was theatre, film, radio,
newspapers, or the novel. We are now grappling with how traditional media's

power has lost the capability of shaping broad swaths of public opinion in the face of the Web and social networks. Our stories are now told minute by minute, second by second. They represent highly isolated echo chambers of self-actualizing knowledge making wherein the members of the community decide, through a decentralized system of upvoting (likes, loves, retweets, re-posts), what is durable and true.

In perhaps the most extreme case of this phenomenon, the early 2000s have seen a resurgence of flat earth conspiracy theories. The more radical the belief, the more ardently those beliefs are held, and the more exclusive the member-ship in a given knowledge community. We are not only discussing "alternative facts" or the former president's assertions about the size of the crowd at his inauguration: we are also discussing a widespread cultural shift toward blend-ing real people, policies, and politics within a mediated experience of reality mixed with fiction. In his television series *Who Is America?*, comedian Sasha Baron Cohen flips this blending of real entertainment with fictional enter-tainment by interviewing real political personalities. Baron Cohen's fictional personas have needled real public figures by playing to their own eagerness to please the crowd and to validate their opinions through the media. The in-teractions are fun to watch precisely because of the tragic irony involved; the persons ridiculed by Baron Cohen are, like classical tragic heroes, only aware of their mistakes once it is too late. The audience is left laughing at the rupture between real and fictional political discourses. This is not merely a question of fake or real, because nothing here can be split so cleanly. Our mediated experi-ence has now allowed for a radical flattening of expertise and the wholesale deregulation of knowledge production. Opinion is now easily confused with scholarship. Political positions are masquerading as knowledge. Beliefs now define community, both online and in the real world.

It is belief, after all, that animates a world unmoored from fact and expert opinion. As yet another sign of the times, the environment that governed Edward S. Herman and Noam Chomsky's famed 1988 book, *Manufacturing Con-sent*, has taken on an extreme character of radical polarity and division. Social media has managed to commodify their notion of "flak" as a kind of propa-gandistic political entertainment. From Westboro Baptist Church, the National Rifle Association, and Friends of Coal to Alex Jones's website *InfoWars* and the Reddit subgroup */r/The_Donald*, every controversial or polarizing group has an online presence, a "base," and a belief system. "God hates homosexuals," "teachers need guns," and "coal is clean" are the logical absurdities of our age. And trolling, animated by aligning hate, need, and identity, has become an act of religious or patriotic devotion. "Call out culture" is sustained by the cruel pleasures of destroying an online life (Brooks 2019). Policing who is in and who is out matters more than what is true. The sensation of saying something wrong, both logically and socially, has an emotional appeal that contains its own pleasures, tinged with religious zealotry. In this context, it is less surprising that one of former president Trump's first actions was to declare January 20 the "National Day of Patriotic Devotion" to commemorate his own inauguration in the habit and tone of religious fervour. There is a certain orgiastic passion that emerges from such fealty to pathetic responses. The cultural logic of bullying has become the personal battlefield of individuals so deeply invested in the tenets of political affiliation that harming others is seen as merely another price of membership.

At the level of the nation-state and subnational hostile forces, social media has been weaponized in other ways. The use of social media by ISIS to spread fear and recruit fighters worldwide is directly accessible on YouTube and goes far beyond the capacities of some nations to disseminate propaganda. In a report prepared for NATO's Strategic Communications Centre of Excellence, Jeff Giesea (2015) describes this kind of weaponized social media as one that, while sharing elements of manufactured consent from the twentieth century, is better described as psychological warfare for digital natives. This new mechanism for influencing large populations online has now been collected under the neologism "memetic warfare," which Giesea defines in the following way:

> [I]t should be thought of as broader and more strategic than "weaponize trolling." Memetic warfare, as I define it, is competition over narrative, ideas, and social control in a social-media battlefield. One might think of it as a subset of "information operations" tailored to social media. Information operations involve the collection and dissemination of information to establish a competitive advantage over an opponent. (Giesea 2015, 69)

The lack of narrative is significant. Narrative is a fundamental structure in human understanding that, in all but the most avant-garde versions, demands some kind of logic. A mind governed by narrative coherence demands a reasonable thread of causality. Rational connection between moments allows for coherence and a logical unfolding of events over time. Narrative coherence is a kind of real-time fact checking. It's a sniff test we all possess. Memetic warfare's rejection of narrative removes rational understanding from the communications strategy and allows for bad-faith, hostile actors to simply take up digital space. By dominating the conversation on social media, hostile entities can influence others to act on their behalf. They can steer the conversation toward real-world outcomes that matter to them.

The case for the broad applicability of social media in realms of social, political, and cultural concerns is seemingly obvious but difficult to summarize because we are dealing with an inherently networked phenomenon. A set of concerns in one realm may be radically different elsewhere, whether those concerns are about asymmetrical cyberwarfare between nation-states and terrorist groups or covert conspiratorial propaganda campaigns to influence the vaccination habits of citizens from various countries. In the case of such hostilities, individuals may be the subject of supervision and coercion by their own government and corporations they trust.

In a now well-known article published in the *Proceedings of the National Academy of Sciences of the United States of America* (*PNAS*), a team of Facebook's Core Data Science researchers reported on how they were able to manipulate the emotions of hundreds of thousands of Facebook users by showing them content that was either sad or happy (Kramer, Guillory, and Hancock 2014). In the article "Experimental Evidence of Massive-Scale Emotional Contagion through Social Networks," the authors explain how users were then more inclined to share or repost content that was also sad or happy, depending on Facebook's throttling of content. As the authors go on to state rather plainly:

> The experiment manipulated the extent to which people (N=689,003) were exposed to emotional expressions in their News Feed. This tested whether exposure to emotions led people to change their own posting behaviors, in particular whether exposure to emotional content led people to post content that was consistent with the exposure—thereby testing whether exposure to verbal affective expressions leads to similar verbal expressions, a form of emotional contagion. (Kramer, Guillory, and Hancock 2014, 8788)

The results of the paper eventually resulted in a public apology and an "editorial expression of concern and correction" from the journal some weeks later (Verma 2014; Goel 2014). This episode is certainly an example of how peer review is capable of authorizing and validating unethical research, but the need to retract peer-reviewed articles has been a perennial problem since the Enlightenment and the codification of research reporting practices: rational discourse allows for errors because rationality demands ongoing revision and correction.

Facebook's experiment in "emotional contagion" used the biological metaphor of virulence associated with malicious software, but had it turned back on its own human creators. Unsurprisingly, however, this scandal in no way curtailed Facebook's involvement in broad social manipulation. The Facebook–Cambridge Analytica scandal, which exposed Facebook's profiteering in election meddling in the 2016 U.S. elections, is just the most obvious example. Among other misuses of Facebook around the world, the Rohingya Muslims of Myanmar have been the target of genocidal campaigns on the platform (Wong, Safi, and Rahman 2017); the American alt-right movement has use the platform to organize "unite the right" rallies, such as the one at Charlottesville, Virginia, that resulted in the death of Heather Heyer (Kelly 2017); and there are well documented examples of how Russia is using Facebook in the elections of its regional neighbours (Satariano 2019). The use of social media data in election meddling is only growing as products such as Facebook's Social Graph Search open personal information to those eager to influence scores of individuals. However, Social Graph Search includes data from persons who are not even on Facebook, because anyone who uploads their contacts to the platform is giving Facebook the tools to track activities of those with no account (Graph Search 2019).

Despite these vast systems designed and used to influence individuals on a massive scale, the targeted individuals may not actually do as the influencer intends. The now infamous 2017 Fyre Festival, an attempt to create the next Coachella-like phenomenon by selling young people an elite music festival experience on social media, ended in absurd failure as the reality of hosting thousands on a remote tropical island failed to match the memetic fantasy. Individuals are still possessed of free will and a critical sensibility. The great power of critique and literacy is best expressed in a free society. We can simply choose not to enter into a manipulative relationship with a social media platform. However, there are systems in place in China that legally curtail freedoms using similar profiling and data collecting. The Social Credit System is now a reality for millions (Hvistendahl 2017), and thousands of individuals are having their travel abroad, access to certain schools, approval of loans, and social activities curtailed based on their social credit (Galeon 2017). Western countries would likely pride themselves on not allowing such impositions on personal freedoms, but the system is not dissimilar to that of credit ratings. Of course, the invisible hand at work with one's credit rating is merely *less authoritarian* than China's Social Credit System.

Still, it seems that those personal freedoms are all too readily given up in the West as well. Lifestyle decisions guided by a desire for a long and happy life will drive consumers to exchange personal privacy for finely tuned and personal influences. In 2016, Google released a video for the Selfish Ledger, "a constantly evolving representation of who we are" (Patch 2018). Google is seeking to apply an understanding of "epigenetics, inheritance, and memetics" to create a species-level data model of human interaction, allowing it to understand an individual so completely that it can anticipate needs, wants, and goals through an intergenerational modelling and manipulation of our actions. "Desirable" behaviours can be selected and expressed, but *whose* desires will be selected is an open question. Perhaps the individual user will be fully enfranchised and will use the system to achieve a truly greater sense of self-knowledge and self-improvement. Google may be building a brave promise to humanity and the digital fulfillment of the great Greek imperative *gnōthi seauton*, "know thyself." Also, perhaps, this influence will be used by the owner of the system, Google, to benefit itself. If Google is able to influence individuals, intergenerationally, for its own good while also benefiting users, we run the risk of allowing an inherently manipulative system to take root in every aspect of our economy and society. Our most significant successes in life may one day be intimately linked to a machine learning system that is helping us get a job, find a spouse, have a family, be healthy, and live a long and happy life. If we feel good, would we even mind? We are content to count steps with pedometers and measure our heart rate to become more fit. Perhaps one day we will also take direction on the most trivial of actions so that we can be better people. While this line of thought is likely wild speculation, perhaps one day a system embedded within Google Docs will recommend that an author close a paragraph and move to a new, more productive topic.

Humans are, after all, content to influence each other on social media today. In the run-up to the 2016 U.S. elections, several incidents occurred that underscored our surprising trust in social interactions—a level of trust highlighted by the way in which social media engagements became real-world, often violent engagements. Combined with the acceptance of the reasonable reliability of content online, the ability to make sense of facts and stories has radically shifted. Although Wikipedia was launched in 2001, it did not become a global force until 2007, when it broke the top-ten list of most popular websites. The emergence of a sense of mediated community understanding in the early 2000s has reshaped political, social, and cultural assumptions. Scholarly communications and publishing, including teaching and creative outputs associated with the academy, have not been immune to these transformations. As a supremely traditionalist cultural institution, the university has also been changed by the emergence of social media. Knowledge is now being produced online in these ad hoc networks of social and cultural commentators. Crowdsourcing has emerged as a legitimate way to generate knowledge about often highly local or highly obscure sociocultural topics. The logic of Wikipedia has spread onto platforms such as Yelp, Google and Amazon reviews, and other consumer-oriented forums where the collective authorizing of products, places, and experiences has led to a degree of trust in non-expert opinion. The gradual erosion of public trust in expert opinion is a phenomenon due in part to academic distance from the experiences of daily lives and the high cost of maintaining and engaging an elite professoriate. Outside the academic social media filter bubble looms an uncomfortable truth: the general public is no longer reliant on scholarly opinion to shape its world view.

There is a market for ideas. The value of those ideas comes in the form of academic positions, employable students, and social prestige. But market forces are at work within the academy, and we have not fully come to terms with the shift. In the same way that the emergence of reality TV after the 2007 writers' strike changed the way small-screen content was generated, our sense of fact and truth has been radically shaken by this remediation of our social reality. The university has been an institutional resource for economic, social, and cultural training—one in which academic opinion has been respected under the mantle of expertise. The tension between ill-informed opinion, or *doxa*, and educated knowledge, or *episteme*, is as old as classical Greek rhetoric. An opinion that has been honed by many years or decades of careful study has always been deemed more valuable than an uninformed opinion. Social media, however, has enabled and encouraged crowdsourcing of opinion, which has in turn made opinion very cheap and plentiful. Academic opinion, it turns out, doesn't amount to much in this environment. What if a Reddit comment thread yields better results than an expert opinion honed by PhD-level training? Where do we go from here, as an academy and as a society?

Social knowledge creation promises to include the mechanisms that have transformed traditional television and film industries. Academic communities, after all, tell stories too. The stories we tell are informed and inspired by a pursuit of fact and reliable knowledge, but we must reassert this value in real time. We have a duty to make this information accessible and actionable for anyone with an Internet connection. Social knowledge creation promises the return of Enlightenment ideals of real, compassionate ways of knowing. Making knowledge should not hold some arbitrary fealty to a specific media type, most obviously the paradigm of print. We also have a responsibility to perform and inform a culture of knowing true and real facts that are *prospective* and leading, rather than prescriptive and demeaning. In the midst of division and anger online, we should rise above the flame wars and be the agents of change we want to see in the world.

The authors of this volume have all held fast to a position of *generosity*. Generosity is a soothing balm for our times. As Anne Balsamo (2011) suggests in *Designing Culture: The Technological Imagination at Work*, "intellectual generosity" is the "foundational ethical principle of multidisciplinary collaboration" (163). In "Putting the Human Back into the Digital Humanities: Feminism, Generosity, and Mess," Losh et al. (2016) cite Balsamo in suggesting that this generosity animates our "feminist antiracism" in digital humanities. In the years since 2016, it is all too easy to append to this generosity an anti-fascist ethos that rejects corporate or governmental control over our digital social spheres. This generosity must do more than incite cries of further division or call out the perceived ethical failures of others. It must welcome them into a healing relationship in which real, rational ideas can be shared.

There are several banners under which we can productively gather this sensibility. Open Access is a promise to share knowledge freely. Open Source is an ability to build upon software. Open Data promises to make data sets public and discoverable. Open Pedagogy or Open Educational Resources promises to share teaching materials, methods, and approaches in the interest of building a more cohesive and dynamic classroom environment. The promise of such generosity, of compassion and forgiveness, allows for new ideas to be heard above the din of mere partisanship and tribalism.

The desire to open the places, systems, and infrastructure that disseminate knowledge is a primary motivation of social knowledge creation. There is an openness within the social that is emulated online, and this online sensibility is rapidly being manifested in our physical spaces. During the publication of this book, one of the authors mused about the public life of ideas that would be possible if we merely socialized in libraries:

**erin glass**
@erinroseglass

Follow

what if public libraries were open late every night and we could engage in public life there instead of having to choose between drinking at the bar and domestic isolation

4:02 PM - 23 Feb 2019 from San Diego, CA

48,876 Retweets  223,833 Likes

3.1K      49K      224K

What if public libraries became public houses? What if the libidinal energy of a bar scene could be harnessed to debate and discuss issues and ideas? What if social spaces became spaces of knowledge creation? Glass is pointing to the potential of taking the logic of social media and making it manifest. The intimacy of friendship mixed with public space, held together in the ferment of ideas, is fertile ground for dialogue and debate. This vision of being social, with media, is so appealing that Glass's tweet went viral. As of this writing, Glass's tweet had gathered some 224,000 likes and 49,000 retweets, numbers which grew even greater after none other than Alexandria Ocasio-Cortez (Member of the U.S. House of Representatives from New York's 14th District) retweeted it for an additional 77,000 likes and 13,000 retweets. These are influential ideas that are playing a role in shaping the political priorities of a generation, and they gain influence by being validated online, in real time.

In turning now to the collection of essays at hand, it is appropriate that we begin with the technologies that have shaped this twenty-first-century media landscape. The collection is split into three parts. The first two parts contain essays of varying length approaching social knowledge creation in a variety of ways, while the third part contains a lengthy annotated bibliography for others interested in taking up further work. The essays in Part 1 emerged from a gathering at the University of Victoria in 2015 and represent some of the first attempts to define social knowledge creation. They also represent shorter interventions into the social media landscape before the political events discussed above.

Christian Vandendorpe's contribution, "The Page: Its Past and Future in Books of Knowledge," represents a grounding reminder of the legacy of manuscript and print culture. In Vandendorpe's history of the page, "the main building block of the codex," we are reminded of how the "soul" of the book format was developed and refined over time. This primordial element of literacy and knowledge dissemination still shapes our imagination as we think through word processing, web pages, Wikipedia, and the paper pages we continue to read today.

The sobering awareness of how past media shapes our new media is a consistent facet of this collection. John Barber's "Digital Radio and Social Knowledge Creation in the Humanities" explores the potential of a familiar technology—when converted into digital form—to enable two-way communication and thus "facilitate social knowledge creation." Radio is, after all, based in sound and human speech, our oldest form of communication. Drawing on the work of Bertolt Brecht and Marshall McLuhan, as well as contemporary scholarship, Barber goes on to discuss digital platforms such as YouTube, Ustream, and other emerging audio networks, positing a model of future radio that is engaged, interactive, and based on conversation.

In each of these contributions, social knowledge creation appears to open new communities and new spaces for critique. Randa El Khatib's "Collocating Places and Words with TopoText" examines efforts to link the Stanford Named Entity Recognition (NER) engine, which is capable of identifying place names from plain text, to automatic cartography using Google Maps. Analysis of Thackeray's *Vanity Fair* is presented as an example of "geocriticism"—a way "to facilitate a deeper engagement with the spatiality of a text through a placial focus." Similarly, Alex Christie, in partnership with the Implementing New Knowledge Environments (INKE) and Modernist Versions Project (MVP) research groups, describes how historical maps based on early twentieth-century novels can be productively distorted to see where and how characters move across fictional and real space. In his "Open Source Interpretation Using Z-axis Maps," Christie conducts geospatial emphasis of works such as Djuna Barnes's *Nightwood* using the Stanford NER tagger. By rendering the NER results through a historic map, we are offered a vision of how modern novels characterized the urban landscape.

Within these essays, there is also an interest in exploring distortions of reality in an effort to learn historical truths. In Juliette Levy's "'Digital Zombies in the Academy': At the Intersection of Digital Humanities and Digital Pedagogy," we learn how an online game, *Digital Zombies*, is used to teach history students to become more effective researchers. By reading a false history of a zombie war in *World War Z*, students are encouraged to discern between reliable, fact-based research and less authoritative online sources. In the process, they also learn how to use their library, and how librarians can help them find what they need to complete their assignments.

As evinced by the *Digital Zombies* project discussed above, student participation and engagement are key components of the scholarship collected in this volume. In Part 2, we encounter essays that focus on pedagogy and student participation from several perspectives. We see how socially participatory online research and teaching emerges at the institutional level, the infrastructure level, and the digital project level. These categories have emerged in recent years as fundamental aspects of digital humanities practice, and these works distinctively place pedagogy and student experiences at their centre.

In Jacob Heil and Ben Daigle's "Projects to Pedagogy: On the Social Infrastructure of Consortial Collaboration in Digital Scholarship," we learn about the commitment to community required to develop an emerging digital humanities community in a formalized curricular structure within a large consortium of liberal arts colleges in Ohio (the "Ohio Five"). Heil and Daigle remind us that, despite the prominent rise of digital humanities *within* the humanities, a transformation of our institutions and curriculum is still very much underway. There is a connection here, as well, to the *Digital Zombies* project, which required students to meet and work with their librarians: the Ohio Five initiative began with funding to build a "Next Generation Library" system among the members, and continued with ongoing collaboration among library, faculty, and administrative staff. A team-centered approach was crucial in helping "to build good will among all parties involved."

Continuing in the liberal arts context, "Rethinking Social Knowledge Creation in the Liberal Arts: The History and Future of Domain of One's Own" offers us an inside view of the inspiration and motivation for developing a cornerstone digital humanities project. Inspired by and named after Virginia Woolf's *A Room of One's Own*, the Domain of One's Own initiative demonstrated the power of digital literacy and student agency by simply giving students their own websites and domain names. Martha Burtis, Nigel Haarstad, Jess Reingold, Kris Shaffer, Lee Skallerup Bessette, Jesse Stommel, and Sean Michael Morris collectively describe the process of bringing this service to students, and how this transformed education at the University of Mary Washington in Fredericksburg, Virginia.

Turning from institutions and infrastructure to individual initiative, the collection takes up the perspective of early career and graduate student research. In "Waste at the Temple of Knowledge: A Personal Reflection on Writing, Technology, and the Student Public to Come," Erin Glass offers a tremendously engaging, up-close look into the life of a graduate student. She recounts how she decided to write her dissertation on a variety of social media platforms, performing her exploration of social media in a public way that lends transparency and honesty to the all-too-often romanticized experience of graduate education. Along the way, we are offered a view into a twenty-first-century version of American Naturalism, in which a "digital detox" stands in place for a Thoreauvian escape from urban life.

John R. Ladd, also a graduate student at the time of writing at Washington University in St. Louis, offers us a detailed and tremendously intriguing view of the life cycle of a very well-known digital humanities project, *Six Degrees of Francis Bacon*. Ladd's "Reassembling the Bacon: Crowdsourcing Historical Social Networks in the Redesign of *Six Degrees of Francis Bacon*" describes the process of redesigning a complex user interface for the network data derived from the correspondence of Francis Bacon. In the era of the digital "social network," Ladd shows us the original "social network" as the complex web of connections and interconnections between Bacon and his contemporaries in English society, politics, business, and literature. The Bacon project, in turn, creates networks of researchers who add information to a crowdsourced repository of knowledge facilitated by technology. In describing this fascinating project, Ladd offers us a compelling argument for the long-standing importance of social networks in understanding our political and cultural legacies.

The "project" remains a central organizing concept within digital humanities research, and these projects are increasingly turning their focus toward better understanding social relations in research contexts. In "Shaping New Models of Interaction in Open Access Repositories with Social Media," Luis Meneses, Alyssa Arbuckle, Hector Lopez, Belaid Moa, Richard Furuta, and Ray Siemens describe how the logic of social media, in tandem with growing Open Access (OA) research repositories, has created the opportunity to mine humanities research in ways that have previously been impossible. Access to research remains a fundamental concern for many groups, both inside and outside the academy, and the Social Media Engine framework developed by this team is helping to improve discoverability and sharing, particularly of "OA academic publications that are mentioned in social media streams." It is remarkable to see a platform designed by humanists, for humanists, compete with large corporate publishers and champion OA publishing by simply allowing it to be found more easily.

In "Social Knowledge Creation in the Digital Humanities: Case Studies," by Cara Marta Messina, Sarah Connell, Julia Flanders, Caroline Klibanoff, and Sarah Payne, several case studies from Northeastern University's Digital Scholarship Group (DSG) are discussed. Central to their activities is the Design for Diversity Toolkit, which has been developed to "support social justice, particularly in connection with the representation of gender, race, sexuality, class, and indigeneity in digital humanities and cultural heritage projects and collections." The essay also discusses the Intertextual Networks project, an initiative focused on intertextuality in early women's writing being developed in tandem with Women Writers Online. By designing pedagogical and research tools with diversity in mind, the DSG confronts a range of issues and concerns that are fundamental to the public practice of humanities research today.

This collection represents a survey of current critical thought on social media and social knowledge creation in the humanities. It represents the range of tools, methods, and approaches needed to discuss this multifaceted and fast-moving sphere of influence in our research and in our academic communities. Central to all these contributions, however, is the theme of generosity. There is a sense of sharing that comes all too naturally to humanistic scholars concerned with issues of justice, equality, and democracy. The sensibility that inspires humanists to give away their hard-won research and freely give their time to students, institutions, publishers, and colleagues is mirrored in the best parts of social media. When we give generously of ourselves, social platforms become rich, even beautiful, representations of our humanity online. In a world where personal data is harvested like a raw material and individuals are targeted in politically motivated campaigns of coercion and control, the humanistic impulse to give becomes politically urgent, radical, and necessary. In her essay "'This Is Why We Fight': Defining the Values of the Digital Humanities," Lisa Spiro (2012) reaffirms the goal of digital humanities: to promote the best of the humanities through "inspired acts of generosity and heroism" (21).[5] The essays collected here represent a continuation of this heroic tradition. Societies can gain cohesion through a common understanding of fact. Beyond limited views of political party as a proxy for belonging, let us reaffirm the core humanistic values of social justice and common cultural understanding. We pursue these values *not* because they are a cornerstone of our belief systems

[5] Spiro quotes from *The Digital Humanities Manifesto 2.0*, published by the UCLA Mellon Seminar in Digital Humanities in 2009 (http://manifesto.humanities.ucla.edu/2009/05/29/the-digital-humanities-manifesto-20/).

and ways of belonging. Instead, we pursue these values because they are never settled and always warrant greater reflection, empathy, and compassion.

WORKS CITED

Anderson, Benedict. 1983. *Imagined Communities: Reflections on the Origin and Spread of Nationalism*. London: Verso.

Arbuckle, Alyssa, Aaron Mauro, and Daniel Powell, eds. 2017. *Social Knowledge Creation in the Humanities: Volume 1*. Toronto: Iter Press; Tempe: Arizona Center for Medieval and Renaissance Studies.

Balsamo, Anne. 2011. *Designing Culture: The Technological Imagination at Work*. Durham, NC: Duke University Press.

Blickley, Leigh. 2018. "10 Years Ago, Screenwriters Went on Strike and Changed Television Forever." *Huffington Post*, February 12. https://www.huffingtonpost.ca/entry/10-years-ago-screenwriters-went-on-strike-and-changed-television-forever_n_5a7b3544e4b08dfc92ff2b32.

Bloom, Harold. 1997. *The Anxiety of Influence: A Theory of Poetry*. 2nd ed. New York: Oxford University Press.

Bradner, Eric. 2017. "Conway: Trump White House Offered 'Alternative Facts' on Crowd Size." *CNN*, January 23. https://www.cnn.com/2017/01/22/politics/kellyanne-conway-alternative-facts/index.html.

Brooks, David. 2019. "The Cruelty of Call-Out Culture." *New York Times*, January 14. https://www.nytimes.com/2019/01/14/opinion/call-out-social-justice.html.

Galeon, Dom. 2017. "China's 'Social Credit System' Will Rate How Valuable You Are As a Human." *Futurism*, December 2. https://futurism.com/china-social-credit-system-rate-human-value/.

Ghosh, Shona, and Jake Kanter. 2019. "Google Says Data Is More Like Sunlight Than Oil, One Day after Being Fined $57 Million over Its Privacy and Consent Practices." *Business Insider*, January 22. https://www.businessinsider.com/google-data-is-more-like-sunlight-than-oil-france-gdpr-fine-57-million-2019-1.

Giesea, Jeff. 2015. "It's Time to Embrace Memetic Warfare." *Defence Strategic Communications* 1(1): 68–76. https://doi.org/10.30966/2018.RIGA.1.4.

Goel, Vindu. 2014. "Facebook Tinkers with Users' Emotions in News Feed Experiment, Stirring Outcry." *New York Times*, June 29. https://www.nytimes.com/2014/06/30/technology/facebook-tinkers-with-users-emotions-in-news-feed-experiment-stirring-outcry.html.

Graph Search (@graphsearcher). 2019. "Introducing Graph." Facebook. https://www.facebook.com/graphsearcher.

Haberman, Clyde. 2016. "Lives and Profits in the Balance: The High Stakes of Medical Patents." *New York Times*, December 11. https://www.nytimes.com/2016/12/11/us/retro-report-medical-patents-profits.html?_r=0.

Handel, Jonathan. 2011. *Hollywood on Strike! An Industry at War in the Internet Age*. Los Angeles: Hollywood Analytics.

Herman, Edward S., and Noam Chomsky. 1988. *Manufacturing Consent: The Political Economy of the Mass Media*. New York: Pantheon Books.

Hvistendahl, Mara. 2017. "Inside China's Vast New Experiment in Social Ranking." *Wired*, December 14. https://www.wired.com/story/age-of-social-credit/.

Kelly, Heather. 2017. "Hate Groups on Facebook: Why Some Get to Stay." *CNN Money*, August 8. https://money.cnn.com/2017/08/17/technology/culture/facebook-hate-groups/index.html.

Kramer, Adam D. I., Jamie E. Guillory, and Jeffrey T. Hancock. 2014. "Experimental Evidence of Massive-Scale Emotional Contagion through Social Networks." *PNAS* 111(24): 8788–90. https://doi.org/10.1073/pnas.1320040111.

Latour, Bruno. 1988. *The Pasteurization of France*. Translated by Alan Sheridan and John Law. Cambridge, MA: Harvard University Press.

———. 2005. *Reassembling the Social: An Introduction to Actor-Network-Theory*. New York: Oxford University Press.

Losh, Elizabeth, Jacqueline Wernimont, Laura Wexler, and Hong-An Wu. 2016. "Putting the Human Back into the Digital Humanities: Feminism, Generosity, and Mess." In *Debates in the Digital Humanities 2016*, edited by

Matthew K. Gold and Lauren F. Klein, 92–103. Minneapolis: University of Minnesota Press.

Moore, Mark. 2018. "Giuliani: 'Truth Isn't Truth.'" *New York Post*, August 19. https://nypost.com/2018/08/19/giuliani-truth-isnt-truth/.

Pariser, Eli. 2011. *The Filter Bubble: What the Internet is Hiding from You.* New York: Penguin.

Patch, Anthony. 2018. "Google's Selfish Ledger Is an Unsettling Vision of Silicon Valley Social Engineering." *YouTube*, May 18. https://www.youtube.com/watch?v=fvUN6Cbogfo.

Satariano, Adam. 2019. "Facebook Identifies Russia-Linked Misinformation Campaign." *New York Times*, January 17. https://www.nytimes.com/2019/01/17/business/facebook-misinformation-russia.html.

Shaw, David. 2017. "The Rise of Stupid." *Medium*, June 29. https://medium.com/@davidshawTV/the-rise-of-stupid-64b1b9f407d9.

Spiro, Lisa. 2012. "'This Is Why We Fight': Defining the Values of the Digital Humanities." In *Debates in the Digital Humanities*, edited by Matthew K. Gold, 16–34. Minneapolis: University of Minnesota Press.

Terras, Melissa. 2012. "The Impact of Social Media on the Dissemination of Research: Results of an Experiment." *Journal of Digital Humanities* 1(3): n.p.

Verma, Inder M. 2014. "Editorial Expression of Concern and Correction: Experimental Evidence of Massive-Scale Emotional Contagion through Social Networks." *PNAS* 111(29): 10779. https://doi.org/10.1073/pnas.1412469111.

Wong, Julia Carrie, Michael Safi, and Shaikh Azizur Rahman. 2017. "Facebook Bans Rohingya Group's Posts As Minority Faces 'Ethnic Cleansing.'" *The Guardian*, September 20. https://www.theguardian.com/technology/2017/sep/20/facebook-rohingya-muslims-myanmar.

Zuboff, Shoshana. 2015. "Big Other: Surveillance Capitalism and the Prospects of an Information Civilization." *Journal of Information Technology* 30(1): 75–89. https://doi.org/10.1057%2Fjit.2015.5.

———. 2019. *The Age of Surveillance Capitalism: The Fight for a Human Future at the New Frontier of Power.* New York: PublicAffairs.

# The Page: Its Past and Future in Books of Knowledge

## Christian Vandendorpe
### University of Ottawa

As we are now fully engaged in the digital culture, it is quite appropriate to examine the unravelling of the codex and its consequences. I shall focus on the page, which is the main building block of the codex, its DNA, its soul. Across the centuries, the changes made to the page have affected the appearance, the functionalities, and the usability of the codex. After following some of these transformations across history, this article will explore the future of the page in digital format.

The definition of a page is quite straightforward: a page is one side of a leaf of paper or parchment, or any other material that is able to receive a text or illustrations and be part of a set. The word "page" comes from the Latin word *pagina*, which designates a column of writing. *Pagina* itself is derived from the verb "*pangere*," meaning "to mark out the boundaries," which is essentially the function of the page, because "writing necessitates the marks of its own limits" (Zali 1999, 23). The Latin verb also means "to plant vines in a vineyard," which has given rise to the vineyard metaphor of the text, first explicitly made by Pliny the Elder, and quite frequent in the Middle Ages, inspiring Ivan Illich's book on Hugh of St. Victor, *In the Vineyard of the Text* (1993).

**Figure 1. Papyrus roll, 1st century CE. British Museum, Pap. 115.**

The vine metaphor is particularly appropriate because, in a papyrus scroll (Figure 1), the *pagina* corresponds to the column of text. In most scrolls, the column width varies from 6 to 8 cm in length, and holds about 25 to 45 lines, with an intercolumn margin of 2 to 2.5 cm (Mak 2011, 11). These proportions "remain remarkably stable" (Johnson 2004, 55). It should be noted that,

ISBN 978-1-64959-008-4 (paper) ISBN 978-1-64959-009-1 (pdf) ISBN 978-1-64959-084-8 (epub)

*New Technologies in Medieval and Renaissance Studies 8* (2022) 25–41

contrary to a common misconception, the volumen unrolls horizontally, unlike the vertical standing *rotulus*, which served essentially for public proclamations in theatrical, liturgical, or administrative settings, and in which the page encompassed the total length of the roll.

The page changed drastically, and took on its present meaning, with the advent of the codex in the Roman Empire at around the first century CE. The codex was initially a gathering of thin wooden tablets, bound by strings and coated with coloured wax (Figure 2). Being easy to erase, these tablets were used for drafts or school exercises (Zali 1999, 37; Mak 2001, 13). In the first century, wood was replaced by papyrus, and then by parchment. With parchment, it was possible to use both sides of the page. The folding of the sheet in two or in four, and the subsequent binding of the sheets, produced the codex. The page thus became an autonomous unit as well as part of a totality.

**Figure 2. Wax tablet, 1st century CE. Toledo, Spain (personal photo).**

In this new format, the book gained in density; it was much easier to handle than the scroll, and, moreover, freed the reader's hands. Since the codex could stay open on any particular pairing of pages (called an *opening*), new possibilities for conveying visual information in the text emerged. As a result, "the readable gradually move[d] into the realm of the visible" (Vandendorpe 2009, 30). This shift accentuated the tension between two antagonistic yet complementary sources of absorbing information: the acoustic-verbal dimension of language and the visibility of text.

The notion of "a page" has always implied a space carefully demarcated for inscribing and reading. As such, it has been called "a temple made of writing where reading will be practised" (Zali 1999, 23). Through the course of centuries, scribes, illuminators, typographers, printers, and publishers perfected the various components of the page in order to better attract readers and entice them to delve into the text.

**Figure 3. Codex of Lindisfarne, 710-720 CE. British Library.**

The richness of the visual dimension was the main characteristic of the illuminated manuscripts produced during the medieval era. Scriptoria (literally "places for writing") were established in monasteries, which developed a very efficient technique for the production of illuminated codices. One of the earliest of these was the *Vergilius Vaticanus*, or Vatican Virgil (ca. 420), followed by thousands of bibles, missals, and psalters designed to reinforce the appeal of the gospel by their sheer beauty, as exemplified by the Lindisfarne Gospels of the early eighth century (Figure 3) or the Book of Kells (ca. 800). In these books, illustration took precedence over the text. Thus, in the chain of book production, one of the most important functions was that of the *rubricator*, who added illustrations—notably incipits, which were ornamental initials or passages written in red ink in order to draw them to the attention of the reader. The text itself was part of the illustration and was required to obey its rule; this subordinate status of the text could be seen, for example, in the filling in of lines, whose purpose was to transform the whole page into a kind of beautiful picture.

Around the thirteenth century, the organization of the page gained in complexity. Demands for clarity and coherence in scholarly editions led to a rethinking of the *ordinatio*, or structure, of the codex. The original text and its glosses were organized on the same page, with a clear distinction established between them. Initials at the beginnings of verses or of important sections were frequently coloured. In a column of text, a pilcrow (paragraph mark) indicated the beginning of a new development. Running titles became a current practice. Importantly, thirteenth-century scribes "introduced the analytic table of contents as a guide to the *ordinatio* and to facilitate the readers' access to component parts of a work" (Parkes 1976, 122).

The visual appeal of the layout was not forgotten, however: during the same century, the French architect Villard de Honnecourt devised the ideal layout of the double page of the book, giving to the various margins specific proportions based on the golden ratio (Figure 4). This layout is still relevant today. As the great Canadian typographer Robert Bringhurst has written: "To give the reader a sense of direction, and the page a sense of liveliness and poise, it is necessary to break this inexorable sameness and find a new balance of another kind. Some space must be narrow so that other space may be wide, and some space emptied so that other space may be filled" (Bringhurst 2008, 163). Thanks to these developments, the page gained in autonomy at the expense of the book's linearity (Demarcq 1999, 66), signalling the beginning of a new era. As noted by Parkes, "the late medieval book differs more from its early medieval predecessors than it does from the printed books of our own day" (Parkes 1976, 135). We can see this typical layout in an incunabulum of St. Thomas Aquinas's *Summa Theologica*, published in 1477 (Figure 5).

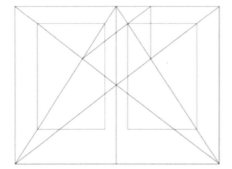

Figure 4. Villard de Honnecourt, "Canon de division harmonieuse," 13th century.

Figure 5. Incunabulum of Aquinas's Summa, 1477. Queen's University.

## *The* Polyanthea

Written by Domenico Nani Mirabelli in 1503, the *Polyanthea* is an anthology of citations classified in about one thousand articles on a variety of moral and theological subjects, as well as others of general interest: friendship, marriage, old age, grammar, memory, war, health, the zodiac, and so on. For example, the article on marriage is divided into twelve questions, such as: "Should someone marry or not?," "At what age?," and "Is beauty an important consideration?" Most topics contained a series of citations carefully chosen from a variety of authors and revered sources. As Ann Blair notes: "The early *Polyanthea* served in part as a dictionary of hard words, offering in addition to the major articles, many very short ones, with just a definition, a Greek etymology, and one or even no quotation as an example" (Blair 2010, 178).

One of the first general reference works produced for the printed book market, the *Polyanthea* was to be found in every great library. The British Museum has ten copies from different editions, one of which was owned by Henry VIII (Blair 2010, 182).

This bestseller was published in many cities (Lyon, Paris, Venice, Cologne, Frankurt, and Basel, for example), and had at least 44 editions between 1503 and 1681. Interestingly, the book gradually grew in content, since some publishers made important additions; it thus went from 430,000 words in 1503 to more than 2.5 million by 1619 (Blair 2010, 125). Clearly, according to the old etymology, the author was also the "*auctor*," a term derived from the Latin verb *augere*, meaning "to grow, to augment." This phenomenon is not dissimilar to the remarkable expansion of Wikipedia, as we shall discuss later.

**Figure 6. Title page of *Polyanthea*, 1503.**

The *Polyanthea* is a particularly interesting tool for following the evolution of ideas and printing across two centuries. In the first edition, published in Savona (Italy), the title page contains only the title, presented in the form of a triangular cul-de-lampe (Figure 6). This disposition may look odd to us, especially since some words are hyphenated without necessity. As Walter Ong points out, however, this was not unusual: "Auditory dominance can be seen strikingly in such things as early printed title pages, which often seem to us crazily erratic in their inattention to visual word units. Sixteenth century title pages very commonly divide even major words, including the author's name, with hyphens, presenting the first part of a word in one line and the latter part in smaller type" (Ong 1982, 118). At that time, reading did not focus on the visual aspect of the words grasped globally, but was still based on oral practices: the presentation of the text was independent of its semantic aspect.

Just after the preface, the table of contents—taking up no fewer than sixteen pages—lists all the entries of the dictionary. It may seem strange to us to see an alphabetical table in a dictionary, but it was a sure sign of modernity and reader-friendly publishing. This concept was not new, however, as indexing had become popular as of the beginning of the thirteenth century (Blair 2010, 36).

Following the table of contents, we find the first page of actual content, which is also a kind of title page, since there is an image enhancing the figure of the author, Nani Mirabelli, shown in the company of important ecclesiastical figures, notably the Pope (Figure 7). The author was rector of schools and archpriest of the cathedral in Savona. He also served as papal secretary.

Next, we find the first entry in the florilegium, which is the word "Abstinence," illustrated by almost three columns of quotations from such authorities as Augustine, Ambrose, Seneca, Aristotle, Cicero, and many others. At the beginning of the article, a full page is dedicated to an analytical table of the various meanings of the word "abstinence"

**Figure 7. *Polyanthea*, 1503. First page of content.**

(Figure 8). This table is called a *divisio* in Latin, a term that Ann Blair translates as a "branching diagram." Made of "squiggly brackets," the *divisio* was already common in medieval sermon manuals (Blair 2010, 145). In *Polyanthea*, the diagrams take many of their divisions from Aquinas's *Summa*. The medieval French scholastic philosopher Peter Abelard (1079–1142), as well as Hugh of St. Victor and Ramon Lull in the thirteenth century, underlined the importance of this device since it was supposed to help the reader memorize. In the medieval era, reading itself was a way to expand one's memory (Illich 1993, 35). In the colophon, Nani proudly mentions the presence of

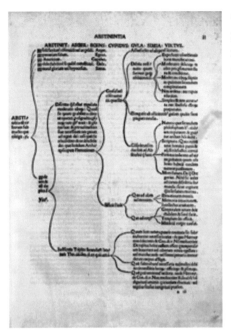

**Figure 8. Analytical table of the concept "Abstinence" in the *Polyanthea*, 1503.**

these analytical tables as an aid to memory: "[You have] some material ramified in trees so that you commit it more easily to the chest of memory."

Interestingly, the analytical tables no longer appear in the 1600 edition, published in Lyon. Memory no longer had the same paramount importance, thanks to the massive availability of printed books. In 1580, Michel de Montaigne had already noted that he preferred a "tête bien faite plutôt que tête bien pleine." By 1600, we are decidedly in the modern era.

By examining the various editions of the *Polyanthea*, one can see how the printed book progressed to its modern form, abandoning such characteristics of the manuscript, for example, as the colophon. Throughout the sixteenth century are introduced the title page, the printer's mark, and pagination in Arabic numerals, and the Roman typeface is widely adopted instead of the Gothic, at least in France and Italy. By around 1600, the cluttered pages of the sixteenth century are replaced by a clean layout quite consistent with the ideal of regularity facilitated by typography. Italics begin to be used for differentiating certain words, although it will only be at the start of the eighteenth century, with the unfinished *Biblioteca universale sacro-profano* by Vincenzo Coronelli (1701–1707), that the use of italics for the titles of books becomes a standard practice.

The layout of the book evolves in accordance with changes in reading goals and readers' habits. By creating a closed space, the page facilitates the engagement of the reader with the text. Its uniform layout is particularly helpful for prolonged immersion because it symbolically shuts out the external world. A stable layout of *openings* or paired pages is most efficient for summoning the activation of spatial memory and for a close study of long texts.

Moreover, the book as a collection of pages offers the promise of a totality of meaning.

## The Ephemeral Triumph of Liquid Text

With the advent of the Web, a new revolution, much more important than the invention of printing or even the transition from the scroll to the codex, is affecting the book. And it is developing very quickly. In digital format, text gains many new characteristics that generations of readers across the centuries did not even dream of, such as portability, ubiquity of access, hyperlinking, interactivity, as well as full and permanent indexation.

At the same time, the old codex has also found its digital avatar. Digitization has made millions of books reachable by almost everybody from everywhere. With 25 million books digitized in October 2015, Google Books is the extreme illustration of the will to avoid losing the books accumulated in great libraries, as was the case when the scroll was abandoned in favour of the codex. For some books, you can even turn the pages as if they were real, particularly on the Internet Archive (https://archive.org/index.php) and the British Library website (http://www.bl.uk/manuscripts/Default.aspx).

Scholars interested in Old English know the *Vercelli Book*, an anthology of Old English prose and verse that dates back to the late tenth century. You can now browse all of the pages of this manuscript both in single or double page format. But the digital edition offers new possibilities that go well beyond the printed book: in addition to a search engine and a magnifying-glass zoom function, you can display a page of the manuscript at left and its diplomatic transcription at right. In sum, the codex, in digital format, is gaining new life with new features that make research easier.

But text created in digital format has known a difficult start. We can trace the origin of digital text to the work of Claude Shannon, who in 1945 abstracted the idea of the message from its physical details and reduced text to a mere sequence of characters. In the model of communication he later published with Warren Weaver, he described "noise" as "everything that corrupts the signal, predictably or unpredictably," and assigned to it a prominent place in his theory of information (Gleick 2011, chap. 7).

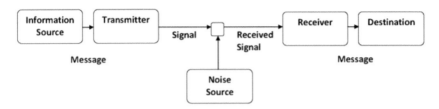

**Figure 9. Shannon-Weaver Model of Communication (1949).**

Shannon's mathematical theory of information (Figure 9) allowed the processing of text by computers and gave text the fluidity necessary to adapt to any device. But this fluidity was gained at the expense of the visual components of the page, which were reduced to "noise" and thus seen as quite expendable. When the World Wide Web Consortium (W3C) set the standard for the Web, it recommended that text in HTML be displayed running from one side of the browser window to the other, filling the screen: the size of the monitor or of the browser window were, by default, the true container of text.

By reducing text to a stream of bits, the engineers dismissed the tradition of the page as a semantic space designed to ensure a maximum of readability. Commenting on this situation, an expert in the history of written language remarked: "With the computer, we risk letting ourselves be convinced that all writing can be reduced to a pattern of black dots on a screen" (Harris 1994, 141; translation). In the first years of the Web, this "de-mediation" of the text was seen as a positive step forward, and a sure method to break away from the printed book. The page was supposed to be superseded by hyperlinks that made the old designs obsolete. In the 1990s, most experts thus avoided the word "page" and preferred to use terms like *space* (Moulthrop 2017), *lexia* (Landow 1992, 3), *texton* (Aarseth 1997, 62), or *screen* (Vandendorpe 2009, 137). Even today, in Microsoft Word, the Web Layout fills up the window of text from left to right without any margins.

As research on the mechanics of reading has made abundantly clear, the reader's eye does not follow a continuous linear path, but proceeds by "rapid movements" (saccades) and "short stops" (fixations). A skilled reader can move her eyes in about a quarter of a second, during which an average of 7 to 9 characters are acquired (see Wikipedia, "Eye movement in reading"). The longer the line, the more frequently a saccade may jump to another line by mistake. Faced with very long lines of text, readers react by speeding up their eye movements, and will sometimes be content with skimming the text, focusing only on the beginnings of the lines and on a few words here and there. This is why the column of text, from the oldest scrolls to the modern tabloids, rarely exceeds 80 characters per line. The shorter the line, the more appealing it will be for the common reader.

As monitors became larger, a full-screen web page could easily count hundreds of characters, which is not ideal for reading. When I pointed to this problem, I sometimes got the answer that I could easily resize the page by resizing the browser window. But when you do that, the tabs at the top of the browser are reduced to almost nothing: it is decidedly not user-friendly to force readers to constantly resize their browser window according to the sites they are visiting.

It took several years for publishers to realize that they could not decently display books and articles in the absence of limits, and that the white margins surrounding the text were not useless space to be dispensed with; on the contrary, they helped to recreate the page as a container and delimited the text, allowing the eye to rest from the tension caused by reading.

It is interesting to study how the layout of the page has evolved in online newspapers over the last twenty years. This can be done thanks to the Internet Archive's Wayback Machine (https://archive.org/web/), which allows us to visit the digital past. Figure 10 shows a screen copy of the *Globe and Mail*, dated September 16, 2001, in which the text fills a central column with no fixed length.

Figure 10. The *Globe and Mail*, September 16, 2001.

Two years later, the design has changed. The page is enclosed in a box with a fixed length (Figure 11).

**Figure 11. The *Globe and Mail*, June 10, 2003.**

By necessity, editors of newspapers and magazines became aware of the physiology of reading and decided to return to the layout of the printed page, with a column of limited width and white space in the margins. Instead of being displayed at the full width of the browser, text is now generally organized into a fixed-width column of 60 to 90 characters per line, and the box has disappeared.

This is the layout we find today in most newspapers. It has also been adopted by the main platforms for bloggers. Similarly, Google, Yahoo, and MSN display search

**Figure 12. Article in the journal *Terrains/Théories* (open access).**

results in columns of about 1024 pixels in total width, with 800 pixels for text. Most learned journals have also adopted a fixed-width column counting about 75 characters—not very different from the printed page of the codex, or the column of the papyrus.

In the case of the scholarly journal *Terrains/Théories* (https://journals. openedition.org/teth/), the editors have chosen to display the footnotes in the margin at right, just as in the *Polyanthea* five centuries earlier (Figure 12). This layout is certainly more sophisticated and more user-friendly than footnotes positioned at the bottom of the page. Moreover, the numbering of paragraphs will help readers interact with this article much more easily. Looking at these numerous examples, one can now say, without any doubt, that the page has found its new avatars in the digital culture.

*Wikipedia: A Special Case*

Then again, maybe I am being too optimistic. Today, in a sense, the true spirit that inspired the *Polyanthea* is probably best represented by Wikipedia, whose strengths go much further than print encyclopedias thanks to hyperlinks and extensive categorization. Wikipedia's layout, however, did not evolve as other platforms did. One of the reasons may be that it was born in 2001, when engineers were still in exclusive command of Web look and feel. And for a programmer, the building block of text is not the page but the line of code: the wider the window, the easier it is to revise a program and look for a bug. If we compare a Wikipedia page from November 2002 (Figure 13) to one from May 2006 (Figure 14), we can see that there has been some improvement in the readability thanks to the introduction of pictures and subdivisions, as well as a table of contents. But, since then, the design hasn't changed much, except for the introduction of an Infobox.

A newcomer arriving on Wikipedia in 2016 may be struck by the fact that the text still occupies the full length of the window, except for the left margin. This radical departure from the page format adopted by most media today tends to confirm the status of Wikipedia as a work in progress.

One could say that with a long line, the eye is able to scan rapidly through an article, and this is typically what one does with an encyclopedia: we rarely read an article from beginning to end, but rather scan it in order to find specific information. This is also a kind of self-fulfilling prophecy, however, since the layout discourages the user from reading the article, and tends to foster superficial browsing rather than close reading. This is hardly ideal for an enterprise fostering the rise of knowledge.

**Figure 13. Wikipedia, November 30, 2002 (Wayback Machine).**

**Figure 14. Wikipedia, May 17, 2006 (Wayback Machine).**

In order to help readers, Wikipedia does offer the possibility of creating a kind of book with one or various articles by clicking on the link "Create a book" in the left margin. The choices of layout offered are very limited, however: you can choose between the paper size "letter" or its European equivalent. The letter format is fine for printing, but who still prints articles today? Wikisource offers a wider choice of layouts and allows you to download a book in various formats, such as PDF, EPUB, and MOBI.

**Figure 15. Wikipedia article displayed on a laptop with a mobile URL.**

On tablets and mobile applications, Wikipedia articles are designed in a limited-width format. If you use the mobile URL on a laptop, you will access articles in a limited-width format also, as one can see with the article on William Blake (Figure 15). Wikipedia has also developed a skin (called Minerva) that could be applied to existing pages and would reformat all the articles in this new layout.[1]

The smartphone today is the platform of choice for more and more people. As we can see on a page from *Middlemarch* by George Eliot (1819–1880), the column of text displayed on an iPhone Plus counts about forty characters (Figure 16), but the user could choose to make the characters bigger or smaller. The author of this long novel certainly could not have anticipated that her work would one day be read on mobile devices in the most unexpected situations, since many readers today turn to their phone to fill any period of waiting. Thanks to mobile reading, one can say that the page has found a new digital avatar.

### After the Page, the Book

Even if the page, as a fixed-width space designed for reading, is now commonly accepted in its virtual reincarnation, there are still some protocols to

---

[1]  See https://www.mediawiki.org/wiki/Skin:Minerva_Neue.

implement before one can say that the book has been rescued from a widely anticipated death. As noted by Peter Brantley, in order for books to be fully replicated in the digital world, we must address the problems posed by annotation management, ensure perfect compatibility between the dedicated environment of the e-book reader and the Web thanks to HTML5, and, most of all, ensure that the new protocol can "reproduce a core definitional aspect of the traditional book: its self-containment." Both the W3C and the International Digital Publishing Forum (IDPF) are working closely toward that objective. With a new e-book standard, EPUB 3.2, currently in development, "books, magazines, and pamphlets—online or off—will be the peers of any document on the web" (Brantley 2016).

Middlemarch

**Chapter 1**

Since I can do no good
because a woman,
Reach constantly at some-
thing that is near it.

*The Maid's
Tragedy:* BEAU-
MONT AND
FLETCHER.

Miss Brooke had that kind of beauty which
seems to be thrown into relief by poor
dress. Her hand and wrist were so finely
formed that she could wear sleeves not less
bare of style than those in which the
Blessed Virgin appeared to Italian painters;
and her profile as well as her stature and
bearing seemed to gain the more dignity
from her plain garments, which by the side
of provincial fashion gave her the impres-
siveness of a fine quotation from the Bible,
- or from one of our elder poets, - in a paragraph of to-day's newspaper. She was usually spoken of as being remarkably clever,
but with the addition that her sister Celia

10 sur 1712

**Figure 16. A page from *Middlemarch* on a smartphone.**

A medium that has been in use for two thousand years and has produced so many illuminating landmarks for the human mind will continue to be alive in our culture, adapted to convey new inquiries into human nature and to shape the minds of future generations.

WORKS CITED

Aarsth, Espen. 1997. *Cybertext: Perspectives on Ergodic Literature.* Baltimore and London: Johns Hopkins University Press.

Baudin, Fernand. 1994. *L'Effet Gutenberg.* Paris: Éditions du Cercle de la librairie.

Blair, Ann M. 2010. *Too Much to Know: Managing Scholarly Information before the Modern Age.* New Haven, CT, and London: Yale University Press.

Brantley, Peter. 2016. "Books, in a browser." *Medium,* May 14. https://medium.com/@naypinya/books-in-a-browser-375df76207ce#.qkd9tbisy.

Bringhurst, Robert. 2008. *The Elements of Typographic Style.* Vancouver: Hartley and Marks.

Demarcq, Jacques. 1999. "L'espace de la page, entre vide et plein." In *L'Aventure des écritures: La page,* edited by Anne Zali, 65–103. Paris: Bibliothèque nationale de France.

Gleick, James. 2011. *The Information: A History, a Theory, a Flood.* New York: Random House.

Harris, Roy. 1994. *La sémiologie de l'écriture.* Paris: CNRS.

Illich, Ivan. 1993. *In the Vineyard of the Text. A Commentary to Hugh's* Didascalicon. Chicago: University of Chicago Press.

Johnson, William A. 2004. *Bookrolls and Scribes in Oxyrhynchus.* Toronto: University of Toronto Press.

Landow, George P. 1992. *Hypertext: The Convergence of Contemporary Critical Theory and Technology.* Baltimore and London: Johns Hopkins University Press.

Laufer, Roger. 1982. "L'espace visuel du livre ancien." In *Histoire de l'édition française,* edited by Henri-Jean Martin, Roger Chartier, and Jean-Pierre Vivet, vol. 1, 579–601. Paris: Promodis.

Mak, Bonnie. 2011. *How the Page Matters.* Toronto: University of Toronto Press.

Moulthrop, Stuart. 2017. "Intimate Mechanics: One Model of Electronic Literature." *Hyperrhiz: New Media Cultures* 17. https://doi:10.20415/hyp/017.e03.

Ong, Walter. 1982. *Orality and Literacy: The Technologizing of the Word.* New York: Routledge.

Parkes, Malcolm Beckwith. 1976. "The Influence of the Concepts of *Ordinatio* and *Compilatio* on the Development of the Book." In *Medieval Learning and Literature: Essays Presented to Richard William Hunt*, edited by J.J.G. Alexander and M.T. Gibson, 115–41. Oxford: Clarendon Press.

Vandendorpe, Christian. 2009. *From Papyrus to Hypertext: Toward the Universal Digital Library.* Translated by Phyllis Aronoff and Howard Scott. Urbana and Chicago: University of Illinois Press.

Zali, Anne, ed. 1999. *L'Aventure des écritures: La page.* Paris: Bibliothèque nationale de France.

# Digital Radio and Social Knowledge Creation in the Humanities

John F. Barber

Washington State University Vancouver

*Introduction*

During the Social Knowledge Creation in the Humanities conference, held in association with the 2015 Digital Humanities Summer Institute, social networks were explored as sites for knowledge creation and sharing while social media and open source online communities/networks were positioned as increasingly valuable models for collaboratively creating shared bodies of knowledge. Conference participants were asked to consider these questions: How might we conceptualize social knowledge creation and communication? What existing tools and platforms might stimulate knowledge creation across communities? In the digital turn, what practices might we undertake for collaborative creation, communication, and consumption of social knowledge in the humanities?

With such a focus, a good starting point might be to ask how social knowledge is created and shared. In *A Social History of Knowledge*, historian Peter Burke argues that knowledge is created by institutions and groups of people, rather than individuals. As a result, there is always a plurality to knowledge, different forms that develop concurrently and intersect and play with one another. Furthermore, he says, the social production of knowledge is always connected to the economic and political environments in which it develops (Burke 2012, 2000).

Burke argues the history of social knowledge creation is long and characterized by the involvement of various agents and elements and a focus on intellectuals. These ideas are explored by others. Terry Eagleton (2010), for example, says that literature has a historical role in social development and nation-building in England and elsewhere. Nancy Fjällbrant (1997) details the history of the scientific journal as developing from a desire by researchers to share their findings with others in a cooperative forum. Along with journals, university presses have been considered primary forms of knowledge dissemination and sharing (Jagodzinski 2008). Adrian Johns (1998) explores the history of printing, especially the social apparatus and construction of

ISBN 978-1-64959-008-4 (paper) ISBN 978-1-64959-009-1 (pdf) ISBN 978-1-64959-084-8 (epub)

*New Technologies in Medieval and Renaissance Studies* 8 (2022) 43–55

print and how it has been used socially. Rather than a single culture, evolving from a deterministic cause-and-effect relationship with any historical factor or cause, Johns says that multiple print cultures have evolved, each local in character. Thomas Streeter (2011) examines how various historical and cultural contexts have contributed to the Internet as a socially constructed complex of multiple networks (technological, economic, and political) that foster openness concurrently with connectivity. Finally, Lisa Gitelman (2006) notes the absence of a singular, ubiquitous media. Instead, she says, media are plural, social communication structures that evolve with surrounding publics.[1]

This essay explores how one medium, digital radio, might facilitate social knowledge creation. In pursuing this idea, I will first outline the potential of radio, based in sound, to connect peoples separated by time and distance and provide a context for information creation and communication. This potential has been largely unfulfilled because, throughout its history, traditional (analog) radio has functioned as a one-to-many broadcast medium. But, with its content, transmission, and reception digitized, radio can become a two-way communication medium in which creators and consumers are seen as "interactors" (Saiz 2011) meeting in online social radio contexts, creating new knowledge through their discussions of "social objects" (Dubber 2013, 111–12).

In conclusion, I posit social, digital radio networks as both context and practice for collaborative creation, communication, and consumption of social knowledge in the humanities.

## The Potential of Radio

Susan Merrill Squier's edited collection, *Communities of the Air: Radio Century, Radio Culture* (2003), explores ways in which radio, as both a technological and a social practice, was constructed by, and in turn helped to shape, twentieth-century Anglo-American society and culture.

---

[1] Alyssa Arbuckle, Nina Belojevic, Matthew Hiebert, and Ray Siemens, working with Shaun Wong, Derek Siemens, Alex Christie, Jon Saklofske, Jentery Sayers, and the INKE and ETCL Research Groups, have prepared three annotated bibliographies focusing on social knowledge creation. The first focuses on social knowledge creation and conveyance; the second, on game design models for digital social knowledge creation, and the third, on social knowledge creation tools. See Arbuckle et al. 2014.

The essays in this collection provide introduction to Andrew Dubber's discussion of radio as a collection of different, but related, phenomena. Radio is an institution, he says; an organizational structure; a category of media content with its own characteristics, conventions, and tropes; a series of professional practices and relationships; and more. As a result, radio work, content, technologies, or cultures should not be considered as single subjects or processes, but rather as part of an ecology, especially within the digital media environment in which radio is increasingly situated (Dubber 2015).

At radio's heart, following Marshall McLuhan, we expect to find sound, specifically the sound(s) of speech. McLuhan argues that each new medium subsumes as its content the older medium it replaces. For example, "the content of writing is speech, just as the written word is the content of print, and print is the content of the telegraph" (McLuhan 1964, 23–24). The content of speech, says McLuhan is the nonverbal process of thought.

The sound of speech, for McLuhan, is primary. Speech, with its origins in abstract thought and orality, is the oldest medium, and the most prevalent form of human communication. Subsumed by writing, printing, and other media, including radio, speech claims a presence in almost all media (Levinson 1999). As James O'Donnell notes, "the manuscript was first conceived to be no more than a prompt-script for the spoken word, a place to look to find out what to say ... to produce the audible word" (O'Donnell 1998, 54).

McLuhan argues that every medium can be asked a "tetrad"—four questions/laws—regarding its impact. One question deals with amplification: "What aspect of society or human life does the medium enhance or qualify in the culture?" Another asks, regarding retrieval, "What does the medium remove from the past, from the realm of the previously obsolesced and put back center stage?" Following McLuhan's tetrad, radio amplifies/enhances oral communication across distance and retrieves some of the pre-literate [pre-writing] prominence of orality (McLuhan 1975, 1977; McLuhan and McLuhan 1988; McLuhan and Powers 1989, 9).

For McLuhan, radio resonates as a tribal drum, its magic weaving a web of kinship and prompting involvement (McLuhan 1964, 259, 260). Radio affords tremendous power as "a subliminal echo chamber" in which to evoke memories/associations long forgotten or ignored (McLuhan 1964, 264). As a "fast hot medium," radio provides accelerated information throughput, thus contracting the world to village size (McLuhan 1964, 265). In this global village, people once again live in oral contexts (McLuhan 1962, 31). Issues and peoples are no longer separate or unrelated. Instead, people depend on talking with one another to create and communicate community knowledge (McLuhan 1964, 20, McLuhan and Fiore 1967, 63).

The potential of radio, with speech as its content, therefore comes from its ability to promote connection(s) and conversations between peoples separated by time and distance. Radio, says McLuhan, offers a "world of unspoken communication between writer-speaker and the listener" (McLuhan 1964, 261).

## The Problem with Radio

The potential of radio, then, seems quite powerful. But, in 1932, just three decades after the introduction of radio as the first new medium of the twentieth century, artist, composer, and playwright Bertolt Brecht observed that radio "is one-sided when it should be two." A radio station, said Brecht, broadcasts its content to many listeners simultaneously, but provides no opportunity for listeners to respond. Despite this problem, Brecht contended that radio could be "the finest possible communication apparatus in public life" if only it "knew how to receive as well as transmit, how to let the listener speak as well as hear, how to bring him into a relationship instead of isolating him. On this principle the radio should step out of the supply business and organize its listeners as suppliers" (Brecht 1964, 51).

## Responses to the Problem

Brecht imagined radio as an apparatus for collaboration, communication, and creation, used daily by people to connect with one another, share thoughts, and create knowledge. As to how to achieve this vision, he provided no details. We can, however, imagine responses to Brecht's challenge. For example, George Gilder, predicting future television, says that technological advances will allow individuals using inexpensive and prolific equipment to produce and broadcast a diversity of rich and engaging television programming via their own channels. The linear model of television programming, one program following another at specific times, produced and broadcast by a few corporations, will be replaced, as will programming targeted to the lowest common denominator. Since anyone can broadcast, the audience becomes actively involved in both the creation and consumption of content (Gilder 1992, 40–41).

YouTube (www.youtube.com) may be the first example of Gilder's prediction. Launched in February 2005, this video-sharing website allows anyone to upload, view, and share video content created with their own equipment.

Registered users can maintain exclusive content channels. Anyone can create, upload, and share a video response to user-generated content.

## *"Stations of Distribution" and "Protagonists of Information"*

How does this apply to radio? Gilder's predictions about television and YouTube's modeling of a social, video distribution platform can be found in streaming, on-demand, social audio networks like AudioBoom, SoundCloud, and MixCloud. All offer global opportunities for active engagement with the production and consumption of user-generated audio content. Following from these models, the widespread availability of digital audio recording, editing, and sharing technologies could move radio away from fixed, one-to-many broadcast models to what Johns calls "stations of distribution," systems in which audio is created and shared by anyone. Simply put, every mobile device loaded with audio production and sharing software could become a radio station (Johns 2010, 261).

Participants in this scenario, according to Carmen Peñafiel Saiz, become "interactors," or "protagonists of information," tuning in their favourite music, news, information, advice, and political views from trusted (non-corporate) broadcasts, channels, or other sources. They create and share rich responses, re-mixed and personalized audio pastiches cross-pollinated from divergent user-generated content sources. Interactors, says Saiz, become parallel broadcasters, with the opportunity to contribute as much or more to the digital radio programming spectrum as a commercial station (Saiz 2011, 67).

## *Radio as a Social Network*

Interactors, as both collaborative creators and consumers, are able to interrupt, influence, and/or customize the program stream, all while conversing with each other (Burnett and Marshall, 2003). As a result, "composer, performer, and audience converge in the playing subject [users]" (Stockburger 2009, 122). This collapse of distinction suggests a less hierarchical and more decentralized model of media production, where interactors enjoy increased ability to "answer back" by producing their own media (Poster 1995, 33). Interactors—or, as Sherry Turkle calls them, "players"—enjoy unprecedented participation in the process of creating and consuming content. Writing about Multi-User Domains (MUDs), Turkle remarks that "as players participate, they become authors not only of text but of themselves, constructing new selves through social interaction" (Turkle 1997, 12).

The ramifications, however, can be mixed, according to Janet Murray. "Giving the audience access to the raw materials of creation runs the risk of undermining the narrative experience," she says. "Nevertheless, calling attention to the process of creation in this way can also enhance narrative involvement by inviting readers/viewers to imagine themselves in the place of the creator" (Murray 1997, 40).

Murray goes on to say that this kind of narrative experience "involves the sustained collaborative writing of stories that are mixtures of the narrated and the dramatized and that are not meant to be watched or listened to but shared by the players as an alternate reality they all live in together" (Murray 1997, 44).

Given this ability to create and consume content, digital radio may promote many-to-many full access sharing of rich and diverse aural content between participants in social audio networks characterized by interaction and collaboration. Rather than corporations, digital radio will be in the hands of individuals, or communities, interactors who will place value on selection, relevance, trust, and sense-making. Combined with on-demand functionalities for content manipulation, digital radio suggests potential for promoting two-way social knowledge creation.

*Social Networks*

Social knowledge creation may be focused in social networks, defined by danah m. boyd and Nicole B. Ellison as structured relationships, composed of individuals tied by one or more types of interdependency: friendship, common interests, beliefs, and/or knowledge (boyd and Ellison 2007). Example social networks include Facebook, Twitter, Instagram, and LinkedIn. All are communities of like-minded people. Each promotes collaboration, communication, and creation among their members, all generally focused on shared content. As Brecht lamented, the one-to-many broadcast model of traditional radio does not promote the listener's ability to contribute content. What Brecht imagined for radio, a site for social collaboration, communication, and creativity, may be provided by digital radio, which seems well situated to encourage collaborative social networks in which members will, according to Jesse Walker, "withdraw from the thick smoke of mediation and interact more directly, more convivially, with others" (Walker 2001, 11).

*Talking about "Social Objects"*

Historically, radio is a culture and a medium based on sound(s) consciously collected (curated) and broadcast as related knowledge modalities (programs) for the purpose of interpreting and distributing information to a broad public. No provision is made for listeners to participate in, contribute to, or create the program stream. With its affordances and features, digital radio might promote the ability of people to engage in conversation about shared content in social networks.

How might this work? Well, as Cory Doctorow observes, conversation is the mainstay of social networks. "Conversation is king," he says. "Content is just something to talk about" (Doctorow 2006, n.p.). Knowledge, according to David Weinberger, emerges for public and social thought/conversations. In the process, authority is transferred from central sources (editors, content providers, broadcasting corporations, etc.) to individuals. But this process, as Weinberger notes, has already moved beyond individuals: "Knowledge— its content and its organization—is becoming a social act" (Weinberger 2007, 133). Authority comes from enabling the group to explore differences and diverse viewpoints "to get past the biases of individuals" (146). Social knowing changes the *who* and *how* of knowing, more than the *what* of knowledge (144). Knowledge exists in the gaps, in the connections, between the contributors and their individual standpoints and passions in lively, public conversations in online social networks. Getting to the knowledge requires active engagement, "because social knowing, like the global conversations that give rise to it, is never finished" (147).

For Weinberger, in talking about something we are making it explicit, imbued with socially agreed-upon knowledge. Clay Shirky agrees, noting that social knowledge creation is an outcome of online collaboration and conversation (Shirky 2008). To briefly describe this process, participants in social audio networks upload and share their audio content. Listeners respond to what they hear with interpretations, connections, suggestions. The original creators, in turn, respond with their visions and explanations for chosen practices. The back and forth conversation produces knowledge. The remixed sound artefacts, the subject of this collaborative knowledge making, become "social objects" (Dubber 2013, 111–12).

For Jyri Engeström (2005) and Hugh MacLeod (2007), social objects are focal points around which conversations occur. Social objects are shared to promote conversation. Social objects may not shape or relate to what conversation does evolve, but they are the reason or meaning for the conversation. The importance of any social object lies not with itself, but rather the conversations that it promotes. These conversations create a shared knowledge base regarding the social object. The conversations, not the social object, represent visions of human situation and agency.

Regarding knowledge making, Yrjö Engeström (2000) says that object-oriented activities (conversations about social objects) are also social activities based on the ways by which learning and knowledge are generated and shared, what meanings are derived in relation to the object and the actors, and whatever norms/regulations apply to the context.

Conversations about social objects need not be *about* those objects, nor do conversations have to follow a particular agenda intended or imposed by the creators of the social objects. Content creators share content that is remixable and sharable, content that derives value from the number of ways it can be incorporated in different discussions. As a result, ideas and discussions are driven by the use of social objects constructed from raw materials, such as audio files (Dubber 2013, 17).

*Putting It All Together*

Both Dubber and Squier imply social collaboration as affecting the cultural object we call radio, as well as its impact. Responses to Brecht's challenge regarding the potential of radio, imply individuals creating and sharing ideas and knowledge. This social knowledge creation is facilitated through speech, the content of radio, according to Paul Levinson (1981) and Marshall McLuhan (McLuhan 1964, 23–24).

Current mobile devices converge and combine multiple technologies, offering multiple features and affordances. One result is that computing devices, like mobile telephones/wireless tablets, become individual "stations of distribution" with which digital content can be created and shared by anyone (Johns 2010, 261) using inexpensive and prolific equipment (Gilder 1992). Protagonists of information or interactors (Saiz 2011), provide personalized content (Burnett and Marshall 2003) beyond the parameters of traditional media. This content can be shared, discussed, and/or remixed in social networks, communities of like-minded peoples able to communicate with each other (boyd and Ellison 2007). Everyone is involved in the act of listening (Bull and Back 2003), immersed as we are in "a world of sound" (Smith 2003, 127) in which sound provides "a modality of knowing and being in the world" (Feld 2003, 226). Sound prompts us to rethink how we relate to others, ourselves, and the spaces and places we inhabit (Bull and Back 2003, 3–4).

Fragmentation of programming (Gilder 1992), including humanities topics (Dubber 2013), results. Interactors could create and share a variety of inquiries into a variety of subjects, architecture, art, literature, music, theatre, for example. Digital radio broadcast streams that are and remain relevant survive and succeed (Shirky 2008; Doctorow 2006). Interactors enjoy unprecedented participation in the process of creating and consuming content (Turkle 1997). This enhances narrative involvement by positioning interactors as creators (Murray 1997). Knowledge creation becomes a social act, fostered by global discussion and conversations moving beyond individual bases (Weinberger 2007, 133–47).

As on-demand streaming and downloading become standard features of the Internet, digital radio interactors focus on collecting, collating, contextualizing, curating, and connecting the best possible social knowledge creation experiences (Saiz 2011). These experiences are valued for their selection, relevance, trust, context, and sense-making. The result: narratives that present shared realities for interactors (Murray 1997).

Models for social knowledge creation are provided by YouTube, Audioboo, SoundCloud, and MixCloud. These examples suggest that radio, as a medium with speech as its content (McLuhan 1964), and as an ecology of related but different phenomena (Dubber 2013), with its content, production, transmission, and reception digitized, becomes an extended oral context for social knowledge creation, a "global village" (McLuhan and Powers 1989), an "answer back" social network (Poster 1995).

## Conclusion and Future Directions

In this essay, I argue that digital radio promotes social knowledge creation in the humanities through two-way collaborative conversations based in social audio networks. In such networks, narrative, as a prevalent form of information, entertainment, and communication, is foregrounded. Adaptive and personal narrative, narrative as a method of knowledge capture, narrative as a lens for identity, narrative as a form of interaction, and/or narrative as a transdisciplinary or transmedia endeavor all invite further exploration.

Furthermore, digital radio, digital sound(s), and digital information have no fixed material form, so we must rethink how to create and share information beyond traditional constraints and familiar assumptions, and how to organize it without limiting categories. As individuals of the digital turn, we no longer just find information. Rather, collaboratively, we can make it find us. I have suggested prototypes for collaborative, social contexts in which information may find us, as humanistic interactors involved in discussions of human nature and the human condition. I have described these contexts as engendered by digital radio and as promoting the social creation of new knowledge. How to create and sustain these contexts of social knowledge creation in the humanities encourages further discussions. The results suggested, as provided by digital radio, may be surprising and rewarding—and certainly worth investigating.

WORKS CITED

Arbuckle, Alyssa, Nina Belojevic, Matthew Hiebert, and Ray Siemens, with Shaun Wong, Derek Siemens, Alex Christie, Jon Saklofske, Jentery Sayers, and the INKE and ETCL Research Groups. 2014. "Social Knowledge Creation: Three Annotated Bibliographies." *Scholarly and Research Communication* 5(2). https://src-online.ca/index.php/src/article/view/150.

boyd, danah m., and Nicole B. Ellison. 2007. "Social Network Sites: Definition, History, and Scholarship." *Journal of Computer-Mediated Communication* 13(1): 210–30. https://academic.oup.com/jcmc/article/13/1/210/4583062.

Brecht, Bertolt. 1964. "The Radio as an Apparatus of Communication." In *Brecht on Theatre: The Development of an Aesthetic*, translated and edited by John Willett, 51–53. New York: Hill and Wang. http://telematic.walkerart.org/telereal/bit_brecht.html. [First published as "Der Rundfunk als Kommunikationsapparat" in *Blätter des Hessischen Landestheaters Darmstadt* 16 (July 1932).]

Bull, Michael, and Les Back, eds. 2003. *The Auditory Culture Reader*. Oxford and New York: Berg.

Burke, Peter. 2000. *A Social History of Knowledge: From Gutenberg to Diderot*. Cambridge: Polity Press.

———. 2012. *A Social History of Knowledge II: From the Encyclopédie to Wikipedia*. Cambridge: Polity Press.

Burnett, Robert, and P. David Marshall. 2003. *Web Theory: An Introduction*. London and New York: Routledge.

Doctorow, Cory. 2006. "Disney Exec: Piracy Is Just a Business Model." *BoingBoing,* October 10. http://www.boingboing.net/2006/10/10/disney-exec-piracy-i-html.

Dubber, Andrew. Radio in The Digital Age: A book (and some associated observations). http://radiointhedigitalage.com/book/.

Dubber, Andrew. 2013. *Radio in the Digital Age.* Cambridge: Polity Books.

Eagleton, Terry. 2010. "The Rise of English." In *The Norton Anthology of Theory and Criticism,* edited by Vincent B. Leitch, 2140–46. New York: W.W. Norton.

Engeström, Jyri. 2005. "Why Some Social Network Services Work and Others Don't—Or: The Case for Object-Centered Sociality." *Zengestrom,* April 13. http://www.zengestrom.com/blog/2005/04/why-some-social-network-services-work-and-others-dont-or-the-case-for-object-centered-sociality.html.

Engeström, Yrjö. 2000. "Activity Theory as a Framework for Analyzing and Redesigning Work." *Ergonomics* 43(7): 960–74.

Feld, Steven. 2003. "A Rainforest Acoustemology." In *The Auditory Culture Reader,* edited by Michael Bull and Les Back, 223–39. Oxford and New York: Berg.

Fjällbrant, Nancy. 1997. "Scholarly Communication—Historical Development and New Possibilities." In *Proceedings of the IATUL Conferences,* Paper 5. Lafayette, IN: Purdue University Library.

Gilder, George. 1992. *Life after Television.* New York: W.W. Norton.

Gitelman, Lisa. 2006. *Always Already New: Media, History, and the Data of Culture.* Cambridge, MA: MIT Press.

Jagodzinski, Cecile M. 2008. "The University Press in North America: A Brief History." *Journal of Scholarly Publishing* 40(1): 1–20.

Johns, Adrian. 1998. *The Nature of the Book: Print and Knowledge in the Making.* Chicago: University of Chicago Press.

———. 2010. *Death of a Pirate: British Radio and the Making of the Information Age.* New York: W.W. Norton.

Levinson, Paul. 1981. "Media Evolution and the Primacy of Speech." Paper presented at the Annual Meeting of the Speech Communication Association (Anaheim, CA, November 12–15, 1981). https://eric.ed.gov/?id=ED235510.

———. 1999. *Digital McLuhan: A Guide to the Information Millennium.* New York: Routledge.

MacLeod, Hugh. 2007. "More Thoughts on Social Objects." *GapingVoid*, October 24. http://www.gapingvoid.com/Moveable_Type/archives/004265.html.

McLuhan, Marshall. 1962. *The Gutenberg Galaxy: The Making of Typographic Man.* Toronto: University of Toronto Press.

———. 1964. *Understanding Media: The Extensions of Man.* New York: McGraw-Hill.

———. 1975. "McLuhan's Laws of the Media." *Technology and Culture* 16(1): 74–78.

———. 1977. "Laws of the Media." *Et cetera* 34(2): 173–79.

McLuhan, Marshall, and Quentin Fiore, with Jerome Agel. 1967. *The Medium is the Massage: An Inventory of Effects.* New York: Bantam Books.

McLuhan, Marshall, and Eric McLuhan. 1988. *Laws of Media: The New Science.* Toronto: University of Toronto Press.

McLuhan, Marshall, and Bruce R. Powers. 1989. *The Global Village: Transformations in World Life and Media in the 21st Century.* New York: Oxford University Press.

Murray, Janet H. 1997. *Hamlet on the Holodeck: The Future of Narrative in Cyberspace.* New York: Free Press.

O'Donnell, James J. 1998. *Avatars of the Word: From Papyrus to Cyberspace.* Cambridge, MA: Harvard University Press.

Poster, Mark. 1995. *The Second Media Age.* Cambridge: Polity.

Saiz, Carmen Peñafiel. 2011. "Radio and Web 2.0: Direct Feedback." In *Radio Content in the Digital Age: The Evolution of a Sound Medium*, edited by Angeliki Gazi, Guy Starkey, and Stanislaw Jedrzejewski, 61–70. Bristol and Chicago: Intellect.

Shirky, Clay. 2008. *Here Comes Everybody: The Power of Organizing without Organizations.* New York: Penguin Press.

Smith, Bruce R. 2003. "Tuning into London c. 1600." In *The Auditory Culture Reader,* edited by Michael Bull and Les Back, 127–35. Oxford and New York: Berg.

Squier, Susan Merrill, ed. 2003. *Communities of the Air: Radio Century, Radio Culture.* Durham, NC: Duke University Press.

Stockburger, Axel. 2009. "An Audience of One: Sound Games as a Specific Form of Visual Music." In *Audio.Visual: On Visual Music and Related Media,* edited by Cornelia Lund and Holger Lund, 116–24. Stuttgart: Arnoldsche Art Publishers.

Streeter, Thomas. 2011. "Introduction." In *The Net Effect: Romanticism, Capitalism, and the Internet,* 1–17. New York: New York University Press.

Turkle, Sherry. 1997. *Life on the Screen: Identity in the Age of the Internet.* New York: Touchstone.

Walker, Jesse. 2001. *Rebels on the Air: An Alternative History of Radio in America.* New York: New York University Press.

Weinberger, David. 2007. *Everything is Miscellaneous: The Power of the New Digital Disorder.* New York: Henry Holt and Co.

# Collocating Places and Words with TopoText

## Randa El Khatib
### University of Toronto Scarborough

## Introduction

The software prototype presented in this article—TopoText[1]—is an attempt at translating an interdisciplinary spatial methodology, geocriticism, into concrete digital functionalities through critical interpretation processes. By transmediating[2] spatial content expressed in textual form into GIS-based visualizations in the form of digital maps, the digital artifact functions as a prism through which the text can be deformed in order to give rise to novel interpretations.[3] At the same time, a second transmediation occurs by translating literary cartographies created by authors into visual literary geographies created by readers through a combination of text analysis, natural language processing, and digital mapping. Within the framework of prototyping as theory, the findings of TopoText are meant to carry out geocriticism's central aim: to facilitate a deeper engagement with the spatiality of a text through a placial focus.[4] This article details the prototyping process of TopoText, provides examples of how it can be applied to the study of literary space, and reports on how some functionalities were enhanced in the second version—TopoText 2.0.

## Geocriticism

Geocriticism—a term first coined by Bertrand Westphal (2011)—is an interdisciplinary approach to the study of literature that includes a spatial or geographical dimension. A geocritical approach adopts a multifocal and

---

[1] The collaboration on TopoText (https://github.com/rkhatib/topotext) was initiated at the American University of Beirut (AUB) by David Wrisley (English Department), Wassim El-Hajj, and Shady Elbassuoni (Computer Science Department). The prototype was designed by Randa El Khatib and coded by Julia El Zini, with Bilal Abi Farraj, Houda Nasser, Shadia Barada, and Yasmin Kadah in Mohammad Jaber's Software Engineering class.

[2] The process of shifting from one medium to another. On transmediation, see Eide 2015, 146.

[3] On deformance, see Samuels and McGann 1999.

[4] See Hardy 2000, 85.

ISBN 978-1-64959-008-4 (paper) ISBN 978-1-64959-009-1 (pdf) ISBN 978-1-64959-084-8 (epub)
*New Technologies in Medieval and Renaissance Studies* 8 (2022) 57–71

geocentred perspective to explore the significance of a place, whether real or fictional (Westphal 2011, 114). That place can therefore be viewed from more than one dimension or perspective, or as represented in a variety of genres such as travel brochures, historical texts, newspapers, or literary works. Geocriticism combines numerous subjective representations of a central placial focus in order to gain a richer historical or literary comprehension of the place in question. By doing so, the methodology encourages a geocentric focus on the place of scholarly inquiry rather than a more traditional ego-centric approach that prioritizes the subject (the person or character) in the text (Westphal 2011, 111).

Elaborating on the conceptual difference between space and place is Yi-Fu Tuan, who argues that place not only signifies a unit of location within the larger frame of space, but also "a reality to be clarified and understood from the perspectives of the people who have given it meaning" (Tuan 1979, 387). By extending the focus beyond the name of the place to the different meanings given to it through textual narratives, the digital geocritical methodology outlined in this paper accommodates both placial and spatial explorations.

TopoText draws inspiration from Westphal, who argues that a multifocal approach would require working with many texts simultaneously—meaning that a branch of geocritical research would necessarily be both digital and collaborative. Building on this notion, TopoText explores the broader concept of geocriticism through a collaborative prototyping process, and embodies concrete elements of the methodology in its functionalities. Engaging with georiticism is also Robert Tally, who argues that there are two kinds of spatialities in a literary work—literary cartography and literary geography. He explains literary cartography by drawing a parallel between the act of writing and the act of mapping: "Like the mapmaker, the writer must survey territory, determining which features of a given landscape to include, to emphasize, or to diminish" (Tally 2012, 45). From this perspective, writers act as mapmakers in creating a fictional world of their choosing, selecting what elements of that world they want to represent in their writing. Literary geography is what is at play at the receiving end of the spectrum. It refers to the reader who focuses on the spatiality of a text by being conscious of how spatial configurations change over time and how this affects literature, keeping in mind that space is a formation of history, "and the history of spatial formation often overlaps with the history of narrative forms" (Tally 2012, 80). While literary geography offers a way to explore texts from a spatial perspective, digital mapping probes the forms it can take and offers a visual entry point through a cartographic medium.

## Theoretical Framework

The concept of prototyping employed in this article conceives of a digital prototype as a theory and of prototyping as a thought experiment to advance our understanding of a scholarly topic. Stephen Ramsay and Geoffrey Rockwell explain "theory" from a humanities perspective as that which "promises deeper understanding of something already given, like historical events of a literary work. To say that software is a theory is to say that digital works convey knowledge the way a theory does, in this more general sense" (Ramsay and Rockwell 2012, 77). The authors draw a parallel between the process of prototyping and the act of writing, arguing that the decisive feature classifying scholarship as such is whether the work proves to be a worthwhile or insightful intervention in the field rather than the particular medium in which it is presented, which has traditionally been expressed in textual form. A similar perspective on prototyping in the digital humanities is proposed by Alan Galey and Stan Ruecker, who lay the foundation for a more formal acknowledgement of prototypes as original contributions to knowledge in themselves. They propose various criteria by which to peer review a prototype, singling out that, like effective academic writing, it ought to be "contestable, defensible, and substantive," and elaborate on how each of these applies within a prototyping framework (Galey and Ruecker 2010, 412).[5] The process of designing a digital artifact, according to the authors, could simultaneously be used for critical interpretation.

Digital prototypes can, more generally, offer novel frameworks for interpreting works. A second way of conceiving of digital artifacts as theories, according to Ramsay and Rockwell, is by approaching them as "hermeneutical instruments through which we can interpret other phenomena. Digital artifacts, like tools, could then be considered as 'telescopes for the mind' that show us something in a new light" (Ramsay and Rockwell 2012, 79). Drawing on Christian Bök's interpretation of Alfred Jarry's concept of pataphysics, Ramsey describes pataphysics as "the apotheosis of perspectivism—a mode, not of inquiry, but of *being*, which refuses to see the relativity of perspective as a barrier to knowledge" (Ramsay 2011, 21). He continues building on Bök's work, specifically Bök's interpretation of Paul Feyerabend's anarchic science—"that, however obsolete or indiscrete any theory might at first

---

[5] Terminology adopted from Booth, Colomb, and Williams 2008, on the components of a good thesis.

appear, every theory has the potential to improve knowledge in some way" (as cited in Bök 2002, 25). This notion rests on the premise of the article: that digital research prototypes can function as thought experiments that advance knowledge, not unlike scholarly writing.

The aforementioned framework also suggests that prototypes can serve as a way of altering the form of a work in order to look at it from different angles, evoking Lisa Samuels and Jerome McGann's notion of deformance (1999).[6] Deformance facilitates a critical interpretive act and can give rise to novel meanings that may have remained unseen in the original form of the text. Switching to a GIS-based interpretation of literary spatiality is an attempt to play on this uncanny representation of literary place in order to create novel forms of knowledge production and interpretation. In literary geography, "the critical reader becomes a kind of geographer who actively interprets the literary map in such a way as to present new, hitherto unforeseen mappings" (Tally 2012, 79). Actually mapping these literary places is its own manifestation of literary geography that reconstructs the literary cartography of the author in an altered, or deformed, manner.

*TopoText*

TopoText was created through collaboration between the English and Computer Science departments at the American University of Beirut (AUB) in an undergraduate Software Engineering course. The collaboration was initiated as a pedagogical experiment in order to facilitate communication between humanities and computer science students, and to provide opportunities for student-led digital humanities tool development that would have immediate practical application in the field. The development of TopoText was carried out by providing several teams of four or five students with identical lists of potential functionalities of a geoparsing and text analysis software prototype. Based on this information and some guidance, each team developed their own version of the prototype, after which the most utile in terms of functionality and research potential was selected for application in a literary context.

The software prototype was built by remixing features of open-source tools. After inputting a text in plain text (.txt) format, TopoText matches all unambiguous place names with geographical coordinates and displays them on a map interface using the Stanford Named Entity Recognition (NER) Tagger.

---

[6] See Travis 2016 for a description of the application of deformance in a mapping context.

Matching is carried out using the Google Maps Platform and placed onto a Google Maps Engine basemap. Coordinated with the map are text analysis and concordance tools that display the context in which the place names occur and allow manipulation of the content for analysis (see Figure 1). Manipulation of text is carried out by collocating place-name occurrences and words that appear around them using Wordle (Feinberg 2014). Users can specify the number of words to collocate around a place name, and can categorize them according to part of speech with the embedded Stanford Part-of-Speech (POS) Tagger, which extracts nouns, verbs, adjectives, or adverbs. These collocations can be localized to the specific passage in which the place name appears, or generated across the entire text by counting the most frequent word collocations around a selected place name.

The target users for this tool are researchers conducting a geospatial analysis of a work and exploring topics that occur around specific place names in or across texts. No technical background is required for using TopoText, nor does it require a steep learning curve; it was purposely designed to provide a quick and easy entry point from which to conduct a spatial analysis that could help guide further spatial investigations. In addition, users can upload any type of plain text in English, French, German, or Spanish; this option facilitates a multifocal approach and makes potential applications of the tool available to different disciplines.

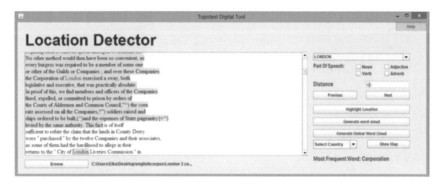

**Figure 1. TopoText 1.0 interface.**

Simply put, the prototype allows users to locate patterns and trends in relation to places and to trace how they evolve over time. Resulting maps provide a more concrete understanding of the spatial scope of the work, which is often far more encompassing than close reading might suggest. For example, Figure 3 is an automatically generated map of William Thackeray's

Vanity Fair that counts hundreds of place-name mentions in the novel, the full span of which is difficult to hold in the mind's eye. Tracing place name occurrences helps facilitate research questions—where specific clusters of place names are found, for example, and what causes interest in that area at a specific time or with a certain author. The scope of the map can be navigated from one of fine granularity (such as a specific neighbourhood) to a province or country, and all the way to an entire world map. By adjusting the scope of the text analysis component, users can dissect the entire text or zone into specific passages. In TopoText, the unit of analysis is the word; computational methods collocate words (either by all the words in a text, words grouped by parts of speech, or most frequent words) in relation to place name occurrences in a text.

A straightforward application of TopoText, by way of example, would be an investigation of Charles Dickens's portrayal of London throughout his writing career, and whether or how his description of the city changed as his career advanced. There are multiple ways to approach this—either by going on a case-by-case basis by running each novel through TopoText, or by comparing his descriptions of London in his early career with those of later works. If a curious word-place collocation appears, the user can switch to the concordance tool in order to do a close reading of a passage to further advance or contradict an argument or observation.

**Figure 2. Word-place collocations surrounding "London" in a selection from Charles Dickens's *Oliver Twist*.**

A text analysis of Dickens's *Oliver Twist* (1838) will illustrate the latter method. In this novel, many collocations reflect the theme of industrialization and population increase, such as *traffic, increased, population, busy, street, bustle, sound, roar, tumult, noise,* and *discordant* (see Figure 2). By tracing the rest of Dickens's novels using this method, it becomes evident that this topic remains a backdrop in most of his urban fiction. Nearly thirty years later, in his final completed work *Our Mutual Friend* (1865), Dickens repeats this topic, evident in multiple word-place collocations related to urbanization. By switching to the concordance tool and going through relevant collocations related to the topic, one quickly finds an episode in which the wealthy Mr. Podsnap and a "meek" stranger argue over the reason for the "destitution and neglect" in London. Mr. Podsnap settles his side of the argument by saying: "You know what the population of London is, I suppose" (168). While the backdrop of urbanization in a 19th-century London-based novel is a straightforward observation, this method can geared towards a more specific research inquiry that is multifocal and geocentered. Let us take another example. According to Pat Hudson (2014), "the acceleration of proletarianisation, urbanization, technological and organizational change in both culture and industry may well have enhanced the formation of classes during the industrial revolution" (202), which became evident in the growing socio-economical split between East and West London. Hudson's idea is further reinforced by Lyn H. Lofland (1985), who argues that the segregation of the classes and strong associations of socioeconomic status with location resulted in people becoming evaluated by where they are encountered rather than by how they look or interact with others. This segregation is often reflected in Victorian urban novels. For example, Arthur Morrison, in the opening paragraph of The Tales of Mean Streets (1894), writes about the East End:

> This street is in the East End. There is no need to say in the East End of what... It is down through Cornhill and out beyond Leadenhall Street and Aldgate Pump, one will say: a shocking place, where he once went with a curate; an evil plexus of slums that hide human creeping things, where filthy men and women live on penn'orths of gin, where collars and clean shirts are decencies unknown, where every citizen wears a black eye, and none ever combs his hair. (1)

Using TopoText, we can trace the most frequent word-place collocations with East End and West End London in a small corpus of Victorian novels to see if word-place collocations generally associated with each hold across works based in London. The novels used in this study are: Ella Hepworth Dixon's The Story of a Modern Woman (1895); Charles Dickens's David Copperfield (1850), Little Dorrit (1857), A Tale of Two Cities (1859), and Great

Expectations (1861); Oscar Wilde's The Picture of Dorian Gray (1891); Robert Louis Stevenson's The Strange Case of Dr. Jekyll and Mr. Hyde (1903); George Gissing's New Grub Street (1891) and Nether World (1903); Marie Corelli's The Soul of Lilith, Vol. 1.(1892), Israel Zangwill's Children of the Ghetto (1895); Vernon Lee's (pseudonym of Violet Paget) Vanitas (1892); Arthur Morrison's Tales of Mean Streets (1895) and To London Town (1899); and Arthur Conan Doyle's The Study in Scarlet (1904) and The Sign of the Four (1904).

First, by running the novels through TopoText, we can identify some of the most popular places associated with each region. In the corpus, these places for the East End are: Whitechapel, Aldgate, Wapping, Mile End, Poplar, Limehouse, Bow, Bromley-by-Bow, Stepney, Shadwel, Cornhill, Leadenhall Street, Tottenham Court Road, and Dean Street. The main places associated with West London in this corpus are: St. Mary Axe, Harbour Lane, Strand, Piccadilly Circus, Oxford Street, Regent Street, Piccadilly, St. James's Park, Old Street, Whitecross Street, Barbican, Long Lane, Smithfield, Bartholomew's Hospital, Thames Embankment, Waterloo Bridge and the Temple Pier. Wordplace collocations for each of these places almost instantly associates the East End with negative connotations, such as crime, dirt, drunkenness, or more extreme forms of intoxication. One would expect that the literary representation of this dichotomy would sharply juxtapose the poverty of the East with the wealth of the West. What the result of the collocations in this corpus point to, however, is that the wealth of the West is more subtly expressed than the poverty of the East, and that themes more closely associated with the East End such as crime and poverty, also appear in West End settings, albeit more rarely than in its counterpart. The main collocations with places in the West End are related to cleanliness, reputation, education, and wandering through the city. These quick results can serve as an entry point into a more robust spatial analysis of Victorian urban fiction.

By using TopoText, researchers can quickly filter through spatial analysis and move between word-place collocations and the concordance tool to identify what works or passages are suitable for closer investigation. This contextualization helps transform points on a map into points of inquiry by providing different narratives and collocations associated with them.

*Geocoding Challenges*

Some noteworthy challenges in the prototyping phase arose mainly from the inherent limitations associated with both automation and close reading. In other words, there was a compromise that had to be made in favour of either speed or accuracy. Automatic geocoding—the process of connecting a location with its corresponding geographical coordinates—bypasses what is considered to be one of the most tedious aspects of digital mapping, or any large data-driven research for that matter: namely, the gathering and assembling of data for accuracy and for readability by digital tools. Automatic parsing methods, however, introduce a set of limitations, especially in terms of accuracy. At present, most automatic geocoding methods do not disambiguate between a place name that corresponds to more than one geographical location and the chosen location itself; the point that actually appears on the map is determined by an invisible ad hoc algorithm that can be incorrect. These types of limitations are often inherent in black box tools.

Figure 3—a visualization of a map of William Thackeray's *Vanity Fair* automatically generated by TopoText—illustrates this difficulty. Although the majority of the matching is accurate, some of the points are misplaced, such as those that appear in Australia and New Zealand but are actually locations in England with the same names. A majority of place names actually refer to more than one location, which makes complete accuracy in automatic matching hard to achieve. Most current geocoding techniques, moreover, do not handle spelling variations well, and can locate and map place names only by their standardized spellings. This limits automatic digital mapping to more contemporary texts or texts with modernized spelling, typically from the nineteenth century onward, with a higher level of accuracy in regions with rich GIS data.

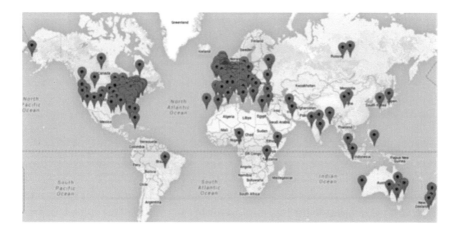

**Figure 3. A world map of William Thackeray's *Vanity Fair* automatically generated by TopoText.**

Some open access tools that carry out automatic geocoding are the UCLA Web Geocoder and the Google Sheets add-on Geocode by Awesome Table. The former is a tool that geocodes addresses in the United States and the United Kingdom, as well as locality-level entries from other countries; however, it is not meant for geocoding city or country names, which is more common for spatial inquiry. Geocode by Awesome Table is an easy-to-use add-on in Google Sheets that automatically geocodes place names or addresses. While it is a quick and easy fix, it is not meant to be used with a large spreadsheet since it has a daily limit (1,000 lines unless upgraded) and the geocoding happens on a line-by-line basis; users can follow the process as the geo-coordinates appear, one after the other, in the spreadsheet. Like TopoText 1.0, both of these tools are black boxed, making it unclear how the matching process is actually taking place. Additionally, both require structured data (i.e., the place names must already be extracted), whereas TopoText goes through the whole geoparsing process—locating and extracting place names, then linking them to geographical coordinates. This limits the scholarly application of the two other tools for those working with unstructured or historical text.

One robust system that carries out the entire geoparsing process is the Edinburgh Geoparser. This open-source tool automatically identifies place names, and is linked to a number of gazetteers such as GeoNames and Unlock to disambiguate references and to provide a list of potential locations that a place name could be referring to (such as London, England; London, Ontario; London, Ohio, and so on). Results can be demonstrated on a Google Map, as with TopoText. Transparent geocoding was also a goal for TopoText, and has been realized in the second version. Although Edinburgh Geoparser has more powerful computational strength than TopoText, it also has a much steeper learning curve, and is thereby geared towards a different audience.

*TopoText 2.0*

After reflecting on how TopoText 1.0 carried out this particular interpretation of geocriticism, and on how to address the aforementioned limitations, the team designed a second iteration.[7] In particular, we considered how to open the automatic geocoding and text analysis processes to correct mismatched points, and to include unstructured text that further contextualizes

---

[7] The design of TopoText 2.0 (https://github.com/rkhatib/topotext/tree/v2 ) was led by Randa El Khatib (University of Victoria) and coded by Julia El Zini (AUB). Team members include David Wrisley (New York University of Abu Dhabi), Mohamad Jaber (AUB), and Shady Elbassuoni (AUB).

places beyond word-place collocations and the concordance tool. While the first iteration focused on rendering geocritical terms into computational tasks, the second version opens the black box for more accuracy and for human intervention. Switching between the concordance and word-place collocations supported multiple approaches to reading the text; however, neither of them are open or interactive in a way that supports human input.

TopoText 2.0 supports collaborative knowledge production by allowing researchers to continuously populate the data sets with new entries in the form of annotations that appear directly on the map interface. All maps and the data set can be exported, shared, and explored offline. Additionally, Topotext 2.0 has a "human-in-the-loop" option that allows researchers to participate in the post-matching phase of the geocoding process by correcting potential mismatches; this "correction" is made by updating the generated list of alternative locations that share the same place name (see Figure 4). Including the human-in-the loop functionality significantly improves on TopoText 1.0, as well as Web Geocoder and Geocode by Awesome Table, since the user, rather than the machine, is in control of the matching process. In its geocoding process, TopoText 2.0 more closely resembles the Edinburgh Geoparser in that it provides a list of alternative locations. However, the second iteration follows the objective of the first—to be accessible to scholars with no technical background.

|   | A | B | C | D | E | F |
|---|---|---|---|---|---|---|
| 1 | Location Name | Country | X | Y | Weight | Annotation |
| 2 | Turin | Italy | 45.07049 | 7.68682 | 3 | Moryson reache |
| 3 | Turin | Canada | 49.96674 | -112.51852 | 3 | Moryson reache |
| 4 | Turin | United States | 33.32651 | -84.63576 | 3 | Moryson reache |
| 5 | Ceres | Argentina | -29.881 | -61.94504 | 1 | While travelling |
| 6 | Ceres | Italy | 45.31336 | 7.38961 | 1 | While travelling |
| 7 | Ceres | Australia | -38.16667 | 144.26667 | 1 | While travelling |
| 8 | Ceres | South Africa | -33.36889 | 19.31095 | 1 | While travelling |
| 9 | Ceres | Brazil | -15.2735 | -49.64455 | 1 | While travelling |
| 10 | Ceres | United Kingdom | 56.29382 | -2.97357 | 1 | While travelling |
| 11 | Ceres | United States | 37.59493 | -120.95771 | 1 | While travelling |
| 12 | Ceres | East Timor | -8.75361 | 125.23389 | 1 | While travelling |
| 13 | Ceres | Cuba | 22.88722 | -81.19889 | 1 | While travelling |
| 14 | Ceres | Philippines | 14.62667 | 121.11777 | 1 | While travelling |

**Figure 4. The TopoText 2.0 CSV output has a "human-in-the-loop" option to correct mismatched entries by moving the accurate location and its geocoordinates to the top of its place-name entry.**

Aiming to cover a wider scholarly scope, the API was switched from Google, which primarily deals with modern place names, to GeoNames, one of the largest open gazetteers, which includes historical place names and alternative place name spellings. By doing so, TopoText facilitates spatial analysis of text that appears in less standard language, such as pre-modern or early modern texts, translated texts, or texts that refer to places by their alternative place name spellings. It also counts the number of times a place name is mentioned (under the "weight" category in Figure 4) and renders the size of the entry on the map to correspond to its weight ratio. Finally, TopoText 2.0 allows users to export the geoparsed data, along with the annotations and other relevant information, into a separate CSV file that can be reused on other platforms.

*Conclusion*

Both versions of TopoText are prototypes created for the interpretation of texts through a geocritical framework, one that is multifocal and geocentred; they support plain text input and provide context through world-place collocations, direct context in the concordance tool, and explanatory annotations displayed directly on the map interface. Designed for wide application, TopoText enables work to be carried out in multiple languages and supports the geoparsing of historical texts, all with no technical knowledge required. The prototype generates a customizable digital literary geography from texts, and, in accordance with Westphal's prediction, this interpretation of geocriticism is both digital and collaborative.

TopoText is a form of critical inquiry into modes of spatial representation and meaning formation through deformance and pataphysical criticism. The prototype ultimately attempts to reconstruct geocriticism in digital terms, in which design-related decisions are made through critical interpretive acts. As Ramsay (2011, 31) states: "The computer revolutionizes, not because it proposes an alternative to the basic hermeneutical procedure, but because it reimagines that procedure at new scales, with new speeds, and among new sets of conditions. It is for this reason that one can even dare to imagine such procedures taking hold in a field like literary criticism." Digital mapping through software prototypes is one way of manifesting a visual literary geography that can advance spatial explorations and enhance our experience of the literary text.

WORKS CITED

Awesome Gapps. n.d. "Geocode by Awesome Table." Google Sheets Add-on.

Bök, Christian. 2002. *'Pataphysics: The Poetics of an Imaginary Science*. Evanston., IL: Northwestern University Press.

Booth, Wayne C., Gregory G. Colomb, and Joseph M. Williams. 2008. *The Craft of Research*. 3rd ed. Chicago: University of Chicago Press.

Corelli, Marie. 1892. The Soul of Lilith, Vol. 1. London: Richard Bentley and Son.

Dickens, Charles. 1894. *A Tale of Two Cities*. Boston: Houghton Mifflin.

———. 1850. *David Copperfield*. London: Bradbury and Evans, 1850.

———. 1868. *Great Expectations*. Boston: Books, Inc.

———. 1880. *Little Dorrit*. Boston: Estes & Lauriat.

———. 1838. *Oliver Twist*. London: Richard Bentley.

———. 1865. *Our Mutual Friend*. New York: Harper & Brothers.

Dixon, Ella Hepworth. 1895. *The Story of a Modern Woman*. Leipzig: Bernhard Tauchnitz.

Doyle, Arthur. 1904. *A Study in Scarlet, The Sign of the Four*. London: Harper & Bros.

Edinburgh Language Technology Group. n.d. "Edinburgh Geoparser." https://www.ltg.ed.ac.uk/software/geoparser/.

Eide, Øyvind. 2015. *Media Boundaries and Conceptual Modelling: Between Texts and Maps*. London: Palgrave Macmillan.

Feinberg, Jonathan. 2014. "Wordle." http://www.wordle.net/.

Galey, Alan, and Stan Ruecker. 2010. "How a Prototype Argues." *Literary and Linguistic Computing* 25(4): 405–24.

GeoNames. n.d. "GeoNames." http://geonames.org/.

Geospatial UCLA. n.d. "Web Geocoder." https://gis.ucla.edu/geocoder/.

Google Developers. n.d. "Google Maps Platform." https://cloud.google.com/maps-platform/?&sign=1.

Gissing, George. 1891. *New Grub Street.* London: Smith, Elder.

———. 1903. *The Nether World.* London: Smith, Elder.

Hardy, Stephen P. 2000. "Placiality: The Renewal of the Significance of Place in Modern Cultural Theory." *Brno Studies in English* 26: 85–100. http://hdl.handle.net/11222.digilib/104271.

Hudson, Pat. 2014. *The Industrial Revolution.* London: Bloomsbury Publishing.

Jarry, Alfred. 1965. *Selected Works of Alfred Jarry.* Edited by Roger Shattuck and Simon Watson Taylor. New York: Grove Press.

Lee, Vernon. 1892. *Vanitas.* London: William Heinemann.

Lofland, Lyn H. 1985. *A World of Strangers: Order and Action in Urban Public Space.* Long Grove, IL: Waveland Press, Inc.

Morrison, Arthur. 1895. *Tales of Mean Streets.* Boston: Roberts Brothers.

———. 1899. *To London Town.* Leipzig: Bernhard Tauchnitz.

Ramsay, Stephen. 2011. *Reading Machines: Toward an Algorithmic Criticism.* Urbana: University of Illinois Press.

Ramsay, Stephen, and Geoffrey Rockwell. 2012. "Developing Things: Notes Toward an Epistemology of Building in the Digital Humanities." In *Debates in the Digital Humanities*, edited by Matthew K. Gold, 75–84. Minneapolis: University of Minnesota Press. http://dhdebates.gc.cuny.edu/debates/text/11.

Samuels, Lisa, and Jerome McGann. 1999. "Deformance and Interpretation." *New Literary History* 30(1): 25–56.

Stanford Natural Language Processing Group. 2006. "Stanford Named Entity Recognizer." https://nlp.stanford.edu/software/CRF-NER.html.

Stevenson, Robert. 1903. *The Strange Case of Dr. Jekyll and Mr. Hyde.* New York: Charles Scribner's Sons.

Tally, Robert T., Jr.. 2012. *Spatiality.* New York: Routledge.

Thackeray, William Makepeace. (1848) 2008. *Vanity Fair.* London: Bradbury and Evans. Reprint, Project Gutenberg.

Travis, Charles, 2016. "Bloomsday's Big Data: GIS, Social Media and James Joyce's *Ulysses.*" In *Literary Mapping in the Digital Age*, edited by David Cooper, Christopher Donaldson, and Patricia Murrieta-Flores, 102–21. New York: Routledge.

Tuan, Yi-Fu. 1979. "Space and Place: Humanistic Perspective." In *Philosophy in Geography*, edited by Stephen Gale and Gunnar Olsson, 387–427. Dordrecht: Springer Netherlands.

Westphal, Bertrand. 2011. *Geocriticism: Real and Fictional Spaces.* Translated by Robert T. Tally, Jr. New York: Palgrave Macmillan.

Wilde, Oscar. 1891. *The Picture of Dorian Grey.* London: Ward, Locke.

Zangwill, Israel. 1892. *Children of the Ghetto.* London: William Heinemann.

# Open Source Interpretation Using Z-axis Maps

Alex Christie

Brock University

with the INKE and MVP Research Groups

## *Introduction: Interpretive Visualizations and the Question of Scale*

As humanities data begins to scale, the question of reconciling data visualization with subjective interpretation comes increasingly to the fore. While the graphical display of large-scale data sets makes trends and currents in literary history and culture visible, the complex and subjective nature of humanities data can make the representative accuracy of such a display problematic. As Johanna Drucker (2011) argues: "rendering *observation* (the act of creating a statistical, empirical, or subjective account or image) as if it were *the same as the phenomena observed* collapses the critical distance between the phenomenal world and its interpretation, undoing the basis of interpretation on which humanistic knowledge production is based."

Taking up the argument that visualizations do not express objective facts, but are interpretive objects in their own right that merit further investigation and analysis, our team set out to visualize geodata from early twentieth-century novels through warped three-dimensional z-axis maps. This project considers how the question of scale plays out through, and can perhaps reconcile, the tension between visualization and theoretical interpretation of a graphical display. Presenting this data in 3D, the maps use varying modes of (carto)graphical display to express different cultural currents through which historical and literary data points may be organized, including spatial phenomena such as population density, wealth distribution, and zoning. Visualizing the same data points through multiple geographic expressions of cultural experience makes scale a question of theoretical multiplicity rather than epistemological certainty.

This paper outlines the means and methods of visualizing multiple literary interpretations both in theory and in practice. In what follows, I present z-axis findings at the convergence of social knowledge creation with critical making; I then argue that this convergence can scale through a process of open source interpretation, by which multiple members of a scholarly

ISBN 978-1-64959-008-4 (paper) ISBN 978-1-64959-009-1 (pdf) ISBN 978-1-64959-084-8 (epub)

*New Technologies in Medieval and Renaissance Studies 8 (2022) 73–81*

community use openly available texts and maps to produce different z-axis visualizations that express linked, interpretive results.

**Figure 1. Z-axis map of Djuna Barnes's *Nightwood*.**

*Z-axis Research: Literary Maps for Theoretical Interpretation*

Z-axis research is a 3D geospatial project conducted through Implementing New Knowledge Environments (INKE) and the Modernist Versions Project (MVP), with work ongoing by both myself and Katie Tanigawa in the Electronic Textual Cultures Lab (ETCL) (funded by SSHRC and in collaboration with Compute Canada). The project has two main premises: first, that GIS-specific maps rely on contemporary understandings of geography often at odds with those expressed in literary and historical documents; and, second, that cultural heritage maps express those historical understandings of space, to which literature of the same period responds. Proceeding from these two premises, z-axis maps anchor geographic data taken from modernist novels in contemporary cartographical expressions of the cities in which they are set, affording historically and culturally specific forms of geospatial expression and interpretation. The project digitizes cultural heritage maps of modern cities and then warps and deforms those maps in 3D according to geographic data taken from specific modernist novels. Rather than charting the geographic locations mentioned in the novel, the results visualize the spatial experience of the modern city described by the novel.

Maps created to date have analyzed the Dublin of James Joyce, the Paris of Djuna Barnes and Jean Rhys, and the London of Virginia Woolf's *Mrs. Dalloway*. The first phase of research creation involved making maps of Dublin and Paris by hand, the method and further findings for which are discussed in "Mapping Modernisms Z-Axis : A Model for Spatial Analysis in Modernist Studies" and "Arguing through Archival Objects: A Z-Axis Method for 3-D-Printed Interpretation." The second phase of map creation, which is currently underway and discussed here, focuses on London and explores a method for scaling up interpretation from the level of the individual map to collections of maps set in the same city. While these maps demonstrate the convergence of critical making with geospatial analysis, they also offer modes of interpretive analysis of interest to modernist literary scholars.

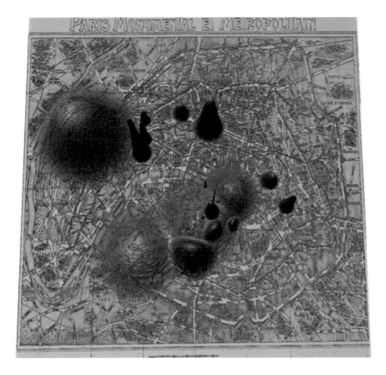

**Figure 2. Z-axis map of Djuna Barnes's *Nightwood*.**

Mapping multiple novels set in the same city and period allows a community of scholars to address shared research questions that appear only at scale. In *Nightwood* and *Quartet*, Djuna Barnes and Jean Rhys, respectively, describe the experience of living on the social and economic margins of 1930s Paris. With this interpretive context in mind, the z-axis maps of these two novels use an interwar tourist map that privileges tourist locations over the common (or *populaire*) areas often frequented by the novels' characters (Christie et al. 2014). Barnes's *Nightwood* focuses on the experience of lesbian and homosexual characters who live in Paris's Latin Quarter. The z-axis map of Barnes's novel (Figures 1 and 2) visualizes the role class plays in the queer experience of 1930s Paris. Each instance of warping on the z-axis map corresponds to a geographic area described in the novel, with the radius of the effect corresponding to the specificity of the geographic reference. The map reveals a Paris that is highly divided by class—references tend to be more specific on the wealthy right bank (north of the river Seine), while the left bank areas inhabited by Barnes's queer characters (south of the Seine) are often referenced vaguely. From this perspective, the z-axis map visualizes the wealthy right bank as a zone of sexual confinement and constraint and the left bank as containing zones of possibility, indeterminacy, and freedom (this interpretation is visible in the features of the warped map). Inspired by modernist theories of space that focus on different cultural uses and appropriations of the same urban geography, the z-axis maps visualize specific cultural and theoretical currents and trends in the modern metropole. Here, scale or pattern is a question of theory and interpretation, leaving further forms of analysis open through which scholars can engage in a process of social knowledge creation.[1]

**Figure 3. Z-axis map of Jean Rhys's *Quartet*.**

---

[1] For further information on social knowledge creation, see Arbuckle et al. 2014.

Creating additional maps set in the same city and decade begin a collective investigation of the trends and patterns in a given city as described by literature of the period. While Djuna Barnes describes a poor Paris that offers spaces of sexual freedom, Jean Rhys describes a Paris that traps and torments its impoverished inhabitants. Katie Tanigawa (Christie et al. 2014) argues that unlike Barnes's characters, who roam the Latin Quarter indeterminately, Rhys's protagonist, Marya, hops between multiple specific bars and cafés in her attempt to find a place of belonging on the margins of Parisian society. Ultimately, Marya's impoverished status makes Paris a social and psychological prison in which she cannot escape exploitation at the hands of those with wealth and power, epitomized through her experience of *la Place Denfert-Rochereau*, which was originally called *la Place d'Enfer* (the place of hell) (Christie et al. 2014).

While the *Nightwood* map visualizes zones of sexual freedom and liberty, the *Quartet* map (Figure 3) expresses sexual exploitation and imprisonment in the interwar period. Taken together, both maps express different social and cultural currents in Paris between the wars; they are not mutually exclusive, but rather call for a process of mutual interpretation. This collaborative interpretation functions through our written analyses of the z-axis maps, as well as through the maps themselves—the warped aesthetic of the Barnes map and the fragmented and disjointed aesthetic of the Rhys map both enable the spatial interpretations discussed above.[2]

## Scaling Up Together: Z-axis Research as a Social Knowledge Enterprise

When read alongside each other, the z-axis maps of *Nightwood* and *Quartet* begin to address a research question that can only be answered at scale: how does modernist literature characterize the geographic experience of poverty in interwar Paris? This question requires the work of a community, including digital humanists with geospatial and data visualization techniques, as well as literary scholars with deep content expertise on authors and novels contemporary to the two mapped here. The z-axis maps invite scholars to further interpret mapped results by transforming and remixing existing z-axis maps and their data, scaling up interpretive discovery by situating it as a social knowledge enterprise. This process applies an open source model to scholarly interpretation—it makes z-axis materials, techniques, and findings *openly* available so that scholars can use shared research *sources* to either reproduce or respond to each other's interpretive findings.[3] For instance, a

---

[2] For further reading on the z-axis mapping project, see Christie et al. 2014 and 2015.

[3] For more on open source development, and its applications beyond software environments, see OpenSource.com 2019.

Barnes scholar might determine that Barnes's references are less vague than I believe them to be and produce an alternate map by modifying my data; this would, in turn, express an alternate interpretation and map that responds to my own. Still another scholar might express my Barnes data through a different map, perhaps considering the role churches and religion play in Barnes's queer city. These examples demonstrate a vision of scale in which not only scholarly conclusions but the interpretive apparatus and methodology of the project are made replicable through an open source approach to data sets and workflows. Here, the question of complex and subjective humanities data functioning at scale is simply a digital revisitation of the traditional task of uniting multiple scholarly voices in a given disciplinary community.

There is no singular graph or visualization that accesses the truth of impoverished Paris in the 1930s, since that experience can only be addressed through trend and pattern; just as a graph charts trends across multiple points, so too can constellations of multiple z-axis maps chart patterns in modernist geospatial expression. Scholars see interpretations operating at scale every time they attend a conference or read a special issue or edited collection, and subjective visualizations can operate at scale by taking the same social knowledge approach already present in traditional humanities infrastructure. (To be sure, this is but one possible way in which visualizations might scale; there are many forms this process may take, and all merit exploration and investigation.) This open source model for interpretation invites scholars to scale a project by addressing theoretical issues that can only be answered at the level of the disciplinary community. Such a model requires open source code—in our case, the z-axis online mapping tool, which allows scholars to rapidly produce, edit, and share z-axis maps online.

The foremost question the z-axis project seeks to address is how specific sets of modernist authors describe a given city in a given decade. For instance, how does modernist literature characterize London after World War I? Are there meaningful differences between the experience of urban poverty in Paris and London in the 1930s? In order to address large research questions such as these, the z-axis project, through its collaboration with Compute Canada, is developing an online mapping tool that allows any scholar to produce and share a warped 3D map with minimal technical requirements or expertise.

*Open Source Interpretation: The Z-axis Mapping Tool*

To facilitate the open source expansion of z-axis findings, the INKE-MVP team is developing a z-axis tool with Compute Canada at http://zaxis. uvic.ca/. Currently, the tool allows the automated production of warped,

3D maps of novels set in modernist London (see Figure 4). Users can choose between out-of-copyright novels that come pre-included with the tool or upload their own novel by copy-pasting the text or uploading a .txt file. The tool then identifies place names in the text using the Stanford Named Entity Recognizer (https://nlp.stanford.edu/software/CRF-NER.html), and users are presented with an interface for refining the list of place names generated by the tool. This human intervention stage allows users to shape the geographic data directly without expertise in geoparsing or XML–TEI editing; it offers an accessible interface through which scholars can accept, reject, or modify geographic tag data based on their interpretation of the novel at hand. The frequency of mentioned locations is then used to warp digitized historical maps using the Compute Canada WestGrid servers. At present, the tool allows users to choose between 1930 and 1966 maps of London (an expanded selection of maps is currently in development). Users can dynamically visualize how geographic references change as the reader progresses through the novel, animating the map in time by selecting a word range for the visualization. In this way, users can dynamically visualize how the space of London actively shifts and changes in time throughout the novel, using the tool to explore connections between time and space.

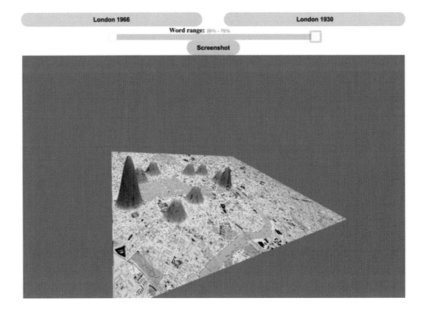

**Figure 4. Virginia Woolf's *Mrs. Dalloway* mapped with the z-axis tool.**

The z-axis tool enables scholars to produce their own interpretive z-axis maps with ease, allowing for the creation of multiple versions and visions of literary cities at specific historical moments. Through this social production of z-axis maps, the INKE-MVP team will use the open source z-axis tool to turn z-axis research over to scholars and scholarly organizations, such as the modernist studies community. Recasting z-axis mapping as a collaborative and community-driven endeavour allows the team to address a key research question in modernist literary studies that can only be answered at scale: how does modernist literature characterize the geographic experience of London between World Wars I and II, or in other historical periods? The answers we produce collaboratively—expressed through a series of modifiable maps, data sets, and interpretations—will then be open for other scholars to change, modify, and expand. The scale of our guiding research question therefore goes hand in hand with a corollary scale of knowledge production and dissemination, through conference workshops, online publications of our findings, and open and remixable interpretive data visualizations.

The shareable and scalable z-axis findings produced using the tool express what Alyssa Arbuckle and I refer to as "self-sustaining knowledge production chains" (Arbuckle and Christie 2015). These chains form when the open source research output of one scholar creates material for other scholars to reuse and repurpose in the creation of new data and findings (which both respond to the original theory while leaving the door open to new research production). Such knowledge production chains traverse disciplinary and institutional boundaries, as the z-axis map produced by a modernist literary scholar may be of interest to cartographers, geographers, desktop fabricators, and so on. Similarly, the transformation of cultural heritage materials offers multimodal output for hybrid publications, interactive visualizations, and the display of library collections. These cross-disciplinary production chains, and the scalable research questions through which they operate, are the fruits of open source interpretation. By repositioning research replicability at the site of interpretive methodology, open source interpretation affords a model of scale in which complex data and subjective graphs may be socially modified, remixed, and transformed. Ultimately, interpretive data visualization can scale by socially expanding the interpretive methods that shape and grow humanities data sets. Just as z-axis maps reveal social currents in the modernist city, so too does social knowledge creation cultivate and expand humanities research through trends and patterns in scholarly findings.

WORKS CITED

Arbuckle, Alyssa, Nina Belojevic, Matthew Hiebert, and Ray Siemens, with Shaun Wong, Derek Siemens, Alex Christie, Jon Saklofske, Jentery Sayers, and the INKE and ETCL Research Groups. 2014. "Social Knowledge Creation: Three Annotated Bibliographies." *Scholarly and Research Communication* 5(2). https://src-online.ca/index.php/src/article/view/150.

Arbuckle, Alyssa, and Alex Christie, with the ETCL, INKE, and MVP Research Groups. 2015. "Intersections Between Social Knowledge Creation and Critical Making." *Scholarly and Research Communication* 6(3). https://src-online.ca/index.php/src/article/view/200.

Barnes, Djuna. 1936. *Nightwood.* London: Faber and Faber.

Brendle-Moczuk, Daniel, Alex Christie, Colin Jones, Belaid Moa, Stephen Ross, and Katie Tanigawa. 2015. "Z-Axis Mapping Tool." http://zaxis.uvic.ca/.

Christie, Alex, Adèle Barclay, Stephen Ross, Jentery Sayers, Katie Tanigawa, Belaid Moa, and the INKE–MVP research team. 2015. "Arguing through Archival Objects: A Z-Axis Method for 3-D-Printed Interpretation." *The Modernist Versions Project.*

Christie, Alex and Katie Tanigawa. 2016. "Mapping Modernism's Z-Axis: A Model for Spatial Analysis in Modernist Studies." In Shawna Ross and James O'Sullivan, eds. *Reading Modernism with Machines: Digital Humanities and Modernist Literature.* Palgrave Macmillan.

Christie, Alex, Stephen Ross, Jentery Sayers, Katie Tanigawa, and the INKE–MVP research team. 2014. "Z-Axis Scholarship: Modeling How Modernists Wrote the City." *The Modernist Versions Project.*

Drucker, Johanna. 2011. "Humanities Approaches to Graphical Display." *Digital Humanities Quarterly* 5(1). http://www.digitalhumanities.org/dhq/vol/5/1/000091/000091.html.

OpenSource.com. 2019. https://opensource.com/resources/what-open-source.

Rhys, Jean. 1969. *Quartet.* Originally published as *Postures* [London: Chatto and Windus, 1928]. London: Deutsch.

# "Digital Zombies in the Academy": At the Intersection of Digital Humanities and Digital Pedagogy

Juliette Levy

University of California, Riverside

A substantial amount of literature exists on just what constitutes the "digital humanities."[1] The scholarly debate taking place in these pages includes the nature of pedagogy in the digital humanities, and recently this has been elevated to a discussion of what digital pedagogy is, or if it even exists.[2] Digital pedagogy and digital humanities are both fields and terms under construction, and trying to define them will inevitably constrain their definitions. In this paper I want to discuss an approach to instruction that is rooted in both digital humanities and digital pedagogy via the use of games, which may help in identifying how the digital humanities and digital pedagogy have and can change our understanding of their traditional, non-digital antecedents. I have used games and meaningful play to teach a humanities class that engaged students in digital tools and collaborative practice, combining digital humanities, traditional humanities instruction, innovative pedagogy, and digital pedagogy.

## All Pedagogy Is Digital Pedagogy

The question of whether digital pedagogy is even a thing stems from statements to the effect that there is no digital pedagogy—there is only pedagogy, and tools that go with it. Digital pedagogy, as seen from this perspective, comprises the digital tools and platforms that accompany pedagogy, with an implication that good pedagogy will rely on a variety of tools, technology, and platforms. Essentially, what this suggests is that the digital component does not change pedagogy; it's simply another tool among many in the teaching repertoire.

Let me be clear: using digital tools in a class IS digital pedagogy. Let's take the most extreme case of digital pedagogy, the online class. Teaching a class

---

[1] See, to name a few: Gold and Klein 2016; Unsworth 2002; Svensson 2009; Bartscherer and Coover 2011; and Nowiskie 2011.

[2] See Losh 2014 and Friend et al. 2015a and 2015b.

ISBN 978-1-64959-008-4 (paper) ISBN 978-1-64959-009-1 (pdf) ISBN 978-1-64959-084-8 (epub)

*New Technologies in Medieval and Renaissance Studies* 8 (2022) 83–97

online requires a consciousness about what the medium does, and to be effective, an online class needs to take that medium into account. In a face-to-face class, one that perhaps uses clickers for engagement in a large lecture class, or online discussion boards, or even one in which the students are simply using laptops to take notes—all of that constitutes a digital environment. So even if the students are connected to the Web via their laptops, the class has a digital component, and effective pedagogy in this context will have to take the digital into account. Or let's imagine a classroom without laptops or Web access, a classroom in which the faculty member is lecturing to a large or small contingent of students taking notes with pads and pencils. Even in that context, the digital will permeate, because once the students leave the class, they will check their learning management system (LMS) to see the next assignment, or go online to access a source via the library's virtual private network (VPN). Today, then, whether one is using a little, a lot, or no digital technology in one's classes, all pedagogy is to a greater or lesser extent digital.[3]

Contrary to the technology-enhanced future presented by Mark Bauerlein (2015), who sees students as "the dumbest generation" and professors as useless, I don't think technology spells doom. Neither do I think it's a panacea. But I do think that if we don't engage with technology as more than a tool in the classroom, we undermine the purpose of pedagogy in the classroom. Engaging with technology doesn't mean we need to give every student an iPad, or do the opposite and ban all technology in the classroom. It doesn't mean we need to flip classrooms, or post lectures to blogs. These are all questions that are worth exploring, but secondary. The key to good pedagogy has always been to engage students and to let them learn actively, whether they are using pencils, blackboards, or iPads. Good pedagogy focuses on the learner, and in order to do that we need to consider the digital environments, affects, and affordances that learners learn in. And today's learning environments are digital, by design or by default.

The concept of "user experience," borrowed from the world of design, is the concept that usability, accessibility, and enjoyment are key factors in the success of any product. It's a key concept in digital product development, because if the end user does not understand how to use the tool, or does not understand its purpose, they will stop engaging with the tool or platform. User-centred design is the process through which a product is developed by thinking about the user. In academia, instructional design offices have

---

[3] Sean Michael Morris (2014) makes the case for this perspective eloquently.

highlighted the concern for user design because of the many digital tools that they offer to support instruction, but the real equivalent to user design in pedagogy would be to develop a syllabus by thinking about the student, or with the student, rather than starting with the content.

## Gamification: From Homo Ludens *to the Humanities*

So how do games fit into this narrative of digital pedagogy? Where and how do games intersect with the digital humanities? Games matter not just because they may very well be the dominant cultural form of the twenty-first century,[4] but also because they allow us to observe learning in a non-academic context. The incursion of games into non-game environments has given rise to the concept of "gamification," in which game thinking and game mechanics are used in non-game contexts to engage users in solving problems.

The theory of gamification is not new; its theoretical forefather, Johan Huizinga, wrote *Homo Ludens* in 1949, and this book was central to Roger Caillois's *Les Jeux et les Hommes* (1958),[5] both foundational texts that explore the various forms of play and their connection to social and cultural structures. In the twenty-first-century context, the notion of games in education developed with online games as the primary focus. The fields of psycholinguistics, literacy and cognitive neuroscience, and education are pushing hardest in the direction of exploring games for cognitive purposes. Mimi Ito at the University of California (UC) Irvine, James Paul Gee at Arizona State University, and Daniel Schwartz at Stanford University are but a few of the scholars working on how online/video games intersect and inform learning; Susanne Lohmann, a political science professor at UCLA, uses games to teach her course on moral judgments.

Scholarly literature on gamification—and there is a vast amount[6]—describes the variety and overwhelming success of games used in education and business. Within a broad spectrum of strategies, gamification exercises generally use a player's natural instincts to compete, discover, explore, and win/close to draw them into accomplishing set tasks in the game. Gamification has received enormous attention of late because it promises an easy path to generating data and information about learners and users. It is also widely misunderstood and oversimplified. There may be two reasons why

---

[4] See Zimmerman 2013.

[5] Translated as *Man, Play and Games*; see Caillois 2001.

[6] To name but a few seminal texts: Kapp 2012; Sheldon 2011; Gee 2003; and Gee 2005.

gamification is the buzzword of the moment: first, in its commercial applications, behavioural incentives of play have been knitted into data-generating projects; second, as an educational tool, it has permeated competency-based training, both in the scholastic (K-12) and corporate training contexts.

In the commercial context, for example, runners using an app such as Nike+, which connects to a chip in their sneakers, are both adding a competitive and play-like edge to their morning jog *and* providing massive amounts of data on usage and location to Nike. Their experience is no different from that of people who check into a favourite coffee shop via their Facebook app: they may be moving closer to a free latte, but they are also sharing information about themselves with both Facebook and the coffee shop. The latter example really isn't a game; it is instead a behavioural incentive that, as in the case of the runner using Nike+, generates personal data. It is also, in the words of Ian Bogost (2011), "bullshit." Bogost is not using the expletive simply to be crass; he is referencing Harry Frankfurt (2005), for whom bullshit is something "used to conceal, to impress or to coerce," which this sort of gamification does. Not surprisingly, many administrators and managers perk up at the possibility of gamifying any aspect of the relationship with their end users or clients (or students). Bogost is probably right that "gamification" of this kind is a deceptive word, and that it is actually closer to what he calls "exploitationware"—because, as he sees it, there is no game, no mystery, no magic in "gamification." I hesitate to take such a strong stance, however. The gamification of a learning experience can be a complex project, and calling it "bullshit" is an oversimplification that risks missing some real advantages of using games in learning.[7]

## The Benefits of Badges

"Badging" is a core mechanism of gamification by which users receive badges for the completion of tasks, which allows them to track their progress visually. Math learning games, library games, and any course that uses badges to replace certificates of completion are all part of the badging trend. Digital badges were originally conceived of to break down assignments and learning activities into smaller parts, to pace the learning, and to allow repeated trial and error without major consequences on the final grade. It is hard to argue against this pedagogical logic. Digital badges, it is often argued, add an element of play to the learning and reemphasize that the purpose of the

---

[7] Although I do have to hand it to Bogost when it comes to corporate reward games (promoted, for example, with the title "For the Win"): he is spot on the scatological essence of those exercises.

exercise is to learn, no matter how many attempts it takes: the reward will be claimed when it is earned.[8] The power of this proposition has led a significant part of the Digital Media Hub at UC Irvine to be dedicated to the development and exploration of badging in education.

The benefits of badging, and any of the tools built into online games, is the immediate response they provide to users. There is never any doubt as to where in the game a player is, or how well (or poorly) the player is doing. In an educational game, real time response mechanisms such as badging also benefit faculty members and advisors; not only can they provide immediate responses on student skills and learning, but they provide access to an enormous variety of possible responses and assessments that go far beyond those produced by the traditional midterm and final exam. In short, digital badges help both students and instructors visualize the learning goals in a class, and they provide both the student and the instructor with transparency about the student's path toward achieving the competencies outlined in the learning goals. This is where digital badges start intersecting with the digital humanities.

Transparent pedagogy and games are keenly connected; in transparent pedagogy, the learning goals and outcomes are communicated clearly and in advance, as are the decisions that lead to those learning goals. Students are involved in the course as participants in the content, but they are also engaged in the structure. The emphasis in transparent pedagogy is not on punitive grading but on iterative exercises, short and frequent feedback loops, and collaborative assignments. Transparent pedagogy overturns much of the hierarchy that traditional classrooms adopt by default, and speaks to the student rather than to the syllabus. The transparency that badges can confer, therefore, as well as the iterative process by which students can earn a badge, all speak to a philosophy of teaching in which students are stakeholders in the learning process rather than subjects of it. This is very much how many digital humanities courses are being taught and modelled, and how much of the praxis of digital humanities is learned.

Games and transparency are further entwined in the work of Jane McGonigal (2011).[9] For better or worse, McGonigal sees in games the potential to save the world. She is, interestingly, no great believer in badges, even if she is probably the most emphatic advocate for the beneficial power of online games,

---

[8] See the Digital Badges efforts by the MacArthur Foundation (n.d.).
[9] See also McGonigal's website at http://janemcgonigal.com/play-me/.

and she is backed up in this by other digital media and games scholars.[10] She also doesn't much like the term "gamification," not just because, as Bogost said, gamification coerces players into doing something they wouldn't otherwise do, but because the spirit of games is not one of coercion.

Games are voluntary. Yet games very often get us to do things we wouldn't do if they weren't also fun. The principle of any sport is closely tied to this. Would we kick a small ball while running across a field alone? Probably not. It's the game in the sport that gets us back on the field, even if it's the health benefit of cardio exercise that makes us live long enough to enjoy it. And there are plenty of "serious" games (called "serious" because their purpose is not just to entertain, but to inform and/or educate). Among the leaders in this field is Games for Change, a non-profit which catalyzes social change through games, and has some of the biggest names in the "games for learning" community on its board (McGonigal herself, James Paul Gee, Eric Zimmerman, Drew Davidson, and Tracy Fullerton, to name a few).

The debate over the value and applicability of the term "gamification" and the use of tools such as badges in games is of course ongoing, as is the debate about games as games vs games as education. Game players and game scholars like to remind educators that every time they design a game that will teach players/students something specific, something the player wouldn't normally or voluntarily do, they are not designing a game, they are designing a curriculum. I maintain my position that the two are not contradictory, and that games—with their implied trial and error dynamic, the ambiguity, as Brian Sutton-Smith (1997) would say, of the very purpose of the game as well as the uncertainty that is inherent in games—represent the very emotions and incentives that the best type of pedagogy does to generate engagement and commitment in students.

The rest of this paper will present *Digital Zombies*, a hybrid pedagogical research experience for students that was developed, using game design as a model, with two explicit goals: first, to teach historical research and writing skills, and, second, to teach it to more than one hundred students at a time.

---

[10] See Ito et al. 2009.

Digital Zombies: *Game or Educational Tool?*[11]

*Digital Zombies* is a meaningful play project in which students learn a series of skills that I consider to be essential to success at the university, but are also what the university should be able to guarantee that students learn. The game structure was set up to create a large, collaborative community of learners, where learning was embedded in the community, where successes were visible and celebrated, and where failures were part of the community experience. Participants would be required to strategize and learn to overcome obstacles collaboratively, and, if possible, spend more time than usual doing research not because it was assigned, but because they were enjoying it. Scholars might enjoy research, or archives and data sets, but they were not the target audience of this game. To conjure up fun and pleasure in doing the work, then, games became the strategy. *Digital Zombies* was created to confer experience and knowledge via a game, a game that was meaningful to those playing it.[12]

The process of doing, making, and praxis is a significant part of the digital humanities, and one that arguably distinguishes digital humanities from many other disciplines in the traditional humanities. However, applying this to a history class was complicated by the fact that learning history by doing history isn't really obvious. How do you actually "do" history? Historians write history, which is our version of "doing," and we spend hours in archives to "do" this. How do we replicate this experience for undergraduate students? How can we inject an active learning component into the tasks that compose our craft, and essentially trap us in archives for years?

The traditional lecture does not convey this act clearly enough, and guiding students in research projects is difficult when class sizes swell. The personal learning experience cannot withstand the weight of a large class, which leads students to feel less connected to the faculty member and the material, and

---

[11] *Digital Zombies* was first formulated in 2014 during a workshop at the University of Victoria's Digital Humanities Summer Institute (DHSI). This is where the first ideas about a learning game involving zombies, the library, and digital and analog primary source materials took shape. Team members included Steve Anderson (a doctoral candidate in American history at the University of California, Riverside), and Andrew Keenan and Matt Bouchard (both doctoral candidates at the University of Toronto's Faculty of Information), developed these ideas collaboratively. Together we articulated the logic of the game's design, the roots of meaningful play, and the identity and branding of *Digital Zombies* itself. This collaboration continues to the present day.
[12] See Salen and Zimmerman 2003.

because large classes are onerous to grade, the syllabus for a large class rarely includes room for iterative assessments, short feedback loops, or creativity.

*Digital Zombies* was born from this realization: that the traditional large lecture class is not a very engaging environment, and that it is largely passive. Even at its best, it is a sub-optimal learning environment—and in order to change this we needed to rethink our approach to teaching large classes. Previous courses had made it clear that despite their familiarity with digital technology, most students did not know how to engage with or use digital resources and methods appropriately. And despite their familiarity with the location of our campus libraries and their most comfortable napping nooks, students rarely knew how to research library collections. *Digital Zombies* was created and developed to let humanities students learn in situ—to engage them in a game-like scenario that unfolded partly in a library, that fostered critical thinking about the library's role in their research, and that taught them how to do research in both a physical and a digital environment.

*Digital Zombies* (static webpage at https://digitalzombies.ucr.edu/) is a scalable and interactive learning tool designed to address the significant preparedness needs of twenty-first-century students and humanities scholars. Using the principles of game design, it breaks down independent research activities into a series of smaller tasks that follow sequentially in a historical narrative around a fictional "digital zombie outbreak."

I used Max Brooks's *World War Z: An Oral History of the Zombie War* (2006) as the foundational text for a course on historical research methods for historians. This course is a lower division, writing-intensive class cross-listed with a course required for graduation, and it is also a requirement for the history major. The course guides students on the use of maps, photographs, letters and diaries, newspapers, and other items, and connects each of these sources to relatively well known historical events: maps and Columbus's voyages, early photographs of the Mexican Revolution and Brazilian plantations, diary entries by an eighteenth-century colonial American midwife and twentieth-century revolutionary Che Guevara, and letters by Charles Darwin and Abigail Adams. This is a class on research methods, so the content needed to be relatively well known, allowing the focus to remain on the exploration of the sources that gave rise to this knowledge.

It may seem contradictory to develop this curricular plan around a fictional history of a zombie war, but *World War Z* is written as an oral history that uses a significant amount of primary sources and ties its origin story to verifiable events. The zombie theme also fit in with a behaviour observed among many students: their overreliance on completely unreliable digital sources and websites for research. Being in the digital world but not of it, it seemed to me, doomed students (and any digital citizen) to a minimal experience of the world. And so the term "digital zombies" was born.

*Digital Zombies* was a dual success in achieving both learning and teaching goals: it generated excitement among students about doing research, and among instructors about teaching core research skills in the library. Its game-like environment enhanced the student's experience of a humanistic research project, transforming the library from a musty napping place with computer banks to the location of all that mattered in a student's life (during the duration of the course, at least!). It also put librarians back in the path of a majority of students, who mostly were unaware that librarians were there to help them.

One of the many "missions" each student had to complete was to meet with a librarian, ask the librarian what the special collections were and why the library was organized the way it was, and maybe take a selfie with the librarian. The purpose of the exercise, of course, was to get students into the library and to engage with the most knowledgeable people in the library, but it also generated a wellspring of unintended comments about librarians. Students did not just post their selfies; they posted their selfies with comments about how wonderful the librarians they had spoken to were, about how the librarians who had assisted them were now their best friends. For many students, the assignment stopped being an assignment and became a part of their own discovery of an important place on campus, and the people who worked there, people they had not conceived of as helpful or useful until then.

Apart from exploring the library, students actually enjoyed the tasks assigned to them, and the library saw a significant increase in visits and usage. Not only were students in the library more often, they were also all over the library. More books were being checked out. Virtual collections were being accessed, and obscure special collections items requested. And once the barrier between librarians and students had been breached, librarians were involved in multiple stages of the research projects.

*Digital Zombies* demonstrates the logic that underlies this intersection of games and humanities. In this project, students interact with physical and digital built environments, provoking interactions with people, physical and digital or digitized library materials, search engines, and social media. The game ties libraries into a specific course curriculum, making libraries and librarians an integral part of the exploration of digital narratives, collaborative and individual writing, and also hybrid research methods, all of which successfully engages students beyond the traditional classroom experience. The game is an innovative narrative exercise that erases the boundaries between the physical and the digital. Students are asked to perform both simple and complex tasks—from identifying the exits of their library, to geolocating a specific book (by call number, but also with their smartphone compass if they have it), to using their library's VPN access to find books through WorldCat and JStor. They are asked to find books pertaining to specific tasks considered vital in an apocalyptic context (the zombie war), and required to explain the logic of their decisions and choices. If a student chooses to be in the "infectious diseases task," they need to justify the use of a book on the 1914 flu pandemic. They will then have to explore primary sources of that period, and compare the various perspectives they have gained to what Wikipedia says about the 1914 flu pandemic—and they will be invited to edit that Wikipedia article if they think it necessary.

At each of these stages, students get feedback, and credit for completing tasks, and at each stage they learn the skills that carry them to the next task. Being assessed is not the purpose of the assignments: completing the assignment is the purpose. Students get assessed in a more traditional way by preparing a final report, which requires them to use all the skills they have been learning and using throughout each task. In short, this final report would be impossible to complete if the previous tasks had not been completed and perfected. The final two-part report asks students to write self-assessments of what they have learned, then to take a critical position on Max Brooks's book—and then to support that critique with the primary and secondary sources they have been learning about in the class and learning to find and use in the library.

There is additionally a heavy digital component to the course: digital submissions and rubrics, multimodal feedback (via mobile platforms, online office hours, and discussion boards), contact with librarians both in the library and via the on-call assistance accessible at all hours, and the virtual collections students have to work with, as well as their engagement with social media and Wikipedia to assess their findings with those of the rest of their digital outlets. Beyond the different tools and assessments allowed by the digital format, the course structure and game it relies on force a transparency that is otherwise much rarer, and harder to manage in a large lecture class.

The learning outcomes of *Digital Zombies* are both specific and broad. Specifically, they lead the student to the library to perform tasks that ultimately teach them how to find and evaluate scholarly sources and to become an expert in a historical field of their choosing. The questions and tasks students work on help them develop critical thinking and research skills, and expose them to the physical context (the library) in which curiosity is welcomed and is one of the key currencies of success. Broadly, the learning outcomes present us with students who are able to navigate in and between the digital and the physical world, who can respond to the affordances of each, whose relationship to these worlds is so compatible that they no longer feel distressed or disturbed by the differences in affect that a technological shift can create, but instead respond to the shift as neutrally as when they step up a staircase or open a door.

The successful outcome of *Digital Zombies* has relied as much on the scaffolding of the game as it has on the endless patience and generosity of librarians, who may occasionally have been caught off-guard by scores of students asking to take selfies with them. The responses from both the students and the librarians were overwhelming, positive, and encouraging. Students expressed having enjoyed the research project, reported how useful it was in completing research assignments in other classes, and shared how gratifying it was to discover that librarians "are actually really nice"—thereby proving that we were meeting the goals of both meaningful play and learning.[13]

### A Future for Games in the (Digital) Humanities and Pedagogy?

There is an element of role-playing in *Digital Zombies*, but its narrative does not replicate the conditions of other educational role-playing games such as, for example, *Mission US* (PBS LearningMedia n.d.) or *Pox and the City* (Stockton University n.d.). The play in *Digital Zombies* is closer to the games Jane McGonigal has developed, such as her *Find the Future* game in the New York Public Library (McGonigal et al. 2011). *Digital Zombies*, like *Find the Future*, relies on players and students to develop their own narratives of history within flexible research parameters. In *Digital Zombies*, students learn skills that are acquired through meaningful social interaction and challenging game dynamics. The student's task in *Digital Zombies* is not to reenact history, but to discover how history is written.

*Digital Zombies* has some overlap with other library games, but as many librarians have told us, games organized by the library have a significant drawback: participation is entirely voluntary, perhaps so much so that there

---

[13] The three quotations in this paragraph come from evaluations given at the end of the course held in the Spring and Summer quarter of 2015.

is little room for iteration or assessment. In order to be successful at scale, educational games must include an incentive structure that leads to large-scale participation. By integrating the strengths of the library with the robust pedagogy and assessment structures of the classroom, *Digital Zombies* has created a meaningful experience that broadens scholarly horizons for everyone involved.[14]

The hybrid nature of *Digital Zombies* also solves a crucial problem and need in the current higher education curriculum, in which "academic digital literacy" is a highly valued learning goal but is difficult to teach, especially if it is not integrated into a course or part of an explicit academic curriculum. The hybrid nature of *Digital Zombies* also addresses another problem of the twenty-first century: how to understand and utilize the physical library in a digital age. *Digital Zombies* puts students in an active learning environment, helping them see the logic and value of information organized within the physical library as well as digital space. It teaches students how to use library resources, how to search for and evaluate online sources, and how best to utilize digital and non-digital materials. Ultimately, *Digital Zombies* is a case study for the kind of game that has specific pedagogical outcomes, that uses digital and non-digital realms interchangeably.

## Concluding Thoughts

*Digital Zombies* could not function at the scale in which it does in a fully physical environment, and it would not work in a traditional pedagogical context of punitive grading and few high-stakes assignments. It has been a powerful example of transparent pedagogy and student agency in a classroom that would otherwise be too large to facilitate these goals. Additionally, traditional learning goals were achieved: students learned how to do effective research and how to write a convincing research paper, and they did it at scale, in a context that allowed for personalized and targeted interventions by teaching assistants and faculty, as well as interactions between students, and obviously the many librarians who supported the game.

Pedagogy has changed in the digital age, and this transformation must be embraced rather than ignored. *Digital Zombies* does just that—as a unique example of digital pedagogy's intersection with the digital humanities, at scale.

---

[14] *Digital Zombies* has a successful track record. As of publication, close to 1000 students have completed the *Digital Zombies* game, and each year, at least 100 more will play it in my class.

WORKS CITED

Bartscherer, Thomas, and Roderick Coover. 2011. *Switching Codes: Thinking Through Digital Technology in the Humanities and the Arts.* Chicago: University of Chicago Press.

Bauerlein, Mark. 2015. "What's the Point of a Professor?" *New York Times,* May 9. http://nyti.ms/1Ernu1O.

Bogost, Ian. 2011. "'Gamification Is Bullshit.'" *The Atlantic,* August 9. https://www.theatlantic.com/technology/archive/2011/08/gamification-is-bullshit/243338/.

Brooks, Max. 2006. *World War Z: An Oral History of the Zombie War.* New York: Three Rivers Press.

Caillois, Roger. 1958. *Les Jeux et les hommes: Le Masque et le vertige.* Paris: Gallimard.

———. (1961) 2001. *Man, Play, and Games.* Trans. Meyer Barash. Chicago: University of Chicago Press.

Frankfurt, Harry. 2005. *On Bullshit.* Princeton, NJ: Princeton University Press.

Friend, Chris, et al. 2015a. "Digital Pedagogy, Part 1." Podcast, August 8. http://hybridpedagogy.org/digital-pedagogy-part-1/.

———. 2015b. "Digital Pedagogy, Part 2." Podcast, September 13. http://hybridpedagogy.org/digital-pedagogy-part-2/.

Games for Change. 2004. http://www.gamesforchange.org/.

Gee, James Paul. 2003. *What Video Games Have to Teach Us about Learning and Literacy.* New York: Palgrave Macmillan.

———. 2005. "Learning by Design: Good Video Games as Learning Machines." *E-Learning and Digital Media* 2(1): 5–16.

Gold, Matthew K., and Lauren F. Klein, eds. 2016. *Debates in the Digital Humanities 2016.* Minneapolis and London: University of Minnesota Press.

Huizinga, Johan. (1949) 2014. *Homo Ludens: A Study of the Play-Element in Culture.* Eastford, CT: Martino Fine Books.

Ito, Mizuko, et al. 2009. *Living and Learning with New Media: Summary of Findings from the Digital Youth Project.* John D. and Catherine T. MacArthur Foundation Reports on Digital Media and Learning. Cambridge, MA: MIT Press.

Kapp, Karl M. 2012. *The Gamification of Learning and Instruction: Game-Based Methods and Strategies for Training and Education.* San Francisco: Pfeiffer.

Losh, Elizabeth. 2014. *The War on Learning: Gaining Ground in the Digital University.* Cambridge, MA: MIT Press.

MacArthur Foundation. n.d. *Digital Badges.* https://www.macfound.org/programs/digital-badges/.

McGonigal, Jane. 2011. *Reality is Broken: Why Games Make Us Better and How They Can Change the World.* New York: Penguin Press.

McGonigal, Jane, with Natron Baxter Applied Gaming and Playmatics. 2011. *Find the Future: The Game.* Created for the Centennial of the New York Public Library. https://www.nypl.org/blog/2011/04/01/jane-mcgonigal-and-nypl-present-find-future-game.

Morris, Sean Michael. 2014. "Digital Pedagogy: A Case of Open or Shut." Blog post, September 24. http://www.seanmichaelmorris.com/digital-pedagogy-a-case-of-open-or-shut/.

Nowviskie, Bethany, ed. 2011. *#Alt-Academy:* A *Media Commons* Project. http://mediacommons.org/alt-ac/.

PBS LearningMedia. n.d. *Mission US: An Interactive Way to Learn History.* http://www.mission-us.org.

Salen, Katie, and Eric Zimmerman. 2003. *Rules of Play: Game Design Fundamentals.* Cambridge, MA: MIT Press.

Sheldon, Lee. 2011. *The Multiplayer Classroom: Designing Coursework as a Game.* Boston: Cengage Learning.

Stockton University. n.d. *Pox and the City.* http://loki.stockton.edu/~games/PoxFinal/Pox.html.

Sutton-Smith, Brian. 1997. *The Ambiguity of Play.* Cambridge, MA: Harvard University Press.

Svensson, Patrik. 2009. "Humanities Computing as Digital Humanities." *Digital Humanities Quarterly* 3(3). http://www.digitalhumanities.org/dhq/vol/3/3/000065/000065.html.

Unsworth, John. 2002. "What is Humanities Computing and What is Not?" Talk delivered at the Maryland Institute for Technology in the Humanities, University of Maryland, October 5, 2000. Republished online by *Forum Computerphilologie,* Universität Würzburg, November 8. http://computerphilologie.uni-muenchen.de/jg02/unsworth.html.

Zimmerman, Eric. 2013. "Manifesto for a Ludic Century." *Kotaku*, September 9. https://kotaku.com/manifesto-the-21st-century-will-be-defined-by-games-1275355204.

# Projects to Pedagogy: On the Social Infrastructure of Consortial Collaboration in Digital Scholarship

Jacob Heil
Davidson College

Ben Daigle
University of Dayton

## Introduction

In *The New Education*, distinguished cultural history and technology scholar Cathy Davidson posits that traditional models of higher education require an overhaul. University, she argues, must be redesigned "beyond the inherited disciplines, departments, and silos … providing an array of intellectual forums, experiences, programs, and projects that push students to use a variety of methods to discover comprehensive and original answers" (Davidson 2017, 13). In this paper, we take a look at one innovative educational model that was launched with just such a goal in mind: the Digital Projects and Pedagogies initiative at the Five Colleges of Ohio (the "Ohio Five").

For some twenty-five years, the libraries of these five colleges have created—in their centrally located spaces—the discipline-agnostic environment necessary to foster research and teaching, making visible the good work of individual departments and institutions that might otherwise have been siloed and obscured from view. Most recently, the Ohio Five have taken on an initiative to foster pedagogical projects that engage with digital methods or technologies. This initiative views such projects in three basic ways: first, they require the expertise of various campus stakeholders; second, these stakeholders include students, faculty, librarians, and technologists; and third, equitable partnerships yield the most robust results. These projects, in other words, begin and end as socially created knowledge born out of multiple disciplinary approaches while remaining focused on pedagogical and research goals.

The multidisciplinary efforts of the Digital Projects and Pedagogies initiative mark a point in an ongoing process by which we acknowledge, explicitly and implicitly, that the nature of our work is evolving even as we press forward. The work discussed here is by way of retrospective glance; it traces the

ISBN 978-1-64959-008-4 (paper) ISBN 978-1-64959-009-1 (pdf) ISBN 978-1-64959-084-8 (epub)
*New Technologies in Medieval and Renaissance Studies* 8 (2022) 99–122

thinking that underpins our own evolution, but is rooted in this particular moment in that evolution. Additionally, ours is not a description of tools or projects that facilitate socially created knowledge, but rather an account of the intellectual, technical, and institutional frameworks that have shifted over time, making room for academic work that is, at its core, socially created. While we cannot presume to prescribe, we hope that our descriptions may resonate with many who are working within or alongside their modern academic libraries. We have defined, then redefined, what we mean by "digital liberal arts," "digital scholarship," and whatever new framing mechanisms we use to guide our work; we have endeavoured to build a shared capacity for our work by leveraging the wonderfully various skills and perspectives of our component collaborators; and we have lobbied the administrative structures that value and evaluate the work of these collaborators.

While these efforts are very much a work in progress, we find ourselves in a watershed moment that bears reflection. Our efforts have grown into consortial initiatives—stamped with the imprimatur of the Ohio Five's presidents and its academic committee, comprising a body of deans and chief academic officers—to explore the future of this process-based, transdisciplinary, socially driven work and the ways in which we might prepare our students for the "world in flux" of Cathy Davidson's subtitle. In what follows, we will outline a bit of how we have arrived at this moment as a way of contextualizing what we see as three distinct phases in the evolution of our efforts. This context may provide a useful framework for others who find themselves on a similar continuum. Further, we will offer a kind of reflective analysis of these phases and their development: what we have learned along the way and how we might do things differently. Finally, we will project forward to our potential futures as a way of giving the most complete snapshot of our collective intellectual and situational frameworks in this moment of institutional change.

## Background and Context

In the 1990s, the libraries of Denison University, Kenyon College, Oberlin College, Ohio Wesleyan University, and the College of Wooster—as yet unconsolidated entities—found themselves balancing the prestige of their physical collections against the expanding footprint that those collections demanded. At a time when the dominant metric of a library's value was the number of volumes on its shelves, the same problem plagued (and, in some cases, continues to plague) research libraries everywhere. Both local ownership as a marker of prestige, and single authorship as the dominant credential in scholarly humanities publishing, were becoming antiquated models. And in neither case, as we know too well, can the centre hold: while human knowledge is expansive, libraries, insofar as they are containers, can only ever be finite. Surprisingly, however, a study by the Andrew W. Mellon Foundation reports even as expanding print collections were growing untenable, research libraries still preferred to maintain local ownership over as much published scholarly material as their budgets would permit (Cummings and Mellon Foundation 1992, 142). This environment helped to spawn a perfect storm out of which the Five Colleges of Ohio would grow. First, as a necessary corrective, a joint venture of research university libraries and the Ohio Department of Education—the OhioLINK cooperative—entered into an agreement with the library software company Innovative Interfaces, Inc. to develop and implement a unique union library system that would later become the OhioLINK Central Catalog. Meanwhile, the library directors at Denison, Kenyon, Oberlin, Ohio Wesleyan, and Wooster were each hatching plans to independently confront the existential paradox of space-delimited ranking by plugging into the newly-formed OhioLINK. Finally, and according to local lore, it was around this time that William G. Bowen, then president of the Andrew W. Mellon Foundation and a Denison University graduate and trustee, discussed an even more granular joint library system among those five colleges with former Kenyon College president Philip Jordan. Bowen, whose Mellon Foundation had reported on the unsustainable direction of library collections, emphasized the necessity of residential colleges to leverage economies of scale to survive in the face of rising costs (Middleman 2005, 5–6).

With the Mellon Foundation's focus set on encouraging new models of collaboration and resource sharing, and OhioLINK's statewide system under development, the Five Colleges of Ohio began to take shape. In June 1995, these five colleges received an $840,000 grant from the Mellon Foundation to create a shared library system, develop a governance structure, incorporate the consortium, and study the use of shared digital images. This grant, along with all of the intellectual and sweat equity invested by the colleges, launched the libraries on a path of continuous collaboration. CONSORT (Colleges of Ohio Networked System for Online Research and Teaching), a shared library system, was born. While the collaboration required the libraries to sacrifice some autonomy and control over the data, practices, and in some cases, services, the rewards were worth the cost: vastly increased access to research materials, shared labour, and shared costs.

As in any collaboration, however, reaching that reward was not possible without struggle, disagreement, and conflict—all of which are, arguably, essential conditions for thinking differently about entrenched practices. Oberlin College, for example, ultimately did not participate in the shared CONSORT library system. The Oberlin library had already migrated to a new system developed by Innovative Interfaces, Inc., and had pledged to join the OhioLINK consortium independently. Because the library's collection was significantly larger than those of the other four libraries, there were concerns about a potential burden on the staff processing a disproportionately large volume of materials to be lent out consortially (Middleman 2005, 22). Still, Oberlin remained invested in the idea of the consortium as such, and became a founding member of the Ohio Five. Even though the shared library system was not an endeavour in which they would participate, the college joined its sister schools on a number of shared initiatives focused on library collaboration and, as the consortium matured, on projects that connected the libraries more directly to their partners in teaching and learning, the faculty. Even from its early days the constituent parties recognized the ways in which they might be stronger together.

Indeed, the Ohio Five libraries have a strong record of collaborative projects that have sought to connect the work of libraries directly to the teaching and learning on our campuses. These are social, political, and sometimes very personal endeavours that require the libraries, as initiators of the collaboration, to navigate campus politics and interdepartmental conflict, and also to confront long-held perceptions of what a librarian does and what a library is. If the value of the library is not its volumes, then what is it? This is a question the Ohio Five libraries have confronted many times over through a series of successive collaborations funded largely by the Mellon Foundation.

These collaborations continued with a $475,000 award from the Mellon Foundation in 2000 to strengthen the teaching of information literacy in the liberal arts curriculum. Projects undertaken for this grant firmly established the librarian liaison model across all five libraries, and provided the context for librarians to assert their value as partners in teaching and as collaborators in the design of new assignments and courses.

A $600,000 award from the Mellon Foundation in 2009 launched the libraries' collaborative digital initiatives with a two-year project entitled *Next Steps in the Next Generation Library: Integrating Digital Collections into the Liberal Arts Curriculum*. This grant leveraged the relationships developed between librarian liaisons and their faculty colleagues to identify and digitize collections with application to particular courses or assignments. It also broadened the scope of the librarian-faculty relationship, moving beyond information literacy toward the co-creation of curricular resources. The success of this initiative brought many important structural questions to the fore, such as how to ensure that libraries and the skills of those working in libraries evolve along with technology, how to assess the use and efficacy of digital collections as curricular resources, and how to develop the technical infrastructure necessary to sustain a digitization program and the preservation of objects they produce.

In 2013, the Ohio Five libraries doubled down on the assertion that digital projects, specifically the process of teaching with and through them, are necessarily collaborative endeavours: they began work on a new initiative entitled *Digital Collections: From Projects to Pedagogy and Scholarship*, supported by a $775,000 award from the Mellon Foundation. This initiative shifted the focus away from identifying and exposing local collections through digitization and instead invited faculty to share ideas for digital projects with the potential to engage students as co-creators of new collections and active curators and stewards of the intellectual work they contributed to those projects. In recognition of the collaborative nature of these projects, the libraries intentionally sought to broaden collaboration, moving beyond the one-to-one pairing of librarian to faculty member on the same campus to the development of larger teams including libraries, faculty members, instructional technologists, and students. In addition, the project sought to encourage collaboration between faculty across campuses. As in the previous grant, this initiative brought home to the Ohio Five many of the questions and debates under discussion in the humanities disciplines writ large, namely debates about authorship and the qualities of digital scholarship, how to assess the impact of digital pedagogy on student learning, and how to evaluate student work.

It is noteworthy that the record of collaboration by the Ohio Five extends well beyond the libraries. While the libraries were indeed the spark that catalyzed the consortium, many other concurrent collaborations have been underway since its formation. In 1996, while the libraries were implementing their shared library system, the Mellon Foundation awarded $750,000 to language faculty across the five colleges to explore the application of emerging technology to language instruction and foster the design of new courses. In 2006, a faculty-led initiative to evaluate student development in the areas of creative and critical thinking was supported by a generous $300,000 grant from the Teagle Foundation; in 2015, Teagle awarded a second grant to the Ohio Five for $280,000 to support a faculty initiative on greater curricular coherence, an initiative designed to develop structures for students to gain a more coherent and holistic understanding of their educational experiences. In 2015, the Mellon Foundation awarded a generous $2 million grant to support development of a program that paired postdoctoral fellows from The Ohio State University with language departments on the Ohio Five liberal arts campuses for instruction in languages not widely taught.

We offer this history of collaborative endeavours not simply to chronicle the activities of the Ohio Five since its origins in the mid-1990s, but as context for the description that follows of our evolving approaches to establishing institutional structures that foster digital scholarship and pedagogy in the liberal arts. As the Ohio Five launched into its first coordinated effort to develop curricular digital projects, there was already an existing and robust social network in place established by earlier collaborations that fostered productive relationships between the libraries and the faculty of each college. The evolutionary phases of our planning and implementation, from our earliest initial digital initiatives through to the present, represent a coherent arc that culminates in a sort of "social knowledge" built through iterations of experimentation and reflection and propagated by members of the consortium to others throughout the network.

## Phases of Collaboration

Building on the groundwork of the collaborations established with the advent of the Ohio Five, library personnel began, in the consortium's second decade, to lay the foundations of their specifically digital endeavours. In reflecting on these efforts—in thinking through the ways in which we might helpfully frame them for a wide audience—we have come to rely on the perfunctory method of metamorphic phases. These phases will map to the digitally-informed Mellon grants of 2009 and 2013, but we will be less interested here in outlining the activities of those grants than in articulating our retrospective understanding of the thinking that informed the development of those grants. In other words, we would like to work through the intellectual and infrastructural contexts out of which those grant projects grew rather than the projects as such. Implicit here is the notion that, even though the boon of grant funding is a relatively common connection among institutions exploring digital scholarship, the terms and conditions of grant-funded efforts will necessarily differ. These idiosyncrasies are enough to suggest that we might more helpfully abstract out our mindset from our methods.

In the balance of this section, then, we will work through three phases we have identified in the development of our digital scholarship efforts: a material phase, a human phase, and an institutional phase. These may also be thought of—loosely, and respectively—as our past, our present, and our future, although such temporal boundaries obscure the fact that the work is ongoing and on a continuum. In practice, our "present" is equal parts "near past" and "near future." While phases mark the passage of time merely as a matter of course, we do see this work as having evolved, one phase necessarily growing from that which preceded it. If we belabour these caveats, it is because we want to be careful not to prescribe. These are not "best practices," or even "practices," but rather a narrative account of how we arrived at where we are from where we started. The stories, we hope, will sound familiar enough to spawn further conversations as well as local explorations.

(i) Material Phase

We refer here to a "material" phase that is as much metaphor as actual matter. On the one hand, as the work of the Ohio Five libraries transitioned from building digital literacies in the early 2000s into building digital collections on our respective campuses in 2009, the work was very much centred on the transformation of material archival objects—documents, museum artifacts, works of art, magnetic tape—into digital surrogates. As the Next-Generation Library (NGL) efforts got underway, the grant narrative focused on the "curriculum development program for faculty, who will partner with librarians to identify, build, and integrate digital collections into their courses" (Five Colleges of Ohio 2009, 6). At its core, then, lay the digital collections, but only as the product of a process by which material objects on our campuses were identified, digitized, and curated to comprise these collections.

It is important to note that the authors of the grant define the working relationship between "teaching" faculty and librarians—some of these librarians were faculty and others were not—as a "partnership." Such a framework reshapes much of the discourse around these academic relationships, shifting from an explicit support model into a collaboration between academic peers. Whether or not this framing was deliberate, it does the rhetorical work of asserting the librarians' intellectual and professional stake in the endeavours, a move that implicitly, at least, pushes against perceived inequities in the working relationships between librarians and disciplinary faculty.[1] As we will discuss below, however, the execution of the NGL grant efforts, in many

---

[1] We would not argue that these are in exactly the same spirit, but we see similar resistance in the responses of Porter (2014) and Nowviskie (2014) to the OCLC report on libraries and digital humanities centres (Schaffner and Erway 2014). While the distinction in these pieces is between the librarian and the "DH academic" rather than a "faculty" writ large, we would posit that the arguments about librarians' subject expertise and intellectual stake in projects resonate in our reading of the NGL grant language here.

cases, only underscored these inequities; we would like to suggest that this focus on the material has something to do with it.

While the framing language surrounding the "Next-Generation Library" always begins with "an emphasis on partnerships between faculty and librarians to integrate digital resources into the curriculum," then, the work itself is firmly seated in the mechanisms that support the digital resources more than they might foster the partnerships as such. These mechanisms comprise the kind of materiality to which we alluded in the opening of this section. We distinguish the "actual matter"—a readily tangible materiality—from the figurative because the latter, although it does not obviously take up material space in the world, is nonetheless important in the development of these efforts.

Of course, we do not suggest that digital technologies are abstract entities, made up solely of energy carried along the "ethernet" and stored in "the cloud." They do take up space on earth: server farms exist, routers and switches direct signals, and fiber optics carry the Internet around the globe. We are thinking, instead, about the tension inherent in Bruno Latour's notion of "idealist materialism" (Latour 2007). For Latour, the fixation on the "material" object, as it were, obscures any true materiality of a thing—to use Latour's theoretical frame—that is as equally imbricated in the milieu of its creation as it is a result of the process of assembly. In our formulation, we are casting our privileging of technical infrastructure as an idealist materialism that, in practice, if without malice, obscures the political and social conditions out of which that infrastructure grows. Indeed, even as the NGL grant affirms "partnerships between faculty and librarians," the combination of objects and technical infrastructure makes up the fabric of the grant: the NGL grant would "enhance access to the scholarly output," "enrich [library staff's] technological sophistication and ability to envision and implement innovative efforts," provide "a digital infrastructure program," and "create The Five Colleges of Ohio Digital Collections Portal [http://www.ohio5.org/portal/tag/wooster/]," a website for sharing projects and documentation (Five Colleges of Ohio 2009, 6). These are the material (if you will) conditions from which collaboratively curated collections will grow.

Attention to the material necessities that undergird the work of the grant is, of course, necessary for the success of the endeavour. Indeed, institutional repositories were adopted to improve and mediate access to the output of scholars in the Ohio Five. In addition, the tools for digitization—scanners, cameras, conversion devices—were purchased, and librarians were trained to use these tools to transform physical objects into bits and bytes. Perhaps most importantly, best practices were researched and articulated, workflows were established and published, virtual and actual locations were created for virtual and actual objects, and humans were identified who could facilitate the work of digitizing the collections. All of these features are not just necessary for the mechanisms of digitization, but in fact fundamental aspects of responsible digital librarianship.

The focus of what we are describing as the first phase of our efforts, then, was on building material infrastructure. Though trailblazing in our consortium, the framing justification (Five Colleges of Ohio 2009, 3) relied on the now-staid truisms of academic computing and digital librarianship: "Digitization improves access to [special collections and archival] resources"; "open access to scholarly resources is an essential aspect of next-generation library development"; "today's students ... are digital natives who have never known a time when the Internet did not exist"; and "today's faculty 'manage' their courses online, teach with a wide variety of technologies, and produce and communicate the results of their research to colleagues in ways that are digitally based." The clarion call of the grant, then, was for the participants—both faculty and students—to leverage familiarity with digital tools and technologies, leading to increased openness and access to campus resources and scholarship. The grant's outreach, in other words, was predicated upon minimizing anxieties associated with technologies through simultaneous appeals to the technologically familiar and the digitally good. As reported to our granting agencies, we fulfilled the promises of our charge: much technical infrastructure was established and many invested humans were identified, partnerships were forged, and the material successes were made manifest in the multiple, smaller-scale projects that turned physical objects into curated digital collections.[2] These successes showed the way forward: leveraging the established human and technical infrastructures "to transition from a model focused on the traditional digital reformatting of materials to designing projects that fully integrate the functionalities offered by today's technologies, enable researchers to interact with their materials in new ways, and deepen student engagement."[3] The authors of the next Ohio Five grant application

---

[2] One might see the project discussed by Flynn, Oyler, and Miles (2015) as an example of infrastructure establishment; the collections integration initiative as one way in which stakeholders were identified and partnerships forged; and the Oberlin College Ethnographic Collection (http://www2.oberlin.edu/library/digital/ocec/) as a digitization project that continues to evolve.

[3] Ohio Five grant application for *Digital Collections: From Projects to Pedagogy and Scholar-*

would frame these efforts as "digital scholarship," and while we will discuss the shape of these efforts in more detail in the subsequent phase, it is worth noting here that the framework for the efforts necessarily and appropriately shifts from material infrastructure to more explicitly critical engagements with "the digital"—a shift away from Latour's idealistic materialism toward a more fully realized accounting of the work we were doing. The development that we can trace through the rhetorical frames is natural and intuitive.

By way of transition to the next, "Human" phase of our processes, it should be noted that the execution of the latter grant was informed by the experiences of the librarians working on the earlier one. The NGL grant process was focused more on establishing the necessary parts to make various digitization shops run than on the needed investment in human capital to run those shops. The work became arduous, and the divisions of labour only seemed to underscore perceived inequities rather than alleviate them. The second phase of the grant—and the driving impulse for the Pedagogy and Scholarship grant—was therefore focused on the project team as a collection of stakeholders, each of whom contributed a unique and equally valuable perspective. Although "the project" remained the basic unit of our endeavours, it was in practice the project team that formed the core of our achievements.

(ii) Human Phase

We call this "the Human Phase," perhaps reluctantly, because it marked a shift in perspective from the "things" of Ohio Five digital scholarship to the humans and thought that comprised Ohio Five digital culture. Both necessitated a kind of building, as we will see, but the character of each construction was qualitatively unique. Of course, identifying this phase as specifically "human" does not suggest that other stages of the initiative failed to focus on the people involved. However, only through a retrospective lens can we see that our work was about building culture rather than collections or other projects. The balance of this section will discuss the ways in which we worked toward this, both in theory and in practice.

In the fall of 2013, as we were establishing the protocols and procedures for the Pedagogy and Scholarship grant, the Digital Humanities universe that was informing our practices was occupied by a figurative thread of useful conversation about the ways in which this work was being done. Earlier in the year, a panel at the annual meeting of the Modern Language Association (MLA) explored "The Dark Side of Digital Humanities," and specifically "the impact of digital humanities on research and teaching in the humanities in higher education—the question of how digital humanities will impact the future of the humanities in general."[4] By 2013, the community also had a shared primer: the first number of the *Debates in the Digital Humanities* series had been published the previous year. In that first edition, Julia Flanders—a librarian and digital humanist from the antecedent era known as "humanities computing"—engaged with "the novel forms of academic practice that even conventional academics find themselves undertaking when they embark on a digital project," as well as "the question of what 'knowledge work' really is and where its boundaries lie" (Flanders 2012). In the same year, Miriam Posner had written a widely circulated blog post (2012) about "the 'make digital humanities happen' postdoctoral fellowship."

Who does this work, and in what segments of the academy is this work done? What are the labour structures that specifically foster the kind of engaged digital scholarship to which we aspire? These questions, when abstracted out, orbit around the concept of the project team and the people who comprise it. Indeed, as a part of the DH/DS zeitgeist of that moment, Miriam Posner (2014) argues that academics empowered to do so should "Commit to DH people." She advocates calls for fellows rather than calls for projects, and muses: "What if the group wasn't (just) faculty? What if it was a mixed group of faculty, librarians, technologists, and students? How much healthier that would be than reinscribing academic hierarchies, which are just so exhausting." While it is not entirely obvious when one looks at our workflow, this centring of the ideas and relationships that people forge—and precisely the kinds of participants about whom she is excited—was the true North of our compass.

In our project workflow, the process did indeed flow through the project idea; these were the kernels that grew into project teams. Individuals, notably faculty, would submit their ideas, at whatever stage of development; this would activate a process by which the Ohio Five Digital Scholar contacted the local grant liaison—a librarian—to plan the next steps. It was in these subsequent steps that we demonstrated a focus on the local communities of practice. The project team was then assembled from various stakeholders on that campus. These typically included education technologists (or the equivalent), a liaison librarian, the faculty member, the digital scholar, and a student who was identified by one of the team members as standing to benefit from and contribute to the project team. This model worked under three

---

[4] One can read more about this framing in Chun, Grusin, Jagoda, and Raley (2016), as well as a fuller accounting in Grusin (2014).

assumptions: (1) projects could not, and should not, happen in a vacuum; (2) there were probably stakeholders on campus better equipped than any one member of the team to shepherd portions of these projects; and (3) organizing these stakeholders would make both process and projects more efficient.

On a very practical level, our project teams—comprised as they were of persons with varying sets of experience—leveraged the expertise that we had on campus. As noted before, the earlier grant was framed primarily as a partnership between libraries and the non-library faculty; these project partnerships needed to grow, along with the projects themselves, beyond digitization. As the workflow was in development the Ohio Five Digital Scholar was keen on including, specifically, educational technology groups with a history of working with faculty on technology-based projects. Additionally, students would lend valuable insights from the ground floor, as it were; it was important to consider fully how their peers might experience the pedagogical projects that were being proposed. In some cases the students on the project teams were in fact technical experts in a particular process and, thus, found ways to lead from within. As an example of a collaboration between French and Francophone Studies and Computer Science (CS), the CS student was the team member best equipped to wrestle with Optical Character Recognition (OCR) processes and corrective algorithms. More than this, though, his contributions gave him project-based experience that he could add to his CV.[5]

No less practical, but perhaps more specific to our small campuses, the team-centred approach to project development helped to build good will among all parties involved. On the one hand, the project leads—the teaching faculty—could witness a microcosm of a widely-reaching investment in the innovative pedagogies with which they wanted to experiment. On the other hand, such investments in technology-based innovative pedagogies have been in the purview of campus educational technologists; by articulating the value of these perspectives in the context of a collaborative endeavour, our model did its best to minimize the perception of domain encroachment. The general philosophy and rhetorical bent in our team formation is that all parties, students included, must have the space to articulate their intellectual stake in any given project; with this as a starting point we could then stage the processes and identify the partners most invested in each stage. Finally, such careful articulations invited good will in the librarian team members by

---

[5] You can read more about this project as the Digital Scudéry case study in Mauro et al. 2017.

modelling the ways in which the work would be distributed, alleviating (with time) any residual fallout from perceived inequities in the preceding grant.

Finally, as we reflect on the trajectory of our efforts, a significant long-term effect of the team-based approach is that it amplified the important conversations we were having on our campuses about the nature of this work. By broadening the census of people who had a stake in these efforts and by starting from the notion that the work was necessarily collaborative, we broadened the pool of perspectives on our campuses and in the consortium. When we understand that the projects were actually the by-product of this kind of critical engagement with digital scholarship rather than its point, we are able to frame the intellectual efforts therein: we centre the collaboratively-conceived questions rather than the projects they drive. The result is a culture of Ohio Five digital scholarship predicated upon this critical and collaborative relationship with technologies and projects.

It is this critical turn, if you will, in our framing of the consortial and local digital endeavours that positions us to move into the next phase of our work. If we are to expand these efforts into their next natural iteration, we need structures that reward students and faculty in the currencies that matter to them: courses taught and credits earned. In other words, we need curricular frameworks that create meaningful space for digitally focused courses and evaluative structures that encourage experimentation in humanistic research and teaching. Critical engagement is not just an intellectual exercise, but a way of thinking through technologies by practising with technologies. By shifting our scholarly proximity to "digital scholarship," we resituate the conversations so that they are more clearly aligned with the missions of our colleges, all of which guide us in helping students become informed and responsible citizens. This is the kind of work that presidents, deans, and academic officers can get behind.

At least, this seems to be the case: our campuses are working individually and collectively to pursue these structures and curricular frameworks. This pursuit will be the focus of what we identify here as a third phase of our development: the institutional phase. Before articulating the details of this latter phase, an accounting of "where we are now," it is worth pausing to underscore the ways in which our work has been informed by a social knowledge feedback loop. Certainly, individuals are bound by the laws of time and space—one can only do what one is able to do in and of oneself. But by creating channels that allow individual efforts to inform the trajectory of the whole, progress can be made in a way that is not just more representative but also more resilient. Social knowledge creation, in other words, is not just about the ways in which our work at this moment is very often necessarily collaborative, but about the ways in which our efforts are fundamentally interwoven. Some of this is intentional, of course, but we want to suggest here that much is imperceptible, just beyond our ken. It is this kind of social knowledge creation that makes up the fabric of our digital culture, overcomes inertia, and prepares us, as a matter of course, for institutional change.

(iii) Institutional Phase

Libraries have been the main drivers of the programmatic digital humanities endeavours at the Ohio Five to date, resulting in visible changes to both technical infrastructure and personnel. Librarians specializing in digital collections and curation are now in place at each college; consortial positions have been restructured and expanded to provide more centralized support for coordinating digital initiatives; and many lasting partnerships have formed between librarians, faculty, and technologists across the consortium. This collaboration has fostered development of curriculum-driven digital projects, as well as experimentation with new pedagogies that aim to cultivate critical engagement with and through digital media and technologies.

Even as the libraries have developed significant experience and capacity to support digital scholarship and pedagogy, however, questions linger about the staying power of these new pedagogies, and the extent to which the colleges' library-led digital initiatives might be more broadly integrated into the curricula through expanded partnerships with faculty interested in developing more digitally-inflected courses and assignments. There are some obvious limitations on how deeply these initiatives can be integrated into the curriculum without faculty champions to share in ownership over their development. If we do indeed subscribe to the notion that our collaborative projects are true partnerships involving faculty, librarians, technologists, and students, each contributing unique strengths toward the creation of something new, the initiative requires not only joint participation but joint ownership over its development and its future.

After two successive grants designed to foster curriculum-driven digital collections and pedagogical digital projects, the "real, transformative value" of digital humanities to which Muñoz (2016) refers had not been made clear to all stakeholders in the Ohio Five. The prevailing perception among our chief academic officers and presidents was that these library-initiated projects were largely concerned with developing collections related to faculty research and scholarship. Although it was clear that students were engaged as contributors, the types of engagement and the nature of their contributions had not been articulated in a way that resonated strongly with our administrators. This perception, coupled with the inevitable uncertainty around the terms "digital scholarship" and "digital humanities," had our deans and provosts wondering about the place of digital humanities in the liberal arts.

Alexander and Davis address this question in their call and response critique from the 2012 edition of *Debates in the Digital Humanities,* asking: "Should Liberal Arts Campuses Do Digital Humanities?" Although we may now question that question, so to speak, we must remember that they wrote their chapter at a time when investment in the digital humanities was focused on the idea and seeming necessity of a "digital humanities centre"—something that represented a prohibitive cost for most small private liberal arts colleges. It was not at all obvious how these colleges could "do digital humanities" in an environment with far fewer resources for faculty development and technical infrastructure, and less focus on scholarship as the institutional mission and priority. While their article does acknowledge that centres established at liberal arts institutions such as Hamilton College and Occidental College may serve as transitional infrastructure to bridge the concept of "Big DH" (Gustafson-Sundell 2013) with the more pedagogically focused liberal arts, they articulate a liberal arts approach to digital humanities characterized by the application of problem-based learning and an emphasis on process over product. Time and experience have since led to a further discussion about the digital humanities on liberal arts campuses, thereby elevating conversations among DH practitioners about the impacts of digital humanities pedagogy. The contributions by Mauro and by Jakacki and Faull to the volume *Doing Digital Humanities* (Crompton, Lane, and Siemens 2016) serve to extrapolate DH-inflected pedagogy from a more general digital pedagogy by emphasizing the foregrounding of critical reflection, project-based pedagogy, and student agency in the making of digital projects that engage them directly in the methods of humanistic inquiry.

Problem-based learning and a focus on process over product—which we had been practising all along, although we had not yet widely adopted a shared language to express it—have surfaced as the resonant points in our internal discourse with faculty colleagues and academic officers about the value of the projects developed. It is this explicit reference to student learning and process that has shifted the conversation in our consortium from faculty-centred digital scholarship toward undergraduate engagement with technology as both a tool for knowledge creation and the subject of critical inquiry itself. This critical turn toward student learning and the curricula of our liberal arts campuses is in fact the culmination of our successive grants. We have progressed from a focus on developing digital collections to a focus on pedagogy and undergraduate scholarship, as the title of our grant foretold we would.

Toward the end of the grant period for *Digital Collections: From Projects to Pedagogy and Scholarship*, conversations about how to sustain engagement led, for the first time, to a series of constructive discussions between the Library Committee (a consortial committee made up of all five library directors) and the Academic Committee (a committee of the consortium's provosts and associate deans). Through these conversations, the libraries aimed to clarify the value of digital humanities pedagogy, to better articulate students' contributions to the projects, and to elevate discussions about the barriers to growth and experimentation throughout the consortium. One might immediately assume that finances are the primary challenge to growth—after all, projects do require funds. In our liberal arts context, however, projects have been relatively inexpensive, and in some cases developed entirely with in-kind contributions from librarians and technologists. Time is really our scarcest resource, and when that scarcity is coupled with uncertainty about the value of this work in the eyes of the institution, especially for those not yet tenured, project ideas are deferred and growth is stunted.

Storytelling has served an important role in these discussions. It was not enough to describe the transformative value of digital humanities pedagogy in the abstract when we were seeking tangible results: changes in the curricula of our institutions; formalized experiential opportunities for students in the humanities; and institutional support for both digital scholarship and teaching innovation manifested in changes to tenure and promotion review guidelines. Without clarity on the value of this kind of project-based digital pedagogy, these conversations could have easily stalled. Stories about projects, their goals, and their outcomes have served as compelling illustrations. We offer a few of those here by way of example.

- In the fall of 2015, Jennifer Hayward, an English professor at the College of Wooster, began work on *elsewhere.anywhere*, a relatively simple blog-based project to showcase writing by students in her course "Writing Travel." The project was heavily influenced by Laurie McMillin's *AWAY: Experiments in Travel and Telling* (http://awayjournal.org/), a similar blog-based student journal developed a year earlier for her "Writing

About Travel" course at Oberlin College. While both projects had basic technical platforms, they challenged students to consider their audiences more critically in the process of writing for a public Web.

• A slightly more advanced project, entitled *Ciudad Juárez: Urban Art and Poetry* (https://ciudadjuarezartandpoetry.org/), was initiated by Juan Armando Rojas of Ohio Wesleyan University in collaboration with instructional technologist David Soliday at the 2015 Institute for Liberal Arts Digital Scholarship (ILiADS). This website interrogates violence, femicide, and other sociopolitical issues of the U.S.-Mexico border region through creative works of art and poetry. The project's use of Omeka and its Neatline platform were influenced in large part by *Mapping the Martyrs* (https://mappingthemartyrs.ohio5.org/), a project led by David Eastman, formerly of Ohio Wesleyan University. Eastman's project was a collaborative initiative involving one of the authors of this chapter and a student; it required Eastman's students to research, collect, and present evidence of Christian martyr stories and situate them within a historical geography to examine them as evidence in relation to each other spatially and temporally. After graduating, the student who developed the Neatline exhibit for the project went on to work as a consultant on Rojas's *Ciudad Juárez: Urban Art and Poetry* project, lending her experience with the platform.

• *The Expanding Archive: Denison LGBTQ Past / Present / Future* (http://www.expandingarchives.org/), a collaboration between professor Sheila Wilson ReStack, librarian Shannon Robinson, and student Orpheus Peng of Denison University, is a digital archive of materials related to the university's Queer Studies program. Peng developed a custom theme for the Omeka platform on which this project was based. His work was later adapted by another student, Zach Phillips-Gary, at the College of Wooster in his own work as a collaborator on *Women in Sport and Physical Education at the College of Wooster* (http://www.ohio5.org/woosterwomeninsport/), also an Omeka-based project, initiated by physical education professor Brenda Meese.

• As a final story, we offer an example from our inaugural Five Colleges of Ohio Post-Baccalaureate Fellow in Digital Scholarship Olivia Geho. After working as a student under her mentor, English professor Regina Martin, on a project titled *Literature and Professional Life: A Digital Life Stories Archive* (http://ohla.info/toolkit/faculty-project-archive/

oral-history-with-communities-of-practice/literature-and-profession-al-life-a-digital-life-stories-archive/), Geho graduated from Denison University in 2016 and subsequently returned to the Ohio Five in her current position. Geho has been a critical voice in our communications with administrators about the value of collaborative, project-based digital pedagogy for students; she has come to embody that value in practice, demonstrating how she has applied her liberal arts experience to learn new technologies and evaluate their relevance and application to humanistic questions.

Stories of collaborative curricular projects such as those above,[6] and a clearer articulation of their value to students, were compelling enough for the deans and provosts serving on the Five Colleges of Ohio Academic Committee to endorse the formation of the Ohio Five Digital Scholarship Task Force in the fall of 2017. This group, co-led by Alexia Hudson-Ward, Azariah Smith Root Director of Libraries at Oberlin College, and Catherine Dollard, Associate Provost for Academic Affairs and Professor of History at Denison University, was charged with defining digital scholarship and digital literacy in a liberal arts context and charting a path forward for the consortium built on the experience of the previous two grants.

The Ohio Five Digital Scholarship Task Force comprised a collaborative, cross-departmental, and cross-campus group of faculty, librarians, and technologists. All contributed as equal partners to a conversation about the transformative value of project-based digital scholarship and pedagogy to the teaching and learning on our campuses, but also to an honest interrogation of the barriers to experimentation and the challenges to deeper integration in the colleges' curricula.

In a rare joint meeting of the Ohio Five Library Committee, Academic Committee, and college presidents in the summer of 2018, the Digital Scholarship Task Force offered five recommendations for the consortium

---

[6] Each of these stories serves to highlight the network quality of the consortium, as well as the ways in which actors within that network serve to influence each other and provide validation for each other's work in the absence of institutional structures and rewards that might otherwise lend legitimacy to those contributions. The openness of one project, and the transparency of its process, can have a strong generative effect on the network, giving other projects licence to move from concept to reality in a way that might not have happened had their processes remained hidden until complete.

which led to a robust and constructive discussion about future directions. Those recommendations were:

1. Develop student fellowships and post baccalaureate opportunities to position students for success during and beyond college.
2. Give faculty the resources to infuse digital practices in their courses by exploring digital lab options and summer pedagogy institutes.
3. Strive for sustainability by developing rewards for faculty and staff service to the consortial enterprise and/or a shared consortial position.
4. Create an information hub for practitioners that includes toolkits, rubrics, documentation, and templates.
5. Promote our distinctiveness by sharing the impact and outcomes of our projects with our higher education community, including faculty and prospective students.

The conversation that accompanied these recommendations was broad and instructive. Deans expanded on these recommendations, proposing new ideas for cohorts of digital student fellows, and at least one president wondered aloud what an Ohio Five designation or credential denoting digital competency might look like. At a time when the leaders of our liberal higher education organizations in the United States are compelled to publicly defend the value of a liberal arts education (Association of American Colleges and Universities 2018), this conversation could easily have taken a different tone. Participants could have spent their time discussing how a consortial "digital liberal arts" program could be a solution to poor job prospects for humanities majors, but instead, the participants in this group focused their thinking on how to best cultivate more critically engaged digital citizens.

We credit Sarah Bolton, president of the College of Wooster, for providing a useful framework to help us organize our thinking about the task force recommendations and ways in which we might map our activities. She described these activities as a triangle, with its three points representing digital literacy, digital scholarship, and digital citizenship. This "Bolton Triangle" might suggest an implied hierarchical structure, in which a learner progresses sequentially through stages of increasing nuance and complexity toward some level of mastery, but one could also interpret this framing as cyclical, or even non-linear, since one's civic engagement could easily influence scholarship that uncovers new literacies yet to be fully developed.

With this new framework in hand, and with the enthusiastic endorsement of our administrators to continue developing plans for a broader consortial program, members of the Ohio Five Digital Scholarship Task Force sought to expand the membership of those contributing to the thinking and planning of what this new program might look like. By August 2018, the task force had assembled a group of almost forty participants representing faculty, librarians, technologists, career services staff, museums, and institutional researchers. In a brainstorming session, members of this highly collaborative and passionate group gave identity to this emerging consortial initiative and named it CODEX (https://codex.ohio5.org), an acronym for the Five Colleges of Ohio Collaborative for Digital Engagement and Experience.

## The Near Futures of Consortial Collaboration

CODEX is the outgrowth of both our *Next-Generation Library* and *Digital Collections: From Projects to Pedagogy and Scholarship* initiatives. It represents a holistic approach to cultivating critical engagement with technology for engaged citizenship. It aims to bolster, and in some cases interrogate, institutional structures that are either absent or lacking in order to signal the explicit support of those engaged in curricular or co-curricular projects using or critiquing digital technologies.

The members of this new collaborative have organized themselves around the five recommendations put forth to administrators by the Digital Scholarship Task Force, condensing these into three focused but overlapping working groups with charges focused on curriculum development, student opportunities, and the need for an information and assessment hub.

The CODEX Curriculum Development Working Group has been charged with exploring the development of structural programs, such as pedagogy institutes, digital labs, and faculty fellowships that address the need among faculty for time and space to develop, test, and implement new digital pedagogies with supportive colleagues in a consortial environment. The CODEX Student Opportunities Working Group will explore the development of opportunities for liberal arts undergraduate students across disciplines to engage in experiential learning that foregrounds digital technologies as both a mode of knowledge creation and the subject of critical inquiry. Lastly, the CODEX Information Hub and Assessment Working Group will explore the development of a repository of information, toolkits, and models that serves as both a reference for practitioners and a guide for faculty or staff responsible for assessing digital research or digital pedagogies—a critical gap at several of our campuses. Each group is led by two co-chairs who, collectively, comprise the CODEX Steering Committee and are supported by one member of the Ohio Five consortial staff.

The breadth of the CODEX initiative and the support in principle from our administrations bodes well for its future, and while we are encouraged by the collective attention to institutional structural issues, it would be disingenuous to suggest that the initiative has reached a state of institutionalization. Cohen (2017) offers three characteristic properties of programs or initiatives that might be said to have become institutionalized. As he suggests, initiatives that begin as experimental, custom projects ultimately need to be routinized to lower the barriers to participation and to achieve scalable support and maintenance. Similarly, practices that at one point are considered "new," "disruptive," or "innovative" must become normalized, such that they come to be perceived as completely ordinary and, indeed, "unremarkable." Lastly, he suggests that programs need to be depersonalized such that their existence does not depend exclusively upon the efforts and reputations of their founding champions. In other words, people should be able to come and go without dooming the initiative to collapse.

Cohen's suggestions take on additional nuance in a consortial context. They raise questions about precisely what institution they refer to. Do they describe the individual institutions or the consortium itself? In 2017, the Ohio Five went through a period of extraordinary transition that would have threatened a less connected organization. Our founding executive director retired and three of our five library directors, including the principal investigator of the Digital Pedagogy and Scholarship grant, transitioned to new positions at other institutions. Upon her arrival, our new executive director conducted a series of interviews with key stakeholders throughout the consortium to explore the question "Are we one, or are we five?" These conversations revealed that our members do not see the consortium as an institution but rather a community of five institutions united, at their core, by their collaborations rather than their infrastructure. It is through these collaborations that ideas and knowledge are spread throughout the community, and it is precisely this community that lends heft to new initiatives that might otherwise languish indefinitely as the call to arms of one or a small group of practitioners working alone within an institutional context.

The EDUCAUSE Center for Analysis and Research (ECAR) working paper "Building Capacity for Digital Humanities" (2017) offers a variety of models for fostering and sustaining digital humanities practices, providing a helpful frame through which to consider the value of community, particularly a community of members from different institutions, in building that capacity and overcoming local institutional challenges. One such model is the "consortial model," in which "the energy, knowledge, and community generated through these networks can feed back into each individual institution by demonstrating to upper-level administrators the importance, vitality, and broader interest in digital humanities." The Ohio Five CODEX initiative embodies this model in that it leverages a socially constructed knowledge of practice to expand the knowledge and experience in the community.

Our account of the emerging CODEX initiative is very much the "near future" of our narrative, and as such there is some hesitation that accompanies its retelling here, since there is much uncertainty about the details of its eventual enactment. However, in keeping with the spirit of this volume and with the promotion of social knowledge creation, we share this open window on a process, rather than the opaque final product of our collective efforts, in hopes that it may prove instructive to others and productive to us. In truth, there is no final product. Our story is one of continuously working toward something which, only in the act of working toward it, has become clearer and more embedded in the fabric of our institutions.

WORKS CITED

Alexander, Bryan, and Rebecca Frost Davis. 2012. "Should Liberal Arts Campuses Do Digital Humanities?: Process and Products in the Small College World." In *Debates in the Digital Humanities*, edited by Matthew K. Gold, 368–89. Minneapolis: University of Minnesota Press.

Association of American Colleges and Universities. 2018. "Joint Statement on the Value of Liberal Education by AAC&U and AAUP." AAC&U website, May 31. https://www.aacu.org/about/statements/2018/joint-statement-value-liberal-education-aacu-and-aaup.

Chun, Wendy Hui Kyong, Richard Grusin, Patrick Jagoda, and Rita Raley, 2016. "The Dark Side of the Digital Humanities." In *Debates in the Digital Humanities 2016*, edited by Matthew K. Gold and Lauren F. Klein, 493–509. Minneapolis: University of Minnesota Press.

Cohen, Dan. 2017. "Institutionalizing Digital Scholarship (or Anything Else New in a Large Organization)." *DanCohen.org*, November 29. http://dancohen.org/2017/11/29/institutionalizing-digital-scholarship-or-anything-else-new-in-a-large-organization/.

Cummings, Anthony M., and the Andrew W. Mellon Foundation. 1992. *University Libraries and Scholarly Communication: A Study Prepared for the Andrew W. Mellon Foundation.* Washington, DC: Association of Research Libraries.

Davidson, Cathy. 2017. *The New Education: How to Revolutionize the University to Prepare Students for a World in Flux.* New York: Basic Books.

EDUCAUSE Center for Analysis and Research. 2017. "Building Capacity for Digital Humanities: A Framework for Institutional Planning." EDUCAUSE website, May 30. https://library.educause.edu/ resources/2017/5/building-capacity-for-digital-humanities-a-framework-for-institutional-planning.

Five Colleges of Ohio. 2009. "Next-Generation Library (NGL) proposal to the Andrew W. Mellon Foundation." November 6. https://docs.google. com/viewer?a=v&pid=sites&srcid=ZGVmYXVsdGRvbWFpbnxvaDVuZX h0Z2VuZXJhd GlvbmxpYnJhcnl8Z3g6ZjcyM2ZkZTNlMDAxZDAy.

Flanders, Julia. 2012. "Time, Labor, and 'Alternate Careers' in Digital Humanities Knowledge Work." In *Debates in the Digital Humanities,* edited by Matthew K. Gold, 292–308. Minneapolis: University of Minnesota Press. http://dhdebates.gc.cuny.edu/debates/text/26.

Flynn, Stephen X., Catalina Oyer, and Marsha Miles. 2015. "Using XSLT and Google Scripts to Streamline Populating an Institutional Repository." *code{4}lib journal* 19. https://journal.code4lib.org/articles/7825.

Grusin, Richard. 2014. "The Dark Side of Digital Humanities: Dispatches from Two Recent MLA Conventions." *Differences* 25(1): 79–92.

Gustafson-Sundell, Nat. 2013. "On Remembering There Are Librarians in the Library." dh+lib Mini-Series, June 19. https://acrl.ala.org/ dh/2013/06/19/on-remembering-there-are-librarians-in-the-library/.

Jakacki, Diane, and Katherine Faull. 2016. "Doing DH in the Classroom: Transforming the Humanities Curriculum Through Digital Engagement." In *Doing Digital Humanities: Practice, Training, Research,* edited by Constance Crompton, Richard J. Lane, and Ray Siemens, 358–72. London and New York: Routledge.

Latour, Bruno. 2007. "Can We Get Our Materialism Back, Please?" *Isis* 98(1): 138–42.

Mauro, Aaron. 2016. "Digital Liberal Arts and Project-Based Pedagogies." In *Doing Digital Humanities: Practice, Training, Research*, edited by Constance Crompton, Richard J. Lane, and Ray Siemens, 373–83. London and New York: Routledge.

Mauro, Aaron, Daniel Powell, Sarah Potvin, Jacob Heil, Eric Dye, Bridget Jenkins, and Dene Grigar. 2017. "Toward a Seamful Design of Networked Knowledge: Practical Pedagogies in Collaborative Teams." *Digital Humanities Quarterly* 11(3): 303–14. http://www.digitalhumanities.org/dhq/vol/11/3/000322/000322.html.

Middleman, Louis. 2005. *Broadening Common Ground: The Five Colleges of Ohio, Inc. Celebrates a Decade of Accomplishment.* Oberlin, OH: Five Colleges of Ohio.

Muñoz, Trevor. 2016. "Recovering a Humanist Librarianship through Digital Humanities." In Laying the Foundation: Digital Humanities in Academic Libraries, edited by John W. White and Heather Gilbert, 3–14.. West Lafayette, IN: Purdue University Press.

Nowviskie, Bethany. 2014. "Asking for It." Personal blog, February 8. http://nowviskie.org/2014/asking-for-it/.

Porter, Dot. 2014. "What if We Do, In Fact, Know Best?: A Response to the OCLC Report on DH and Research Libraries." *dh+lib*, February 12. https://acrl.ala.org/dh/2014/02/12/what-if-we-do-in-fact-know-best-a-response-to-the-oclc-report-on-dh-and-research-libraries/.

Posner, Miriam. 2012. "The Digital Humanities Postdoc." *Miriam Posner's Blog*, May 7. http://miriamposner.com/blog/the-digital-humanities-postdoc/.

———. 2014. "Commit to DH People, Not DH Projects." *Miriam Posner's Blog*, March 18. http://miriamposner.com/blog/?s=commit+to+DH+people.

Schaffner, Jennifer, and Ricky Erway. 2014. "Does Every Research Library Need a Digital Humanities Center?" Dublin, OH: OCLC [Online Computer Library Center] Research. https://www.oclc.org/research/publications/library/2014/oclcresearch-digital-humanities-center-2014-overview.html.

# Rethinking Social Knowledge Creation in the Liberal Arts: The History and Future of Domain of One's Own

Martha Burtis, Nigel Haarstad, Jess Reingold, Kris Shaffer,
Lee Skallerup Bessette, Jesse Stommel, and
Sean Michael Morris

Virginia Woolf's 1929 essay "A Room of One's Own" began its life in two papers she had presented on the topic of "women and fiction." Anticipating her audiences' puzzlement about "a room of one's own," she explained that "a woman must have money and a room of her own if she is to write fiction" (Woolf 1935, 6). Later, she recounted what happened when she went to a (fictional) Oxbridge university library in hopes of consulting a manuscript copy of William Makepeace Thackeray's novel *Esmond*. "Here I was," she wrote, "actually at the door which leads into the library itself"—but that was as far as she got:

> I must have opened it, for instantly there issued, like a guardian angel barring the way with a flutter of black gown instead of white wings, a deprecating, silvery, kindly gentleman, who regretted in a low voice as he waved me back that ladies are only admitted to the library if accompanied by a Fellow of the College or furnished with a letter of introduction. (Woolf 1935, 12)

Clearly, even an ostensibly public institution such as a university library could not provide Woolf with the "room" she required, whether that was room to write, to read, to do research, or simply to reflect. Almost a century after Woolf wrote her essay, however, the University of Mary Washington (UMW) in Fredericksburg, Virginia, began an initiative to provide all members of its community with their own "rooms": rooms in the online realm. Taking its cue from both the title and philosophy of Woolf's essay, the Domain of One's Own project was launched in 2013.

In an online question-and-answer essay about the connection between Woolf's work and the UMW project, Debra Schleef (2016) asks, "What does it mean, both literally and figuratively, to have a room of one's own?" As she then explains:

ISBN 978-1-64959-008-4 (paper) ISBN 978-1-64959-009-1 (pdf) ISBN 978-1-64959-084-8 (epub)
*New Technologies in Medieval and Renaissance Studies* 8 (2022) 123–138

> Woolf's room with a lock, and resources (the famous "500 pounds a year," but also education, time, and access), provides a place within which the figurative can flower. Similarly, a domain is more than a delimited internet space with your name on it—it is a figurative room that provides time, creative license, and a space to express oneself freely.

When the idea for this project originated in 2007, therefore, it seemed appropriate to suggest that what a student in the twenty-first century needed in order to be a digital citizen was a digital space, a digital "room" of her own.

*Domain of One's Own: How It Works, and How It Has Grown*

The Domain of One's Own (DoOO) initiative at UMW gives all students, faculty, and staff the opportunity to receive a domain name with hosted web space, both of which are provided free of charge during their time at the university. Importantly, however, names can be chosen from one of four basic top level domains: .com, .net, .org, and .info. UMW thus provides online identities that would be available outside the academic environment—unlike those of other schools, at which the university or college is identifiable because its name is embedded in the URL. When students or faculty/staff members leave UMW, they can move their websites to commercial hosting services, but must then assume responsibility for payment.[1]

For its primary users, the students, the DoOO project was formulated with four goals in mind:

1. Provide students with the tools and technologies to build out a digital space of their own.
2. Help students appreciate how digital identity is formed.
3. Provide students with curricular opportunities to use the Web in meaningful ways.
4. Push students to understand how the technologies that underpin the Web work, and how that impacts their lives.

Domain of One's Own enables students, especially those who do not yet have an online presence, to establish themselves on the Web. Templates, as well as tools and resources such as cPanel and WordPress, allow them to become

---

[1] See "Signing Up on Domain of One's Own" (https://umw.domains/signing-up-on-domain-of-ones-own/) for complete instructions. DoOO websites are not hosted on campus, but by a local company, Reclaim Hosting.

familiar with the technology they need to build and customize their sites. Faculty members have access to both course and blog templates. Guides to various digital tools and media, as well as migration instructions for those about to leave UMW, are provided.

Launched as a pilot project with 116 domains, DoOO expanded in the fall of 2014 to provide free domains and hosting not only to every student, but to every member of the UMW community. The Digital Knowledge Center, which offered peer tutoring, also opened in the fall of 2014, and has since provided more than 400 DoOO tutorials; a faculty development project has been popular as well, with seventy participants registered over the course of three years.

DoOO's extraordinary growth can be measured in real numbers: by the fall of 2018, it had 2,422 active domains, with as many as 850 sign-ups in a single year. The project has garnered national and international attention;[2] more than forty other schools have DoOO-inspired initiatives, while individual faculty members at more than a hundred schools have implemented DoOO at the course level.

As ambitious and groundbreaking as it is, a project such as Domain of One's Own presents its own set of challenges and questions. Just getting back to basics, for example, what is the digital? What are the liberal arts? What happens at their intersection? What possibilities and what frictions arise? The concept of digital liberal arts is continuing to be defined, with a handful of initiatives underway at various institutions across the country—at Middlebury College in Vermont, and at Whittier and Occidental Colleges in California, among others. All are facing the challenge of preparing their students (and preparing faculty members to prepare their students) for digital citizenship in the rapidly evolving twenty-first century.

How can the liberal arts be infused ethically into initiatives such as Domain of One's Own—not to mention full online learning, and continuing education? How do we ensure that digital spaces, digital "rooms," are spaces students choose to make, to inhabit, to learn within, and perhaps to continue learning within once they graduate? How do we address privacy and security concerns? To answer these questions, we find ourselves looking back even as we look forward. In offering a version of the project's history, we cannot merely present a chronology; rather, we start here with an exploration of

---

[2] See Bessette 2016.

the origins and genealogy of the project, in order to capture its spirit, and to look toward its future.

*Origins, Precursors, and Open Source Experimentation*

The origins of Domain of One's Own coincide with the origins of the Web in higher education. When the Web arrived on our campuses in the mid- to late 1990s, it was already a powerful force that was washing over society. In every field, in every industry, in both the personal and the professional sphere, many were trying to stay afloat and figure out its meaning. It seems only reasonable to assume that in the domain of education, a domain that is entirely about the creating, building, and sharing of knowledge and learning, this new force of creation and knowledge-sharing could be fully and authentically realized.

In hindsight, we may well ask why educators could not see the power that this new medium was affording them, and were not immediately drawn to it—as a platform for transformational teaching, a space for public research and dissemination of knowledge, a place for collaboration on an entirely new level. At the dawn of the Internet age, however, this was easier said than done. If the cultural transition from print/analog to online/digital was one issue, the commercial paradigm shift was another. The Web hit higher education at a critical moment when we were already struggling with doing our work less like schools and more like businesses; the tech industry and its vendors had already begun to infiltrate academia with promises of how technology could help us achieve this goal.

The learning management system (LMS) developed as a teaching and course delivery tool in the late 1990s, and some early examples were actually born in the higher education environment: WebCT (University of British Columbia, 1995), Web Course in a Box (Virginia Commonwealth University, 1995), and CourseInfo (Cornell University, 1996). Blackboard, which is now used in some 100 countries around the world, was founded in 1997, and merged with CourseInfo to form the present company. Its rival Canvas is much newer, but also a worldwide phenomenon.

Courses have long been the way higher education has measured itself, and the way it has organized its administrative processes. But we would argue that with the greater adoption of administrative systems, higher education doubled down on that unit of measure—a failure of imagination, if you will, that identifies the *course* as the basic academic unit of measure rather than the *person*. Yet even if the course was established as a standard measurement, schools nevertheless valued the notion that each individual professor had the freedom to enact and explore the topic at hand, within that course, using the pedagogies of his or her own choosing. And, by extension, presumably the tools and technologies of his or her own choosing. When a learning management system goes beyond merely providing administrative and management features, however, and offering features designed (perhaps badly) to build community, share information, and collaborate with others, it is obviously influencing pedagogy.

It is easy to think that a tool can be defined by its basic functionality: the discussion board, the wiki page, synchronous chat, the quiz builder. But all of these tools are far more complex. They've been designed and coded and engineered by companies to provide functionality in particular ways. And that design and code guides both students' and instructors' experiences through their use.

Let's say someone told you that from now on, when you conduct a discussion in your classroom, you are bound by a series of rules, procedures, and steps. You must follow these rules at all times, and everyone else at your institution must as well. From now on, every classroom discussion at your school must be conducted using these same rules, procedures, and steps. If you don't like them, you will have to wait and see if the next update addresses your concerns. You would probably balk at this suggestion—and you should. But rules, procedures, and steps are exactly what code defines, and when we fail to acknowledge this we fail to see the pedagogical power that LMS technology can have in our classroom.

As the Web evolved into the 2000s, we were no longer restricted to the LMS. Not only were there many more tools from which we could choose, but the tools themselves had been developed using open source technology—applications to create websites in many different flavours: blogs, discussion forums, media galleries, and wikis. There were even open source learning management systems, such as the Sakai Project platform that first appeared in 2005. Additionally, we were working in a space in which we could learn to build our own tools if we wanted to, or at the very least could adapt the tools we had. And most of us started our own blogs around that time, as did many of our colleagues; WordPress, launched in 2003, is still one of the most popular blogging services worldwide.

Working with open source tools such as WordPress made possible all the things imagined back in the 1990s, and provided an opportunity to create alternatives to the LMS: learning environments that did not need to follow a standardized methodology. Open source culture was infused with a different set of values and beliefs: collaborative construction, iteration, fast prototyping, extensibility, and, of course, openness.

The Domain of One's Own project grew out of this open source experimentation. It is based on the belief that students should have a web space in which they can publish their (best) academic work, a space they can control, a space they can take with them after graduating. And like the open source concept itself, DoOO is revolutionary. As Audrey Watters (2015) says, "Giving students their own digital domain is a radical act."

The goal of DoOO is to help students think critically about their place on the Web, and a series of point and click tasks with instrumental outcomes does not help them move in that direction. But as Andrew Rikard (2015) notes: "Until students see this domain as a space that rewards rigor and experimentation, it will not promote student agency." The best domains do not fall into the cracks of formal assignments and assessment; rather, they subvert and even defy attempts at schooliness. A domain at its most "academically rigorous" doesn't overtly betray its origin as a graded set of tasks assigned by a teacher. Rikard continues: "The domains project isn't revolutionary to the traditional classroom, but it is revolutionary to a classroom reimagined around public scholarship, student agency, and experimentation."

### Building a Website Block by Block, Skill by Skill

In contrast to a traditional educational platform such as the LMS, Domain of One's Own enables faculty, staff, and students to gain "more control over their scholarship, data, and digital identity" (Watters 2015). But what does this mean? In a Web filled with third-party advertisers, social media platforms (with fake accounts), bots, and shady analytics companies all grabbing data, there is increasingly little space on the Web to call your own, a space where your content and information stays with you.

While it is nearly impossible to create quarantined places on the Web, there is a way to cultivate a presence, a digital identity, away from the presets and pressures of platforms that require inputting personal information. DoOO gives faculty, students, and staff the opportunity to inhabit a corner of the Web as a human rather than an account number—and the freedom to express and present themselves in any way they can imagine.

An integral part of this process is the development of flexible, adaptable modules—a series of DoOO Building Blocks.[3] The current modules are:

- Digital Identity
- Digital Privacy and Security
- Understanding the Web
- What is a Domain?
- Digital Citizenship
- Copyright, Fair Use, Creative Commons
- Data Ownership and Usage
- Representation (gender, race, culture, orientation)

Each module includes an overall goal, a handful of carefully selected readings, discussion questions, and activities for students, as well as an instructor guide and a "Customize it!" section. The goal of the "Digital Identity" module, for example, is to "[i]ntroduce concepts about how online identity is created, managed, and represented." Readings include an article about how much personal information can be found in public documents accessible on the Web. The activity section invites students to Google themselves and write a third-person biography based on what they have found.

Readings tackle the various challenges and potential pitfalls of life in the digital age. Topics covered by readings include: how a Google search works (Understanding the Web); the rules of Twitter (Digital Citizenship); what being "Internet famous" means (Digital Citizenship); why women are attacked by online trolls (Representation); and online anonymity (Data Ownership and Usage). As the module system grows and evolves over time, it can easily add new topics, activities, and questions of concern and interest: cyberbullying, crowdsourcing (and crowdsourcing fraud), the limits of free speech, the rise of the Instagram influencers.

In addition to the modules, the DoOO project includes a variety of resources to help with the actual building process: cPanel, to manage the account; WordPress and its Gutenberg Editor, to create and manage content; a guide to the creation of subdomains and subdirectories; and links to digital tools for everything from audio and video editing to maps and 3D printing. Faculty members have access to templates for both blogs and course sites.

WordPress, the most common tool used on Domain of One's Own, exemplifies the value of the skills learned by DoOO participants. This content

---

[3] See https://umw.domains/modules/ for more information on each module.

management system is popular not just at UMW, but across the Web. But even if it weren't that popular, or even if another open source tool were to overtake it in popularity in the next four years, the experience of learning it would retain its value when applied to other systems and online spaces. Consider some of the skills students learn by working with WordPress:

- identifying an audience;
- honing a voice;
- designing, building, and organizing an online space;
- considering the interplay between design and content;
- mixing media to create compelling narratives;
- understanding how Web applications work "under the hood" and how databases and scripts interact;
- adapting sites to consider accessibility and universal design;
- connecting disparate online spaces so they relate to each other as a synthesized whole;
- adapting a site as it grows and develops in new directions;
- responding to comments, and finding other spaces and sites on which to comment;
- learning how search engines rank sites, and the impact of search engine algorithms on how others find our own sites.

Domain of One's Own, then, aims to provide students with the opportunity to take critical control of their digital identities and to develop advanced digital literacy skills—in an organic and meaningful way that continues to appreciate in value.

### Terms of Service / Data and Privacy Issues

Giving UMW students, faculty, and staff their own domains may be a revolutionary idea, but it cannot be implemented without ground rules. The terms of service governing Domain of One's Own were written to give community members agency and ownership over their websites, as well as to provide transparency about what the project represents.[4] Following an overview of the project are the policies that apply to all users:

- Users of the system are expected to abide by all federal and state law (including copyright and intellectual property law) as well as by UMW's Network and Computer Use Policy, UMW's honour code, and UMW's

---

[4] The full document can be seen at http://umw.domains/terms-of-service.

statement of community values. UMW may remove any content that is found to be in violation of any of these laws, policies, or standards.

- Domains may not be used for nonprofit or for-profit businesses or organizations, and may not act as gateways for financial transactions. In addition, domains may not be used for events that are non-recurring or do not involve the UMW community.
- UMW may terminate this project at any time. Users will be given the opportunity to take personal ownership of their domains and export all of their content if the project should end.

One important aspect of DoOO is student data, a significant amount of which is collected through the program. How is this data, both institutional and personal, being used—and, more importantly, protected? If an influential administrator somewhere asks a new employee to produce a report that seems to violate the privacy or humanity of faculty or students, what incentive does that employee have to say "no"? Should they? Some of the points that have come up in discussion of this topic at UMW follow below.

## A Strong Safety Culture and Stop-Work Policies

The U.S. Occupational Safety and Health Administration (OSHA) has described a strong safety culture as one of "shared beliefs, practices, and attitudes," one in which "everyone feels responsible for safety and pursues it on a daily basis."[5] Establishing norms, telling stories, and feeling empowered to bring up concerns are just a few of the ways this might manifest itself. Although OSHA's definition was created with physical safety in mind, it transfers easily to the idea of institutional data ethics.

Stop-work policies are a natural extension of a strong safety culture. These policies started in our assembly lines and on oil rigs. If any member of the team sees something that seems unsafe or out of place, that worker has the authority to stop the entire assembly line until the issue is addressed. Applied to data ethics, this is simply a more formal and robust implementation of a strong data safety culture.

## Inserting Ethics into Policies

This seems obvious, but is worth reflection. Clear policies help empower individuals with stop-work authority by reducing ambiguity. The DoOO project

---

[5] OSHA factsheet, quoted in Haarstad 2016. This factsheet is no longer accessible on the OSHA website (https://www.osha.gov/).

has clear and concise rules meant to safeguard sensitive data. UMW students and faculty have an expectation that their personal data will remain private, and that those of us who handle their data will treat them with respect and dignity. Those ethical expectations do not always accompany the policies themselves, which are usually a list of prohibited actions. Our policies (at UMW and across all educational institutions) could be bolstered by illuminating the ethical and ideological underpinnings from which they are derived.

## Following IRB Rules for Institutional Data

Institutional review boards (IRBs), which review research involving human subjects to ensure that it is carried out ethically, are valuable models for the level of accountability required to deal with data collection. IRBs came into being following the passage of the 1974 National Research Act and the release of the 1978 Belmont Report on ethics in health care research.

The UMW Institutional Review Board (https://provost.umw.edu/irb/) must review and approve any human subject research by a member of the university community, whether student, faculty, or staff. By the same token, all students, faculty, and staff participating in the DoOO project have the right to protection of their institutional data. All community members must be treated as human beings, not just as data points. And because the IRB's membership is drawn from among various units across the university, it can provide a more objective space for evaluation and dissent in cases of complaint or dispute.

## Is All of This Really Necessary?

All of the above notwithstanding, personal privacy and freedom must be balanced against the ability of faculty and administrators to actually run an effective institution. A vast and growing amount of institutional data requires a formalized approach to the values and ethics that govern how it is used. To that end, Domain of One's Own is as fraught as it is successful. At every step of the way—even now—working with domains is anything but simple. Questions abound: What do we do about assessment? Should domains even be curricular? What do we do with old domains after students graduate? Do we know if we are hosting inappropriate material? What sorts of freedoms should be encouraged, what sorts of ethics should be maintained?

Indeed, the Domain of One's Own project should make us nervous. It should keep us on edge. We should look at it every year, every semester, and wonder if it can or should continue. Yet ultimately the problems and challenges of

Domain of One's Own are also its joys, for to work with DoOO requires an openness to the project itself, and to the students and teachers and others who use it, explore it, defy its immediate constrictures. In other words, the very best part of DoOO has less to do with the Web and more to do with how we as humans encounter the questions it raises.

### Seeing the Web through the Domain Lens

We need to push for an approach to the Web as a space that begs of us an interpretive approach. Much as when, in our specific disciplines, we learn how to interpret text, research, data, stories, art, we need to approach the Web as an object of this kind of interrogation and consideration. The Web is not merely the content we read or view, and not merely the sites we browse or post on. It is a multifaceted space that reflects human society in a number of ways:

- as a structured space, coded and built by humans with identities, biases, leanings and agendas;
- as an evolving space, one we will have to always be chasing after in order to understand where it might be headed next;
- as a commodified space, in which corporations make a great deal of money through retail sales, advertising, content dissemination, digital services, etc.;
- as a political space in which power and access is not evenly distributed, and where people and groups will always attempt to consolidate and reinforce those power differentials;
- as neither an inherently good or bad space—one that can, through its marvels and monstrosities, provide amazing and terrible experiences;
- as neither streamlined nor straightforward or predictable—as messy, chaotic, wonderful, and awful.

This is the Web we need to grapple with, for our students' sakes as well as our own. And there is still so much work we have to do. We can begin at the level of individual platforms and applications, but the discussion can't end there.

Take WordPress, for instance. As discussed above, this popular content management system is used to create DoOO websites, enabling students to learn digital literacy skills that they can later export to other environments. WordPress is also part of the larger ecosystem of the open or "indie" Web movement, "an effort to create a web that's not so dependent on tech giants ... a web that belongs not to one individual or one company, but to everyone."[6] Indie's difficult-to-define mystique makes it great for marketing. But educators, particularly those espousing innovative and critical pedagogies, have to cut through the hype and expose the ideology, the practice, the data collection and data retention policies, the intended (or unintended but foreseeable) ends of each technology—even WordPress. Uncritically celebrating any tool or platform keeps us from finding these answers.

Aspects of ownership, control, and cost abound on the Web, and certainly on Domain of One's Own. While the students using DoOO have ultimate control of their Web space, faculty members give (and often grade) assignments within that space. And while the apps students can install in their hosting space are open source, some were made by indie developers and some by corporations. Domain of One's Own schools typically contract with a for-profit web hosting provider, such as Reclaim Hosting, and deal with other for-profit companies along the way, such as domain registrars.

Of course, nothing is bad because it costs money, just as no company is bad because it is for-profit (which is simply the default disposition under U.S. law). However, the degree to which students, instructors, the institution, the hosting company, the registrar, etc. own, rent, and control the data on a student's "own" domain is a complex issue, and one that deserves unpacking and engaging with a high degree of nuance—especially because it is a core part of the digital literacy that programs like Domain of One's Own are intended to foster.

When students leave the university and are faced with a decision about keeping (and paying for) their domain on their own or letting it go, there are real financial implications for the space that they *own*. UMW, as a small, public institution, does not have the means to keep paying for the domain names and server space once the student leaves the institution. But it is another moment of agency for the student, who gets to decide what to do with that Web presence (and all of that personal data) upon graduation.

After four years of immersion in the DoOO environment, then, the student's final act—and assignment, if you will—is whether to leave the digital "room" of the university, or to move it into the "real world," in which the student can apply all that he or she has learned and absorbed. Domain of One's Own, in the end, is more than just a digital platform—it is a *liberatory* digital platform. It is a platform that has taught its participants "to build out a digital

[6] See Finley 2013.

space of their own," to forge their own digital identities, to learn all they can about the Web, and to take their places in its wider world as fully functioning but always self-aware digital citizens. In this experiential learning environment, the point is about praxis.

## Digital Identity and Student Agency

The concept of Domain of One's Own is founded in the work of educators, pedagogues, and activists such as John Dewey, Paulo Freire, Seymour Papert, and bell hooks, all of whom push back against traditional institutional and instrumental educational frameworks. Freire's concept of praxis, in particular, has informed the project. In his seminal work *Pedagogy of the Oppressed* (1970), which sets out his concept of liberatory pedagogy, he explains "praxis" as a process that begins with an idea or experience and translates it into purposeful action. Praxis, in turn, must lead to transformation and liberation, an outcome realized through working to resolve problems. For Freire, as Mary Breunig (2011, 60) notes, "a problem-posing method of education that values the importance of student experience and a dialogical method of teaching and learning whereby the student and the teacher are mutually engaged in the production of knowledge and the process of teaching and learning can aid in a person's liberation."

When we encourage UMW students to build domains of their own, we are locating their freedom in a space close to our own. How does this change, how does this diminish, the voices that students speak in when we're not watching? When we're not providing them with a platform we've built? In other words, does Domain of One's Own work toward creating an open channel between what students are saying—what's important to them, what comes deliberately from their lived experiences—and what school asks them to say?

In "A Room of One's Own," Virginia Woolf explored and defined what a woman in early twentieth-century England needed to become a writer: resources, and a space of her own. Kept outside the Oxbridge library because she was a woman, she offered this pointed response: "Lock up your libraries if you like; but there is no gate, no lock, no bolt that you can set upon the freedom of my mind" (Woolf 1935, 114). Seventy years later, bell hooks wrote about being, and speaking, on the outside—not just as a woman but as a woman of color "located in the margin" (hooks 1989, 23). The margin, however, is a realm of possibility,

> a site one stays in, clings to even, because it nourishes one's capacity
> to resist. It offers one the possibility of a radical perspective from

> which to see and create, to imagine alternatives, new worlds. (hooks 1989, 20)

Speaking from the margin is a subversive act, even as it is a liberatory one and an intervention. With a room of her own, Virginia Woolf wrote fiction that stirred and shook the literary world. She did not say what we wanted her to say, but rather broadcast what she had been saying all along, despite our ears. With domains of their own, students can speak from the margins—the margins of their social locations as female, Black, Latinx, disabled, queer, trans ... and as students.

By creating their own domains, of course, students move up from the margins through their very first act: choosing a domain name. This choice establishes digital identity, and cannot be changed after signup; as the UMW guidelines state, "You should choose a domain name that you feel you can live with for some time." In supporting students during this process, UMW emphasizes agency, and a moment of taking ownership: participants should be able determine for themselves how they wish to be known and found on the Web. Many participants automatically choose their name, or some variation thereof; others may be inspired by culture or tradition, or by a specific interest. And while some students may spend little or no time choosing a domain name, others will select a name that is deeply reflective of who they are and what they would like to become; they are more likely to see their domain as an online "room of their own" in which they can grow both in school and in the world after graduation.

In addition to the domain name, the DoOO project provides that "room," that online space, for students to build and build within. When the project first started, one of the things frequently imparted to students was that the Web was not something that shaped them, but something *they* were shaping. Resources such as WordPress, Gutenberg Editor, and software for audio-video editing and storymapping were available, but the stories could only be told by their creators. In reversing Marshall McLuhan's frequently quoted statement that "we shape our tools and then our tools shape us" (Culkin 1967, 70)[7] students have demonstrated their agency and independence as digital citizens.

---

[7] Although McLuhan became famous for this statement, it was first coined by his friend John Culkin of Fordham University: "We shape our tools and thereafter our tools shape us." See Culkin 1967.

Five years into the Domain of One's Own project, the UMW community and its support staff are still learning, evolving, asking questions, and solving problems. The process is ongoing: praxis is a work in progress. But the project has attempted to create, and to foster, something unique: a space that truly embodies a spirit of student self-determination and agency even as it exists within the academy, the Web, and society as a whole.

We can't expect that just building a new system will magically change our teaching practices. Pedagogy requires a never-ending commitment and curiosity, an awareness of potential dangers, and an openness to possibilities. Who does the system serve? What data does it collect? Who profits? What hierarchies does it reinforce or disrupt? Who does it allow under the hood? What is its default configuration? What pedagogies does that configuration make possible? What are the risks to students and teachers in subverting the system? Asking these questions, and getting started on answering them, is the future of Domain of One's Own, the next chapter of its (our) history.

WORKS CITED

Bessette, Lee Skallerup. 2016. "Assembling Resources on Domain of One's Own." University of Mary Washington (UMW) Division of Teaching and Learning Technologies, blog post, September 23. http://umwdtlt.com/assembling-resources-on-domain-of-ones-own/.

Breunig, Mary. 2011. "Paulo Freire: Critical Praxis and Experiential Education." In *Sourcebook of Experiential Education: Key Thinkers and Their Contributions*, edited by Thomas E. Smith and Clifford E. Knapp, 56–63. New York and London: Routledge.

Culkin, John. 1967. "A Schoolman's Guide to Marshall McLuhan." *Saturday Review*, March 18, 51–53, 70–72.

Finley, Klint. 2013. "Meet the Hackers Who Want to Jailbreak the Internet." *Wired*, August 14. https://www.wired.com/2013/08/indie-web/.

Haarstad, Nigel. 2016. "Musings on Ethical Policies of Institutional Data." University of Mary Washington (UMW) Division of Teaching and Learning Technologies, blog post, September 7. http://umwdtlt.com/musings-on-ethical-policies-of-institutional-data/.

hooks, bell. 1989. "Choosing the Margin as a Space of Radical Openness." *Framework: The Journal of Cinema and Media* 36: 15–23.

Rikard, Andrew. 2015. "Do I Own My Domain if You Grade It?" *EdSurge*, August 10. https://www.edsurge.com/news/2015-08-10-do-i-own-my-domain-if-you-grade-it.

Schleef, Debra. 2016. "Who's Afraid of Domain of One's Own?" University of Mary Washington (UMW) Division of Teaching and Learning Technologies, blog post, June 3. http://umwdtlt.com/whos-afraid-domain-ones/.

Watters, Audrey. 2015. "The Web We Need To Give Students." *Bright Magazine*, July 15. https://brightthemag.com/the-web-we-need-to-give-students-311d97713713.

Woolf, Virginia. 1935. *A Room of One's Own*. London: Hogarth Press.

# Waste at the Temple of Knowledge:
# A Personal Reflection on Writing, Technology, and the Student Public to Come

Erin Rose Glass

DigitalOcean

*You must write, and read, as if your life depended on it. That is not generally taught in school.*

—Adrienne Rich (1993, 32)

## In Pursuit of the Life of the Mind

Toward the end of my graduate education I did something that many academics, myself included, would likely look upon in horror. I began to post drafts of my dissertation chapters on a variety of online writing platforms and—grabbing every social media microphone within reach—loudly solicited feedback from what I called my "fourth committee member," the general public. I was hardly the first person to use the Web to circulate academic work in progress for public review. But these were not polished drafts of a respected, published, and employed professor. Instead, they were living representations of a struggle to understand and overcome an academic requirement designed to judge whether a student is fit to join a community of scholars. The dissertation process, of course, is supposed to be a struggle, or a "hazing ritual," as William Pannapacker observes (Patton 2013), but admitting its difficulty is also in some sense to admit defeat. To be a "real" intellectual, a "real" scholar, or at least a serious contender for one of the dwindling tenure track jobs, one's academic writing must perform Olympian feats of disciplinary expertise, sublime originality, and an aristocratic ease with narrative control. Or at least it can feel that way. For a long time, I suspected that my struggle to achieve these qualities was peculiar to my own shortcomings, and that I would have to hide this struggle if I wanted to join the community of respected and employed scholars. But over the course of my grauate education, for reasons I will recount in this essay, I began to question whether this perceived private flaw might in fact have broad social significance. However "natural" it may be, the student's sense of intellectual inferiority works brilliantly in maintaining a culture of student silence.

ISBN 978-1-64959-008-4 (paper) ISBN 978-1-64959-009-1 (pdf) ISBN 978-1-64959-084-8 (epub)
*New Technologies in Medieval and Renaissance Studies* 8 (2022) 139–167

A culture of student silence is one in which the insecurities, struggles, and divergent perspectives of student life are kept hidden in pursuit of performing an academic ideal. Maximillian Alvarez has written eloquently about the myths that shape our academic unconsciousness, causing many to doubt their own abilities while feeling compelled to perform confidence in front of others. "These fronts, airs, and pretenses give a venerable glow to everything in academe, " he observes, and "confirm your worst fears—that your colleagues and role models know way more than you do and are more fit for this work than you are" (2017). Alvarez, like other critics of academia such as Pannapacker and Marc Bousquet, see these myths as helping to enable and hide an exploitative academic labour system. Recent writing about sexual harassment of graduate students by professors has pointed to other forms of student exploitation that are exacerbated by a culture of student inferiority and isolation (Chu 2018). A culture of student silence, however, is also one in which students would rather have the intellectual validation of their superiors than share knowledge-making practices with their peers or the public. It should strike one as curious, for example, that in a day and age when social media companies make billions from rampant sharing of personal content related to everyday life, student writing is typically anxiously guarded or trashed. As students privately toil to gain admittance to an abstract community of scholars, they waste one of the greatest opportunities students have ever had to forge a serious intellectual public for themselves.

There is an exciting movement underway in theorizing and cultivating public forms of humanities research. Kathleen Fitzpatrick, one of this movement's advocates, has argued that public engagement is necessary for public support for the humanities. "The more we close our work away from the public and the more we refuse to engage in dialogue across the boundaries of the academy," she argues, "the more we undermine that public's willingness to fund our research and our institutions" (2012 n.p.). There are also many educators who use public virtual spaces such as Wikipedia or blogs to facilitate class discussion and assignments. These public-facing initiatives are invaluable steps for humanities research and teaching, but they do not constitute—at least not at this moment—a genuine, sustainable, discoverable, and self-reflective public open to the contribution of any student voice. However unrealistic, it was this sort of public I hungered for—and not just for my own writing, but for all the millions of unread words produced by students every year. Of course, I could not create such a public on my own, but I could make a gesture in its direction by posting my dissertation drafts for public review.

Announcing the project in a blog post on HASTAC (https://www.hastac. org/), I offered four questions to help explain why I would choose to expose myself in such a manner:

- To what extent can the general public participate in and benefit from the production of a dissertation?
- How might the private and anxiety-ridden processes of education be transformed into a public good and social joy?
- Are the imperfect artifacts of learning to be hidden and disposed of as shameful waste, or might they provide fertile soil for the cultivation of a global learning community?
- Could the form of the dissertation itself blossom into something more vibrant and responsive to today's world in the process?

I called the project #SocialDiss, supplied it with its own eponymous hashtag, and then proceeded to carry out a PR campaign for what felt like an "ill-form'd offspring of my feeble brain," to borrow a phrase from the poet Anne Bradstreet (1969, 40). For the next year, I posted drafts and reflections via platforms and tools including Google Docs, Twitter, Facebook, Hypothes.is, Medium, the HASTAC website, the Modern Language Association's Humanities Commons, CommentPress, Academia.edu, and my personal website, as well as Social Paper, a networked writing platform I had co-developed at the City University of New York (CUNY) Graduate Center. It's likely, I thought somewhat hopefully, that no one would click. But as notifications, likes, retweets, favourites, hits, comments, and other signs of networked engagement began to alert me that folks were in fact clicking—and in fact many more than I had expected—the old fears reappeared. Would I be run out of the academy for the drafts' hasty claims, clunky sentences, and grammatical stumblings, of which I was sure there were many? Would I lose the respect of my academic peers, social communities, and academic job search committees for so shamelessly and relentlessly promoting my intellectual dirty laundry? And could such a dissertation possibly contain anything of merit if written by an author so willing to embrace the technology of the shallows?

And yet those outcomes no longer seemed the worst possible fate of a graduate education. By the time I had begun the dissertation process, I had seen multiple ways that health, family, financial, and psychological issues were exacerbated by academic life, and I was no longer as hopeful as I had been that drive and discipline would protect me. It wasn't as if I hadn't been warned. While applying to graduate school, I came across the viral online video, "So You Want to Get a PhD in the Humanities" (Allison 2010), which satirized the bleak prospects of pursuing an academic career and resonated with so many academics that the *Chronicle of Higher Education* wrote a piece on its popular reception (Parry 2011). In the video, a student requests a letter of recommendation for graduate school from a professor who strongly urges her to not to apply. "You will teach fifty kids in one semester while reading thousands of pages a week and writing hundreds of pages for your jaded professors who are contemplating suicide daily," the professor warns the student. "You will work on average sixty-five hours a week trying to publish an obscure article that no one cares about in an obscure scholarly journal article that nobody will read just so you can put it on your CV." The student, however, is impervious to the professor's advice, insisting that she wants "to be a college professor," that she wants "to live a life of the mind." The professor retorts, "You cannot seriously be this stupid," before agreeing to write the letter. In 2018, the video has been watched almost one million times.

In a recent report, the Survey of Earned Doctorates found that of the 5,600 recipients of doctorate degrees in the humanities in 2015, fewer than 44 per cent found employment or continued on to postgraduate study. Relatedly, the American Association of University Professors (AAUP) found that as of 2016, 73 per cent of instructional positions at all U.S. universities combined were not tenure track (2018).

Facing such bleak career prospects, is it stupidity—as the professor in the YouTube video claims—to pursue a graduate degree in the humanities? Or is there something of social and cultural interest about this obstinate quest for the "life of the mind" and the belief that institutions can cultivate that life in a way that individuals on their own can't? "Graduate school was—at least for me—an opportunity to look at the world as it is without flinching and to imagine the world anew as a better place that we could all discover together," English professor Min Hyoung Song writes. "This is a hopeless idealism that the business of higher education is often quick to beat flat" (2018, 408).

In a follow-up animation entitled, "So You Want to Get a PhD in the Humanities: Nine Years Later," we see the former undergraduate congratulated by a professor for her brilliant dissertation before finding out her only job prospect is to compete with high school students for a half-time receptionist's position in the history department. Though her writing had been favourably received by professors, it was powerless to bring about a world in which it might continue. It was representative of a type of writing that disempowers the humanities as surely as it disempowers the student. How did we come to so jealously guard this practice? Why do beliefs about the life of the mind seem to assure its obsolescence?

## Literature as Ghost Institution

I wonder if the student of the YouTube video, like myself, had grown up with the strange and unquenchable desire to write, and whether that desire was linked in some way to her own particular brand of "hopeless idealism." Maybe, in her early years, the practice of reading and writing offered a pleasing mode of self-development or recognition by teachers and friends. Or maybe, as George Orwell (2000, 1) explained his own early inclination for the craft, a "facility with words and a power of facing unpleasant facts" helped her make up for feeling "isolated and undervalued" and a "failure in everyday life." There is no telling what configuration of historical, cultural, psychological, and educational forces go into the making of the aspirational writer, but there is evidence of her prolific existence in the industry of creative writing programs and books. For example, a recent study by the British public opinion company YouGov (Dahlgreen 2015) found that the number one desired job in Britain is being an author: 60 per cent of the 15,000 poll respondents said they would prefer this occupation above all others, with librarians and academics coming in as the second and third most desired occupations. It is good to work among books; it is best to also be writing them.

Jean Guerrero's recent book *Crux: A Cross-Border Memoir*, published in 2018, provides further glimpses into this modern compulsion. Although the memoir specifically focuses on growing up on the San Diego-Tijuana border while dealing with a mentally unstable father, it also offers a portrait of the author's relationship to reading and writing. From her very first encounter with the written word, reading and writing function as a kind of ghost institution, a seemingly immaterial association that offers relief from the formal institutions of schooling while instilling an intractable (and perhaps unconscious) dependence on them. "I hated school," the narrator recounts of her introduction to it. "We had to sit for hours on stiff chairs, wasting our bodies, wasting our lives. ... But then the teachers taught us to read and write long sentences" (Guerrero 2018, 44). She then describes how reading and writing transformed school from a prison to a "utopia" with their ability to provide "vivid escapes" that yielded "full-body 3-D experiences ... due to the high-voltage power of strings of texts connecting with my brain" (45). The narrator also recounts the way this early encounter with writing provided the thrill of creating and destroying imaginative worlds through words alone. "Writing," she observes, "became a godlike experience" (45). In middle school, reading and writing gave her the sense of inclusion in an imagined community, protecting her from the alienation she felt around others. While browsing in the library, she discovers a science fiction book series about a group of children called the Animorphs who are trying to save humanity from a group of brainwashing aliens. "I became convinced," she writes, "that the Animorphs would come find me, to incorporate me into their meaningful group" (62), and begins to pity others in her life who "were Controllers, victims of Yeerk mind control" (63). In high school, reading and writing become a way of transforming negative life experiences. A teacher, knowing the author's complicated relationship with her father, gives her Mary Karr's *The Liars' Club*, telling her that she, too, can "turn bad things into good things" (152). For better or worse, reading and writing also contribute to the narrator's sense of self. After reading Fyodor Dostoyevsky's *Notes from the Underground*, she describes thinking of herself as "a female version of the antisocial narrator—hateful of others due to mental superiority" (157).

There are too many anecdotes to detail here, but in each of them, the practice of reading and writing offers transcendent powers to transform the present situation, at least in the mind of the writer. Describing her reasons for choosing a career in journalism, Guerrero writes: "Narrative non-fiction felt like a superpower. I could lasso the whole wide world into paragraphs, cage it up in language" (155). Her description of reading and writing, of course, is very different from academic versions of these activities, and there are certainly many academics who would not relate to Guerrero's formative experiences with them. Nonetheless, Guerrero's experiences struck me as deeply relevant for thinking about the situation of the humanities and higher education in the twenty-first century. On one hand, her story details one example of how the influence of the humanities is still felt with passion in an age when they are often bemoaned as besieged or in their death throes. And it is interesting to consider, even if literature is largely portrayed as antithetical or outside of institutionalized education (Guerrero does not, for example, mention the MFA program in which she worked on the memoir in the memoir itself), that the narrator's encounters with literature are often facilitated through the social body of these institutions or that higher education at large has no doubt played a significant role in fostering literary culture. On the other hand, Guerrero's intense and near-spiritual identification with the writerly life shares commonalities with many writers studied in English and literature departments, from Herman Melville to Audre Lorde. Even if not all graduate students in literature share this identification, it is not unthinkable that at least some are drawn to literary study because they do.

I, at least, was driven to graduate school in search of a home for this lifelong practice of reading and writing, and once there, met many others who shared this drive. For many of us, reading and writing before graduate school had served as a sort of ghostly temple, a cult of the imagination, that promised transcendence from social realities and godlike perceptions through all of its falsehoods. No form of knowledge was too broad for its halls—literary knowledge was of course relevant, but so were history, philosophy, the sciences, gossip, magic, cooking, or anything that else that showed up in the writer's experience. And no linguistic form was too obscure or too subjective as its method—it was up to the writer herself to determine the language and style that would most "correctly" express her literary vision. Its community was mainly the dead, writers who had achieved immortality through their words, which offered solace to lonely worshippers. Worship in this temple could sometimes provide material rewards, such as favourable recognition by English teachers from secondary school to college, and the ability to impress others with written communication. But above all, it was a sense of divinity, or that "godlike experience" described by Guerrero, which motivated the practice. These temples seemed to put us in touch with our highest selves, our most sacred realities. Its pursuit would be worth all costs. For Guerrero, as she recounts in her memoir, it took her close to death.

## Writing in the Dark

In a similar experience to that of Guerrero, literature's appearance in my life seemed partly divine: no infrastructure seemed to support it—it simply showed up, often through personal connections, cherished moments, and dear friends in the nooks and crannies of institutional life. Literature was connected to school, but it was also against it. For reasons that weren't entirely clear, reasons which were continuously reflected upon, changing, and evolving, writing was an activity upon which—to paraphrase the epigraph of this essay—one's life depended (Rich 1993, 32). As an undergraduate, I majored in English, but when it came time to write course papers, the act of writing suddenly felt alien and repellant. "I write entirely to find out what I'm thinking, what I'm looking at, what I see and what it means," Joan Didion once remarked. "What I want and what I fear" (Didion 2000, 20). The university, however, did not seem to help me find out what I was thinking; for some reason, writing authentically and writing for course requirements always felt diametrically opposed. When I graduated in 2006, I had the luck of acquiring a full-time journalism job, a suitable profession—or so I had hoped—to complement my writing interests. I was happy to escape the university and had no intention of ever returning for graduate school. I would look for other ways to write as if my life depended upon it.

But as the world filled with ever more digital connectivity over the course of the next few years, journalistic writing began to feel like little more than clickbait production, and my mind its slavish analogue. Technology, I sighed like so many others in the midst of that first decade of the twenty-first century, was antithetical to thought, creativity, and care. Abandoning job, friends, electricity, and plumbing, I unplugged. I moved across the country to a shack in the middle of the woods where the lack of connectivity held, at last, the promise of a space in which to live deliberately, to read and write. It seemed the natural path for the aspiring writer. As C.P. Snow observed, "western intellectuals have never tried, wanted, or been able to understand the industrial revolution, much less accept it. Intellectuals, in particular literary intellectuals, are natural Luddites" (Snow 1998, 22). If I wanted to write, to be a "real writer, I thought then perhaps I should also reject the new technologies of my time.

Nights were extraordinarily dark, like puddles of black paint poured over your eyes. In the purity of the woods, I turned to candles as a means to light my writerly path. This situation, however, turned out to be no less ideal for the life of the mind than a world of buzzing cell phones and digitally-fractured attention. Each night, the light of the candle drew an assortment of winged creatures to the shack's windows, against which they would thump in crazed repetition. These were not your polite suburban moths or other gentle evening insects, but wild forest dwellers that appeared sometimes as large as my hand as their half-lit bodies thudded against the glass. The one-room shack had been built decades before without the use of electric tools, and the holes left by this low-tech construction method welcomed the more determined creatures inside. I ducked and cursed liked a madwoman as moths darted about my head, worried that at any moment one might tip the candle and cause the shack to burst into flames. Why again, I wondered, did I consider the candle, the pencil, and the paper I was using to write in the woods any less "technological" than electricity, keyboards, and software I had fled from, and what special quality did I think they achieved? Nature has been said to teach writers many things. Those moths were one of the many ways during that year that nature taught me—relentlessly and indel-ibly—that much of what I had assumed about writing, its proper tools, and its ideal rooms was completely and ridiculously wrong.

My teachers, however, insisted that I hang on—that pain, isolation, and struggle were the filters that separated real writers from the chaff. "I will write in spite of everything, absolutely," Franz Kafka declared to his diary at a moment when its pursuit seemed impossible given his work and personal commitments. "It is my struggle for self preservation" (Kafka 1965, 75). "It is necessary to accept the loneliness, to lose one's dread of it," Galway Kinnell replied in an interview. "Without the loneliness there can be no poetry" (Kinnell 1978, 11). "The poet is in labor," Denise Levertov wrote. "She has been told that it will not hurt but it has hurt so much that pain and struggle seem, just now, the only reality" (Levertov 1973, 17). "Search for the reason that bids you write," Rainer Maria Rilke advised a young poet. "Find out whether it is spreading out its roots in the deepest places of your heart, acknowledge to yourself whether you would have to die if it were denied to you to write." (18). Near the end of his letter he notes that "it is enough ... to feel that one could live without writing: then one must not attempt it at all" (Rilke 1954).

To not be a writer, however, would be a sort of death. And so I tried to love my solitude and sing out with the pain it caused me in forms I hoped might one day be publishable. I continued, against all common sense, to write in the woods. Seasons passed as I attempted to finish various writing projects while working farm jobs and growing, despite myself, more and more depressed. Words piled up as my sense of connection to the world thinned. Ironically, the more I wrote in those dark woods, the more disconnected I felt from my desire to write in the first place. What were these hundreds of pages, I wondered, if they were never to be read by anyone? What if I never published? Writing might need solitude but it also needed a reader. "All writers are nourished by the sense of having an audience—or, in the exceptional cases, like that of William Blake, by faith that the audience will someday be found," Malcolm Cowley writes. "If they lose that feeling it is as if they had been deprived of some essential food; often they suffer from psychosomatic complaints that sometimes prove fatal and almost always they stop writing" (Cowley 1958, 139). Without such nourishment, my writing began to seem like nothing more than a transcription of lost time.

As Hannah Arendt reminds us (1998, 38), the Greeks considered a life spent in the privacy of "'one's own' (idion), outside of the world of the common, (as) 'idiotic' by definition." Indeed, my quest for intellectual development began to fee very idiotic, and I began to question my subconscious motives. What was I doing? "I was really isolated when I wrote this novel," the novelist Ottessa Moshfegh recounts in an interview (2018), "but I didn't realize that I was trying to escape my life." I looked up one day from the fields and saw a young boy from the Amish community, famous for its rejection of technology, pulling a motorized tiller with a horse. At that moment, I realized, there was no natural line determining what was natural and what was technological. That line is always constructed by humans. Perhaps it was time to try to choose my tools not due to arbitrary notions of naturalness, but according to the life I hoped to bring about.

When I returned from the woods, the life I had once lived was gone. Although my retreat had cost relatively little, it was in the end—professionally, emotionally, and socially—a very expensive experiment. The only job I could find was part-time bussing work for a restaurant whose opening I had once reviewed. The hundreds of pages of writing I had produced sat unread, a relic of lost time and sadness. "The most depressed, pitiful, and sordid lot has been that of writers," the psychoanalyst Edmund Bergler once claimed. "The majority are poor, never achieve material success, are habitually misunderstood, struggle along, either scornfully making a poor living in some tangential profession (journalism, copywriting in advertising concerns, teaching, clerking, et cetera) or being lifelong parasites" (quoted in Cowley 1958, 137). And yet, still, I could not quit. Throughout the day, I would find myself compulsively writing short fragments on the backs of recycled menus, receipts, and other scraps of restaurant ephemera. "A day without writing," as Simone de Beauvoir once complained, "tasted like ashes" (Sanos 2016, 78). Perhaps, I thought, I should reconsider the university. Wasn't that a place where one could read and write for a living? I began auditing graduate courses and tried to befriend every graduate student who would give me time. I had once been suspicious of these academic pursuits, thinking them too narrow-minded and too isolated within the sheltered space of the academy to be meaningful and satisfying. Now I wanted to try to participate in the university's conversations, on its own terms, if it would only open itself back up to me.

There are so many walls, however, separating the university from the rest of civilian life. Some of these boundaries are material, such as the lack of access to university library privileges or academic journals without a university affiliation. "Information is power," Aaron Swartz writes in his Guerilla Open Access Manifesto. "But like all power, there are those who want to keep it for themselves. The world's entire scientific and cultural heritage, published over centuries in books and journals, is increasingly being digitized and locked up by a handful of private corporations" (Swartz 2008). The mentality trickled down into casual academic communication practices. Whatever papers graduate students were always working on, well, it wasn't like I could just ask to see them! Even in casual conversation, it felt as if there was some wall between their institutionally sanctioned pursuit of intellectual life and my own eager hobbling. If I wanted to "feed at the banquet of knowledge," as Swartz eloquently put it in his Manifesto, I would have to become a member of the ivory tower myself.

One of the things I hoped to come to understand through graduate school was the madness that led me into the woods: I would write about poets who rejected the world and its technologies in one way or another in order to pursue their art. What purpose did they give their writing—its process and products—in the face of this rejection? What did they hope that their writing might achieve? And how might these impulses (as they show up in writers today) be redirected, given the world's evolving opportunities and challenges? Like the student in the YouTube video "So You Want to Get a PhD in the Humanities," I asked college professors from my undergrad days who surely didn't remember me to write letters of recommendation, and smiled patiently when some warned me to reconsider. At last, I thought, I will have the proper space to read and write.

## Writing in the Temple of Knowledge

It is true that academic work in the humanities involves a great deal of writing. I knew, entering the program, that it would not be the same type of writing I had attempted in the woods. Academic knowledge-making practices, since the birth of the modern university in the late nineteenth century, have largely aspired to an objective ideal, employing writing as a medium for making neutral, universally valid, archivable, and permanent forms of knowledge, or what was once commonly referred to as "brick(s) in temple of wisdom" (Russell 2002, 71–72). This use of writing in the academy may seem natural, but in fact, as Sharon Crowley (1998), James Berlin (1987), David Russell (2002), and many other historians of composition have shown, academic writing in U.S. institutions of higher education has been a site of ideological struggle for well over a hundred years. In both the production and teaching of academic writing, scholars and educators have championed diverse forms of academic writing that prioritize other goals, such as personal and aesthetic expression, the display of taste or distinction, the cultivation of character, or effecting social change. Still, the objective ideal dominates the modern research university and has profoundly shaped its research practices, library infrastructure, and evaluation standards. As an undergraduate, I had found this temple too cold, too self-satisfied, and too narrow to lend meaning to my own experiences. But now, humbled by my pursuit of writing in the woods, I prepared myself for the challenge of adopting the logic and the language of the academy, to try my own hand at producing bricks fit for this temple.

The production of bricks, however, turned out not to be so simple. While academic term papers were treated as a straightforward task, I found myself completely baffled by their purpose. In theory, I understood that they were meant to present an original argument, but when I sat down to produce them I could not understand, at least not the way I had understood writing in the woods, what the purpose of such an argument would be. If writing did not shake the reader and open up new truths ungraspable by reason alone, then I did not know what it was for. The solution to this problem, I thought, would be to write more, to find the answer to the reason for writing the term paper in writing the term paper itself. For brief moments, ideas would thrill before me, the whole New York City skyline shining with the purpose and possibility of the writing to come. At last, I would claim my own spot in the temple! But then, as I attempted to anchor these thrills into language, their edges would fade, and I would write even more, words verging on nonsense, words that made up sentences that never ended, desperate to capture even a piece of what had seemed so real and so important. "Anyone moderately familiar with the rigours of composition will not need to be told the story in detail," the narrator observes in Virginia Woolf's novel *Orlando*. This story, the narrator continues, is one in which the writer

> wrote and it seemed good; read and it seemed vile; corrected and tore up; cut out; put in; was in ecstasy; in despair; had his good nights and bad mornings; snatched at ideas and lost them; saw his book plain before him and it vanished; acted people's parts as he ate; mouthed them as he walked; now cried; now laughed; vacillated between this style and that; now preferred the heroic and pompous; next the plain and simple; now the vales of Tempe; then the fields of Kent or Cornwall; and could not decide whether he was the divinest genius or the greatest fool in the world. (Woolf 1956, 82)

I wrote and I wrote and I wrote, chiselling out papers from the great mass of words I had accumulated at the end of every semester into that required term paper. The words felt like blight, writing like a disease. In a series of interviews published about women's experiences in the academy, one graduate student lamented: "At the end, the finished project just kills me. I mean, I'm almost physically ill when I complete it" (Kirsch 1993, 45). I held onto the words of this anonymous past graduate student as a treasure—they were one of the few signs that I was not the only one who found academic writing a near traumatizing activity. Other students groaned about their various paper deadlines, but never betrayed the same sort of terror I felt awaited me with every writing exercise. A postdoc, self-assured, successful, told me he never worked after five o'clock, never worked on weekends. I, on the other hand, stayed in the library every night until it closed while the rest of my life withered, and still it was not enough time. It seemed far more important to write than it was to live—after all, I thought, this writing was my last chance for a life where one might think and not just live. When our papers were returned with feedback, I hung onto every word of the professor's comments. As Adam Szetela notes (2018), academic life is a "dehumanizing" process, one in which we're told not to worry if our "health, hobbies, friendships, and other aspects of ... life fall to pieces in the process." These little marks had to stand in for the life I had exchanged to produce those papers. It was an awful lot of bricks for no temple.

"A teacher," however, is—as Peter Elbow (1998) observes—"usually too good a reader. ... He [sic] isn't really listening to you. He usually isn't in a position where he can be genuinely affected by your words. He doesn't expect your words actually to make a dent on him. He doesn't treat your words like real reading. He has to read them as an exercise. He can't hold himself ready to be affected unless he has an extremely rare, powerful openness" (127). My teachers were remarkably generous with their feedback, but even so, for structural reasons, it is rare that these exchanges can be seen as equivalent to real dialogue. There are too many students, too few professors. And while professors have read a thousand student papers before, deeply trained in the mistakes, anxieties, clumsiness, and mistaken assumptions inherent in student writing, students have no exposure to this literature. Cruelly, they have very little awareness that many of their attempts at original thought or authoritative style are so cliché that *McSweeney's Internet Tendency* regularly publishes parodies of them.[1]

Over the decades, many educators have recognized the value of providing student audiences for student writing, something for which Elbow argues in his book *Writing Without Teachers* (first published in 1972). As Danica Savonick (2018) argues, "having students write not just for the professor, but for an audience beyond the classroom teaches them the power of their voices and stories. It helps them understand that they are critical participants in longer, ongoing conversations, and that learning offers an opportunity to contribute to the public and social good." Despite the fact that educators in many different contexts have demonstrated the value of these methods, however, they have never seemed to reach widespread acceptance and have to be rediscovered anew by educators time and time again. For example, compositionists have experimented with forms of networked writing in the classroom since the early 1980s (Wresch 1984, Hawisher et al. 1996), yet it was not until my

---

[1] See, for example, Wu 2014.

second year of graduate school that I had heard of the practice. Today, when I set up course blogs for undergraduate classes, most students tell me that they've never been asked to write regularly for their peers in a class setting.

And so, as I was attempting to produce bricks of authoritative knowledge for some courses, other courses made the modest requirement that we extend the class discussion by posting short reflections on the course blog. The assignment provoked a sea of intense but dimly understood feelings in me. As I could only articulate much later, I sensed that the opportunity to write for other students might have something to offer. I was uneasy, though: what would writing in such a context achieve? Was it the type of writing that I thought worth my time? And why would it be worth reading the posts of my peers, who had no expert point of view to offer? Some sort of inner snobbery persisted, shaped by an educational system that often valued individual competition and prestige over community and collaboration.

The first course that required this activity was entitled "The Meaning of Media," taught by the brilliant textual scholar David Greetham. In my first post (Glass 2012), I reflected on arguments about whether literary and cultural production would continue without the protection of copyright. "It's always seemed to me that some of the best art came from conditions where there was very little interest in material reward," I wrote. "My bookshelf swears that writers write because the gods whispered or the zeitgeist blew or the emotions spontaneously overflowed and for health's sake had to be drained twice weekly through paper and pen release. There is a long and cherished tradition of alleged material apathy in the history of writers, stemming most notably from the Romantics who championed the authentic and ideal as opposed to the material and commercial." Would all of this come to a grinding halt if writers were no longer paid according to the amount of copies of their work they sold? And what did it mean for artistic production that it was now much easier for any individual with a network connection to share their work with the masses? Turning to another form of cultural production, I argued, "If the pop star disappears because the immense, wealth-dependent machine required for such a delicate specimen dries up, than she will be replaced by a new type of artist, the artist of the public domain. I look forward to her arrival." It would be the student of the public domain, however, for whose arrival I would come to spend the rest of my graduate education preparing.

*Waste as a Thwarted Student Public*

Nadine Gordimer once observed that "the lack of a means to distribute is another form of censorship" (Rich 1993, 28). But the means to distribute requires more than just media; it requires the collective will to distribute and receive in ways that are sensitive to the needs of the community. When I began posting on course blogs I felt the disorienting pressures of conflicting rhetorical situations converge and compete. In theory, online writing environments opened up the exciting opportunity to transform student writing into a socially meaningful experience. In practice, however, these types of online exchange did not live up to the comparatively vibrant, highly-engaged exchanges that I saw happening between academics on commercial social media platforms such as Facebook and Twitter. Although online student writing activities are often championed as modes of engaging the public, more often than not they are in fact simply the posting of student writing on a publicly accessible domain. In other words, a thousand public student blogs do not a public make. There can, of course, still be a great deal of value in course blogs that enables students to engage with one another's writing. But publics, as Hannah Arendt, Michael Warner, and others have observed, consist of much more than mere publicity—they are complex social configurations with very particular sets of attributes. Arendt, for example, argues that a public realm exists only by virtue of its "permanence." As she writes, "if the world is to contain a public space, it cannot be erected for one generation and planned for the living only; it must transcend the life-span of mortal men" (Arendt 1998, 55). Although this may seem an extreme requirement for qualifying a student public, publics are often defined as configurations whose durability and scale of circulation extend beyond the participation of any one of its members.

For Warner, this duration and scale is necessary, as a public is "is a social space created by the reflexive circulation of discourse" (2002, 62). He continues: "No single text can create a public. Nor can a single voice, a single genre, even a single medium. All are insufficient to create the kind of reflexivity that we call a public, since a public is understood to be an ongoing space of encounter for discourse. Not texts themselves create publics, but the concatenation of texts through time" (62). Additionally, for Warner, this circulation must occur among strangers: "A public is always in excess of its known social basis. It must be more than a list of one's friends. It must include strangers" (55). The ongoing circulation of reflexive texts among strangers "convinces us that publics have activity and duration" (68), and enables "confidence that the discourse will circulate along a real path" (75).

For both Arendt and Warner, then, typical online student writing activities do not in fact constitute or engage with a genuine public, as their texts do not typically circulate beyond the members and duration of the course. Although we may find occasional examples of student writing that does in fact find an audience beyond the class, these exceptions still do not constitute the rich, reflexive, intertextual, and durational discourse that define publics for Warner. A student public, by Warner's definition, would not exist until students were citing other students (at least some of whom they did not know) in public forms of writing that they had confidence would also "circulate along a real path" to inform future discourse from this student public. Interestingly, then, writing that sought to participate in the context of a student public would be qualitatively different from any other type of student writing (even publicly accessible writing), given that it would be crafted to reflect on concrete utterances of a student public while seeking, as Warner describes, to "extend its circulation" (75) within that student public. This does not mean that a student public would be segregated from a general public, but that regardless of its engagement with the broader public, the student public would remain discoverable and reflexive to itself.

Certainly, not all student writing should be forced to engage in such a public, or need even be shared beyond the exchange between student and professor. Learning, especially learning to write, is a vulnerable activity that requires various stages of privacy. Our word "essay," after all, is based on the French word for "attempt," as used by Michel de Montaigne in the sixteenth century to describe his book of written reflections. But, ultimately, writing is a tool for participating in public discourse: even when one uses it in private spaces, its character is profoundly shaped by its public existence. Teaching students to write without having them engage a public is like teaching a bird to flap its wings without ever allowing it to leave the ground. But just as a bird cannot learn to fly by imagining a sky, a student cannot engage a student public if it does not yet exist. As it stands, the existence of such a student public has been hindered by a number of technical, cultural, and organizational reasons. Most online student writing, even if publicly accessible, is effectively siloed in course blogs or other content management systems. There is little technical infrastructure in place that promotes the reflexive circulation of student writing beyond the members of the course, nor are there social practices (such as required assignments) that would encourage students to seek out and reflect on student discourse. Furthermore, student writing is a very particular type of discourse, beset with its own sensitivities, reputations, self-regard, materialities, and complex set of goals that make it very different from conventional species of discourse we find circulating in the public sphere, such as news articles, opinion pieces, and blog posts on permanent sites.

Student writing is profoundly vulnerable; it exposes the student to various forms of authoritative analysis, discipline, and sorting. As Brainerd Kellogg, an instructor at Brooklyn Polytechnic, wrote in 1893: "One's English is already taken as the test and measure of his culture—he is known by the English he keeps." He continued: "To mistake his words (even to mispronounce them or to speak them indistinctly), to huddle them as a mob into sentences, to trample on plain rules of grammar, to disregard the idioms of the language,—these things all or severally, *disclose the speaker's intellectual standing.* One's English betrays his breeding, tells what society he frequents, and determines what doors are to open to him or be closed against him" (quoted in Crowley 1998, 97–98, emphasis added). Kellogg's statement may be well over a century old, but the belief that writing provides a lens from which to view the intellect, class, and potential (in short, the worth) of the writer is still alive and well. Today, we judge college applicants, job applicants (Martin-Lacroux and Lacroux 2017), and potential romantic partners (Wells 2015) by their writing skills. "I am astounded," complained a commenter named William, writing in response to an online article on college essay mills, "at the number of grammar and spelling errors in these comments from people who apparently think they are intelligent enough to post an opinion" (Ruff and Costello 2009). David Foster Wallace (2005) observed the prevalence of this judgmental regard of language in his description of "SNOOTS," a group of people he described as "Grammar Nazis, Usage Nerds, Syntax Snobs, the Language Police" (69). "In ways that certain of us are uncomfortable about," he wrote, "SNOOTs' attitudes about contemporary usage resemble religious/political conservatives' attitudes about contemporary culture. We combine a missionary zeal and a near-neural faith in our beliefs' importance with a curmudgeonly hell-in-a-handbasket despair at the way English is routinely defiled by supposedly educated adults" (70–71). For better or worse, language habits are routinely used as a means to socially locate the speaker.

For those who have absorbed the principles of what stands accepted today as "good writing," a SNOOTish standard of language in the classroom or the public sphere works to their advantage. For others, whose race, class, gender, ability, available free time, or any other aspect of identity hinders this absorption, this standard can cause humiliation and discrimination. "Writing is exposure," a graduate student referred to as Ms. Dannon observed in an interview about women's experiences with academic writing in 1993. "It's like being naked and you can't fake it with a lot of things. When you write it down, you're pretty naked and you're alone. There's no one else there, and it's just you, raw meat" (Kirsch 1993, 45). The educator Ira Shor (1980) has written about ways in which working-class students often refrain from talking in the classroom, given the way their use of language would "betray their inferior class-background" (74). As he argues, "silence is a form of defense as well as resistance—it prevents the enemy from knowing what you think or feel, and using it against you" (73). "Because a power struggle surrounds the use of words in every institution of life, there are tense rules and high prices to pay for talking" (72).

It is interesting to note, however, that this power struggle affects professional scholars as well. In her argument for producing academic writing in public, Kathleen Fitzpatrick writes: "Even more frighteningly, perhaps, we'll have to become willing to expose some of our process in public, to allow our readers—and our colleagues—to see some of the bumps and false starts along the way. This, I confess, is the aspect of my argument that I find the most alarming" (Fitzpatrick 2011, 70). Given the challenge of negotiating different types of vulnerabilities in the academy, then, it is unsurprising that many students would choose to restrain their communication, or to write in insincere ways that leave them as little exposed as possible. These vulnerabilities, which exist even in the private space of an analog class, grow exponentially in assignments for which students are asked to write in publicly accessible digital spaces. As Savonick (2018) cautions, "We also have to be careful in encouraging students to join these conversations ... because public writing always entails the risk of exposure, because students live complicated lives that may require the cover of confidentiality, and because the digital leaves traces everywhere."

Digitally-archived student writing is also vulnerable to future misuse, such as by trolls, potential employers, insurance companies or the state. The digital medium transforms writing into an object that can be preserved indefinitely and might have a greatly different use value than the one its author intended. Online writing is easily preserved, archived, organized, searched, instrumentalized, shared, circulated, analyzed, and even monetized. Even writing shared in private contexts can be hacked, leaked, subpoenaed, or scrutinized in ways the author didn't initially anticipate. When people write online, they never know how that information may be used against them later on, wittingly or not. For example, an individual might be fired for political sentiments expressed in private texts, as was seen in the case of former FBI agent Peter Strzok (Goldman and Schmidt 2018). Or someone might be revealing a propensity for developing Alzheimer's, such as suggested by a study on its correlation with early linguistic ability (Snowdon et al. 1996).[2] As Joshua Gruenspecht, a cybersecurity expert at the Center for Democracy and Technology, notes, "mass digital storage ... has significantly increased the chances that records of any given document exist and is increasingly unifying the locations in which those records can be found" (2011, 544). Given this vulnerability, it may seem unwise to advocate for the formation of a student public that would expose an entire generation to future forms of undesired scrutiny.

The idea of a student public seems preposterous to many of those who are most acquainted with it. Social media is filled with examples of professors bemoaning the poor quality of student writing. The Tumblr and Twitter accounts *Shit My Students Write*, for example, post short snippets of comically bad (and often offensive) student writing, which regularly receives thousands of "favorites." On the very same social media platforms, students often express cheerful agreement about the quality of their work, demonstrating mastery in digital communication through networked boastings, viral tutorials, crowdsourced requests, and convivial complaints related to the practice of "bullshitting" the student paper. On YouTube, for example, "bullshit" is taken up as topic of voluntary instruction by and for students in videos such as "How to BS an Essay" (Rob's Rants 2016) with 22,977 views and counting, presented next to a feed of related videos with titles like "How to Bullshit an Essay" (answerly 2011) and "How to Bullshit Your Way Through an Entire English Paper" (xxThroughThePainxx 2011).

In more serious but less viral venues of scholarly discourse, composition scholars theorize the economic causes and political consequences of "student bullshit" (Perelman 2012 427), applaud it as a rightful act of resistance in alienating educational structures (Cruz n.d.), and defend its unexpected and positive learning outcomes (Smagorinsky et al. 2010; Eubanks and Schaeffer 2008). The phenomenon is, as one writing centre director laments, "unfortunately, nothing new" (Griffin 2015); in fact, it was recognized at least as early as 1963 in Harvard education professor William G. Perry's condemnation of student "bulling," a practice he defines as presenting "evidence of an understanding of form in the hope that the reader may be deceived into supposing a familiarity with content" (Perry 1963, 7). Ken Macrorie also noted the phenomenon more than forty years ago, describing it as "Engfish," a "bloated, pretentious language [... found] in the students' themes, ... A feel-nothing, say-nothing language, dead like Latin, devoid of the rhythms of contemporary speech" (Macrorie 1970, 18).

---

[2] I thank Dr. Oliver Duke-Williams for drawing my attention to this issue.

Student writing is thought to be so horrible that one professor wrote a satiric ode on *McSweeney's* entitled "I Would Rather Do Anything Else Than Grade Your Final Papers." In this piece, Robin Lee Mozer writes: "I would rather go back to the beginning of the semester like Sisyphus and recreate my syllabus from scratch while simultaneously building an elaborate class website via our university's shitty web-based course content manager and then teach the entire semester over again than grade your goddamn Final Papers" (2016).

If student writing is so horrible, one might wonder why it should be worthy of a public. Unlike professional forms of writing, which deserve formal practices of transmission and preservation, student writing is typically treated like a waste product in the production of literate citizens. But as composition scholars such as Macorie have pointed out, the quality of student writing may be more of a reflection of the context in which they are trained to write than the potential of student writing itself. We have built temples to manage student writing (learning management systems such Blackboard, for example), temples to discipline student writing (such as plagiarism checkers like Turnitin), and temples to mine the information capital of student writing (such as Google Docs), but we have not designed temples that would grant student discourse the dignity to "circulate along a real path" when it was ready and to protect itself when needed. We have not worked with students to change our inherited assumptions about the proper tone, form, and citation practices of student writing into experiments about methods for fostering public student discourse. While some virtual spaces may allow forms of peer exchange, they are not designed in earnest to foster a student public, nor are they accompanied by pedagogical strategies that foster reflexive discourse across the bounds of the classroom and the academic term. Critiques of online student discussion being just as fake, as expressed in a recent Tweet currently "liked" almost six thousand times and retweeted almost two thousand times (Hoyt 2018), must be understood as reflective of current methods for facilitating peer exchange rather than indicative of the potential of a student public under more conducive conditions.

Turnitin, the online plagiarism detection tool, boasts that its service has been used to check some thirty million student papers. That is, thirty million student papers are sitting on its servers, unread by anything but the computer. Wouldn't it be nice, I wondered, if all those words might be held differently? Not captured and filtered and disciplined, but put into dialogue with one another through technology, experimentation, encouragement, and care? Perhaps, repurposed and rewoven, those words could tell us something very important. Alone, I was just as incapable of creating such a public as I was of creating its technology. I could, however, at the very least, address my personal fears. I wrote a little poem:

> & so
> what if i
> do inscribe my
> errors into
> posterity?

## Writing the Student Public to Come

In the "Interactive Technology and Pedagogy" course" I took, we were required to come up with a pitch for a project that engaged with issues related to technology and education. I came up with the idea for Social Paper (https://socialpaper.commons.gc.cuny.edu/), a tool that might help provide infrastructure for a student public that transcended courses, academic terms, disciplines, and institutions. It was intended, so to speak, to be a temple that gave dignity to student writing, a place to transform what is effectively treated as waste into an influential, self-aware, and self-determining public. I wanted to build a platform that attended specifically to the needs and sensitivities of student writing while also incorporating functionalities and tactics from commercial social media platforms that encouraged participation and engagement. A centralized platform for sharing and commenting on student writing, for example, could potentially develop a network large enough that, like Facebook and Twitter, provided a broad, engaged, and durable community in which student writing might circulate. Activity feeds would help make student papers and student comments visible to the broader community. Granular privacy settings for each individual paper, such as those on Google Docs, would allow students to share work only at their level of comfort and hopefully build, at their own pace, the confidence to participate in such a student public. And, above all, it was important to me that this tool would be developed as a public good rather than yet another instrument of surveillance capitalism, and ideally with the participation of other students. As my dissertation work focused on the way software use in schools often teaches students to passively accept their design, functionality, and policies, I was excited about the prospect of implementing a form of writing technology that incorporated student governance and design.

With great luck, I had the privilege of working at CUNY with English professor Matthew K. Gold, urban education graduate student Jennifer Stoops, and the Commons in A Box software development team on creating a beta version of Social Paper with funding from the National Endowment for the Humanities.

Of course, given the reality of software development, especially within the context of higher education, the beta version of Social Paper that we released in 2016 was a dialed-down version of the original vision. I had planned all along to post my dissertation drafts on the platform to try to experiment with the possibilities of bringing a student public forward. However, when my drafts were at last ready to share, I realized that my experiment might be even more fruitful if I posted my drafts in different virtual spaces as a means to explore how different platform functionality, networked communities, and written forms might influence public engagement with the drafts. It was in this spirit that I came up with the idea for #SocialDiss. This project, however, was not intended as an instructive model for others to emulate, but rather as a project to contribute to the conversation and interest in public forms of student work. As I describe in more detail elsewhere (Glass, forthcoming), it served its purpose well. I was overcome with the amount of intellectual exchange the project created among my peers, the new professional connections it made, and the ways it opened up new conversations about these intellectual topics with those in my familial and social circles. At the same time, the project also helped hone my understanding of some of the drawbacks of the methods I used to put my work in the public sphere.

As students, professors, and researchers with varying academic and social backgrounds, we come with different sets of beliefs, anxieties, and hopes about what academic writing can and should be. Many, I am certain, will not relate to some of the anxieties about academic writing I've described, or the arguments I've attempted to make. Before I went to the woods, I, too, had strongly believed that beauty, original insight, and superior intellectual perspective were the most important truths that writing might achieve. I have tried to recount how I came to see that writing practices also create other types of important truths but in unexpected ways: they can isolate us in our pursuit for individual success or alternately, through intentional organization, they can create more supportive, dialogic, and empowered communities. I have also tried to shine light on the way the different spaces in which we write (and the social dynamics that they embody) reflect and reinforce our ideologies about writing. Beauty, originality, and intellectual quality need not be sacrificed to in order to support more community-oriented writing practices, but they will be utterly transformed. As human society faces ever greater political, environmental, economic, and social challenges, it seems time to question the dominance of teaching and using academic writing only as a tool for self reflection, advancing arguments, and demonstrating one's learning and character. For if we are to meaningfully address the world's pressing challenges, we need writing to do much more, such as to inspire and enable collective action, to advance genuine and productive dialogue between divergent viewpoints, and to help counteract forms of loneliness, insecurity, and hate that are rampant in modern life. Locked away in individual assignments or scattered in fragmented sites of the web, there is little opportunity for students to explore or even become aware of the potential power of their speech. To my mind, the question is not whether students are capable of producing writing that merits public attention—we'll never know that in their current writing conditions. The more vital question instead is what sort of space would enable student writing to accrue dignity, collective awareness, public engagement, and purpose over time? And in building this new temple of knowledge, could academic life more fruitfully attend to the challenges of the twenty-first century?

WORKS CITED

Allison, Leslie. 2010. "So You Want to Get a PhD in the Humanities." *YouTube*, October 25. https://www.youtube.com/watch?v=obTNwPJvOI8.

Alvarez, Maximillian. 2017. "Writing Better Won't Cure Your Academic Woes." *Chronicle of Higher Education*, April 23. http://www.chronicle.com/article/Writing-Better-Won-t-Cure/239832.

American Association of University Professors (AAUP). 2018. "Data Snapshot: Contingent Faculty in US Higher Ed." *AAUP Updates*, October 11. https://www.aaup.org/news/daa-snapshot-contingent-faculty-us-higher-ed#.XLKZQ9h7mpo.

answerly. 2011. "How to BS an Essay." *YouTube*, December 5. https://www.youtube.com/watch?v=pjavmXxEOos.

Arendt, Hannah. 1998. *The Human Condition*. 2nd ed. Chicago: University of Chicago Press.

Benton, Thomas H. 2010. "The Big Lie About the 'Life of the Mind.'" *Chronicle of Higher Education*, February 8. https://www.chronicle.com/article/The-Big-Lie-About-the-Life-of/63937.

Berlin, James A. 1987. *Rhetoric and Reality: Writing Instruction in American Colleges, 1900–1985*. Carbondale: Southern Illinois University Press.

Bousquet, Marc. 2008. *How the University Works: Higher Education and the Low-Wage Nation.* New York: New York University Press.

Bradstreet, Anne. 1969. Poems of Anne Bradstreet. Edited with an introduction by Robert Hutchinson. New York: Dover Publications.

Carr, Nicholas. 2010. *The Shallows: What the Internet is Doing to Our Brains.* New York: W.W. Norton.

Chu, Andrea Long. 2018. "I Worked With Avital Ronell. I Believe Her Accuser." *Chronicle of Higher Education*, August 30. https://www.chronicle.com/article/I-Worked-With-Avital-Ronell-I/244415.

Cowley, Malcolm. 1958. *The Literary Situation.* New York: Viking Press.

Crowley, Sharon. 1998. *Composition in the University: Historical and Polemical Essays.* Pittsburgh: University of Pittsburgh Press.

Cruz, Joshua. n.d. "Resisting Reproduction in Writing: Bullshit as Subversive Tactic and Game." http://www.academia.edu/23683462/Resisting_Reproduction_in_Writing_Bullshit_as_Subversive_Tactic_and_Game.

Curtis, John W., and Saranna Thornton. 2014. "Losing Focus: The Annual Report on the Economic Status of the Profession, 2013–14." *Academe* 100(2): 4–17.

Dahlgreen, Will. 2015. "Bookish Britain: Literary Jobs are the Most Desirable." *YouGov*, February 15. https://yougov.co.uk/news/2015/02/15/bookish-britain-academic-jobs-are-most-desired/.

Didion, Joan. 2000. "Why I Write." In The Writer on Her Work, edited by Janet Sternburg, rev. ed., vol. 1, 17–26. New York: W.W. Norton.

Elbow, Peter. 1998. *Writing Without Teachers.* 2nd ed. New York: Oxford University Press.

Eubanks, Philip, and John D. Schaeffer. 2008. "A Kind Word for Bullshit: The Problem of Academic Writing." *College Composition and Communication* 59(3): 372–88.

Fitzpatrick, Kathleen. 2011. *Planned Obsolescence: Publishing, Technology, and the Future of the Academy.* New York: New York University Press.

————. 2012. "Giving It Away: Sharing and the Future of Scholarly Communication." Personal blog, January 12. https://kfitz.info/giving-it-away/.

Glass, Erin R. 2012. "BANKSY + THE ART OF THE PUBLIC DOMAIN." *Meaning of Media,* February 13. http://meaningofmedia2012.blogspot.com/2012/02/banksy-art-of-public-domain-boyle.html.

————. Forthcoming. "#SocialDiss: Transforming the Dissertation into Networked Knowledge Production." In *The Digital Dissertation: History, Theory, Practice,* edited by Virginia Kuhn and Kathie Gossett. Forthcoming database and eBook project.

Goldman, Adam, and Michael S. Schmidt. 2018. "F.B.I. Agent Peter Strzok, who Criticized Trump in Texts, is Fired." *New York Times,* August 13. https://www.nytimes.com/2018/08/13/us/politics/peter-strzok-fired-fbi.html.

Griffin, Kathi R. 2015. "Avoiding 'Academic Bullshit': Meeting Disengaged Students Where They Are." Jackson State University, Richard Wright Center for Writing, Rhetoric, and Research, blog post, April 8. http://www.jsums.edu/wrightcenter/2015/04/08/avoiding-academic-bullshit-meeting-disengaged-students-where-they-are/.

Gruenspecht, Joshua. 2011. "'Reasonable' Grand Jury Subpoenas: Asking for Information in the Age of Big Data." *Harvard Journal of Law and Technology* 24(2): 543–62.

Guerrero, Jean. 2018. *Crux: A Cross-Border Memoir.* New York: Random House.

Hall, Gary. 2016. *The Uberfication of the University.* Minneapolis: University of Minnesota Press.

Hawisher, Gail E., Paul LeBlanc, Charles Moran, and Cynthia L. Selfe. 1996. *Computers and the Teaching of Writing in American Higher Education, 1979–1994: A History.* Norwood, NJ: Ablex Publishing Corporation.

Hoyt, Issy. 2018. "There's nothing more fake than a college students reply to a classmate's discussion post." Tweet, September 5. https://twitter.com/issyhoyt/status/1037375101371654144?lang=en.

Jaschik, Scott. 2017. "The Shrinking Humanities Job Market." *Inside Higher Ed,* August 28. https://www.insidehighered.com/news/2017/08/28/more-humanities-phds-are-awarded-job-openings-are-disappearing.

Kafka, Franz. 1965. *The Diaries of Franz Kafka*. Edited by Max Brod. New York: Schocken Books.

Kinnell, Galway. 1978. *Walking Down the Stairs: Selections from Interviews*. Ann Arbor: University of Michigan Press.

Kirsch, Gesa E. 1993. *Women Writing the Academy: Audience, Authority, and Transformation*. Published for the Conference on College Composition and Communication. Carbondale and Edwardsville: Southern Illinois University Press.

Levertov, Denise. 1973. *The Poet in the World*. New York: New Directions.

Macrorie, Ken, comp. 1970. *Uptaught*. New York: Hayden Book Co.

Martin-Lacroux, Christelle, and Alain Lacroux. 2017. "Do Employers Forgive Applicants' Bad Spelling in Résumés?" *Business and Professional Communication Quarterly* 80(3): 321–35.

Moshfegh, Ottessa. 2018. "On Writing as a Rite of Passage." From a conversation with Yasi Salek. *The Creative Independent*, July 16. https://thecreativeindependent.com/people/ottessa-moshfegh-on-writing-as-a-rite-of-passage/.

Mozer, Robin Lee. 2016. "I Would Rather Do Anything Else Than Grade Your Final Papers." *McSweeney's Internet Tendency*, May 2. https://www.mcsweeneys.net/articles/i-would-rather-do-anything-else-than-grade-your-final-papers.

National Science Foundation, National Center for Science and Engineering Statistics. 2017. *Doctorate Recipients from U.S. Universities: 2015*. Special Report NSF 17-306. Arlington, VA. https://www.nsf.gov/statistics/sed/2017/nsf17306/.

Orwell, George. 2000. *George Orwell: An Age Like This, 1920–1940*. Vol. 1 of *The Collected Essays, Journalism, and Letters of George Orwell*, edited by Sonia Orwell and Ian Angus. Boston: Nonpareil Books.

Pannapacker, William. 2011. "So You Want to Get a PhD in the Humanities: Nine Years Later." *YouTube*, January 25. https://www.youtube.com/watch?v=obTNwPJvOI8.

Parry, Marc. 2011. "So You Think an English Professor's Life Is a Cartoon." *Chronicle of Higher Education*, January 16. https://www.chronicle.com/article/So-You-Think-an-English/125954.

Patton, Stacey. 2013. "The Dissertation Can No Longer Be Defended." *Chronicle of Higher Education*, February 11. https://www.chronicle.com/article/The-Dissertation-Can-No-Longer/137215.

Perelman, Les. 2012. "Mass-market Writing Assessments as Bullshit." In *Writing Assessment in the 21st Century: Essays in Honor of Edward M. White*, edited by Norbert Elliot and Les Perelman, 425–37.

Perry, William G., Jr. 1963. *Examsmanship and the Liberal Arts: An Epistemological Inquiry.* Cambridge, MA: President and Fellows of Harvard College. https://bsc.harvard.edu/files/bsc/files/bsc_pub_-_examsmanship_and_the_liberal_arts.pdf.

Rich, Adrienne. 1993. *What is Found There: Notebooks on Poetry and Politics.* New York: W.W. Norton.

Rilke, Rainer Maria. 1954. *Letters to a Young Poet.* New York: W.W. Norton. http://www.lettersofnote.com/2012/07/letter-to-young-poet.html.

Rob's Rants. 2016. "How to Bullshit an Essay." *YouTube*, May 5. https://www.youtube.com/watch?v=f2_fnt9QwSQ.

Ruff, Bob, and Carol Costello. 2009. "Educating America: Cheating on Papers is a Booming Web Business." CNN, *American Morning*, December 30. http://am.blogs.cnn.com/2009/12/30/cheating-on-papers-is-a-booming-web-business/.

Russell, David R. 2002. *Writing in the Academic Disciplines: A Curricular History.* 2nd ed. Carbondale: Southern Illinois University Press.

Sanos, Sadrine. 2016. *Simone de Beauvoir: Creating a Feminist Existence in the World.* New York and Oxford: Oxford University Press.

Savonick, Danica. 2018. "Why I Teach with HASTAC: Platforms as Critical Pedagogy." HASTAC blog post, August 7. https://www.hastac.org/blogs/danicasavonick/2018/08/07/why-i-teach-hastac-platforms-critical-pedagogy.

Shor, Ira. 1980. *Critical Teaching and Everyday Life.* Montreal and New York: Black Rose Books.

Smagorinsky, Peter, Elizabeth Anne Daigle, Cindy O'Donnell-Allen, and Susan Bynum. 2010. "Bullshit in Academic Writing: A Protocol Analysis of a High School Senior's Process of Interpreting Much Ado about Nothing." *Research in the Teaching of English* 44(4): 368–405. https://eric.ed.gov/?id=EJ886404.

Snow, C.P. 1998. *The Two Cultures.* Introduction by Stefan Collini. Cambridge and New York: Cambridge University Press.

Snowdon, D.A., S.J. Kemper, J.A. Mortimer, L.H. Greiner, D.R. Wekstein, and W.R. Markesbery. 1996. "Linguistic Ability in Early Life and Cognitive Function and Alzheimer's Disease in Late Life: Findings from the Nun Study." *JAMA* 275(7): 528–32.

Song, Min Hyoung. 2018. "Viet Thanh Nguyen and the Scholar–Public Intellectual." *PMLA* 133(2): 406–12.

Swartz, Aaron. 2008. "Guerilla Open Access Manifesto." https://openaccessmanifesto.wordpress.com/guerilla-open-access-manifesto/.

Szetela, Adam. 2018. "Feeling Anxious? You're Not the Only One." *Chronicle of Higher Education*, April 13. https://www.chronicle.com/article/Feeling-Anxious-You-re-Not/243117.

Wallace, David Foster. 2005. "Authority and American Usage." In *Consider the Lobster, and Other Essays,* 66–127. New York: Little, Brown.

Warner, Michael. 2002. "Publics and Counterpublics." *Public Culture* 14(1): 49–90.

Wells, Georgia. 2015. "What's Really Hot on Dating Sites? Proper Grammar." *Wall Street Journal,* October 1. https://www.wsj.com/articles/whats-really-hot-on-dating-sites-proper-grammar-1443746849.

Woolf, Virginia. 1956. *Orlando: A Biography.* New York: Harcourt Brace Jovanovich.

Wresch, William. 1984. *The Computer in Composition Instruction: A Writer's Tool.* Urbana, IL: National Council of Teachers of English.

Wu, Jon. 2014. "A Generic College Paper." *McSweeney's Internet Tendency,* September 14. https://www.mcsweeneys.net/articles/a-generic-college-paper.

xxThroughThePainxx. 2011. "How to Bullshit Your Way Through an Entire English Paper." *YouTube*, November 12. https://www.youtube.com/watch?v=mv8LszVl4TY.

Zuboff, Shoshana. 2015. "Big Other: Surveillance Capitalism and the Prospects of an Information Civilization." *Journal of Information Technology* 30(1): 75–89.

# Reassembling the Bacon: Crowdsourcing Historical Social Networks in the Redesign of *Six Degrees of Francis Bacon*

## John R. Ladd
### Washington and Jefferson College

Beyond the fact that his name makes for a snappy project title, Francis Bacon is a well-chosen poster child for an early modern social network project.[1] As scientist, essayist, politician, and courtier, Bacon participated in most of the political, scientific, literary, and cultural developments that concern present-day scholars. Bacon's most famous quotation—*scientia potentia est*, knowledge is power—calls to mind the many advancements of the Renaissance as well as the ways in which both power and knowledge were deployed in the service of colonial violence. But appropriately, the phrase itself is not Bacon's invention: the social artifact is the result of intertextual transmission and mutation. He borrowed the aphorism from a variety of classical and medieval sources, and it was Thomas Hobbes in *Leviathan* (1651) who transmuted the phrase into its commonly quoted form years later.[2] Even at his most famous and most quotable, Bacon was shaped by the social world around him.

An extension of the "knowledge is power" principle for both Bacon's world and our own might be "social knowledge is power."[3] Certainly someone who rose to the position of Lord Chancellor of England saw the value of who-you-know for obtaining and retaining power. And in our twenty-first-century social media age, vast networks of social information are wielded by political

---

[1] Of course our play on this phrase is itself the result of a long chain of relationships. The "Six Degrees of Kevin Bacon" game, in which people try to connect any actor to Kevin Bacon by no more than six shared film acting credits, is a reference to the idea that all people are connected by only "six degrees of separation." This notion, popularized by John Guare's 1990 play of the same name, is drawn from the "small world" principle of network analysis and was first set forth by Frigyes Karinthy. For more, see Barabási 2002.

[2] For a detailed discussion of the several places in which Bacon uses this phrase, see García 2001.

[3] I am far from the first to suggest this, and Grewal (2008) offers a comprehensive historical view of this phenomenon.

leaders, tech entrepreneurs, and multinational corporations. The digital networks we all now live and work with every day can make our lives easier,
by suggesting a new Facebook friend or something to watch on Netflix, but
unchecked misuse of social networks can have disastrous effects. This was
recently evident in the now infamous Cambridge Analytica scandal, in which
a private data firm working for a specific political party used Facebook without users' permission in order to influence the 2016 U.S. presidential election
(Rosenberg, Confessore, and Cadwalladr 2018). In Bacon's aphorism, the term
"potentia" is ambiguous; Bacon, and those who repeated and simplified the
phrase after him, do not clarify whether the power that knowledge creates is
political, theological, or economic. Certainly the advancements of the seven-
teenth century saw various kinds of power deployed mainly to preserve the
interests of the already powerful. With this in mind, in our own historical moment, we would do well to ask what kinds of power social knowledge makes
available, and for whom. Examining the social structures of the past can help
us to better understand how large systems of power are built and maintained.

*Six Degrees of Francis Bacon* is a project that catalogues social information
about the early modern period using digital crowdsourcing; in doing so, it interrogates both the potential and the limits of social networks in early modern England and on today's social Internet. Some background on the project:
*Six Degrees* was started in 2011 by Christopher Warren of Carnegie Mellon
University (CMU) and Daniel Shore of Georgetown University. The goal was
to create a data set that included as much information as possible about who
knew whom in Britain, 1500 to 1700, and to allow scholars to share their
own specialized knowledge of relationships in that period. From the start, it
made sense to have a web application in which historical social relationships
could be recorded by the scholars who knew them best, but a website that
was merely an empty canvas for scholars to fill up with their research was
an uninviting prospect: how would scholars know where to begin? The *Six
Degrees* team decided to begin with an existing database of social information—the prose biographies, themselves full of scholars describing social relations among historical figures, in the *Oxford Dictionary of National Biography*
(*ODNB*). Using a method of statistical inference combined with text mining,[4]
*Six Degrees* was able to create a starting data set based on the *ODNB*'s large
source of secondary material. After that, led by then-research fellow and
now co-principal investigator Jessica Otis, they created a website to display
the statistically-inferred network and invite scholars to add to and edit the
connections that the text mining process produced. This site, the *Six Degrees*

---

[4] For more detail on this process, see Warren et al. 2016.

of *Francis Bacon* Beta, launched in 2015, and since then scholars around the world have been able to add their knowledge to the database (with verification from a team of dedicated curators).

In 2017, the *Six Degrees* team, by then joined by myself and Scott Weingart, revisited the site's principles and design to create a stable, long-term version of the web application. In the two years that the beta site was live, we learned a lot about how a networked community of scholars work with *Six Degrees* data, and how that scholarly network of contributors interacts with the historical networks visualized on the site. The new site, which launched in November 2017, takes into account common user behaviours and desired new features, and it provides a richer series of views into the social life of early modern England. The major takeaway from this year-long process was that to create an accurate network of the people who lived and worked together in sixteenth- and seventeenth-century Britain, it was necessary to rely on overlapping contemporary networks: of the people who created the new site, of the scholars and editors who wrote the *ODNB*, and of the larger community of early modernists who interacted with the *Six Degrees* site daily. While it is impossible to go through every change made to the interface during the year-long redesign process, a number of specific design decisions— comprising both the exploration and contribution features available on *Six Degrees*—highlight the ways in which the affordances of networks and the needs of scholars influenced the site's new features.

## The Team (Design + Humanities)

Before turning to these features, I first want to recognize the contributions that many people from a diverse array of fields made to the redesign process. This is about more than just giving credit—although a lot of credit is due to many people. *Six Degrees* is a collaborative project to its core, and it relies on the contributions of scholars and professionals from a variety of disciplines. I have already mentioned the main team of Warren, Shore, Otis, Weingart, and myself. We received a generous National Endowment for the Humanities (NEH) Implementation Grant, from the Office of Digital Humanities, that not only made my position with *Six Degrees* possible, but allowed us to bring in a number of other experts in different fields. We supplemented our in-house expertise in digital history and literary studies with the expertise of the team at DensityDesign, led by Politecnico di Milano professor Paolo Ciuccarelli.[5]

---

[5] Along with Ciuccarelli, the DensityDesign team that worked on our project comprised Tommaso Elli, Michele Mauri, and Michele Invernizzi. DensityDesign has been instrumental in a number of marquee digital humanities projects in the last several years,

David Newbury contributed his experience in web development as well, re-fining and streamlining the site's application programming interface (API). We also benefited from the advice and help of CMU's wider community of de-signers, web developers, and humanities scholars. This collaboration across disciplines has in many ways been the key to the success of *Six Degrees* as a project. The early stages of the project relied on collaboration with statisti-cians and computer scientists, and in this later stage it was crucial to get the help of web developers and designers—not just to execute the humanities scholars' vision for the project, but to construct a shared vision of what the project could and should accomplish.

This shared plan first took shape during a week-long Design Sprint event, in which we split up into intellectually diverse teams to tackle specific areas of the site. Common in development and design disciplines, a sprint is a short period of intense work in which the full team gathers to make headway on large parts of a project before settling in to a longer-term working rhythm. So the collaboration began at the sprint but continued all year long, as I co-ordinated work and code coming in from Milan, Washington, D.C., Los An-geles, and Pittsburgh. In working on *Six Degrees*, the core team learned a lot about the advantages of working with experts in web design. Decisions about the appearance of visualizations, basic user interactions, and even fonts and colours could be grounded in decades of experience. For the designers and developers, the humanities issues at stake on the site presented unique challenges that they rose to meet. How can scholarly reputation and credit be preserved in a crowdsourcing interface? How can you create a beautiful, simplified visualization that fulfills scholarly expectations for citation and information density? How can you streamline scholarly collaboration while still making the verification and curation of submissions rigorous? We could not have begun to answer these questions without working across disciplin-ary boundaries, and the ultimate changes made to the site are better for it. For example, our network density filter, described in more detail later in this essay, was a direct result of in-person discussions during the design sprint, growing out of a combination of the designers' desire for a readable network graph and the historians' desire for specificity and completeness.

*Exploration*

The vast majority of visitors to *Six Degrees* are not there to contribute to the site's data—they visit the site to explore the network. This presented two

including *Mapping the Republic of Letters*, *Palladio*, and *RAWGraphs*.

challenges for the redesign team: to make movement between exploration and contribution as easy as possible and to emphasize the many ways in which users can visualize and explore the site's data. To the latter point, we completely overhauled the site's network visualizations and added a number of new visualization paradigms to the site's existing node-link diagrams.[6] These changes to the exploration interface fell under three general critical categories: a productive emphasis on scholarly (un)certainty, employment of the flexibility of network visualizations, and the integration of groups as a category overlaying networks.

I mentioned above that the *Six Degrees* data set began with a statistical inference process run on *ODNB* articles. This process produced a data set of proposed relationships between names that appeared in the *ODNB*, and each relationship was assigned an algorithmic confidence measure, from 0 to 100 per cent—a measure of the algorithm's degree of certainty over whether the relationship existed.[7] These confidence measures were preserved in the data for each relationship on the site; you can click on an edge—a line representing a relationship in the network visualization—and see how sure the original computational process was about this relationship's existence. These inferred edges were only meant to be a start, a first prospective step toward increasing scholarly confidence in a specific set of historical relationships. The site has always invited scholars to enter their own confidence of a relationship existing, on the same 0 to 100 scale, when they update an existing edge or add a new one.

In a sense, all historical relationships are inferred from available evidence. From the evidence of period documents or accounts of events, historians and literary scholars posit the past existence of a relationship by inference. By extending this uncertainty to algorithms as well as human contributors, *Six Degrees* makes this inference process explicit. *Six Degrees* is not simply a database of historical relationships, but a database of different degrees of certainty about the past existence of such relationships. In some cases we are very certain that a relationship existed, and in others we have some sense that it could have been, but the available evidence limits our confidence.

---

[6] Briefly, our technology stack includes a PostgreSQL database with a Ruby on Rails application for APIs and an AngularJS application for the front end. All visualizations were made using D3.js. The original *Six Degrees* web application was built entirely in Ruby on Rails, but for the redesign Angular gave us more flexibility.

[7] On the site, we retained only relationships that had a confidence of 10 per cent or above, so 10–100 per cent is the full visible range.

When asked to either raise or lower the algorithm's confidence about a relationship (or to create a new relationship and add confidence sui generis),
scholars must engage with their own degree of certainty. The confidence
measures on the site are thus a useful aid to further inquiry and the product
of important historical work.

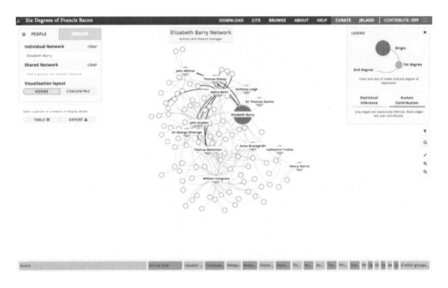

Figure 1. The network of actress and theatre manager Elizabeth Barry.

Figure 2. Relationship types and confidence values of the connection
between Katherine Jones and Lucius Cary.

On the original site, you could see confidence measures after clicking on an edge. Because of the importance of confidence to the site's raison d'être, however, we wanted a way of visualizing the distinction between algorithmic and human confidence, to alert contributors to edges that needed human attention and to give a sense of how much of the network had been curated. Now, when you visit the site, edges that have been only inferred statistically are grey. When an edge has been human-curated, it turns black (Figure 1). The full set of relationship types and confidence values is still just a click away (Figure 2). The effect of this change is that it's instantly clear which parts of the network need attention, and which are already sites of productive scholarly debate. We do not separate computer and human to make a value judgment between one and the other—the algorithm was, after all, designed by humans with experience in both history and statistics—but showing a distinction between the two reduces confusion about how this crucial part of the site operates and highlights the main way scholars can intervene in the data and in the further growth and maintenance of the *Six Degrees* network.

Meaningful colours for edges was just one of many ways we updated and extended the site's node-link network diagrams, the visual representation that most people instantly think of when they hear the word "network." Despite the ubiquity of force-directed node-link diagrams—what *Six Degrees* has dubbed the "Hooke graph" (Ladd 2017)—a network is not tied to any one visual representation. A network is a data structure that represents a series of relationships between entities. Often those entities are represented as circles (called nodes or vertices), and the relationships between them are represented as lines (called links or edges). That data structure, however, can be represented in any number of ways, as a table of values, a matrix, or a tree, to name a few examples. Certain pieces of information on *Six Degrees*—such as the overall number of connections around prominent individuals—are best represented by the traditional network diagram, but other data points, such as the type or duration of a relationship, need other representations such as the timelines we use in multiple places in the new design.

In our redesign we took advantage of the flexibility of network representation to help users get the most out of the site's visualizations. For example, when users search for an individual person, they see that person's immediate network—the people immediately connected to them and the others connected by two degrees. If the individual is well-known, such as Francis Bacon or Aphra Behn, the number of nodes in the graph can quickly become visually overwhelming. On the beta site, we were only able to represent part of each network in order to produce readable graphs. The redesigned site includes a concentric network view, which arrays the nodes in a circle around the individual for whom the user searched (Figure 3).

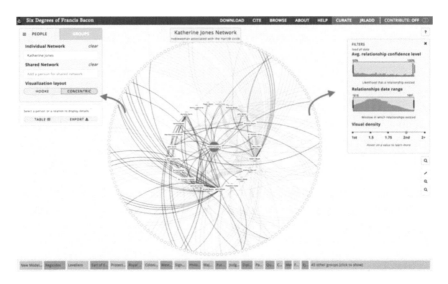

**Figure 3. Concentric view of Katherine Jones's network.**

Another way in which *Six Degrees* makes crowded networks easier to read is through the use of filters. The complexity of graphs can be reduced through our unique "Visual Density" filter, which lets users select the amount of nodes and edges (based on their distance from the searched-for individual) that they would like to view. Additional sliding filters for confidence percentages (see above) and relationship date range allow the user to pull a sliding window across the view to see how a network changes over time or by scholarly certainty. This makes the information encoded within an edge accessible to users in a visual way.

Networks are a flexible format; nodes are entities, and edges are relations, and by switching between which entities and relations are represented, you can visualize a huge range of complex systems. Because nodes in a network can be positioned anywhere so long as the connections are all present, we were able to create a shared network view that allows users to search for two figures and see them as distinct poles in a network of mutual acquaintances (Figure 4). Because the nodes and edges of a network can describe any kind of entity and any kinds of relationships, we could create a network of groups in which each node represents a group and each edge represents members shared between those groups. And because our network visualizations were interactive, we could allow various kinds of click and double-click behaviours for navigating quickly through many different networks—a feature that became important for contribution as well. Rather than tying our visualizations to a single, static representation, the *Six Degrees* visualization can be adapted to a range of scholarly uses, facilitating navigation through the site and research on the figures it visualizes.

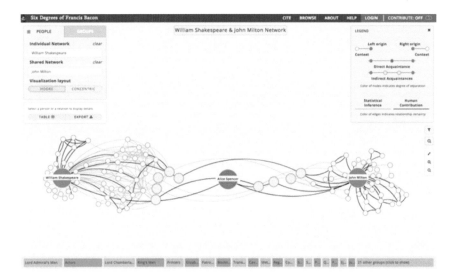

**Figure 4. Shared Network visualization of William Shakespeare and John Milton.**

The last major exploration change from the beta design to the new site was the introduction of visualizations for groups. From the beginning of the project, *Six Degrees* has collected data on a category of association we call, simply, "groups," and which includes early modern organizations (such as the Royal Society or Patrons of the Mermaid Tavern), occupations (such as Judges or Midwives), and modern scholarly categories (such as Elizabethan Playwrights). These groups do not fit into the *Six Degrees* network schema—the relation between members of a group is not the same as the social relations that *Six Degrees* represents as an edge. You can be part of a group without having any relation, direct or indirect, with other members. We realized quickly, therefore, that group information would have to be represented differently. Rather than choose one representation, we again took advantage of the network tools at our disposal to create multiple ways for the user to interact with group data.

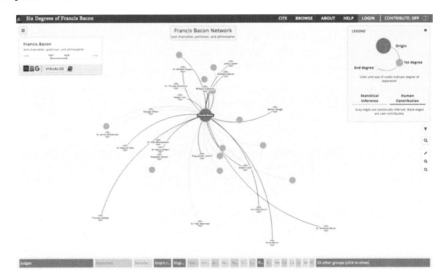

**Figure 5. Francis Bacon, selected to show his membership in specific groups.**

When a user views a network of people—either the individual network or the shared network—a bar of groups is shown at the bottom of the page, with bubbles for groups proportional in size to the number of group members shown in the current view (Figure 5). Then, when you mouse over or click on a particular person, the Groups Bar is highlighted with the groups of which that person is a member. Conversely, when you mouse over a group bubble, the members of the group are highlighted in the graph. This is a quick way to view, without switching to a new page, the ways in which the social relationships a user is looking at are related to the group associations of those same people. This view treats group data as a kind of overlay or filter on existing networks.

It is sometimes necessary, of course, to view group data on its own. When users search for a specific group, they can choose two representations for group data. The first is a *node-link diagram* (Figure 6) in which the nodes represent members of the group and any person who is connected to at least one group member. The connections themselves are the typical social relationships visible in the other graphs. This allows a user to quickly see whether any group members knew one another. The other visualization of a group is the *timeline* (Figure 7), in which users can browse a scrollable timeline that shows the lifespan of each group member and the duration they spent as group members. Unlike the network diagram, which focuses on relationships, this visualization gives a quick sense of the way groups develop and change over time.

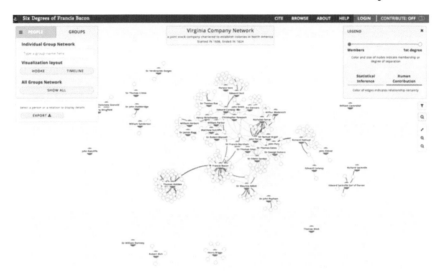

Figure 6. Network visualization (node-link diagram) of a specific group: the Virginia Company.

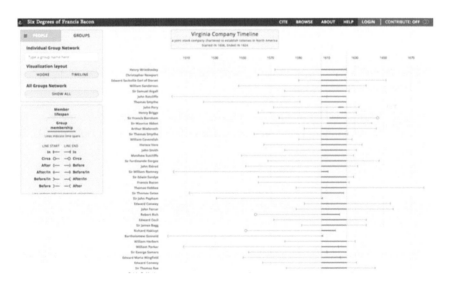

Figure 7. Timeline visualization of a specific group: the Virginia Company.

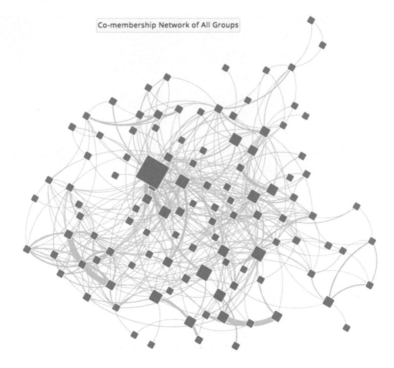

**Figure 8. Network visualization showing the co-membership network of all groups (node labels not shown).**

Finally, as I mentioned above, we made it possible to view all groups at once, for a bird's-eye view of early modern society (Figure 8). In our only node-link diagram in which nodes do not represent people, the square nodes in the All Groups visualization represent each group as a whole, and the size of the node denotes the number of members of each group. The edges, meanwhile, represent the number of members that two groups share. If two groups share at least one member, they are connected by an edge, and the edge is thicker depending on the number of shared members. This graph gives the user a quick overview of how the many different groups of the early modern period, both scholarly and historical, interacted with one another. And because this visualization naturally raises questions about the makeup of individual groups, we've made it easy to move from this meta-visualization to the individual group graphs.

The main goal of *Six Degrees* has always been to help scholars share their knowledge of historical social relationships and to make those relationships easily accessible to researchers. While the exploration features described above may not initially seem related to contribution, we realized that giving scholars a better sense of the ways in which our data was put together gave them greater purchase on how to contribute to the data set. It is much easier to visualize what to add when you can easily see all that is available and where the gaps are. The new exploration features made this possible, and once these features had been decided on we were able to turn our attention to a total overhaul of the site's contribution interface.

## Contribution

*Six Degrees* refers to its contribution system not as crowdsourcing but as *scholarsourcing*. Rather than making everything on the site fully changeable by the public, as it would be on a wiki, *Six Degrees* requires that every submission be reviewed by an expert curator. This prevents any one user from altering the network far outside of scholarly consensus, and ensures that the site remains a reliable resource. It also means that the system for contribution has two tiers: *direct contribution*, in which a user can add a person or group, or add/update a relationship, and *curation*, in which approved curators can review submissions and fine-tune changes to the data. In order for *Six Degrees* to work properly as a living data set, both systems have to work smoothly.

One potential bottleneck occurs when user submissions stack up in a curation dashboard for long periods of time without getting approved, and this can happen when there are too few curators. Even before the latest redesign we had been working on this issue. CMU undergraduates in Information Systems, working with Jessica Otis, developed a system by which users with more than 100 approved contributions would become curators on the site. A small meter on the user's profile lets them know how close they are to the threshold. This process not only makes sure there are enough trusted curators to manage the load of submissions—since, as more submissions come in, more people can be made curators—it encourages our already most enthusiastic users to make it to the next level. For the redesign, we gave a new face to this system, but under the hood it works the same as it always has, allowing every submission to be reviewed by an expert.

While many good principles for contribution were already in place before the redesign, we still had big plans for improvement. Chiefly, we wanted to streamline the primary mechanics of contribution and make them more engaging for the user. When an early modernist lands on a *Six Degrees* network page, they are likely to see a network that in some way doesn't comport with their knowledge of the period. This is by design. As mentioned above, the initial inferred *Six Degrees* data set was meant to be a starting point for inquiry and an enticement to contribution of scholarly knowledge. Perhaps someone is missing from the graph that the scholar knows should be there, or perhaps a relationship the scholar is sure existed has only a 30 per cent confidence level. When that moment arises, users instinctively want to correct their view of the network so that it matches their knowledge of history. In the beta interface, if you wanted to contribute to the data, you had to leave the visualization and fill out a web form on a separate page. The new person or relationship would not show up in the visualization until after the change was approved by a curator, which could sometimes take a day or two. This arrangement was less than ideal for scholars whose intention was, in some sense, to correct the visualization they were viewing.

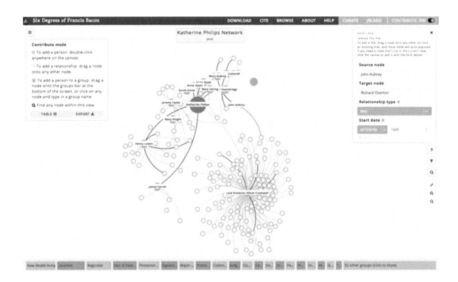

**Figure 9. Katherine Philips's network viewed in Contribute Mode.**

At the top of our priority list for the redesign was a contribution interface that allowed users to work directly with the visualization. Now you can enter a new Contribute Mode by clicking a switch at the top of the page. When in this new user mode, a simple double-click on the canvas creates a new node on the page, with a more compact form that allows the user to enter all the necessary information. To add a new relationship or edit an existing one, the user can simply drag one node onto another. In this way, as the user works, the visualization itself changes to look like the network that the scholar had in mind.[8]

---

[8] Group additions work similarly. To add a person to a group, drag a node to the

This also changes the flow of contributions from a single contribution at a time, through a form, to a series of related contributions—maybe even a whole mini-network about which the scholar has important information to add. Once the user is finished with a set of contributions, they can all be submitted for curation. Although submitting the changes resets the graph to the original state (until the changes are approved and they become a permanent addition to the network), the scholar has had a chance to see how the network will look once the contributed changes are in place.

Rather than asking our users to use two different ways of thinking for exploration of and contribution to the *Six Degrees* data, contribution through the network visualization itself lets data use and data curation blend into one. It becomes much clearer to users what effect their changes will have on the final product, and it encourages them to share knowledge in a way that matches their experience of the information they are currently viewing. Contribution through visualization emphasizes the collaboration that takes place on the site: scholars not only add information that becomes visualized, they are responsible, through their work, for expanding the visualized network itself.

Although we aimed to make the contribution process as easy for scholars as possible, the information that is being shared is far from simple. The process of adding a person is fairly straightforward (simply enter a name, date range, and some additional information), but adding or updating a relationship is a more complex intellectual task. The goal of *Six Degrees* is to contain as many social relationships as possible, but what is a relationship as defined on *Six Degrees*? Again, this is something that the project has grappled with since its inception, and as the first data was being collected, the *Six Degrees* team was determining how relationships could be categorized.

Eventually we landed on a list of relationship types. Since all relationships on *Six Degrees* are undirected or reciprocal (for an explanation of this and other network concepts, see Ladd et al. 2017), relationship types typically work in pairs: Parent of/Child of, Patron of/Client of, etc. These relationship types also fit into categories, which include Affective, Educational/Intellectual, Kinship, Labour/Professional, Legal/Commercial, Political, Religious, and Spatial.[9]

---

groups bar. To add a new group, double-click on the All Groups visualization to create a new square node.

[9] Because these categories often overlap, some relationship types belong to more than one category.

Many contributions to *Six Degrees* are updates to relationships that take an initial, statistically inferred edge and add information to it. This usually includes a new confidence rating, changes to the date range, and an assigned relationship type. All statistically inferred edges default to the "Has met" relationship type, but users have already made great strides in adding texture to the data by filling out the nature of many of those relationships. For example, the network of Sidney-family noblewoman and patron Katherine Hastings now includes "sibling of," "patron of," "correspondent of," and more relationship types that better describe the many complex social networks to which Hastings belonged.[10] We made sure these relationship types were easy to add in the redesign (Figure 10). When in Contribute Mode, the user can simply click on an existing edge to add a relationship type (the same form comes up when they add a new edge). They can then select their relationship type from the available options. We include the relationship categories along with the types in the menu, so the user can see all levels of categorization at the contribution stage.

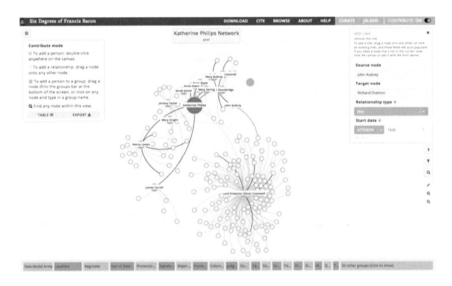

**Figure 10. Adding a relationship type in Contribute Mode.**

---

[10] These relationship types, and a decent portion of the relationships themselves, were added by Catherine Medici at a recent *Six Degrees* add-a-thon (an event at which users are invited to upload new contributions to the site), part of the *Early Modern Digital Agendas* seminar on Network Analysis at the Folger Shakespeare Library.

The relationship ontology for *Six Degrees* has been talked about at greater length in other venues (see Langmead et al. 2016, for example), but it remains a crucial part of the site's data infrastructure. We have aimed to build a shared resource that shows not only whether certain relationships existed but also, as much as possible, the nature of those relationships.

The final major change to contribution did require an interface separate from the network visualization. At *Six Degrees* we're grateful to be part of a growing community of early modern network scholars. Since the project started, we have had the opportunity to collaborate with many people in the field who are building their own network data sets, especially at two "add-a-thon" events we've hosted at Carnegie Mellon and the Folger Shakespeare Library. There are already many scholars who have well-curated early modern network data sets of their own;[11] as evidenced by the enthusiasm for *Six Degrees* at these events, and the excitement around network analysis as the theme for the recent *Early Modern Digital Agendas* seminar in summer 2017 (Ahnert 2017), there are likely to be many more of these data sets in the near future.

Lots of time and work goes into curating these smaller network data sets, often to advance a particular argument for a presentation or publication. Once those initial goals have been reached, *Six Degrees* wants to make sure that this data is easily discoverable by other scholars. To that end, we developed an interface for easily uploading an entire network data set at once, as a CSV file. This involved a detailed form system, so that at every step along the way of the contribution process, users have full control over the data they are uploading and can provide all the information necessary for it to be a part of *Six Degrees*. And where the Contribute Mode is designed best for one to twenty contributions at a time, the Upload interface can handle hundreds of contributions at once without requiring a lot of extra drudgery from the user.

This interface in particular raises the question of scholarly credit, one we've done a lot of thinking about during the beta period and in the redesign. We believe *Six Degrees* can be a responsible home for data sets that are "finished" and might otherwise have difficulty reaching interested scholars, but we want to make sure that our users always know the provenance of a particular piece of information. That's true of a scholar who has only contributed

---

[11] Notable examples include Ruth and Sebastian Ahnert's Protestant letter network (Ahnert and Ahnert 2015), much of which has been incorporated into *Six Degrees*, and Claude Willan's network of John Locke's correspondence (Willan 2011–16).

a single person to the data set and of a digital humanities professional who has uploaded a data set with hundreds of people and relationships (Figure 11). The site respects user privacy and doesn't display a full user profile to all other users, but for each data point on the site, the username of the contributor is displayed along with any outside citation that was added when the data was entered. *Six Degrees* recognizes contributions on the site as scholarly work that deserves credit, and we want the site to serve as a record of how the data set came to be in the shape that it is now.

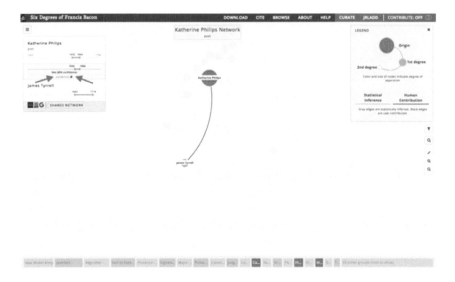

**Figure 11. The relationship between James Tyrrell and Katherine Philips, crediting the scholar who added the relationship.**

*Data Sharing*

While we have invested a lot in the particulars of this new site and its presentation of data, it is important to acknowledge that even the sturdiest web platforms have a short shelf life due to the fast-moving progress of web technologies. One way we have combatted this is by moving our site from a proprietary web hosting service to servers at Carnegie Mellon University Libraries, which has committed to preserving the site for the foreseeable future. We have also worked, however, to make it as easy to get data out of the site as it is to bring data in through contribution, and we have partnerships with outside data preservation groups to make sure that the *Six Degrees* data far outlasts even this brand-new site.

On the original site, you could download the *Six Degrees* data in large batch-es—a single file that includes data on all the people in *Six Degrees* as well as a series of files that include all the relationship data. Many of our users have remarked on the usefulness of *Six Degrees* as a name authority file, in addi-tion to its network features, and we wanted to make sure we preserved that usefulness on the new site. You can still download all the people of *Six Degrees* in one comma-separated value file, and the file updates weekly to include the newest people that have been added to the database. We also streamlined the relationship data so that it is also available in a single file, making it much easier to download, share, and process data. Tools like Gephi and NetworkX make it simpler than ever for scholars to process large amounts of network data, and by making the full data available for download, interested schol-ars can calculate network metrics and visualize the *Six Degrees* data in ways specific to their own projects. To facilitate this, we published a *Programming Historian* tutorial last year that walks readers step-by-step through using NetworkX, a Python library, to calculate network metrics (with a sample data set from *Six Degrees*).

Since we provide so many different views of the data on the new site, we also took data exports a step forward. On every page, an export button al-lows users to download the exact data set used to generate that view. This means there are now hundreds of already-curated data subsets ready for download at the simple click of a button—previously, users would have to download the full data set and make a subset themselves. This feature is par-ticularly powerful with the group network views: a user can download just the group of Quakers or judges with one click. This data is downloadable in the JSON format that generates the page view (rather than as a CSV), but we are also working on a tool that will easily convert these files to make them more readable. While having the full data set available is necessary for many larger projects, we hope that the ability to recreate these smaller data sets will facilitate smaller projects as well.

Data exports go hand in hand with data preservation, and *Six Degrees* works to make its data widely but also continuously available regardless of the site's longevity. The best way to do this is through partnerships that store and serve *Six Degrees* data outside of the *Six Degrees* platform. Over the lifetime of the project, there has long been interest in making *Six Degrees* informa-tion available as linked open data (LOD). Network data is especially suited for this because LOD treats all information as a series of linked relationships, and its open nature would allow our data set to talk to many other overlap-ping data sets (such as the *ODNB* data itself) that include additional helpful information. Thanks to the work of Andrew Gray, the *Six Degrees* data set of people is now available as part of Wikidata, the publicly available online knowledge base.[12] What this means is that it is now possible to search for other kinds of information, such as country of origin or other geographic data, alongside the information already stored in *Six Degrees*. Wikidata and LOD are exciting because they preserve data but also add extra functionality that would be cumbersome to incorporate into the *Six Degrees* website itself.

We have, in addition, partnered with the Folger Shakespeare Library to make *Six Degrees* data available as part of their Miranda online platform. This is an ongoing process, but we are excited about the possibilities of having *Six Degrees* data alongside information about the Folger's impressive early modern collections and data from other early modern digital humanities projects. The Folger is important as a site of data preservation because it will make the *Six Degrees* data set more easily discoverable by the group of early modern historians, literary scholars, art historians, and musicologists most likely to benefit from easy access to this information.

The last piece in the data preservation puzzle at *Six Degrees* has to do with properly recording and storing our methods, as well as all the data we have collected. To this end all the code used to create *Six Degrees* is open source and available in two GitHub repositories. The first, called "sdfb_network," includes all the code for the original named-entity recognition and statistical inference process we used to create the core data set. This code was recently streamlined and reorganized by *Six Degrees* collaborator David Walling as part of our year-long updates to the project. If a scholar had a new set of documents and wanted to create a similar network using the same methods, that could be done from start to finish using the code in this repository.

The second repository contains all the code for the *Six Degrees* website, and is named simply "sdfb." This includes both the code for the front-end visualizations of the site and the back-end application programming interface (API). The repository has everything a scholar would need to recreate the *Six Degrees* site for a new data set, and we have had several scholars express interest in using our code to create versions of *Six Degrees* for different time periods or geographic areas. The code for the redesigned site has also been modularized as much as possible, so that someone interested in a part of our project can reuse code without having to remake the parts of the project they don't need. For example, much of the visualization code is available in

---

[12] Wikidata is a part of the Wikimedia Foundation, so it is related to—but not the same as—Wikipedia.

separate files, so that others could adapt our network visualizations into different applications.

By keeping the data and code for the project open, *Six Degrees* hopes to be a starting point for scholars interested in network analysis and visualization. And by making the full project available in these various ways, scholars can build on the work we have done while familiarizing themselves with the rewards and challenges of working with network data at scale.

## The Power of Networks and Networks of Power

Throughout the redesign process we were motivated by the desire not only to make the site easier to use, but to help scholars see how early modern figures fashioned themselves through their relationships with others. Although the social networks of today might look different from those of the past, we would still recognize the early modern ways of negotiating one's own position within a network—reaching out to new people through mutual acquaintances, passing messages across long distances, forging new relationships as one's influence grows. Recent scholarship provides many examples of early modern people navigating their personal and professional networks in these ways. Ruth and Sebastian Ahnert (2015) have written about martyrs' importance within Protestant letter networks, and Evan Bourke (2017) has shown the centrality of Katherine Jones within the Hartlib Circle.[13] The people of early modern England seemed to understand implicitly how to operate within their social networks, and without the language we use to describe those networks today.

Twentieth- and twenty-first-century sociology and critical theory has provided us with an array of terms to describe social networks unavailable to early modern thinkers. Although their theories are opposed, both Pierre Bourdieu (1993) and Bruno Latour (2005) describe interlocking systems of social interaction, whether as "fields" or as "actor-networks." Latour, through actor-network theory (ANT), may have done the most to popularize the term "network" in early twenty-first-century intellectual discourse. The more diffuse, rhizomatic actor-networks, however, do not share so much in common with the structured maps of human interaction that make up contemporary social network analysis. A more precise theoretical approach to the quantitative methods that make up network analysis might be Randall Collins's

---

[13] Samuel Hartlib was an early modern intellectual who maintained a large network of contacts and correspondents. For more on his network and Philips's role in it, see Bourke 2017.

*The Sociology of Philosophies* (1998), which traces the history of philosophical thought as a series of networked negotiations of knowledge creation. Collins's approach, alongside key works of network analysis such as Granovetter's "The Strength of Weak Ties" (1973), have built up a vocabulary for social networks in literature and history.

It is tempting to add that one of the reasons we know more about networks today is due to the many technological social networks we actively participate in each day. But Facebook, Twitter, and other "social networking" platforms often conceal networks themselves in favor of feeds and streams that rely on an invisible social network to which the user is never privy. As we have learned in a series of increasingly unsettling revelations,[14] it is often advertisers and the state that benefit from this hidden data, handed over without our knowledge by the companies who claim to value our interactions and our privacy. A Facebook user who visits the site every day to keep up with friends and family will never see a visualization of the full network, and will likely never understand the power Facebook maintains by withholding that bird's-eye view of the network. Social media users are network actors, but are seldom prompted to think critically about the networks in which they are acting.

An excellent illustration of this phenomenon is in Facebook's known use of "shadow profiles." Facebook has so much information about its users and their habits within its network that it is able to infer the existence of a particular person who is not a member of Facebook at all. This practice uses Facebook data—as well as data from other sources to which Facebook has access—to imagine persons outside of Facebook who must exist based on the social patterns of the Facebook users who know them (Hautala 2018). Even those who explicitly opt out of participating in Facebook's platform are identified and catalogued within its network. It can be hard to imagine how Facebook does this unless you can picture the vast web of interaction that Facebook can view at its whim, and how easy it can be to fill in the gaps when someone in that web is missing.

The gap of knowledge between those who run social networking sites and those who participate in them represents a larger power differential between everyday social interactions and those who clandestinely collect and hoard information about those interactions. The most recent example concerns the many shortcomings of sites such as Facebook and Twitter—the sale

---

[14] Revelations that, again, began with Rosenberg, Confessore, and Cadwalladr's *New York Times* piece (2018), and have since become an ever-growing scandal for Facebook.

or leaking of sensitive data to advertisers and governments, the failure to adequately address harassment on their platforms, and knowing inaction in the face of calculated trolling and influence campaigns. But the clandestine collection of personal and relationship data has long been the practice of the modern surveillance state, which collects and keeps hidden information on the interactions of its citizens. In his recent book *F.B. Eyes* (2015), William J. Maxwell records how the FBI kept secret files on African-American authors of the early twentieth century and even engaged in a kind of criticism of those authors' work; this is just one of many examples of the state spying on its own citizens and then using that knowledge as a tool of oppression. There are plenty more recent examples of this phenomenon; incidents in which massive amounts of data from the National Security Agency (NSA) and other parts of the U.S. intelligence community have been made public has shown that secretly recording and storing social information has become accepted national policy (at least until the public finds out). Although it is true to say that we know more about networks today and how they work, that knowledge is often leveraged against us by powerful governmental or private interests.

While it was once thought that mere participation in broader social networks, usually online, would lead to a more open society and better living, recent political events and the behaviour of large media organizations has shown that to be somewhat wishful thinking. As social networks become a more well-known way of understanding social interaction, however, better knowledge of those networks could help people to navigate them more skillfully and to resist those who would use network data against them. This is where the *Six Degrees* redesign fits into these larger issues. By making the often hidden machinery of networks directly visible, users are invited to be full participants in a dialogue about the historical networks visualized and the scholarly networks that create them. Rather than presenting our users with a list or feed or prose description of facts about social interaction, *Six Degrees* visualizes the structure of those interactions. We extend this principle in the redesign by allowing users to fill in the gaps in our network with their own scholarly knowledge, and because the entire network is visualized for them, users do so with much greater knowledge about what such contributions will do to the web of knowledge as it currently exists.

The phrase "knowledge is power" has become cliché, a way of expressing confidence in the positive effects of spreading information without examining the power imbalances that are created when knowledge is withheld, misused, or otherwise disingenuously deployed. The danger is the same with social networks—that society takes for granted the ways in which the study of and technology for networks can be used to facilitate greater communication and connection among people while ignoring the ways in which the powerful can leverage networks to increase their own power. A first step toward remedying this is to make it easier for people to understand their own networks. Techniques such as those employed in the *Six Degrees* redesign can make visible many hidden features of social networks: visual flexibility, representations of uncertainty, and ontologies of relationship types, to name a few. One of the contributions to early modern studies made by *Six Degrees* is to make the web of historical social interactions visible in a way that is consistent with up-to-date sociological, historiographic, and critical theory. And a well-designed *Six Degrees* is a knowledge interface that crowdsources scholarship as it provides a guide to understanding the social systems of the past and present.

## WORKS CITED

Ahnert, Ruth. 2017. "Report from the Field: Network Analysis." *The Collation,* October 10. https://collation.folger.edu/2017/10/report-network-analysis/.

Ahnert, Ruth, and Sebastian E. Ahnert. 2015. "Protestant Letter Networks in the Reign of Mary I: A Quantitative Approach." *ELH* 82(1): 1–33.

Barabási, Albert-László. 2002. *Linked: The New Science of Networks.* Cambridge, MA: Perseus Publishing.

Bourdieu, Pierre. 1993. *The Field of Cultural Production: Essays on Art and Literature.* New York: Columbia University Press.

Bourke, Evan. 2017. "Female Involvement, Membership, and Centrality: A Social Network Analysis of the Hartlib Circle." *Literature Compass* 14(4). doi:10.1111/lic3.12388.

Collins, Randall. 1998. *The Sociology of Philosophies: A Global Theory of Intellectual Change.* Cambridge, MA, and London: Belknap Press of Harvard University Press.

García, José María Rodríguez. 2001. "Scientia Potestas Est — Knowledge is Power: Francis Bacon to Michel Foucault." *Anglia: Journal of English Philology* 119(1): 1–19. doi:10.1515/ANGL.2001.1.

Granovetter, Mark S. 1973. "The Strength of Weak Ties." *American Journal of Sociology* 78(6): 1360–80.

Grewal, David Singh. 2008. *Network Power: The Social Dynamics of Globalization.* New Haven, CT: Yale University Press.

Hautala, Laura. 2018. "Shadow Profiles: Facebook Has Information You Didn't Hand Over." *CNET*, April 11. https://www.cnet.com/news/shadow-profiles-facebook-has-information-you-didnt-hand-over/.

Ladd, John. 2017. "'Ut Tensio Sic Vis': Introducing the Hooke Graph." *Six Degrees of Francis Bacon*, April 10. http://6dfb.tumblr.com/post/159420498411/ut-tensio-sic-vis-introducing-the-hooke-graph.

———— et al. 2017. "Exploring and Analyzing Network Data with Python." *The Programming Historian*, August 23. https://programminghistorian.org/en/lessons/exploring-and-analyzing-network-data-with-python.

Langmead, Alison, et al. 2016. "Towards Interoperable Network Ontologies for the Digital Humanities." *International Journal of Humanities and Arts Computing* 10(1): 22–35. https://www.euppublishing.com/doi/abs/10.3366/ijhac.2016.0157.

Latour, Bruno. 2005. *Reassembling the Social: An Introduction to Actor-Network-Theory.* Oxford and New York: Oxford University Press.

Maxwell, William J. 2015. *F.B. Eyes: How J. Edgar Hoover's Ghostreaders Framed African American Literature.* Princeton, NJ: Princeton University Press.

Rosenberg, Matthew, Nicholas Confessore, and Carole Cadwalladr. 2018. "How Trump Consultants Exploited the Facebook Data of Millions." *New York Times*, March 17. https://www.nytimes.com/2018/03/17/us/politics/cambridge-analytica-trump-campaign.html.

Warren, Christopher N., et al. 2016. "Six Degrees of Francis Bacon: A Statistical Method for Reconstructing Large Historical Social Networks." *Digital Humanities Quarterly* 10(3). https://hcommons.org/deposits/item/mla:989.

Willan, Claude. 2011–16. "Visualizations of Locke's Correspondence Network."
    Stanford Digital Repository. https://purl.stanford.edu/gx970nw8882.

# Shaping New Models of Interaction in Open Access Repositories with Social Media

Luis Meneses, Alyssa Arbuckle, Hector Lopez, Belaid Moa, Richard Furuta, and Ray Siemens

*Introduction*

The methods for representing documents and disseminating knowledge are changing—more so if we consider that the definition of a paper as an academic publication is becoming inadequate for the dissemination of research. Leggett and Shipman (2004) present their arguments for the necessity of an interactive scholarly communication research agenda by briefly reviewing the rapid development of alternative authoring and publishing models. On the other hand, social media has gained added relevance, given its potential to transform the scholarly communication system (Sugimoto et al. 2016). In general, social media has not been considered as integral to the composition and workflow of digital collections.

We have been addressing this situation by developing a framework that introduces social media into the context of an open access (OA) repository. We have named this framework the Social Media Engine. This framework aims to instigate public engagement and social knowledge creation (Arbuckle, Mauro, and Powell 2017)—by matching readers with OA academic publications that are mentioned in social media streams—and relies on the gathering and analysis of harvested, indexed, and rendered corpora.

The fundamental concepts behind our framework and its Social Media Engine can be explained using three points, which are illustrated in Figure 1. First, our framework yields a list of topics related to individual entries and articles in the corpus by applying textual analysis techniques, such as term frequency–inverse document frequency (Tf-Idf) (Baeza-Yates and Ribeiro-Neto 1999), and topic modelling (Blei, Ng, and Jordan 2003). Second, our engine connects readers and publications by monitoring social media for trending topics and returning links to OA publications that can be used to feed and enrich the discussion. Finally, our engine identifies trending papers on social media by looking at the number of times papers on social science topics are shared, saved, liked, or commented on. Figure 2 shows a user scenario that outlines the processes and workflow of the Social Media Engine.

ISBN 978-1-64959-008-4 (paper) ISBN 978-1-64959-009-1 (pdf) ISBN 978-1-64959-084-8 (epub)
*New Technologies in Medieval and Renaissance Studies 8 (2022) 195–217*

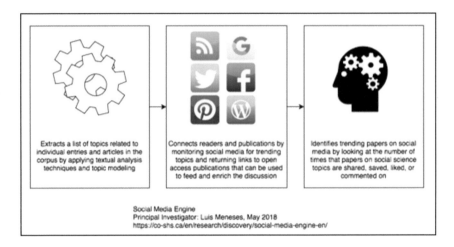

**Figure 1. Fundamental concepts behind the Social Media Engine.**

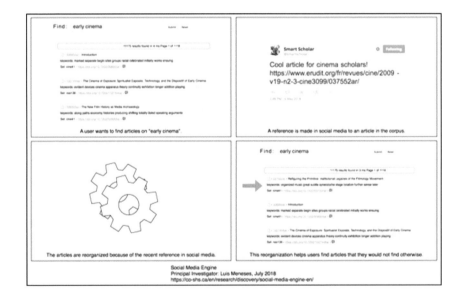

**Figure 2. User scenario outlining the processes and workflow of the Social Media Engine.**

In our previous presentations we addressed the implications that our framework introduces in terms of user engagement, changing some of the preconceived notions in digital libraries by making repositories more dynamic and consequently switching the patterns of interaction in OA repositories

(Meneses, Arbuckle, Moa, et al. 2017; Meneses et al. 2017; Meneses et al. 2018). In this paper, we expand on how social media has shaped new models of interaction, which we base on the increased accessibility of OA repositories. More specifically, we focus on how social media and online conversations can bridge the gap between a user's intention and a search interface, allowing the users of OA repositories to access documents that they would otherwise have difficulty finding. Finally, we discuss this increased accessibility and its implications within the context of the humanities.

## Context: Open Social Scholarship

An important, contextual component of our work is the INKE Partnership for Networked Open Social Scholarship (Siemens et al. 2011, 2009). Our partnership brings together researchers and stakeholders at the forefront of computing in the humanities, text analysis, information studies, usability, and interface design to advance understanding of and resolve crucial issues in the production, distribution, and widespread engagement of digital scholarship in Canada. We explore ways to implement the progressive Canadian OA and open source policies in ways that make sense for research professionals and society at large, working together toward the successful realization of robust, inclusive, participatory, and publicly engaged digital scholarship, which we call "networked open social scholarship." This exploration is undertaken by cultivating dialogue and developing speculative and innovative models and prototypes for online, multimodal knowledge environments in order to challenge, interpret, extend, and reflect on contemporary reading, writing, and research practices.

Networked open social scholarship involves creating and disseminating research and research technologies to a broad audience of specialists and active non-specialists in ways that are accessible and significant. As a concept, open social scholarship has grown from roots in OA—affording greater accessibility to the results of research (Suber 2012; Willinsky 2006)—as well as open scholarship movements, contemporary online practices, and public-facing "citizen scholarship." Networked open social scholarship includes: (i) developing, sharing, and implementing research in ways that consider the needs and interests of both academic specialists and communities beyond academia; (ii) providing opportunities to co-create, interact with, and experience openly available cultural data; (iii) exploring, developing, and making public tools and technologies under open licences to promote wide access, education, use, and repurpose; and (iv) enabling productive dialogue between academics and non-academics.

Following these central values, the overall goal of the INKE Partnership is to understand, embody, model, and facilitate engaged, participatory digital scholarship and knowledge in Canada. We bring together digital humanities researchers and leading national organizations on a shared, active foundation of scholarly communication, OA, digital publishing, data management, knowledge mobilization, social knowledge creation, and community engagement. Our interrelated objectives are to: (i) strengthen and solidify open scholarly communication, interaction, engagement, and training among researchers, organizations, institutions, and the public; (ii) discover and share how to effectively create and mobilize knowledge within and between research, administrative, policy, and other communities; (iii) collaborate to adapt, develop, and disseminate digitally oriented, innovative, and inclusive open networked scholarship and technologies; and (iv) engage a diverse public via accessible, interactive methods and through alternative modes of communication.

Overall, we aim to provide answers to research questions such as:

- How do we model networked open social scholarship practices and behaviour?
- How can we avoid the consequences of inaccessible research data?
- What development approaches to workflows, technologies, publications, protocols, policies, and initiatives best foster and encourage openness?
- How do we promote, study, and archive engagement with cultural data?
- How can we leverage existing resources within libraries and cultural institutions across Canada to provide regular opportunities for mentorship and training in networked open social scholarship?

In the following section of this paper we will describe the related work relevant to our framework that sets the stage toward the decomposition and analysis of the first research question, which deals with modelling networked open social scholarship practices and behaviours.

*Related Work*

Collaborative projects are starting to become strong alternatives toward making research accessible to a larger audience by focusing on the quality of article content (Kittur and Kraut 2008) and the project's viability as a venue for academic publishing (Xiao and Askin 2012). Along the same lines, crowdsourced projects lack the paywalls that can restrict access to content, fostering collaborative interactions while allowing users to search for information online (Bozzon, Brambilla, and Ceri 2012; Brambilla et al. 2017). Collaborative projects share some similarities with open access publishing platforms, serving as a space for knowledge dissemination (Pfister 2011). Additionally, these approaches toward data sharing, collaborative web tools, and social media have made an impact on the sustainability of data (Jeffrey 2012). The possibilities that crowdsourced projects and collaborative tools introduce toward research access, dissemination, sustainability, and public engagement make them important in our review.

Social media tools offer researchers a different approach to their workflow, and introduce platforms for showcasing their research to a greater audience. In this sense, social media has applications throughout the research life cycle (Nicholas and Rowlands 2011), influencing the use of traditional scholarly information sources (Tenopir, Volentine, and King 2013) and the knowledge creation process (Majchrzak et al. 2013) while attracting the attention of a greater audience (Schrier 2011). Not only do social media tools help bridge the communication gaps between scholars, but they can help make connections between ideas by providing interaction methods that highlight the work from other scholars and allow users to find results (Evans, Kairam, and Pirolli 2010). Keeping all of this in mind, social media tools such as Twitter and Facebook are becoming highly integrated into the research and knowledge creation processes.

Search user interfaces can provide a front-end mechanism that allows users to retrieve documents from a repository. Considering that a user's information needs change during the process of formulating and carrying out a series of queries, accessible and intuitive user interfaces are needed to allow users timely and adequate access to information. Previous work on general practices for interface design are a result of extensive experimentation and testing (Hearst 2009), whereas user behaviour can be driven by a user's background (Alharbi, Smith, and Mayhew 2013). Furthermore, a user's behaviour can suggest different ways in which interfaces can be redesigned to make searching for information more effective (Rose 2006). These two factors contribute toward our analysis of models of interaction.

To summarize, the survey of previous work on crowdsourced and collaborative tools, social media, and search user interfaces that we have outlined in this section highlights the potential for new models of interaction that would facilitate research access, dissemination, and public engagement. As we previously mentioned, social media tools are becoming highly integrated into the research and knowledge creation processes. In our opinion, this integration contributes toward the need for investigating alternative models of interaction with repositories. In the following section we will describe the background for our work, the initial assumptions we used, and the steps we took in our initial analysis.

*Background and Initial Analysis*

We started our analysis by developing an understanding of our document collection. Érudit (https://www.erudit.org/) is a digital repository of social sciences and humanities publications (Érudit Consortium 2019). This collection consists mostly of scholarly and cultural journals (100 and 30 respectively), theses, books, proceedings, and technical reports. The documents are diverse in content and span 35 disciplines, including the arts, engineering, education, cinema, demography, law, theology, history, sociology, and women's studies, among others. As of February 2017, the collection consisted of 174,269 documents divided into 169 sets.

We proceeded to download the complete set of descriptive metadata through Érudit's Open Archives Initiative Protocol for Metadata Harvesting (OAI-PMH) API. The OAI-PMH interface presents the documents as PDFs, which can be quite problematic to parse. Alternatively, a full text working set of the source materials was provided to us from Érudit's development platform. Since these documents were in XML format, we created a parser using Python's Beautiful Soup library (Richardson 2015) to pull the text from the markup elements. Using this parser, we found that 57 documents did not have full text associated with them, making their impact negligible when compared to the collection as a whole.

The majority of the articles in the repository are in French, and efforts to procure more articles in English by the Érudit Consortium are currently underway. To get a better sense of the document distribution, we ran a language detection process based on Google's language detection algorithms (Danilak 2017) on the full-text articles. We found that 91 per cent of the documents were in French, 8.6 per cent in English, and the remaining 0.4 per cent in other languages. This analysis of the corpus is important, as it allows us to grasp an overall understanding of the collection and set a foundation toward implementing solutions that can deal with diverse documents in multiple languages. Our future plans include analyzing and ingesting other document collections, namely the Public Knowledge Project (PKP) (Owen and Stranack 2012).

After downloading and parsing, we proceeded to further our initial understanding of the corpus from Érudit. More specifically, we were interested in how the descriptive metadata correlated and aligned with the full text contained in the documents. Upon analyzing the corpus, we found that 19 per cent of the documents had metadata descriptions and full text that were in the same language (i.e., both metadata description and document text in French). We then attempted to quantify the correlation for each description and its corresponding full text using three techniques: topic modelling with Latent Dirichlet allocation (LDA), Tf-Idf, and resemblance with Jaccard coefficient (Broder 1997). Out of the three, topic modelling and Tf-Idf had the best performance, clustering the full text with the description in most of the cases. This was a result we expected, as the terms in Tf-Idf are not indirectly inferred and come from the text in the document corpus. We will explore the implications of using these similarity measures in the discussion section of this paper.

## System Architecture

Our framework consists of three main components, which are hosted under Compute Canada's WestGrid server infrastructure (WestGrid 2019): (i) a keyword extraction module; (ii) a social media mining component, and (iii) a search engine. These components and their corresponding interactions are illustrated in Figure 3, and will be described in more detail in the following sections of this paper.

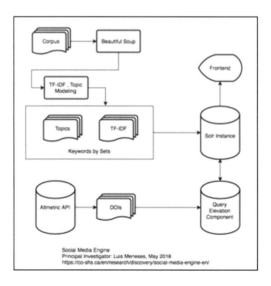

**Figure 3. System diagram for the Social Media Engine.**

## Keyword Extraction: Search Engine Alignment

After our initial analysis and definition of the system architecture, we started to include topic modelling in our analysis. We performed topic modelling using the implementation of LDA available in Gensim (Řehůřek 2019) by dividing the corpus into its different OAI-PMH sets and checking if the results of the analysis aligned with our overall understanding of the corpus. As a part of this stage of the study, we worked on retrieving documents from the corpus using the terms that were unique for each topic. For testing purposes, we proceeded to increase the granularity of the sample, and used documents from an OAI-PMH set labeled "rabaska96"; this set contained 792 documents exclusively in French. We modelled these documents into 15 topics and extracted the terms that were unique for each topic. Given that this was part of our preliminary analysis, we are not including a list of topics or keywords, but we do focus on our results in the evaluation and discussion sections of this paper.

We used Whoosh (Chaput 2016), an open source search engine built with Python (Rossum 1995), to test if the documents from each topic could be retrieved using their identifying features, which in this case corresponded to their unique terms. We found that the documents in the set were being matched using only the unique terms gathered from the topic modelling. Furthermore, these findings support our hypothesis that unique terms extracted from each topic can be used to boost certain facets of the query. Consequently, we hypothesized at this point that these unique terms would facilitate the re-ranking of the results.

## Modelling the Corpus

During this phase, we also started experimenting with parallel computing solutions based on Apache Spark (Apache Software Foundation 2018) and its implementation of LDA clustering. Our previous approaches used Python, which is a single threaded programming language. There are several solutions to this problem, but Spark is likely the best. In this sense, Compute Canada's WestGrid server infrastructure was well suited for a Spark Cluster. The use of parallelization brought two advantages: a substantial increase in speed and a more robust codebase—by-products of the optimization to afford parallelism.

The documents were ingested into a Spark Dataframe and preprocessed with five steps before undergoing the modelling stage. First, the text in each document was tokenized and lower-cased. Second, tokens that contained non-alphanumeric characters were removed. Third, tokens that had less than four characters were removed as well. Fourth, we removed proper names from the corpus. To achieve this, we downloaded Comma-Separated Values (CSV) files containing first names (both male and female) and last names from the 1990 U.S. Census site (US Census Bureau 2014). The files were then parsed and transformed into a reusable Python list with 91,910 entries. Finally, we created a list of stop words that consisted of one-third of the most common terms, which was appended to the proper names from step 4. This preprocessing, along with multiple iterations per model, allowed us to obtain appropriate terms that referenced the topics as results.

Taking advantage of the speed increase through parallelization, we were able to model the entire corpus, which we separated into sets to ensure the scalability of our approach. We modelled the 174,212 documents into 169 sets, and further clustered the documents into 20 topics per set with 100 iterations per model. For the most part, we were able to identify terms that could be linked specifically to each individual OAI-PMH set. The results from modelling the documents gave us a set of terms that could be used to cluster each set and a probability distribution for each document, which we saved as XML files for convenience. As described in the evaluation section of this paper, we used these terms and probability distribution to perform a simple evaluation.

*Mining Social Media*

Connecting readers with publications and monitoring social media to identify trending topics are fundamental aspects of our framework. However, these two points are complex research problems on their own. To streamline this complicated process and provide our framework with a greater level of abstraction, we decided to use Altmetric.com (Altmetric LLP 2017) for our social media mining. Altmetric.com is a web service that monitors several social media streams (including wikis, scholarly blogs, Twitter, and Facebook), thereby helping scholars get a better overview of their scholarly content. More importantly, Altmetric's API provides some level of granularity in searching, including by date and DOI range. Finally, we used Pyaltmetric (Earp 2017) to query Altmetric's API by using and creating sets of XML files that could be parsed by the search engine component of our prototype.

It is worthwhile to note the implications of using an external web service. The level of abstraction we achieved can be seen as an advantage. On the other hand, we have no control over how Altmetric harvests and processes social media content and produces its results. We will expand on these points in the discussion section of this paper.

*Search Engine Component*

We used Apache Solr (Apache Software Foundation 2019b) as the search engine for our framework; Solr is a robust open source enterprise search platform based on Apache Lucene (Apache Software Foundation 2019a). Ingesting the document corpus into Solr is done through XML files and by defining a schema, which defines the fields and metadata that will be used for searching. Given the robustness of Solr, ingesting Érudit's corpus into a core was not a difficult process: we had to specify an adequate configuration and find a directory location to store the document index. More importantly, Solr's Query Elevation Component allowed us to boost specific search results depending on their mentions in social media: the rankings of the documents were altered and boosted using sets of keywords that matched both social media and the documents in our corpus.

The biggest challenge in using Solr is finding an adequate front end. It is a very common practice to develop a custom front end for searching and browsing a collection, as several programming libraries for interfacing with Solr's API exist. We initially decided to use a customized version of the Velocity Response Writer, a Solr front end based on Apache's Velocity Project (Apache Software Foundation 2016), to provide us with the user interfacing functionality we needed. We have currently moved to a new front end that uses Python and Flask (Ronacher 2019) to query our Solr instance. The main advantage of using this framework and its templating system is that it allows us to implement new features without much overhead. Figure 4 shows a screenshot of the Social Media Engine user interface.

**Figure 4. Screenshot of the Social Media Engine user interface.**

## Automated Evaluation

We used a simple ranking function to evaluate our results. This ranking function was based on adding the Tf-Idf values to the documents, which were calculated using the terms obtained from the topic modelling for each set as a vocabulary. The output from this ranking was calculated for each set, and, as before, the results for the ranking per set were saved in XML files.

In the end, we performed ranking calculations for three sets of terms: the first using the terms from the topic modelling, the second using terms gathered using Tf-Idf, and the third using a combination of topic modelling and Tf-Idf terms. In the third case, duplicated terms were removed to avoid overlap.

Using this simple ranking function, the Tf-Idf terms provided better rankings over the topic modelling terms. This was expected to some extent, given that the terms came from the documents themselves. On the other hand, the terms from the topic modelling also came from the documents, but they conveyed different information regarding the overall "aboutness" of the collection. This "aboutness" is important, especially since we were not aiming for higher values of precision (which were very specific to a formulated query), but higher recall (i.e., better document coverage for a given set of keywords). Figure 5 provides a representation of the average rankings for each OAI-PMH set.

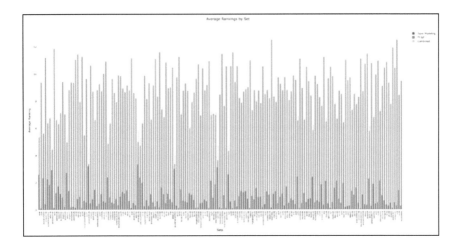

**Figure 5. Average rankings by OAI-PMH Set.**

Ultimately, we believe that a more thorough evaluation is needed to assess our findings. This thoroughness can be obtained by running a user study; however, a user study introduces a new layer of complexity, as elaborated on below.

*User Evaluation*

The type of research that we have outlined in this paper requires a user study to test its validity and applications. We currently have plans for two phases of user studies. Phase 1 consists of a preliminary qualitative study, whereas phase 2 is a more formal and exhaustive quantitative user study that will be administered over the Web.

1. First Phase

The target population for phase 1 comprises researchers, post-doctoral fellows, graduate research assistants, and other individuals who work with open access collections. The participants for phase 1 will be chosen because of their expertise in OA collections. Thus, the participants for phase 1 could potentially include researchers and other individuals associated with the project. This phase of the study is mostly exploratory, and the participants will be interviewed: they will be asked a series of questions regarding their interactions with social media and OA collections. The responses recorded from the participants will provide context for the next phase of our user study.

## 2. Second Phase

The target population for phase 2 is more general, and involves individuals who have used search engines on a daily basis. The participants for phase 2 will not be chosen based on any salient characteristics. The purpose of this phase is to understand the alignment and the connections between social media and the documents in OA collections. As can be inferred from its purpose, the population is ideally composed of individuals who have connections and/or experience with OA document collections, although this background is not entirely necessary to complete our assessment. In this phase, the participants will be asked to complete a set of tasks involving finding information using a specific search engine. A set of questions is provided to the participants to evaluate the search tasks. In a departure from the methods used in the previous phase, the participants will not be interviewed during phase 2; instead, questions will be administered using a web-based adaptive questionnaire.

The two phases of user studies will provide participants with an opportunity to reflect on the ways in which they interact with social media and open access collections, which may be useful to them as they reflect on their use of online technologies. In terms of society, our findings will provide descriptions for best practices to facilitate the development of large open access corpora. Finally, the conclusions obtained from these user studies will also help advance the knowledge base regarding the implications that new interactions with social media can bring within the context of the humanities.

## Implications

First, we argue that integrating social media into the workflow of an open access repository is timely and needed, especially when considering that social media has shaped new models of interaction and knowledge distribution. Rowlands et al. show how social media has found applications within the research life cycle at different stages, from identifying possible research opportunities to disseminating findings (Nicholas and Rowlands 2011). According to this study, the most popular uses for social media tools in an academic setting were to satisfy interactions—perfectly fitting the purposes of our framework.

Second, we acknowledge that social media and online conversations have allowed the users of OA repositories to access documents they would otherwise have difficulty finding. To illustrate this scenario, Wang et al. compared the differences in the impact between OA and non-OA articles (Wang et al. 2015). This study finds that authors who publish OA have a citation advantage, especially when considering how social media helps increase the number of views of OA articles. Wang et al. also found that OA articles held an advantage not only in total downloads, but also in long-term, sustained downloads, compared to their non-OA counterparts. Our work aims to expand on this increased accessibility within the context of the humanities.

Third, the Social Media Engine can be perceived as a collaborative academic search engine. Similarly, Chen et al. have introduced CollabSeer, a search engine for discovering potential collaborators for a given author or researcher (Chen et al. 2011). Their results show that CollabSeer can effectively suggest prospective collaborators by performing an analysis of the network structure. Indeed, the merging of social media interaction with a search engine on an OA corpus lets users add documents back into ongoing discussions. This becomes especially important since it has been proven that social activity can improve the performance of a recommendation system (Konstas, Stathopoulos, and Jose 2009). However, the representation of items and semantics has to be taken into account (Lops, de Gemmis, and Semeraro 2011). Our framework is collaborative, but in a different sense.

Fourth, our framework affords a multidisciplinary crossover through search query results and academic social interaction with scholars from other fields. Taking into account that a user's research interest can remain unchanged for some time depending on the scope of a given study, this crossover can help users find publications that they wouldn't normally consider otherwise. Our framework is designed to highlight ongoing social media trends in the resulting search patterns in research papers, which might bring details about related articles by other scholars—for example, overlaps between social sciences and the humanities, among other fields. Furthermore, our engine is expected to include the functionality of reinserting relevant articles into the discussion, which brings the multidisciplinary interaction to a full circle.

Fifth, our framework can lead to improvements in the delivery of direct and indirect scholarly communications. A study by Letierce et al. (2010) showed that Twitter conference streams provided the context to identify trending topics by combining the amount of tweets posted with the conference hashtags and URLs, along with other hashtags and retweets. This study also focused on understanding the tagging habits of scientists on Twitter, revealing that tagging content leads mainly to messages and collaboration between peer researchers. This last point directly affects the interaction of users of our framework, as it directly influences how search results are ranked and displayed, increasing the visibility of academic articles and motivating researchers to distribute their work via OA repositories (Lovett et al. 2017). Additionally, our framework has the potential to promote content diversification and improve the classification methods in a corpus to allow curators to get a better sense of their collection.

Sixth, we will elaborate on the potential for creating other frameworks that focus on other facets of social media and altmetrics. Sugimoto (2015) presents some of the challenges that altmetrics have faced as a result of the focus of funding agencies on the impact of research beyond academia. While the idea of altmetrics is to offer different measures of how scholarship is produced and disseminated, most altmetrics scholarship focuses specifically on the journal article metrics from a few platforms. Lastly, there is the concern of goal displacement—an inevitable by-product of the promotion of altmetrics. Libraries have begun to incorporate altmetrics into institutional repositories, and to provide guidance to researchers on how to document altmetrics on their CVs for the purposes of promotion, tenure, and merit evaluation. This, in turn, would mean that an article has more value if it has a higher altmetric score, and therefore that the reputation of a scholar is proportional to the number of mentions of their articles.

Finally, we considered using a different strategy involving caching query results to improve query effectiveness (Fagni et al. 2006). We discarded this strategy, since these manipulations could complicate the integration of other repositories into our framework. Along these lines, we plan to integrate the Public Knowledge Project (PKP) into the workflow of our framework in the near future. PKP presents a challenge because it is stored throughout different repositories rather than in a central location. However, integration of PKP would benefit from further study and attention, especially when taking into account the characteristics of different publishing venues (Kenner 2014).

## Discussion

Finding a way to evaluate our results was a difficult task. We debated between the two obvious alternatives for evaluation: automated numerical methods versus running a user study with human subjects. Automated numerical methods are convenient, accurate, and inherently replicable. Their implied convenience comes with a cost, however: their accuracy can hinder the modelling of behaviours and thinking of human subjects. User studies, on the other hand, can portray a better image of behaviours and user intentions—but they are both time- and resource-intensive. In the end, we decided to compromise and find a balance between the two alternatives. The automated numerical methods provided us with the necessary feedback to lead us into the next stage of our research, while two rounds of user testing, as planned, will further validate our findings.

Although the terms obtained with Tf-Idf provided better results in the clustering by ranking, we do not discard the validity of the terms obtained with topic modelling. As stated earlier, we believe that these terms provide an additional layer of metadata, which introduces the potential for an alternative method for their classification. More importantly, we believe that the combination of the terms obtained using Tf-Idf and topic modelling provides a layer of metadata that is very rich in its entropy, measured in regard to the amount of information it conveys. Moreover, we hypothesize that this metadata layer can be used to dynamically reorganize a digital collection and align it with current trends in social media. We plan to explore this last hypothesis in future iterations of our work that involve modelling trends in social media and testing the alignment of these trends with our document corpus.

Another point that demands our attention is the use of Altmetric.com's API for identifying trends in social media. Using this API does streamline our approach, as identifying ongoing trends in social media is a complex problem in itself. More so—and because of its difficulty—it does fall outside the scope of our research. On the other hand, the level of abstraction that we achieved forced us to use Altmetric as a "black box" (a method in which its output is produced without us knowing its inner workings), something that could potentially hinder our overall outcome if the API methods are flawed.

There are risks associated with a long-term dependency on an external API. For example, the API could skew its output unintentionally, which would compromise the integrity of our processes; it could change its output schema, requiring adjustments in our social media mining component; or, in the worst case scenario, it could stop working as a service altogether. In this sense there is real value in having an end-to-end solution. Unfortunately, the increased complexity of mining social media makes this impractical. Does scholarly inquiry require this type of solution? We believe it is not necessary at this point. However, the utility of altmetrics as an alternative to measure research impact is becoming more accepted. Unfortunately, scholars are starting to game the system in an attempt to gain self-promotion by exaggerating their scores, thus affecting the value of their research impact (Adie 2013).

Still, we believe that social knowledge is resilient (to some extent) to this kind of influence, as open social knowledge creation practices tend to correct outliers and erroneous data over time. Additionally, Altmetric is considered a reputable source, and offers other research institutions access to its API, which provides some assurance as to the soundness of the metadata they provide. In an ideal scenario, we would have used a harvester that we or our research partners had developed. Given that a custom solution does not exist, we decided to compromise.

## Conclusions and Future Work

We have elaborated on three points in this paper. First, we described the implementation of a prototype for our system. Second, we discussed how our methods allow users of OA repositories to incorporate information from online conversations into their search tasks, with the potential to access documents that they would otherwise have difficulty finding. Finally, we expanded on this increased accessibility and its implications within the context of the humanities.

In terms of aligning keywords with sets of documents using textual analysis techniques, we found that some techniques were more effective than others (notably Tf-Idf over topic modelling). However, their effectiveness is relative in this case. We concluded that one of the more complicated aspects of our study was its assessment. For this purpose, we have carried out automated testing, and two rounds of user studies are scheduled for the near future. Nonetheless, the results that we obtained do prove that sets of documents align with different sets of keywords. This has provided us with the necessary groundwork to match documents with ongoing trends in social media.

Through our research, we have developed a clear understanding of our document collection and points of inflection to align its more prominent features with sets of keywords. In the future deliverables of our work, we will focus on the evaluation of techniques and technologies for extracting features from social media, which will potentially afford us greater possibilities when reorganizing our document collection. Further, we will perform test cases on the alignment of these social media indicators with the models that we have extracted from our document corpus. Finally, we are also invested in integrating other OA repositories into the workflow of our framework, allowing us to investigate further the possibilities of our research.

WORKS CITED

Adie, Euan. "Gaming Altmetrics." 2013. *Altmetric* blog post, September 18. https://www.altmetric.com/blog/gaming-altmetrics/.

Alharbi, Abeer, Dan Smith, and Pam Mayhew. 2013. "Web Searching Behaviour for Academic Resources." In *Proceedings of 2013 Science and Information Conference*, 104–13. Bradford, UK: Science and Information (SAI) Organization. https://ieeexplore.ieee.org/document/6661724.

Altmetric LLP. 2017. "Altmetric." https://www.altmetric.com/.

Apache Software Foundation. 2016. "The Apache Velocity Project." http://velocity.apache.org/.

———. 2018. "Apache Spark: Lightning-fast unified analytics engine." http://spark.apache.org/.

———. 2019a. "Welcome to Apache Lucene." https://lucene.apache.org/.

———. 2019b. "Apache Solr." http://lucene.apache.org/solr/.

Arbuckle, Alyssa, Aaron Mauro, and Daniel Powell, eds. 2017. *Social Knowledge Creation in the Humanities : Volume 1.* Toronto: Iter Press; Tempe: Arizona Center for Medieval and Renaissance Studies.

Baeza-Yates, Ricardo, and Berthier Ribeiro-Neto. 1999. *Modern Information Retrieval.* Harlow, UK: Addison-Wesley Longman.

Blei, David M, Andrew Y. Ng, and Michael I. Jordan. 2003. "Latent Dirichlet Allocation." *Journal of Machine Learning Research* 3: 993–1022.

Bozzon, Alessandro, Marco Brambilla, and Stefano Ceri. 2012. "Answering Search Queries with CrowdSearcher." In *Proceedings of the 21st International Conference on World Wide Web* (*WWW '12*), 1009–18. New York: ACM. https://doi.org/10.1145/2187836.2187971.

Brambilla, Marco, Jordi Cabot, Javier Luis Cánovas Izquierdo, and Andrea Mauri. 2017. "Better Call the Crowd: Using Crowdsourcing to Shape the Notation of Domain-Specific Languages." In *Proceedings of the 10th ACM SIGPLAN International Conference on Software Language Engineering (SLE 2017)*, 129–38. New York: ACM. https://doi.org/10.1145/3136014.3136033.

Broder, Andrei Z. 1997. "On the Resemblance and Containment of Documents." In *Proceedings of the Compression and Complexity of Sequences 1997 (SEQUENCES '97)*, 21–29. Washington, DC: IEEE [Institute of Electrical and Electronics Engineers]. https://www.cs.princeton.edu/courses/archive/spring13/cos598C/broder97resemblance.pdf.

Chaput, Matt. 2016. "Whoosh 2.7.4: Fast, pure-Python full text indexing, search, and spell checking library." April 3. https://pypi.python.org/pypi/Whoosh/.

Chen, Hung-Hsuan, Liang Gou, Xiaolong Zhang, and Clyde Lee Giles. 2011. "CollabSeer: A Search Engine for Collaboration Discovery." In *Proceedings of the 11th Annual International ACM/IEEE Joint Conference on Digital Libraries (JCDL '11)*, 231–40. New York: ACM. https://doi.org/10.1145/1998076.1998121.

Danilak, Michal. 2016. "Langdetect 1.0.7: Language detection library ported from Google's language-detection." October 3. https://pypi.python.org/pypi/langdetect.

Earp, Will. 2014. "Pyaltmetric: Python Wrapper for Altmetric API v1 (version 0.2.0)." September 23. https://github.com/wearp/pyaltmetric.

Érudit Consortium. 2019. "Érudit." https://www.erudit.org/.

Evans, Brynn M., Sanjay Kairam, and Peter Pirolli. 2010. "Do Your Friends Make You Smarter?: An Analysis of Social Strategies in Online Information Seeking." *Information Processing and Management* 46(6): 679–92. https://doi.org/10.1016/j.ipm.2009.12.001.

Fagni, Tiziano, Raffaele Perego, Fabrizio Silvestri, and Salvatore Orlando. 2006. "Boosting the Performance of Web Search Engines: Caching and Prefetching Query Results by Exploiting Historical Usage Data." *ACM Transactions on Information Systems (TOIS)* 24(1): 51–78. https://doi.org/10.1145/1125857.1125859.

Hearst, Marti A. 2009. *Search User Interfaces.* New York: Cambridge University Press.

Jeffrey, Stuart. 2012. "A New Digital Dark Age? Collaborative Web Tools, Social Media and Long-Term Preservation." *World Archaeology* 44(4): 553–70. https://doi.org/10.1080/00438243.2012.737579.

Kenner, Ali. 2014. "Designing Digital Infrastructure: Four Considerations for Scholarly Publishing Projects." *Cultural Anthropology* 29(2): 264–87. https://doi.org/10.14506/ca29.2.05.

Kittur, Aniket, and Robert E. Kraut. 2008. "Harnessing the Wisdom of Crowds in Wikipedia: Quality Through Coordination." In *Proceedings of the 2008 ACM Conference on Computer Supported Cooperative Work (CSCW '08)*, 37–46. New York: ACM. https://doi.org/10.1145/1460563.1460572.

Konstas, Ioannis, Vassilios Stathopoulos, and Joemon M. Jose. 2009. "On Social Networks and Collaborative Recommendation." In *Proceedings of the 32nd International ACM SIGIR Conference on Research and Development in Information Retrieval (SIGIR '09)*, 195–202. New York: ACM. https://doi.org/10.1145/1571941.1571977.

Leggett, John J., and Frank M. Shipman III. 2004. "Directions for Hypertext Research: Exploring the Design Space for Interactive Scholarly Communication." In *Proceedings of the Fifteenth ACM Conference on Hypertext and Hypermedia (HYPERTEXT '04)*, 2–11. New York: ACM. https://doi.org/10.1145/1012807.1012812.

Letierce, Julie, Alexandre Passant, John G. Breslin, and Stefan Decker. 2010. "Understanding How Twitter is Used to Spread Scientific Messages." In *Proceedings of the Web Science Conference WebSci10: Extending the Frontiers of Society*, edited by Wendy Hall et al. http://www.johnbreslin.org/files/publications/20100426_webs2010c.pdf.

Lops, Pasquale, Marco de Gemmis, and Giovanni Semeraro. 2011. "Content-Based Recommender Systems: State of the Art and Trends." In *Recommender Systems Handbook*, edited by Francesco Ricci, Lior Rokach, Bracha Shapira, and Paul B. Kantor, 73–105. New York: Springer.

Lovett, Julia A., Andrée J. Rathemacher, Divana Boukari, and Corey Lang. 2017. "Institutional Repositories and Academic Social Networks: Competition or Complement? A Study of Open Access Policy Compliance vs. ResearchGate Participation." *Journal of Librarianship and Scholarly Communication* 5(1). https://doi.org/10.7710/2162-3309.2183.

Majchrzak, Ann, Samer Faraj, Gerald C. Kane, and Bijan Azad. 2013. "The Contradictory Influence of Social Media Affordances on Online Communal Knowledge Sharing." Journal of Computer-Mediated Communication 19(1): 38–55. https://doi.org/10.1111/jcc4.12030.

Meneses, Luis, Alyssa Arbuckle, Hector Lopez, Belaid Moa, Richard Furuta, and Ray Siemens. 2018. "Aligning Social Media Indicators with the Documents in an Open Access Repository." Paper presented at the INKE Victoria Gathering 2018, Victoria, BC, January 10.

Meneses, Luis, Alyssa Arbuckle, Hector Lopez, Belaid Moa, and Ray Siemens. 2017. "Social Media Engine." Paper presented at the Open Cyberinfrastructure for the Humanities and Social Sciences Workshop 2017, Montreal, October 25.

Meneses, Luis, Alyssa Arbuckle, Belaid Moa, Richard Furuta, and Raymond Siemens. 2017. "Towards a More Context Aware Digital Library: Implications in the Humanities." Paper presented at the Joint CSDH/ SCHN and ACH Digital Humanities Conference 2017, Toronto, May 29.

Nicholas, David, and Ian Rowlands. 2011. "Social Media Use in the Research Workflow." *Information Services and Use* 31(1–2): 61–83. https://doi. org/10.3233/ISU-2011-0623.

Owen, Brian, and Kevin Stranack. 2012. "The Public Knowledge Project and Open Journal Systems: Open Source Options for Small Publishers." *Learned Publishing* 25(2): 138–44. https://doi.org/10.1087/20120208.

Pfister, Damien Smith. 2011. "Networked Expertise in the Era of Many-to-Many Communication: On Wikipedia and Invention." *Social Epistemology* 25(3): 217–31. https://doi.org/10.1080/02691728.2011.578306.

Řehůřek, Radim. 2019. "Gensim: Topic Modelling for Humans." https:// radimrehurek.com/gensim/.

Richardson, Leonard. 2019. "Beautiful Soup." http://www.crummy.com/ software/BeautifulSoup/.

Ronacher, Armin. 2019. "Flask: Web Development, One Drop at a Time." http://flask.pocoo.org/.

Rose, Daniel E. 2006. "Reconciling Information-Seeking Behavior with Search User Interfaces for the Web." *Journal of the American Society for Information Science and Technology* 57(6): 797–99. https://doi.org/10.1002/asi.20295.

Rossum, Guido van. 1995. "Python Tutorial." Technical Report CS-R9526. Amsterdam: Centrum voor Wiskunde en Informatica (CWI). https://ir.cwi.nl/pub/5007/05007D.pdf.

Schrier, Robert A. 2011. "Digital Librarianship and Social Media: The Digital Library as Conversation Facilitator." *D-Lib Magazine* 17 (7/8). https://doi.org/10.1045/july2011-schrier.

Siemens, Ray, Teresa Dobson, Stan Ruecker, Richard Cunningham, Alan Galey, Claire Warwick, Lynne Siemens, et al. 2011. "HCI-Book? Perspectives on E-Book Research, 2006–2008 (Foundational to Implementing New Knowledge Environments)." *Papers of the Bibliographical Society of Canada / Cahiers de La Société Bibliographique du Canada* 49(1): 35–89. https://jps.library.utoronto.ca/index.php/bsc/article/view/21941.

Siemens, Ray, Claire Warwick, Richard Cunningham, Teresa Dobson, Alan Galey, Stan Ruecker, Susan Schreibman, and INKE Team. 2009. "Codex Ultor: Toward a Conceptual and Theoretical Foundation for New Research on Books and Knowledge Environments." *Digital Studies/Le Champ Numérique* 1 (2). https://doi.org/10.16995/dscn.270.

Suber, Peter. 2012. *Open Access.* Cambridge, MA: MIT Press.

Sugimoto, Cassidy R. 2015. "'Attention Is Not Impact' and Other Challenges for Altmetrics." *The Wiley Network*, June 24. https://hub.wiley.com/community/exchanges/discover/blog/2015/06/23/attention-is-not-impact-and-other-challenges-for-altmetrics.

Sugimoto, Cassidy R., Sam Work, Vincent Larivière, and Stefanie Haustein. 2016. "Scholarly Use of Social Media and Altmetrics: A Review of the Literature." *arXiv.org*: 1608.08112 [CS]. http://arxiv.org/abs/1608.08112.

Tenopir, Carol, Rachel Volentine, and Donald W. King. 2013. "Social Media and Scholarly Reading." *Online Information Review* 37(2): 193–216. https://doi.org/10.1108/OIR-04-2012-0062.

United States Census Bureau. 2014. "Frequently Occurring Surnames from Census 1990 – Names Files." https://www.census.gov/topics/

population/genealogy/data/1990_census/1990_census_namefiles.
html.

Wang, Xianwen, Chen Liu, Wenli Mao, and Zhichao Fang. 2015. "The Open
Access Advantage Considering Citation, Article Usage and Social Media
Attention." *Scientometrics* 103(2): 555–64. https://doi.org/10.1007/
s11192-015-1547-0.

WestGrid. 2019. "WestGrid: Compute Canada Regional Partner." https://
www.westgrid.ca.

Willinsky, John. 2006. *The Access Principle: The Case for Open Access to Research
and Scholarship.* Cambridge, MA: MIT Press.

Xiao, Lu, and Nicole Askin. 2012. "Wikipedia for Academic Publishing:
Advantages and Challenges." *Online Information Review* 36(3): 359–73.
https://doi.org/10.1108/14684521211241396.

# Social Knowledge Creation in the Digital Humanities: Case Studies

Cara Marta Messina, Sarah Connell, Julia Flanders,
Caroline Klibanoff, and Sarah Payne

## Introduction

The peculiar professional and organizational space of the "digital humanities centre" has been much studied in recent years, with a focus on how such centres are managed and funded, where they are situated institutionally, and what their role in the digital research ecology is or should be. More recently, as such spaces are becoming commonplace and well-naturalized as part of the humanities ecology, they are being called upon to host the experiments of that ecology: crossovers and partnerships between pedagogy, tool-building, research, public outreach, and mentoring. In this article, we focus on Northeastern University's Digital Scholarship Group (DSG) as an exemplar of this organizational genre, to explore the role that social knowledge creation plays both in the group's own regular operations and in its function within the institution.

DSG is in many ways typical of the "digital humanities centre" or "digital scholarship group," as characterized in surveys such as Diane Zorich's 2008 study or Nancy Maron and Sarah Pickle's 2014 report on "Sustaining the Digital Humanities." It is an applied research group located (as is now common) within a library, and it builds on the library's established role in gathering, synthesizing, and disseminating knowledge, while helping to move work even further in social directions through activities such as transcribathons, Wikipedia editathons, and crowd-sourced data-gathering and enhancement. DSG also has an increasing pedagogical role as the university explores experiential education at the graduate level, focused on digital humanities. And, like many digital scholarship centres, DSG has primary responsibility for developing and maintaining expertise and core infrastructure for building, supporting, and publishing digital research projects. Social knowledge creation is thus built into the group's foundational activities at a deep level.

What do we mean by "social knowledge creation"? Previous studies using the term have focused on formal processes of scholarly communication such

ISBN 978-1-64959-008-4 (paper) ISBN 978-1-64959-009-1 (pdf) ISBN 978-1-64959-084-8 (epub)
*New Technologies in Medieval and Renaissance Studies* 8 (2022) 219–244

as scholarly editing, peer review, and open access publishing.[1] Our focus in this article is on both "social knowledge" and "social creation": on the ways in which shared knowledge emerges through specific working processes that include not just shared decision-making or planning, but also longer-term processes of communication and trust-building that play out over time and create durable ecologies with wide-ranging effects. We are interested in how knowledge is instantiated in humans and human processes as well as in documents, and we consider a wide variety of documents that include not only artefacts recognizable as "scholarship" but also documentation, discussions in workplace chat forums such as Slack, project blog posts, and shared note-taking. This article is itself an exemplar: it was collaboratively written by a team that includes the DSG director, other DSG staff, and graduate students with roles in DSG's regular work and grant-funded projects. The writing process involved interviewing each member to elicit insights about the project case studies, followed by a shared drafting and revision process. The "we" that speaks here is a collective voice, but at various points it draws on individual perspectives.

This article is broken into four case studies that model the work processes of the DSG: the writing of this article, the CERES toolkit, the Design for Diversity initiative, and finally the Intertextual Networks project. A few particular themes run through these reflections. Process matters a great deal (as the phrase "knowledge *creation*" reminds us), and we seek to document specific work processes that influence how students and faculty learn to take on varied roles and forms of expertise. Mentorship also matters tremendously, but that term describes a broad spectrum of relationships and actions: what forms of mentorship genuinely empower students, help to build trust, and create space for them to operate as true collaborators? Finally, we are concerned with the ways in which these kinds of digital projects ask us to be attentive to terms such as "scholarship" and "work" (terms which come from the two different professional frameworks that intersect at the DSG), and to avoid distinctions that devalue some kinds of labour and elevate others. These case studies illustrate how effective social knowledge creation is supported by forms of professional credit and responsibility; the creation

---

[1] For example, Daniel Powell's 2016 University of Victoria dissertation, "Social Knowledge Creation and Emergent Digital Research Infrastructure for Early Modern Studies," looks in particular at digital infrastructure for scholarly editing and scholarly communication; the description of the previous volume in this series highlights "peer-review, open access publishing, tenure and promotion, mentorship, teaching, collaboration, and interdisciplinarity." See Arbuckle, Mauro, and Powell 2017.

of collegial working relationships between students, faculty, and staff; and even the use of physical space.

*About the Digital Scholarship Group*

Housed within Northeastern University's main library, the Digital Scholarship Group (DSG) has brought together expertise and resources across disciplines since 2014. The DSG is both a centralized resource for digital scholarship and an applied research team; we seek out new tools and methods, test them on real-world projects, and make them available to the Northeastern community. In addition to working with centres, departments, and individual scholars within Northeastern, the group has also established collaborative partnerships with peer organizations and researchers outside the university, including grant-funded research, open source software development, and pedagogical materials and methods.

The DSG's full-time staff is composed of individuals with backgrounds in digital humanities, library sciences, and information technology, in addition to more specific areas of expertise such as data visualization, geographic information systems (GIS), text encoding, and linguistics. This broad range of disciplinary knowledge is core to its success, allowing the DSG to offer services ranging from grant-writing support to GIS, data visualization, and grant-writing consultations as well as to conduct research on subjects such as diverse interface design, digital repository systems, and text encoding. In a university with no central departmental hub for digital humanities work, the DSG and its space—the Digital Scholarship Commons (DSC)—fill this need as a place in which faculty, students, and staff can come together to collaborate on projects and utilize resources.

The DSG's commitment to student employment is notable. Paid student employees serve as project managers, coordinators, encoders, and research assistants, giving them considerable work experience on real scholarly projects as well as additional entries for their resumés. Students are often encouraged to produce scholarly texts about their everyday DSG work, bridging the gap between academic scholarship and professional experience (as in this article, for example). Students can work on a variety of projects, and interact with faculty and staff across the university in a professional role. This enables them to serve as conduits for other students, faculty, and departments to the resources available at the DSG, helping to spread the word and bring in more projects and collaborations.

For DSG as an "applied research group," social knowledge creation is also a prompt for experimentation. We are interested in ways of creating stronger working relationships (in project teams, planning groups, and conversational spaces) that bridge faculty, staff, student, and community roles. In particular, we focus intensively on ways of involving students in DSG's work as colleagues, co-authors, researchers, contributors, teachers, learners, and co-investigators. This experimentation is driven by a desire for ethical labour practices in research and projects, as well as pedagogical motives, but also has an element of design: developing procedures for collaboration that can accommodate these roles also reinforces other good practices such as documentation, transparency, consensus-based decision-making, and strong training programs that make their value felt throughout the organization.

*Writing This Article*

In writing this article, we modelled the DSG's approach to collaborative scholarship and social knowledge production; we use this article as our first case study to demonstrate the process of social knowledge creation. The writing team included five people—faculty, staff, and graduate student employees—who wear multiple hats on campus and can therefore speak to the far-reaching tendrils of the DSG's work across the university. Each contributor brought a different perspective to considering social knowledge creation. In a series of meetings, the group reflected on the ways in which knowledge has been produced through processes just like these. The meetings were held in one of DSG's informal meeting spaces, familiar to all of the coauthors and one in which they were placed on an equal footing as they shared their perspectives on the DSG's work from the standpoint of social knowledge creation.

After brainstorming sessions to decide on the overall structure of the article, we chose to conduct individual interviews with each other to use as a source of inspiration and consensus as we wrote. For the first step, we agreed on a set of questions about the DSG's work processes and the effect they have:

- Describe the DSG project and your role in this project.
- What are the most important aspects of the project's structure, from the standpoint of social knowledge creation? How did those aspects of the structure come about?
- What specific tools, practices, and spaces are most central to the ways in which the project constructs knowledge socially?

- How does knowledge circulate and get used within the project team? Between the project team and others?
- What did you find most difficult or challenging about social knowledge creation (i.e., sharing/disseminating knowledge and arriving at shared knowledge)?
- What transferable skills have you gathered in the course of this project, specifically around social knowledge creation? What is the most important thing you've learned?
- Can you identify a specific moment or action that best represents social knowledge creation taking place within this project?

After agreeing on the questions, the contributors meditated on their potential answers before meeting again to conduct the actual interviews. The interview format provided approximately 15 to 20 minutes for each interviewee to answer questions while one contributor played the role of the interviewer and the other contributors took notes. This process allowed each person to speak individually, while providing an opportunity for sharing ideas and building consensus.

Using these interview responses, each contributor wrote a section of the article. Once the first draft was finished, we reviewed all the sections, provided comments and suggestions, and used each other's ideas to come up with themes that appeared throughout the sections. This method required us to be aware of each other's writing processes as well as our collaborators' virtual space on the document; we made an effort to respect and validate each other's writing while also challenging each other to produce the best versions of our sections. The article thus sought to represent all of the authors' perspectives while also providing a collaborative synthesis, following an equitable process.

*CERES*

The first case study that demonstrates the role of social knowledge creation in everyday DSG practices is the Community-Enhanced Repository for Engaged Scholarship (CERES) project. CERES began as a way to meet technical needs regarding storage of digital objects and integration of those objects into project websites. While CERES is a digital tool, the DSG's approach in training others to use CERES and supporting existing CERES projects makes CERES more than just a form of technology. CERES is also a site of social knowledge creation that involves multiple participants across various institutional positions. Using CERES as a case study highlights the DSG's commitment to reciprocity, flexibility, self-reflection, and horizontal rather than hierarchical knowledge production.

CERES, which was developed by the DSG in 2014, functions as an application program interface (API) between Northeastern's Digital Repository Service (DRS) and a WordPress site. In other words, projects store their data—which could be images or text files, for example—in the DRS. Projects then build site content using the WordPress interface. CERES allows users to pull items directly from the DRS while working within WordPress to create digital exhibits.

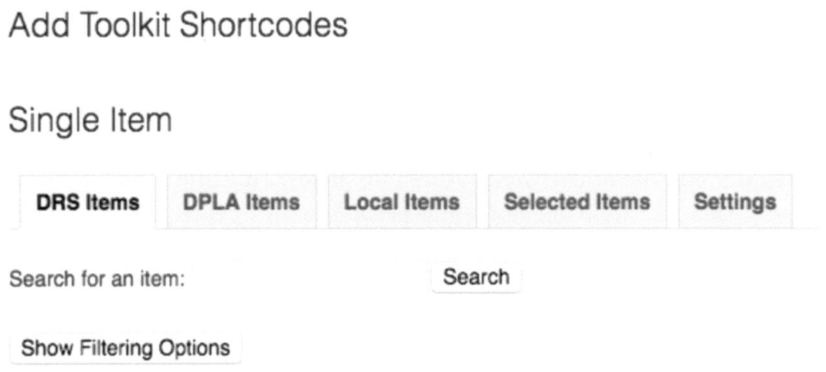

## Add Toolkit Shortcodes

### Single Item

| DRS Items | DPLA Items | Local Items | Selected Items | Settings |

Search for an item:                    Search

Show Filtering Options

**Figure 1. CERES editing interface: screenshot of adding a single item shortcode from the DRS.**

Within the CERES editing interface, users have access to a library of pre-defined code segments ("shortcodes") that can generate dynamic timelines, maps, and image galleries drawing on repository data without requiring technical knowledge on the part of the user (see Figure 1). By developing digital publications using CERES, projects are able to store their research materials and digital objects in the DRS, where files are preserved and maintained for future users and project members. The DSG issued its first call for proposals for CERES projects in February 2015, and now has more than twenty-five projects in various stages of completion and six projects that have been completed.

While there are many long-term projects that use CERES, several instructors at Northeastern have chosen to use CERES in the classroom as well, demonstrating the pedagogical potential of the tool. In these instances, instructors receive a CERES installation at the beginning of the semester, which typically functions as the website for the class as a whole. Either individually or in small groups, students create exhibits on the site that advance a narrative or argument and combine text with audio/visual material.

Classrooms are not simply given a CERES installation and then cut loose, however. Instead, classrooms receive support and training throughout the semester with various members of the DSG as part of a scaffolding that is built into the work from early planning stages to final publication. Both the initial proposal for a CERES site and the site installation involve conversations with the DSG's metadata librarians and staff. During the semester, classrooms typically participate in two technical workshops led by a graduate research assistant (RA). The RA usually provides technical support throughout the semester as well. Using CERES in the classroom thus involves a high level of collaboration across disciplines and institutional positions. Administrators, staff, faculty, undergraduates, and graduate students all participate in developing and maintaining the site. While the logistics of a CERES site inherently involve many participants, each participant is also influential in producing a final product or publishable site. The necessity of these different participants creates a model of knowledge production that is more horizontal than hierarchical. While the DSG staff does provide more mentorship to graduate RAs, no one person is unilaterally distributing knowledge to the rest of the group; rather, many voices from many institutional positions and ranks contribute to the site and student exhibits.

Additionally, we have found that training sessions, in the classroom especially, are more productive when students are asked to participate in deciding how CERES can be used to create an effective online exhibit. Rather than using a top-down pedagogical approach to show students how to perform various technical functions in CERES, it is important to marry the technical processes with the actual narrative or argument students may wish to convey with their content. Instead of telling students what to do and how to create an exhibit, we find it is more effective to demonstrate the technical steps and then ask them, for example, how different shortcodes might affect the argument of an exhibit and why they might choose one shortcode over another. Doing so allows the training session to be more of a reciprocal exchange of knowledge than a top-down dissemination of technical know-how. By allowing for experimentation and engaging all participants, even those new to CERES, the training sessions function as a particularly fruitful arena for social knowledge creation.

As with other digital tools and collaborative knowledge production, working with CERES is not without its challenges. Members of the DSG often have to manage the ambitions of a project or classroom within the technical limitations of the tool. This often involves establishing a reasonable scope for the project, particularly if the project is confined to one semester. And with one graduate RA providing the bulk of the technical training and support, additional support structures must be built into the classroom environment to prevent that graduate student from becoming overwhelmed by the work. Sarah Payne, the RA for the 2017–2018 academic year, reflected that she avoided becoming overwhelmed with technical support by designating two or three more technically proficient students as the first line of support, followed by the instructor, then herself. The CERES documentation, created by members of the DSG, became essential for scaffolding the technical support. Payne found that, when supplied with the documentation, students and instructors were often able to troubleshoot many of the questions that arose and were better able to solve problems themselves than to have someone else do it for them. Thorough documentation is thus essential for CERES projects to run smoothly, and while we feel confident in our documentation, we also do not consider the documentation static or finished. Instead, we continually look for ways to expand or revise the documentation in response to the needs of projects and classrooms.

To demonstrate how social knowledge creation works with CERES, it's helpful to look at a specific instance of collaboration that we felt had both successes and challenges: the creation of documentation regarding "advanced topics" related to CERES and the subsequent training session on those topics. In the initial stages of a CERES project, the designated research assistant at the DSG leads the project team through a training session, which largely focuses on the basics of WordPress and CERES. Topics include creating a new page, using shortcodes, designing layouts, and customizing colours and fonts. During the Fall 2017 semester, we found that many project teams were interested in more complex interactions with CERES. In one of our biweekly meetings, members of the DSG decided it would be useful not only to expand the CERES documentation to include more advanced topics, but also to lead a training session on advanced topics. One project in particular requested training on more specialized topics, and in conjunction with the project team, we planned to hold an advanced training session for them at the end of the Fall semester.

The selection of "advanced" topics was a collaborative decision. Amanda Rust, the Associate Director of the DSG, first sent an email to several of us who work with CERES in order to crowdsource ideas for the documentation and training on advanced topics. These topics were based not only on suggestions from various projects, but also on our own individual observations as to where the CERES documentation could be expanded. Together we decided to focus on the various WordPress widgets (a basic training session typically covers only two or three widgets). Widgets are different from shortcodes in that they enhance the functionality of the WordPress site. Commonly used widgets include clickable buttons that link to other pages or social media accounts, a contact form, and multiple widgets that change the display of posts. Additional advanced topics included the affordances of posts and pages and when to use one over the other; creating and styling side menus; advanced formatting and customization options; and how to use the tagging feature to optimize a website. We also expected that the project team attending the training would bring its own troubleshooting questions as well. Rather than plan highly structured training, we wanted to allow the project team to decide what topics would be most useful for them. While we were prepared to discuss the aforementioned advanced topics, we planned to start the training by writing possible topics on a whiteboard, including any suggestions from the project team, and then allowing them to decide where they wanted to start. The more flexible approach to the training session is indicative of the DSG's commitment to ensuring that knowledge production is a collaborative effort.

During the training session, then, we wrote a list of potential topics on the whiteboard and asked for suggestions. One of the suggestions was that we go over how to use the CERES shortcodes, which is heavily emphasized during basic training and was not, to our minds, an "advanced topic." Keeping with our plan to let the project team take the initiative, we began by focusing on the shortcodes, which we thought would be a quick refresher. Instead, however, it became evident that familiarity with CERES differed widely among the project members. While some members seemed proficient using shortcodes, others required a more deliberate, step-by-step demonstration. What we had planned as advanced topics training ended up focusing largely on shortcodes and creating exhibits. Payne, who led the training, found that the advanced session was ultimately quite similar to basic training, but noted the importance of meeting the project where it was at rather than pushing advanced topics that some participants were not yet prepared to work with.

In our next biweekly meeting, members of the DSG expressed some ambivalence regarding the training. On the one hand, we had allowed the project members to take the lead in terms of what they wanted to learn, and we were successfully able to cover the information requested. On the other hand, we suspected that the training was not as useful for those with more experience with CERES, and we did not end up discussing many of the advanced topics we had planned for. In retrospect, it might have been more useful to divide the project team based on members' proficiency and what they were most interested in learning. For example, since we had multiple members of the DSG present, we could have divided the project team into those who required a refresher on basic topics and those who felt equipped to work on more advanced topics. The training was a lesson in flexibility in terms of not being tied to a rigid structure for a training session, but also recognizing that project teams contain varying technical proficiencies. We felt it was important to accommodate a range of technical experience, particularly in a workshop aimed at covering advanced topics. Although the training was not exactly what we had planned, we still produced valuable documentation. Afterward, we circulated the notes that had been prepared for the training in order to solicit feedback before adding the notes to the formal documentation on the DSG's website. The subsequent self-reflection within the DSG, as well as an understanding of our documentation as continually evolving, allowed us to improve our approach to social knowledge production within the context of training sessions.

The structure for getting started with a CERES site, and the subsequent training, technical support, and site development, necessitates a high level of communication and collaboration. Whether the CERES site serves a long-term project or a semester-long class, the development and maintenance of the site involves a range of participants from undergraduates to professors and library staff. In this process, no one person is more essential than another; all participants are necessary to produce a successful site or exhibit. Additionally, the structure of the technical training sessions themselves aims to involve students in the knowledge production of the site. Through the involvement of many participants, continual attention to documentation, and flexibility in our approach to training sessions, CERES has become one successful instance of the DSG's commitment to social knowledge production.

*Design for Diversity*

While the working community for CERES was comparatively small and focused on institutional colleagues, other DSG projects have operated in a much wider sphere and have posed a different kind of challenge in social knowledge creation. One of the most ambitious of these is the Design for Diversity (D4D) initiative, for which an Institute for Museum and Library Services (IMLS) National Forum Grant was awarded to the DSG in September 2016.[2] The work for D4D began in early 2017 and continued until the end of Summer 2018.

[2] To learn more about Design for Diversity, visit https://dsg.neu.edu/research/design-for-diversity.

D4D has engaged practitioners at Northeastern and other institutions in collaboratively building a learning toolkit focused on designing information systems and work practices that support social justice, particularly in connection with the representation of gender, race, sexuality, class, and indigeneity in digital humanities and cultural heritage projects and collections. The project was inspired by two parallel concerns: first, a theoretical question prompted by the work of scholars such as Tara McPherson, Michelle Caswell, and Moya Bailey, asking about the role of race and power in the design of technical and information systems; second, a practical question prompted by DSG's work with projects focused on marginalized communities and cultures, asking how DSG's systems might avoid replicating systemic marginalization and disempowerment (following the lead of projects such as Mukurtu, the content management system discussed below). DSG sought funding for an initiative that would synthesize current research and expertise in information science (IS), software development, digital humanities (DH), library and archival practice, museum studies, and other domains, and produce an opportunity for open conversation. The project's foundational premise is that knowledge and information representation and dissemination are not objective, but rather socially constructed choices made by groups of people; this premise follows the discourse in DH that tools, data models, code, and information systems express particular politics.

The D4D project was framed as a two-year undertaking focused on two Forum events, with outcomes disseminated through a Learning Toolkit to be hosted by DSG in partnership with the Arlington, VA-based Digital Library Federation.[3] Work on D4D began in early 2017, led by a planning team that included Julia Flanders and Amanda Rust (the two principal investigators), Sarah Sweeney (the Digital Repository Manager at Northeastern Libraries), and Cara Marta Messina, a graduate student in the Northeastern English Department, who was hired as the Research Associate in Summer 2017 to help plan the event, take on administrative tasks, conduct research about similar work done in IS and DH, and serve as a main point of contact for event participants. Central to the planning group's work was the design of both the Forum events themselves and the authoring and review processes for the toolkit, to ensure that these would be collaborative, inclusive, and transparent in their goals.

The opening Forum event took place in October 2017. By this point, the D4D grant team had decided to produce not only a white paper based on the

---

[3] The beta version of the Design for Diversity Learning Toolkit can be seen at https://des4div.library.northeastern.edu/.

event as originally intended, but also the Learning Toolkit. In this toolkit, the D4D team imagined several different resources: readings and exemplary projects from practitioners doing similar work; case studies created for D4D; and classroom activities and assignments called "study paths," based on the previous resources. The Core Design Group (CDG), a group of national practitioners with expertise ranging from user experience to museum studies, were provided with honoraria to come together and begin drafting these study paths. A Critical Review Partners (CRP) group was invited to review the study paths, case studies, and other potential documents included in the toolkit. An additional Research Assistant, Des Alaniz, was hired in early Summer 2018 to assist with the final stretch of the grant; Messina and Rust took on teaching roles to introduce Alaniz to D4D practices and encouraged Alaniz to include their own expertise. Finally, in August 2018, D4D hosted a closing Forum event to review the toolkit materials with a larger group, including potential users, as well as a writing sprint to invite other writers to contribute to the toolkit. At the conclusion of the grant, the D4D grant team is gathering user feedback as teachers and practitioners explore the contents of a prototype toolkit site.

The year and a half from when the grant work started to when the closing Forum occurred demonstrates the necessary longevity needed to run collaborative projects and foster social knowledge creation. The grant team chose to apply for an IMLS National Forum Grant because the Forum aspect was focused on crowdsourcing, democracy, and collaboration. Because the grant team wanted to advocate for responsible and ethical practices when working with digital or digitized cultural heritage materials, we also recognized the necessity of implementing these practices in the planning of the Forum and the creation of the Learning Toolkit. Instead of taking a top-down approach in which knowledge is imparted to a person or group of people, the grant team utilized a horizontal approach, viewing ourselves and the people we worked with as learners in some areas of knowledge and experts in others; the grant team acted as a *platform* to disseminate knowledge instead of imparting it. In order to actually implement this approach, constant communication and iterative review processes were needed. These review processes ranged from reading scholarship on responsible practices to sitting down with practitioners already implementing these practices into their everyday work (such as members of the Digital Library Federation, and the Peabody Essex Museum in Salem, MA). For instance, the team created a Zotero bibliography with almost four hundred readings across the disciplines.[4]

---

[4] The Zotero bibliography created by Design for Diversity is available at https://www.

The creation of the toolkit's beta website took almost the entire year and a half as we asked multiple practitioners in one-on-one meetings and during the October opening Forum event what they wanted to see, invited people with diverse expertise to join the CDG, created and revised documents to help guide the writers of the toolkit materials while continuing to revise as we received feedback, reached out to the CRP to review materials written by the grant team and the CDG, and more. As Moya Bailey stated during the opening Forum, building collaborative relationships focused on a common goal requires *time* and *transparency*; working toward a common goal does not automatically lead to trust. The grant team attempted to build trust with our collaborators—particularly the CDG—by inviting them to provide suggestions and feedback on all areas of event planning and material creation, then attempting to implement those suggestions in ways that still kept the original grant goal in mind. An essential element of social knowledge creation in the D4D project was thus the establishment of transparency by negotiating and responding to feedback from many different kinds of contributors.

From the perspective of social knowledge creation, this project was extremely ambitious, and a number of specific challenges are worth examining in more detail. One of the points of tension for the grant team was negotiating between our own design ideas and the feedback we received from our collaborators. We wanted to concentrate on democratic collaboration while still maintaining that the goal of this democracy was a product: the toolkit. Although the D4D team strove to invite collaborators and provide compensation for their ideas and labour, the final choices made throughout the project occurred in one of the DSG offices on the third floor of the Northeastern Library. The grant team constantly negotiated between our original visions and the visions of the D4D collaborators, discussing how the feedback we received aligned with our goals, made us rethink our goals, or made us rework how we were approaching our goals.

At a meeting early in the grant period, for example, staff from the Native American Fellowship Program at the Peabody Essex Museum reminded us that the communities who have been colonized and marginalized are already doing the work of decolonizing archives, museums, and libraries, but do not necessarily have opportunities to intervene in the design, purchase, or configuration of the technical tools for that work. They thus directed our attention to a deeper problem for D4D to explore: not simply the redesign of tools, or the retraining of tool designers, but the creation of critical tool

---

zotero.org/groups/1341761/design_for_diversity_working_bibliography.

design processes involving those who have the greatest knowledge of de-colonization and the greatest stake in its results. In that sense, the larger collaborative process producing the materials for the toolkit included more local cycles of insight and readjustment. The design choices, topics, and case studies had been developed mostly on a smaller collaborative scale by the grant team, and informed by layers of review from the D4D community and beyond.

Another key challenge was the question of how to create an advocacy toolkit that could be accessible and applicable across different disciplines, expertise, positions, and identities. During their presentation at the Opening Forum in October 2017, Trevor Muñoz, Catherine Knight Steele, and Purdom Lindblad advocated for "de-centering" expertise, viewing collaboration as not only working together, but highlighting strengths and learning from each other's perspectives. This "de-centering" framework became central for the D4D grant team, in terms of not just expertise, but also identities. Focusing on identities became important because identity and experience are closely in-tertwined; we wanted to work with a team that had diverse experiences and could use those to foster stronger, more equitable conversations. The grant team itself was fairly homogenous in race, profession, and location. Because this homogeneity was acknowledged within the grant team and in external conversations, however, our goal when approaching certain conversations and events was to leave with new knowledge, perspectives, and ideas. When the call for the CDG was sent out, for example, we paid particular attention to inviting practitioners from different Information Science professions and diverse identities. We de-centered our own expertise in order to focus on and make room for diverse knowledge, expertise, and experience.

A third challenge, then, became how to continue to foster a space for pro-ductive, focused conversations in which these knowledges could thrive. Space—both the virtual and intellectual space of the collaborative encoun-ter, and the physical spaces that supported it—was a crucial design issue for the D4D initiative. Navigating and taking advantage of space—as discussed throughout this article—became central for this project's social knowledge creation. These spaces included physical spaces on the Northeastern campus in the DSG, and other areas for group events; virtual communication spaces on Google Drive, BlueJeans, Twitter, and email; and finally physical spaces outside campus, such as our meeting at the Peabody Essex Museum.

The design of the two Forum events was a particularly important challenge in creating effective collaborative spaces that could operate both physically and virtually. First, we wanted to show our gratitude and commitment to the Forum participants by making the physical and virtual space as comfortable and accommodating as possible. We researched best practices for inclusive and equitable events, including name tags with space to add pronouns, clear instructions for access to Northeastern's all-gender bathrooms and important resources such as lactation rooms, food to accommodate different dietary needs, wheelchair accessible space, and more. We tried to remember that the participants were attending an all-day event two days in a row to share their knowledge with us; we wanted to build spaces in both the physical auditorium and the sharing of information that reflected our participants' needs and let them know we were thinking of them. The experience of the opening Forum provided additional insight and opportunity for improvement: making sure the "pronoun" section on the badges was large enough to read, for example, and providing longer breaks. The physical space was also augmented in important ways with accompanying virtual spaces. At both Forums, a live stream and an actively monitored Twitter feed expanded the body of participation to include people outside the room. To support people who might need visual guidance to pair with the auditory conversations and presentations, we encouraged Forum participants to take notes using a Google Document created for each table; these notes were made publicly available during the Forum. The design choices made by the grant team during the Forums and other meetings were guided by an awareness of the diversity of abilities, learning styles, interests, and identities; we wanted to acknowledge that range, and to ensure that all participants felt their presence validated and their contributions valued. In addition, we took specific measures to anticipate participants' needs (through questions in the registration process about special needs, and through careful listening at the event) and to meet those needs through provision of unisex bathrooms, lactation facilities, food options, and furniture arrangements. In some cases we were not able to fully meet specific needs, but feedback on the events suggests that participants did recognize and respond to the overall intention.

During her interview for this article, Cara Marta Messina reflected on one of the individual challenges she faced as a graduate student taking on an integral role in a larger grant-funded project for the first time. Messina originally believed that merely asking a few questions and providing some readings, such as the original foundational readings chosen by the grant team,[5] would

---

[5] The annotated foundational readings list created by the Design for Diversity grant team is available at https://dsg.neu.edu/research/design-for-diversity/documents/foundational-readings/.

inspire new knowledge; because of the diversity of people's experiences and backgrounds, however, everyone's attention was focused on different areas. In January 2018, for example, the grant team hosted an event for the CDG; one of the goals of the event was to bring the group together, discuss the genre and template of the "study path," and begin drafting those study paths. Messina realized that simply asking, "What do you think about this?" or "What would you do?" to this group of passionate and brilliant practitioners would yield excellent answers, but answers far too varied to create a common space in which to actually begin producing materials for the toolkit. On the other hand, providing a strict agenda might lead to a clear outcome, but not one that would reflect the values of D4D or allow for diverse expertise.

When the grant team invited Kim Christen of Washington State University to speak at the CDG event, we hoped to inspire conversations about practices actually implemented in the field, with CDG members bringing in their own knowledge and expertise instead of molding their writing around Christen's talk. As the group began writing, however, almost all their study paths revolved around Mukurtu,[6] the content management system Kim Christen had helped produce. Halfway through the first day of the event, the grant team decided to step back and try to rework the second day, focusing instead on imagining the study path genre so that it reflected CDG members' own expertise.

Messina reflected that putting together this event, and learning to be flexible, was one of her biggest challenges and one of the most important skills she learned. In the early months of working for D4D, Messina believed democratic conversations and changes would happen by merely inviting a group of diverse experts to speak and do work. The first issue associated with this is compensation for labour; marginalized people across genders, races, ethnicities, sexualities, and abilities are typically expected to put in the labour of educating others and doing the work to make changes. Thankfully, the initial grant was enough to fund and compensate for the CDG's labour. The second issue, which arose mainly after the CDG was chosen, was that changes and conversations do not just happen—the way to construct, disseminate, and inspire knowledge creation comes from creating a work plan and agenda to act as a catalyst without silencing perspectives.

---

[6] The Mukurtu content management system (http://mukurtu.org/) is "a grassroots project aiming to empower communities to manage, share, narrate, and exchange their digital heritage in culturally relevant and ethically-minded ways." See http://mukurtu.org/about/.

The in-person conversations and spaces have broken ground in shifting the theoretical frameworks and beginning to produce materials, but it has been the D4D virtual spaces in which these theoretical foundations were actually implemented. We relied on collaborative writing tools and created listservs to support communication between the grant team and the different D4D communities. The Core Design Group, particularly, has used collaborative authoring tools such as Google Docs to produce study paths and comment on each other's work. The grant team also relied on collaborative authoring and reviewing processes, circulating draft materials for review to the CDG, Critical Review Partners, and Advisory Board, revising based on their feedback, and sharing the updated draft for further review. This iterative process encouraged extensive conversation and revision.

No amount of time or energy could capture the immense wealth of knowledge and expertise the D4D grant team encountered along its journey. As grant team members constantly took steps back and assessed their relationship with the project, how they were articulating project choices to the larger community, and whether their practices reflected their theoretical and ethical foundations, there was bound to be a sense of vulnerability. Messina found some conversations difficult with respect to her own lack of knowledge in both the Information Science field and larger social and political experiences. Nevertheless, she wanted to hear from as many practitioners as possible about whose knowledge, and what materials, needed to be included by the grant team. The workflow slowed down the production of materials, challenging the grant team to allow space for diverse knowledges and expertise to flourish.

*Intertextual Networks*

The final example of social knowledge creation in which the DSG has been involved is Intertextual Networks, a three-year research project funded by a grant from the National Endowment for the Humanities (NEH) and focused on intertextuality in early women's writing. In October 2016, the Women Writers Project (WWP) began work on this initiative, assembling a team of fifteen research collaborators at various institutions. Each collaborator began pursuing a project related to intertextuality and the texts in Women Writers Online (WWO), to be published in the WWP's open access publication series, *Women Writers in Context*.[7] We have also begun identifying quotations and citations across the entire WWO collection, linking these textual references

---

[7] *Women Writers in Context* is the Women Writers Project's open access publication series: see https://wwp.northeastern.edu/context/.

to a comprehensive bibliography of sources. The connections between these strands are central to the Intertextual Networks project; we have developed processes to ensure that WWP staff, research collaborators, and the encoding team tasked with identifying and cataloguing the 6,400 titles and 12,000 quotations in the WWO collection can complete the independent aspects of their work while communicating and collaborating effectively with other members of the project.

Some very brief background may be helpful here. Women Writers Online is a collection of more than four hundred texts written, translated by, or attributed to women, primarily published in print and in English from 1526 to 1850. These texts are encoded according to the standards of the Text Encoding Initiative (TEI)[8] and published through the WWO interface.[9] The Intertextual Networks project draws on the information available in the WWO collection's encoding, such as the identification of titles and quotations with <title> and <quote> elements. We are programmatically extracting these titles and quotations, developing a bibliography of all the textual references in WWO using the TEI's provisions for bibliographic encoding, then linking each individual instance in WWO to this bibliography; in this way, for example, we can identify *A Midsummer Night's Dream*, *A Midſummer Night's Dream*, *Midsummer-night's Dream*, and *Dream* as references to the same play. We have two staff members currently focused on the day-to-day work of the project, and a team of five graduate encoders.

In developing work processes to complete this bibliographic endeavour, the Intertextual Networks team has been able to draw on the WWP's established practices for training and documentation, along with an approach to student labour that positions graduate and undergraduate encoders as equal collaborators with staff toward a shared goal. Because it is crucial that our markup remain consistent, despite the many layers of complexity at stake in bibliographic encoding for a diverse collection of early texts, we have extensive training processes, weekly meetings, and detailed documentation. Asking encoders to understand the whole system of work, rather just than the concrete tasks in front of them, takes more initial time, but also means that the work we can do is more consistent and better able to address the inherent

---

[8] Information about the Text Encoding Initiative (TEI) is available at https://tei-c. org/. For more on the basics of text encoding, see Flanders, Bauman, and Connell 2016.

[9] The Women Writers Online interface can be seen at https://wwp.northeastern.edu/ wwo/.

complexity at stake. For the Intertextual Networks project, this approach took a few specific forms: first, all the encoders on the project learned the basics of marking up texts for WWO, and encoded a short text to contextualize their primary task of locating and developing bibliographic entries for the texts referenced in WWO. We also approached all of our tool development in a collaborative spirit, with encoders and WWP staff working together to create the platforms used for different phases of bibliographic development. In allocating tasks, we prioritize skill building over exigency; as Sarah Connell said in her interview, "when a new project comes up, we don't just think about who can do it in that minute but also who could learn how to do it, so that encoders are continuously expanding the skills they can apply to our collaborative work." More broadly, we have a set of built-in processes that provide space for encoders to contribute their expertise to our shared efforts in knowledge creation, ranging from tags that allow encoders to mark individual texts as being unusual or interesting to an encoder-edited internal documentation system.

A brief example will illustrate some of these practices and their outcomes. In the second year of the project, we added a new team of encoders, one of whom, Kenneth Oravetz, joined the group as part of a research fellowship at Northeastern's NULab for Texts, Maps, and Networks, a centre for digital humanities and computational social science. The fellowship includes an independent research project, for which Oravetz decided to develop a genre taxonomy for the WWP's bibliography of referenced texts. At this point, we had reviewed all but a handful of the titles named in WWO and had developed an XML bibliography with basic publication details for those texts (title, author, publication date and location, and publisher for most, as well as translator, editor, and other information where relevant). Oravetz's project was focused on genre and the XML bibliography, but we asked him to encode a short text of his own and to meet regularly with the rest of the Intertextual Networks and WWO encoding teams, so that his work would be connected with and informed by the rest of the work we were doing.

Student meetings at the WWP are typically devoted to discussing the questions our encoders bring in from their work, so it was entirely typical that Oravetz said he had a few questions at the start of one meeting several weeks after he had begun labelling the genres of texts in the bibliography. Once we began working through his questions, however, it was clear that many were not focused solely on the genre project,[10] but instead were engaging

---

[10] For example, questions focused on genre included how best to tag a possibly satirical

substantively with the bibliography itself. Oravetz had located publication details for several texts that previous encoders had been unable to find; he flagged several minor inconsistencies in the ways we were handling publication locations; and he even identified a handful of cases in which we needed to discuss making changes to the encoding in the WWO collection—interventions that he was able to make because he was familiar with WWO encoding and with our ongoing conversations about bibliographic development. The observations that Oravetz made throughout his genre-identification project were invaluable in the extensive review that we conducted a short time later when we had finished identifying the remainder of the titles. As this instance indicates, the knowledge that we create at the WWP is necessarily social because projects like Intertextual Networks would not be possible without the involvement of multiple well-informed collaborators who possess a deep understanding of the project's goals and infrastructures.

As this example also suggests, the processes we have built for our bibliographic development are multilayered and complex. Our tools are designed to shift as the work we do shifts—and, at every point in this ongoing tool development, WWP staff have collaborated closely with the encoders who use these processes. At the start of the bibliography project, we extracted the contents of the 6,400 <title> elements in WWO and performed some regularization to account for minor variations in spelling and punctuation. This allowed us to determine that we had 1,400 distinct references to titles that appeared more than once and/or within citations. Because we were working to identify more than a thousand references, representing the contents of approximately 4,500 <title> elements,[11] we needed a work process that allowed encoders to efficiently enter information in a shared workspace. In this phase, Google Sheets worked well for basic textual entries, with an XML bibliography for the more complex cases, such as translations and periodicals.

We devoted significant time in our first few meetings to discussing the spreadsheet and the XML bibliography, working together to refine our uses of these. We adopted colour coding as a basic work-tracking mechanism during one of the initial meetings; we also added several new columns for information that encoders were encountering in their work and that we had

---

occult reference text, and whether or not we could identify a text that we had not been able to locate as a play, based on the fact that all of the other texts listed in the same advertisement were dramas.

[11] As these figures indicate, a great many titles in the WWO collection are referenced multiple times.

not initially anticipated. We took a similar approach in the second phase of bibliographic development, which covered the 1,800 titles that were named only once and without any citation information. Because additional context from around the title references tended to be more necessary in identifying them, and because we had at that point tested our data modelling and information gathering practices to the point that these were much more stable, we decided to shift to a web interface that allows encoders to focus on adding information for one text at a time, with dropdowns, text entry fields, checkboxes, and other web-based mechanisms for entering the information that we had been collecting in the spreadsheet.

The tools that we use for social knowledge creation at the WWP are designed to be highly responsive to changing work environments, which requires us to set aside time for incremental adjustments and adaptations—and also means that we must have very detailed documentation and occasionally need to review and update the data we are producing. For instance, we added checkboxes to flag duplicate entries, entries complex enough to require handling with the XML bibliography, and cases in which encoding interventions would be needed in the WWO textbase itself. In this phase, we also adjusted our processes based on input from the encoders, such as when we added a flag that encoders could use to mark individual texts as being particularly noteworthy, to make it easier to retrieve these in future research and publications on the project. We also added flags for encoders to mark texts they had questions about, along with a sorting feature on the main list of texts, to make it easier to review and discuss all of the encoders' questions during our weekly meetings. As noted above, there are substantial costs in time and other resources to this approach, but knowledge creation at this scale and complexity demands these types of intensively responsive and collaboratively refined processes.

We have recently completed another phase of the project by linking entries for all the titles named in WWO to the individual <title> elements in the textbase. For this phase, we shifted tools again, moving fully into the XML bibliography for proofing and deduplication. As part of this review— and as we have done at all the transitional points in this project—we also paused to take stock of where we might need to make adjustments to our processes. This equally reflexive and responsive approach, while admittedly very resource-intensive, is necessary because the project we have taken on is a difficult one. The TEI has extensive provisions for encoding information about texts, but developing detailed and consistent bibliographies is challenging, especially when working from texts that were published well before citation practices were standardized in any way. Despite the wealth of information now available online, we have also struggled with finding any records at all for many of the texts referenced in WWO. And the sheer numbers have made our work a challenge: with a bibliography of more than 3,200 entries cataloguing approximately 3,800 individual biblical references, and 6,400 titles named across a generically diverse collection of more than 400 texts from a period of over 300 years, maintaining consistency is no small task. However, approaching our bibliographic development as a practice of social knowledge creation by a team of equally involved collaborators with complementary—and continuously expanding—levels of expertise has helped us to address the inherent difficulty in this project.

Our collaborative work processes have also helped to mitigate some staffing challenges we have faced; in the first year of the project, one of our two encoders graduated at the end of the year, causing inevitable disruption in our progress. In the next year, we hired four graduate encoders, which meant that most of the students on the project during the second year were relatively new to our work. We were able to navigate this transition fairly smoothly, however, because Lara Rose—the encoder who remained on the team after the first year of the project—took on a leadership role in training the new students. Rose also made substantive additions to our internal documentation, and has become the encoding team's mentor and first point of contact when questions come up or when students need to learn how to handle more complex bibliographic cases. Rose was well equipped to take on this role because she is a motivated scholar with extensive experience in using XML for literary analysis—but also because she has been working at the WWP for several years in an environment that prioritizes building encoders' skills and supporting their collaboration in every aspect of our shared work. Fostering this kind of environment for social knowledge creation requires considerable—and continuous—attention, thought, and effort, but the work that the WWP does would not be possible without it.

### Conclusions

What these case studies illustrate is how important forms of knowledge creation can result not only from the pursuit of research intentions, but also from interactions that might seem incidental to those intentions, such as the conduct of training activities or the structure of a classroom encounter. As a result, the structure of those interactions matters a great deal and requires its own attention to design. Cara Marta Messina's analysis of the Design for Diversity project describes how the iterative processes of conversation, review, negotiation, and revision were instrumental in producing a more inclusive and fully realized plan for the project. This process was informed by what Moya Bailey has called the "ethics of pace": a research process that includes explicit allowance for what look like false starts or cyclic processes of self-examination. Similarly, Sarah Connell's account of the WWP shows how it operates as a space for producing competent teams that are well-practised and comfortable at processes of learning and decision-making, a form of social knowledge creation that is foundational to the project's more visible research activities. Sarah Payne's description of CERES in the classroom illustrates how the positioning of the tool, the teacher, the consultant, and the class affects how learning takes place through social processes.

The "social knowledge" that is so important to projects such as these is not only a product or outcome, but also an architectural principle with four crucial points. First, the work of social knowledge creation is strongly relational, based on interdependence and sustained interaction. Second, it is because of this relationality that while individual participants are not interchangeable, they are also not indispensable in a social knowledge workspace because of the ways in which knowledge is shared and used within the collaborative group. Third, documentation plays a crucial role in supporting both persistence and accumulation of shared knowledge, which can serve as a principle of intellectual continuity as individual members come and go, making such workspaces more resilient despite regular changes in staff (as is typical for organizations in which students play a key role). Finally, the habits of social knowledge praxis are an important part of the professional acculturation that students and staff take with them to other organizations.

Several practical lessons have emerged from the projects described in these case studies. For one thing, social knowledge creation requires iteration and patience so as to avoid premature closure. While a more conventional work practice might use structures of delegation ("downward") and reviewing/ approval ("upward") to produce outcomes efficiently, social knowledge creation as described here uses horizontal and networked structures ("outward" or "across") to iteratively contribute to and revise outcomes based on consensus. These are time- and resource-intensive practices that require not only the ethical pacing described above, but also an extra investment in mentorship, documentation, and the establishment of a culture of trust. Furthermore, organizing projects around social knowledge creation also entails a different approach to the division of responsibility. While it is typical in information technology organizations to centralize and specialize technical expertise and responsibility, these projects support social knowledge creation by sharing both technical knowledge and responsibility across levels of seniority and roles (including students, staff, and faculty) and establishing spaces of authority for each participant (as illustrated, for instance, in the CERES classroom example). This diversification of responsibility in turn depends on a stronger investment in the mutually reinforcing activities of training, mentorship, documentation, and the development of tools and systems that invite meaningful intervention at multiple levels of expertise. These investments are significant, but they carry important benefits in addition to the work of social knowledge creation: stability, sustainability, consistency and quality of work, flexibility in collaboration, potential for broader and easier uptake of tools, and greater intelligibility of research output through supporting documentation.

All of these practices depend on trust, and these case studies have illustrated in practical terms the specific measures undertaken here to establish working environments characterized by trust. It may be helpful here, however, to pay closer attention to some specific modes and practices of trust, to highlight that trust-building is not just a generalized social aim ("we should trust each other!") but a process carried out through specific decisions and actions. Some of these trust activities entail delegation or diminution of one's own role to allow others a more significant role: for instance, trusting someone to accomplish an essential task, trusting someone to represent your views or interests, trusting someone to act on behalf of the group. We might term this "transitive trust"—the willingness to allow someone else to occupy a role of competency or action that we would normally prefer to occupy ourselves.

When the WWP empowers its graduate students to write documentation, this delegation requires the full-time staff to set aside anxiety about possible errors or inefficiencies, and trust both that the training process has equipped students to do a good job and that the students are equally invested in the results and will know when to seek help. This trust is an important aspect of mentorship because it declines to infantilize the students by over-supervising them. Other kinds of trust activities involve trusting others' intentions, candour, or good will (and demonstrating the same in return): for instance, acknowledging mistakes, avoiding assumptions of ulteriority, being thoughtful in the presence of vulnerability. These actions are essential in creating a collaborative environment where energy is not wasted being on guard, and where participants feel comfortable taking risks, resulting in more imaginative work and a happier working environment. We might term this "ethical trust" or "compassionate trust" in that it is founded on an assumption of shared ethical and compassionate action and intentions within the group.

All of these forms of trust operate multidirectionally—"up," "down," and "sideways" within organizational hierarchies—and when they are working well, they tend to diminish the tendency of those hierarchies to stratify and separate roles and work activities.

We conclude with a few final reflections on how these practices of social knowledge creation put some of the central value terms of digital humanities into a different light. If we test our collaborative practices against the goals articulated here, we find that many common forms of collaboration—although certainly "social" in some sense—operate in ways that leave the individual participants unaltered, such that although the collaborative product (a book, article, project, event) is a form of social knowledge, the collaborative group itself is not. The best outcomes, in the projects described above, resulted from much greater degrees of interdependency, and required an element of vulnerability from the participants that was deeply challenging and often difficult to learn. These more intense collaborative formations also put pressure on the concept of expertise and its role in establishing systems of authority, responsibility, and accountability. Individual expertise, whether in the form of domain knowledge, technical competence, or practical experience, does not have a simple or direct impact on the social knowledge creation within the group: it must be successfully transmitted, negotiated, consumed, and disseminated so that it can be used by the group rather than remaining available only to individual members. Expertise still has a role to play, but as an enrichment to the learning and working environment rather than as a mark of authority or personal distinction. As a result, the establishment of the social knowledge creation *environment* as a working space structured around trust and shared responsibility is critical in enabling expertise to play a positive role, and to avoid having expertise function solely as a marker of power and authority differentiation. When present and future scholars, administrators, and practitioners are taught how to create such working spaces, these environments have the potential for a transformative effect on the academy.

The Intertextual Networks project has been made possible in part by a major grant from the National Endowment for the Humanities: Exploring the human endeavor. The Design for Diversity project was made possible in part by the Institute of Museum and Library Services. The views, findings, conclusions or recommendations expressed in this article do not necessarily represent those of the National Endowment for the Humanities or the Institute of Museum and Library Services.

WORKS CITED

Arbuckle, Alyssa, Aaron Mauro, and Daniel Powell, eds. 2017. *Social Knowledge Creation in the Humanities: Volume 1*. Toronto: Iter Press; Tempe: Arizona Center for Medieval and Renaissance Studies.

Bailey, Moya. 2015. "#transform(ing)DH Writing and Research: An Autoethnography of Digital Humanities and Feminist Ethics." *Digital Humanities Quarterly* 9(2). http://www.digitalhumanities.org/dhq/vol/9/2/000209/000209.html.

Caswell, Michelle. 2014. "Seeing Yourself in History: Community Archives and the Fight Against Symbolic Annihilation." *The Public Historian* 36(4): 26–37. http://tph.ucpress.edu/content/36/4/26.

Flanders, Julia, Syd Bauman, and Sarah Connell. 2016. "Text Encoding." In *Doing Digital Humanities: Practice, Training, Research*, edited by Constance Crompton, Richard J. Lane, and Ray Siemens, 104–22. London and New York: Routledge.

hooks, bell. 2000. *Feminist Theory: From Margin to Center*. 2nd ed. Cambridge, MA: South End Press.

Maron, Nancy L., and Sarah Pickle. 2014. "Sustaining the Digital Humanities: Host Institution Support Beyond the Start-up Phase." *Ithaka S+R*, June 18. https://sr.ithaka.org/wp-content/uploads/2015/08/SR_Supporting_Digital_Humanities_20140618f.pdf.

McPherson, Tara. 2012. "Why Are the Digital Humanities So White? Or Thinking the Histories of Race and Computation." In *Debates in the Digital Humanities*, edited by Matthew K Gold, 139–60. Minneapolis: University of Minnesota Press. http://dhdebates.gc.cuny.edu/debates/text/29.

Zorich, Diane M. 2008. "A Survey of Digital Humanities Centers in the United States." CLIR Publication No. 143. Washington, DC: Council on Library and Information Resources. https://www.clir.org/wp-content/uploads/sites/6/pub143.pdf.

# Open Social Scholarship Annotated Bibliography

Randa El Khatib, Lindsey Seatter, Tracey El Hajj, and Conrad Leibel, with Alyssa Arbuckle, Ray Siemens, Caroline Winter, and the ETCL and INKE Research Groups

Electronic Textual Cultures Lab, University of Victoria

Corresponding Author: Lindsey Seatter

**Abstract**: This annotated bibliography responds to and contextualizes the growing 'Open' movements and recent institutional reorientation toward social, public-facing scholarship. The aim of this document is to present a working definition of open social scholarship through the aggregation and summation of critical resources in the field. Our work surveys foundational publications, innovative research projects, and global organizations that enact the theories and practices of open social scholarship. The bibliography builds on the knowledge creation principles outlined in previous research by broadening the focus beyond conventional academic spaces and reinvigorating central, defining themes with recently published research.

**Keywords**: community; open; scholarship; social; technology

The bibliography is reprinted with permission of *KULA: Knowledge Creation, Dissemination, and Preservation Studies.*

ISBN 978-1-64959-008-4 (paper) ISBN 978-1-64959-009-1 (pdf) ISBN 978-1-64959-084-8 (epub)
*New Technologies in Medieval and Renaissance Studies 8 (2022) 245–510*

# Contents

# Introduction: Open Social Scholarship, Theory and Practice

In his monograph *A Social History of Knowledge* (2000), Peter Burke defends the sociality of knowledge by conducting a systematic look at knowledge production from the early modern period until today. Burke argues that knowledge is always plural, and demonstrates this multiplicity by exploring knowledge production in religious, scholarly, and governmental institutions. Similarly, in *The Nature of the Book* (1998), Adrian Johns uncovers the social history of print by drawing attention to the various, often unseen labours of knowledge construction. Like Burke, Johns argues that there is no singular stream of print culture, but rather that such knowledge is defined by its wide-ranging influences and manifold features. Where Johns focuses on print culture, Christine Borgman examines the digital turn in *Scholarship in the Digital Age: Information, Infrastructure, and the Internet* (2007). Despite a shift in medium, Borgman echoes Johns in her assertion that the inherent social elements of scholarship continue to endure. The persevering social qualities of knowledge—over both time and place—are highlighted by each of these seminal works. As Burke, Johns, Borgman, and others suggest, knowledge persists beyond the borders of the university and has the ability to negotiate diverse spaces, institutions, and communities.

These central tenets of sociality and openness ground open social scholarship as a concept. Open social scholarship enables the creation, dissemination, and engagement of research by specialists and non-specialists in accessible and significant ways. Because the production of knowledge does not occur solely in standard academic spaces, such as university classrooms or institutional libraries, knowledge dissemination must be comprehensive and public facing. By placing an emphasis on community-driven initiatives, open social scholarship highlights outreach and partnerships in an attempt to bridge the gap between the practices of the university and the goals of the community.

Over the last few years, the importance of open social scholarship within higher education institutions and aligned research groups has become clear. From 2014 to 2018 the Implementing New Knowledge Environments (INKE; https://inke.ca) Partnership hosted gatherings for international scholars curated around ideas of open knowledge models, scholarly partnerships, and new modes of production in the university. The proceedings from the 2014, 2015, and 2016 conferences were published in the journal *Scholarly and Research Communication*, and the 2017 proceedings are also forthcoming in *KULA:*

*Knowledge Creation, Dissemination, and Preservation Studies*. These proceedings address topics related to open, digital scholarship: partnerships, prototypes, creativity, implementation, interfaces, audience, initiatives, and sustainability. The forward-facing, networked knowledge production discussed in these collections—by scholars including John Maxwell, Ray Siemens, Susan Brown, and Constance Crompton—is also reflected in this bibliography.

In order to encompass the broad field of open knowledge production and circulation, this bibliography extends its focus beyond academic contexts to the multifarious manifestations of community-based research, including citizen science and citizen-scholar projects. Projects are documented in this bibliography as examples of how academic researchers can benefit from partnering with active citizen scholars, such as the large crowdsourced initiative *Transcribe Bentham* and the Canadian-based *Linked Modernisms* (Causer and Terras 2014; Ross, Christie and Sayers 2014). The increasingly popular citizen science and citizen scholarship movements draw attention to research partially or wholly conducted by non-experts, typically volunteers who receive the training necessary to collect and interpret data for a specific research purpose. Many of the resources included in this bibliography address the challenges of public scholarship and use case studies to explore how to develop an ethical, collaborative, and dialogic university-community partnership (Cantor and Lavine 2006; Silka and Renault-Caragianes 2007).

This bibliography also considers the role of open knowledge and technology in community partnerships and global activism. The advent of digital technology has created unprecedented opportunities to mobilize crowds and rapidly share information with a wide, public audience. The effect of these technological advancements can be recognized in a number of notable movements, such as Black Lives Matter and #MeToo. The growth of cyberactivism and use of online tools, such as Twitter, in social protest has had a significant impact on promoting political activism, mobilizing certain portions of society, and enhancing dissemination potentials for activist causes (Sandoval-Almazan and Gil-Garcia 2014). Online platforms provide an opportunity to make social justice movements more visible, and the merging of social justice initatives with online technologies has made knowledge more dynamic. This bibliography considers how technologies facilitate knowledge management and mobilization, as well as how specialized research can play an active role in burgeoning global justice movements.

## Intent and History of the Bibliography

The 'Open Social Scholarship Annotated Bibliography' was compiled in 2015–2016 by a collaborative team at the Electronic Textual Cultures Lab (ETCL).[1] This document was inspired by two previous annotated bibliographies authored by ETCL members in collaboration with the INKE Research Group: the initial 'Social Knowledge Creation: Three Annotated Bibliographies' (Arbuckle et al. 2014) and an updated version, 'An Annotated Bibliography of Social Knowledge Creation' (Arbuckle et al. 2017). The 2014 publication provided a snapshot of contemporary scholarship, initiatives, and research technologies related to social knowledge creation. The later iteration of the bibliography updated the materials with publications authored between 2013 and 2016 and expanded its scope by including resources on crowdsourcing, open access, public humanities, digital publishing, and collaborative games. The 2017 bibliography also provided a definition of social knowledge creation: 'acts of collaboration in order to engage in or produce shared cultural data and/or knowledge products' (Arbuckle et al. 2017, 29). This bibliography builds further on the research collected in these two surveys by updating and adding recently published materials on common topics, including crowdsourcing, the history of knowledge production, and the 'Open' movements. Additionally, this bibliography collates several entirely new sections that demonstrate the broader, more outward-facing focus of this document, including 'Community Engagement' and 'Action and Activism.' Given the overlap in subjects, theories, and practices between 'An Annotated Bibliography of Social Knowledge Creation' and the 'Open Social Scholarship Annotated Bibliography,' replicated entries have been marked with a cross symbol (+). This bibliography aims to capture a particular moment in the open social scholarship movement. Since its compilation, the field has shifted and expanded. As such, this bibliography is necessarily not exhaustive, and future iterations would benefit from an even wider scope that includes additional and even more diverse open social scholarship resources. In particular, this material could be expanded to include literature on open social scholarship

---

[1] The Electronic Textual Cultures Lab (ETCL) is a research lab at the University of Victoria, Victoria, Canada, directed by Dr. Ray Siemens. It serves as an intellectual hub for about 20 local faculty, staff, students, and visiting scholars. Through a series of highly collaborative relationships, the ETCL's international community comprises more than 300 researchers. The ETCL welcomes more than 800 students per year through their organization of the annual Digital Humanities Summer Institute (DHSI) and INKE.

in minority communities, which has grown in prominence since this document's conception.

The authors of the 'Open Social Scholarship Annotated Bibliography' enacted social knowledge creation practices in the assemblage of this bibliography by collaboratively setting the intellectual direction of the work, compiling resources, and annotating them. Research was carried out on platforms that facilitate collaborative research, including Google Drive (https://www.google.com/drive/) and Zotero (https://www.zotero.org/). As scholarship in this area is being rapidly and continually produced, it is important to note that this bibliography is a snapshot of the topics covered, not an exhaustive list. Some resources belong to more than one delineated category, in which case duplicated entries have been marked with two asterisks (**) after their first appearance.

The intention of this document is to present a working definition of open social scholarship through the aggregation and summation of critical resources in the field. As the environmental scan demonstrates, open knowledge practices date back hundreds of years. The exchange of scholarly information can be observed in the publication of historical journals, the development of public libraries, and, contemporarily, through access to online resources and the various 'Open' movements: Open Access, Open Source, Open Education, and Open Data. The iterative dialogue between academic, alternative-academic, and community-based audiences is central to the principles of open social scholarship. For this reason, the bibliography pays particular attention to models for university-community partnerships through crowdsourcing or other forms of collaboration. Further, this bibliography demonstrates that open social scholarship practices are not only present in institutional, formal scholarship but also manifest increasingly in grassroots social movements. The objectives of this bibliography are to draw together various examples of knowledge output and to highlight their points of intersection.

*Section I. Forms of Open Knowledge*

The 'Forms of Open Knowledge' section addresses the circulation of open knowledge in digital and non-digital environments. The entries in this section are divided into categories that showcase different forms of knowledge creation and dissemination, including historical instances of open knowledge, major shifts in knowledge production in the Western world, and contemporary manifestations of knowledge creation in the digital medium. Included authors share the conviction that access to knowledge is a universal human right. Resources in this category tie some of the early instances of open knowledge to the development of public libraries. Other, more contemporary forms of open knowledge are explored in the context of scholarly communication, as well as open access and open source movements beyond academia. The infrastructure of these movements has been built through the commitment of organizations such as the European Organization for Nuclear Research (CERN, responsible for the open protocols of the Internet) and the Free Software Movement (defense for the stability of open structures). A general increase in access to knowledge on a global scale is one of the defining characteristics that distinguishes the contemporary world from that of previous generations (Kelty 2008).

The majority of the 163 entries in this section were published after 2000; each of the five categories showcase between 12 to 48 annotations:

1. Forms of Open Knowledge and their History
2. New Modes of Scholarly Communication
3. Open Access
4. Open Source
5. Open Data

Some of the key historical moments in the formation and cementing of open knowledge are addressed in the 'Forms of Open Knowledge and their History' category, including the development of the public library system in the Western world; the switch to journals from private letters as a means of sharing knowledge; and the rise of the philosophy of public access in seventeenth-, eighteenth-, and nineteenth-century institutions. The second category, 'New Modes of Scholarly Communication,' traces the evolution of scholarly communication with the advent of the digital age, focusing on the means by which knowledge is produced and disseminated as a result of open access culture. 'Open Access' is the movement and practice addressed in the third category, which aligns itself with the ideology that knowledge is a human right and should be accessible to anyone with Internet access. This position is justified by authors who offer practical paths for successfully implementing open access in a capitalist society. By collating resources related to the umbrella term 'Open Source,' the fourth category generally refers to the practice of openly sharing, modifying, and reusing software code. Initiatives such as the Free Software Movement and the Open Source Movement have played an important role in the current structure of the Internet and continue to be prominent voices defending the interest of users in contemporary debates about the accessibility of the Web (Kelty 2008). This category also includes the development of Open Source programming, from its origins in Linux and Apache to its potential for collaborative software development (Godfrey and Tu 2000; Hars and Ou 2001; Lerner and Tirole 2002). Resources range from the theoretical to the technical to the political. The fifth and final category, 'Open Data,' includes resources that debate making research data publicly available and usable. This category also explores the motivations for institutions and researchers to openly publish, or refrain from publishing, their data (Murray-Rust 2008; Piwowar and Vision 2013).

*Section II. Community-Based and Collaborative Forms of Open Knowledge*

This section addresses collaborative forms of knowledge production in contemporary society and the ubiquity and accessibility of digital tools that facilitate knowledge production. Instead of focusing on collaborations within field-specific or academic contexts, publications in this section focus on interdisciplinary collaborations, on university–community collaborations, and on knowledge production by citizens not affiliated with universities, including crowdsourcing, citizen science, and citizen scholarship. These modes of research have drastically expanded the scope of questions that can be asked. Although the steepest increase in citizen science is seen in the social sciences, it contributes to other disciplines as well. The Cornell Lab of Ornithology (CLO), for example, focuses on environmental studies projects and has been practicing citizen science for more than twenty years. The CLO has thousands of participants gathering tens of millions of observations each year, demonstrating the power of crowdsourcing and the impact of nonacademic participants on research projects. In their article "Citizen Science: A Developing Tool for Expanding Science Knowledge and Scientific Literacy," CLO researchers provide a model for setting up a successful citizen science project (Bonney et al. 2009). While the article evinces that open social knowledge was being practised long before the digital age, its focus is on how open knowledge is currently practised and systematized. For example, many funding agencies require research organizations and individuals to have a public-facing element to their projects. This can be enacted in multiple ways, such as having community members involved in the project (through citizen science or crowdsourcing) or by openly publishing the data and results.

The 123 entries in this section are divided into five categories with between 12 and 50 annotations each:

1. Community Engagement
2. Citizen Science

3. Crowdsourcing
4. Collaborative Scholarship
5. Groups/Initiatives/Organizations Discussing Open Social Scholarship

The 'Community Engagement' category focuses on university representatives who are invested in creating and maintaining partnerships with community members, often in the form of goal-oriented projects that benefit the broader society. Resources in this section detail the benefits of these partnerships—both for the university and the community—as well as challenges that may arise during this collaboration and how to overcome them. In order to ensure that working with outside groups is professionally rewarding, authors argue that university administrations need to formally recognize university–community partnerships. A number of resources also discuss the role of technology in community engagement and collaboration. The 'Citizen Science' category includes research initiatives that are partially or wholly conducted by nonscientists, in most cases by volunteers who receive the necessary training to collect and interpret data for a targeted research investigation. The authors generally argue that the rise of citizen science is due to advances in technology that allow the collection of data by non-professionals. Another factor is that funding agencies are increasingly seeking the public's approval of scientific research endeavours, since taxpayer dollars often fund these initiatives. Moreover, authors unanimously agree that, if done properly, citizen science can go a long way in educating the public, supporting scientific research, and improving the ecological environment through targeted nature-based research. The third category, 'Crowdsourcing,' refers to projects built on information gathered by large groups of individuals through digital means. Crowdsourced data is quickly becoming a common element of many academic projects. The resources collected in this category define crowdsourcing and offer a rich depiction of existing crowdsourcing practices, as well as suggestions for optimal implementation. The 'Collaborative Scholarship' category addresses the rise of disciplinary and interdisciplinary research partnerships. An extended study of collaboration throughout the life cycle of the seven-year INKE project is communicated through a series of articles that explore how this collective evolved over time and offer advice about how to develop and maintain productive team relationships, how to effectively integrate new team members into a project, and how to deal with unexpected challenges that may arise in collaborative environments (Siemens 2012a, 2012b, 2013, 2014, 2015, 2016). Overall, this category serves as a solid starting point for those preparing to launch collaborative projects. Finally, the 'Groups/Initiatives/Organizations

Discussing Open Social Scholarship' category catalogues those who are currently active and engaging with open social scholarship. Advocacy for open access to information is the most dominant trend among the groups listed.

*Section III. Knowledge in Action*

Resources in this category investigate how knowledge is mobilized and implemented in real-world settings. Instead of defining knowledge as static—something that sits on shelves and in machines—authors in this category trace the dynamism of knowledge and how it is made useful to others. This focus can also be seen as a shift away from overly specialized niches of knowledge to a more practical approach that investigates to what end knowledge is created and to what extent it is utilized. This section also addresses and assesses the impact of technology on society at large, including the public voice in political movements and decisions. It explores how technology facilitates communication and mobilizes crowds—both virtually and in real life—to partake in various actions and activist movements. The role of technology and open knowledge in facilitating social justice in various scenarios is also addressed.

The 76 entries in this section are divided into five categories with between 9 and 24 annotations each:

1. Knowledge Mobilization
2. Data Management
3. Prototyping
4. Social Justice and Open Knowledge Facilitated by Technology
5. Action and Activism

The 'Knowledge Mobilization' category includes works that reference the dissemination of research output, as well as knowledge engagement by groups outside of the pertaining research team. Notably, Colin R. Anderson and Stéphane M. McLachlan advocate for knowledge mobilization as a practice that opposes the models of knowledge transfer that often reign in academic environments and manifest a hierarchical transmission of knowledge (2015). This top-down structure is challenged by giving voice to typically marginalized groups—mostly those outside of academia—by establishing productive channels of communication (Anderson and McLachlan 2015). Authors in this category acknowledge the value of implementing knowledge mobilization strategies and delve into possibilities, problems, and solutions, using concrete examples that employ a variety of theoretical frameworks. The 'Data Management' category hones in on effective methods for organizing data and documents through the application of systematic mechanisms. Collected and annotated resources in this category address metadata and database management, as well as data visualization. Overall, the core foci of this section are data life cycles, infrastructural mechanisms, and effective governance of digital information. Scholarly prototyping, a field that has proliferated over the last two decades, is addressed in the 'Prototyping' category. By experimenting with conventional forms of scholarly communication, the research prototypes in this category offer alternative modes of production, presentation, and dissemination that are supported by the digital medium. Although they have different end goals, all the prototypes in this category are experimental and innovative in their respective fields. The 'Social Justice and Open Knowledge Facilitated by Technology' category engages with the effects of the digital medium on social justice operations. Authors argue that open knowledge is a tool for social justice and demonstrate how it can advance diverse scholarly fields, as well as society more generally. Overall, this category explores the various technologies and approaches that enable the development of open knowledge and social justice. Finally, the 'Action and Activism' category describes how digital media impact the scope, outreach, and visibility of activist groups and movements.

## Reference List

Anderson, Colin R., and Stéphane M. McLachlan. 2015. "Transformative Research as Knowledge Mobilization: Transmedia, Bridges, and Layers." *Action Research* 14(3): 295–317. DOI: https://doi.org/10.1177/1476750315616684.

Arbuckle, Alyssa, Nina Belojevic, Tracey El Hajj, Randa El Khatib, Lindsey Seatter, and Raymond G. Siemens, with Alex Christie, Matthew Hiebert, Jon Saklofske, Jentery Sayers, Derek Siemens, Shaun Wong, and the INKE and ETCL Research Groups. 2017. "An Annotated Bibliography of Social Knowledge Creation." In *Social Knowledge Creation in the Humanities*, edited by Alyssa Arbuckle, Aaron Mauro, and Daniel Powell, 29–264. Toronto: Iter Press; Tempe: Arizona Center for Medieval and Renaissance Studies.

Arbuckle, Alyssa, Nina Belojevic, Matthew Hiebert, and Ray Siemens, with Shaun Wong, Derek Siemens, Alex Christie, Jon Saklofske, Jentery Sayers, and the INKE and ETCL Research Groups. 2014. "Social Knowledge Creation: Three Annotated Bibliographies." *Scholarly and Research Communication* 5(2): n.p. DOI: https://doi.org/10.22230/src.2014v5n2a150.

Arbuckle, Alyssa, Alex Christie, Lynne Siemens, Aaron Mauro, and the INKE Research Group, eds. 2016. Special issue. *Scholarly and Research Communication* 7(2/3): n.p. http://src-online.ca/index.php/src/issue/view/24.

Bonney, Rick, Caren B. Cooper, Janis Dickinson, Steve Kelling, Tina Phillips, Kenneth V. Rosenberg, and Jennifer Shirk. 2009. "Citizen Science: A Developing Tool for Expanding Science Knowledge and Scientific Literacy." *BioScience* 59(11): 977–84. DOI: http://dx.doi.org/10.1525/bio.2009.59.11.9.

Borgman, Christine L. 2007. *Scholarship in the Digital Age: Information, Infrastructure, and the Internet.* Cambridge, MA: MIT Press.

Burke, Peter. 2000. *A Social History of Knowledge: From Gutenberg to Diderot.* Cambridge: Polity Press.

Cantor, Nancy, and Steven D. Lavine. 2006. "Taking Public Scholarship Seriously." *Chronicle of Higher Education* 52(40): B20. https://www.chronicle.com/article/Taking-Public-Scholarship/22684.

Causer, Tim, and Melissa Terras. 2014. "Crowdsourcing Bentham: Beyond the Traditional Boundaries of Academic History." *International Journal of Humanities and Arts Computing* 8(1): 46–64. DOI: http://dx.doi.org/10.3366/ijhac.2014.0119.

Godfrey, Michael W., and Qiang Tu. 2000. "Evolution in Open Source Software: A Case Study." In *Proceedings of the International Conference on Software Maintenance (ICSM'00)*, 131–42. Washington, DC: IEEE Computer Society. http://svn-plg.uwaterloo.ca/~migod/papers/2000/icsm00.pdf.

Hars, Alexander, and Shaosong Ou. 2001. "Working for Free?—Motivations of Participating in Open Source Projects." In *Proceedings of the 34th Annual Hawaii International Conference on System Sciences (HICSS '01)*, 7014. Washington, DC: IEEE Computer Society.

Johns, Adrian. 1998. *The Nature of the Book: Print and Knowledge in the Making.* Chicago: University of Chicago Press.

Kelty, Christopher M. 2008. *Two Bits: The Cultural Significance of Free Software.* Durham, NC: Duke University Press.

Lerner, Josh, and Jean Tirole. 2002. "Some Simple Economics of Open Source." *The Journal of Industrial Economics* 50(2): 197–234. DOI: https://doi.org/10.1111/1467-6451.00174.

Murray-Rust, Peter. 2008. "Open Data in Science." *Serials Review* 34(1): 52–64. http://www.tandfonline.com/doi/abs/10.1080/00987913.2008.10765152.

Piwowar, Heather A., and Todd J. Vision. 2013. "Data Reuse and the Open Data Citation Advantage." *PeerJ* 1:e175. DOI: https://doi.org/10.7717/peerj.175.

Ross, Stephen, Alex Christie, and Jentery Sayers. 2014. "Expert/Crowd-Sourcing for the *Linked Modernisms Project*." *Scholarly and Research Communication* 5(4): n.p. DOI: https://doi.org/10.22230/src.2014v5n4a186.

Sandoval-Almazan, Rodrigo, and J. Ramon Gil-Garcia. 2014. "Towards Cyberactivism 2.0? Understanding the Use of Social Media and Other Information Technologies for Political Activism and Social Movements." *Government Information Quarterly* 31(3): 365–78. http://doi.org/10.1016/j.giq.2013.10.016.

Siemens, Lynne. 2012a. "Understanding Long-Term Collaboration: Reflections on Year 1 and Before." *Scholarly and Research Communication* 3(1): n.p. DOI: https://doi.org/10.22230/src.2012v3n1a48.

———. 2012b. "Firing on All Cylinders: Progress and Transition in INKE's Year 2." *Scholarly and Research Communication* 3(4): n.p. DOI: https://doi.org/10.22230/src.2012v3n4a72.

———. 2013. "Responding to Change and Transition in INKE's Year Three." *Scholarly and Research Communication* 4(3): n.p. DOI: https://doi.org/10.22230/src.2013v4n3a115.

———. 2014. "Research Collaboration as 'Layers of Engagement': INKE in Year Four." *Scholarly and Research Communication* 5(4): n.p. DOI: https://doi.org/10.22230/src.2014v5n4a181.

———. 2015. "'INKE-cubating' Research Networks, Projects, and Partnerships: Reflections on INKE's Fifth Year." *Scholarly and Research Communication* 6(4): n.p. DOI: https://doi.org/10.22230/src.2015v6n4a198.

———. 2016. "'Faster Alone, Further Together': Reflections on INKE's Year Six." *Scholarly and Research Communication* 7(2/3): n.p. DOI: https://doi.org/10.22230/src.2016v7n2/3a250.

Silka, Linda, and Paulette Renault-Caragianes. 2007. "Community-University Research Partnerships: Devising a Model for Ethical Engagement." *Journal of Higher Education Outreach and Engagement* 11(2): 171–83.

# I. Forms of Open Knowledge

## 1. Forms of Open Knowledge and Their History

Many institutions have historically privileged the open circulation of knowledge. The resources in this category include historiographical accounts of the development of the public library system in the Western world, with a particular focus on the United Kingdom and the United States (Besser 2004; Hamlyn 1946; Harris 1999; Jordan 2015; Kelly 1966, 1973). Historically, it was the *Philosophical Transactions* (1665), the world's oldest and longest running scientific journal, that pioneered the debates and arguments involved in the decision of making privately circulated knowledge accessible to a public predominantly interested in partaking in this knowledge acquisition (Willinsky 2006b). Resources detail the rise of the philosophy of public access in seventeenth-, eighteenth-, and nineteenth-century institutions. Open knowledge is a historically based value system with a long tradition (Hamlyn 1946), and the historical publications included exemplify how knowledge was discussed and debated through publication. A number of the resources were written in response to previous research or as a means of summarizing an ongoing debate, thereby emphasizing the conversational foundations of the publications. Overall, this category demonstrates a strong British and American commitment to circulating knowledge products broadly (Besser 2004).

### A. Annotations

+Besser, Howard. 2004. "The Past, Present, and Future of Digital Libraries." In *A Companion to Digital Humanities*, edited by Susan Schreibman, Ray Siemens, and John Unsworth, 557–75. Oxford: Blackwell.

Besser provides a history of digital libraries and argues for their continued importance in humanities disciplines. Libraries, archives, and museums can use high quality digital surrogates of original material from different repositories so that they appear to be catalogued within the same collection. The author notes that libraries have long upheld ethical traditions, clientele service, stewardship, and sustainability in addition to facilitating use of their collections. Besser details the philosophies of metadata. To correct current problems facing digital libraries, the author suggests that Web architecture should no longer violate conventional library practices of providing relative location information for a work, as this impinges on the ability of users to access the material.

+Burke, Peter. 2000. *A Social History of Knowledge: From Gutenberg to Diderot.* Cambridge: Polity Press.
Burke discusses the various agents and elements of social knowledge production, with a specific focus on intellectuals and Europe in the early modern period (until ca. 1750). He argues that knowledge is always plural, and that various types of knowledge develop, surface, intersect, and play concurrently. Burke relies on sociology, including the work of Émile Durkheim, and critical theory, including the work of Michel Foucault, as a basis on which to develop his own notions of social knowledge production. He acknowledges that the church, scholarly institutions, the government, and the printing press have all had a significant effect on knowledge production and dissemination—often affirmatively, but occasionally through restriction or containment. Furthermore, Burke explores how both 'heretics' (humanist revolutionaries) and more conventional academic structures developed the university as a knowledge institution.

Eisenstein, Elizabeth L. 1979. *The Printing Press as an Agent of Social Change.* 2 vols. Cambridge: Cambridge University Press.
Eisenstein highlights the role of the printing press as an agent of social change by adopting a historical approach that investigates the shift from script to print. She studies the implications of this transformation on three specific time periods: the Renaissance, the Reformation, and the rise of modern science. One of the central thoughts of the book is what Eisenstein terms the 'Unacknowledged Revolution' that took place after the invention of the printing press, a time when public access to print media facilitated the growth of public knowledge and formulation of individual thought. Another achievement of print was the standardization and preservation of previous knowledge, which was a much more challenging endeavour in the manuscript generation. According to Eisenstein, this shift marked a crucial step in the development of humankind. By focusing on dissemination, standardization, preservation, and their effects on historical processes, Eisenstein provides a coherent argument about the social effects of the historical transition to the print medium.

Hamlyn, Hilda M. 1946. "Eighteenth-Century Circulating Libraries in England." *The Library* 5(3–4): 197–222. DOI: https://doi.org/10.1093/library/s5-I.3-4.197.
Hamlyn refers to several articles on circulating libraries of the eighteenth century, noting that the number of these libraries increased from 1740 to 1800, despite claims to the contrary. The author provides a brief history of

the selling of the British Library after John Bell's bankruptcy, as well as the creation of Francis Noble's circulating library. She notes that, during this period, business management became essential: fixed subscription rates were introduced, catalogues were published, and records of borrowers were kept. The accumulation of large fortunes by William Lane's library indicates that circulating libraries were a prosperous enterprise in the eighteenth century, and that the increase of book lending by subscription is evidence of their popularity.

**Harris, Michael H. 1999. *History of Libraries in the Western World*. 4th ed. Lanham, MD: Scarecrow Press.**
Harris traces the history of libraries throughout the Western world. He defines the library as a collection of graphic materials arranged for relatively easy use, cared for by an individual, and available to a number of persons. His history includes early religious and governmental archives, and spans the centuries from ancient Babylonian and Assyrian libraries to modern American and European ones. The study takes social, economic, and political conditions into account in understanding why these libraries flourished. Theological collections are given prominence; Harris considers temple collections, as well as the more recognizable theological forms in contemporary America.

**+Johns, Adrian. 1998. *The Nature of the Book: Print and Knowledge in the Making*. Chicago: University of Chicago Press.**
Johns, a self-professed historian of printing, seeks to reveal a social history of print: a new, more accurate exploration of how print, and thereby knowledge, developed. His account of print includes acknowledging the labours of those involved in the printing process, as well as their understandings and anxieties surrounding print and publication. With a distinct focus on the history of science, he explores the social apparatus and construction of print, as well as how print has been used socially. Notably, Johns constructs his argument in firm opposition to Elizabeth Eisenstein's earlier work on print culture (1979; annotated above); he argues that there is no singular 'print culture' as such, but rather various print cultures that are all local in character. For Johns, the wide-ranging influence of print is manifold, multiple, and not implicit in a deterministic cause and effect relationship with any single historical factor or trigger.

**Jordan, Mary Wilkins. 2015. "Public Library History on the Lewis and Clark Trail."** *Public Library Quarterly* **34(2): 162–77. DOI: https://doi.org/10.1080/01616846.2015.1036709.**

Jordan follows the Lewis and Clark Trail to visit public libraries from Saint Louis to the Pacific Ocean, finding that they consider local history and genealogy of high importance, while they de-emphasize knowledge of their own histories. She notes that Benjamin Franklin is credited with starting the first public subscription library (The Library Company of Philadelphia) in 1731, and that this type of library tended to be supported and used by white males looking for education and entertainment. In the early twentieth century, women's clubs often created travelling libraries to share ideas and knowledge among communities. In her visits to these libraries, Jordan explored the physical structures, watched the patrons, and surveyed different library services, specifically querying who used them and why. Noting that 28 per cent of the libraries had paper handouts about the library's history, she concludes that public library history belongs to the community, and that it is the responsibility of each library to collect and share its history.

**Kelly, Thomas. 1966.** *Early Public Libraries: A History of Public Libraries in Great Britain Before 1850.* **London: Library Association.**

Kelly studies the origins of the British public library system from the medieval period until immediately before the Public Libraries Act of 1850. The author summarizes what is known about medieval archives in Britain and discusses the wholesale destruction and dispersion of these materials in Scotland and England following the Reformation. After the Reformation, university institutions, such as Cambridge and Oxford, were the primary holders of library materials in Britain. According to Kelly, the printing press also had a substantial effect on the archives, as it drove down public use of cathedral and institutional collections. The author concludes with chapters on the nineteenth century, which detail the rise of national libraries across Europe on a broad scale and the foundation of the British Museum Library in England. The 1850 Public Libraries Act is generally considered to be the main force behind the creation of more substantial public collections for the future. Kelly, however, contends that this was nothing more than a rhetorical exaggeration of policies already in place in England at that time.

**Kelly, Thomas. 1973.** *A History of Public Libraries in Great Britain, 1845–1965.* **London: Library Association.**

Kelly studies the organization, social history, and policies surrounding public libraries in Britain following the 1850 Public Libraries Act up until the 1970s. He focuses on library organization, annual reports, job descriptions, and salaries of librarians in order to determine the social environment of these institutions at the turn of the century. Kelly devotes a chapter to 'the Age of Carnegie,' during which industrialist Andrew Carnegie's grants enabled local authorities to undertake the labour of library provision throughout Britain; he then discusses the period between the First and Second World Wars, when new legislation in 1919 brought about 'the birth of the county libraries.' Government reports and policies illuminate various developments and reforms throughout the twentieth century, and the economic challenges of the postwar era. Detailed appendices include information on early (pre-1850) initiatives to create and fund public libraries in Britain.

McLuhan, Marshall. 1962. *The Gutenberg Galaxy: The Making of Typographic Man*. Toronto: University of Toronto Press.

McLuhan traces the ways in which mental outlook, expression, and various forms of experiences have been modified by the phonetic alphabet and by printing, as well as their effects on forms of thought and social structures. He argues that contemporary means of media and communication have resulted in the 'global village,' a term describing a feeling of connectedness that resembles a village-like setting. According to McLuhan, the relationship between humankind and technology is two-way, and technology actively partakes in reinventing humankind. He points to the popularization of literacy and movable type and their extensive effects on culture and society; according to McLuhan, these technologies have given rise to nationalism, standardization, and the assertion of rationalism, among other significant developments. Although this book focuses on mechanical technology, McLuhan argues that the new 'electric galaxy' has long ago moved into the Gutenberg galaxy, and that this shift subtly introduces an element of the grotesque into contemporary life.

+Siemens, Raymond G. 2002. "Scholarly Publishing at its Source, and at Present." In *The Credibility of Electronic Publishing: A Report to the Humanities and Social Sciences Federation of Canada*, compiled by Raymond G. Siemens, Michael Best, Elizabeth Grove-White, Alan Burk, James Kerr, Andy Pope, Jean-Claude Guédon, Geoffrey Rockwell, and Lynne Siemens. TEXT Technology 11(1): 1–128. https://web.archive.org/web/20151012065051/https://web.viu.ca/hssfc/Final/Overview.htm.

Siemens's introduction to this report focuses on the rethinking of scholarly communication practices in light of new digital forms. He meditates on this topic through the framework of *ad fontes*—the act, or conception, of going to the source. Siemens argues that scholars should look at the source, or genesis, of scholarly communication. The source, for Siemens, goes beyond the seventeenth-century inception of the academic print journal to include less formal ways of communicating and disseminating knowledge, such as verbal exchanges, epistolary correspondence, and manuscript circulation. In this way, scholars can look past the popular, standard academic journal and into a future of scholarly communication that productively involves varied scholarly traditions and social knowledge practices.

**Willinsky, John. 2006b. "History." In *The Access Principle: The Case for Open Access to Research and Scholarship*, 189–207. Cambridge, MA: MIT Press.**
Willinsky draws a parallel between the rise of the printing press and the evolution of the book in the digital age, specifically in relation to access and means of knowledge dissemination. He argues that open access in scholarship and research has a certain 'back-to-the-future' form in that it draws on historical traditions to extend knowledge circulation. This parallel is demonstrated through a description of the formation of the scientific journal *Philosophical Transactions* (1665) and the debates and arguments involved in the decision to make scientific discourse open to the larger public, a public eager to partake in this knowledge acquisition. Willinsky relates the founding of this first journal to new forms of scholarly communication and open access made possible by the digital turn, pointing to the increased participation of various peoples all over the world in this mode of knowledge production. Willinsky acknowledges that, similar to the debates surrounding Philosophical Transactions, various debates have taken and will continue to take place with this shift in knowledge communication. He calls for the need to continuously improve the quality and value of access, as well as the exploration of its various potentialities.

### B. Reference List

Besser, Howard. 2004. "The Past, Present, and Future of Digital Libraries." In *A Companion to Digital Humanities*, edited by Susan Schreibman, Ray Siemens, and John Unsworth, 557–75. Oxford: Blackwell.

Burke, Peter. 2000. *A Social History of Knowledge: From Gutenberg to Diderot.* Cambridge: Polity Press.

Eisenstein, Elizabeth L. 1979. *The Printing Press as an Agent of Social Change.* 2 vols. Cambridge: Cambridge University Press.

Hamlyn, Hilda M. 1946. "Eighteenth-Century Circulating Libraries in England." *The Library* 5(3–4): 197–222. DOI: https://doi.org/10.1093/library/s5-I.3-4.197.

Harris, Michael H. 1999. *History of Libraries in the Western World.* 4th ed. Lanham, MD: Scarecrow Press.

Johns, Adrian. 1998. *The Nature of the Book: Print and Knowledge in the Making.* Chicago: University of Chicago Press.

Jordan, Mary Wilkins. 2015. "Public Library History on the Lewis and Clark Trail." *Public Library Quarterly* 34(2): 162–77. DOI: https://doi.org/10.1080/01616846.2015.1036709.

Kelly, Thomas. 1966. *Early Public Libraries: A History of Public Libraries in Great Britain Before 1850.* London: Library Association.

———. 1973. *A History of Public Libraries in Great Britain, 1845–1965.* London: Library Association.

McLuhan, Marshall. 1962. *The Gutenberg Galaxy: The Making of Typographic Man.* Toronto: University of Toronto Press.

Siemens, Raymond G. 2002. "Scholarly Publishing at its Source, and at Present." In *The Credibility of Electronic Publishing: A Report to the Humanities and Social Sciences Federation of Canada,* compiled by Raymond G. Siemens, Michael Best, Elizabeth Grove-White, Alan Burk, James Kerr, Andy Pope, Jean-Claude Guédon, Geoffrey Rockwell, and Lynne Siemens. *TEXT Technology* 11(1): 1–128. https://web.archive.org/web/20151012065051/https://web.viu.ca/hssfc/Final/Overview.htm.

Willinsky, John. 2006b. "History." In *The Access Principle: The Case for Open Access to Research and Scholarship,* 189–207. Cambridge, MA: MIT Press.

## 2. New Modes of Scholarly Communication

Recent decades have witnessed an exponential shift in modes of research production and dissemination from primarily print-based formats to digital media. Switching to digital modes of scholarly communication has resulted in various discourses and experimentations that address and explore optimal ways of knowledge creation, access, and representation. The digital medium has also motivated a novel scope of knowledge outreach fueled by open access advocacy and practices by numerous scholars and scholarly groups, as seen in the increasing shift to open access journals. One example is *Scholarly and Research Communication*, a journal that addresses ways of facilitating collaborations and discussions around the future of scholarly publishing, such as introducing open peer review systems and open access publishing (Arbuckle, Crompton, and Mauro 2014). Some of these methods are enacted in the open networked peer review and publishing system CommentPress (Fitzpatrick 2007). This category addresses the digital book in its historical, current, and potential future forms (Bath, Schofield, and the INKE Research Group 2015; Fjällbrant 1997; Shearer and Birdsall 2002; Siemens 2002). A central component in current scholarly communication involves experimenting with and building alternative forms of digital scholarly editions, such as social and visualization-based editions (Crompton, Arbuckle, and Siemens, with the Devonshire Manuscript Editorial Group 2013; Saklofske and Bruce 2013). Together, the resources explore the evolution of knowledge production and dissemination, and speculate about potential directions for this form of scholarly communication.

### A. Annotations

**Adema, Janneke. 2010. "Overview of Open Access Models for eBooks in the Humanities and Social Sciences." OAPEN Project Report. http:// project.oapen.org/images/documents/openaccessmodels.pdf.**
Adema provides an overview of current open access publishing models being experimented with by organizations and institutions in the humanities and social sciences. The author intends to find strategies for making open access book publishing a sustainable enterprise, with funding and profit for all parties involved. Adema explores a variety of business models and publishing processes that make up what she terms the 'experimental phase' of open access book publishing. She touches on the motives—both monetary and missionary—behind the open access movement, compares various presses and press partnerships, and explores the different practices and collaborations that make open access sustainable.

+Andersen, Christian Ulrik, and Søren Bro Pold. 2014. "Post-digital
  Books and Disruptive Literary Machines." *Formules: Revue des créations formelles* 18: 164–83.
Andersen and Pold explain that the book is now 'post-digital,' and provide
various examples of innovative and common textual artifacts to support this
claim. They argue that the infrastructure around electronic publications has
been normalized and integrated fully into international reading, writing,
and consumption practices. Andersen and Pold emphasize the capitalism
inherent in current mainstream digital text platforms, such as Amazon; they
detail and vouch for attempts to counter the controlled, corporate, and user-
objectifying electronic text ecosystem.

Arbuckle, Alyssa, Alex Christie, Lynne Siemens, Aaron Mauro, and
  the INKE Research Group, eds. 2016. Special issue. *Scholarly and
  Research Communication* 7(2/3): n.p. http://src-online.ca/index.
  php/src/issue/view/24.
Arbuckle, Christie, and Siemens dedicate the introduction of this special issue to an exploration of the topics discussed in the 'New Knowledge Models:
Sustaining Partnerships to Transform Scholarly Production' INKE gathering
of 2016. The editors explain that the conversations addressed aspects of digital scholarship including creativity, implementation, institutional interface,
opportunities, challenges, audience, initiatives, and sustainability. They
claim that digital technology has enhanced the dissemination of contemporary scholarly practice, all the while acknowledging that the technological
changes in knowledge production are not new concepts. In addition, 'new
models for knowledge production blend more traditional forms of scholarly
inquiry with digital modes and methods' (n.p.). Furthermore, the editors address how cultural institutions are changing their views on how to best to
serve the public at large, with digital scholarship in mind. They conclude by
emphasizing that open social sharing of scholarship constructs a community
that contributes to maintaining a critical mass of thought through its diversity of strength and interests.

+Arbuckle, Alyssa, and Alex Christie, with the ETCL Research Group, INKE
  Research Group, and MVP Research Group. 2015. "Intersections
  Between Social Knowledge Creation and Critical Making."
  *Scholarly and Research Communication* 6(3): n.p. DOI: https://doi.
  org/10.22230/src.2015v6n3a200.
Arbuckle and Christie outline the practices of digital scholarly communica-
tion (moving research production and dissemination online), critical making

(producing theoretical insights by transforming digitized heritage materials), and social knowledge creation (collaborating in online environments to produce shared knowledge products). In addition to exploring these practices and their principles, the authors argue that combining these activities engenders knowledge production chains that connect multiple institutions and communities. Highlighting the relevance of critical making theory for scholarly communication practice, Arbuckle and Christie provide examples of theoretical research that offer tangible products for expanding and enriching scholarly production.

+Arbuckle, Alyssa, Constance Crompton, and Aaron Mauro. 2014. Introduction: "Building Partnerships to Transform Scholarly Publishing." *Scholarly and Research Communication* 5(4): n.p. http://src-online.ca/index.php/src/issue/view/18.
Arbuckle, Crompton, and Mauro introduce the INKE Gathering special issue of *Scholarly and Research Communication* by exploring the topics discussed during the 2014 'Building Partnerships to Transform Scholarly Publishing' gathering, which aimed to facilitate collaborations and discussions around the future of scholarly publishing. They emphasize the importance of open peer review systems and open access online publishing to the evolution of technology and programming standards. The editors also address the question of knowledge mobilization, which is taking place online and contributing to how the humanities are currently being measured. Referencing the content of the issue, the editors discuss how digital innovations are affecting the terms of academic publishing as well as the collaborative and interdisciplinary aspect of the humanities and how it is flourishing within digital environments. They conclude on the note that the INKE 2015 gathering will facilitate a continuation of these conversations.

Arbuckle, Alyssa, Nina Belojevic, Matthew Hiebert, and Ray Siemens, with Shaun Wong, Derek Siemens, Alex Christie, Jon Saklofske, Jentery Sayers, and the INKE and ETCL Research Groups. 2014. "Social Knowledge Creation: Three Annotated Bibliographies." *Scholarly and Research Communication* 5(2): n.p. DOI: https://doi.org/10.22230/src.2014v5n2a150.
Arbuckle, Belojevic, Hiebert, and Siemens, with Wong, Siemens, Christie, Saklofske, Sayers, and the INKE and ETCL research groups, provide three annotated bibliographies anchored in social knowledge creation. As they note, their project seeks 'to provide a transient representation of interrelational research areas,' and emphasizes '(re)shaping processes that produce knowledge' (n.p.). The authors address the work's intent, highlighting the

importance of collaboration and open source. They discuss the principles to which this bibliography adheres, addressing topics such as the book, print, remediation of culture, and interaction and collaboration. In addition, they explore the importance of digital tools and gamification to the practice of social knowledge creation. The three main parts of this document are social knowledge creation and conveyance, game-design models for digital social knowledge creation, and social knowledge creation tools. Each of these sections begins with an introduction that presents an overview of the section's content and ends with a complete alphabetical list of selections.

Association of Universities and Colleges of Canada–Canadian Association of Research Libraries Task Force on Academic Libraries and Scholarly Communication. 1997. "The Changing World of Scholarly Communication: Challenges and Choices for Canada—Final Report of the AUCC–CARL/ABRC Task Force." *Canadian Journal of Communication* 22(3): n.p.

The AUCC-CARL/ABRC Task Force on Academic Libraries and Scholarly Communication claims that advances in electronic communication influence knowledge creation and communication, which in turn affect the state of scholarly communication. The authors generate a series of recommendations to help ensure that 'Canadian scholarship flourishes in the global network of knowledge dissemination of the future' (n.p.). These recommendations address local and national action for raising awareness, implementing best practices, establishing an electronic communications infrastructure, building a distributed digital library, supporting electronic publishing, creating an appropriate copyright environment, and renewing the academic reward system.

+Bath, Jon, Scott Schofield, and the INKE Research Group. 2015. "The Digital Book." In *The Cambridge Companion to the History of the Book*, edited by Leslie Howsam, 181–95. Cambridge: Cambridge University Press.

Bath and Schofield reflect on the rise of the e-book by contemplating the various moving parts involved in its history and production. They focus on, and contribute to, the scholarly engagement with e-books, and they provide a comprehensive survey of theorists, including Johanna Drucker, Elizabeth Eisenstein, N. Katherine Hayles, Matthew Kirschenbaum, Jerome McGann, D.F. McKenzie, and Marshall McLuhan. Bath and Schofield integrate these theorists into a larger argument suggesting that both a nuanced understanding of book history and a comprehensive familiarity with digital scholarship are necessary to fully grasp the material and historical significance of the e-book. The authors conclude with a call to book history and digital humanities specialists (a.k.a. 'scholar-coders') to collaborate and develop new digital research environments together.

**Belojevic, Nina. 2015. "Developing an Open, Networked Peer Review System."** *Scholarly and Research Communication* **6(2): n.p. DOI: https://doi.org/10.22230/src.2015v6n2a205.**

Belojevic presents the Personas for Open, Networked Peer Review wireframe prototype: an open, networked peer review model initiated by Belojevic and Jentery Sayers in 2013 that was further developed by the Electronic Textual Cultures Laboratory (ETCL) in partnership with University of Victoria Libraries, the Humanities Computing and Media Centre, and the Public Knowledge Project. In this environment, articles undergo open peer review and can be commented on by a specific group of reviewers or the public. The prototyping process followed an approach similar to the one described in Katie Salen and Eric Zimmerman's *Rules of Play: Game Design Fundamentals* (2003), which outlines common game design principles. Belojevic describes how the project moved from iterative prototyping to agile development, an approach that permits researchers to break down the project into smaller chunks. This approach allows stakeholders to ensure that their goals are being met at every stage, and allows scholars and researchers to maintain the quality of the project. Further research will focus on determining the aspects of agile development adaptable by the project in order to facilitate a balance between project development and deliverables, while being flexible enough to pursue and integrate novel insights that may appear during the prototyping process.

**+Borgman, Christine L. 2007.** *Scholarship in the Digital Age: Information, Infrastructure, and the Internet.* **Cambridge, MA: MIT Press.**

Borgman lays out research questions and hypotheses concerning the evolving scholarly infrastructure and modes of communication in the digital environment. She deduces that the inherent social elements of scholarship endure, despite new technologies that alter significantly the way scholarship is performed, disseminated, and archived. Scholarship and scholarly activities continue to exist in a social network of varying actors and priorities. Notably, Borgman focuses on the 'data deluge'—the increasing amount of generated data and data accessed for research purposes. The influences of large data sets, as well as how these data sets will be preserved in keeping with library and archival conventions, are of particular significance. Overall, Borgman synthesizes the various aspects of contemporary scholarship, and reflects on the increasingly pervasive digital environment.

+Bowen, William R., Constance Crompton, and Matthew Hiebert. 2014. "Iter Community: Prototyping an Environment for Social Knowledge Creation and Communication." *Scholarly and Research Communication* 5(4): n.p. DOI: https://doi.org/10.22230/src.2014v5n4a193.

Bowen, Crompton, and Hiebert discuss the features and challenges of Iter Community, a collaborative research environment. They also discuss *A Social Edition of the Devonshire Manuscript*, focusing on its human and computer social engagement. The authors organize the article into three sections: (1) a historical and conceptual framework of Iter Community; (2) an update on the state of Iter Community (at writing), and (3) a perspective on *A Social Edition of the Devonshire Manuscript.* They conclude that Iter Community's vision is to provide a flexible environment for communication, exchange, and collaboration, which will evolve with its participants' priorities and challenges.

Brown, Susan, and John Simpson. 2014. "The Changing Culture of Humanities Scholarship: Iteration, Recursion, and Versions in Scholarly Collaboration Environments." *Scholarly and Research Communication* 5(4): n.p. DOI: https://doi.org/10.22230/src.2014v5n4a191.

Brown and Simpson discuss versions and versioning in contemporary scholarship, archiving, and data preservation. They present dynamic textuality, collaborative textuality, granulated and distributed textuality, and interdependent textuality. They also discuss technical considerations in order to highlight the cyclical influence between culture and technology (sections study control, cost, collaboration, conflicts and management, and representation, mostly within the context of digital texts). Brown and Simpson explain that collaborative digital objects are subject to modification, remediation, and revision, as 'textuality is increasingly granular, distributed, and interdependent' (n.p.). The authors conclude that the dynamic aspect of the culture of scholarship allows the community to contribute to the sustainability of cultural scholarship and records.

Brown, Susan, and John Simpson. 2015. "An Entity By Any Other Name: Linked Open Data as a Basis for a Decentered, Dynamic Scholarly Publishing Ecology." *Scholarly and Research Communication* 6(2): n.p. DOI: https://doi.org/10.22230/src.2015v6n2a212.

Brown and Simpson propose that linked open data enables more easily navigable scholarly environments that permit better integration of research materials and greater interlinkage between individuals and institutions. They frame linked open data integration as an ecological problem in a complex system of parts and relationships. The different parts of the ecology co-evolve and change according to the relationships in the system. The authors suggest that tools are needed for establishing automated conditions; for evaluating the provenance, authority, and trustworthiness of linked open data resources; and for developing tools that facilitate corrections and enhancements. The authors explain that an ontology negotiation tool would be a most valuable contribution to the Semantic Web. Such a tool would represent an opportunity for collaboration between different sectors of the knowledge economy, and would allow the *Semantic Web* to develop as an evolving space of knowledge production and dissemination.

Cohen, Daniel J. 2010. "Open Access Publishing and Scholarly Values." Personal blog post, May 27. https://dancohen.org/2010/05/27/open-access-publishing-and-scholarly-values/. Archived at https://perma.cc/78MH-PK43.

Cohen builds on the notions of the supply and demand side of scholarly communication, as well as the value system of scholars, in order to make a case for increasing open access scholarship and being more receptive to scholarship that does not adhere to the conventional academic publishing system. According to Cohen, the four sentiments that stand in the way of embracing open access scholarship are impartiality, passion, shame, and narcissism. Cohen discusses impartiality in relation to the pressure scholars feel to publish in established, toll access venues for a number for reasons, including legitimate concerns such as career growth. He argues that open access publishing can take place in parallel to more conventional forms of academic publishing. Cohen also criticizes the commercial apparatus of the publishing system for taking advantage of scholars and their labour and passion, which is expressed in writing. He argues for the need to reorient the ways in which scholarship is produced and published in order to increase access, and also to break the chain within a system that is exploiting academics. Cohen argues that the act of accepting certain aspects of digital media and rejecting others is a 'shameful hypocrisy' (n.p.)—first, by using the digital medium as the primary source for research yet avoiding it as a means of publishing and, second, talking about access and the need for academics to be more inclusive but avoiding the existing necessary steps toward implementing these notions in practice. Finally, the narcissistic factor is related to the reputability of publishing in typical venues; Cohen counters this by saying that open access publishing is likely to get better readership and to spread ideas more widely, and could also be added to the CV. The author concludes by inviting us to envision and enact a more straightforward and virtuous model for scholarly communication.

Crompton, Constance, Alyssa Arbuckle, and Raymond G. Siemens, with the Devonshire Manuscript Editorial Group. 2013. "Understanding the Social Edition Through Iterative Implementation: The Case of the *Devonshire MS* (BL Add MS 17492)." *Scholarly and Research Communication* 4(3): n.p. DOI: https://doi.org/10.22230/src.2013v4n3a118.

Crompton, Arbuckle, and Siemens address the process of building a digital social edition of a manuscript that involves consultation with, and contribution from, various communities. The article is based on a case study of *A Social Edition of the Devonshire Manuscript*, a Wikibooks edition of the first known miscellany that features women and men writing together in English. Since the *Social Edition* is published on Wikibooks, it includes a traceable revision history and is available for collaborative work. The Wikibooks platform also provides a safety net in case users tamper with the content in bad faith; the authors detail a user incident that was easily reversible due to the Wikibooks versioning options. Work on the *Social Edition* involved a series of consultations with various communities and advisory boards, primarily through Skype and Iter-based interactions, but also through social network platforms such as Twitter. Researchers in the Electronic Textual Cultures Lab (ETCL) often carried out suggested changes to the Wikibooks edition that arose from these consultations. Indeed, one of the primary outcomes of this process was a rethinking of the editor's authority on a project that also involved citizen scholars and a number of researchers contributing to the work to different extents. The authors regard this project as an example of a process-driven digital social edition that practises traced versioning and involves various communities working and contributing to a project that is, in its own way, meaningful to all. This is done in conjunction with experimentation with the digital medium.

+Crompton, Constance, Raymond G. Siemens, and Alyssa Arbuckle, with the INKE Research Group. 2015. "Enlisting 'Vertues Noble & Excelent': Behavior, Credit, and Knowledge Organization in the Social Edition." *Digital Humanities Quarterly* 9(2): n.p. http://www.digitalhumanities.org/dhq/vol/9/2/000202/000202.html.

Crompton, Siemens, and Arbuckle consider the gender factors involved in social editions, drawing on their experience developing *A Social Edition of the Devonshire Manuscript*: a Wikibooks edition of the sixteenth-century multi-author verse miscellany discussed above. The authors argue that while the Wikimedia suite can often devolve into openly hostile online spaces, Wikimedia projects remain important for the contemporary circulation of knowledge. The key, for the authors, is to encourage gender equity in social behaviour, credit sharing, and knowledge organization in Wikimedia, rather than abandoning it in favour of a more controlled collaborative environment for edition production and dissemination.

**Dumova, Tatyana. 2012. "Social Interaction Technologies and the Future of Blogging." In** *Blogging in the Global Society: Cultural, Political and Geographical Aspects*, **edited by Tatyana Dumova and Richard Fiordo, 249–74. Hershey, PA: IGI Global.**
Dumova addresses the social potential of blogging—specifically, the ways in which blogs permit people to engage in social interactions, build connections, and collaborate with others. She argues that blogging should not be studied in isolation from the social media clusters that function together to sustain each other. She also notes that blogging is an international phenomenon, since more than 60 per cent of all blogs created after the 1990s are written in languages other than English. Dumova broadly traces the development of blog publishing platforms. She concludes that network-based peer production and social media convergence are the driving forces behind the current transformation of blogs into increasingly user-centric, user-driven practices of producing, searching, sharing, publishing, and distributing information.

**Eve, Martin Paul. 2015. "Open Access Publishing and Scholarly Communication in Non-Scientific Disciplines."** *Online Information Review* **39(5): 717–32. DOI: https://doi.org/10.1108/OIR-04-2015-0103.**
Eve presents an overview of the current open access debate in non-scientific (non-STEM) disciplines, arguing that non-STEM disciplines have consistently lagged behind in their approach to open access policies and practices. He attributes this gap to a variety of economic and cultural factors, arguing that these specific challenges or objections have stunted the growth of open access in these disciplines. Eve suggests that his article is far too short and biased to do justice to the complexity of the issues he raises; however, it is his hope that his insights will spur action and critical appraisal from the community at large. Academia must consider what is needed from a scholarly communications infrastructure and simultaneously build pragmatic and non-damaging transition strategies in order to utilize open access dissemination to its full advantage.

**+Fitzpatrick, Kathleen. 2007. "CommentPress: New (Social) Structures for New (Networked) Texts."** *Journal of Electronic Publishing* **10(3): n.p. DOI: http://dx.doi.org/10.3998/3336451.0010.305.**
Fitzpatrick meditates on the current state and future possibilities of electronic scholarly publishing. She focuses her consideration on a study of

CommentPress, a digital scholarly publishing venue that combines the hosting of long texts with social network features. Fitzpatrick argues that community and collaboration are at the heart of scholarly knowledge creation—or at least they should be. Platforms such as CommentPress acknowledge the productive capabilities of scholarly collaboration, and promote this fruitful interaction between academics. Although Fitzpatrick admits that CommentPress is not the only, or best, answer to the questions of shifting scholarly communication, she celebrates its emergence as a service for the social interconnection and knowledge production of authors and readers in an academic setting.

+Fitzpatrick, Kathleen. 2011. *Planned Obsolescence: Publishing, Technology, and the Future of the Academy.* New York: New York University Press.
Fitzpatrick duly surveys and calls for a reform of academic publishing. She argues for more interactivity, communication, peer-to-peer review, and a significant move toward digital scholarly publishing. Fitzpatrick demonstrates how the current mode of scholarly publishing is economically unviable. Moreover, tenure and promotion practices based primarily on institutional modes of scholarly publishing need to be reformed. Fitzpatrick acknowledges certain touchstones of the academy (peer review, scholarship, sharing ideas), and how these tenets have been overshadowed by priorities shaped, in part, by mainstream academic publishing practices and concepts. She details her own work with CommentPress, and the benefits of publishing online with an infrastructure that enables widespread dissemination as well as concurrent reader participation via open peer review.

+Fjällbrant, Nancy. 1997. "Scholarly Communication—Historical Development and New Possibilities." In *Proceedings of the IATUL Conferences.* West Lafayette, IN: Purdue University Libraries. http://docs.lib.purdue.edu/iatul/1997/papers/5/.
In order to study the widespread transition to electronic scholarly communication, Fjällbrant details the history of the scientific journal. Academic journals had emerged in seventeenth-century Europe, and the first of these, the *Journal des Sçavans,* was published in 1665 in Paris. The first learned societies (such as the Royal Society in London and the Académie des Sciences in Paris) were primarily concerned with the dissemination of knowledge, and the scholarly journal developed out of a desire by researchers to share their findings with others in a cooperative forum. Fjällbrant lists other contemporaneous forms of scholarly communication, including the letter, the scientific book, the newspaper, and the anagram system. The journal,

however, emerged as a primary source of scholarly communication because it met the needs of various stakeholders: the general public, booksellers and publishers, libraries, authors who wished to make their work public and claim ownership, the scientific community invested in reading and applying other scientists' findings, and academic institutions that required metrics for evaluating faculty.

**Grumbach, Elizabeth, and Laura Mandell. 2014. "Meeting Scholars Where They Are: The Advanced Research Consortium (ARC) and a Social Humanities Infrastructure."** *Scholarly and Research Communication* **5(4): n.p. DOI: https://doi.org/10.22230/src.2014v5n4a189.**
Grumbach and Mandell investigate the Advanced Research Consortium (ARC) infrastructure in the context of scholarly engagement, focusing on digital project peer review, aggregation and search, and outreach services. The authors emphasize the importance of meeting scholars where they are for the sake of success and productivity. They also outline the histories of Nineteenth-Century Scholarship Online (NINES) and ARC, showing how these projects have assisted the scholarly community through the areas of focus listed above. The article concludes with a note that the ARC nodes' directors are not necessarily digital humanists, which helps bring together conventional scholarly and new digital infrastructures.

**+Jones, Steven E. 2014. "Publications." In** *The Emergence of the Digital Humanities*, **147–77. New York and London: Routledge.**
Jones explores the current state of scholarly publishing and the role of the digital humanities. He argues that now, more than ever, academic practitioners are able to take the means of producing scholarly work into their own hands. Rather than relying on scholarly communication systems already in place, researchers can now experiment with different modes, media, and models of publication. Jones considers digital publishing and engagement of academic work to be symptomatic of the deep integration and interplay of computational methods with contemporary scholarship in general, and with digital humanities in particular.

**+Lane, Richard J. 2014. "Innovation through Tradition: New Scholarly Publishing Applications Modelled on Faith-Based Electronic Publishing and Learning Environments."** *Scholarly and Research Communication* **5(4): n.p. DOI: https://doi.org/10.22230/src.2014v5n4a188.**
Lane explores the popular eTheology platforms Olive Tree and Logos, and the possibilities for the uptake of their information management and design

models. He details the advantages of popular, or non-academic, digital knowledge spaces, and argues for their potential application to secular electronic publishing. The most advantageous element of this proposal may be the suggestion to tailor applications to communities of users—which Olive Tree and Logos do, as described in the article—in order to develop a more integrated and dynamically engaged scholarly publishing system that includes user analysis.

Lewis, Vivian, Lisa Spiro, Xuemao Wang, and Jon E. Cawthorne. 2015. *Building Expertise to Support Digital Scholarship: A Global Perspective.* Arlington, VA: Council on Library and Information Resources. https://www.clir.org/pubs/reports/pub168/pub168.

Lewis, Spiro, Wang, and Cawthorne investigate the necessary expertise for robust and sustainable digital scholarship (DS). The authors list the components of expertise, laying out their methods (such as site selection and interviews) and findings (including analysis, study limitations, and challenges). They discuss the skills, competencies, and mindsets important for digital scholarship, and list the factors upon which digital scholarship depends. Additionally, the authors study the characteristics of organizations that enable continuous learning to nurture expertise and knowledge creation. They examine DS expertise in a global context, the role of the research library and campus computing, and the challenges faced by digital scholarship organizations. Based on their observations of successful programs, the authors offer some recommendations for digital scholars, leaders of digital scholarship organizations, university and host organizations, organizations that fund digital scholarship, and the digital scholarship community. They conclude that sharing and communication among individuals allows for remarkable learning in digital scholarship.

Liu, Alan. 2007. "Imagining the New Media Encounter." In *A Companion to Digital Literary Studies*, edited by Ray Siemens and Susan Schreibman, 3–25. Oxford: Blackwell.

Liu introduces a volume edited by Siemens and Schreibman that brings together narratives about the new media encounter, as told from the perspectives of scholars, theorists, and practitioners working in the intersection of literary studies and digital new media. He offers a narrative of the origin and development of new media and its encounters with sociopolitical, historical, and subjective registers, ultimately claiming that its dynamic and manifold nature elicits numerous encounter narratives. Liu draws on a number of central theorists to point to the manifold, often juxtaposing characteristics of new media that further complicate its clear-cut definition. Given this context, Liu explains that the goal of this volume is to introduce the various stories of the new media encounter, and the messiness and imaginative possibilities integral to it. Essays in this volume fall under three main sections—'Traditions,' 'Textualities,' and 'Methodologies'—and work together to address the potentials of new media in scholarly and cultural contexts.

+Lorimer, Rowland. 2013. "Libraries, Scholars, and Publishers in Digital Journal and Monograph Publishing." *Scholarly and Research Communication* 4(1): n.p. DOI: https://doi.org/10.22230/src.2013v4n1a43.

Lorimer briefly details the last forty years of scholarly publishing to explicate the current state of affairs. He asserts that a reorganization of the academic publishing infrastructure would greatly encourage forthright contributions to knowledge, especially concerning academic journals and monographs. The splitting of the university press from the university (except in name), coupled with funding cuts and consequent entrepreneurial publishing projects, has hampered the possibilities of academic publishing. By integrating all of the actors of digital scholarly communication in an inclusive collaboration—libraries, librarians, scholars on editorial boards, technologically-inclined researchers, programmers, digital humanists, and publishing professionals—digital technology could offer significant benefits for the future of scholarship and knowledge creation.

+Lorimer, Rowland. 2014. "A Good Idea, a Difficult Reality: Toward a Publisher/Library Open Access Partnership." *Scholarly and Research Communication* 5(4): n.p. DOI: https://doi.org/10.22230/src.2014v5n4a180.

Lorimer comments on the state of scholarly publishing in Canada. He offers thorough insight into the financial, social, and cultural obstacles that arise as academic institutions move toward an open access model of knowledge mobilization. Lorimer argues that although the *idea* of open access is desirable to academic and academic-aligned researchers, practitioners, and organizations, the *reality* of a complete open access model still requires considerable planning and implementation. Lorimer emphasizes the importance of long-term thinking in supporting Canada's research libraries as open access hubs of orderly, sustainable, and productive information.

+Maxwell, John W. 2014. "Publishing Education in the 21st Century and the Role of the University." *Journal of Electronic Publishing* 17(2): n.p. DOI: http://dx.doi.org/10.3998/3336451.0017.205.

From his perspective within the Canadian Centre for Studies in Publishing at Simon Fraser University, Maxwell ruminates on the current state of university-level training in publishing studies, as well as its future role. He considers the shifting economy, and the rise of digital media and practices, as major factors influencing the current Canadian academic and non-academic publishing scene. Maxwell suggests that the university has a pivotal role to play in reinvigorating publishing by encouraging a supportive community of practice as well as openness to creativity, innovation, and flexibility. Overall, Maxwell underlines the importance of academic publishing studies in the evolving publishing scene.

+Maxwell, John W. 2015. "Beyond Open Access to Open Publication and Open Scholarship." *Scholarly and Research Communication* 6(3): n.p. DOI: https://doi.org/10.22230/src.2015v6n3a202.
Maxwell calls for radical openness in scholarly publishing—that is, moving beyond the ideas of open access toward a cultural transformation. He argues that as the humanities are reimagined in the light of digital media, there is an increasing need for old practices to be thrown away instead of merely reconceived. For Maxwell, the print-based journal economy relies on limited access in order to maintain a profit. The economics of open access, however, could adapt a new system of openness to shifting market demands, opened by the Web, that depend upon interconnection and interlinkage. Maxwell turns to agile publishing and its mission statement of 'release early, release often' as an example of a more open movement. He asks whether scholarly work can be remixed, combined, reassembled, taken apart, and inscribed through an iterative process. Maxwell asserts that education, publishing, and scholarship can all be cultures of transformation.

+O'Donnell, Daniel, Heather Hobma, Sandra Cowan, Gillian Ayers, Jessica Bay, Marinus Swanepoel, Wendy Merkley, Kelaine Devine, Emma Dering, and Inge Genee. 2015. "Aligning Open Access Publication with the Research and Teaching Missions of the Public University: The Case of the Lethbridge Journal Incubator (If 'if's and 'and's were pots and pans)." *Journal of Electronic Publishing* 18(3): n.p. DOI: http://dx.doi.org/10.3998/3336451.0018.309.
O'Donnell et al. present a research mission summary for the group behind the Lethbridge Journal Incubator, and detail how this project provides graduate students with early experience in scholarly publishing. The Lethbridge Journal Incubator trains graduate students in technical and managerial aspects of journal production under the supervision of scholar-editors and professional librarians. The project introduces students to the core elements of academic journal production workflows and provides training in copyediting,

preparation of proofs, document encoding, and the use of standard journal production software. Using circle graphs, the authors demonstrate the significant increase in research time devoted to production tasks that improve research ability or knowledge. For O'Donnell et al., the key innovation of the Lethbridge Journal Incubator is its alignment of journal production sustainability with the educational and research missions of the university. The authors attribute the slow growth of open access to attitudes among those who pay for the production and dissemination of research. By unlocking the training and administrative support potential of the production process, the Lethbridge Journal Incubator promotes access within the University of Lethbridge.

+Powell, Daniel, Raymond Siemens, Matthew Hiebert, Lindsey Seatter, and William R. Bowen. 2015. "Transformation through Integration: The Renaissance Knowledge Network (ReKN) and a Next Wave of Scholarly Publication." *Scholarly and Research Communication* 6(2): n.p. DOI: https://doi.org/10.22230/src.2015v6n2a199.

Powell, Siemens, Bowen, Hiebert, and Seatter explore the first six months of the Andrew W. Mellon-funded Renaissance Knowledge Network (ReKN). The authors focus on the potential for interoperability and metadata aggregation of various Renaissance and early modern digital projects. They examine how interconnected resources and scholarly environments might integrate publication and markup tools. Powell et al. consider how projects such as ReKN contribute to the shifting practices of contemporary scholarly publishing. For a detailed exploration of the planning phase of ReKN, please see Powell, Siemens, and the INKE Research Group (2014), annotated above.

+Powell, Daniel, Ray Siemens, and the INKE Research Group. 2014. "Building Alternative Scholarly Publishing Capacity: The Renaissance Knowledge Network (ReKN) as Digital Production Hub." *Scholarly and Research Communication* 5(4): n.p. DOI: https://doi.org/10.22230/src.2014v5n4a183.

Powell, Siemens, and the INKE Research Group report on the status of the Renaissance Knowledge Network (ReKN), an Advanced Research Consortium node. ReKN is a large-scale collaborative project that spans the University of Victoria, the University of Toronto, and Texas A&M University. The authors detail the planning phase of ReKN, a project that aims to centralize and integrate research and production in a single online platform that will serve the specific needs of early modern scholars. The authors are working to develop and implement ReKN as a dynamic, holistic scholarly environment. For a further update, please see Powell, Siemens, and Bowen, with Hiebert and Seatter (2015), annotated below, an article that reflects on the first six months of ReKN development.

**Price, Kenneth M., and Raymond G. Siemens, eds. 2013. *Literary Studies in the Digital Age*. New York: Modern Language Association.**
Price and Siemens bring together an anthology of essays that address the changing modes of knowledge production and dissemination in the digital age. In their introduction, the editors offer an explanation of digital humanities and digital literary studies and how they developed historically, as well as their present form and the various branches and opportunities that stem from them. They highlight some of the significant aspects of digital humanities, such as the ability to bridge theory and practice, as well as the collaborative element at the heart of most research carried out in the field. The editors also point to the various aspects that have been affected by the digital turn, such as textual editing, access to primary materials, and the development of online databases that can feed various projects, among others. The essays also address various ways in which computers can assist literary studies and the ways in which these technologies can deal with humanities-oriented questions and concerns.

**Saklofske, Jon. 2014. "Exploding, Centralizing and Reimagining: Critical Scholarship Refracted Through the NewRadial Prototype." *Scholarly and Research Communication* 5(2): n.p. DOI: https://doi.org/10.22230/src.2014v5n2a151.**
In light of the focus of the Implementing New Knowledge Environments (INKE) research team on the ways in which digital environments affect the production, dissemination, and use of established venues for academic research, the NewRadial prototype has been extended for further investigation of this research direction. NewRadial is a data visualization environment that was originally designed as an alternative way to encounter and annotate image-based databases. It allows users to engage with humanities data outside of scholarly paradigms and the linear nature of the printed book, and encourages user contributions through collective commentary rather than isolated annotation. This prototype investigates a number of questions, such as whether the aforementioned venues can coexist in their present form, the ways in which scholarship can be visualized through time and space, how critical ideas are born and evolve, and whether the collaborative elements of alternate reality games (ARGs) and massively multiplayer online role-playing games (MMORPGs) can be adopted into the peer review process

and secondary scholarship. This prototype is a response to the established view of a finished work existing in a print-based format and is, rather, a way of experimenting in an interactive and dynamic digital environment that invites dialogue and collaborative curation—as well as numerous alternative narrative opportunities.

Saklofske, Jon, with the INKE Research Team. 2016. "Digital *Theoria, Poiesis,* and *Praxis*: Activating Humanities Research and Communication through Open Social Scholarship Platform Design." *Scholarly and Research Communication* 7(2/3): n.p. DOI: https://doi.org/10.22230/src.2016v7n2/3a252.

Saklofske states that although research has drastically changed in the last two decades, scholarly communication has remained relatively stable, adhering to standard scholarly forms of publication as a result of materialist economies. Saklofske argues for the necessity of innovating digital means of scholarly communication with *theoria, poiesis,* and *praxis* in mind. He offers a number of case studies that experiment with unconventional ways of carrying out research that utilize these concepts, among which is the NewRadial prototype: an online environment that brings in secondary scholarship and debate, in which outside information can be added to and visualized with the primary data without affecting the original databases. NewRadial is taken as a model for other spaces that facilitate dynamic organization and centralized spacing as an alternative solution to typical, isolated forms of monographs and linear narrativization. Saklofske, a proponent of open social scholarship, argues that this type of scholarship is an essential part of the transformation of scholarly research and communication in a way that would take advantage of the digital medium, rather than propagate conventional forms of knowledge creation into this environment. This type of research platform is also more inclusive and public-facing.

+Saklofske, Jon, and Jake Bruce. 2013. "Beyond Browsing and Reading: The Open Work of Digital Scholarly Editions." *Scholarly and Research Communication* 4(3): n.p. DOI: https://doi.org/10.22230/src.2013v4n 3a119.

Saklofske and Bruce detail NewRadial, an Implementing New Knowledge Environments (INKE) prototype scholarly edition environment. The prototype draws together primary texts, secondary scholarship, and related knowledge communities into a social digital scholarly edition. NewRadial provides an open, shared workspace where users may explore, sort, group, annotate, and contribute to secondary scholarship creation collaboratively.

**Schreibman, Susan, Ray Siemens, and John Unsworth, eds. 2004. *A Companion to Digital Humanities*. Oxford: Blackwell.**
Schriebman, Siemens, and Unsworth edit a collection of essays by practitioners who both address the digital humanities as a separate discipline in a volume for the first time and think of the ways in which the discipline connects to more standard humanities practices. The collection presents various disciplinary perspectives on the digital humanities and describes evolving modes of scholarly research. According to the editors, one of the main principles uniting the various subfields of the digital humanities is that they are as concerned with the practical application of knowledge to concrete environments as they are with the theoretical. Together, the essays offer a historical record of how digital humanities has been practised and has evolved over the past half-century, its present state, and its potential futures. The editors believe that the discipline has the potential to work with human records on an unprecedented scale, and to recognize patterns and connections that would have otherwise remained unnoticed.

**Shearer, Kathleen, and Bill Birdsall. 2002. "The Transition of Scholarly Communications in Canada." http://www.moyak.com/papers/scholarly-communications-canada.pdf.**
Shearer and Birdsall analyze the impact of technology and economy on the scholarly communication process and outline a conceptual framework for the latter, along with corresponding actors, drivers, and issues. They start by addressing the scholarly communication system, and emphasize the economic and social importance of knowledge. The authors also discuss the actors within the process, which they categorize as researchers, publishers, libraries, and users. Shearer and Birdsall identify technology, globalization, economics, changing patterns of research, increasing quantity of scholarly publications, and public policy as 'external forces [on], or drivers' of, the system (4). They address issues such as changing knowledge needs, alternative publishing models, copyright, licensing, intellectual property, interoperability and technical infrastructure, and access and retrieval. The authors conclude that there are many transformations occurring in the scholarly communication system that may have various impacts yet to become clear, which calls for a multidisciplinary research agenda.

**+\*\*Siemens, Raymond G. 2002. "Scholarly Publishing at its Source, and at Present." In *The Credibility of Electronic Publishing: A Report to the Humanities and Social Sciences Federation of Canada*, compiled by Raymond G. Siemens, Michael Best, Elizabeth Grove-White, Alan Burk, James Kerr, Andy Pope, Jean-Claude Guédon, Geoffrey**

Rockwell, and Lynne Siemens. *TEXT Technology* 11(1): 1–128. https://web.archive.org/web/20151012065051/https://web.viu.ca/hssfc/Final/Overview.htm.

Siemens's introduction to this report focuses on the rethinking of scholarly communication practices in light of new digital forms. He meditates on this topic through the framework of *ad fontes*—the act, or conception, of going to the source. Siemens argues that scholars should look at the source, or genesis, of scholarly communication. The source, for Siemens, goes beyond the seventeenth-century inception of the academic print journal to include less formal ways of communicating and disseminating knowledge, such as verbal exchanges, epistolary correspondence, and manuscript circulation. In this way, scholars can look past the popular, standard academic journal and into a future of scholarly communication that productively involves varied scholarly traditions and social knowledge practices.

**Siemens, Raymond G., and David Moorman, eds. 2006.** *Mind Technologies: Humanities Computing and the Canadian Academic Community.* **Calgary: University of Calgary Press.**

Siemens and Moorman edit a collection of essays that result from an awareness of the increasing role of the computer in the academy and its central role in enhancing humanities research and pedagogy in particular. The collection focuses on how scholars in Canada utilize computational methods, described here within the Humanities Computing framework, in the arts and humanities. This collection was preceded by various discussions and planning events, one of the most central and recent being the Mind Technologies conference sessions hosted by the Consortium for Computing in the Humanities/ Consortium pour ordinateurs en science humaines (COCH/COSH) and the Social Sciences and Humanities Research Council of Canada (SSHRC) at the University of Toronto. The essays describe the various terminologies and research directions that fall within Humanities Computing, and offer a broad range of applications in academic contexts.

**Siemens, Raymond G., Claire Warwick, Richard Cunningham, Teresa Dobson, Alan Galey, Stan Ruecker, Susan Schreibman, and the INKE Research Group. 2009.** "*Codex* Ultor: Toward a Conceptual and Theoretical Foundation for New Research on Books and Knowledge Environments." *Digital Studies / Le champ numérique* 1(2): n.p. DOI: http://doi.org/10.16995/dscn.270.

Siemens, Warwick, Cunningham, Dobson, Galey, Ruecker, Schreibman, and the INKE Research Group investigate the 'conceptual and theoretical foundations for work undertaken by the Implementing New Knowledge Environments research group' (n.p). They address the need for designing new knowledge environments, taking into consideration the evolution of reading and writing technologies, the mechanics and pragmatics of written forms of knowledge, and the corresponding strategies of reading—as well as the computational possibilities of written forms due to emerging technology. The authors highlight the importance of prototyping as a research activity, and outline corresponding research questions that target the experiences of reading, using, and accessing information, as well as issues of design. They discuss their research methods, which include digital textual scholarship, user experience evaluation, interface design prototyping, and information management. Siemens et al. conclude that the various reading interface prototypes produced by INKE allow a transformation of engagement methods with reading materials.

Siemens, Raymond G., Teresa Dobson, Stan Ruecker, Richard Cunningham, Alan Galey, Claire Warwick, and Lynne Siemens. 2011. "HCI-Book? Perspectives on E-Book Research, 2006–2008 (Foundational to Implementing New Knowledge Environments)." *Papers of the Bibliographical Society of Canada / Cahiers de la Société bibliographique du Canada* 49(1): 35–89. http://web.uvic.ca/~siemens/pub/2011-HCI-Book.pdf.

Siemens, Dobson, Ruecker, Cunningham, Galey, Warwick, and Siemens examine the book in various domains as the electronic book emerged, with a specific focus on the role and importance of digital and analog books in humanities scholarship. They contextualize electronic book research, aiming to understand and describe principles of humanistic interaction with knowledge objects. The authors lay out core strategies for designing those objects, and study principles of evaluation and implementation of new technologies. They also investigate human-computer interaction possibilities and those of the electronic book. The authors take various elements into consideration, including audience, interface and design, and form and content. When studying readers and users, the authors consider user studies and usability assessment, the importance of user studies in the humanities, and previous studies of humanities users. They also examine features of books and e-books, such as tangibility, browsability, searchability, referenceability, hybridity, sustainability, and access—and investigate uses of books and e-books, as well as digital archives. The authors' research also examines aspects of the books and e-books (material, symbolic, and formal), and develops prototypes in various directions. They conclude by noting that team members, having worked together for six years, have been able to create the relationships and processes necessary to work through the challenges of multidisciplinary research collaborations.

+Stein, Bob. 2015. "Back to the Future." *Journal of Electronic Publishing* 18(2): n.p. DOI: http://dx.doi.org/10.3998/3336451.0018.204.
Stein considers the digital book as a *place* rather than an object or tool—a place where readers gather, socially. He details the experiments with social platforms conducted at his Institute for the Future of the Book, including the creation of an online social edition of McKenzie Wark's *Gamer Theory* (2007), and their current work with SocialBook. SocialBook is an online, collaborative reading platform that encourages readers to comment on the text and interact with each other. Stein makes reference to historic social reading practices, and infers that platforms such as SocialBook are closely aligned to these traditions.

Stranack, Kevin. 2008. *Starting A New Scholarly Journal in Africa*. Public Knowledge Project. https://pkp.sfu.ca/files/AfricaNewJournal. pdf.
Stranack outlines the factors involved in starting a high-quality, sustainable academic journal. He situates this discussion within an African context, arguing that African knowledge production is crucial for local African communities and for the academic community at large. He presents the benefits of starting a journal on personal, institutional, disciplinary, and national levels, and addresses certain challenges involved, such as the necessary financial input and the need for time and people willing to dedicate themselves to such an undertaking. Stranack's discussion spans the types of existing journals and methods, economic models for journals, the open access versus limited access debate, and tips on how to promote and sustain a successful journal. He concludes by highlighting the merit of a journal that makes valuable contributions to academic society at large.

+Vandendorpe, Christian. 2012. "Wikisource and the Scholarly Book." *Scholarly and Research Communication* 3(4): n.p. DOI: https://doi. org/10.22230/src.2012v3n4a58.
Vandendorpe contemplates Wikisource, a project of the Wikimedia Foundation, as a potential platform for reading and editing scholarly books. He comes to this conclusion after considering what the ideal e-book or digital knowledge environment should look like. For Vandendorpe, this artifact must be available on the Web; reflect the metaphor of a forest of knowledge, rather than a container; situate the reader at the centre of the experience; and be

open, reliable, robust, and expandable. Wikisource, the author concludes, has the potential to meet these criteria: it enables quality editing and robust versioning, and has various display options. That being said, Vandendorpe also outlines areas of development necessary for Wikisource to become an ideal candidate for hosting this type of knowledge creation.

+Van de Sompel, Herbert, Sandy Payette, John Erickson, Carl Lagoze, and Simeon Warner. 2004. "Rethinking Scholarly Communication: Building the System that Scholars Deserve." *D-Lib Magazine* 10(9): n.p. DOI: http://dx.doi.org/10.1045/september2004-vandesompel.
Van de Sompel, Payette, Erickson, Lagoze, and Warner ruminate on transforming scholarly communication to better serve and facilitate knowledge creation. They primarily target the current academic journal system; for the authors, this system constrains scholarly work, as it is expensive, difficult to access, and print-biased. The authors propose a digital system for scholarly communication that more effectively incorporates ideals of interoperability, adaptability, innovation, documentation, and democratization. This proposed system would be implemented as a concurrent knowledge production environment instead of as a mere stage, annex, or afterthought for scholarly work.

Veletsianos, George. 2015. "A Case Study of Scholars' Open and Sharing Practices." *Open Praxis* 7(3): 199–209. DOI: https://doi.org/10.5944/openpraxis.7.3.206.
Velatsianos addresses the extent of open scholarship in institutions that lack a formal infrastructure to support such research. This is carried out through a case study on a public, not-for-profit North American institution (referred to in the paper as Tall Mountain University), specifically by working with faculty members. According to the case study, there are a number of ways in which open scholarship is carried out, with certain practices being favoured over others; some examples include open access manuscripts and educational resources, social media, and open teaching/pedagogy. The author also found that some faculty members publish their materials openly on the Internet without attaching open licences, and that the settings of the platform, as well as the institutional protocols, also affect the extent to which the material is accessible. Despite these findings, Veletsianos states that open scholarship is still a relatively narrow practice at the institution. The author outlines possible limitations of the research, such as open practices that may not have been revealed in the case study and possible limitations of Google Scholar (the search engine used for this research) that may prevent the study from being exhaustive. Overall, the study is descriptive, and does not address the motivations behind practising open scholarship.

## B. Reference List

Adema, Janneke. 2010. "Overview of Open Access Models for eBooks in the Humanities and Social Sciences." OAPEN Project Report. http://project.oapen.org/images/documents/openaccessmodels.pdf.

Andersen, Christian Ulrik, and Søren Bro Pold. 2014. "Post-digital Books and Disruptive Literary Machines." *Formules: Revue des créations formelles* 18: 164–83.

Arbuckle, Alyssa, Alex Christie, Lynne Siemens, Aaron Mauro, and the INKE Research Group, eds. 2016. Special issue. *Scholarly and Research Communication* 7(2/3): n.p. http://src-online.ca/index.php/src/issue/view/24.

Arbuckle, Alyssa, and Alex Christie, with the ETCL Research Group, INKE Research Group, and MVP Research Group. 2015. "Intersections Between Social Knowledge Creation and Critical Making." *Scholarly and Research Communication* 6(3): n.p. DOI: https://doi.org/10.22230/src.2015v6n3a200.

Arbuckle, Alyssa, Constance Crompton, and Aaron Mauro. 2014. Introduction: "Building Partnerships to Transform Scholarly Publishing." *Scholarly and Research Communication* 5(4): n.p. http://src-online.ca/index.php/src/issue/view/18.

Arbuckle, Alyssa, Nina Belojevic, Matthew Hiebert, and Ray Siemens, with Shaun Wong, Derek Siemens, Alex Christie, Jon Saklofske, Jentery Sayers, and the INKE and ETCL Research Groups. 2014. "Social Knowledge Creation: Three Annotated Bibliographies." *Scholarly and Research Communication* 5(2): n.p. DOI: https://doi.org/10.22230/src.2014v5n2a150.

Association of Universities and Colleges of Canada–Canadian Association of Research Libraries Task Force on Academic Libraries and Scholarly Communication. 1997. "The Changing World of Scholarly Communication: Challenges and Choices for Canada—Final Report of the AUCC–CARL/ABRC Task Force." *Canadian Journal of Communication* 22(3): n.p.

Bath, Jon, Scott Schofield, and the INKE Research Group. 2015. "The Digital Book." In *The Cambridge Companion to the History of the Book*, edited by Leslie Howsam, 181–95. Cambridge: Cambridge University Press.

Belojevic, Nina. 2015. "Developing an Open, Networked Peer Review System." *Scholarly and Research Communication* 6(2): n.p. DOI: https://doi.org/10.22230/src.2015v6n2a205.

Borgman, Christine L. 2007. *Scholarship in the Digital Age: Information, Infrastructure, and the Internet.* Cambridge, MA: MIT Press.

Bowen, William R., Constance Crompton, and Matthew Hiebert. 2014. "Iter Community: Prototyping an Environment for Social Knowledge Creation and Communication." *Scholarly and Research Communication* 5(4): n.p. DOI: https://doi.org/10.22230/src.2014v5n4a193.

Brown, Susan, and John Simpson. 2014. "The Changing Culture of Humanities Scholarship: Iteration, Recursion, and Versions in Scholarly Collaboration Environments." *Scholarly and Research Communication* 5(4): n.p. DOI: https://doi.org/10.22230/src.2014v5n4a191.

————. 2015. "An Entity By Any Other Name: Linked Open Data as a Basis for a Decentered, Dynamic Scholarly Publishing Ecology." *Scholarly and Research Communication* 6(2): n.p. DOI: https://doi.org/10.22230/src.2015v6n2a212.

Cohen, Daniel J. 2010. "Open Access Publishing and Scholarly Values." Personal blog post, May 27. https://dancohen.org/2010/05/27/open-access-publishing-and-scholarly-values/. Archived at https://perma.cc/78MH-PK43.

Crompton, Constance, Alyssa Arbuckle, and Raymond G. Siemens, with the Devonshire Manuscript Editorial Group. 2013. "Understanding the Social Edition Through Iterative Implementation: The Case of the *Devonshire MS* (BL Add MS 17492)." *Scholarly and Research Communication* 4(3): n.p. DOI: https://doi.org/10.22230/src.2013v4n3a118.

Crompton, Constance, Raymond G. Siemens, and Alyssa Arbuckle, with the INKE Research Group. 2015. "Enlisting 'Vertues Noble & Excelent': Behavior, Credit, and Knowledge Organization in the Social Edition." *Digital Humanities Quarterly* 9(2): n.p. http://www.digitalhumanities.org/dhq/vol/9/2/000202/000202.html.

Dumova, Tatyana. 2012. "Social Interaction Technologies and the Future of Blogging." In *Blogging in the Global Society: Cultural, Political and Geographical Aspects,* edited by Tatyana Dumova and Richard Fiordo, 249–74. Hershey, PA: IGI Global.

Eve, Martin Paul. 2015. "Open Access Publishing and Scholarly Communication in Non-Scientific Disciplines." *Online Information Review* 39(5): 717–32. DOI: https://doi.org/10.1108/OIR-04-2015-0103.

Fitzpatrick, Kathleen. 2007. "CommentPress: New (Social) Structures for New (Networked) Texts." *Journal of Electronic Publishing* 10(3): n.p. DOI: http://dx.doi.org/10.3998/3336451.0010.305.

———. 2011. *Planned Obsolescence: Publishing, Technology, and the Future of the Academy.* New York: New York University Press.

Fjällbrant, Nancy. 1997. "Scholarly Communication—Historical Development and New Possibilities." In *Proceedings of the IATUL Conferences.* West Lafayette, IN: Purdue University Libraries. http://docs.lib.purdue.edu/iatul/1997/papers/5/.

Grumbach, Elizabeth, and Laura Mandell. 2014. "Meeting Scholars Where They Are: The Advanced Research Consortium (ARC) and a Social Humanities Infrastructure." *Scholarly and Research Communication* 5(4): n.p. DOI: https://doi.org/10.22230/src.2014v5n4a189.

Jones, Steven E. 2014. "Publications." In *The Emergence of the Digital Humanities,* 147–77. New York and London: Routledge.

Lane, Richard J. 2014. "Innovation through Tradition: New Scholarly Publishing Applications Modelled on Faith-Based Electronic Publishing and Learning Environments." *Scholarly and Research Communication* 5(4): n.p. DOI: https://doi.org/10.22230/src.2014v5n4a188.

Lewis, Vivian, Lisa Spiro, Xuemao Wang, and Jon E. Cawthorne. 2015. *Building Expertise to Support Digital Scholarship: A Global Perspective.* Arlington, VA: Council on Library and Information Resources. https://www.clir.org/pubs/reports/pub168/pub168.

Liu, Alan. 2007. "Imagining the New Media Encounter." In *A Companion to Digital Literary Studies,* edited by Ray Siemens and Susan Schreibman, 3–25. Oxford: Blackwell.

Lorimer, Rowland. 2013. "Libraries, Scholars, and Publishers in Digital Journal and Monograph Publishing." *Scholarly and Research Communication* 4(1): n.p. DOI: https://doi.org/10.22230/src.2013v4n1a43.

Lorimer, Rowland. 2014. "A Good Idea, a Difficult Reality: Toward a Publisher/ Library Open Access Partnership." *Scholarly and Research Communication* 5(4): n.p. DOI: https://doi.org/10.22230/src.2014v5n4a180.

Maxwell, John W. 2014. "Publishing Education in the 21st Century and the Role of the University." *Journal of Electronic Publishing* 17(2): n.p. DOI: http://dx.doi.org/10.3998/3336451.0017.205.

———. 2015. "Beyond Open Access to Open Publication and Open Scholarship." *Scholarly and Research Communication* 6(3): n.p. DOI: https://doi.org/10.22230/src.2015v6n3a202.

O'Donnell, Daniel, Heather Hobma, Sandra Cowan, Gillian Ayers, Jessica Bay, Marinus Swanepoel, Wendy Merkley, Kelaine Devine, Emma Dering, and Inge Genee. 2015. "Aligning Open Access Publication with the Research and Teaching Missions of the Public University: The Case of the Lethbridge Journal Incubator (If 'if's and 'and's were pots and pans)." *Journal of Electronic Publishing* 18(3): n.p. DOI: http://dx.doi.org/10.3998/3336451.0018.309.

Powell, Daniel, Raymond Siemens, Matthew Hiebert, Lindsey Seatter, and William R. Bowen. 2015. "Transformation through Integration: The Renaissance Knowledge Network (ReKN) and a Next Wave of Scholarly Publication." *Scholarly and Research Communication* 6(2): n.p. DOI: https://doi.org/10.22230/src.2015v6n2a199.

Powell, Daniel, Ray Siemens, and the INKE Research Group. 2014. "Building Alternative Scholarly Publishing Capacity: The Renaissance Knowledge Network (ReKN) as Digital Production Hub." *Scholarly and Research Communication* 5(4): n.p. DOI: https://doi.org/10.22230/src.2014v5n4a183.

Price, Kenneth M., and Raymond G. Siemens, eds. 2013. *Literary Studies in the Digital Age.* New York: Modern Language Association.

Saklofske, Jon. 2014. "Exploding, Centralizing and Reimagining: Critical Scholarship Refracted Through the NewRadial Prototype." *Scholarly and Research Communication* 5(2): n.p. DOI: https://doi.org/10.22230/src.2014v5n2a151.

Saklofske, Jon, with the INKE Research Team. 2016. "Digital *Theoria, Poiesis,* and *Praxis*: Activating Humanities Research and Communication through Open Social Scholarship Platform Design." *Scholarly and*

*Research Communication* 7(2/3): n.p. DOI: https://doi.org/10.22230/src.2016v7n2/3a252.

Saklofske, Jon, and Jake Bruce. 2013. "Beyond Browsing and Reading: The Open Work of Digital Scholarly Editions." *Scholarly and Research Communication* 4(3): n.p. DOI: https://doi.org/10.22230/src.2013v4n3a119.

Schreibman, Susan, Ray Siemens, and John Unsworth, eds. 2004. *A Companion to Digital Humanities*. Oxford: Blackwell.

Shearer, Kathleen, and Bill Birdsall. 2002. "The Transition of Scholarly Communications in Canada." http://www.moyak.com/papers/scholarly-communications-canada.pdf.

Siemens, Raymond G. 2002. "Scholarly Publishing at its Source, and at Present." In *The Credibility of Electronic Publishing: A Report to the Humanities and Social Sciences Federation of Canada*, compiled by Raymond G. Siemens, Michael Best, Elizabeth Grove-White, Alan Burk, James Kerr, Andy Pope, Jean-Claude Guédon, Geoffrey Rockwell, and Lynne Siemens. *TEXT Technology* 11(1): 1–128. https://web.archive.org/web/20151012065051/https://web.viu.ca/hssfc/Final/Overview.htm.

Siemens, Raymond G., and David Moorman, eds. 2006. *Mind Technologies: Humanities Computing and the Canadian Academic Community*. Calgary: University of Calgary Press.

Siemens, Raymond G., Claire Warwick, Richard Cunningham, Teresa Dobson, Alan Galey, Stan Ruecker, Susan Schreibman, and the INKE Research Group. 2009. "*Codex* Ultor: Toward a Conceptual and Theoretical Foundation for New Research on Books and Knowledge Environments." *Digital Studies / Le champ numerique* 1(2): n.p. DOI: http://doi.org/10.16995/dscn.270.

Siemens, Raymond G., Teresa Dobson, Stan Ruecker, Richard Cunningham, Alan Galey, Claire Warwick, and Lynne Siemens. 2011. "HCI-Book? Perspectives on E-Book Research, 2006–2008 (Foundational to Implementing New Knowledge Environments)." *Papers of the Bibliographical Society of Canada / Cahiers de la Société bibliographique du Canada* 49(1): 35–89. http://web.uvic.ca/~siemens/pub/2011-HCI-Book.pdf.

Stein, Bob. 2015. "Back to the Future." *Journal of Electronic Publishing* 18(2): n.p. DOI: http://dx.doi.org/10.3998/3336451.0018.204.

Stranack, Kevin. 2008. *Starting A New Scholarly Journal in Africa.* Public Knowledge Project. https://pkp.sfu.ca/files/AfricaNewJournal.pdf.

Vandendorpe, Christian. 2012. "Wikisource and the Scholarly Book." *Scholarly and Research Communication* 3(4): n.p. DOI: https://doi.org/10.22230/src.2012v3n4a58.

Van de Sompel, Herbert, Sandy Payette, John Erickson, Carl Lagoze, and Simeon Warner. 2004. "Rethinking Scholarly Communication: Building the System that Scholars Deserve." *D-Lib Magazine* 10(9): n.p. DOI: http://dx.doi.org/10.1045/september2004-vandesompel.

Veletsianos, George. 2015. "A Case Study of Scholars' Open and Sharing Practices." *Open Praxis* 7(3): 199–209. DOI: https://doi.org/10.5944/openpraxis.7.3.206.

## 3. Open Access

The open access movement has infiltrated many aspects of today's world and has been increasingly advocated for in academic settings, often under the banner of access to knowledge as a human right that should be openly available rather than hidden behind paywalls. The objective of this category is to present critical publications that focus on the accessibility of information, primarily scholarly research. Authors approach open access from two different vantage points: either by focusing on open access as a theory or as a fundamental human right (Anderson 1998; Suber 2004), or treating open access as a practical problem and offering suggestions on how to successfully implement its principles in a capitalist society (Asmah 2014; Ayris et al. 2014; Kingsley 2013). Several articles explore the perception of open access publishing in order to establish why scholars might shy away from sharing their research in this type of venue (Cohen 2010; Coonin and Younce 2009; Gaines 2015; Rodriguez 2014). Overall, these studies found that despite the community's agreement to open access publishing and understanding of its benefits, free information is seen as less prestigious and therefore less valuable when it comes to academic promotions and tenure. The majority of publications discuss the roles of scholars and libraries in the open access movement, but some also touch on the importance of policy-makers and the larger community in advocating for change.

### A. Annotations

**\*\*Adema, Janneke. 2010. "Overview of Open Access Models for eBooks in the Humanities and Social Sciences." OAPEN Project Report. http://project.oapen.org/images/documents/openaccessmodels. pdf.**
Adema provides an overview of current open access publishing models being experimented with by organizations and institutions in the humanities and social sciences. The author intends to find strategies for making open access book publishing a sustainable enterprise, with funding and profit for all parties involved. Adema explores a variety of business models and publishing processes that make up what she terms the 'experimental phase' of open access book publishing. She touches on the motives—both monetary and missionary—behind the open access movement, compares various presses and press partnerships, and explores the different practices and collaborations that make open access sustainable.

**Anderson, Charles. 1998. "Universal Access—Free and Open Access—It Depends ..."** *Reference & User Services Quarterly* 38(1): 25–27.

Anderson provides a brief editorial introduction to the tradition of open access values, arguing that the values of open access are anything but new. He asserts that the entire public library movement was founded on the ideas of open access, and asks how much progress has been made since then. For Anderson, it is necessary that attitudes around open access change in order to stimulate progress. It is not enough to simply provide a workstation or to secure resources; the individuals working in the institutions have to believe in the importance of open access principles.

**Asmah, Josephine. 2014. "International Policy and Practice on Open Access for Monographs." Federation for the Humanities and Social Sciences. http://www.ideas-idees.ca/sites/default/files/aspp-oa-appendix.pdf.**

Asmah presents an overview of international open access policies and practices. The objective of this report is to inform the Federation for the Humanities and Social Sciences to what extent international government policies address open access, especially in terms of open access monographs. Asmah begins with a history of the open access movement and a summary of the importance of open access ideologies. She conducts a survey of open access policies across global markets and gives a brief but detailed summary on how various countries handle open access issues (including Austria, the United Kingdom, Australia, Belgium, France, the United States, Japan, and South Africa). These countries were chosen specifically to represent the organizations that Asmah considers to be the major global open access players. She concludes by suggesting a position for Canada in the open access movement.

**Ayris, Paul, Erica McLaren, Martin Moyle, Catherine Sharp, and Lara Speicher. 2014. "Open Access in UCL: A New Paradigm for London's Global University in Research Support."** *Australian Academic & Research Libraries* 45(4): 282–95.

Ayris, McLaren, Moyle, Sharp, and Speicher address the benefits and challenges of open access publishing for a research university. While open access publishing provides an unprecedented opportunity for scholars to disseminate their research globally, it also presents numerous barriers for institutions, such as funding start-up costs and the need to balance roles and measure success. The authors provide insight on how to overcome these challenges from their positions as employees of the University College London (UCL). Ayris et al. argue that popular discourse discouraging open access, or presenting it in a negative light, is often factually incorrect. They provide evidence that free publications from UCL are widely disseminated, financially viable, and of outstanding quality. The authors assert that open access is an opportunity, not a threat, to research universities. By developing open access policies, constructing open access repositories, and establishing a gold standard open access press, universities can reap the rewards of open access publishing.

**Bailey, Charles W., Jr. 2007. "Open Access and Libraries."** *Collection Management* **32(3–4): 351–83.**
Bailey examines the major components of the open access movement. He analyzes the validity of open access strategies, discusses the rationale behind the open access movement, addresses the movement's impact on libraries, and considers whether and how open access policies will transform jobs. Bailey takes up several open access case studies, including the Berlin Declaration, as a means of describing the field. He defines open access as freely available, online literature that is royalty free and can be used with minimal restrictions. While acknowledging that the open access movement is only one of many potential solutions to the serious problems libraries face when it comes to scholarly communication and research support, Bailey argues that it is a very important one and that the voices of libraries need to be more prominent in the debate. He believes that if libraries were to embrace open access to a greater degree, graduate students could be involved in creating new, valuable, and authoritative digital resources.

**Björk, Bo-Christer. 2004. "Open Access to Scientific Publications—An Analysis of the Barriers to Change?"** *Information Research* **9(2): n.p. http://informationr.net/ir/9-2/paper170.html.**
Björk asserts that the rise of the Internet has changed how information is disseminated. While the methods may have changed, the economic ramifications of scholarly publishing have stayed the same, creating a need to rethink the current publishing system. Björk proposes an open access system, and defines open access as the means to information that can be read and shared for noncommercial purposes without any payments or restrictions. He also acknowledges that systems are difficult to change; legal barriers, a lack of infrastructure, and the need to develop a new business model stand in the way. While most people recognize the need for an open access system, it will take more than simple awareness for the system to be implemented.

**Bohannon, John. 2013. "Who's Afraid of Peer Review?"** *Science* **342: 60–65. DOI: www.doi.org/10.1126/science.342.6154.60.**
This article details an experiment in which a spoof paper was submitted to a myriad of open access journals, with the results of this experience used as

evidence for the lack of thorough, robust peer review. Bohannon submitted this spoof paper, using a fake name and institution, to relevant online journals. The spoof paper was designed to be mundane, with obvious flaws in its methodology. At the time of publication, Bohannon had submitted the paper to 304 journals. More than half of the journals (157) accepted the paper, 98 journals rejected the paper, and the remaining 49 journals had not responded. Only 36 of the submissions generated any type of review comments that recognized the fatal flaws in the experiment's methodology; ultimately, 16 of those papers were still accepted despite the poor reviews. Bohannon closes the article by suggesting that open access journals might not be to blame for these deficiencies, and that the same result might have been produced if conducted with subscription journals.

**Canadian Association of Research Libraries. n.d. "Open Access." Canadian Association of Research Libraries. http://www.carl-abrc. ca/advancing-research/scholarly-communication/open-access/.**
The Canadian Association of Research Libraries (CARL) advocates for open access because of the benefits it grants users, primarily open access to reading and utilizing knowledge. This mode of dissemination benefits funding agencies, since their investment has a maximized return, as well as the researchers, since their scholarship is distributed to a wider audience. CARL aligns its principles with the Budapest Open Access Initiative (BOAI) Declaration and the Berlin Declaration on Open Access to Knowledge in the Sciences and Humanities. From BOAI, CARL adopts and propagates the practice of publishing scholarly literature in open access. It also follows the Berlin Declaration in its decision to publish all original scientific research results and related data and metadata in open access. Thus, CARL's vision applies to the output of the scholarly work it funds, with criteria emphasizing that copyright is met and that the product is consistent with highest peer review standards. CARL continues to work to implement open access standards, and to deal with the challenges that arise with this type of knowledge dissemination.

**Chan, Leslie. 2004. "Supporting and Enhancing Scholarship in the Digital Age: The Role of Open-Access Institutional Repositories." *Canadian Journal of Communication* 29(3): 277–300. https://www.cjc-online.ca/index.php/journal/article/view/1455/1579.**
Chan argues that the key goal of open access is to maximize the impact of research by reaching the largest number of readers possible. This impact can be measured by counting citation references connected to specific articles. Chan summarizes a study of 190 journals conducted by the Institute

of Scientific Information, which found that those with open access and those with proprietary access showed no difference in impact. However, Chan argues that the data is invalid because the study took up the journal itself, not the individual article, as its unit of measurement. Conducting his own research, Chan finds that there was, in fact, an impact factor difference of 300 per cent in favour of open access articles. For Chan, knowledge is a public good, and must be distributed as openly as possible.

Chang, Yu-Wei. 2015. "Librarians' Contribution to Open Access Journal Publishing in Library and Information Science From the Perspective of Authorship." *Journal of Academic Librarianship* 41(5): 660–68. DOI: https://doi.org/10.1016/j.acalib.2015.06.006.
Chang examines how librarian authors participate in open access publishing. In particular, the author studies librarians who contribute articles to journals in the field of library and information science. Chang's case study took up 19 open access library and information science journals in which 1,819 articles were published between 2008 and 2013. Of these articles, 55.6 per cent of the authors were librarians (the next highest category was scholars at 33.5 per cent), and 53.7 per cent of the articles were co-authored or collaborative. The majority of these partnerships were librarian–librarian collaborations, but librarian–scholar co-authorships ranked second highest. Overall, the results demonstrate that open access publishing offers an opportunity for librarians to move from the more typical research support role into more of a knowledge creation role. Chang concludes that more authors need to publish on open access platforms in order to survive.

**Cohen, Daniel J. 2010. "Open Access Publishing and Scholarly Values." Personal blog post, May 27. https://dancohen.org/2010/05/27/open-access-publishing-and-scholarly-values/. Archived at https://perma.cc/78MH-PK43.
Cohen builds on the notions of the supply and demand side of scholarly communication, as well as the value system of scholars, in order to make a case for increasing open access scholarship and being more receptive to scholarship that does not adhere to the conventional academic publishing system. According to Cohen, the four sentiments that stand in the way of embracing open access scholarship are impartiality, passion, shame, and narcissism. Cohen discusses impartiality in relation to the pressure scholars feel to publish in established, toll access venues for a number for reasons, including legitimate concerns such as career growth. He argues that open access publishing can take place in parallel to more conventional forms of academic

publishing. Cohen also criticizes the commercial apparatus of the publishing system for taking advantage of scholars and their labour and passion, which is expressed in writing. He argues for the need to reorient the ways in which scholarship is produced and published in order to increase access, and also to break the chain within a system that is exploiting academics. Cohen argues that the act of accepting certain aspects of digital media and rejecting others is a 'shameful hypocrisy' (n.p.)—first, by using the digital medium as the primary source for research yet avoiding it as a means of publishing and, second, talking about access and the need for academics to be more inclusive but avoiding the existing necessary steps toward implementing these notions into practice. Finally, the narcissistic factor is related to the reputability of publishing in typical venues; Cohen counters this by saying that open access publishing is likely to get better readership and to spread ideas more widely, and could also be added to the CV. The author concludes by inviting us to envision and enact a more straightforward and virtuous model for scholarly communication.

**Coonin, Bryna, and Leigh Younce. 2009. "Publishing in Open Access Journals in The Social Sciences and Humanities: Who's Doing It and Why." Paper presented at the *ACRL Fourteenth National Conference*. http://www.ala.org/acrl/sites/ala.org.acrl/files/content/conferences/confsandpreconfs/national/seattle/papers/85.pdf.**
Coonin and Younce survey 918 authors who published in open access humanities and social science journals in 2007 and 2008 in order to study the demographics and perceptions of open access. A total of 339 individuals responded to the survey. The respondents ranked peer review as the most important factor in choosing a journal, with reputation and suitability ranking second and third. The authors who published the most over the calendar year also published the most articles in open access journals. Approximately 15 per cent of the respondents were unaware of open access publishing, and more than 50 per cent saw open access journals as having less prestige. Further, author processing charges (APCs) often obstruct publication, as authors or their institutions are sometimes expected to levy fees to publish in open access journals, and these costs discourage many from seeking this type of publication venue. Overall, Coonin and Younce observe that the humanities and social sciences have been slower at integrating open access publishing than the scientific disciplines.

**\*\*Eve, Martin Paul. 2015. "Open Access Publishing and Scholarly Communication in Non-Scientific Disciplines." *Online***

*Information Review* **39(5): 717–32. DOI: https://doi.org/10.1108/OIR-04-2015-0103.**

Eve presents an overview of the current open access debate in non-scientific (non-STEM) disciplines, arguing that non-STEM disciplines have consistently lagged behind in their approach to open access policies and practices. He attributes this gap to a variety of economic and cultural factors, arguing that these specific challenges or objections have stunted the growth of open access in these disciplines. Eve suggests that his article is far too short and biased to do justice to the complexity of the issues he raises; however, it is his hope that his insights will spur action and critical appraisal from the community at large. Academia must consider what is needed from a scholarly communications infrastructure and simultaneously build pragmatic and non-damaging transition strategies in order to utilize open access dissemination to its full advantage.

**Fund, Sven. 2015. "Will Open Access Change the Game? Hypotheses on the Future Cooperation of Libraries, Researchers, and Publishers." *Bibliothek Forschung und Praxis* 39(2): 206–9. DOI: https://doi.org/10.1515/bfp-2015-0025.**

Fund provides a general outline of the potential for open access to enlarge the scope of conversations in the scientific community. He compares the open access journal industry to the music industry since the turn of the century and to the personal computing industry of the past several decades. In 2008, Spotify introduced a completely new business model that questioned the mechanism of buying music altogether, and the music industry could not continue its former economic policies. He argues that the biggest hurdle for the breakthrough of open access is not the absence of publication channels, or a lack of cooperation at the publisher's end, but the imminent structure of the library system, its decision-making mechanisms, and the circulation of funds.

**Gaines, Annie M. 2015. "From Concerned to Cautiously Optimistic: Assessing Faculty Perception and Knowledge of Open Access in a Campus-Wide Study." *Journal of Librarianship & Scholarly Communication* 3(1): 1–40. DOI: https://doi.org/10.7710/2162-3309.1212.**

Gaines argues that, while the academic community has a solid understanding of what open access is, very little research has gone into examining individuals' impressions of open access publishing platforms. She surveys faculty members at one university in hopes of gathering data to fill in this information gap. A total of 240 surveys were administered, and 54 respondents (23 per cent) returned completed surveys. The majority of these respondents were from the sciences. Overall, the respondents had very little practical knowledge about open access: most knew what it was, but could not differentiate between types of platforms. The respondents indicated that the three key motivations in choosing a publication venue were prestige, impact, and personal recommendations. They felt that open access journals were unreliable and did not hold as much academic value. Policy is cited as a major roadblock, as many institutions do not have promotion and tenure guidelines that allow open access articles. Fear and misinformation resulted in a general lack of motivation to publish in open access spaces.

Gargouri, Yassine, Chawki Hajjem, Vincent Larivière, Yves Gingras, Les Carr, Tim Brody, and Stevan Harnad. 2010. "Self-Selected or Mandated, Open Access Increases Citation Impact for Higher Quality Research." *PLOS One* 5(10): n.p. DOI: https://doi.org/10.1371/journal.pone.0013636.

Gargouri, Hajjem, Larivière, Gringras, Carr, Brody, and Harnad compare the impact of open access (OA) and non-open access articles that have been archived in a repository due to self-selection or to journal mandate. They challenge the OA Advantage hypothesis, which claims that articles published in OA according to self-selection are cited significantly more than those that are published because of mandate. According to the hypothesis, the articles that researchers choose to archive are their 'best' work, or articles with the widest scope or most applicable research, which naturally leads to higher citation hits. By adopting a social science approach to test this claim, Gargouri et al. conduct a comprehensive study of journals that contain articles from all the aforementioned categories. The study found that there is actually no reduction in the OA Advantage for mandated OA articles (60 per cent) in comparison to self-selected OA articles (15 per cent). Another finding is that the impact or number of citation hits was not affected by whether the article was published through self-selection or mandate; the main increase of exposure results from being published in OA. Overall, authors of this article disprove the OA Advantage hypothesis, and point to how publishing in OA is a productive means for increased exposure.

Government of Canada. 2015b. "Tri-Agency Open Access Policy on Publications." *Science and Technology for Canadians.* http://www.science.gc.ca/default.asp?lang=En&n=F6765465-1.

The 'Tri-Agency Open Access Policy on Publications' web page begins with a preamble that discusses the importance of agencies, such as the Social

Sciences and Humanities Research Council (SSHRC), in advancing research. It highlights the role played by barrier-free access to research and knowledge, as well as how the Internet has contributed to open access, multi-disciplinary, and collaborative scholarship. The policy objective and policy statement address peer-reviewed journal publications (online repositories and journals) and publication-related research data. The document also provides information about the implementation date, compliance with the policy, and a policy review, and concludes with links to additional information resources.

**Hampson, Crystal. 2014. "The Adoption of Open Access Funds Among Canadian Academic Research Libraries, 2008–2012."** *The Canadian Journal of Library & Information Practice & Research* **9(2): 1–14. DOI: https://doi.org/10.21083/partnership.v9i2.3115.**
Hampson discusses and analyzes the adoption of open access publishing funds—allocated monies set aside to support the open publication of scholarly research—at Canadian institutional libraries. She explores the emergence of this policy by studying surveys published between 2007 and 2012 in light of the Innovation Diffusion Theory (IDT) to determine whether these types of funds are becoming standard at Canadian academic research institutions. According to the results, the trend of open access funds in Canada closely resembles the S-curve anticipated in positive IDT studies. Overall, Hampson argues that this demonstrates a pressure for continual support of open access funds and the need to closely evaluate the effectiveness of these monies. Hampson's research forms part of the conversation that is pushing for the continued adoption of open access funds among Canadian academic research institutions.

**Heath, Malcolm, Michael Jubb, and David Robey. 2008. "E-Publication and Open Access in the Arts and Humanities in the UK."** *Ariadne* **54: n.p. http://www.ariadne.ac.uk/issue/54/heath-et-al/. Archived at https://perma.cc/NKM4-E3T5.**
Heath, Jubb, and Robey present an overview of the role of e-monographs, e-texts, and other e-books in arts and humanities-related disciplines. E-monographs are still relatively unpopular for open access publication in the humanities since many people find these difficult to read and prefer the printed form. The survey uses as its principal object the activities of the UK's Arts and Humanities Research Council (AHRC) and the Research Information Network (RIN) to highlight a range of issues with open access monographs, journals, repositories, electronic publication of theses, and data publication. The authors point to the success of JSTOR as an open access repository,

although it is well known that JSTOR requires libraries to pay a substantial subscription fee for access. The survey suggests that there is limited, slow progress to changing attitudes toward electronic publication. The academic community needs to develop a broader and more well-informed dialogue about what its needs are with regard to digital publication, and the issues endemic to publishing a monograph electronically.

+Kingsley, Danny. 2013. "Build It and They Will Come? Support for Open Access in Australia." *Scholarly and Research Communication* 4(1): n.p. DOI: https://doi.org/10.22230/src.2013v4n1a39.
Kingsley reflects on Australia's adoption and support of open access policies over the last decade. He pays particular attention to the building of open access infrastructure, repositories, mandates, and funding bodies, and provides a full history of Australia's open access movement. Kingsley uses the collected citation information as a test case for exploring the effectiveness and efficiency of open access publication. Finally, he concludes by providing some suggestions for improvement. Kingsley argues that developing an open access advocacy body, altering and updating the language of the current mandates, and introducing requirements for using open access platforms could help move Australia into the next phase of adopting this movement.

Kitchin, Rob, Sandra Collins, and Dermot Frost. 2015. "Funding Models for Open Access Digital Data Repositories." *Online Information Review* 39(5): 664–81. DOI: https://www.doi.org/10.1108/OIR-01-2015-0031.
Kitchin, Collins, and Frost outline financial models for digital open access repositories that are not funded by a core source. The authors discuss a list of challenges to open access, including Christine Borgman's 'dirty little secret': despite the promotion of open data sharing, not much sharing is actually taking place.[2] The authors propose that creating open access data repositories is not enough for attitudes in academia to change; substantial cultural changes in research practices must take place, and researchers should be encouraged to deposit their data as they complete research. The survey covers 14 potential funding streams for open access research data repositories. The authors argue that the lack of full, core funding and a direct funding stream through payment-for-use pose considerable financial challenges to the directors of such repositories. The collections that are maintained without funding are

---

[2] See Christine L. Borgman (2012), "The Conundrum of Sharing Research Data," *Journal of the American Society for Information Science and Technology* 63(6), 1059.

in significant danger of being lost to 'digital decay' and other technological challenges.

**Laakso, Mikael, and Bo-Christer Björk. 2012. "Anatomy of Open Access Publishing: A Study of Longitudinal Development and Internal Structure."** *BMC Medicine* **10(124): n.p. DOI: https://doi. org/10.1186/ 1741-7015-10-124.**

Laakso and Björk measure the volume of scientific articles published in full, immediate open access journals. They take account of longitudinal internal shifts in the structure of open access publishing concerning revenue models, publisher types, and relative distribution among scientific disciplines between 2000 and 2011. The analysis is quantitative in method, and includes open access publisher output across geographic regions, number of articles by different publisher types, and disciplines. The survey creates a chart of all the articles indexed in Scopus and categorizes them according to year published, and whether they were published in full immediate open access journals, hybrid form, or delayed open access publications. The authors question whether open access will become the mainstream model for journal article publication, and if new entrants into the field, such as the Public Library of Science (PLOS) and BioMed Central (BMC), will take over the market ground lost by the publishers.

**+**Lorimer, Rowland. 2014. "A Good Idea, a Difficult Reality: Toward a Publisher/Library Open Access Partnership."** *Scholarly and Research Communication* **5(4): n.p. DOI: https://doi.org/10.22230/ src.2014v 5n4a180.**

Lorimer comments on the state of scholarly publishing in Canada. He offers thorough insight into the financial, social, and cultural obstacles that arise as academic institutions move toward an open access model of knowledge mobilization. Lorimer argues that although the *idea* of open access is desirable to academic and academic-aligned researchers, practitioners, and organizations, the *reality* of a complete open access model still requires considerable planning and implementation. Lorimer emphasizes the importance of long-term thinking in supporting Canada's research libraries as open access hubs of orderly, sustainable, and productive information.

**Lowe, Megan W. 2014. "In Defense of Open Access: Or, Why I Stopped Worrying and Started an OA Journal."** *Codex* **2(4): 1–11.**

Lowe outlines the general principles of open access publishing and discusses and defends the merits of her own production: *Codex*, a peer-reviewed open access journal focused on academic libraries and librarianship. *Codex* operates by giving its authors full rights, except that the journal retains the right of first publication. Lowe claims that Bohannon's 2013 study (annotated above) draws rather broad conclusions regarding peer review of open access journals, and that authors seeking publication in open access journals should examine other venues, such as *Codex*. She declares that it is a mistake to pit the conventional model of publishing against the open access model. Furthermore, Lowe asserts, librarians should act as advocates for what open access means, and share knowledge of its benefits with new patrons. *Codex* was started with the aim of helping librarians demystify the publication process, and giving new authors a chance to publish and gain experience in the field. She acknowledges issues of occasional fraud and scandal in open access publications, but argues that prioritizing accountability of information providers and upholding publisher ethics will help open access become a mainstream vehicle for scholarly production.

+**Maxwell, John W. 2015. "Beyond Open Access to Open Publication and Open Scholarship." *Scholarly and Research Communication* 6(3): n.p. DOI: https://doi.org/10.22230/src.2015v6n3a202.

Maxwell calls for radical openness in scholarly publishing—that is, moving beyond the ideas of open access toward a cultural transformation. He argues that as the humanities are reimagined in the light of digital media, there is an increasing need for old practices to be thrown away instead of merely reconceived. For Maxwell, the print-based journal economy relies on limited access in order to maintain a profit. The economics of open access, however, could adapt a new system of openness to shifting market demands, opened by the Web, that depend upon interconnection and interlinkage. Maxwell turns to agile publishing and its mission statement of 'release early, release often' as an example of a more open movement. He asks whether scholarly work can be remixed, combined, reassembled, taken apart, and inscribed through an iterative process. Maxwell asserts that education, publishing, and scholarship can all be cultures of transformation.

+McGregor, Heidi, and Kevin Guthrie. 2015. "Delivering Impact of Scholarly Information: Is Access Enough?" *Journal of Electronic Publishing* 18(3): n.p. DOI: http://dx.doi.org/10.3998/3336451.0018.302.

McGregor and Guthrie write on open access from their perspective at ITHA-KA, a not-for-profit organization that focuses on the wide dissemination of knowledge and is most well known for JSTOR, a large-scale digital library service. They argue that free access alone is not sufficient for ensuring the broad dissemination, uptake, and impact of knowledge. The authors then shift focus from access to what they term 'productive use,' and they outline a series of conditions that they deem necessary for a scholarly resource to be considered effective from a knowledge-building perspective. These conditions include literacy, technology, awareness, access, know-how, and training. McGregor and Guthrie conclude that a sustained commitment to these conditions will inevitably heighten scholarly impact and bring the world one step closer to the goal of universal access to knowledge.

+Meadows, Alice. 2015. "Beyond Open: Expanding Access to Scholarly Content." *Journal of Electronic Publishing* 18(3): n.p. DOI: http://dx.doi.org/10.3998/3336451.0018.301.

Meadows argues that open access should merely be the beginning of new trends of openness and access to scholarly resources. She summarizes and evaluates a series of public, low-cost access initiatives started between 1990 and 2014, including Access to Research; Electronic Information for Libraries; the International Network for Access to Scientific Publications; the New School for Social Research's Journal Donation Project; patientACCESS; and Research for Life. Meadows argues that these initiatives are valuable for publishers because they increase access to, and usage of, content beyond core markets. While Meadows acknowledges that open access is definitely not a one-size-fits-all challenge, publishers, small businesses, and medium enterprises all have something to gain from the movement: the opportunity to engage new audiences.

Ober, Josiah, Walter Scheidel, Brent D. Shaw, and Donna Sanclemente. 2007. "Toward Open Access in Ancient Studies: The Princeton-Stanford Working Papers in Classics." *Hesperia* 76(1): 229–42. https://www.jstor.org/stable/25068017.

Ober, Scheidel, Shaw, and Sanclemente present the history of open access publication in Classics and Ancient Studies. Launched in 2005, the Princeton/Stanford Working Papers in Classics (PSWPC) provides open access to a range of publications by faculty, postdoctoral fellows, visiting scholars, and, with permission, graduate students from Princeton and Stanford Universities in an online database. The authors cite both the Perseus Project and the *Bryn Mawr Classical Review* as two early digital projects in classics that have become standard points of reference for ancient studies. The PSWPC allows scholars to circulate pre-publication works for popular reception, although these are non-reviewed and rely solely on the reputations of the authors who have submitted them. Ober et al. note that the certification process has been observed as the primary distinguishing asset of non-open access publication. Inadvertently, they argue that quality standards, determined by users rather than by a few editors, provide evidence in favour of open access in humanities and social science departments. The PSWPC was developed in order to encourage other departments at the two universities to consider open access and digital circulation as economical resources for university publication.

+**O'Donnell, Daniel, Heather Hobma, Sandra Cowan, Gillian Ayers, Jessica Bay, Marinus Swanepoel, Wendy Merkley, Kelaine Devine, Emma Dering, and Inge Genee. 2015. "Aligning Open Access Publication with the Research and Teaching Missions of the Public University: The Case of the Lethbridge Journal Incubator (If 'if's and 'and's were pots and pans)." *Journal of Electronic Publishing* 18(3): n.p. DOI: http://dx.doi.org/10.3998/3336451.0018.309.**

O'Donnell et al. present a research mission summary for the group behind the Lethbridge Journal Incubator, and detail how this project provides graduate students with early experience in scholarly publishing. The Lethbridge Journal Incubator trains graduate students in technical and managerial aspects of journal production under the supervision of scholar-editors and professional librarians. The project introduces students to the core elements of academic journal production workflows and provides training in copyediting, preparation of proofs, document encoding, and the use of standard journal production software. Using circle graphs, the authors demonstrate the significant increase in research time devoted to production tasks that improve research ability or knowledge. For O'Donnell et al., the key innovation of the Lethbridge Journal Incubator is its alignment of journal production sustainability with the educational and research missions of the university. The authors attribute the slow growth of open access to attitudes among those who pay for the production and dissemination of research. By unlocking the training and administrative support potential of the production process, the Lethbridge Journal Incubator promotes access within the University of Lethbridge.

**Organisation for Economic Cooperation and Development (OECD). 2015. "Making Open Science a Reality." *OECD Science, Technology and Industry Policy Papers* 25. Paris: OECD Publishing.**

The Organisation for Economic Cooperation and Development states that open science represents an effort toward making accessible publicly funded research in digital format, and provides a rationale for open science. The authors discuss key actors in open science, including researchers, government ministries, research funding agencies, universities and public research institutes, libraries, repositories, data centres, private nonprofit organizations and foundations, private scientific publishers, and businesses. They also examine policy trends in open science, which could be mandatory rules, incentives, or funding. Their main findings include statements that approach open science as a means and not an end. The authors also explore open access to scientific publications and define open access in an exploratory manner by looking at it from various perspectives, with an interest in its legal implications.

**Peekhaus, Wilhelm, and Nicholas Proferes. 2015. "How Library and Information Science Faculty Perceive and Engage with Open Access." *Journal of Information Science* 41(5): 640–61. DOI: https:// doi.org/10.1177/ 0165551515587855.**

Peekhaus and Proferes conduct the first systematic exploration of North American library and information science faculties' awareness of, attitudes toward, and experience with open access scholarly publishing. Following a thorough literature review, the authors argue that the sustained annual growth in journals in the past five decades has resulted in a contemporary multibillion-dollar scholarly publishing industry dominated by a handful of commercial behemoths that receive resources and funding from the wealthiest higher education institutions. Their survey indicates that while 80 per cent of respondents had submitted an article to a subscription-based journal in the last year, only 37 per cent had done the same in an open access journal. Further, just over half of the respondents had ever published with an open access journal. In terms of using institutional repositories, 35 per cent of the respondents had deposited an article. Overall, engagement with open access is related to perceptions of faculty rank and promotion. While experience with open access platforms alleviates some concerns, a substantial bias remains.

**Pinfield, Stephen. 2015. "Making Open Access Work: The 'State-of-the-Art' in Providing Open Access to Scholarly Literature." *Online Information Review* 39(5): 604–36. DOI: https://doi.org/10.1108/ OIR-05-2015-0167.**

Twenty years into the movement, Pinfield examines the challenges that still plague open access scholarship. Despite the growth of open access, Pinfield asserts that barriers to universal acceptance remain, namely significant levels of disinterest, suspicion, and scepticism among researchers. Much of the debate among open access advocates and other people, he argues, assumes that different types of open access frameworks—such as green (repositories) versus gold (journals)—are rivals. The author believes that popular understanding of open access needs to be further developed, and uses the Research Information Network's 2014 report as a framework for understanding the problems of accessibility, availability, usage, and financial sustainability of open access publication. Overall, the key issue of open access is transforming policy into practice—it is not a question of whether or not information should be open, but rather a question of how.

Prelinger, Rick. 2007. "Archives and Access in the 21st Century." *Cinema Journal* 46(3): 114–18. DOI: https://www.doi.org/10.1353/cj.2007.0027.

Prelinger seeks to understand how moving images problematize archival practices, and how the archive can reconcile legacy practices with new cultural functions. He outlines the history of the archive's role in film preservation, and how access to film materials has largely been conceded to Web services such as YouTube and the Internet Archive. Open access, for Prelinger, is an important asset for film studies, since the field is of great interest to nonacademic audiences as well. The author is sceptical, however, as he does not see open access as a career-enhancing alternative for scholars who publish in comparatively expensive and limited access journals. Digital literacy goes hand-in-hand with rethinking access and copyright for the film archive. Prelinger argues that archival ethics should generally favour use over the fear of abuse, and that archives should cease to be wholesale repositories relying on presenters, producers, and scholars to distribute the knowledge contained within them.

Rath, Prabhash Narayana. 2015. "Study of Open Access Publishing in Social Sciences and its Implications for Libraries." *DESIDOC Journal of Library & Information Technology* 35(3): 117–83. DOI: https://www.doi.org/10.14429/djlit.35.3.8720.

Rath discusses how, in India, the open access movement was initially confined to science, technology, and medical fields. Rath's study identifies and analyzes 60 open access social science journals in India. Most of Rath's findings consist of quantitative data compiled from the Directory of Open Access Journals (DOAJ; https://doaj.org/), and he notes that only 15 out of 60 open access journals in the social sciences were published under a Creative Commons licence in India. Rath concludes with several recommendations: that social science departments in India make publicly funded research available via open access, that research institutes encourage and fund their own repositories, that scholars deposit post-print copies of their research papers, and that a central advisory board monitor open access journals and encourage scholars to submit research papers to select publications in order to increase visibility of Indian publications worldwide.

RECODE Project Consortium. 2014. "Policy Recommendations for Open Access to Research Data." https://zenodo.org/record/50863/files/recode_guideline_en_web_version_full_FINAL.pdf.
The Policy RECommendations for Open Access to Research Data in Europe (RECODE) Project Consortium provides an overview of the RECODE project and introduces the five interdisciplinary case studies in open access research data that helped in the examination of important challenges. The report includes a summary of the project findings and general recommendations. In addition, it studies targeted policies for funders, research institutions, data managers, and publishers, and provides practical guides for developing policies. The report also includes resources to further the policy development processes and their implementations. The authors conclude with a list of grouped resources and project partners.

Rodriguez, Julia. 2014. "Awareness and Attitudes about Open Access Publishing: A Glance at Generational Differences." *Journal of Academic Librarianship* 40(6): 604–10. DOI: https://doi.org/10.1016/j.acalib.2 014.07.013.
Rodriguez surveys faculty members at a mid-size American university to determine the current awareness and perception of open access publishing. The majority of the respondents were from the faculties of arts, humanities, and social sciences. Overall, the data demonstrates a growing trend toward self-reported knowledge of open access accompanied by very little engagement with open publishing: while 61.7 per cent of the respondents knew what open access was, only 28.2 per cent had published in an open access venue. This demonstrates a gap between attitude and behaviour, a gap Rodriguez attributes to habits and institutional culture. In order to bridge this divide, she suggests educating faculty members early and revisiting this discussion often.

+San Martin, Patricia Silvana, Paolo Carolina Bongiovani, Ana Casali, and Claudia Deco. 2015. "Study on Perspectives Regarding Deposit on Open Access Repositories in Context of Public Universities in the Central-Eastern Region of Argentina." *Scholarly and Research Communication* 6(1): n.p. DOI: https://doi.org/10.22230/src.2015v6n1a145.
San Martin, Bongiovani, Casali, and Deco survey and present qualitative statistics on the needs and practices of disseminating scholarly work through

open access institutional repositories in Argentina. Their findings address issues of usability, navigation, and accessibility across three institutional repositories at Argentinean universities. In an online survey conducted by the authors, some 1,000 individuals from the three universities responded to their queries about using open access institutional repositories, with 81 per cent having a positive attitude toward freely disseminating their scholarly works. However, barriers of interface design, organization, terminology, and inconsistent metadata requirements prevented the use of the system. The authors propose a new prototype in order to help alleviate these issues.

**Snijder, Ronald. 2015. "Better Sharing Through Licenses? Measuring the Influence of Creative Commons Licenses on the Usage of Open Access Monographs."** *Journal of Librarianship & Scholarly Communication* **3(1): 1–21. DOI: https://doi.org/10.7710/2162-3309.1187.**
Snijder measures the influence of Creative Commons licences on the usage of open access monographs. He suggests that there is, in fact, no evidence that making books available under open access licences results in more significant download numbers than personal use licences. For Snijder, the application of open licences to books cannot, on its own, result in more downloads. Open licences pave the way for other intermediaries to offer new discovery and aggregation services. Snijder's study breaks away from the tradition of work on open licences by measuring the effects of free licences; he focuses on the implications of freely licensing open access monographs as opposed to discussing the legal frameworks surrounding copyright law and the Creative Commons.

**Suber, Peter. 2004. "Open Access Overview." Last modified December 5, 2015.https://legacy.earlham.edu/~peters/fos/overview.htm.**
Suber presents an introduction to open access, which he defines as literature that is digital, online, free of charge, and free of most copyright/licensing restrictions. The open access campaign allows authors to give access to information to the public without requiring any fees. In this same vein, many open access initiatives focus on publicly funded research. There are two types of open access: gold (open access journals) and green (open access repositories). Both types of open access are compatible with peer review and, in fact, peer review is insisted upon in many open access venues. Suber also sees open access as well suited to copyright, revenue, print, preservation, prestige, quality, and career involvement. For Suber, open access is not a business model; it is a type of access that works to serve the interests of many diverse groups.

Suber, Peter. 2005. "Promoting Open Access in the Humanities."
*Syllecta Classica* 16: 231–46. DOI: https://www.doi.org/10.1353/
syl.2005.0001.
Suber examines how humanities and social science scholars can promote
open access within their own disciplines. He identifies some of the roadblocks of open access publishing in the humanities and social sciences, and
proposes avenues to circumvent these barriers. Despite the Internet creating an opportunity for low-cost distribution of knowledge, the humanities
and social sciences have been slow to take up open access practices. Suber
argues that this is due to a number of factors: high cost of journals, low funding of research, high rejection rates of journals, low demand for open access
(compared to the sciences), and copyright issues. Suber suggests that the
following practices be used to navigate or circumnavigate these issues: use
software to manage costs of peer review, do without copyeditors, encourage
universities to pay processing fees, experiment with retroactive peer review,
explore open access archiving, and publish open access books.

Tananbaum, Greg. 2014. "North American Campus-Based Open Access
Funds: A Five-Year Progress Report." Scholarly Publishing and
Academic Resources Coalition (SPARC). https://sparcopen.org/
wp-content/uploads/2016/01/OA-Fund-5-Year-Review.pdf.
Tananbaum provides an overview of the successes and challenges of campus-
based open access funds across North America. The report provides quantitative data to show how the funds have encouraged authors to get involved
with open access publishing. It also includes a qualitative analysis of successes, challenges, level of satisfaction, and communication with faculty and
administration. The author notes that launching funds at more institutions
will highlight the impact of this mechanism on scholarly communication,
and adds that 'SPARC anticipates an ongoing involvement in campus-based
Open Access Funds' (5).

Vandegrift, Micah, and Josh Bolick. 2014. "'Free to All': Library
Publishing and the Challenge of Open Access." *Journal of
Librarianship & Scholarly Communication* 2(4): 107–16. DOI: https://
doi.org/10.7710/ 2162-3309.1181.
Vandegrift and Bolick examine the role of library publishing in the open
access movement. From the outset, Vandegrift and Bolick maintain that
libraries should identify as 'library publishers' and not 'publishing libraries' in order to keep in line with the 'free to all' policy. Further, the authors
assert that clear distinctions should be made between university publishers,

libraries, and commercial publishers. They argue that the goal of the library publisher should be to produce high quality scholarship that can be accessed by anyone. The authors see the primary issue facing open access as a question of alliance rather than compliance, and one that demands publishers to reconsider open access as a freedom, rather than a requirement or restriction. Moving toward this open access policy as a core principle of library publishing could shift allegiances, dissolve organizational categories, influence policy, and grow the community.

**\*\*Veletsianos, George. 2015. "A Case Study of Scholars' Open and Sharing Practices." *Open Praxis* 7(3): 199–209. DOI: https://doi. org/10.5944/openpraxis.7.3.206.**
Veletsianos addresses the extent of open scholarship in institutions that lack a formal infrastructure to support such research. This is carried out through a case study on a public, not-for-profit North American institution (referred to in the paper as Tall Mountain University), specifically by working with faculty members. According to the case study, there are a number of ways in which open scholarship is carried out, with certain practices being favoured over others; some examples include open access manuscripts and educational resources, social media, and open teaching/pedagogy. The author also found that some faculty members publish their materials openly on the Internet without attaching open licences, and that the settings of the platform, as well as the institutional protocols, also affect the extent to which the material is accessible. Despite these findings, Veletsianos states that open scholarship is still a relatively narrow practice at the institution. The author outlines possible limitations of the research, such as open practices that may not have been revealed in the case study and possible limitations of Google Scholar (the search engine used for this research) that may prohibit the study from being exhaustive. Overall, the study is descriptive, and does not address the motivations behind practising open scholarship.

**Waters, Donald J., and Joseph S. Meisel. 2007. "Scholarly Publishing Initiatives." In *The Andrew W. Mellon Foundation: 2007 Annual Report*, 31–45. New York: Andrew W. Mellon Foundation. https://mellon. org/media/filer_public/42/76/4276ef43-d0b2-42e5-8747-e63d-b6a7bd68/2007.pdf.**
Waters and Meisel summarize the findings of the 2007 annual report of scholarly publishing initiatives. The Mellon Foundation began two initiatives in 2007: the first aimed to increase the capacity of university presses to publish first books by junior scholars in fields with constrained opportunities;

the second sought to strengthen the substantive relationship between home institutions and university presses. Waters and Meisel briefly outline historical concerns about the roles and functions of university presses, and efforts to support scholarly publishing. They acknowledge early projects, such as Johns Hopkins University Press's *Project Muse*, as well as the 1998–99 Mellon Foundation's establishment of *Gutenberg-e* and *History E-Books*, which tested the hypothesis that monographs authored for electronic media would be cheaper to produce than those authored for print media. The goal of the two initiatives aforementioned is to strengthen both humanistic scholarship and the institutions upon which it depends.

Willinsky, John. 2003. "The Nine Flavours of Open Access Scholarly Publishing." *Journal of Postgraduate Medicine* 49(3): 263–67.
Willinsky delves into the digital life of scholarly journals that was sparked approximately 340 years after their inception in print. He states that in 2000, nearly 75 per cent of journals had online editions, and nearly 1,000 peer reviewed journals appeared only in digital form. Although the ease of accessing information is unprecedented, however, institutions are simply unable to keep up with their own production of published research—no university can afford to provide access to all information. Willinsky turns to open access by first arguing that it is not a single economic model but rather a collection of economic models that fit different situations. He concludes by categorizing and detailing what he refers to as the nine viable flavours of open access scholarly publishing: e-print archive, unqualified open access journal, dual mode, delayed open access, fee-based edition, partial open access, per-capita open access, open-access lite, and cooperative access.

Willinsky, John. 2006a. *The Access Principle: The Case for Open Access to Research and Scholarship*. Cambridge, MA: MIT Press.
Willinsky argues that open access scholarship is a tradition that goes back to ancient collections, such as the fabled library of Alexandria, and then to the establishment of massive public libraries in nineteenth-century America. He argues that digital publishers are responsible for exploring new technologies and economic models to improve public access to materials. Willinsky uses the *New England Journal of Medicine* as an example of a publisher that grants open access to issues six months after they are published and, on the first Monday of the month, makes the issue immediately accessible at no cost digitally. His discussion focuses on definitions of opening the scholarly community, access, copyright, a history of associations, economic factors, cooperative scholarship, development, the role of the public, the influence

of politics, and the establishment of rights, as well as methods of reading and indexing open access materials. Willinsky concludes his study with an index of different models for open access publication, a chart that includes scholarly association budgets, journal management economies, and sections on indexing serial literature and creating metadata for journal cataloguing.

Willinsky, John. 2007. "What Open Access Research Can Do for Wikipedia." *First Monday* 12(3): n.p. https://firstmonday.org/ojs/ index.php/fm/article/viewArticle/1624/1539.
Willinsky interrogates the degree to which Wikipedia entries cite or reference scholarship, and whether this research is generally available to readers in open access format. The author is interested in whether contributors are taking advantage of the growing amount of open access research available to them. To study this, Willinsky randomly selected 100 Wikipedia entries, which reference 168 resources. Of those 168 resources, only 2 per cent point to open access scholarly research. Given these findings, Willinsky argues that more can be done to enhance Wikipedia, and to bolster the current state of knowledge provided by the online encyclopedia. Wikipedia, Willinsky argues, should be used as a platform to springboard open access initiatives and circulate materials in an accessible way for the entire Internet community. If the platform were to become more of an entry point, researchers and scholars would have greater motivation to make their work open access.

Yang, Zheng Ye (Lan), and Yu Li. 2015. "University Faculty Awareness and Attitudes towards Open Access Publishing and the Institutional Repository: A Case Study." *Journal of Librarianship & Scholarly Communication* 3 (1): 1–29. DOI: https://doi. org/10.7710/2162-3309.1210.
Yang and Li study the awareness of Texas A&M University (TAMU) faculty regarding open access publishing. The authors assess their attitudes toward and willingness to contribute to institutional repositories, and investigate their perceptions of newer open access trends and resources. The survey results suggest that tenured faculty have a higher engagement rate with open access journals in their fields. A lack of awareness, however, surrounds processes to deposit materials in institutional repositories: 84 per cent of respondents did not know the institutional repository deposit process at all. Similarly, a quarter of the respondents indicated that they did not know enough about open access to form an opinion on institutional repositories and could not see depositing their work as counting toward merit raises, tenure and promotion, or annual evaluation. Attitudes remain the greatest barrier toward increasing open access publication in academic settings.

## B. Reference List

Adema, Janneke. 2010. "Overview of Open Access Models for eBooks in the Humanities and Social Sciences." OAPEN Project Report. http://project.oapen.org/images/documents/openaccessmodels.pdf.

Anderson, Charles. 1998. "Universal Access—Free and Open Access—It Depends …" *Reference & User Services Quarterly* 38(1): 25–27.

Asmah, Josephine. 2014. "International Policy and Practice on Open Access for Monographs." Federation for the Humanities and Social Sciences. http://www.ideas-idees.ca/sites/default/files/aspp-oa-appendix.pdf.

Ayris, Paul, Erica McLaren, Martin Moyle, Catherine Sharp, and Lara Speicher. 2014. "Open Access in UCL: A New Paradigm for London's Global University in Research Support." *Australian Academic & Research Libraries* 45(4): 282–95.

Bailey, Charles W., Jr. 2007. "Open Access and Libraries." *Collection Management* 32(3–4): 351–83.

Björk, Bo-Christer. 2004. "Open Access to Scientific Publications—An Analysis of the Barriers to Change?" *Information Research* 9(2): n.p. http://informationr.net/ir/9-2/paper170.html.

Bohannon, John. 2013. "Who's Afraid of Peer Review?" *Science* 342: 60–65. DOI: www.doi.org/10.1126/science.342.6154.60.

Canadian Association of Research Libraries. n.d. "Open Access." Canadian Association of Research Libraries. http://www.carl-abrc.ca/advancing-research/scholarly-communication/open-access/.

Chan, Leslie. 2004. "Supporting and Enhancing Scholarship in the Digital Age: The Role of Open-Access Institutional Repositories." *Canadian Journal of Communication* 29(3): 277–300. https://www.cjc-online.ca/index.php/journal/article/view/1455/1579.

Chang, Yu-Wei. 2015. "Librarians' Contribution to Open Access Journal Publishing in Library and Information Science From the Perspective of Authorship." *Journal of Academic Librarianship* 41(5): 660–68. DOI: https://doi.org/10.1016/j.acalib.2015.06.006.

Cohen, Daniel J. 2010. "Open Access Publishing and Scholarly Values." Personal blog post, May 27. https://dancohen.org/2010/05/27/

open-access-publishing-and-scholarly-values/. Archived at https://perma.cc/78MH-PK43.

Coonin, Bryna, and Leigh Younce. 2009. "Publishing in Open Access Journals in The Social Sciences and Humanities: Who's Doing It and Why." Paper presented at the *ACRL Fourteenth National Conference.* http://www.ala.org/acrl/sites/ala.org.acrl/files/content/conferences/confsandpreconfs/national/seattle/papers/85.pdf.

Eve, Martin Paul. 2015. "Open Access Publishing and Scholarly Communication in Non-Scientific Disciplines." *Online Information Review* 39(5): 717–32. DOI: https://doi.org/10.1108/OIR-04-2015-0103.

Fund, Sven. 2015. "Will Open Access Change the Game? Hypotheses on the Future Cooperation of Libraries, Researchers, and Publishers." *Bibliothek Forschung und Praxis* 39(2): 206–9. DOI: https://doi.org/10.1515/bfp-2015-0025.

Gaines, Annie M. 2015. "From Concerned to Cautiously Optimistic: Assessing Faculty Perception and Knowledge of Open Access in a Campus-Wide Study." *Journal of Librarianship & Scholarly Communication* 3(1): 1–40. DOI: https://doi.org/10.7710/2162-3309.1212.

Gargouri, Yassine, Chawki Hajjem, Vincent Larivière, Yves Gringas, Les Carr, Tim Brody, and Stevan Harnad. 2010. "Self-Selected or Mandated, Open Access Increases Citation Impact for Higher Quality Research." *PLOS One* 5(10): n.p. DOI: https://doi.org/10.1371/journal.pone.0013636.

Government of Canada. 2015b. "Tri-Agency Open Access Policy on Publications." Science and Technology for Canadians. http://www.science.gc.ca/default.asp?lang=En&n=F6765465-1.

Hampson, Crystal. 2014. "The Adoption of Open Access Funds Among Canadian Academic Research Libraries, 2008–2012." *The Canadian Journal of Library & Information Practice & Research* 9(2): 1–14. DOI: https://doi.org/10.21083/partnership.v9i2.3115.

Heath, Malcolm, Michael Jubb, and David Robey. 2008. "E-Publication and Open Access in the Arts and Humanities in the UK." *Ariadne* 54: n.p. http://www.ariadne.ac.uk/issue/54/heath-et-al/. Archived at https://perma.cc/NKM4-E3T5.

Kingsley, Danny. 2013. "Build It and They Will Come? Support for Open Access in Australia." *Scholarly and Research Communication* 4(1): n.p. DOI: https://doi.org/10.22230/src.2013v4n1a39.

Kitchin, Rob, Sandra Collins, and Dermot Frost. 2015. "Funding Models for Open Access Digital Data Repositories." *Online Information Review* 39(5): 664–81. DOI: https://www.doi.org/10.1108/OIR-01-2015-0031.

Laakso, Mikael, and Bo-Christer Björk. 2012. "Anatomy of Open Access Publishing: A Study of Longitudinal Development and Internal Structure." *BMC Medicine* 10(124): n.p. DOI: https://doi.org/10.1186/1741-7015-10-124.

Lorimer, Rowland. 2014. "A Good Idea, a Difficult Reality: Toward a Publisher/Library Open Access Partnership." *Scholarly and Research Communication* 5(4): n.p. DOI: https://doi.org/10.22230/src.2014v5n4a180.

Lowe, Megan W. 2014. "In Defense of Open Access: Or, Why I Stopped Worrying and Started an OA Journal." *Codex* 2(4): 1–11.

Maxwell, John W. 2015. "Beyond Open Access to Open Publication and Open Scholarship." *Scholarly and Research Communication* 6(3): n.p. DOI: https://doi.org/10.22230/src.2015v6n3a202.

McGregor, Heidi, and Kevin Guthrie. 2015. "Delivering Impact of Scholarly Information: Is Access Enough?" *Journal of Electronic Publishing* 18(3): n.p. DOI: http://dx.doi.org/10.3998/3336451.0018.302.

Meadows, Alice. 2015. "Beyond Open: Expanding Access to Scholarly Content." *Journal of Electronic Publishing* 18(3): n.p. DOI: http://dx.doi.org/10.3998/3336451.0018.301.

Ober, Josiah, Walter Scheidel, Brent D. Shaw, and Donna Sanclemente. 2007. "Toward Open Access in Ancient Studies: The Princeton-Stanford Working Papers in Classics." *Hesperia* 76(1): 229–42. https://www.jstor.org/stable/25068017.

O'Donnell, Daniel, Heather Hobma, Sandra Cowan, Gillian Ayers, Jessica Bay, Marinus Swanepoel, Wendy Merkley, Kelaine Devine, Emma Dering, and Inge Genee. 2015. "Aligning Open Access Publication with the Research and Teaching Missions of the Public University: The Case of the Lethbridge Journal Incubator (If 'if's and 'and's were pots and pans)." *Journal of Electronic Publishing* 18(3): n.p. DOI: http://dx.doi.org/10.3998/3336451.0018.309.

Organisation for Economic Cooperation and Development (OECD). 2015. "Making Open Science a Reality." *OECD Science, Technology and Industry Policy Papers* 25. Paris: OECD Publishing.

Peekhaus, Wilhelm, and Nicholas Proferes. 2015. "How Library and Information Science Faculty Perceive and Engage with Open Access." *Journal of Information Science* 41(5): 640–61. DOI: https://doi.org/10.1177/0165551515587855.

Pinfield, Stephen. 2015. "Making Open Access Work: The 'State-of-the-Art' in Providing Open Access to Scholarly Literature." *Online Information Review* 39(5): 604–36. DOI: https://doi.org/10.1108/OIR-05-2015-0167.

Prelinger, Rick. 2007. "Archives and Access in the 21st Century." *Cinema Journal* 46(3): 114–18. DOI: https://www.doi.org/10.1353/cj.2007.0027.

Rath, Prabhash Narayana. 2015. "Study of Open Access Publishing in Social Sciences and its Implications for Libraries." *DESIDOC Journal of Library & Information Technology* 35(3): 117–83. DOI: https://www.doi.org/10.14429/djlit.35.3.8720.

RECODE Project Consortium. 2014. "Policy Recommendations for Open Access to Research Data." https://zenodo.org/record/50863/files/re-code_guideline_en_web_version_full_FINAL.pdf.

Rodriguez, Julia. 2014. "Awareness and Attitudes about Open Access Publishing: A Glance at Generational Differences." *Journal of Academic Librarianship* 40(6): 604–10. DOI: https://doi.org/10.1016/j.acalib.2014.07.013.

San Martin, Patricia Silvana, Paolo Carolina Bongiovani, Ana Casali, and Claudia Deco. 2015. "Study on Perspectives Regarding Deposit on Open Access Repositories in Context of Public Universities in the Central-Eastern Region of Argentina." *Scholarly and Research Communication* 6(1): n.p. DOI: https://doi.org/10.22230/src.2015v6n1a145.

Snijder, Ronald. 2015. "Better Sharing Through Licenses? Measuring the Influence of Creative Commons Licenses on the Usage of Open Access Monographs." *Journal of Librarianship & Scholarly Communication* 3(1): 1–21. DOI: https://doi.org/10.7710/2162-3309.1187.

Suber, Peter. 2004. "Open Access Overview." Last modified December 5, 2015. https://legacy.earlham.edu/~peters/fos/overview.htm.

———. 2005. "Promoting Open Access in the Humanities." *Syllecta Classica* 16: 231–46. DOI: https://www.doi.org/10.1353/syl.2005.0001.

Tananbaum, Greg. 2014. "North American Campus-Based Open Access Funds: A Five-Year Progress Report." Scholarly Publishing and Academic Resources Coalition (SPARC). https://sparcopen.org/wp-content/uploads/2016/01/OA-Fund-5-Year-Review.pdf.

Vandegrift, Micah, and Josh Bolick. 2014. "'Free to All': Library Publishing and the Challenge of Open Access." *Journal of Librarianship & Scholarly Communication* 2(4): 107–16. DOI: https://doi.org/10.7710/2162-3309.1181.

Veletsianos, George. 2015. "A Case Study of Scholars' Open and Sharing Practices." *Open Praxis* 7(3): 199–209. DOI: https://doi.org/10.5944/openpraxis.7.3.206.

Waters, Donald J., and Joseph S. Meisel. 2007. "Scholarly Publishing Initiatives." In *The Andrew W. Mellon Foundation: 2007 Annual Report*, 31–45. New York: Andrew W. Mellon Foundation. https://mellon.org/media/filer_public/42/76/4276ef43-d0b2-42e5-8747-e63db6a7bd68/2007.pdf.

Willinsky, John. 2003. "The Nine Flavours of Open Access Scholarly Publishing." *Journal of Postgraduate Medicine* 49(3): 263–67.

———. 2006a. *The Access Principle: The Case for Open Access to Research and Scholarship.* Cambridge, MA: MIT Press.

———. 2007. "What Open Access Research Can Do for Wikipedia." *First Monday* 12(3): n.p. https://firstmonday.org/ojs/index.php/fm/article/viewArticle/1624/1539.

Yang, Zheng Ye (Lan), and Yu Li. 2015. "University Faculty Awareness and Attitudes towards Open Access Publishing and the Institutional Repository: A Case Study." *Journal of Librarianship & Scholarly Communication* 3(1): 1–29. DOI: https://doi.org/10.7710/2162-3309.1210.

## 4. Open Source

Open source is an umbrella term that generally refers to the practice of sharing, modifying, and reusing software code freely, and houses a number of initiatives, such as the free software and open source movements. These initiatives have a rich history; they are responsible for the open structure of the Internet and serve as prominent voices in the defence of user interest in contemporary Internet policy debates, such as the battle over privacy-related issues (Kelty 2008). This category covers materials related to the development of open source programs, from its origins with Linux and Apache to its potential for collaborative software development (Godfrey and Tu 2000; Hars and Ou 2001; Lerner and Tirole 2002). The resources range from the theoretical to the technical and political. Many of the articles focus on Apache and Linux as the primary models for economic success in the open source software community. In this category, the open source software model is frequently juxtaposed with the commercial model, represented by Microsoft, to reveal comparative successes and areas of improvement (West 2003). Overall, this category traces the historical development of open source and speculates about its potential directions.

### A. Annotations

**Bastian, Mathieu, Sebastien Heymann, and Mathieu Jacomy. 2009. "Gephi: An Open Source Software for Exploring and Manipulating Networks." In *Proceedings of the Third International AAAI Conference on Weblogs and Social Media*, 361–62. Palo Alto, CA: Association for the Advancement of Artificial Intelligence (AAAI). https://www. aaai.org/ocs/index.php/ICWSM/09/paper/view/154/1009.**
Bastian, Heymann, and Jacomy describe the development of their open software tool, Gephi, which is used for graph and network analysis. The software presents large networks in real time using a 3D render engine. This technique uses the graphic card while leaving the CPU memory free for other computing. The user interface is structured into workspaces, through which algorithms, filters, or tools can be easily added, even by those with little programming experience. Visualization modules can be exported as SVG or PDF files, and Rich SVG Export—a powerful SVG exporter—is included with Gephi. Dynamic networks can be played in Gephi as movie sequences. The architecture of the software is interoperable, and data sources can be created easily to communicate with existing software, third party databases, and Web services. The authors note that they are searching for better ways to adapt the

user interface to users' needs. The program has successfully been used for Internet link and semantic network case studies.

**Bonaccorsi, Andrea, and Cristina Rossi. 2003. "Why Open Source Software Can Succeed."** *Research Policy* **32(7): 1243–58. DOI: https:// doi.org/10.1016/S0048-7333(03)00051-9.**
Bonaccorsi and Rossi discuss the questions of motivation, coordination, and diffusion raised by the emergence of open source software. They note that hierarchical coordination emerged without proprietary rights, yet open source systems are diffused in environments dominated by proprietary standards. The authors attempt to understand how an immense group of unpaid programmers have advanced open source technology to its present stage. The hobbyist groups and hacker culture, which consists of programmers trained in engineering and physics fields, are noted as the primary groups participating in the development of open source software. This hybrid business model—whereby companies and software houses produce software, give it away to customers free of charge, and shift the value toward additional services (packaging, consultancy, maintenance, updating, and training)—is suggested as a productive alternative. The recent tendency for open source programs to become more user-friendly will enable even wider diffusion into increasingly broad communities.

**Bruns, Axel. 2008.** *Blogs, Wikipedia, Second Life, and Beyond: From Production to Produsage.* **New York: Peter Lang.**
Bruns's book on blogs, Wikipedia, Second Life, and other virtual landscapes discusses how creative, collaborative, and ad hoc engagement with content in user-led spaces is no longer accurate. Instead, user-led content production is built on iterative and evolutionary development models in which large communities make a number of very small incremental changes to established knowledge bases. He uses the concept of 'produsage' to describe changes to user-led content management systems. The comparative significance of distinction between producers and users of content has faded over time. The opening chapters detail open source software development; later chapters move to case studies of news blogs, citizen journals, Wikipedia, and what he terms the 'produsage of folksonomies,' referring to knowledge structures that encapsulate economic environments of their own. He discusses 'produsage' in terms of education, video games, and creative structures, and concludes with a chapter on how democracy itself can be re-examined in light of the 'produsage' structure.

**Childs, Merilyn, and Regine Wagner. 2015. "Open Sourced Personal, Networked Learning and Higher Education Credentials." In *Open Learning and Formal Credentialing in Higher Education*, edited by Shirley Reushie, Amy Antonio, and Mike Keppell, 223–44. Hershey, PA: IGI Global.**

Childs and Wagner claim to present an *Imaginarium* in their article, which they define as a type of place dedicated to imagination that may struggle to exist in institutional reality. The authors use imaginary reconstruction (fiction writing in research spaces) to construct a plausible and comprehensible text that offers an alternative to current institutional thought and practice. The text weaves in and out of fiction, with the first sections discussing global citizenship and research performed by the United Nations. The authors stage their semi-fictional discussion at the 46th triennial Australian Labor Party National Conference of December 3, 2011. A same-sex marriage protest in support of dropping queer-phobic Australian legislation occurs outside of the event, and the authors create a character, Ludmilla, to narrate some of their concerns. They follow her involvement in the protest and narrate many of the works she would have encountered prior to that moment in order to provide evidence of the type of person who would benefit from recognition of prior learning (RPL) developments. This includes authentic and service learning, ePortfolios, learning pathways between vocational and university studies, and open learning practices in higher education.

**Chopra, Samir, and Scott Dexter. 2009. "The Freedoms of Software and Its Ethical Uses." *Ethics and Information Technology* 11(4): 287–97. DOI: https://doi.org/10.1007/s10676-009-9191-0.**

Chopra and Dexter explain that the difference between free and proprietary software is that the latter restricts user actions through end user licence agreements, while the former eliminates restrictions on users. The authors explain the concept of free software, discussing software freedom, the Freedom Zero problem, the ethical use of scientific knowledge, and scientific knowledge and property rights. They then discuss community discourse and Freedom Zero (the freedom to use software in any way or for any purpose), explaining that Freedom Zero supports deliberative discourse within the development and user communities. When exploring the ethical uses of software, Chopra and Dexter answer the question of whether Freedom Zero is inaccurate, and whether a free software licensor could be liable for granting Freedom Zero. The authors conclude that Freedom Zero facilitates a broader debate about software's larger social significance.

**Dahlander, Linus, and Mats G. Magnusson. 2005. "Relationships between Open Source Software Companies and Communities: Observations from Nordic Firms."** *Research Policy* **34(4): 481–93. DOI: https://doi. org/10.1016/j.respol.2005.02.003.**
Dahlander and Magnusson consider the relationship between firms and communities with regard to open source software. Open source software is not directly controlled by firms, but resides within communities that form the firms. The authors use Nordic open source software firms as a case study to examine the symbiotic, commensalistic, and parasitic approaches to handling firm-community relationships. Firms release source codes in order to get their product widely adopted, as this increases the likelihood of attracting skilled developers and a higher pace of technological development. The authors collected annual reports, company directories, business and specialist press reports, and home pages to get an idea of the competitive environment, important milestones, and outside perceptions of four firms: MySQL, Cendio, Roxen, and SOT. The authors note that people working within communities share innovations that are often not protected by intellectual copyrights. Firms, in turn, benefit from this, and can create and maintain relationships with these communities.

**Feller, Joseph, and Brian Fitzgerald. 2002.** *Understanding Open Source Software Development.* **Boston: Addison-Wesley Longman.**
Feller and Fitzgerald attempt to understand the success of open source publication. The authors tackle discussions to define the open source software development method: how it works, its sustainability, and what tools can enable it. They provide an overview of different open source software and accompanying licences, a brief history of the open source software movement, a landscape of the organizations currently at the forefront of open source affairs, how to organize open source processes, and the different motivations behind open source development. The authors argue that the hacker ethic has commonalities with the pre-Protestant work ethic motivated by passion and freedom. The authors claim that open source software is more than just a fad, and that it will come to define the industry rather than be a symptom of it.

**Fitzgerald, Brian. 2006. "The Transformation of Open Source Software."** *MIS Quarterly* **30(3): 587–98. DOI: https://www.doi. org/10.2307/25148740.**
Fitzgerald contends that the open source software (OSS) movement has metamorphosed into a mainstream and commercially viable form of publishing, which he labels as OSS 2.0. He argues that describing the open source

community as a collective of supremely talented developers who volunteer their services to develop high quality software is a myth. He characterizes the first phase of the OSS movement as Free Open Source Software (FOSS), and creates charts that illustrate what he sees as the defining characteristics of both the earlier and the developing movements. Fitzgerald discusses aspects of FOSS, including product licensing and support. The discussion then shifts to OSS 2.0--the design and analysis phases of which, according to Fitzgerald, have become more deliberate than FOSS. Market creation strategies, value added service enabling, and product support are discussed. He concludes by suggesting that open source research exacerbates problems when scholars continue to focus their efforts on repeatedly studying project characteristics and developer motivation.

**Godfrey, Michael W., and Qiang Tu. 2000. "Evolution in Open Source Software: A Case Study." In *Proceedings of the International Conference on Software Maintenance (ICSM '00)*, 131–42. Washington, DC: IEEE Computer Society. http://svn-plg.uwaterloo.ca/~migod/papers/2000/icsm00.pdf.**

Godfrey and Tu note that most studies of software evolution since the year 2000 have been performed on systems developed within a single company using standard management techniques. The authors use the open source Linux operating system Kernel as a case study for further investigations. As of the time of writing, Linux included over two million lines of code and did not have a tightly planned development model. The authors use graphs to demonstrate the growth of smaller core subsystems, arch subsystems, and the driver subsystems in Linux over its lifespan. Kernel has been very successful, and the authors comment that the 'black-box' examination has not been enough--researchers must investigate the nature of the subsystems and explore their evolutionary patterns to understand how and why the system as a whole has evolved.

**Hars, Alexander, and Shaosong Ou. 2001. "Working for Free?— Motivations of Participating in Open Source Projects." In *Proceedings of the 34th Annual Hawaii International Conference on System Sciences (HICSS '01)*, 7014. Washington, DC: IEEE Computer Society.**

Hars and Ou discuss the success of the Linux operating system, which has demonstrated the viability of open source software. The authors discuss both internal factors (intrinsic motivation, altruism) and external rewards (future returns, personal needs) that motivate the development of open source software such as the Linux Kernel. The authors briefly discuss the history of open source software, beginning in the 1950s, when software was sold together with hardware, and macros and utilities were freely exchanged in user forums. Hars and Ou create a timeline from the 1950s until the year 2000, when Novell, Real, and other software companies released versions of their products that ran on Linux. The authors also provide pie charts of respondent demographics (programmer types and highest degree earned). Hars and Ou note that the open source movement draws on diverse actors with various motivations, and cannot be attributed to the efforts of one demographic.

Kelty, Christopher M. 2008. *Two Bits: The Cultural Significance of Free Software*. Durham, NC: Duke University Press.

Kelty investigates the history and structure of the Internet with a specific focus on free software, defined as the collaborative creation of software code that is made freely available through a specific use of copyright law. He argues that the open structure of the Internet can be tied to the Free Software Movement, a social movement that formally originated during the development of the GNU/Linux operating system. Kelty categorizes practitioners who participate in these types of social movements as the 'recursive public,' responsible for reorienting power relations around modes of creation and dissemination of a massive body of virtual information. The Free Software Movement binds together lawyers, hackers, geeks, and professionals from all types of disciplines to form the recursive public that is still actively defending users' interest in the maintenance of an open Internet.

Koehn, Philipp, Hieu Hoang, Alexandra Birch, Chris Callison-Burch, Marcello Federico, Nicola Bertoldi, Brooke Cowan, et al. 2007. "Moses: Open Source Toolkit for Statistical Machine Translation." In *Proceedings of the 45th Annual Meeting of the ACL on Interactive Poster and Demonstration Sessions*, 177–80. https://www.aclweb.org/anthology/P07-2045.

Koehn et al. describe their open source toolkit, Moses, which is used for statistical machine translation and was developed due to the perceived lack of openness in machine translation research. Moses integrates confusion network decoding and enables tighter integration of speech recognition and machine translation than other software. Efficient data structures in Moses allow for the exploitation of larger data resources with limited hardware. The software has been downloaded more than one thousand times since its release in March 2007. The authors provide explanations of the factored translation model and confusion network decoding, and conclude with their description of a new SMT decoder that incorporates linguistic features in a consistent and flexible framework.

**Kogut, Bruce, and Anca Metiu. 2001. "Open Source Software Development and Distributed Innovation."** *Oxford Review of Economic Policy* 17(2): 248–64. https://www.jstor.org/stable/23606809.

Kogut and Metiu discuss the open source software production model as one that exploits the distributed intelligence of participants in Internet communities. The authors call these broad communities 'communities of practice.' Kogut and Metiu argue that open source practices avoid the inefficiencies of a strong intellectual property regime and implement concurrent design and testing of modules, thereby saving financial and labour expenditures. Two types of open source models are examined as case studies using a chart that logs different projects, including Zope, Mozilla, MySQL, Python, KDE, GIMP, and GNOME. The authors proceed to a discussion of Linux and its history. Open source is touted as the emergence of a production model ideally suited for properties of information that can be digitally coded and distributed.

**Lakhani, Karim R., and Eric von Hippel. 2003. "How Open Source Software Works: 'Free' User-to-User Assistance."** *Research Policy* 32(6): 923–43. DOI: https://doi.org/10.1016/S0048-7333(02)00095-1.

Lakhani and von Hippel explore how the mundane, but necessary, task of field support is organized in the Apache web server software. They also discuss the motivations of project participants and note that the community has a strong support system. The effort expended by information providers to develop Apache returns direct learning benefits. The authors suggest that the free, voluntary labour of the open source community is often undertaken with the goal of self-education, rather than materialist concerns with capital. A brief history of Apache is provided as well as an analysis of the field support system. The study collects data on questions posted by information seekers, responses to these questions, growth in Apache web server sites, and a survey of the motivations of various respondents for undertaking such work. The authors conclude with the suggestion that it is important to analyze the micro-level functioning of successful open source projects to understand how and why they work.

**Lerner, Josh, and Jean Tirole. 2001. "The Open Source Movement: Key Research Questions."** *European Economic Review* 45(4–6): 819–26. DOI: https://doi.org/10.1016/S0014-2921(01)00124-6.

Lerner and Tirole discuss the general history and cultural impact of the open source movement. The authors discuss major programs, including Linux, Apache, Sendmail, and the Perl language for writing Common Gateway Interface (CGI) scripts. These programs were designed as a standard means of delivering dynamic content on the Web. Lerner and Tirole point out how open source software has challenged economic paradigms of individual incentives, corporate strategies, organizational behaviour, and innovative process. They argue that, contrary to appearances, the open source movement is well accounted for by standard economic theory, and point to areas for further research. The authors examine individual motivations for participating, how people assess good projects and leadership, and how these often mix commercial elements with open source programs. They conclude with discussions of why corporate bodies involve themselves with open source software, and the legal and sociological aspects and influences of the open source software movement.

**Lerner, Josh, and Jean Tirole. 2002. "Some Simple Economics of Open Source."** *The Journal of Industrial Economics* 50(2): 197–234. DOI: https://doi.org/10.1111/1467-6451.00174.

Lerner and Tirole discuss the surge of interest in open source software development. The behaviour of individual programmers and commercial companies is startling and counter-intuitive to accepted theories of capitalist economics. Open source software has diffused rapidly. Examples include the Apache web server and Linux, which, as of 2002, had roughly seven to twenty million users worldwide, with a 200 per cent annual growth rate. The authors provide a breakdown of the history of open source software, beginning with the 1950s. They provide statistics on the demographics of contributors to open source software, and provide table charts of different open source programs studied in their research. Lerner and Tirole note that the development of individual components requires large team work and substantial capital costs. Users in mass market industries are comparatively numerous and unsophisticated, and they deliver few services of peer recognition. Economic theories must be updated to accommodate shifting open source software standards.

**Mockus, Audris, Roy T. Fielding, and James D. Herbsleb. 2002. "Two Case Studies of Open Source Software Development: Apache and Mozilla."** *ACM Transactions on Software Engineering and Methodology* 11(3): 309–46. DOI: https://www.doi.org/10.1145/567793.567795.

Mockus, Fielding, and Herbsleb discuss open source software's capacity to compete and displace common commercial development methods. The authors examine data from the Apache web server and Mozilla browser that includes email archives of source code change history and problem reports. The research team reports on the basic structure of the development process, the number of participants filling each of the major roles, distinctiveness of the roles, importance of core developers, and customer support in open source software. They also provide basic outlines of both Apache and Mozilla's development histories. The study concludes with the suggestion that highly knowledgeable users should experiment in commercial environments with open work assignments in the style of open source software. Further, they argue that the developers and users of a product, rather than a marketing management organization, should choose its new features.

Raymond, Eric S. 2001. *The Cathedral and the Bazaar: Musings on Linux and Open Source by an Accidental Revolutionary*. Rev. ed. Sebastopol, CA: O'Reilly.

Raymond's manifesto for open source social politics begins with an overview of early programmers. This group of programmers— heavily associated with scientific batch computing—assembled before the term 'programmer' entered the vernacular in its present-day meaning. Open source hacker culture developed out of the rise of interactive computing, which would be propagated on the ARPAnet in its early years. The Massachusetts Institute of Technology (MIT), Stanford, and Carnegie Mellon University were important centres of computer science and artificial intelligence research. Raymond details the rise of Unix software, which was considered by commercial developers to be the work of a group of upstarts using primitive tools. The author devotes most of his analysis to the proprietary Unix, the early free Unix, and how Linux brought hacker culture from the fringes of public consciousness to its current prominence.

Roberts, Jeffrey A., Il-Horn Hann, and Sandra A. Slaughter. 2006. "Understanding the Motivations, Participation, and Performance of Open Source Software Developers: A Longitudinal Study of the Apache Projects." *Management Science* 52(7): 984–99. DOI: https://doi.org/10.1287/mnsc.1060.0554.

Roberts, Hann, and Slaughter conduct a study to understand the motivations, participation, and performance of open source software developers. The authors evaluate their model with survey and archival data collected from a longitudinal field study of software developers in the Apache projects. Payment for contributing to Apache projects is positively related to the developer's status motivations, but negatively related to use-value criteria. The authors rely heavily on psychology literature and some analysis of Apache and its contributors.

Rosen, Lawrence E. 2004. *Open Source Licensing: Software Freedom and Intellectual Property Law.* Upper Saddle River, NJ: Prentice Hall PTR.
Rosen's book on open source software licences details the legal frameworks for open source licences and the intellectual property rights by which they are governed. He provides a definition and history of intellectual property, and definitions of software freedom and open source. The following chapters include taxonomies of different licence types, a discussion of academic licences, and a chapter on the GNU general public licence, which helped create a large public commons of software freely available to everyone worldwide. Rosen then discusses Mozilla licences, common public licences, IBM's relation to open source development, and how an open source software firm can choose an open source licence—as well as a guide to open standards. The appendices include the documents to which Rosen refers to throughout the monograph in order to provide additional context.

+Rosenzweig, Roy. 2006. "Can History Be Open Source? *Wikipedia* and the Future of the Past." *Journal of American History* 93(1): 117–46. DOI: https://www.doi.org/10.2307/4486062.
Rosenzweig claims that the field of open source software development is notoriously individualistic, noting that only 6 per cent of more than 32,000 scholarly works indexed since 2000 have more than one author, and less than 2 per cent have three or more authors. The cooperation and freedom of Wikipedia, on the other hand, have transformed it into the most important demonstration of the principles of free and open source software. Rosenzweig discusses Wikipedia as both a tool for historiography and an expression of history itself. Professional historians should pay attention to Wikipedia, because students certainly do. Wikipedia and Linux are alternative models to the hierarchical, commercial model represented by Microsoft as means of producing encyclopedic material and software.

Schloss, Patrick D., Sarah L. Westcott, Thomas Ryabin, Justine R. Hall, Martin Hartmann, Emily B. Hollister, Ryan A. Lesniewski, et al. 2009. "Introducing mothur: Open-Source, Platform-Independent, Community-Supported Software for Describing and Comparing Microbial Communities." *Applied and Environmental Microbiology* 75(23): 7537–41. DOI: https://www.doi.org/10.1128/AEM.01541-09.
Schloss et al. discuss mothur, their comprehensive software package that allows use of a single piece of software to analyze community sequence data. It can be used to trim, screen, and align sequences, as well as calculate distances, assign sequences to operational taxonomic units, and describe the

diversity of eight marine samples. The authors present a table that outlines the features of the software, as well as a flow chart of the number of tags sampled. In the future, the team hopes to develop computational tools to describe and analyze microbial communities. The authors note that although mothur goes a long way toward improving the efficiency of data analysis, researchers should still take care to ensure that their experiments are well designed and thought out and that their results are biologically plausible.

Truscello, Michael. 2003. "The Architecture of Information: Open Source Software and Tactical Poststructuralist Anarchism." *Postmodern Culture* 13(3): n.p. http://pmc.iath.virginia.edu/issue.503/13.3truscello.html.

Truscello examines the discourse of computer programming through Eric Raymond's ethnographical account of the open source software development model (2001, annotated above). He notes that open source is a tactical political philosophy, and analyzes the points of convergence between the history and philosophy of software development and poststructuralist thought. For Truscello, the Internet is emblematic of both the apotheosis of the surveillance society and the dream of anarchistic autonomy, a space increasingly being encroached upon by multinational post-industrial capitalism. The open source movement can create an anarchic space for tactical intervention in the surveillance, and can control society by making the code visible to the greatest number of people. Truscello concludes by noting that cultural theorists have neglected the work of discourse analysis and practices that shape computer programmers and their code.

Von Hippel, Eric, and Georg von Krogh. 2003. "Open Source Software and the 'Private-Collective' Innovation Model: Issues for *Organization Science*." *Organization Science* 14(2): 209–23. DOI: https://doi.org/10.1287/orsc. 14.2.209.14992.

Von Hippel and von Krogh discuss what they see as the two models of innovation in organizational science: the private investment model, which assumes that returns to the innovator result from private goods and efficient regimes of intellectual property protection, and the collective action model, which operates on the assumption that under conditions of market failure, innovators collaborate in order to produce public goods. The authors provide a brief history of open source software and include a few case studies. Von Hippel and von Krogh take these projects as examples of the private-collective innovation models for the industry. The authors conclude with the suggestion that interpretation of subtle matter in organizational science will be aided by contextual and behavioural understanding of project activities, as well as a broad set of data and methods.

Von Krogh, Georg, and Eric von Hippel. 2006. "The Promise of Research on Open Source Software." *Management Science* 52(7): 975–83. DOI: https://www.doi.org/10.1287/mnsc.1060.0560.
Von Krogh and von Hippel discuss how the open source phenomenon has developed utility for research findings in many fields. Research is categorized into three areas: motivations for open source software projects; governance, organization, and the process of innovation in open source software projects; and competitive dynamics enforced by open source software. The authors create a table chart that amalgamates all available research (as of 2006) on open source software. They break this table into research focuses, special issues, and contributions. Open source software contributors have created a new economic model that can spread to other areas of economic and social activity. The authors express pride in having published some of the studies related to open source software.

Von Krogh, Georg, Sebastian Spaeth, and Karim R. Lakhani. 2003. "Community, Joining, and Specialization in Open Source Software Innovation: A Case Study." *Research Policy* 32(7): 1217–41. DOI: https://doi.org/10.1016/S0048-7333(03)00050-7.
Von Krogh, Spaeth, and Lakhani develop an inductive theory of the open source software innovation process. They focus on the creation of Freenet, a project that aims to develop a decentralized and anonymous peer-to-peer electronic file-sharing network. They analyze data from multiple sources documenting the Freenet software development process, and propose relationships among joining script, specialization, contribution barriers, and feature gifts. The authors provide a reference model and graphical overview of the Freenet architecture, as well as a diagram that evaluates project size based on email activity. In conclusion, the authors have noted that there are no empirical studies or solid theory building on the social aspects of software development.

Weber, Steven. 2004. *The Success of Open Source*. Cambridge, MA: Harvard University Press.
Weber's book-length study surveys the success of software and source code that is freely distributed. He discusses how property underpins the social organization of cooperation and production in the digital era, and how older models of production can no longer be followed after the success of systems

such as Linux and Apache. The success of open source software in this highly competitive industry subverts several assumptions about how software firms should be run, as well as the distribution and circulation of product. Weber discusses the history of open source in addition to basic definitions of the field and its methods of distribution, circulation, and production. The interactions between open source software and the disciplines of business and law are also examined, with Weber suggesting that these have all changed drastically with the advent of open source code distribution.

West, Joel. 2003. "How Open is Open Enough? Melding Proprietary and Open Source Platform Strategies." *Research Policy* 32(7) 1259–85. DOI: https://doi.org/10.1016/S0048-7333(03)00052-0.

West discusses how computer platforms provide integrated architectures for hardware and software standards. He examines both proprietary and open source strategies—the extremes of software development. The personal computer brings horizontal platform control, which is arguably more efficient than the vertically integrated structure because it allows the producer of each layer to serve the broadest possible market according to economies of scale. A table that indicates ownership of architectural layers for representative computer platforms as of 1990 is provided. West also evaluates the development of Unix, and how both the open source market and rival firms responded to the Microsoft challenge. The study concludes with a suggestion that the hybrid open source strategies of proprietary platform vendors are more suited to current market conditions, and that further discussion is needed on how open standards affect commercial firms.

West, Joel, and Scott Gallagher. 2006. "Challenges of Open Innovation: The Paradox of Firm Investment in Open Source Software." *R&D Management* 36(3): 319–31. DOI: https://www.doi.org/10.1111/j.1467-9310.2006.00436.x.

West and Gallagher discuss open innovation for the generation, capture, and employment of intellectual property within and by firms. Firms need to find creative ways to exploit internal innovation and incorporate external innovation into their developments. Additionally, they need to find ways to motivate outsiders to supply an ongoing stream of external innovations to supplement their own developments. The paradox is that rival firms could easily manipulate these innovations. However, pooled research, product development, spinouts, selling complements, and attracting donated complements are suggested as strategies to tackle the challenges created by the development of open source software for traditional firms. The authors note that more studies need to be conducted on virtual teams, cultural openness, technological modularization, and public/private collaboration.

## B. Reference List

Bastian, Mathieu, Sebastien Heymann, and Mathieu Jacomy. 2009. "Gephi: An Open Source Software for Exploring and Manipulating Networks." In *Proceedings of the Third International AAAI Conference on Weblogs and Social Media*, 361–62. Palo Alto, CA: Association for the Advancement of Artificial Intelligence (AAAI). https://www.aaai.org/ocs/index.php/ICWSM/09/paper/view/154/1009.

Bonaccorsi, Andrea, and Cristina Rossi. 2003. "Why Open Source Software Can Succeed." *Research Policy* 32(7): 1243–58. DOI: https://doi.org/10.1016/S0048-7333(03)00051-9.

Bruns, Axel. 2008. *Blogs, Wikipedia, Second Life, and Beyond: From Production to Produsage*. New York: Peter Lang.

Childs, Merilyn, and Regine Wagner. 2015. "Open Sourced Personal, Networked Learning and Higher Education Credentials." In *Open Learning and Formal Credentialing in Higher Education*, edited by Shirley Reushie, Amy Antonio, and Mike Keppell, 223–44. Hershey, PA: IGI Global.

Chopra, Samir, and Scott Dexter. 2009. "The Freedoms of Software and Its Ethical Uses." *Ethics and Information Technology* 11(4): 287–97. DOI: https://doi.org/10.1007/s10676-009-9191-0.

Dahlander, Linus, and Mats G. Magnusson. 2005. "Relationships between Open Source Software Companies and Communities: Observations from Nordic Firms." *Research Policy* 34(4): 481–93. DOI: https://doi.org/10.1016/j.respol.2005.02.003.

Feller, Joseph, and Brian Fitzgerald. 2002. *Understanding Open Source Software Development*. Boston: Addison-Wesley Longman.

Fitzgerald, Brian. 2006. "The Transformation of Open Source Software." *MIS Quarterly* 30(3): 587–98. DOI: https://www.doi.org/10.2307/25148740.

Godfrey, Michael W., and Qiang Tu. 2000. "Evolution in Open Source Software: A Case Study." In *Proceedings of the International Conference on Software Maintenance* (*ICSM '00*), 131–42. Washington, DC: IEEE Computer Society. http://svn-plg.uwaterloo.ca/~migod/papers/2000/icsm00.pdf.

Hars, Alexander, and Shaosong Ou. 2001. "Working for Free?—Motivations of Participating in Open Source Projects." In *Proceedings of the 34th Annual Hawaii International Conference on System Sciences (HICSS '01)*, 7014. Washington, DC: IEEE Computer Society.

Kelty, Christopher M. 2008. *Two Bits: The Cultural Significance of Free Software.* Durham, NC: Duke University Press.

Koehn, Philipp, Hieu Hoang, Alexandra Birch, Chris Callison-Burch, Marcello Federico, Nicola Bertoldi, Brooke Cowan, et al. 2007. "Moses: Open Source Toolkit for Statistical Machine Translation." In *Proceedings of the 45th Annual Meeting of the ACL on Interactive Poster and Demonstration Sessions*, 177–80. https://www.aclweb.org/anthology/P07-2045.

Kogut, Bruce, and Anca Metiu. 2001. "Open Source Software Development and Distributed Innovation." *Oxford Review of Economic Policy* 17(2): 248–64. https://www.jstor.org/stable/23606809.

Lakhani, Karim R., and Eric von Hippel. 2003. "How Open Source Software Works: 'Free' User-to-User Assistance." *Research Policy* 32(6): 923–43. DOI: https://doi.org/10.1016/S0048-7333(02)00095-1.

Lerner, Josh, and Jean Tirole. 2001. "The Open Source Movement: Key Research Questions." *European Economic Review* 45(4–6): 819–26. DOI: https://doi.org/10.1016/S0014-2921(01)00124-6.

———. 2002. "Some Simple Economics of Open Source." *The Journal of Industrial Economics* 50(2): 197–234. DOI: https://doi.org/10.1111/1467-6451.00174.

Mockus, Audris, Roy T. Fielding, and James D. Herbsleb. 2002. "Two Case Studies of Open Source Software Development: Apache and Mozilla." *ACM Transactions on Software Engineering and Methodology* 11(3): 309–46. DOI: https://www.doi.org/10.1145/567793.567795.

Raymond, Eric S. 2001. *The Cathedral and the Bazaar: Musings on Linux and Open Source by an Accidental Revolutionary.* Rev. ed. Sebastopol, CA: O'Reilly.

Roberts, Jeffrey A., Il-Horn Hann, and Sandra A. Slaughter. 2006. "Understanding the Motivations, Participation, and Performance of Open Source Software Developers: A Longitudinal Study of the Apache Projects." *Management Science* 52(7): 984–99. DOI: https://doi.org/10.1287/mnsc.1060.0554.

Rosen, Lawrence E. 2004. *Open Source Licensing: Software Freedom and Intellectual Property Law.* Upper Saddle River, NJ: Prentice Hall PTR.

Rosenzweig, Roy. 2006. "Can History Be Open Source? *Wikipedia* and the Future of the Past." *Journal of American History* 93(1): 117–46. DOI: https://www.doi.org/10.2307/4486062.

Schloss, Patrick D., Sarah L. Westcott, Thomas Ryabin, Justine R. Hall, Martin Hartmann, Emily B. Hollister, Ryan A. Lesniewski, et al. 2009. "Introducing mothur: Open-Source, Platform-Independent, Community-Supported Software for Describing and Comparing Microbial Communities." *Applied and Environmental Microbiology* 75(23): 7537–41. DOI: https://www.doi.org/10.1128/AEM.01541-09.

Truscello, Michael. 2003. "The Architecture of Information: Open Source Software and Tactical Poststructuralist Anarchism." *Postmodern Culture* 13(3): n.p. http://pmc.iath.virginia.edu/issue.503/13.3truscello.html.

Von Hippel, Eric, and Georg von Krogh. 2003. "Open Source Software and the 'Private-Collective' Innovation Model: Issues for *Organization Science.*" *Organization Science* 14(2): 209–23. DOI: https://doi.org/10.1287/orsc.14.2.209.14992.

Von Krogh, Georg, and Eric von Hippel. 2006. "The Promise of Research on Open Source Software." *Management Science* 52(7): 975–83. DOI: https://www.doi.org/10.1287/mnsc.1060.0560.

Von Krogh, Georg, Sebastian Spaeth, and Karim R. Lakhani. 2003. "Community, Joining, and Specialization in Open Source Software Innovation: A Case Study." *Research Policy* 32(7): 1217–41. DOI: https://doi.org/10.1016/S0048-7333(03)00050-7.

Weber, Steven. 2004. *The Success of Open Source.* Cambridge, MA: Harvard University Press.

West, Joel. 2003. "How Open is Open Enough? Melding Proprietary and Open Source Platform Strategies." *Research Policy* 32(7) 1259–85. DOI: https://doi.org/10.1016/S0048-7333(03)00052-0.

West, Joel, and Scott Gallagher. 2006. "Challenges of Open Innovation: The Paradox of Firm Investment in Open Source Software." *R&D Management* 36(3): 319–31. DOI: https://www.doi.org/10.1111/j.1467-9310.2006.00436.x.

## 5. Open Data

Open data concerns the availability and accessibility of research data to the public. Research data may include government, university, institutional, corporate, and educational materials (Bradley et al. 2009; Davies 2010; Stadler, Lehmann, Höffner, and Auer 2012). Resources in this category explore why certain researchers do not make their data publicly available, and what motivates institutional attitudes toward open data (Murray-Rust 2008; Piwowar and Vision 2013). Authors are concerned with educating faculty about the importance of preserving research data and metadata, as well as the political implications of free data distribution as opposed to corporate or institutional holdings (Molloy 2011). Many resources address government data and government policies on openness (Davies 2010; Geiger and Lucke 2012; Janssen 2012; Janssen et al. 2012; Kalampokis et al. 2011; Shadbolt et al. 2012). Research in this category examines the effectiveness of open data policies within institutions and various strategies for data management (Bauer and Kaltenböck 2012; Görlitz and Staab 2011). Generally, these articles argue that open data should be published in ways that can be utilized by the public in order to be beneficial.

### A. Annotations

**Anokwa, Yaw, Carl Hartung, Waylon Brunette, Gaetano Boriello, and Adam Lerer. 2009. "Open Source Data Collection in the Developing World."** *Computer* **42(10): 97–99. http://ieeexplore.ieee.org/xpl/articleDetails.jsp?arnumber=5280663&tag=1.**
Anokwa, Hartung, Brunette, Boriello, and Lerer, all members of the Open Data Kit (ODK) development team, present evidence as to how the ODK can be used for accessible data collection in the developing world. The authors suggest that current services are inflexible, closed source, and based on closed standards. When this article was published in 2009, the ODK had not yet been developed as a tool, and the authors provide arguments for funding agencies to give consideration to their proposal. As a case study, the authors discuss AMPATH Kenya, the most comprehensive initiative in the country to combat HIV. AMPATH opted to use the ODK to improve its methods of data collection and retrieval. The ODK research team argues that the ability to collect data is key to the success of many organizations in the developing world.

**Auer, Soren, Christian Bizer, Georgi Kobilarov, Jens Lehmann, Richard Cyganiak, and Zachary Ives. 2007. "DBpedia: A Nucleus for a Web of Open Data." In** *The Semantic Web,* **edited by Karl Aberer, Key-Sun Choi, Natasha Noy, Dean Allemang, Kyung-Il Lee, Lyndon Nixon,**

Jennifer Golbeck, et al., 722–35. Berlin and Heidelberg: Springer. http://link.springer.com/chapter/10.1007/978-3-540-76298-0_52.
Auer et al. outline the basic premises and mission of DBpedia: a community effort to extract structured information from Wikipedia and make the data available for access on the Web. DBpedia provides support for sophisticated queries against Wikipedia data sets. Infobox templates, categorization information, images, geo-coordinates, links to external sites, and various language editions of Wikipedia form the nucleus of information that is extracted and queried. DBpedia operates using three mechanisms: linked data, the SPARQL protocol, and downloadable RDF dumps. Their data sets can be accessed royalty-free via the GNU free-documentation licence. The authors then provide instructions on how to efficiently search through DBpedia to access relevant materials, a list of third-party user interfaces, and a catalogue of related work. In the future, the research team wishes to further automate the data extraction process to increase the currency of DBpedia's data set and to synchronize it with changes in Wikipedia.

Bauer, Florian, and Martin Kaltenböck. 2012. *Linked Open Data: The Essentials*. Vienna: edition mono/monochrom. https://www.reeep.org/sites/default/files/LOD-the-Essentials_0.pdf.
Bauer and Kaltenböck have written a guide for administrators describing how to wisely manage and use linked open data. The guide provides basic definitions that clarify the differences between open data and linked open data. The authors expound on the industrial potential of using the linked approach, and provide advice and examples on how to start a linked open data catalogue. Bauer and Kaltenböck select the reegle.info country profiles, UK legislation, and Open EI definitions as representative of larger linked open data trends. They articulate a vision that depicts how these tools can be used to create the *Semantic Web* of the future. The guide provides links to Web resources, and uses visual graphs to simplify the process of linking and cataloguing data.

Bradley, Jean-Claude, Robert J. Lancashire, Andrew S.I.D. Lang, and Antony J. Williams. 2009. "The Spectral Game: Leveraging Open Data and Crowdsourcing for Education." *Journal of Cheminformatics* 1(9): 1–10. DOI: https://doi.org/10.1186/1758-2946-1-9.
Bradley et al. use The Spectral Game to frame their discussion of leveraging open data and crowdsourcing techniques in education. The Spectral Game is used to assist in the teaching of spectroscopy in an entertaining manner. It was created by combining open source spectral data, a spectrum-viewing tool, and appropriate workflows, and it delivers these resources through the

game medium. The authors evaluate the game in an undergraduate organic chemistry class, and argue that The Spectral Game demonstrates the importance of open data for remixing educational curriculum.

**Brown, Susan, and John Simpson. 2015. "An Entity By Any Other Name: Linked Open Data as a Basis for a Decentered, Dynamic Scholarly Publishing Ecology." *Scholarly and Research Communication* 6(2): n.p. DOI: https://doi.org/10.22230/src.2015v6n2a212.**

Brown and Simpson propose that linked open data enables more easily navigable scholarly environments that permit better integration of research materials and greater interlinkage between individuals and institutions. They frame linked open data integration as an ecological problem in a complex system of parts and relationships. The different parts of the ecology co-evolve and change according to the relationships in the system. The authors suggest that tools are needed for establishing automated conditions; for evaluating the provenance, authority, and trustworthiness of linked open data resources; and for developing tools that facilitate corrections and enhancements. The authors suggest that an ontology negotiation tool would be a most valuable contribution to the Semantic Web. Such a tool would represent an opportunity for collaboration between different sectors of the knowledge economy, and would allow the *Semantic Web* to develop as an evolving space of knowledge production and dissemination.

**Davies, Tim. 2010. "Open Data, Democracy and Public Sector Reform. A Look at Open Government Data Use from Data.gov.uk." *Open Data Impacts*. http://www.opendataimpacts.net/report/.**

Davies explores the use of open government data (OGD) from the United Kingdom website data.gov.uk. He begins with a theoretical discussion of open government data by arguing that the digital turn has undermined the government's monopoly on data processing and interpretation. By contrast, the open data movement aspires to promote transparency and accountability by empowering citizens. In this exploratory case study, Davies details who uses OGD, how OGD is being used, and the potential implications OGD has for the public sector. This empirical study uses a variety of research methods and draws on survey, interview, and participant-observation data. Overall, Davies found that OGD was used by an overwhelmingly male audience with occupations in the private sector, public sector, and at academic institutions. The use of open data generally fell into five categories: data to fact, data to information, data to interface, data to data, and data to service. This study highlights real-world, practical uses of OGD and lays the groundwork for future research to test the adequacy and applicability of Davies's typologies.

Di Noia, Tommaso, Roberto Mirizzi, Vito Claudio Ostuni, Davide Romito, and Markus Zanker. 2012. "Linked Open Data to Support Content-Based Recommender Systems." In *Proceedings of the 8th International Conference on Semantic Systems* (*I-SEMANTICS '12*), 1–8. New York: ACM. DOI: https://doi.org/10.1145/2362499.2362501.

Di Noia, Mirizzi, Ostuni, Romito, and Zanker analyze the open data approach for supporting content-based recommender systems. The research team performs an evaluation of MovieLens, the historical data set for movie recommender systems. The researchers link this data to DBpedia data sets and perform one-to-one mapping. Evidence shows that 298 of 3,952 mappings in MovieLens have no correspondence with DBpedia. Their content-based recommender system leverages the knowledge encoded in the semantic data sets of linked open data with DBpedia, Freebase, and LinkedMDB to collect metadata (such as actors, directors, or genres) on movies.

Geiger, Christian P., and Jörn von Lucke. 2012. "Open Government and (Linked) (Open) (Government) (Data)." *eJournal of eDemocracy and Open Government* 4(2): 265–78. DOI: https://doaj.org/article/0bc5e 4c6a0e84ee3a74c4aa4190c8126.

Geiger and Lucke explore free usage of stored public sector data, arguing that it is not enough to simply put data online; data needs to be considered, weighed, and determined if and where it can be published. The authors describe different types of machine readable and open formats for data. The open data movement currently faces difficulty with different national and international laws about access and transparency. Geiger and Lucke argue that a fair balance between the interests of individual authors, publishers, and the general public must be reached. Misinterpretation by third parties, as well as the structure and culture of the public sector, are further difficulties faced by open data directives. Administrations and individual actors should cooperate with each other to achieve sustainability of open government data communities.

Görlitz, Olaf, and Steffen Staab. 2011. "Federated Data Management and Query Optimization for Linked Open Data." In *New Directions in Web Data Management 1*, edited by Athena Vakali and Lakhmi C. Jain, 109–37. Berlin: Springer. DOI: https://doi. org/10.1007/978-3-642-17551-0_5.

Görlitz and Staab provide tips for federated data management and query optimization for linked open data. For the authors, complex queries are the only means of leveraging the full potential of linked open data. The authors argue that a federation infrastructure is necessary for linked open data, and they provide the architecture for their own model. The basic components for this model are a declarative query language, a data catalogue, a query optimizer, data protocol, result ranking, and provenance information. Data source federation combines the advantages of both centralized repositories and explorative query processing for efficient query execution and returning complete results. This model allows for transparent querying of distributed linked open data sources. The authors suggest that the SPARQL standard does not support all requirements to efficiently process federated queries. To improve these, the authors recommend focusing on join order optimization (the optimization of basic graph patterns).

**Gray, Jonathan. 2015. "Five Ways Open Data Can Boost Democracy around the World."** *The Guardian*, **February 20. https://www.the-guardian.com/public-leaders-network/2015/feb/20/open-data-day-fairer-taxes. Archived at https://perma.cc/2P4P-4V3A.**
Gray provides information on the amount of public resource spending on goods and services per year, and how open data can improve political standards. He argues that open data policies can help protect public resources and expenditures, control corporate lobbyists, fight pollution, and hold politicians accountable. Gray provides evidence of dozens of parliamentary monitoring websites, which are often built by civic hackers to track speeches and votes and to hold politicians accountable to voters. Open data is commensurate with democratic values for Gray, who argues that incorporating such policies will allow for the development of increasingly open and accountable democracies worldwide.

**Gurstein, Michael B. 2011. "Open Data: Empowering the Empowered or Effective Data Use for Everyone?"** *First Monday* **16(2): n.p. https://firstmonday.org/article/view/3316/2764.**
Gurstein is supportive of the open data project but maintains that the impact on poor and marginalized communities must be investigated. Policy should ensure that there is a wide basis of opportunity for effective data use. He uses research on the impact of digitization of land records in Bangalore as evidence of the potential for land surveyors, lawyers, and other high ranking officials to exploit gaps in titles, take advantage of mistakes in documentation, and identify opportunities and targets for crimes. Gurstein creates a seven-point framework for making effective use of open data. This should be combined with training in computer/software use, accessible formatting of data sets, interpretation training, and a supportive advocacy network for the community.

Hartung, Carl, Adam Lerer, Yaw Anokwa, Clint Tseng, Waylon Brunette, and Gaetano Borriello. 2010. "Open Data Kit: Tools to Build Information Services for Developing Regions." In *Proceedings of the 4th ACM/IEEE International Conference on Information and Communication Technologies and Development* (ICTD '10), Article 18. New York: ACM. DOI: https://doi.org/10.1145/2369220.2369236.
Hartung, Lerer, Anokwa, Tseng, Brunette, and Borriello present the development of the Open Data Kit (ODK), which contains four tools: collect, aggregate, voice, and build. The 'collect' platform renders complex application logic and supports the manipulation of data types. 'Aggregate' performs a 'click to deploy' server that supports data upload and storage transfer in the cloud. 'Voice' renders application logic using automated phone prompts to which the user responds with the keypad. 'Build' is a drag and drop application designer that generates logic used by the tools. The ODK was created to empower individuals and organizations and allow them to build services for distributing data in developing countries. The authors provide outlines of tool designs and charts of system architecture, a list of the drivers and clients employed by their program, and a list of organizations that support open source applications such as ODK. The tool uses a modular, extensible, and open source design to allow users to choose tools best suited for their own specific deployments.

Hausenblas, Michael, and Marcel Karnstedt. 2010. "Understanding Linked Open Data as a Web-Scale Database." In *Proceedings of the Second International Conference on Advances in Databases, Knowledge, and Data Applications* (DBKDA 2010), 56–61. Los Alamitos, CA: IEEE Computer Society. DOI: https://doi.org/10.1109/DBKDA.2010.23.
Hausenblas and Karnstedt compare linked open data to relational, web-scale databases. The authors provide general linked data principles and reference the linked open data community project to open their discussion and pose questions regarding the steps that should be taken to migrate parts of the relational database. Hausenblas and Karnstedt maintain that a database perspective is required for linked open data to ensure its acceptance and realize a low-barrier adoption process. The linked open data community needs to create specialized web-scale database engines made for the requirements of the linked open data cloud.

Jain, Prateek, Pascal Hitzler, Amit P. Seth, Kunal Verma, and Peter Z. Yeh. 2010. "Ontology Alignment for Linked Open Data." In *The Semantic Web – ISCW 2010*, edited by Peter F. Patel-Schneider et al., 402–17.

Berlin and Heidelberg: Springer. DOI: https://doi.org/10.1007/978-3-642-17746-0_26.

Jain et al. argue that the Linked Open Data project is a major step in realizing the early open access vision for the Semantic Web. The group discusses its findings on alignment systems available for linked open data, and how they had struggled to find systems that performed satisfactorily. The group suggests that the system they have developed, BLOOMS, outperforms contemporary state-of-the-art ontology alignment systems in linked open data schema. BLOOMS uses the Wikipedia category hierarchy, pre-processes the input ontologies, and post-processes with the assistance of an Alignment API and a reasoner. The research group provides charts that detail specifications for precision and recall rates across several different open data schema ontology alignment programs. The authors then suggest that further inquiries should be made into partonomical relationships and disjointedness on the linked open data cloud.

Janssen, Katleen. 2012. "Open Government Data and the Right to Information: Opportunities and Obstacles." *The Journal of Community Informatics* 8(2): n.p. http://www.ci-journal.net/index.php/ciej/article/view/952.

Janssen provides an overview of the current discussion on open government data and the right to information. She argues that the open government data movement has close ties with the Right to Information movement in their promotion of access to government information as a fundamental right, and of greater availability of data held by government bodies. Janssen argues that access to government information is a key component of any transparency and accountability process for government activities. Transparency results in better-informed citizens who can contribute to governmental processes and express meaningful views with regard to government policy. Janssen concludes that the two movements should be seen as complementary, and argues that they can promote each other through legislation. For example, the European Commission's 2011 open data strategy promoted open data as indispensable for a smart, sustainable, and inclusive economy, and as a strategy to increase accountability.

Janssen, Marijn, Yannis Charalabidis, and Anneke Zuiderwijk. 2012. "Benefits, Adoption Barriers and Myths of Open Data and Open Government." *Information Systems Management* 29(4): 258–68. DOI: https://doi.org/10.1080/10580530.2012.716740.

Janssen, Charalabidis, and Zuiderwijk provide a political analogue to many of the barriers preventing true open data publication. Open government demands that the government give up control and that the public sector undergo considerable transformation. The authors use systems theory to draw attention to the distinctions between systems that are open to their environment and systems that are closed. The authors deem several points of open access rhetoric as myth: that publicizing data will yield benefits, that all information should be unrestrictedly publicized, that publishing public data is the whole of the task, and that every constituent can make use of open data. Finally, the myth that open data will result in open government is refuted. Janssen, Charalabidis, and Zuiderwijk suggest that open data becomes valuable only through use, and that research demands more inquiry into the conversion of public data into services of public value.

Johnson, Jeffrey Alan. 2014. "From Open Data to Information Justice." *Ethics and Information Technology* 16(4): 263–74. DOI: https://doi.org/10.1007/s10676-014-9351-8.

Johnson argues that scholarly discussions of information justice should subsume the question of open data. His article examines the embedding of social privilege in data sets, the different capabilities of data users, and the norms that data systems impose through disciplinary functions. For Johnson, open data has potential to exacerbate rather than alleviate social injustices. Data sovereignty should trump open data, and active pro-social countermeasures need to be taken to ensure ethical practices. Johnson calls for information pluralism, which would embrace rather than problematize the messiness of data. He argues that an information justice movement is vital for drumming up the participation necessary to make information pluralism a reality. Johnson calls for further inquiry into how existing social structures are perpetuated, exacerbated, and mitigated by information systems.

Kalampokis, Evangelos, Efthimios Tambouris, and Konstantinos Tarabanis. 2011. "Open Government Data: A Stage Model." In *Proceedings of the 10th IFIP WG 8.5 International Conference (EGOV 2011)*, edited by Marijn Janssen et al., 235–46. Heidelberg: Springer. DOI: https://doi.org/10.1007/978-3-642-22878-0_20.

Kalampokis, Tambouris, and Tarabinis create a stage model for open government data in this article, asserting that governments have a mandate to enable and facilitate data consumption by both citizens and businesses. A lack of information on available data poses considerable difficulty to the field. The objective of this article is to supplement existing eGovernment stage models by providing a roadmap for open government data reuse and enabling evaluation of relevant initiatives. The stage model is made up of four parts: aggregation of government data, integration of that data, integration of government data with formal non-government data, and integration of government data with formal and social non-government data. Public agencies are advised to make their data easily and quickly available online. The authors recommend that open government data initiatives should be thoroughly studied to identify important data sets for each stage of the model to be identified.

Molloy, Jennifer. 2011. "The Open Knowledge Foundation: Open Data Means Better Science." *PLOS Biology* 9(12): 1–4. http://journals. plos.org/plosbiology/article?id=10.1371/journal.pbio.1001195.

Molloy stipulates that implementing open data allows for initiatives within science-related disciplines to provide new infrastructure that supports data archiving and the development of stronger data management policies. The author suggests that there is little value in making data open and accessible if it is not being used. Molloy provides evidence from a recent collaboration between the Open Data in Science working group, the Joint Information Services Council and *Semantic Web* Applications, and Tools for Life Sciences in creating collections of open publications and data sets through available bibliographic data and crowdsourced summaries of non-open content. An accessible open data approach within the sciences will allow the disciplines to generate a wealth of tools, apps, and data sets to facilitate the discovery and recirculation of data.

Murray-Rust, Peter. 2008. "Open Data in Science." *Serials Review* 34(1): 52–64. http://www.tandfonline.com/doi/abs/10.1080/00987913.2 008.10765152.

Murray-Rust argues for the need of open access publishing initiatives in the sciences and provides an outline of several early initiatives in the field. He discusses concepts such as reuse, mash-up, community norms, and permission barriers. Most of the data filed in chemistry, for example, is published as a collection of facts, and open access publishing could help reorient the method by which data in the sciences is collected. Murray-Rust provides paper extracts with structures from organic chemistry as examples of the types of data that could be openly distributed in the sciences. He concludes his observations with the argument that the sciences should adopt Open Notebook science in parallel with formal publications in order to achieve the goal of liberating old data.

Piwowar, Heather A., and Todd J. Vision. 2013. "Data Reuse and the Open Data Citation Advantage." *PeerJ* 1:e175. DOI: https://doi. org/10.7717/peerj.175.

Piwowar and Vision argue that reusing data and opting for a data management policy that makes use of open citation are effective means of facilitating science. This type of policy allows these resources to circulate and contribute to discussions far beyond their original analysis. The authors discuss the advantages and challenges of making research publicly available. Piwowar and Vision conduct a small-scale manual review of citation contexts and use attribution, through mentions of data accession numbers, to explore patterns in data reuse on a larger scale. The researchers determine that data availability is associated with citation benefit, of which data reuse is a demonstrable component.

**Science International. 2015. *Open Data in a Big Data World*. Paris: International Council for Science (ICSU), International Social Science Council (ISSC), The World Academy of Sciences (TWAS), and InterAcademy Partnership (IAP). https://council.science/cms/2017/04/open-data-in-big-data-world_long.pdf.**
The International Council for Science (ICSU), the InterAcademy Partnership (IAP), the World Academy of Sciences (TWAS), and the International Social Science Council (ISSC), in the accord reached at the first Science International meeting, address the opportunities and challenges of data revolution in the realm of global science policy. They explain the digital revolution as a world-historical event, considering the amounts of data produced and their effect on the research industry. The authors characterize big data by volume, variety, velocity, and veracity. Another important element is linked data and its importance for the Semantic Web. The accord also addresses the open data imperative with regard to various issues, such as the need to maintain the process of 'self-correction,' and problems arising from unsuccessful replication of experiments. Finally, the document lists principles of open data, which include boundaries of openness, enabling practices, and various responsibilities (of scientists; research institutions and universities; publishers; funding agencies; professional associations, scholarly societies, and academies; and libraries, archives, and repositories).

**Shadbolt, Nigel, Kieron O'Hara, Tim Berners-Lee, Nicholas Gibbins, Hugh Glaser, Wendy Hall, and M.C. Schraefel. 2012. "Linked Open Government Data: Lessons from Data.gov.uk." *IEEE Intelligent Systems* 27(3): 16–24. http://eprints.soton.ac.uk/340564/.**
Shadbolt, O'Hara, Berners-Lee, Gibbins, Glasner, Hall, and Schraefel present their findings from the data.gov.uk website and its approach to open data management. They argue that the top-down political culture creates a data monopoly. Transparency in the UK is focused on data.gov.uk, a public data catalogue with thousands of downloadable data sets under permissive open

government licence. The adoption of open government data is important for the linked data web, which can enhance the data discovery processes. The authors suggest that geography provides an intuitive way of aligning data sets.

**Stadler, Claus, Jens Lehmann, Konrad Höffner, and Sören Auer. 2012. "LinkedGeoData: A Core for a Web of Spatial Open Data." *Semantic Web* 3(4): 333–54. DOI: https://doi.org/10.3233/SW-2011-0052.**
Stadler, Lehmann, Höffner, and Auer present their research on the collaborative development of a spatial data web: OpenStreetMap (OSM). They describe how their data is interlinked through the LinkedGeoData project and can be accessed via the Linked Data paradigm. They describe the makeup of OSM, which consists of nodes to represent geographic points with latitude and longitude, as well as the general architecture of the OSM model. The representational state transfer (REST) API gives full access to OSM's nodes and can be combined with RDF/XML, N-Triples, or Turtle. The authors provide a list of browser tools that use LinkedGeoData.

**Vision, Todd J. 2010. "Open Data and the Social Contract of Scientific Publishing." *BioScience* 60(5): 330–31. DOI: https://doi.org/10.1525/bio.2010.60.5.2.**
Vision considers open data and the social contract of scientific publishing. He begins with an appraisal of the scientific enterprise's effectiveness for providing scientists with a means to publish their findings and receive credit for their work. To improve upon these standards, however, Vision believes that data needs to be included in the arrangement, and that the printed page can no longer be the unit of measurement for attributing scholarship and research. Publishers can assist in this process by having journals require data archiving at the time of publication, since un-archived data files are often misplaced, corrupted, and rendered obsolete over time. Vision moves on to a discussion of Dryad, a tool that promotes data citations by assigning unique DOIs and compiling data in a shared repository. He concludes with the suggestion that permanent archives for research data would allow the social contract of publishing to give authors and their data their due.

**Xu, Guan-Hua. 2007. "Open Access to Scientific Data: Promoting Science and Innovation." *Data Science Journal* 6: 21–25. DOI: https://doi.org/10.2481/dsj.6.OD21.**
Xu details open access policies for scientific data in China. In 2002, the Ministry of Science and Technology launched the Scientific Data Sharing program

with 24 participating government agencies. The government of China is expecting to make 80 pervcent of scientific research data available to the general public. Xu notes that relevant laws and regulations need to be established, and authentic data resources need to be further integrated. The author maintains that China is committed to the policy of reform and making information more readily available, especially with regard to shared and open data.

## B. Reference List

Anokwa, Yaw, Carl Hartung, Waylon Brunette, Gaetano Boriello, and Adam Lerer. 2009. "Open Source Data Collection in the Developing World." *Computer* 42(10): 97–99. http://ieeexplore.ieee.org/xpl/articleDetails. jsp?arnumber=5280663&tag=1.

Auer, Soren, Christian Bizer, Georgi Kobilarov, Jens Lehmann, Richard Cyganiak, and Zachary Ives. 2007. "DBpedia: A Nucleus for a Web of Open Data." In *The Semantic Web*, edited by Karl Aberer, Key-Sun Choi, Natasha Noy, Dean Allemang, Kyung-Il Lee, Lyndon Nixon, Jennifer Golbeck, et al., 722–35. Berlin and Heidelberg: Springer. http://link. springer.com/chapter/10.1007/978-3-540-76298-0_52.

Bauer, Florian, and Martin Kaltenböck. 2012. *Linked Open Data: The Essentials.* Vienna: edition mono/monochrom. https://www.reeep.org/sites/default/files/LOD-the-Essentials_0.pdf.

Bradley, Jean-Claude, Robert J. Lancashire, Andrew S.I.D. Lang, and Antony J. Williams. 2009. "The Spectral Game: Leveraging Open Data and Crowdsourcing for Education." *Journal of Cheminformatics* 1(9): 1–10. DOI: https://doi.org/10.1186/1758-2946-1-9.

Brown, Susan, and John Simpson. 2015. "An Entity By Any Other Name: Linked Open Data as a Basis for a Decentered, Dynamic Scholarly Publishing Ecology." *Scholarly and Research Communication* 6(2): n.p. DOI: https://doi.org/10.22230/src.2015v6n2a212.

Davies, Tim. 2010. "Open Data, Democracy and Public Sector Reform. A Look at Open Government Data Use from Data.gov.uk." *Open Data Impacts.* http://www.opendataimpacts.net/report/.

Di Noia, Tommaso, Roberto Mirizzi, Vito Claudio Ostuni, Davide Romito, and Markus Zanker. 2012. "Linked Open Data to Support Content-Based

Recommender Systems." In *Proceedings of the 8th International Conference on Semantic Systems* (*I-SEMANTICS '12*), 1–8. New York: ACM. DOI: https://doi.org/10.1145/2362499.2362501.

Geiger, Christian P., and Jörn von Lucke. 2012. "Open Government and (Linked) (Open) (Government) (Data)." *eJournal of eDemocracy and Open Government* 4(2): 265–78. DOI: https://doaj.org/article/0bc5e4c6a0e84ee3a74c4aa4190c8126.

Görlitz, Olaf, and Steffen Staab. 2011. "Federated Data Management and Query Optimization for Linked Open Data." In *New Directions in Web Data Management 1*, edited by Athena Vakali and Lakhmi C. Jain, 109–37. Berlin: Springer. DOI: https://doi.org/10.1007/978-3-642-17551-0_5.

Gray, Jonathan. 2015. "Five Ways Open Data Can Boost Democracy around the World." *The Guardian*, February 20. https://www.theguardian.com/public-leaders-network/2015/feb/20/open-data-day-fairer-taxes. Archived at https://perma.cc/2P4P-4V3A.

Gurstein, Michael B. 2011. "Open Data: Empowering the Empowered or Effective Data Use for Everyone?" *First Monday* 16(2): n.p. https://firstmonday.org/article/view/3316/2764.

Hartung, Carl, Adam Lerer, Yaw Anokwa, Clint Tseng, Waylon Brunette, and Gaetano Borriello. 2010. "Open Data Kit: Tools to Build Information Services for Developing Regions." In *Proceedings of the 4th ACM/IEEE International Conference on Information and Communication Technologies and Development* (*ICTD '10*), Article 18. New York: ACM. DOI: https://doi.org/10.1145/2369220.2369236.

Hausenblas, Michael, and Marcel Karnstedt. 2010. "Understanding Linked Open Data as a Web-Scale Database." In *Proceedings of the Second International Conference on Advances in Databases, Knowledge, and Data Applications* (*DBKDA 2010*), 56–61. Los Alamitos, CA: IEEE Computer Society. DOI: https://doi.org/10.1109/DBKDA.2010.23.

Jain, Prateek, Pascal Hitzler, Amit P. Seth, Kunal Verma, and Peter Z. Yeh. 2010. "Ontology Alignment for Linked Open Data." In *The Semantic Web – ISCW 2010*, edited by Peter F. Patel-Schneider et al., 402–17. Berlin and Heidelberg: Springer. DOI: https://doi.org/10.1007/978-3-642-17746-0_26.

Janssen, Katleen. 2012. "Open Government Data and the Right to Information: Opportunities and Obstacles." *The Journal of Community Informatics* 8(2): n.p. http://www.ci-journal.net/index.php/ciej/article/view/952.

Janssen, Marijn, Yannis Charalabidis, and Anneke Zuiderwijk. 2012. "Benefits, Adoption Barriers and Myths of Open Data and Open Government." *Information Systems Management* 29(4): 258–68. DOI: https://doi.org/10.1080/10580530.2012.716740.

Johnson, Jeffrey Alan. 2014. "From Open Data to Information Justice." *Ethics and Information Technology* 16(4): 263–74. DOI: https://doi.org/10.1007/s10676-014-9351-8.

Kalampokis, Evangelos, Efthimios Tambouris, and Konstantinos Tarabanis. 2011. "Open Government Data: A Stage Model." In *Proceedings of the 10th IFIP WG 8.5 International Conference* (*EGOV 2011*), edited by Marijn Janssen et al., 235–46. Heidelberg: Springer. DOI: https://doi.org/10.1007/978-3-642-22878-0_20.

Molloy, Jennifer. 2011. "The Open Knowledge Foundation: Open Data Means Better Science." *PLOS Biology* 9(12): 1–4. http://journals.plos.org/plosbiology/article?id=10.1371/journal.pbio.10011952.

Murray-Rust, Peter. 2008. "Open Data in Science." *Serials Review* 34(1): 52–64. http://www.tandfonline.com/doi/abs/10.1080/00987913.2008.10765152.

Piwowar, Heather A., and Todd J. Vision. 2013. "Data Reuse and the Open Data Citation Advantage." *PeerJ* 1:e175. DOI: https://doi.org/10.7717/peerj.175.

Science International. 2015. *Open Data in a Big Data World*. Paris: International Council for Science (ICSU), International Social Science Council (ISSC), The World Academy of Sciences (TWAS), and InterAcademy Partnership (IAP). https://council.science/cms/2017/04/open-data-in-big-data-world_long.pdf.

Shadbolt, Nigel, Kieron O'Hara, Tim Berners-Lee, Nicholas Gibbins, Hugh Glaser, Wendy Hall, and M.C. Schraefel. 2012. "Linked Open Government Data: Lessons from Data.gov.uk." *IEEE Intelligent Systems* 27(3): 16–24. http://eprints.soton.ac.uk/340564/.

Stadler, Claus, Jens Lehmann, Konrad Höffner, and Soren Auer. 2012. "LinkedGeoData: A Core for a Web of Spatial Open Data." *Semantic Web* 3(4): 333–54. DOI: https://doi.org/10.3233/SW-2011-0052.

Vision, Todd J. 2010. "Open Data and the Social Contract of Scientific Publishing." *BioScience* 60(5): 330–31. DOI: https://doi.org/10.1525/bio.2010.60.5.2.

Xu, Guan-Hua. 2007. "Open Access to Scientific Data: Promoting Science and Innovation." *Data Science Journal* 6: 21–25. DOI: https://doi.org/10.2481/dsj.6.OD21.

# II. Community-Based and Collaborative Forms of Open Knowledge

## 1. Community Engagement

Certain university representatives are invested in creating and maintaining partnerships with community members, often in the form of goal-oriented projects that benefit society in some way. This category primarily focuses on university-community partnerships and how they evolve over time. Earlier sources focus on why such collaboration is important and reasons why it should become a common practice in the university (Hart and Wolff 2006; O'Meara, Sandmann, Saltmarsh, and Giles 2011). More recent resources focus on the aftermath of such integration; they discuss the benefits of these partnerships for the university and the community, as well as the obstacles and challenges that arise when representatives of these two groups collaborate, and how to overcome them (Barnes et al. 2009; Butin 2010; McNall, Reed, Brown, and Allen 2009). A central issue addressed is the need for university administrations to adapt to community engagement by appropriately rewarding students and scholars who engage in such work, and to ensure that working with communities is career-enhancing (Pasque et al. 2005; Sturm, Eatman, Saltmarsh, and Bush 2011). There are also a number of resources that discuss the role of technology in community engagement and collaboration. Many authors argue that the use of technology can bring about social and political change, and support civic action (Bennett 2008; Bowdon and Carpenter 2011; Caplan, Perse and Gennaria 2007; Dumova 2012; Jenkins and Deuze 2008; Lin and Atkin 2007; Milakovich 2012). Together, the resources support community engagement as an essential role of the university.

### A. Annotations

Barnes, Jessica V., Emily L. Altimare, Patricia A. Farrell, Robert E. Brown, C. Richard Burnett III, LaDonna Gamble, and James Davis. 2009. "Creating and Sustaining Authentic Partnerships with Community in a Systemic Model." *Journal of Higher Education Outreach and Engagement* 13(4): 15–29. https://files.eric.ed.gov/fulltext/EJ905410.pdf.
Barnes et al. present approaches to community partnerships—developed by and practised at Michigan State University—that focus on community voices and are developmental, dynamic, and systematic in nature. The authors

provide a brief history of university outreach and engagement since the 1980s, as well as a visual diagram of key terms in the university's approach to outreach. This strategy aims to become embedded in stress-asset based solutions, and to build community capacity for collaborative networks. The authors provide a list of challenges in current university partnerships and assess engagement efforts. Future research will examine how scholars, communities and conveners define partnership success.

**Bennett, W. Lance, ed. 2008.** *Civic Life Online: Learning How Digital Media Can Engage Youth.* **Cambridge, MA: MIT Press.**
Bennett, in his introduction to the collection, suggests that younger generations are increasingly disconnected from conventional politics and government. However, the percentage of youth involved in civic engagement in non-governmental areas has increased. He explains that communication channels take many forms, including official communication tools and online social community networks. The collection's authors discuss how online networks can inspire conventional political participation, and how digital technologies can be used to expand the boundaries of politics and public issues. In general, the authors suggest that there is a need for a transparent global debate about how digital media reshapes the expectations and prospects of youth in democratic societies.

**Bowdon, Melody A., and Russell G. Carpenter, eds. 2011.** *Higher Education, Emerging Technologies, and Community Partnerships: Concepts, Models and Practices.* **Hershey, PA: IGI Global.**
Bowdon and Carpenter collect essays from 88 teachers, professors, and community leaders in a book that argues that technologies are being used in increasingly compelling ways to forge partnerships between college students, staff, faculty members, and the communities around them. The authors note that college and high school students are taking a lead in the process of creating valuable partnerships in local and global communities. The chapters include observations on successful partnerships between universities and other groups, as well as on the practical and theoretical meanings that technological tools have for different populations. Other issues addressed include the fact that capacity-building for technology use remains a critical objective in many regions of the world, and that the challenges of online education heighten as it increasingly becomes a staple of academic training.

**Butin, Dan W. 2010.** *Service-Learning in Theory and Practice: The Future of Community Engagement in Higher Education.* **New York: Palgrave Macmillan.**
Butin's book on the theoretical and practical applications of service learning in community engagement covers a variety of topics ranging from the conceptualization of service learning to the establishment of institutional programs that create spaces for service learning in higher education. He provides examples of majors, minors, and certificate programs that encourage service learning at a variety of institutions. The book concludes with suggestions about how higher education institutions can embrace a scholarship of engagement and a discussion of current trends in service learning, as well as the implications that these hold for the future. Butin argues that democratic community engagement is a vital aspect of linking colleges and communities, and that service learning is an established institutional method of encouraging such partnerships.

**Butin, Dan W. 2012a. "Rethinking the 'Apprenticeship of Liberty': The Case for Academic Programs in Community Engagement in Higher Education."** *Journal of College and Character* **13(1): 1–8. DOI: https:// doi.org/10.1515/jcc-2012-1859.**
Butin articulates a model for an 'engaged' campus that he envisions can be practised through academic programs focused on community engagement. Certificate programs, minors, and majors provide a complementary vision for the deep institutionalization of civic and community engagement that can help revitalize what he terms an apprenticeship of liberty for students, faculty, and staff. Butin identifies as a major problem in the institutional 'engagement ceiling' the low institutionalization of sustained investment for civic engagement in education (1). He concludes his study by suggesting that the egalitarian, horizontal, and equally legitimate model of knowledge construction is missing in higher education because academic knowledge and its development, critique, and expansion are understood as the purview of highly specialized researchers. Community engagement, according to Butin, needs to be done in academic spaces that foster and strengthen the very qualities that academics are looking for in community partnerships.

**Butin, Dan W. 2012b. "When Engagement is Not Enough: Building the Next Generation of the Engaged Campus." In** *The Engaged Campus: Certificates, Minors, and Majors as the New Community Engagement,* edited by Dan Butin and Scott Seider, 1–11. New York: Palgrave Macmillan.

Butin discusses the practical applications of majors, minors, and certificate programs within institutions and their potential to reform the relationship between community and institution. It is clear, Butin argues, that the theoretical arguments of the last quarter century have questioned every assumption, enactment, and orientation of community and engagement. He argues that the community engagement movement in its present state still lacks the rigorous scholarship necessary for its incorporation into higher education. The next direction of community engagement in higher education, according to Butin, must engage in efforts at border crossings and must embrace critical academic spaces. This includes moving away from what he sees as an ineffectual model of 'hallway activists' in which theory and practice are disjointed.

Butin, Dan W., and Scott Seider, eds. 2012. *The Engaged Campus: Certificates, Minors, and Majors as the New Community Engagement.* New York: Palgrave Macmillan.

Butin and Seider edit this collection of essays arguing for the vital role of higher education in both citizenship and the creation of rich civic and community life. A central concept to this collection is conceiving the goal of education as an aspirational idea for democracy, as well as personal, social, and political responsibility for a more just and equitable world. Reflection is a major concept and practice in the type of service learning discussed in the essays. The book focuses on service learning programs, experiential learning, and the role of interdisciplinary, active, and engaged research. The editors and authors seek to dismantle the boundaries between action and knowledge and create a model for publicly engaged campuses through certificates, majors, and minors in community partnerships.

Cantor, Nancy, and Steven D. Lavine. 2006. "Taking Public Scholarship Seriously." *The Chronicle of Higher Education* 52(40): B20. https://www.chronicle.com/article/Taking-Public-Scholarship/22684.

Cantor and Lavine claim that today's system of tenure and promotion comes at a high cost to communities and deprives them of relationships with educational partners. The authors note a gap between the appraisal of creative scholars who are committed to the public good and those who are promoted. Portland State University is used as an example of an institution that has accepted the blurred boundaries between research, teaching, and engagement, which are all hallmarks of excellence in public scholarship. It is crucial to the future development of public scholarship that faculty and evaluators not advise junior colleagues to postpone public scholarship if that is where their

interests lie. The institution, the authors argue, needs more flexible definitions of scholarship, research, and creative work.

Caplan, Scott E., Elizabeth M. Perse, and Janice E. Gennaria. 2007.
"Computer-Mediated Technology and Social Interaction." In
*Communication Technology and Social Change: Theory and Implications,*
edited by Carolyn A. Lin and David J. Atkin, 39–57. Mahwah, NJ:
Lawrence Erlbaum Associates.

Caplan, Perse, and Gennaria explore how and why people use instant messaging, email, and chat rooms in a social context. The authors provide a brief
historical background on these technologies, as well as the social implications that result from a change between computer-mediated communication (CMC) and face-to-face communication. The authors find that teens and
young adults provide most of the traffic in computer-mediated social forums.
The reduced amount of non-verbal cues contributes to selectively control-
ling the quantity, quality, and validity of personal information available to
other participants. As computer-mediated social interaction increases in
popularity, physical location will become a less salient predictor of whom
people interact with. Communication scholars need to adapt communication
theories to evolving technologies and changing contexts to understand the
uses and effects of computer-mediated social interaction technologies.

Deuze, Mark, Axel Bruns, and Christopher Neuberger. 2007. "Preparing
for an Age of Participatory News." *Journalism Practice* 1(3): 322–38.
DOI: https://doi.org/10.1080/17512780701504864.

Deuze, Bruns, and Neuberger argue that journalism must rethink and rein-
vent itself in the wake of declining public trust in news. The authors believe
that news journalism will be gathered, selected, edited, and communicated
by professionals, amateurs, producers, and consumers. They include findings from emerging practices in the Netherlands, Germany, Australia, and
the United States. The four case studies used are the American *Bluffton Today,* the Dutch *Skoeps,* the German *Opinio,* and the Australian *On Line Opinion.*
These digital resources, the authors argue, provide clear and workable alternatives to the standard separation of journalists, their sources, and the
public. Due to the highly accessible flow of information available digitally
to the public, journalism can no longer leave large sections of the citizenry
disenfranchised from participation, nor omit valuable insights into political
and social processes.

**Dumova, Tatyana. 2012. "Social Interaction Technologies and the
Future of Blogging." In *Blogging in the Global Society: Cultural,*

*Political and Geographical Aspects,* edited by Tatyana Dumova and Richard Fiordo, 249–74. Hershey, PA: IGI Global.

Dumova addresses the social potential of blogging—specifically, the ways in which blogs permit people to engage in social interactions, build connections, and collaborate with others. She argues that blogging should not be studied in isolation from the social media clusters that function together to sustain each other. She also notes that blogging is an international phenomenon, since more than 60 per cent of all blogs created after the 1990s are written in languages other than English. Dumova broadly traces the development of blog publishing platforms. She concludes that network-based peer production and social media convergence are the driving forces behind the current transformation of blogs into increasingly user-centric, user-driven practices of producing, searching, sharing, publishing, and distributing information.

Gahran, Amy. 2012. "SeeClickFix: Crowdsourced Local Problem Reporting as Community News." *Knight Digital Media Center,* September 19. http://www.knightdigitalmediacenter.org/blogs/ agahran/2012/09/seeclickfix-crowdsourced-local-problem-reporting-community-news.html. Archived at https://perma.cc/ T6NF-EGZX.

Gahran details the benefits of using SeeClickFix, a web-based open access widget used for illuminating local issues, spurring community discourse, and sparking story ideas. Users can also use it to file public reports on local issues and vote for individual reports when they would like to see a specific issue resolved. The widget enables plotting of locations on a Google Map interface so that users within a geographic area can view a list of individual reports in that area. Having this widget on a site makes it easier to stay aware of community-reported issues and maintain greater engagement with the broader geographic area in which the individual or group in question lives.

Hall, Peter V., and Ian MacPherson, eds. 2011. *Community-University Research Partnerships: Reflections on the Canadian Social Economy Experience.* Victoria: University of Victoria. https://ccednet-rcdec.ca/sites/ ccednet-rcdec.ca/files/Comm_Univ_Res_Partnerships_SE.pdf.

Hall and MacPherson edit this collection of essays on various community and university relationships within Canada. The book includes topics on Canadian social economy research partnerships from 2005 to 2011, new proposals for evaluating the research partnership process, respect and learning from communities, and the British Columbia-Alberta research alliance's effects on social economy. The appendices of the collection include region-specific information, such as the BC and Alberta Node and the Atlantic Node. This book focuses on the outcomes of previous grant offers and university-community partnerships, and the role of funding in university-related partnerships.

Hart, Angie, and Simon Northmore. 2011. "Auditing and Evaluating University-Community Engagement: Lessons from a UK Case Study." *Higher Education Quarterly* 65(1): 34–58. DOI: https://doi. org/ 10.1111/j.1468-2273.2010.00466.x.

Hart and Northmore argue that the development of effective tools to audit and evaluate public engagement is still at a formative stage in university communities and public engagement activities—a claim confirmed by the literature search, which was based on articles written in or after the year 2000. The University of Brighton's Corporate Plan is used as a case study for further elaboration, which includes engagement with the cultural, social, and economic life of the localities, region, and nation as its primary precept. According to the authors, this case study demonstrates that back and forth dialogue between practitioners, researchers, and community members is essential to the audit and evaluation process.

Hart, Angie, and David Wolff. 2006. "Developing Local 'Communities of Practice' through Local Community-University Partnerships." *Planning Practice and Research* 21(1): 121–38. DOI: https://doi. org/10.1080/ 02697450600901616.

Hart and Wolff draw on the experiences of local community-university partnership activities at the University of Brighton to offer what they perceive as a pragmatic framework for future community-university partnerships. The authors argue that unless the discussion is framed in a way that shows academics are trying to understand community members, academics will have considerable difficulty in demonstrating the practical application of scholarly knowledge. The Community University Partnership program at the University of Brighton was established in 2003 to enhance the capacity of the community and university for engagement with mutual benefit, and to ensure that the university's resources were fully available to and used by local and sub-regional communities. The authors conclude by addressing both the cultural and spatial dimensions of the terrain and their impact on community-university partnerships within a community of practice framework.

Hiebert, Matthew, Raymond Siemens, William R. Bowen, the ETCL and Iter Advisory Groups, and the INKE Research Group. 2015. "Implementing a Social Knowledge Creation Environment."

*Scholarly and Research Communication* 6(3): n.p. DOI: https://doi. org/10.22230/src.2015v6n3a223.

Hiebert, Bowen, and Siemens introduce Iter Community, a public-facing web-based platform prototyped by the Electronic Textual Cultures Lab (ETCL) and Iter: Gateway to the Middle Ages and Renaissance, with a specific focus on how this platform is geared toward facilitating social knowledge creation. The authors argue that the emerging area of research known as social knowledge creation promotes critical interventions into the more conventional processes of academic knowledge production; this type of research is increasingly made more convenient by emerging technologies that allow research groups to more actively participate in and contribute to the dissemination of their work and communication with other partners. The Iter Community page is meant as a critical intervention into modes of scholarly production and publication, and models how the implementation of functionalities that support social knowledge creation can facilitate novel research opportunities and invite scholars and members of the community to participate in the creation of knowledge. The platform facilitates online knowledge production and dissemination in ways that ultimately enhance research practices and community outreach.

**Holland, Barbara, and Judith A. Ramaley. 2008. "Creating a Supportive Environment for Community-University Engagement: Conceptual Frameworks." In *Engaging Communities, Proceedings of the 31st HERDSA Annual Conference, Rotorua, 1–4 July 2008*, 11–25. http:// www.herdsa.org.au/system/files/Holland%20%26%20Ramaley.pdf.**

Holland and Ramaley argue that the changing nature of knowledge production, global issues, and the role of education affect intellectual strategies, relationships, societal roles, and expectations of how universities prepare students for the workplace. Educational institutions must increasingly embrace multidisciplinary and collaborative frameworks in order to address the evolving community landscape. The study concludes with the authors' recommendation that universities stop using communities as laboratories for research and learning, and rather collaborate with and acknowledge the essential expertise and wisdom that resides in communities. This shift will transform current understandings and prompt academics to understand themselves as learners, and to respect community leaders as experts in their own right.

**Hoy, Ariane, and Matthew Johnson, eds. 2013.** *Deepening Community Engagement in Higher Education: Forging New Pathways.* **New York: Palgrave Macmillan.**
Hoy and Johnson collect diverse essays on approaches to community engagement in higher education that stress the role of students as civic-minded professionals in student development, as well as community-centred approaches for the institution to engage in more productive partnerships with community leaders. The Bonner High-Impact Initiative embraces this and has the goal of transforming curricula, including approaches to engagement and institutional structures and practices. The authors hope to share their methods of engaging with communities as a means of allowing institutions to craft roles for themselves as stewards of place and civic learning, and agents of change. The essays included cover student leadership, pedagogy, institutional architecture, and community partnerships.

**Jenkins, Henry, and Mark Deuze. 2008. "Convergence Culture."** *Convergence: The International Journal of Research into New Media Technologies* **14(1): 5–12. DOI: https://www.doi. org/10.1177/1354856507084415.**
Jenkins and Deuze argue that shifts in communication infrastructure are bringing about contradictory forces between democratization and the concentration of power. The current global digital culture, the authors suggest, should be understood as Lev Manovich's culture of remix and remixability, in which user-generated content exists both within and outside commercial contexts, supporting and subverting corporate control.[3] With the widespread use of mobile Web technologies, media branding choices are being made as frequently in boardrooms as they are in teenagers' bedrooms. Contemporary media operate through a complex web of temporary connections and relationships between media companies and public stakeholders. Liquid differentiation is increasingly the model of corporate production: a formerly linear product is infused with unconventional new media formulas, hybrid genres, and transmedia strategies in its next installment to keep the brand marketable. The authors point to how these diverse forms of media further the capitalist agenda of constructing citizens as individualized and perpetually connected consumers.

---

[3] See Lev Manovich, "Remixability and Modularity" (2005), http://manovich.net/ content/04-projects/046-remixability-and-modularity/43_article_2005.pdf.

Jensen, Klaus Bruhn, and Rasmus Helles. 2011. "The Internet as a Cultural Forum: Implications for Research." *New Media & Society* 13(4): 517–33. DOI: https://doi.org/10.1177/1461444810373531.

Jensen and Helles take up Horace Newcomb and Paul Hirsch's model for studying television as a cultural forum[4] and use that as the frame of reference for studying the Internet. A cultural forum is the most common reference point for public issues and concerns in a particular society. The Internet is a distinctive kind of medium that comprises different communicative genres. The authors find that blogs, social network sites, and other recent genres attract much public and scholarly attention; however, ordinary media users are still inclined to support typical broadcasting methods. While the Internet is displacing television, the authors argue that it will not replace television completely, and that future studies should focus on the plurality of cultural forums in a given society.

Lampe, Cliff, Robert LaRose, Charles Steinfield, and Kurt DeMaagd. 2011. "Inherent Barriers to the Use of Social Media for Public Policy Informatics." *The Innovation Journal* 16(1): Article 6.

Lampe, LaRose, Steinfield and DeMaagd address the barriers to social media use for public policy informatics, arguing that social media has the potential to foster interactions between policymakers, government officials, and their constituencies. The authors refer to this framework as Governance 2.0, and use AdvanceMichigan as a case study. AdvanceMichigan is a social media implementation designed to crowdsource feedback from stakeholders of Michigan State University Cooperative Extension. This organization approaches the education process in such a way that students can apply their knowledge to a range of critical issues, needs, and opportunities. The organization is planning to return to traditional methods for collecting data from stakeholders due to the challenges of crowdsourcing data. The authors conclude with a discussion on how to create compelling technologies tailored to correctly scaled tasks for an audience that is likely to use social media sites.

Lin, Carolyn A., and David J. Atkin, eds. 2007. *Communication Technology and Social Change: Theory and Implications.* Mahwah, NJ: Lawrence Erlbaum Associates.

Lin and Atkin edit this anthology on the significant outcomes of technology adoption and uses. Throughout the volume, authors explain how communication and information technologies facilitate social change. The editors

---

[4] Horace M. Newcomb and Paul M. Hirsch (1983), "Television as a Cultural Forum: Implications for Research," *Quarterly Review of Film Studies* 8(3): 45–55.

organized the essays to enhance the understanding of these social change outcomes by readers, scholars, students, and practitioners from a theoretical standpoint that examines the effects of communication technology on different social environments. The technologies examined by the authors include video and home entertainment, online technology education and entertainment, and cultural attitudes toward paper and electronic documents. The editors argue from the standpoint of social change, namely that advancements in communication technology have shaped political perspectives around the globe toward, for example, the Iraq War.

McNall, Miles, Celeste Sturdevant Reed, Robert Brown, and Angela Allen. 2009. "Brokering Community-University Engagement." *Innovative Higher Education* 33(5): 317–31. DOI: https://doi.org/10.1007/s10755-008-9086-8.
McNall, Reed, Brown, and Allen identify a lack of substantial agreement on the characteristics of effective community-university partnerships for research. This, they argue, is due to a lack of empirical research on the relationship between the characteristics of these partnerships and their outcomes. Qualities of effective partnership include shared leadership, two-way open communication and constructive conflict resolution, participatory decision-making, shared resources, and well-organized meetings with collaboratively developed agendas. The authors use a survey to understand the purposes of these partnerships, as well as their group dynamics. Through their survey, the authors demonstrate that efficient partnership management is related to increased research on a community issue, that collaboratively created knowledge is associated with better service outcomes for clients, and that shared power and resources are adversely correlated with an increase in funding for community partners and organizations.

Milakovich, Michael E. 2012. *Digital Governance: New Technologies for Improving Public Service and Participation.* New York: Routledge.
Milakovich studies the application of digital information and communication technologies and their role in reforming governmental structures, politics, and public administration. He notes that governments are transitioning between electronic government and digital governance, which emphasizes citizen participation and the accessibility of information technology. Organizations have shifted from bureaucracy-centred to customer-centred service operation in order to restore public trust in both governing and corporate bodies. Milakovich contributes several chapters to the social implications of virtual learning, methods of applying digital technologies to governance,

and a discussion of global attitudes and patterns toward digital governance in the international community.

Mortensen, Mette. 2015. "Connective Witnessing: Reconfiguring the Relationship Between the Individual and the Collective." *Information, Communication & Society* 18(11): 1393–1406. https://www.tandfonline.com/doi/abs/10.1080/1369118X.2015.1061574.

Mortensen proposes the term 'connective witnessing' to refer to what she believes is the prevalent form of witnessing today. This witnessing combines personalized political participation with connective action in the recording and sharing of visual documentation. Civic action is chosen as the empirical example for research data, and is connected to the deployment of digital communication technologies by protest movements. The boundaries between these positions are evidently blurred, since the individual witness can speak for the collective on occasion, especially with the use of digital technologies. These technologies also allow for increasing personalization of the political acts of witnessing, and for depersonalizing witnesses into a collective voice. The operation of collective and individual witnessing must be re-evaluated in light of recent mobile and other digital technological development.

O'Meara, Kerry Ann, Lorilee R. Sandmann, John Saltmarsh, and Dwight E. Giles, Jr. 2011. "Studying the Professional Lives and Work of Faculty Involved in Community Engagement." *Innovative Higher Education* 36(2): 83–96. DOI: https://doi.org/10.1007/s10755-010-9159-3.

O'Meara, Sandmann, Saltmarsh, and Giles discuss the professional lives of faculty members and their intimate ties to the academic mission. The authors discuss how the conceptualization of faculty-community engagement influences the questions asked of the institution and the kinds of recruitment, support, and professional growth that it provides in turn. They provide a brief history of institutional community engagement and faculty work since the 1980s. The lack of clear boundaries between the work and lives of publicly engaged scholars necessitates studies, frameworks, and methods that weave faculty work with theories from different social sciences and research methods. Demographics, identities, life experiences, epistemologies, personal goals, institutions, disciplines, and department contexts all influence attitudes toward community involvement in institutional settings. The authors also provide a critique of perspectives used to study faculty community engagement and argue that an approach with multiple lenses is needed, including social, psychological, and cultural dimensions.

Pasque, Penny A., Ryan E. Smerek, Brighid Dwyer, Nick Bowman, and Bruce L. Mallory, eds. 2005. *Higher Education Collaboratives for Community Engagement and Improvement*. Ann Arbor, MI: National Forum on Higher Education for the Public Good. https://files.eric.ed.gov/fulltext/ED515231.pdf.

Pasque, Smerek, Dwyer, Bowman, and Mallory compile the proceedings from the Wingspread Conference on *Higher Education Collaboratives for Community Engagement and Improvement* held on October 27–29, 2004 in Racine, Wisconsin. The conference was convened to examine the current and evolving role of higher education institutions, especially those operating within coalitions, consortia, and state systems, in order to catalyze change on issues that affect communities and society. This event was also designed as a forum for groups with common interests, and consists of a series of working groups with developed partnerships. The issues covered in the proceedings include how faculty can overcome the few incentives and little preparation given to them to engage in community improvement, and how the universities can recognize working with communities as career-enhancing. These discussions focus on university-community relations and their sustainability in the long term.

Silka, Linda, G. Dean Cleghorn, Milago Grullon, and Trinidad Tellez. 2008. "Creating Community-Based Participatory Research in a Diverse Community: A Case Study." *Journal of Empirical Research on Human Research Ethics* 3(2): 5–16. DOI: https://doi.org/10.1525/jer.2008.3.2.5.

Silka, Cleghorn, Grullon, and Tellez use their community-based participatory research group, the Lawrence Research Initiative Working Group (RIWG), as a case study to create guidelines for ethical community-based research. The authors seek to move beyond the problems identified by the Agency for Healthcare Research and Quality and begin to include tribal nations and research centres. The primary focus is to develop an ethical and non-exploitative relationship on the part of the institution. They introduce a set of guiding documents—the RIWG documents—that outline strategies for dealing with the challenges of multiple layers of partners and coping with changing committee memberships, and provide tips for technical research language to help strengthen communication. The research team recommends that other communities adapt the RIWG documents for their own use. They hope to shift understanding toward community decision-making as a necessity rather than a luxury.

Silka, Linda, and Paulette Renault-Caragianes. 2007. "Community-University Research Partnerships: Devising a Model for Ethical Engagement." *Journal of Higher Education Outreach and Engagement* 11(2): 171–83.
Silka and Renault-Caragianes discuss the problems that have previously faced community-university partnerships. These partnerships often involve powerful university scholars with relatively disempowered community members. Funding agencies are now calling for researchers to set up partnerships in order to investigate health disparities in poor urban communities. The challenge currently facing this type of partnership is to move beyond existing guidelines that were not designed to provide ethical guidance, and to work with the community in establishing mutual respect. The research agenda and methods, and the usefulness and purpose of the research, all need to be determined by discussions with the community.

Silka, Linda, and Robin Toof, guest eds. 2011. "International Perspectives on Community-University Partnerships" issue. *Metropolitan Universities* 22(2). Towson, MD: Coalition of Urban and Metropolitan Universities.
Silka and Toof claim that communities struggle to create research guidelines for ethical collaborative research within their localities. The authors use the Mayor's Health Task Force Research Initiative Working Group in Lawrence, Massachusetts, as a case study. The task force addresses research ethics in a community where families struggle with limited resources and face many health disparities. An earlier study on high levels of pollution did not take the concerns of Lawrence-area residents seriously, and was unable to answer the community's questions as to how their approaches to research were selected, who would receive the results, who would own the data, and what would be done with the saliva samples collected. Research committees must involve community members in discussions of how problems should be investigated, and what kinds of purposes the research aims to achieve.

Sturm, Susan, Timothy Eatman, John Saltmarsh, and Adam Bush. 2011. *Full Participation: Building the Architecture for Diversity and Public Engagement in Higher Education.* Catalyst paper, Imagining America: Artists and Scholars in Public Life. http://imaginingamerica.org/wp-content/uploads/2015/09/fullparticipation.pdf.
Sturm, Eatman, Saltmarsh, and Bush's work grew out of the realization that the long-term success of diversity, public engagement, and student success initiatives requires these efforts to be more fully integrated into institutional

settings. They explain their concept of full participation, which is an affirmative value focused on creating institutions that enable people to thrive and realize their capabilities. They note that a lack of integration of diversity, public engagement, and student success efforts in university architecture limits the efficacy and sustainability of the institution's work. The authors argue that public engagement will encourage and enable full participation of diverse groups and communities, which is a critical attribute of legitimate and successful public engagement. The institutions that take account of public engagement enhance the legitimacy, levels of engagement, and robustness of higher education.

Whitmer, Ali, Laura Ogden, John Lawton, Pam Sturner, Peter M. Groffman, Laura Schneider, David Hart, et al. 2010. "The Engaged University: Providing a Platform for Research that Transforms Society." *Frontiers in Ecology and the Environment* 8(6): 314–21. DOI: https://doi.org/10.1890/090241.

Whitmer, Ogden, Lawton, Sturner, Groffman, Schneider, and Hart discuss how solutions to current environmental problems can be developed through collaborations between scientists and stakeholders. Societal partners are active throughout both the research and knowledge transfer processes. They are able to identify problems in conducting research and developing strategies for applying the outcomes of that work. The article provides some examples of science-related programs, including Georgetown University's program on Science in the Public Interest, which promotes direct dialogue with engaged and interested public groups on critical scientific issues. The authors also address topics related to developing a peer community, and sustainability issues in linking knowledge with action. According to the authors, institutions should evaluate faculty by recognizing research and activities that advance scientific knowledge and improve outcomes for human and natural systems.

### B. Reference List

Barnes, Jessica V., Emily L. Altimare, Patricia A. Farrell, Robert E. Brown, C. Richard Burnett III, LaDonna Gamble, and James Davis. 2009. "Creating and Sustaining Authentic Partnerships with Community in a Systemic Model." *Journal of Higher Education Outreach and Engagement* 13(4): 15–29. https://files.eric.ed.gov/fulltext/EJ905410.pdf.

Bennett, W. Lance, ed. 2008. *Civic Life Online: Learning How Digital Media Can Engage Youth.* Cambridge, MA: MIT Press.

Bowdon, Melody A., and Russell G. Carpenter, eds. 2011. *Higher Education, Emerging Technologies, and Community Partnerships: Concepts, Models and Practices.* Hershey, PA: IGI Global.

Butin, Dan W. 2010. *Service-Learning in Theory and Practice: The Future of Community Engagement in Higher Education.* New York: Palgrave Macmillan.

——. 2012a. "Rethinking the 'Apprenticeship of Liberty': The Case for Academic Programs in Community Engagement in Higher Education." *Journal of College and Character* 13(1): 1–8. DOI: https://doi.org/10.1515/jcc-2012-1859.

——. 2012b. "When Engagement is Not Enough: Building the Next Generation of the Engaged Campus." In *The Engaged Campus: Certificates, Minors, and Majors as the New Community Engagement*, edited by Dan Butin and Scott Seider, 1–11. New York: Palgrave Macmillan.

Butin, Dan W., and Scott Seider, eds. 2012. *The Engaged Campus: Certificates, Minors, and Majors as the New Community Engagement.* New York: Palgrave Macmillan.

Cantor, Nancy, and Steven D. Lavine. 2006. "Taking Public Scholarship Seriously." *The Chronicle of Higher Education* 52(40): B20. https://www.chronicle.com/article/Taking-Public-Scholarship/22684.

Caplan, Scott E., Elizabeth M. Perse, and Janice E. Gennaria. 2007. "Computer-Mediated Technology and Social Interaction." In *Communication Technology and Social Change: Theory and Implications*, edited by Carolyn A. Lin and David J. Atkin, 39–57. Mahwah, NJ: Lawrence Erlbaum Associates.

Deuze, Mark, Axel Bruns, and Christopher Neuberger. 2007. "Preparing for an Age of Participatory News." *Journalism Practice* 1(3): 322–38. DOI: https://doi.org/10.1080/17512780701504864.

Dumova, Tatyana. 2012. "Social Interaction Technologies and the Future of Blogging." In *Blogging in the Global Society: Cultural, Political and Geographical Aspects*, edited by Tatyana Dumova and Richard Fiordo, 249–74. Hershey, PA: IGI Global.

Gahran, Amy. 2012. "SeeClickFix: Crowdsourced Local Problem Reporting as Community News." *Knight Digital Media Center*, September 19. http://

www.knightdigitalmediacenter.org/blogs/agahran/2012/09/seeclick-fix-crowdsourced-local-problem-reporting-community-news.html. Archived at https://perma.cc/T6NF-EGZX.

Hall, Peter V., and Ian MacPherson, eds. 2011. *Community-University Research Partnerships: Reflections on the Canadian Social Economy Experience.* Victoria: University of Victoria. https://ccednet-rcdec.ca/sites/cced-net-rcdec.ca/files/Comm_Univ_Res_Partnerships_SE.pdf.

Hart, Angie, and Simon Northmore. 2011. "Auditing and Evaluating University-Community Engagement: Lessons from a UK Case Study." *Higher Education Quarterly* 65(1): 34–58. DOI: https://doi.org/10.1111/j.1468-2273.2010.00466.x.

Hart, Angie, and David Wolff. 2006. "Developing Local 'Communities of Practice' through Local Community-University Partnerships." *Planning Practice and Research* 21(1): 121–38. DOI: https://doi.org/10.1080/02697450600901616.

Hiebert, Matthew, Raymond Siemens, William R. Bowen, the ETCL and Iter Advisory Groups, and the INKE Research Group. 2015. "Implementing a Social Knowledge Creation Environment." *Scholarly and Research Communication* 6(3): n.p. DOI: https://doi.org/10.22230/src.2015v6n3a223.

Holland, Barbara, and Judith A. Ramaley. 2008. "Creating a Supportive Environment for Community-University Engagement: Conceptual Frameworks." In *Engaging Communities, Proceedings of the 31st HERDSA Annual Conference, Rotorua, 1-4 July 2008*, 11–25. http://www.herdsa.org.au/system/files/Holland%20%26%20Ramaley.pdf.

Hoy, Ariane, and Matthew Johnson, eds. 2013. *Deepening Community Engagement in Higher Education: Forging New Pathways.* New York: Palgrave Macmillan.

Jenkins, Henry, and Mark Deuze. 2008. "Convergence Culture." *Convergence: The International Journal of Research into New Media Technologies* 14(1): 5–12. DOI: https://www.doi.org/10.1177/1354856507084415.

Jensen, Klaus Bruhn, and Rasmus Helles. 2011. "The Internet as a Cultural Forum: Implications for Research." *New Media & Society* 13(4): 517–33. DOI: https://doi.org/10.1177/1461444810373531.

Lampe, Cliff, Robert LaRose, Charles Steinfield, and Kurt DeMaagd. 2011. "Inherent Barriers to the Use of Social Media for Public Policy Informatics." *The Innovation Journal* 16(1): Article 6.

Lin, Carolyn A., and David J. Atkin, eds. 2007. *Communication Technology and Social Change: Theory and Implications.* Mahwah, NJ: Lawrence Erlbaum Associates.

McNall, Miles, Celeste Sturdevant Reed, Robert Brown, and Angela Allen. 2009. "Brokering Community-University Engagement." *Innovative Higher Education* 33(5): 317–31. DOI: https://doi.org/10.1007/s10755-008-9086-8.

Milakovich, Michael E. 2012. *Digital Governance: New Technologies for Improving Public Service and Participation.* New York: Routledge.

Mortensen, Mette. 2015. "Connective Witnessing: Reconfiguring the Relationship Between the Individual and the Collective." *Information, Communication & Society* 18(11): 1393–1406. https://www.tandfonline. com/doi/abs/10.1080/1369118X.2015.1061574.

O'Meara, Kerry Ann, Lorilee R. Sandmann, John Saltmarsh, and Dwight E. Giles, Jr. 2011. "Studying the Professional Lives and Work of Faculty Involved in Community Engagement." *Innovative Higher Education* 36(2): 83–96. DOI: https://doi.org/10.1007/s10755-010-9159-3.

Pasque, Penny A., Ryan E. Smerek, Brighid Dwyer, Nick Bowman, and Bruce L. Mallory, eds. 2005. *Higher Education Collaboratives for Community Engagement and Improvement.* Ann Arbor, MI: National Forum on Higher Education for the Public Good. https://files.eric.ed.gov/fulltext/ ED515231.pdf.

Silka, Linda, G. Dean Cleghorn, Milago Grullon, and Trinidad Tellez. 2008. "Creating Community-Based Participatory Research in a Diverse Community: A Case Study." *Journal of Empirical Research on Human Research Ethics* 3(2): 5–16. DOI: https://doi.org/10.1525/jer.2008.3.2.5.

Silka, Linda, and Paulette Renault-Caragianes. 2007. "Community-University Research Partnerships: Devising a Model for Ethical Engagement." *Journal of Higher Education Outreach and Engagement* 11(2): 171–83.

Silka, Linda, and Robin Toof, guest eds. 2011. "International Perspectives on Community-University Partnerships" issue. *Metropolitan Universities* 22(2). Towson, MD: Coalition of Urban and Metropolitan Universities.

Sturm, Susan, Timothy Eatman, John Saltmarsh, and Adam Bush. 2011. *Full Participation: Building the Architecture for Diversity and Public Engagement in Higher Education.* Catalyst paper, Imagining America: Artists and Scholars in Public Life. http://imaginingamerica.org/wp-content/uploads/2015/09/fullparticipation.pdf.

Whitmer, Ali, Laura Ogden, John Lawton, Pam Sturner, Peter M. Groffman, Laura Schneider, David Hart, et al. 2010. "The Engaged University: Providing a Platform for Research that Transforms Society." *Frontiers in Ecology and the Environment* 8(6): 314–21. DOI: https://doi.org/10.1890/090241.

## 2. Citizen Science

Citizen science refers to research that is partially or wholly conducted by nonscientists, typically by volunteers who receive the training necessary to collect and interpret data for a target research investigation. In recent years, citizen science projects have become much more prominent, especially in the social sciences. Authors argue that this is due to the advancement of technology allowing the collection and transfer of data by nonprofessionals, as well as the recent demand by funding agencies to seek the public's approval of scientific research endeavours, since taxpayer dollars often fund these initiatives. One of the central organizations in this field is the Cornell Lab of Ornithology (CLO; https://www.birds.cornell.edu/), which has been practising citizen science for more than twenty years; in this category, CLO researchers provide a model for setting up a successful citizen science project (Bonney et al. 2009). Some of the central issues brought to light in this category revolve around the question of data reliability, which often depends on the clarity of instructions, the type of training, and the level of motivation of participants. Prestopnik and Crowston (2011) propose one way of increasing this motivation through a gaming model that includes a crowdsourcing element; the authors assert that gaming may encourage a more engaged practice and accurate data. Research also addresses the educational role of citizen science for individual participants and the necessary steps that project leaders must take to ensure reaching these goals, as well as the benefits of integrating citizen science in undergraduate curricula (Jordan, Ballard, and Phillips 2012; Oberhauser and LeBuhn 2012). Authors especially encourage making data, results, and their interpretation available for the public in open access (Bonney et al. 2009; Gallo and Waitt 2011), and unanimously agree that if done properly, citizen science can go a long way in educating the public, supporting scientific research, and improving the environment more generally.

### A. Annotations

**Bonney, Rick, Caren B. Cooper, Janis Dickinson, Steve Kelling, Tina Phillips, Kenneth V. Rosenberg, and Jennifer Shirk. 2009. "Citizen Science: A Developing Tool for Expanding Science Knowledge and Scientific Literacy."** *BioScience* **59(11): 977–84. DOI: http://dx.doi.org/10.1525/bio.2009.59.11.9.**
Bonney et al. provide a model for citizen science based on the past two decades of projects run by the Cornell Lab of Ornithology (CLO), an organization that is deeply engaged with environmental studies projects and has had thousands of participants gather tens of millions of observations annually.

The authors assert that citizen science is especially useful in projects that require the gathering of vast amounts of data over the span of many years. They outline the various steps of their model, which involve choosing a scientific question and forming a science-based interdisciplinary team comprising scientists, educators, evaluators, and technologists to lead the project and develop the necessary standards and materials to carry it out. This is followed by recruiting and training citizen participants in the skills required to gather the appropriate data. This data is immediately displayed to the public in open access, after which it is analyzed and interpreted. These results are then disseminated and the outcomes are measured. The authors emphasize the necessity to innovate current data management, scientific analysis, and educational research practices in order to accommodate the growing scope and level of citizen science.

Cooper, Caren B., Janis Dickinson, Tina Phillips, and Rick Bonney. 2007. "Citizen Science as a Tool for Conservation in Residential Ecosystems." *Ecology and Society* 12(2): Article 11. http://www.ecologyandsociety.org/vol12/iss2/art11/.

Cooper et al. address the role that citizen science plays in implementing conservation strategies in residential lands for positive impacts on biodiversity. The authors argue that the value suburban and urban residential lands can contribute to our understanding of ecosystems is only beginning to be acknowledged. They propose a framework for using citizen science in order to gather data that may help gain insight into conservation studies in this newly emerging field. The volunteers gather data, often over long periods of time, based on their training and the research questions set by the science-led team interested in observing certain occurrences, such as watershed-based monitoring. They base their framework on the citizen science model developed at the Cornell Lab of Ornithology, outlined by Bonney et al. (annotated above), and adapt it to their own research question. Phillips et al. conclude that using citizen science in conservation research in residential areas can help not only in tackling scientific questions, but also in implementing and monitoring various management strategies at a large scale, which can eventually result in long-term improvements in the environment.

Gallo, Travis, and Damon Waitt. 2011. "Creating a Successful Citizen Science Model to Detect and Report Invasive Species." *BioScience* 61(6): 459–65. DOI: https://doi.org/10.1525/bio.2011.61.6.8.

Gallo and Waitt describe a citizen science program—the Invaders of Texas—that relies on local volunteers to gather data on invasive weed species in certain parts of Texas. This data is uploaded into a public database, and serves as a point of reference for policymakers, scientists, and resource managers to make various decisions about weed distribution and to be aware of the scope of invasive species at a given time. The volunteers in the citizen science program receive proper training in order to provide detailed information about the target weed, such as its physical attributes, the GPS coordinates of where it was spotted, time of observation, level of damage to the crop, and other information. This information is added to the Invaders of Texas database, an open source Web application with an embedded Google Maps interface that supports exportation in a variety of formats. The authors conclude that making such projects a more common and collaborative endeavour could benefit the ecosystem as a whole.

**Jordan, Rebecca C., Heidi L. Ballard, and Tina B. Phillips. 2012. "Key Issues and New Approaches for Evaluating Citizen-Science Learning Outcomes."** *Frontiers in Ecology and the Environment* **10(6): 307–9. DOI: https://doi.org/10.1890/110280.**
Jordan, Ballard, and Phillips call attention to the educational role of citizen science projects and focus on its importance in developing ecological literacy at the individual, communal, and program levels. The authors are concerned with whether citizen science projects carry out the educational goals they set forth. They argue that team members need to develop an evaluation plan to trace whether project activities allow these learning goals to be achieved, whether the goals are clearly defined, and what the concrete measures of success for both of these points are. Some projects, for example, may vary learning outcomes according to participant engagement, giving long-term volunteers more extensive training. The authors suggest that a more comprehensive approach—one that would take into consideration the wider scope of impacts, ranging from the individual to the community level—should be implemented. They point out that various types of citizen science projects have resulted in positive outcomes for the community, including 'increased social capital, community capacity, and trust between scientists, managers, and the public' (308).

**Mayer, Amy. 2010. "Phenology and Citizen Science."** *BioScience* **60(3): 172–75. DOI: https://www.jstor.org/stable/10.1525/bio.2010.60.3.3.**
Mayer argues that phenology—the relationship between annual events and seasonal changes, such as observing the bloom of flowers—lends itself to citizen science when many people record these observations. On the issue of data quality, evidence from various studies shows that clear and straightforward instructions result in reliable data from volunteers. Mayer discusses various recent and long-term phenology projects, such as the National Ecological

Observatory Network (NEON) and Feedwatcher, with a specific focus on how both projects address the challenge of sustaining ongoing citizen observations. This is an issue in phenology, since it is long-term observations over years that add real value to a project. Another issue is that such long-term research is not compatible with traditional funding agencies, since they often give out shorter term grants than such research requires.

Newman, Greg, Andrea Wiggins, Alycia Crall, Eric Graham, Sarah Newman, and Kevin Crowston. 2012. "The Future of Citizen Science: Emerging Technologies and Shifting Paradigms." *Frontiers in Ecology and the Environment* 10(6): 298–304. DOI: https://doi.org/10.1890/110294.

Newman et al. speculate about the future of citizen science in conjunction with rapidly evolving technologies. They propose suggestions for project managers to integrate technology in a way that would help their research appeal to a wider audience. The authors describe how the various steps of citizen science projects, including 'gathering teams/resources/partners, defining research questions, collecting and managing data, analyzing and interpreting data, disseminating results, and evaluating program success and program outcomes' (299), may change in the years to come. They foresee a future in which technology could allow volunteers to have more agency and responsibility in science projects, and argue that this could eventually balance out the hierarchy between scientists and volunteers into more of a partnership. Newman et al. focus on wireless sensor networks that may help link the laboratory to the environment and help volunteers collect, analyze, and interpret data. They recommend that project managers encourage the use of open data and open source software, and utilize technology in a way that would increase motivation, retention, and ethnic diversity.

Oberhauser, Karen, and Gretchen LeBuhn. 2012. "Insects and Plants: Engaging Undergraduates in Authentic Research through Citizen Science." *Frontiers in Ecology and the Environment* 10(6): 318–20. DOI: https://doi.org/10.1890/110274.

Oberhauser and LeBuhn point to the various benefits of including undergraduate students in citizen science, and advocate for increased citizen science hands-on training during undergraduate years. They argue that the type of learning invoked by citizen science is valuable because it is an inquiry-based practice that encourages students to pose questions, gather and interpret data, and draw conclusions. The authors focus on two citizen science projects, including the Monarch Larva Monitoring Project (MLMP) and the Great Sunflower Project (GSP), in which the students participate in

data collection, data analysis, and the creation of independent or group research projects. The authors are the project managers of these initiatives,
and provide a number of examples of how students behave and learn in such
environments. Students working on these projects range from volunteers to
paid assistants, and are actively engaged in the scientific process rather than
merely performing tedious tasks. Oberhauser and LeBuhn believe that the
three areas of undergraduate studies that would most benefit from citizen
science are data collection, class projects, and research opportunities.

Prestopnik, Nathan R., and Kevin Crowston. 2011. "Gaming for (Citizen)
    Science: Exploring Motivation and Data Quality in the Context
    of Crowdsourced Science through the Design and Evaluation of
    a Social-Computational System." In *Proceedings of the 2011 IEEE
    Seventh International Conference on e-Science Workshops* (*ESCIENCEW
    '11*), 28–33. Washington, DC: IEEE Computer Society. DOI: http://
    doi.org/10.1109/eScienceW.2011.14.

Prestopnik and Crowston discuss the role of gaming in improving the present citizen science model, especially in terms of increasing motivation and
data quality. This is done by presenting Citizen Sort, a social-computational
system that functions as a game for crowdsourced science. According to the
authors, the major challenges of the study include measuring abstract concepts such as the level of user motivation, whereas more tangible attributes
of measurement are related to the quality and completeness of the data set.
The main task of Citizen Sort, when launched, will be to identify whether introducing a gaming element into citizen scholarship will result in a more engaged practice (instead of the somewhat tedious process of gathering data),
or if gaming is distracting or uninteresting in this context. The game itself
will be made in a system assemblage approach, meaning that it will incorporate different features and technologies in order to appeal to users. Users
will be asked to either upload or identify photographed species according to
preset parameters that vary from game to game. Their interaction with the
game will be recorded in order to determine the games that are the most fun
and motivational, and result in the highest data quality; this information will
be used for improving their gaming techniques.

Purdam, Kingsley. 2014. "Citizen Social Science and Citizen
    Data? Methodological and Ethical Challenges for Social
    Research." *Current Sociology* 62(3): 374–92. DOI: https://doi.
    org/10.1177/0011392114527997.

Purdam explores the practical implications of citizen social science in a real
world setting. The volunteers are trained by social scientists to systematically

collect observation data throughout their routine daily lives rather than go out of their way to target the specific focus of the study. The research focus is recording the number of people seen begging in Central London, specifically because London is a densely populated city with a high rate of beggars and limited research in this field. The main concerns raised are in relation to the methodology, quality of the data collected, ethical implications raised by observation of others, presentation of the data, and potential value of a citizen-engaged model for social science research. The various findings of this research are of interest to the social science researchers and policymakers, including international charities and local authorities. The ethical issue of surveillance is strongly acknowledged, especially in terms of what this type of research could mean if it were formalized and the scope increased. However, the authors argue that the form of surveillance in this study adheres to ethical standards since the observers are not spies, and lack political interest in their subjects; as well, the study is based on an ethically approved research design and follows a strict set of instructions. One limitation is the fact that the targets are being observed only for a short time, which fails to provide the researchers with facts that may help improve their situation. Other limitations have been found in the sample size and strategies adopted, and the potential for generalizations to occur. The authors believe that such citizen social science, backed up with new theoretical frameworks, could help with research projects that explore inequality and oppression in a coordinated way.

Rotman, Dana, Jenny Preece, Jen Hammock, Kezee Procita, Derek Hansen, Cynthia Parr, Darcy Lewis, and David Jacobs. 2012. "Dynamic Changes in Motivation in Collaborative Citizen-Science Projects." In *Proceedings of the ACM 2012 Conference on Computer Supported Cooperative Work* (CSCW '12), 217–26. New York: ACM. DOI: https://doi.org/10.1145/2145204.2145238.

Rotman, Preece, Hammock, Procita, Hansen, Parr, Lewis, and Jacobs conduct a study that borrows from a motivational model in order to determine the various incentives of volunteers to participate and perform well in citizen science projects related to ecological scientific research. Although many successful citizen science projects exist, many do not take full advantage of the collaborative possibilities between the scientists and volunteers; hence, studying the motivation of each party and designing an environment that rewards and motivates all parties could drastically improve the field altogether. After conducting the study, the authors found that volunteers were primarily motivated by their curiosity, drive for learning, and desire for conservation, whereas the scientists were primarily motivated by their careers and scientific advancement more generally. They also found that the two most important motivational moments for volunteers are the first encounter with the project and group and the wrapping up of a project, when volunteers decide whether or not to participate in other projects. Finally, the authors also contribute a dynamic model that displays the engagement cycle of the participants throughout the different stages of the project.

Silvertown, Jonathan. 2009. "A New Dawn for Citizen Science." *Trends in Ecology & Evolution* 24(9): 467–71. DOI: https://doi.org/10.1016/j.tree.2009.03.017.

Silvertown calls attention to burgeoning citizen science projects, especially in environmental sciences, and addresses the main underlying reasons for such exponential growth. The first is the availability of tools that facilitate the gathering and dissemination of information to and from the public by the volunteers themselves. The second is the fact that citizen science is carried out by volunteers who bring a diverse set of skills to the project, thereby significantly cutting down on costs. Finally, he states that present funding agencies require scientific research to incorporate an element of project-related outreach, and a means to ensure that the public values taxpayer-funded work; having members of the public directly participate in scientific research allows them to reach this goal. Despite its established roots, dating from the nineteenth century, the author points out that citizen science is underrepresented in formal scientific literature because the term itself is fairly recent and the practice has yet to fit within the standard methods of scientific research that are based on hypothesis testing. He concludes by pointing to guidelines for good practice in citizen science, outlining various challenges that may spring up, and arguing for the benefits of citizen science in large-scale projects.

Wiggins, Andrea, and Kevin Crowston. 2011. "From Conservation to Crowdsourcing: A Typology of Citizen Science." In *Proceedings of the 2011 44th Hawaii International Conference on System Sciences* (*HICSS '11*), 1–10. DOI: https://doi.org/10.1109/HICSS.2011.207.

Wiggins and Crowston discuss citizen science in terms of the common attributes many projects share, and attempt to provide a theoretical sampling that future citizen science projects may rely on. The authors argue that the majority of scholarship on citizen science is invested in describing the process of integrating volunteers into the various levels of scientific research, without taking into account the macrostructural and sociotechnical factors. They believe that this comes at the expense of crucial design and process management. Wiggins and Crowston identify and discuss five distinct typologies witnessed in various citizen science projects: action, conservation, investigation, virtuality, and education. The authors classify these typologies by major goals and the extent to which they are virtual. One of the main motivations for developing these typologies is to describe the existing state of citizen science and to make accessible the necessary conditions for successful citizen science projects.

### B. Reference List

Bonney, Rick, Caren B. Cooper, Janis Dickinson, Steve Kelling, Tina Phillips, Kenneth V. Rosenberg, and Jennifer Shirk. 2009. "Citizen Science: A Developing Tool for Expanding Science Knowledge and Scientific Literacy." *BioScience* 59(11): 977–84. DOI: http://dx.doi.org/10.1525/bio.2009.59.11.9.

Cooper, Caren B., Janis Dickinson, Tina Phillips, and Rick Bonney. 2007. "Citizen Science as a Tool for Conservation in Residential Ecosystems." *Ecology and Society* 12(2): Article 11. http://www.ecologyandsociety.org/vol12/iss2/art11/.

Gallo, Travis, and Damon Waitt. 2011. "Creating a Successful Citizen Science Model to Detect and Report Invasive Species." *BioScience* 61(6): 459–65. DOI: https://doi.org/10.1525/bio.2011.61.6.8.

Jordan, Rebecca C., Heidi L. Ballard, and Tina B. Phillips. 2012. "Key Issues and New Approaches for Evaluating Citizen-Science Learning Outcomes." *Frontiers in Ecology and the Environment* 10(6): 307–9. DOI: https://doi.org/10.1890/110280.

Mayer, Amy. 2010. "Phenology and Citizen Science." *BioScience* 60(3): 172–75. DOI: https://www.jstor.org/stable/10.1525/bio.2010.60.3.3.

Newman, Greg, Andrea Wiggins, Alycia Crall, Eric Graham, Sarah Newman, and Kevin Crowston. 2012. "The Future of Citizen Science: Emerging Technologies and Shifting Paradigms." *Frontiers in Ecology and the Environment* 10(6): 298–304. DOI: https://doi.org/10.1890/110294.

Oberhauser, Karen, and Gretchen LeBuhn. 2012. "Insects and Plants: Engaging Undergraduates in Authentic Research through Citizen Science." *Frontiers in Ecology and the Environment* 10(6): 318–20. DOI: https://doi.org/10.1890/110274.

Prestopnik, Nathan R., and Kevin Crowston. 2011. "Gaming for (Citizen) Science: Exploring Motivation and Data Quality in the Context of Crowdsourced Science through the Design and Evaluation of a Social-Computational System." In *Proceedings of the 2011 IEEE Seventh International Conference on e-Science Workshops (ESCIENCEW '11)*, 28–33. Washington, DC: IEEE Computer Society. DOI: http://doi.org/10.1109/eScienceW.2011.14.

Purdam, Kingsley. 2014. "Citizen Social Science and Citizen Data? Methodological and Ethical Challenges for Social Research." *Current Sociology* 62(3): 374–92. DOI: https://doi.org/10.1177/0011392114527997.

Rotman, Dana, Jenny Preece, Jen Hammock, Kezee Procita, Derek Hansen, Cynthia Parr, Darcy Lewis, and David Jacobs. 2012. "Dynamic Changes in Motivation in Collaborative Citizen-Science Projects." In *Proceedings of the ACM 2012 Conference on Computer Supported Cooperative Work (CSCW '12)*, 217–26. New York: ACM. DOI: https://doi.org/10.1145/2145204.2145238.

Silvertown, Jonathan. 2009. "A New Dawn for Citizen Science." *Trends in Ecology & Evolution* 24(9): 467–71. DOI: https://doi.org/10.1016/j.tree.2009.03.017.

Wiggins, Andrea, and Kevin Crowston. 2011. "From Conservation to Crowdsourcing: A Typology of Citizen Science." In *Proceedings of the 2011 44th Hawaii International Conference on System Sciences (HICSS '11)*, 1–10. DOI: https://doi.org/10.1109/HICSS.2011.207.

## 3. Crowdsourcing

Crowdsourcing projects, typically built on information gathered by large groups of unrelated individuals through digital means, are becoming more common in academia. In this category, authors define crowdsourcing and explore most common trends and essential practices (Carletti et al. 2013; Holley 2010; McKinley 2012). Crowdsourcing projects in the digital humanities typically engage participant contribution by adding to existing resources or creating new ones, especially in terms of charting, locating, sharing, revising, documenting, and enriching materials (Carletti et al. 2013). Some exemplary projects are included, such as the *Transcribe Bentham* project that successfully brings together crowdsourcing and public engagement into a scholarly framework (Causer and Terras 2014), and *Prism*, a textual markup tool that supports multiple interpretations of text through close reading (Walsh et al. 2014). Authors also propose ways to moderate input from users with unknown reliability (Ghosh, Kale, and McAfee 2011). The category provides a rich snippet of existing crowdsourcing practices and offers suggestions for optimal implementation.

### A. Annotations

**Bradley, Jean-Claude, Robert J. Lancashire, Andrew S.I.D. Lang, and Antony J. Williams. 2009. "The Spectral Game: Leveraging Open Data and Crowdsourcing for Education." *Journal of Cheminformatics* 1(9): 1–10. DOI: https://doi.org/10.1186/1758-2946-1-9.**
Bradley et al. use The Spectral Game to frame their discussion of leveraging open data and crowdsourcing techniques in education. The Spectral Game is used to assist in the teaching of spectroscopy in an entertaining manner. It was created by combining open source spectral data, a spectrum-viewing tool, and appropriate workflows, and it delivers these resources through the game medium. The authors evaluate the game in an undergraduate organic chemistry class, and argue that The Spectral Game demonstrates the importance of open data for remixing educational curriculum.

+Carletti, Laura, Derek McAuley, Dominic Price, Gabriella Giannachi, and Steve Benford. 2013. "Digital Humanities and Crowdsourcing: An Exploration." *Museums and the Web 2013 Conference* (MW2013). Silver Spring, MD: Museums and the Web LLC. http://mw2013.museumsandtheweb.com/paper/digital-humanities-and-crowdsourcing-an-exploration-4/.
Carletti, McAuley, Price, Giannachi, and Benford survey and identify emerging practices in current crowdsourcing projects in the digital humanities.

The authors base their understanding of crowdsourcing on an earlier definition of crowdsourcing as an online, voluntary activity that connects individuals to an initiative via an open call (Estellés-Arolas and González-Ladrón-
de-Guevara 2012, annotated below). This definition was used to select the
case studies for the current research. The researchers found two major
trends in the 36 initiatives included in the study: crowdsourcing projects
use the crowd to either (a) integrate/enrich/configure existing resources
or (b) create/contribute new resources. Generally, crowdsourcing projects
asked volunteers to contribute in terms of curating, revising, locating, sharing, documenting, or enriching materials. The 36 initiatives surveyed were
divided into three categories in terms of project aims: public engagement,
enriching resources, and building resources.

+Causer, Tim, and Melissa Terras. 2014. "Crowdsourcing Bentham:
  Beyond the Traditional Boundaries of Academic History."
  *International Journal of Humanities and Arts Computing* 8(1): 46–64.
  DOI: http://dx.doi.org/ 10.3366/ijhac.2014.0119.
Causer and Terras reflect on some of the key discoveries that were made
in the *Transcribe Bentham* crowdsourced initiative. *Transcribe Bentham* was
launched with the intention of demonstrating that crowdsourcing can be
used successfully for both scholarly work and public engagement by allowing
all types of participants to access and explore cultural material. Causer and
Terras note that the majority of the work on *Transcribe Bentham* was undertaken by a small percentage of users, or 'super transcribers.' Only 15 per cent
of the users had completed any transcription, and approximately 66 per cent
of those users had transcribed only a single document—leaving a very select
number of individuals responsible for the core of the project's production.
The authors illustrate how some of the user transcription has contributed
to our understanding of some of Jeremy Bentham's central causes: animal
rights, politics, and prison conditions. Overall, Causer and Terras demonstrate how scholarly transcription undertaken by a wide, online audience
can uncover essential material.

+Causer, Tim, Justin Tonra, and Valerie Wallace. 2012. "Transcription
  Maximized; Expense Minimized? Crowdsourcing and Editing
  *The Collected Works of Jeremy Bentham*." *Digital Scholarship in the
  Humanities* (formerly *Literary and Linguistic Computing*) 27(2): 119–
  37. DOI: http://dx.doi.org/10.1093/llc/fqs004.
Causer, Tonra, and Wallace discuss the advantages and disadvantages of
user-generated manuscript transcription using the *Transcribe Bentham* proj-
ect as a case study. The intention of the project is to engage the public with

the thoughts and works of Jeremy Bentham by creating a digital, searchable repository of his manuscript writings. The authors preface this article by setting out five key factors the team hoped to assess in terms of the potential benefits of crowdsourcing: cost effectiveness, exploitation, quality control, sustainability, and success. Evidence from the project showcases the great potential for open access TEI-XML transcriptions in creating a long-term, sustainable archive. Additionally, users reported that they were motivated by a sense of contributing to a greater good and/or recognition. In the experience of *Transcribe Bentham*, crowdsourcing transcription may not have been the cheapest, quickest, or easiest route, but the authors argue that projects with a longer time scale may find this method both self-sufficient and cost-effective.

Estellés-Arolas, Enrique, and Fernando González-Ladrón-de-Guevara. 2012. "Towards an Integrated Crowdsourcing Definition." *Journal of Information Science* 38(2): 189–200. DOI: http://dx.doi.org/ 10.1177/0165551512437638.
Estellés-Arolas and González-Ladrón-de-Guevara present an encompassing definition of crowdsourcing, arguing that the flexibility of crowdsourcing is what makes it challenging to define. They demonstrate that, depending on perspective, researchers can have vastly divergent understandings of crowdsourcing. By conducting a detailed study of current understandings of the practice, the authors form a global definition that facilitates the distinguishing and formalizing of crowdsourcing activities. Using textual analysis, they identify crowdsourcing's three key elements: the crowd, the initiator, and the process. The authors advance a comprehensive definition that highlights the individuals, tasks, roles, and returns associated with crowdsourcing. They present a verification table, with nine categories, that can be used to determine whether or not an initiative falls into the classification of crowdsourcing. Estellés-Arolas and González-Ladrón-de-Guevara suggest that further research should be done to understand the relationship between crowdsourcing and other associated concepts, such as outsourcing.

+Franklin, Michael J., Donald Kossman, Tim Kraska, Sukriti Ramesh, and Reynold Xin. 2011. "CrowdDB: Answering Queries with Crowdsourcing." In *Proceedings of the 2011 ACM SIGMOD International Conference on Management of Data (SIGMOD '11)*, 61–72. New York: ACM.
Franklin, Kossman, Kraska, Ramesh, and Xin discuss the importance of including human input in query processing systems due to their limitations in

dealing with certain subjective tasks, which often result in inaccurate results. The authors propose using CrowdDB, a system that allows for crowdsourcing input when dealing with incomplete data and subjective comparison cases. The authors discuss the benefits and limitations of combining human effort with machine processing, and offer a number of suggestions to optimize the workflow. Franklin et al. envision the field of human input combined with computer processing to be an area of rich research because it improves existing models and enables new ones.

**Gahran, Amy. 2012. "SeeClickFix: Crowdsourced Local Problem Reporting as Community News." *Knight Digital Media Center,* September 19. http://www.knightdigitalmediacenter.org/blogs/ agahran/2012/09/seeclickfix-crowdsourced-local-problem-reporting-community-news.html. Archived at https://perma.cc/ T6NF-EGZX.

Gahran details the benefits of using SeeClickFix, a web-based open access widget used for illuminating local issues, spurring community discourse, and sparking story ideas. Users can also use it to file public reports on local issues and vote for individual reports when they would like to see a specific issue resolved. The widget enables plotting of locations on a Google Map interface so that users within a geographic area can view a list of individual reports in that area. Having this widget on a site makes it easier to stay aware of community-reported issues and maintain greater engagement with the broader geographic area in which the individual or group in question lives.

+Ghosh, Arpita, Satyen Kale, and Preston McAfee. 2011. "Who Moderates the Moderators? Crowdsourcing Abuse Detection in User-Generated Content." In *Proceedings of the 12th ACM Conference on Electronic Commerce* (EC '11), 167–76. New York: ACM. DOI: https:// doi.org/ 10.1145/ 1993574.1993599.

Ghosh, Kale, and McAfee address the issue of how to moderate the ratings of users with unknown reliability. They propose an algorithm that can detect abusive content and spam, starting with approximately 50 per cent accuracy on the basis of one example of good content, and reaching complete accuracy after a number of entries using machine-learning techniques. They believe that rating each individual contribution is a better approach than rating the users themselves based on their past behaviour, as most platforms do. According to Ghosh, Kale, and McAfee, this algorithm may be a stepping-stone in determining more complex ratings by users with unknown reliability.

+Holley, Rose. 2010. "Crowdsourcing: How and Why Should Libraries Do It?" *D-Lib Magazine* 16(3/4): n.p. DOI: https://www.doi.org/10.1045/march2010-holley.

Holley defines crowdsourcing, and makes a number of practical suggestions to assist with launching a crowdsourcing project. She asserts that crowdsourcing uses social engagement techniques to help a group of people work together on a shared, usually significant initiative. The fundamental principle of a crowdsourcing project is that it entails greater effort, time, and intellectual input than is available from a single individual, thereby requiring broader social engagement. Holley's argument is that libraries are already proficient at public engagement, but need to improve how they work toward shared group goals. Holley suggests ten basic practices to assist libraries in successfully implementing crowdsourcing. Many of these recommendations centre on project transparency and motivating users.

**Lampe, Cliff, Robert LaRose, Charles Steinfield, and Kurt DeMaagd. 2011. "Inherent Barriers to the Use of Social Media for Public Policy Informatics." *The Innovation Journal* 16(1): Article 6.

Lampe, LaRose, Steinfield, and DeMaagd address the barriers to social media use for public policy informatics, arguing that social media has the potential to foster interactions between policymakers, government officials, and their constituencies. The authors refer to this framework as Governance 2.0, and use AdvanceMichigan as a case study. AdvanceMichigan is a social media implementation designed to crowdsource feedback from stakeholders of Michigan State University Cooperative Extension. This organization approaches the education process in a way that students can apply their knowledge to a range of critical issues, needs, and opportunities. The organization is planning to return to traditional methods for collecting data from stakeholders due to the challenges of crowdsourcing data. The authors conclude with a discussion on how to create compelling technologies tailored to correctly scaled tasks for an audience that is likely to use social media sites.

+Manzo, Christina, Geoff Kaufman, Sukdith Punjasthitkul, and Mary Flanagan. 2015. "'By the People, For the People': Assessing the Value of Crowdsourced, User-Generated Metadata." *Digital Humanities Quarterly* 9(1): n.p. http://www.digitalhumanities.org/dhq/vol/9/1/ 000204/000204.html.

Manzo, Kaufman, Punjasthitkul, and Flanagan make a case for the usefulness of folksonomy tagging when combined with categorical tagging in crowdsourced projects. The authors open with a defence of categorization by arguing that classification systems reflect collection qualities while allowing for efficient retrieval of materials. However, they admit that these positive effects are often diminished by the use of folksonomy tagging, which promotes self-referential and personal task organizing labels. The authors suggest that a mixed system of folksonomic and controlled vocabularies be put into play in order to maximize the benefits of both approaches while minimizing their challenges. This is demonstrated through an empirical experiment in labelling images from the Leslie Jones Collection of the Boston Public Library, followed by evaluating the helpfulness of the tags.

+McKinley, Donelle. 2012. "Practical Management Strategies for Crowdsourcing in Libraries, Archives and Museums." Report for the School of Information Management, Faculty of Commerce and Administration, Victoria University of Wellington (NZ), 1–13. http://nonprofitcrowd.org/wp-content/uploads/2014/11/McKinley-2012-Crowdsourcing-management-strategies.pdf.

The purpose of McKinley's report is to review the literature and theory on crowdsourcing, and to consider how it relates to the research initiatives of libraries, archives, and museums. McKinley begins by claiming that burgeoning digital technologies have contributed to an increase in participatory culture. Furthermore, she argues that this is evinced by the growing number of libraries, archives, and museums that use crowdsourcing. McKinley cites five different categories of crowdsourcing: collective intelligence, crowd creation, crowd voting, crowdfunding, and games. By way of conclusion, McKinley makes the following recommendations for crowdsourcing projects: (a) understand the context and convey the project's benefits; (b) choose an approach with clearly defined objectives; (c) identify the crowd and understand its motivations; (d) support participation; (e) evaluate implementation.

+Ridge, Mia. 2013. "From Tagging to Theorizing: Deepening Engagement with Cultural Heritage through Crowdsourcing." Curator 56(4): 435–50. DOI: http://dx.doi.org/10.1111/cura.12046.

Ridge examines how crowdsourcing projects have the potential to assist museums, libraries, and archives with the resource-intensive tasks of creating or improving content about collections. She argues that a well-designed crowdsourcing project aligns with the core values and missions of museums by helping to connect people with culture and history through meaningful activities. Ridge synthesizes several definitions of crowdsourcing to present an understanding of the term as a form of engagement in which individuals contribute toward a shared and significant goal through completing a series of small, manageable tasks; several examples of such projects are used to illustrate her definition. Ridge argues that scaffolding the project by setting up boundaries and clearly defining activities helps to increase user engagement by making participants feel comfortable completing the given tasks. She sees scaffolding as a key component of mounting a successful crowdsourcing project that offers truly deep and valuable engagement with cultural heritage.

+Rockwell, Geoffrey. 2012. "Crowdsourcing the Humanities: Social Research and Collaboration." In *Collaborative Research in the Digital Humanities*, edited by Marilyn Deegan and Willard McCarty, 135–54. Farnham, UK, and Burlington, VT: Ashgate.

Rockwell demonstrates how crowdsourcing can facilitate collaboration by examining two humanities computing initiatives. He exposes the paradox of collaborative work in the humanities by summarizing the 'lone ranger' past of the humanist scholar. He asserts that the digital humanities are, conversely, characterized by collaboration because they require a diverse range of skills. Rockwell views collaboration as an achievable value of digital humanities rather than a transcendent one. He presents case studies of the projects *Dictionary of Words in the Wild* and *Day in the Life of the Digital Humanities* to illustrate the limitations and promises of crowdsourcing in the humanities. Rockwell argues that the main challenge of collaboration is the organization of professional scholarship. Crowdsourcing projects provide structured ways to implement a social, counterculture research model that involves a larger community of individuals.

+Ross, Stephen, Alex Christie, and Jentery Sayers. 2014. "Expert/Crowd-Sourcing for the *Linked Modernisms Project*." *Scholarly and Research Communication* 5(4): n.p. DOI: https://doi.org/10.22230/src. 2014v5n4a186.

Ross, Christie, and Sayers discuss the creation and evolution of the *Linked Modernisms Project*. The authors demonstrate how the project negotiates the productive study of both individual works and the larger field of cultural modernism through the use of digital, visual, and networked methods. *Linked Modernisms* employs a four-tier information matrix to accumulate user-generated survey data about modernist materials. Ross, Christie, and Sayers argue that the resulting information allows serendipitous encounters with data and emphasizes discoverability. *Linked Modernisms* is focused on developing modes of scholarly publication that line up with the dynamic nature of the data and comply with the principles of open access.

+Walsh, Brandon, Claire Maiers, Gwen Nally, Jeremy Boggs, and Praxis Program Team. 2014. "Crowdsourcing Individual Interpretations: Between Microtasking and Macrotasking." *Digital Scholarship in the Humanities* (formerly *Literary and Linguistic Computing*) 29(3): 379–86. DOI: http://dx.doi.org/10.1093/llc/fqu030.

Walsh, Maiers, Nally, Boggs, et al. track the creation of Prism, an individual text markup tool developed by the Praxis Program at the University of Virginia. Prism was conceived in response to Jerome McGann's call for textual markup tools that foreground subjectivity, as the tool illustrates how different groups of readers engage with a text. Prism is designed to assist with projects that blend two approaches to crowdsourcing: microtasking and macrotasking. The tool balances the constraint necessary for generating productive metadata with the flexibility necessary for facilitating social, negotiable interactions with the textual object. In this way, Prism is poised to redefine crowdsourcing in the digital humanities.

**Wiggins, Andrea, and Kevin Crowston. 2011. "From Conservation to Crowdsourcing: A Typology of Citizen Science." In *Proceedings of the 2011 44th Hawaii International Conference on System Sciences* (*HICSS '11*), 1–10. DOI: https://doi.org/10.1109/HICSS.2011.207.

Wiggins and Crowston discuss citizen science in terms of the common attributes many projects share, and attempt to provide a theoretical sampling that future citizen science projects may rely on. The authors argue that the majority of scholarship on citizen science is invested in describing the process of integrating volunteers into the various levels of scientific research, without taking into account the macrostructural and sociotechnical factors. They believe that this comes at the expense of crucial design and process management. Wiggins and Crowston identify and discuss five distinct typologies witnessed in various citizen science projects: action, conservation, investigation, virtuality, and education. The authors classify these typologies by major goals and the extent to which they are virtual. One of the main motivations for developing these typologies is to describe the existing state of citizen science and to make accessible the necessary conditions for successful citizen science projects.

### B. Reference List

Bradley, Jean-Claude, Robert J. Lancashire, Andrew S.I.D. Lang, and Antony J. Williams. 2009. "The Spectral Game: Leveraging Open Data and Crowdsourcing for Education." *Journal of Cheminformatics* 1 (9): 1–10. DOI: https://doi.org/10.1186/1758-2946-1-9.

Carletti, Laura, Derek McAuley, Dominic Price, Gabriella Giannachi, and Steve Benford. 2013. "Digital Humanities and Crowdsourcing: An Exploration." *Museums and the Web 2013 Conference* (*MW2013*). Silver Spring, MD: Museums and the Web LLC. http://mw2013.museumsandtheweb.com/ paper/digital-humanities-and-crowdsourcing-an-exploration-4/.

Causer, Tim, and Melissa Terras. 2014. "Crowdsourcing Bentham: Beyond the Traditional Boundaries of Academic History." *International Journal of Humanities and Arts Computing* 8(1): 46–64. DOI: http://dx.doi. org/10.3366/ijhac.2014.0119.

Causer, Tim, Justin Tonra, and Valerie Wallace. 2012. "Transcription Maximized; Expense Minimized? Crowdsourcing and Editing *The Collected Works of Jeremy Bentham*." *Digital Scholarship in the Humanities* (formerly *Literary and Linguistic Computing*) 27(2): 119–37. DOI: http:// dx.doi.org/10.1093/llc/fqs004.

Estellés-Arolas, Enrique, and Fernando González-Ladrón-de-Guevara. 2012. "Towards an Integrated Crowdsourcing Definition." *Journal of Information Science* 38(2): 189–200. DOI: http://dx.doi.org/ 10.1177/0165551512437638.

Franklin, Michael J., Donald Kossman, Tim Kraska, Sukriti Ramesh, and Reynold Xin. 2011. "CrowdDB: Answering Queries with Crowdsourcing." In *Proceedings of the 2011 ACM SIGMOD International Conference on Management of Data* (*SIGMOD '11*), 61–72. New York: ACM.

Gahran, Amy. 2012. "SeeClickFix: Crowdsourced Local Problem Reporting as Community News." *Knight Digital Media Center*, September 19. http:// www.knightdigitalmediacenter.org/blogs/agahran/2012/09/seeclick-fix-crowdsourced-local-problem-reporting-community-news.html. Archived at https://perma.cc/T6NF-EGZX.

Ghosh, Arpita, Satyen Kale, and Preston McAfee. 2011. "Who Moderates the Moderators? Crowdsourcing Abuse Detection in User-Generated Content." In *Proceedings of the 12th ACM Conference on Electronic Commerce* (*EC '11*), 167–76. New York: ACM. DOI: https://doi.org/ 10.1145/1993574.1993599.

Holley, Rose. 2010. "Crowdsourcing: How and Why Should Libraries Do It?" *D-Lib Magazine* 16(3/4): n.p. DOI: https://www.doi.org/10.1045/ march2010-holley.

Lampe, Cliff, Robert LaRose, Charles Steinfield, and Kurt DeMaagd. 2011. "Inherent Barriers to the Use of Social Media for Public Policy Informatics." *The Innovation Journal* 16(1): Article 6.

Manzo, Christina, Geoff Kaufman, Sukdith Punjasthitkul, and Mary Flanagan. 2015. "'By the People, For the People': Assessing the Value of Crowdsourced, User-Generated Metadata." *Digital Humanities Quarterly* 9(1): n.p. http://www.digitalhumanities.org/dhq/vol/9/1/000204/000204.html.

McKinley, Donelle. 2012. "Practical Management Strategies for Crowdsourcing in Libraries, Archives and Museums." Report for the School of Information Management, Faculty of Commerce and Administration, Victoria University of Wellington (NZ), 1–13. http://nonprofitcrowd.org/wp-content/uploads/2014/11/McKinley-2012-Crowdsourcing-management-strategies.pdf.

Ridge, Mia. 2013. "From Tagging to Theorizing: Deepening Engagement with Cultural Heritage through Crowdsourcing." *Curator* 56(4): 435–50. DOI: http://dx.doi.org/10.1111/cura.12046.

Rockwell, Geoffrey. 2012. "Crowdsourcing the Humanities: Social Research and Collaboration." In *Collaborative Research in the Digital Humanities*, edited by Marilyn Deegan and Willard McCarty, 135–54. Farnham, UK, and Burlington, VT: Ashgate.

Ross, Stephen, Alex Christie, and Jentery Sayers. 2014. "Expert/Crowd-Sourcing for the *Linked Modernisms Project*." *Scholarly and Research Communication* 5(4): n.p. DOI: https://doi.org/10.22230/src.2014 v5n4a186.

Walsh, Brandon, Claire Maiers, Gwen Nally, Jeremy Boggs, and Praxis Program Team. 2014. "Crowdsourcing Individual Interpretations: Between Microtasking and Macrotasking." *Digital Scholarship in the Humanities* (formerly *Literary and Linguistic Computing*) 29(3): 379–86. DOI: http://dx.doi.org/10.1093/llc/fqu030.

Wiggins, Andrea, and Kevin Crowston. 2011. "From Conservation to Crowdsourcing: A Typology of Citizen Science." In *Proceedings of the 2011 44th Hawaii International Conference on System Sciences* (*HICSS '11*), 1–10. DOI: https://doi.org/10.1109/HICSS.2011.207.

## 4. Collaborative Scholarship

Collaborative scholarship in academia is rapidly gaining prevalence, as evinced by the increase in both disciplinary and interdisciplinary research partnerships on individual campuses and across universities. The possibility of virtual correspondence fueled by the Internet is one of the primary catalysts for this development. Authors in this category address the benefits and challenges of collaboration, and suggest essential practices. This category includes an extended study on collaboration throughout the life cycle of a seven-year project, Implementing New Knowledge Environments (INKE). Siemens (2012–2016) reflects on collaboration at the end of every funded year of the project and explores how it evolves over time, how to develop and maintain positive and productive team relationships, how to integrate new team members into a project in the most optimal way, and how to deal with many other challenges that may occur within collaborative environments. Authors also address partnerships in virtual communities and the importance of utilizing platforms designed to facilitate collaboration (Kondratova and Goldfarb 2004). Overall, this category is meant as a solid starting point for those preparing to launch collaborative projects.

### A. Annotations

**\*\*Arbuckle, Alyssa, Nina Belojevic, Matthew Hiebert, and Ray Siemens, with Shaun Wong, Derek Siemens, Alex Christie, Jon Saklofske, Jentery Sayers, and the INKE and ETCL Research Groups. 2014. "Social Knowledge Creation: Three Annotated Bibliographies." *Scholarly and Research Communication* 5(2): n.p. DOI: https://doi. org/10.22230/src.2014v5n2a150.**

Arbuckle, Belojevic, Hiebert, and Siemens, with Wong, Siemens, Christie, Saklofske, Sayers, and the INKE and ETCL research groups, provide three annotated bibliographies anchored in social knowledge creation. As they note, their project seeks 'to provide a transient representation of interrelational research areas,' and emphasizes '(re)shaping processes that produce knowledge' (n.p.). The authors address the work's intent, highlighting the importance of collaboration and open source. They discuss the principles to which this bibliography adheres, addressing topics such as the book, print, remediation of culture, and interaction and collaboration. In addition, they explore the importance of digital tools and gamification to the practice of social knowledge creation. The three main parts of this document are social knowledge creation and conveyance, game-design models for digital social knowledge creation, and social knowledge creation tools. Each of these sections begins with an introduction that presents an overview of the section's content, and ends with a complete alphabetical list of selections.

Brown, Susan. 2016. "Towards Best Practices in Collaborative Online Knowledge Production." In *Doing Digital Humanities: Practice, Training, Research,* edited by Constance Crompton, Richard J. Lane, and Ray Siemens, 47–64. London and New York: Routledge.

Brown addresses the affordances of Web technologies that facilitate collaborative modes of online scholarly knowledge production. She argues that collaboration in the humanities still lags behind natural and social sciences. Brown discusses the key principles researchers ought to consider when choosing a platform for collaborative scholarship, as well as components of work processes and workspaces that help implement these principles into the project. She defines 'best' practices as both the control over scholarly processes that bring together a number of contributors, and those that more optimally address interoperability, preservation, reuse, and the various ethical and professional considerations involved with group work. This article focuses on approaches to systems and standards that enable collaborative knowledge production online rather than on ways to coordinate collaborative relationships.

Crompton, Constance, Cole Mash, and Raymond G. Siemens. 2015. "Playing Well with Others: The Social Edition and Computational Collaboration." *Scholarly and Research Communication* 6(3): n.p. DOI: https://doi.org/10.22230/src.2015v6n3a111.

Crompton, Mash, and Siemens study the use of microdata formats as a means of including larger groups of researchers and editors working on a digital social edition. They also provide readily parsable data about the content of *A Social Edition of the Devonshire Manuscript,* the main object of their study. The authors argue that adopting linked data standards allows for an interconnection between texts and virtual collaboration across projects and scholars. Crompton, Mash, and Siemens explain how Resource Descriptions Framework in Attributes (RDFa) is well suited for academic projects, and elaborate on the idea of encoding for the Semantic Web. They discuss technical decisions that would shift the focus of the encoder on data entry instead of the technical details of encoding. In their conclusion, the authors suggest that with the RDFa enhancement, *A Social Edition of the Devonshire Manuscript* will provoke new research questions about the culture and contexts of the Tudor court.

Kondratova, Irina, and Ilia Goldfarb. 2004. "Virtual Communities of Practice: Design for Collaboration and Knowledge Creation." *Proceedings of the European Conference on Products and Processes Modelling* (*ECPPM 2004*). NRC Publications Archive. https://nrc-publications.canada.ca/eng/view/accepted/?id=9a521a4b-bd4b-43c6-88bf-28288de1b1ff.

Kondratova and Goldfarb discuss knowledge dissemination and collaboration in online communities. They conduct a study on design functionality by looking at portal types that include institutional, governmental and organizational, professional, and social portals. The study includes 80 criteria grouped under content, discussion forum functionality, features, tools and learning modules, search functionality, membership, and topic experts. Based on this study, the authors develop a new template, as they believe that there is need for further similar investigations.

**Rotman, Dana, Jenny Preece, Jen Hammock, Kezee Procita, Derek Hansen, Cynthia Parr, Darcy Lewis, and David Jacobs. 2012. "Dynamic Changes in Motivation in Collaborative Citizen-Science Projects." In *Proceedings of the ACM 2012 Conference on Computer Supported Cooperative Work* (*CSCW '12*), 217–26. New York: ACM. DOI: https://doi.org/10.1145/2145204.2145238.

Rotman, Preece, Hammock, Procita, Hansen, Parr, Lewis, and Jacobs conduct a study that borrows from a motivational model in order to determine the various incentives of volunteers to participate and perform well in citizen science projects related to ecological scientific research. Although many successful citizen science projects exist, many do not take full advantage of the collaborative possibilities between the scientists and volunteers; hence, studying the motivation of each party and designing an environment that rewards and motivates all parties could drastically improve the field altogether. After conducting the study, the authors found that volunteers were primarily motivated by their curiosity, drive for learning, and desire for conservation, whereas the scientists were primarily motivated by their careers and scientific advancement more generally. They also found that the two most important motivational moments for volunteers are the first encounter with the project and group and the wrapping up of a project, when volunteers decide whether or not to participate in other projects. Finally, the authors contribute a dynamic model that displays the engagement cycle of the participants throughout the different stages of the project.

+Siemens, Lynne. 2009. "It's a Team if You Use 'Reply All': An Exploration of Research Teams in Digital Humanities Environments." *Digital Scholarship in the Humanities* (formerly *Literary and Linguistic Computing*) 24(2): 225–33.
Siemens begins by identifying a contrast between conventional humanities research and digital humanities research: while the humanities disciplines have relied on predominantly solo research efforts, digital humanities research involves the collaboration of various individuals with a wide spectrum of skills. She argues that the collaborative nature of academic research communities, especially in the humanities, has been understudied. Her article takes a step toward remediating this gap by examining the results of interviews conducted on the topics of teams, team-based work experiences, and team research preparation. The interview subjects identified both benefits and challenges of team research. Some of the challenges include relationship building with potential for future projects, communication challenges, funding, and team member retention. In conclusion, Siemens articulates a list of five essential practices: (i) deliberate action by each team member; (ii) deliberate action by the project leader; (iii) deliberate action by the team; (iv) deliberate training; and (v) balance between digital and in-person communication.

Siemens, Lynne. 2012a. "Understanding Long-Term Collaboration: Reflections on Year 1 and Before." *Scholarly and Research Communication* 3(1): n.p. DOI: https://doi.org/10.22230/src.2012v3n1a48.
Siemens addresses the advantages and challenges of collaborative work in the first year of the seven-year funded Implementing New Knowledge Environments (INKE) project, a group of 35 researchers from Canada, England, Ireland, and the United States that focus specifically on Interface Design, Textual Studies, User Experience, and Information Management. The study is carried out in an interview format with seven collaborators, including graduate research assistants, researchers, members of the administrative team, and others. Findings indicate that team members share similar views on collaboration, saying that it yields grander research results and helps attain established goals, and that it requires a certain skill set to work together productively. The advantage of collaborative work is that it allows graduate students and researchers to interact with the larger community, and members of the community to learn and acquire various skill sets from each other. Disadvantages involve accountability within the project and to the funding agencies, the time-consuming nature of the project, the necessity of travel for personal meetings, and other potential personal or institutional tensions. Siemens summarizes the benefits and challenges of the first year

of the INKE project, and argues that the skill set acquired by participating in such a project may be useful in future academic and nonacademic work.

**Siemens, Lynne. 2012b. "Firing on All Cylinders: Progress and Transition in INKE's Year 2."** *Scholarly and Research Communication* **3(4): n.p. DOI: https://doi.org/10.22230/src.2012v3n4a72.**
Siemens explores how collaborative practices evolve over the span of a project, using the Implementing New Knowledge Environments (INKE) second year of funded research as a case study. As with the previous study based on year one (Siemens 2012a, annotated below), the study here is carried out through a series of interviews with various INKE researchers and administrators. The results show that INKE's members have developed closer relationships, allowing research to progress; the graduate research assistants also stated that their work experience has deepened their academic and collaborative skills. Some of the major challenges have to do with human resources, and include the difficulty in securing postdoctoral fellows with technical skills and a project manager, mostly due to competition with other disciplines for hiring these professionals. A number of members and sub-research areas were in a period of transition, which resulted in a slight restructuring of the project. Siemens offers a number of potential solutions to the aforementioned challenges and addresses ways to structure the workflow during transitional periods that would help maintain the flow of the project and swiftly integrate newcomers. She ends her article with various recommendations on how to sustain successful collaboration, which include having face-to-face meetings (in formal and informal settings) of geographically distributed team members, utilizing the most optimal methods for knowledge transfer in moments of transition, and taking into account ways in which partner university policies may affect the project and its internal dynamics.

**Siemens, Lynne. 2013. "Responding to Change and Transition in INKE's Year Three."** *Scholarly and Research Communication* **4(3): n.p. DOI: https://doi.org/10.22230/src.2013v4n3a115.**
Siemens addresses the collaborative nature of the Implementing New Knowledge Environments (INKE) project at the closing of the third year of funded research. The purpose of this investigation is to document the nature of collaboration so that teams can benefit in future scenarios from past lessons learned. Also, there is a notable lack of scholarship focused on collaboration despite its increased adoption in the academic sphere. Siemens frames the third year as a transitional one for INKE, since it is the period in which there was a change in sub-research areas, partners, and team members. The

study is conducted through various interviews with team members. and the data analysis is carried out through a ground theory approach. The major observations that emerged in relation to transitional phases and how to best manage them include an acknowledgment that the integration of new team members into a project takes time and that an account of the project and team relationships, as well as project documentation, may be helpful. Other essential parts of this process are formal and informal face-to-face meetings. According to Siemens, the selection of individuals with a collaboration-oriented mindset is useful, since they are more likely to accommodate the short timespan allotted for new team member integration while still meeting research objectives.

**Siemens, Lynne. 2014. "Research Collaboration as 'Layers of Engagement': INKE in Year Four."** *Scholarly and Research Communication* 5(4): n.p. DOI: https://doi.org/10.22230/src.2014v5n4a181.

Siemens discusses the fourth year of the Implementing New Knowledge Environments (INKE) project, and focuses on how the nature of the collaboration over this period of the project has evolved. As with other studies on INKE's collaboration, this one was carried out through a series of interviews with the researchers, graduate researchers, and administrative members of the team using a series of questions that could be extended and which are then analyzed with a ground theory approach. Siemens argues that year four reflects a more mature period of the project in which the nature of collaboration has morphed into a more fulfilling and closely bound relationship: researchers from one area feel more involved with research in other areas, and all team members, including research assistants, recognize their role in an important and rewarding way. Siemens states that a significant development in year four is team members' ability to better balance INKE-related work with outside research, sometimes even having INKE's research drive motivate other work endeavours. One major challenge that still exists is coordinating across four time zones with few windows for possible meeting times. Overall, the interviews demonstrate that the team acknowledges the need and benefits of working together to attain research objectives. Siemens concludes with a set of suggestions for other teams working in a collaborative atmosphere.

**Siemens, Lynne. 2016. "'Faster Alone, Further Together': Reflections on INKE's Year Six."** *Scholarly and Research Communication* 7(2/3): n.p. DOI: https://doi.org/10.22230/src.2016v7n2/3a250.

Siemens addresses the sixth year of the Implementing New Knowledge Environments (INKE) project, namely the collaborative aspect of the long-term, large-scale project as it nears completion (in the seventh year). This study is carried out through a set of semi-structured interviews that are analyzed with a ground theory approach. According to Siemens, the team found collaboration to be a positive and beneficial experience overall, something that was continuously strengthened through face-to-face interactions. Another finding pointed to how large-scale projects are in a constant stage of transition, where the change in pace of the project also affects the pace of work on an individual level and the nature of the collaboration. Recurring challenges that sprang up in earlier years and continued throughout the project include working at a distance with team partners and the hiring and retention of postdoctoral fellows and research assistants. The documentation of this collaborative process and the lessons learned throughout the years are employed as a foundation for the next grant application and future collaborations.

Siemens, Lynne, Ray Siemens, Richard Cunningham, Teresa Dobson, Alan Galey, Stan Ruecker, and Claire Warwick. 2012. "INKE Administrative Structure: Omnibus Document." *Scholarly and Research Communication* 3(1): n.p. DOI: https://doi.org/10.22230/src.2012v3n1a50.

Siemens et al. outline the administrative structure to be executed in the Implementing New Knowledge Environments (INKE) project. The document is meant to serve as an agreement between the various individuals and groups involved in INKE on how members will work with each other over the upcoming years of collaboration to achieve the goals that were outlined in the research application. The article breaks down the administrative structure of the projects and the various groups involved, and presents the guidelines and responsibilities for each group. The groups consist of various researchers and partners, as well as various administrative divisions overlooking and advising the project. The authors also disclose the guidelines concerning intellectual property of knowledge created as part of the project, as well as the adopted policies for co-authoring work within the INKE framework. In the latter part of the document, Siemens et al. include excerpts from the grant application that addresses the broad range of key stakeholder areas, and the project charter that outlines how the work will be disseminated, the future of the project, and the nature of the work between members of INKE.

### B. Reference List

Arbuckle, Alyssa, Nina Belojevic, Matthew Hiebert, and Ray Siemens, with Shaun Wong, Derek Siemens, Alex Christie, Jon Saklofske, Jentery

Sayers, and the INKE and ETCL Research Groups. 2014. "Social Knowledge Creation: Three Annotated Bibliographies." *Scholarly and Research Communication* 5(2): n.p. DOI: https://doi.org/10.22230/src.2014v5n2a150.

Brown, Susan. 2016. "Towards Best Practices in Collaborative Online Knowledge Production." In *Doing Digital Humanities: Practice, Training, Research,* edited by Constance Crompton, Richard J. Lane, and Ray Siemens, 47–64. London and New York: Routledge.

Crompton, Constance, Cole Mash, and Raymond G. Siemens. 2015. "Playing Well with Others: The Social Edition and Computational Collaboration." *Scholarly and Research Communication* 6(3): n.p. DOI: https://doi.org/10.22230/src.2015v6n3a111.

Kondratova, Irina, and Ilia Goldfarb. 2004. "Virtual Communities of Practice: Design for Collaboration and Knowledge Creation." *Proceedings of the European Conference on Products and Processes Modelling (ECPPM 2004).* NRC Publications Archive. https://nrc-publications.canada.ca/eng/view/accepted/?id=9a521a4b-bd4b-43c6-88bf-28288de1b1ff.

Rotman, Dana, Jenny Preece, Jen Hammock, Kezee Procita, Derek Hansen, Cynthia Parr, Darcy Lewis, and David Jacobs. 2012. "Dynamic Changes in Motivation in Collaborative Citizen-Science Projects." In *Proceedings of the ACM 2012 Conference on Computer Supported Cooperative Work (CSCW '12),* 217–26. New York: ACM. DOI: https://doi.org/10.1145/2145204.2145238.

Siemens, Lynne. 2009. "It's a Team if You Use 'Reply All': An Exploration of Research Teams in Digital Humanities Environments." *Digital Scholarship in the Humanities* (formerly *Literary and Linguistic Computing*) 24(2): 225–33.

———. 2012a. "Understanding Long-Term Collaboration: Reflections on Year 1 and Before." *Scholarly and Research Communication* 3(1): n.p. DOI: https://doi.org/10.22230/src.2012v3n1a48.

———. 2012b. "Firing on All Cylinders: Progress and Transition in INKE's Year 2." *Scholarly and Research Communication* 3(4): n.p. DOI: https://doi.org/10.22230/src.2012v3n4a72.

———. 2013. "Responding to Change and Transition in INKE's Year Three." *Scholarly and Research Communication* 4(3): n.p. DOI: https://doi.org/10.22230/src.2013v4n3a115.

————. 2014. "Research Collaboration as 'Layers of Engagement': INKE in Year Four." *Scholarly and Research Communication* 5(4): n.p. DOI: https://doi.org/10.22230/src.2014v5n4a181.

————. 2016. "'Faster Alone, Further Together': Reflections on INKE's Year Six." *Scholarly and Research Communication* 7(2/3): n.p. DOI: https://doi.org/10.22230/src.2016v7n2/3a250.

Siemens, Lynne, Ray Siemens, Richard Cunningham, Teresa Dobson, Alan Galey, Stan Ruecker, and Claire Warwick. 2012. "INKE Administrative Structure: Omnibus Document." *Scholarly and Research Communication* 3(1): n.p. DOI: https://doi.org/10.22230/src.2012v3n1a50.

## 5. Groups/Initiatives/Organizations Discussing Open Social Scholarship

This category presents a list of groups, initiatives, and organizations engaging with some aspect of open social scholarship. Advocacy for open access to information is the most dominant trend among the groups listed. In general, the organizations agree that publicly funded research should be accessible to the wider public and not siloed behind institutional paywalls. Core values of education, the human right to access information regardless of geographical or cultural factors, and collaboration are echoed among many of the initiatives presented in this list. Several of these groups work within a specific geographical region and tailor their outreach to the needs of that particular group (African Commons Project, Alliance of Science Organisations in Germany, FinnOA). Other organizations operate on an international level by appealing to general principles of openness and fairness (IFLA Open Access Taskforce, Max Planck Society, Open Humanities Alliance). Many of the groups mention the Budapest Initiative and the Berlin Declaration as foundational to their mission (Federation for the Humanities and Social Sciences, Open Access Working Group, Canadian Association of Research Libraries). This category brings together groups that advocate for open, collaborative modes of knowledge production and dissemination.

### A. Annotations

Access2Research. 2019. "Access2Research." https://en.wikipedia.org/wiki/Access2Research.
Michael W. Carroll, Heather Joseph, Mike Rossner, and John Wilbanks lead Access2Research, an open access campaign that promotes reform in academic journal publishing. Access2Research is committed to making publicly funded research open access. Significantly, in 2012, the working group launched a petition demanding that the United States government require all journal articles arising from taxpayer-funded research be made openly available.

African Copyright and Access to Knowledge Project. 2019. "African Copyright and Access to Knowledge Project (ACA2K)." https://www.idrc.ca/en/project/african-copyright-and-access-knowledge-network-aca2k.
The African Copyright and Access to Knowledge Project, active from 2007 to 2011, was committed to investigating the relationship between African national copyright environments and access to learning materials. The African Copyright and Access to Knowledge Project probed this relationship within the context of A2K, a framework that protects user access to knowledge. The project conducted five environmental scans of copyright contexts

across African nations and used the collected data to draft country reports, a comparative review, and executive policy briefs.

**Akada Network. 2014. "Akada Network." https://www.facebook.com/akadanetwork/.**
Founded in 2013 by Yemi Makinde, the Akada Network is a nonprofit organization based in Nigeria and the Netherlands. The mission of the Akada Network is to support, promote, and develop higher education and research in Africa with the hope that fostering learning will build community. To achieve this goal, the Akada Network hosts initiatives that facilitate learning, sharing, and collaboration.

**Alliance for Taxpayer Access. 2019. "Alliance for Taxpayer Access." http://www.taxpayeraccess.org.**
The Alliance for Taxpayer Access is a U.S. collective of researchers, practitioners, educators, publishers, and institutions that support barrier-free access to taxpayer-funded research. The Alliance is committed to four principles of open access: taxpayers are entitled to barrier-free access of research they fund, widespread access to published information is foundational to a country's investment in research, information should be shared in cost-effective ways in order to stimulate engagement, and facilitating access will result in information being used by individual taxpayers. The Alliance for Taxpayer Access is directed by the Scholarly Publishing and Academic Resources Coalition (annotated below).

**American Academic & Scholarly Research Center. 2019. "American Academic & Scholarly Research Center." http://aasrc.org.**
Founded in 2007, the American Academic & Scholarly Research Center promotes academic research activities and sustained development of global resources, especially in developing nations. The Center is committed to knowledge innovation, dissemination, and collaboration. To support its mandate of encouraging practical, interdisciplinary research, the American Academic & Scholarly Research Center launched its first journal in 2009 and recently started a second, multilingual journal. The Center hosts annual, international conferences in order to unite likeminded individuals around the aims of the organization.

**Association for Computers and the Humanities. 2019. "Association for Computers and the Humanities." http://ach.org.**
The Association for Computers and the Humanities (ACH) is a digital humanities society. The organization is committed to cultivating professional

communities and disseminating digital humanities research. The Association is based in the United States, but hosts conferences around the world and boasts international membership. ACH, along with the Alliance of Digital Humanities Organizations, publishes three peer-reviewed journals, one of which is open access.

**Australasian Open Access Strategy Group. 2019. "Australasian Open Access Strategy Group." https://aoasg.org.au.**
The Australasian Open Access Strategy Group is committed to four main principles: advocating, collaborating, raising awareness, and building capacity. The organization supports open access outcomes for publicly funded research in Australia and New Zealand. By collaborating with researchers and other organizations, the Australasian Open Access Strategy Group raises awareness of, and support for, open access initiatives.

**Authors Alliance. 2019. "Authors Alliance." https://www.authorsalliance.org.**
The Authors Alliance supports authors who want to engage with their community through reading, helping them harness the power of digital networks to distribute knowledge. The Authors Alliance assists authors in navigating the complexities of print, copyright, and digitization in hopes of maximizing public access and supporting fair use. The organization bridges the gap between the author and the public in order to disseminate knowledge broadly.

**Berkman Klein Center for Internet & Society at Harvard University. 2018. "Harvard Open Access Project." https://cyber.law.harvard.edu/research/hoap.**
The Harvard Open Access Project (HOAP) is committed to opening access to research both within the university and beyond it. By using a combination of consultation, collaboration, and community building, HOAP aims to make knowledge accessible and reusable—maximizing the return on society's investment in innovative research. They developed the Open Access Tracking Project, which uses folksonomy tagging to provide real-time updates on open access and related news. HOAP was launched in 2011 and is supported by the Berkman Center for Internet & Society.

**Bioline International. 2019. "Bioline International." http://www.bioline.org.br.**
Bioline International is a not-for-profit publishing group committed to facilitating open access for residents of developing countries. With a goal of

reducing the South to North knowledge gap, Bioline International provides a distribution platform for peer-reviewed journals to disseminate information on topics such as biodiversity, conservation, health, and international development. Bioline makes it possible for research coming out of developing nations to have a place on the global stage. Some of the journals in the Bioline cooperative include *Zoological Research*, *African Population Studies*, *Rwanda Medical Journal*, and the *Journal of Health, Population, and Nutrition*.

**Canadian Association of Research Libraries. n.d. "Canadian Association of Research Libraries." http://www.carl-abrc.ca.**
The Canadian Association of Research Libraries (CARL) is a federation of 29 of the country's university libraries and two of Canada's national institutions. Members of the CARL community work together to improve access to knowledge; support students, faculty, and researchers; promote sustainable and effective communication; and share best practices. It is CARL's mission to support knowledge creation, dissemination, preservation, and public policy in order to enable broad access to scholarly information.

**Center for Open Science. 2019. "Center for Open Science." https://cos.io.**
Founded in 2013, the Center for Open Science is a nonprofit technology company that provides free and open services in order to increase information inclusivity and transparency while also working to align more closely with the values of scientific research. The Center for Open Science operates on three mission components that guide its development of sound scientific research: openness, integrity, and reproducibility. The Center works with scientists, developers, research institutions, and publishers to build a community and infrastructure that fosters this type of open science.

**Center for the Study of the Public Domain. 2019. "Center for the Study of the Public Domain." Duke University School of Law. https://law. duke.edu/cspd/.**
The Center for the Study of the Public Domain is located at Duke University Law School. While much of the society's contemporary attention, resources, and care has gone into protecting exclusive intellectual property rights, the Center is devoted to balancing economic, cultural, and technological dependencies by focusing on materials in the public domain. Founded in 2002, the Center is part of the university's wider intellectual property program. Its mission is to promote research and scholarship that contribute to open access repositories.

Coalition for Open Access Policy Institutions. 2018. "Coalition for Open
    Access Policy Institutions." https://sparcopen.org/coapi/.
The Coalition for Open Access Policy Institutions (COAPI) unites higher
education institutions across North America with the aim of proliferating
open access to scholarly research. COAPI brings together faculty members
and institutions already committed to open access principles with universities in the process of developing open access policies. This cooperative was
formed with the aim of supporting faculty-led movements to disseminate
research widely and openly. COAPI is a hub and resource for the open access
movement.

Compute Canada. 2014. "Sustainable Planning for Advanced Research
    Computing (SPARC)." News release, June 23. https://www.com-
    putecanada.ca/news/compute-canada-announces-sustainable-
    planning-for-advanced-research-computing-sparc/.
The Canada Foundation for Innovation is renewing Compute Canada's national platform, positioning it as a funding body for domain-specific data
projects with a budget for cyberstructure initiation that is meant to significantly benefit Canada's research community. In preparation for this,
Compute Canada will bring together researchers and institutions to develop
Sustainable Planning for Advanced Research Computing (SPARC), a discussion forum meant to address the types of investments that will position
Canada's leadership in science and innovation, especially those sectors that
rely highly on digital infrastructure. This article discusses the various roles
of SPARC, which focus on providing the necessary support for the growth of
digital infrastructure and the infrastructure necessary for Compute Canada's
upcoming service offering. Compute Canada also outlines the steps it will
take to assemble the appropriate input for SPARC over the summer of 2014.

Confederation of Open Access Repositories. 2019. "Confederation of
    Open Access Repositories." https://www.coar-repositories.org.
The Confederation of Open Access Repositories (COAR) is a not-for-profit organization based in Gottingen, Germany. Founded in 2010, COAR is a global
confederation of more than 100 libraries, universities, research institutions,
government funders, and various other partners. COAR joins together major
research networks and the broader repository community in order to build
capacity, policy, and practices to support global open access. Their mission
is to create an international knowledge commons that enhances accessibility
to and visibility of information.

**European University Association. 2019. "European University Association: The Voice of Europe's Universities." http://www.eua.be.**
The European University Association (EUA) is one of the largest and most comprehensive university collectives. The EUA has more than 850 members across 47 countries representing some 17 million students. It is the vision of the EUA to advance the continued development of culture, society, technology, and economy in Europe. The EUA has a working group devoted to the study of open access policy.

**Federation for the Humanities and Social Sciences. 2019a. "Issues." Federation for the Humanities and Social Sciences / Fédération des sciences humaines. http://www.ideas-idees.ca/issues/open-access-aspp.**
The Federation for the Humanities and Social Sciences is committed to supporting open access. In 2011, the Federation signed the Berlin Declaration and, in 2013, it embarked on a multi-year project to develop open access policy. Initial research, including an international scan of policy and informal discussions with groups across the country, sparked the 2015 writing and adopting of open access principles for the Federation. In 2015, the Federation's executive director at the time, Jean-Marc Mangin, participated in an Implementing New Knowledge Environments (INKE) conference on open scholarship in which he shared the Federation's efforts toward developing an open access policy.

**Federation for the Humanities and Social Sciences. 2019b. "Our Members." Federation for the Humanities and Social Sciences / Fédération des sciences humaines. http://www.ideas-idees.ca/about/members.**
The Federation for the Humanities and Social Sciences is dedicated to the promotion of research and teaching in order to advance toward a more inclusive and democratic society; this is done by supporting research and discussions that deal with critical issues within public and academic contexts. The Federation has a vast networked membership, with more than 160 universities, colleges, and scholarly associations, altogether representing some 91,000 voices of various humanities and social sciences specialists. The three membership types at the Federation are scholarly association members (graduate students and researchers selected for excellent research and leadership qualities); institutional members (universities and colleges); and affiliate members (organizations that have similar agendas to the Federation and are dedicated to enhancing post-secondary education and research).

**FinnOA. 2008. "Finnish Open Access Working Group (FinnOA)." http://www.openaccess.fi/info/english.html.**
Founded in 2003, FinnOA is a collective group that supports and promotes open access to scientific research. From its inception, FinnOA has been committed to a variety of open publication and dissemination platforms that value transparency in scientific publishing. Now, partnered with individuals in academia, libraries, and data management, FinnOA is focused on resolving issues related to open access and publicly-funded research data.

**FORCE11. 2019. "FORCE11." https://www.force11.org.**
FORCE11 ('The Future of Research Communications and e-Scholarship') is a cooperative of scholars, librarians, archivists, publishers, and research funding bodies that have joined together to help facilitate a better means of creating and sharing knowledge. The group was formed as a result of the Future of Research Communications (FORC) Workshop held in Dagstahl, Germany, in August 2011—hence the "11" in its name. Starting as a small community of like-minded individuals, FORCE11 has become a bold and diverse working group in support of open access. The collective leverages information technologies and multimedia in order to reach and educate the greater community, and welcomes new members who value and support its manifesto in favour of openness.

**Foundation for Open Access Statistics. 2013. "Foundation for Open Access Statistics." http://www.foastat.org.**
The mission of the Foundation for Open Access Statistics (FOAS) is to support free software, open access publishing platforms, and reproducible research in statistics. FOAS encourages researchers to make information publicly available online and accessible to members of the academic community at large. The organization publishes the *Journal of Statistical Software*, one of the few open access journals that is free for both authors and readers. FOAS advocates for open source code, and the materials and information necessary to reproduce mathematical results.

**Free Knowledge Institute. 2015. "Free Knowledge Institute." http://freeknowledge.eu.**
The Free Knowledge Institute (FKI) is a collective of networks and communities that support, facilitate, and enable the study, sharing, and collaborative development of free knowledge and free technologies. FKI supports a just, free knowledge society through sustainable collaboration and empowerment. Its mission is to educate people about open access and open source

ideologies so that they can become effective participants and advocates in their own domains. The tenets of the collective include flexibility, collaboration, shared purpose, shared values, and communication.

**German Research Foundation. 2019. "Alliance of Science Organisations in Germany." http://www.dfg.de/en/dfg_profile/alliance/.**
The Alliance of Science Organisations in Germany is a coalition of Germany's top research organizations. The Alliance is committed to developing and implementing new research policies and addressing the challenges young researchers are facing. Members of the Alliance include the Alexander von Humboldt Foundation, the Deutsche Forschungsgemeinschaft (DFG, German Research Foundation), the Fraunhofer-Gesellschaft, the German Academic Exchange Service, the German Council of Science and Humanities (Wissenschaftsrat), the German National Academy of Sciences Leopoldina, the German Rectors' Conference, the Helmholtz Association of German Research Centres, the Leibniz Association, and the Max Planck Society.

**Government of Canada. 2015a. "Digital Canada 150 2.0." Industry Canada. http://www.digitaleconomy.gc.ca/eic/site/028.nsf/eng/home.**
The Minister of Industry presents Digital Canada 150 2.0, a plan that aims to equip all Canadian citizens with the necessary digital skills and tools to succeed in today's world, help individuals and communities by providing opportunities in the global digital economy, and connect and protect Canadians online. The five pillars of Digital Canada 150 are connecting Canadians, protecting Canadians, economic opportunities, digital government, and Canadian content. Their website addresses each of these pillars individually, defines what they mean, and provides updates of recent accomplishments in each of these categories by posting updates, policies, success stories, and other information.

**International Community for Open Research and Education. n.d. "Welcome to ICORE, the International Community for Open Research and Open Education." http://www.icore-online.org.**
The International Community for Open Research and Education (ICORE) aims to support, promote, and enhance open access to research and education worldwide. The overall mission of the community is to re-establish openness, as was default in scholarship starting with the inception of journal publishing and up until as recently as several decades ago. ICORE's five main objectives are to promote open access as a fundamental social objective; to

support the implementation of strategies and services for facilitating open access; to foster cooperation between policymakers, researchers, educators, and students; to facilitate the transfer of current research into the deployment of future research; and to encourage innovative research that benefits the other objectives of the association. ICORE currently supports two active working groups and hosts a workshop series entitled 'Openness for All.'

**International Federation of Library Associations and Institutions. 2011. "IFLA Open Access Taskforce Established." News release, October 11. https://www.ifla.org/news/ifla-open-access-taskforce-established.**
The International Federation of Library Associations and Institutions (IFLA) is committed to facilitating open access and believes that universal, equitable access to information is a critical component of ensuring the well-being of people, communities, and organizations across the globe. IFLA acknowledges that the current model of scholarly production and publication is exclusive and not sustainable. It wants to change the role of libraries to support a sustainable, open access movement. In 2011, IFLA also established a task force dedicated to advocating for the adoption of their open access policies.

**Knowledge Exchange. n.d. "KE: Knowledge Exchange." http://www. knowledge-exchange.info.**
Knowledge Exchange understands that digital technologies open opportunities for advanced research and higher education. It is the vision of the organization that open scholarship be acknowledged and taken up as one of these opportunities. Knowledge Exchange argues that opening up access to scientific research and encouraging collaboration will improve transparency, engender trust, increase effective use of data, and support wider participation in research. The group's mission is to support its five partner organizations on the road to achieving a shared vision of open scholarship.

**Leadership Council for Digital Research Infrastructure. 2014. "'Think Piece' on a DI Roadmap." http://digitalleadership.ca/wp-content/ uploads/ 2014/01/DI-Roadmap-Think-Piece-Jan-2014.pdf.**
The "'Think Piece" on a DI Roadmap' investigates important steps toward 'a robust and sustainable digital infrastructure for research in Canada' (1). The authors address challenges such as governance/coordination, policy and planning framework, and data management within the DI roadmap framework. The authors propose methods to expand on the roles and responsibilities of organizational structures. The first phase of action consists of developing a collaborative national coalition for going forward, implementing

priority working groups, pursuing refinements to the DI funding system, giving priority to the data management pillar of the DI ecosystem, and articulating a value proposition. In the second phase, the authors propose engaging the government and the private sector, expertise and capacity development, middleware and software development, and a need for more structured communications and engagement with research communities and institutions. The authors conclude that there is an ongoing need for an 'engagement with individuals within and external to this network [as it is] critical to communicating and realizing the vision for the sector' (17).

**Lithuanian Research Library Consortium. 2019. "Lithuanian Research Library Consortium." http://www.lmba.lt/en.**
The Lithuanian Research Library Consortium was founded in 2011 and currently comprises 56 members. The cooperative is a member of the Network of Electronic Information for Libraries (EIFL) and supports that organization's open access policies. The open access program objectives are to build a global network of open access journals and repositories; to provide training and education on open access policies; and to motivate scholars, educators, and students to bring these policies into practice. The Lithuanian Research Library Consortium also participates in global open access education events.

**Max Planck Society. 2019a. "Berlin Declaration on Open Access to Knowledge in the Sciences and Humanities." http://openaccess. mpg.de/Berlin-Declaration.**
The Berlin Declaration is considered to be a significant milestone in the Open Access movement. Published in October 2003, the Berlin Declaration addresses the fundamental changes of knowledge distribution since the proliferation of the Internet. The declaration promotes the use of the Internet as a functional instrument of knowledge collection and human reflection. The document specifies measures for policymakers, research institutions, funding agencies, and heritage archives to consider. The mission of the Berlin Declaration is to make information widely and readily available through an Internet-supported, open access paradigm.

**Max Planck Society. 2019b. "Max Planck Society." https://openaccess. mpg.de.**
The Max Planck Society is a co-founder of the international open access movement and was an original supporter of the Berlin Declaration, which celebrated its tenth anniversary in 2013. The Society believes that research should be accessible and free to the public. This stipulates that full text

documents be available, downloadable, searchable, and distributable. The organization's mission is to increase interoperability of open access repositories, to support innovative open access publishing models, and to cooperate with other members of the Berlin Declaration to ensure a smooth and stable transition into a new model of open, scholarly publishing.

**Mediterranean Open Access Network. n.d. "MEDOANET 2012: Mediterranean Open Access Network." http://www.medoanet.eu.**
The Mediterranean Open Access Network (MedOANet) addresses the need for coordinated open access strategies across scientific information organizations in Europe. MedOANet unites six Mediterranean countries (Greece, Turkey, Italy, France, Spain, and Portugal) by enhancing, promoting, and creating open access policies and structures across the collaborative. The consortium is committed to strengthening current open access policies; identifying existing effective open access strategies; engaging policymakers in open access awareness; and producing guidelines for effective implementation of open access policies.

**Open Access India. 2019. "Open Access India." http://openaccessindia. org.**
Open Access India is a community of open access advocates who create awareness of open access policies among graduate students, early career researchers, professors, and policymakers. The collective is committed to the practices of open access, open data, and open education in India. It aims to advocate and educate the public on open access policies and to develop the infrastructure and framework necessary to support those policies. Open Access India believes that making information free and unrestricted will increase community engagement in publicly funded research.

**Open-Access.net. 2019. "Open Access: Free Access to Scientific Information." https://www.open-access.net/startseite/.**
Open-access.net is an information platform that archives the core concepts and main forms of open access research. Its goal is to bundle and disseminate information about open access that is tailored to target groups, specific country policies, and individual scenarios. Some examples of the types of information included in open access packages are a history of the open access movement, examples of open access business models, and a summary of legal issues relating to open access.

**Open Access Network. 2019. "Open Access Network." http://openaccess-network.org.**
The Open Access Network (OAN) is a collaboratory of individuals, organizations, societies, libraries, and institutions committed to working together to make knowledge public. OAN acknowledges the burden of an open access business model and aims to address the problem head-on—beginning with the humanities and social sciences disciplines. OAN recommends broad, transformative solutions that support sustainable, open access practices.

**Open Access Scholarly Publishers Association. 2019. "Open Access Scholarly Publishers Association." http://oaspa.org.**
The Open Access Scholarly Publishers Association is a trade organization established in 2008 with the objective of representing the interests of open access journal publishers across disciplines and around the globe. Its mission is carried out through opening information exchange, advancing open access models, improving education, and promoting innovation. The Open Access Scholarly Publishers Association aims to develop business models, tools, and standards to support a vibrant and sustainable market for open access publishing.

**Open Access Working Group. n.d. "Open Access Working Group." http://access.okfn.org.**
The Open Access Working Group is part of the Open Knowledge Foundation, which works to promote open knowledge in the digital era. The collective comprises individuals who are unhappy with the current status of the fragmented open access movement and with the common misuse of the term 'open access' among groups that do not adhere to its clear definition. The goal of the Open Access Working Group is to re-establish the open access movement according to the terms of the Budapest Open Access Initiative.

**OpenAIRE. 2019. "OpenAIRE." https://www.openaire.eu.**
OpenAIRE envisions itself as a bridge between research stakeholders and the world of scholarly publication. It was created to support the implementation of open access policies through an aggregated repository of open resources. Currently, OpenAIRE is working with 50 partners, from the European Union and beyond, on the OpenAIRE 2020 project. This 3.5-year research and innovation project aims to promote open scholarship and to improve the accessibility, discoverability, and reusability of research publications. The initiative brings together research professionals, organizations, libraries, and data experts in a truly collaborative partnership.

**Open Humanities Alliance. n.d. "Open Humanities Alliance." http:// openhumanitiesalliance.org.**
The Open Humanities Alliance aims to open humanities scholarship to the larger, global community. The Alliance is a collective of people committed to furthering scholarship and learning in the humanities, and overcoming the technical barriers to humanities research. It fosters open access and collaboration by bringing together students, faculty, libraries, and other invested parties to work on open access and scholarly communications initiatives.

**Open Knowledge International. n.d. "Open Knowledge International." https://okfn.org.**
Open Knowledge International is a global, nonprofit network that champions openness using advocacy, technology, and training. Its mission is for everyone to have access to key information, and possess the ability to understand and use it to shape their lives. The network aims for open knowledge to be a foundational concept and for knowledge to create power for the many, not the few. Open Knowledge International works to achieve its aims by developing an international network of individuals, opening up information, and providing stewardship and consulting services.

**Open Scholarship Initiative. 2019. "Open Scholarship Initiative." http:// osiglobal.org/.**
The Open Scholarship Initiative is a global cooperative established with the goal of creating a space for dialogue about, and unification under, open access practices. It unites a group of high-level, international, scholarly publishing decision-makers in a series of annual meetings where ideas can be shared and common, actionable solutions can be established. Their aim is to improve the scholarly publishing system over the course of their 10-year effort (2016–2025).

**\*\*Organisation for Economic Cooperation and Development (OECD). 2015. "Making Open Science a Reality."** *OECD Science, Technology and Industry Policy Papers* **25. Paris: OECD Publishing.**
The Organisation for Economic Cooperation and Development (OECD) states that open science represents an effort toward making accessible publicly funded research in digital format, and provides a rationale for open science. The authors of this paper discuss key actors in open science, including researchers, government ministries, research funding agencies, universities and public research institutes, libraries, repositories, data centres, private nonprofit organizations and foundations, private scientific publishers, and businesses. They also examine policy trends in open science, which could be

mandatory rules, incentives, or funding. Their main findings include statements that approach open science as a means and not an end. The authors also explore open access to scientific publications and define open access in an exploratory manner by looking at it from various perspectives, with an interest in its legal implications.

**Public Knowledge Project. 2019. "Public Knowledge Project." Simon Fraser University Library. https://pkp.sfu.ca.**
The Public Knowledge Project was established in 1998 by John Willinsky at the University of British Columbia. Since its inception, the project has expanded and evolved to include multiple universities in North America, but it is located primarily at Simon Fraser University. The Public Knowledge Project creates open source software, such as Open Journal Systems, Open Monograph Press, and Open Conference Systems. Additionally, it conducts research in order to improve scholarly publishing. The core team is made up of approximately twenty developers, researchers, students, librarians, and staff.

**Ridley, Michael, Clare Appavoo, and Sabina Pagotto. 2014. "Seeing the Forest and the Trees: The Integrated Digital Scholarship Ecosystem (IDSE) Project of the Canadian Research Knowledge Network (CRKN)." Chicago: Association of College & Research Libraries (ACRL). http://www.ala.org/acrl/sites/ala.org.acrl/files/content/conferences/confsandpreconfs/2015/Ridley_Appavoo_Pagotto.pdf.**
Ridley, Appavoo, and Pagotto present the Integrated Digital Scholarship Ecosystem (IDSE) project of the Canadian Research Knowledge Network (CRKN). The CRKN is a partnership of 75 Canadian universities working toward increasing digital content for research in Canada, which has a significant impact on Canadian research and academic libraries. This article relates the findings of a study on digital scholarship within these institutions, focusing specifically on the first phase of the IDSE, an initiative dedicated to advancing research in Canada by exploring the state of the digital landscape. Some important issues addressed in phase one are the role of the library, preservation, development of a research agenda, promotion and tenure, and ways to address and sustain the voice of a community. IDSE, according to the authors, is an ecosystem that helps point out the areas of digital scholarship that need to be addressed.

**Right to Research Coalition. 2017. "Right to Research Coalition." http://www.righttoresearch.org.**
The Right to Research Coalition was founded in 2009 in order to promote open scholarly publishing. The group agrees that no student should be denied

access to information that they need for study on the basis that their institution cannot afford to pay the high subscription fees. It argues that open information improves education, democratizes access, improves the impact of scholarship, and advances research. The Right to Research Coalition now represents almost seven million students across the world. They work to educate and advocate for the universal adoption of open access policies.

**Scholarly Publishing and Academic Resources Coalition. 2019. "SPARC: The Scholarly Publishing and Academic Resources Coalition." http://sparcopen.org.**

The Scholarly Publishing and Academic Resources Coalition (SPARC) aims to democratize access to knowledge by opening up the dissemination of research outputs and educational materials. SPARC works with interested parties to create opportunities to promote change, both in infrastructure and culture, and make 'open' the default for research and education. SPARC has more than 200 members across North America and is closely affiliated with other international open access organizations. The group values collective action and collaboration. Some of its current initiatives include organizing International Open Access Week, creating campus open access policies, and recognizing work in the field with the SPARC Innovator Award.

**Social Sciences and Humanities Research Council. 2019. "*Dialogue*, SSHRC's Newsletter." http://www.sshrc-crsh.gc.ca/about-au_su-jet/publications/dialogue-eng.aspx.**

The Social Sciences and Humanities Research Council (SSHRC) is an organization that represents the interests of both public and private sectors of academia and is a large facilitator of research through grants and fellowships granted to Canadian researchers. SSHRC has a wide network of faculty; postdoctoral, doctoral, and masters students; as well as other researchers and research partnerships. The SSHRC eNewsletter, *Dialogue*, publishes news related to academia and funding, as well as news on various opportunities and deadlines. *Dialogue* also publishes about original research undertaken both in Canada and around the world.

**University of Cambridge. n.d. "Open Access at the University of Cambridge." https://www.cam.ac.uk/research/research-at-cambridge/open-access.**

The University of Cambridge hosts an open access repository of scholarly research outputs, ranging from data sets and media collections to articles and conference presentations. It is the aim of the university that this archive help make scholarship widely accessible. The repository is supported by an

Open Access team and an Open Data team, both of which assist in making research widely and freely available.

**Wikimedia Foundation. 2019. "Wikipedia: About." https://en.wikipedia. org/wiki/Wikipedia:About.**
Wikipedia is a multilingual, online, open access encyclopedia. The foundational principle of Wikipedia is that the encyclopedia is developed from a neutral point of view that anyone can use, edit, and distribute. Wikipedia is written collaboratively, mostly by anonymous volunteers. Since its conception in 2001, Wikipedia has grown into one of the most frequently referenced websites, with more than 38 million articles and 374 million unique visitors each month.

### B. Reference List

Access2Research. 2019. "Access2Research." https://en.wikipedia.org/wiki/Access2Research.

African Copyright and Access to Knowledge Project. 2019. "African Copyright and Access to Knowledge Project (ACA2K)." https://www.idrc.ca/en/project/african-copyright-and-access-knowledge-network-aca2k.

Akada Network. 2014. "Akada Network." https://www.facebook.com/akadanetwork/.

Alliance for Taxpayer Access. 2019. "Alliance for Taxpayer Access." http://www.taxpayeraccess.org.

American Academic & Scholarly Research Center. 2019. "American Academic & Scholarly Research Center." http://aasrc.org.

Association for Computers and the Humanities. 2019. "Association for Computers and the Humanities." http://ach.org.

Australasian Open Access Strategy Group. 2019. "Australasian Open Access Strategy Group." https://aoasg.org.au.

Authors Alliance. 2019. "Authors Alliance." https://www.authorsalliance.org.

Berkman Klein Center for Internet & Society at Harvard University. 2018. "Harvard Open Access Project." https://cyber.law.harvard.edu/research/hoap.

Bioline International. 2019. "Bioline International." http://www.bioline.org.br.

Canadian Association of Research Libraries. n.d. "Canadian Association of Research Libraries." http://www.carl-abrc.ca.

Center for Open Science. 2019. "Center for Open Science." https://cos.io.

Center for the Study of the Public Domain. 2019. "Center for the Study of the Public Domain." Duke University School of Law. https://law.duke.edu/cspd/.

Coalition for Open Access Policy Institutions. 2018. "Coalition for Open Access Policy Institutions." https://sparcopen.org/coapi/.

Compute Canada. 2014. "Sustainable Planning for Advanced Research Computing (SPARC)." News release, June 23. https://www.compute-canada.ca/news/compute-canada-announces-sustainable-planning-for-advanced-research-computing-sparc/.

Confederation of Open Access Repositories. 2019. "Confederation of Open Access Repositories." https://www.coar-repositories.org.

European University Association. 2019. "European University Association: The Voice of Europe's Universities." http://www.eua.be.

Federation for the Humanities and Social Sciences. 2019a. "Issues." Federation for the Humanities and Social Sciences / Fédération des sciences humaines. http://www.ideas-idees.ca/issues/open-access-aspp.

———. 2019b. "Our Members." Federation for the Humanities and Social Sciences / Fédération des sciences humaines. http://www.ideas-idees.ca/about/members.

FinnOA. 2008. "Finnish Open Access Working Group (FinnOA)." http://www.openaccess.fi/info/english.html.

FORCE11. 2019. "FORCE11." https://www.force11.org.

Foundation for Open Access Statistics. 2013. "Foundation for Open Access Statistics." http://www.foastat.org.

Free Knowledge Institute. 2015. "Free Knowledge Institute." http://freeknowledge.eu.

German Research Foundation. 2019. "Alliance of Science Organisations in Germany." http://www.dfg.de/en/dfg_profile/alliance/.

Government of Canada. 2015a. "Digital Canada 150 2.0." Industry Canada. http://www.digitaleconomy.gc.ca/eic/site/028.nsf/eng/home.

International Community for Open Research and Education. n.d. "Welcome to ICORE, the International Community for Open Research and Open Education." http://www.icore-online.org.

International Federation of Library Associations and Institutions. 2011. "IFLA Open Access Taskforce Established." News release, October 11. https://www.ifla.org/news/ifla-open-access-taskforce-established.

Knowledge Exchange. n.d. "KE: Knowledge Exchange." http://www.knowledge-exchange.info.

Leadership Council for Digital Research Infrastructure. 2014. "'Think Piece' on a DI Roadmap." http://digitalleadership.ca/wp-content/uploads/2014/01/DI-Roadmap-Think-Piece-Jan-2014.pdf.

Lithuanian Research Library Consortium. 2019. "Lithuanian Research Library Consortium." http://www.lmba.lt/en.

Max Planck Society. 2019a. "Berlin Declaration on Open Access to Knowledge in the Sciences and Humanities." http://openaccess.mpg.de/Berlin-Declaration.

——. 2019b. "Max Planck Society." https://openaccess.mpg.de.

Mediterranean Open Access Network. n.d. "MEDOANET 2012: Mediterranean Open Access Network." http://www.medoanet.eu.

Open Access India. 2019. "Open Access India." http://openaccessindia.org.

Open-Access.net. 2019. "Open Access: Free Access to Scientific Information." https://www.open-access.net/startseite/.

Open Access Network. 2019. "Open Access Network." http://openaccessnetwork.org.

Open Access Scholarly Publishers Association. 2019. "Open Access Scholarly Publishers Association." http://oaspa.org.

Open Access Working Group. n.d. "Open Access Working Group." http://access.okfn.org.

OpenAIRE. 2019. "OpenAIRE." https://www.openaire.eu.

Open Humanities Alliance. n.d. "Open Humanities Alliance." http://openhumanitiesalliance.org.

Open Knowledge International. n.d. "Open Knowledge International." https://okfn.org.

Open Scholarship Initiative. 2019. "Open Scholarship Initiative." http://osiglobal.org/.

Organisation for Economic Cooperation and Development (OECD). 2015. "Making Open Science a Reality." *OECD Science, Technology and Industry Policy Papers* 25. Paris: OECD Publishing.

Public Knowledge Project. 2019. "Public Knowledge Project." Simon Fraser University Library. https://pkp.sfu.ca.

Ridley, Michael, Clare Appavoo, and Sabina Pagotto. 2014. "Seeing the Forest and the Trees: The Integrated Digital Scholarship Ecosystem (IDSE) Project of the Canadian Research Knowledge Network (CRKN)." Chicago: Association of College & Research Libraries (ACRL). http://www.ala.org/acrl/sites/ala.org.acrl/files/content/conferences/confsandpreconfs/2015/Ridley_Appavoo_Pagotto.pdf.

Right to Research Coalition. 2017. "Right to Research Coalition." http://www.righttoresearch.org.

Scholarly Publishing and Academic Resources Coalition. 2019. "SPARC: The Scholarly Publishing and Academic Resources Coalition." http://sparcopen.org.

Social Sciences and Humanities Research Council. 2019. "*Dialogue*, SSHRC's Newsletter." http://www.sshrc-crsh.gc.ca/about-au_sujet/publications/dialogue-eng.aspx.

University of Cambridge. n.d. "Open Access at the University of Cambridge." https://www.cam.ac.uk/research/research-at-cambridge/open-access.

Wikimedia Foundation. 2019. "Wikipedia: About." https://en.wikipedia.org/wiki/Wikipedia:About.

# III. Knowledge in Action

## 1. Knowledge Mobilization

Knowledge mobilization refers to the dissemination of research output, as well as its uptake by groups other than the researcher or researchers who developed it. Authors in this category acknowledge the gap found between the amount of research produced and how much of this knowledge is actually implemented into practice. They offer a number of strategic knowledge mobilization steps to address this issue, including measures such as developing optimal implementation strategies through planned action theories (Graham, Tetroe, and KT Theories Research Group 2007), strengthening the link between research, policy, and practice (Cooper and Levin 2010), and working through the various theoretical models of knowledge utilization (Landry, Amara, and Lamari 2001). Anderson and McLachlan (2015) advocate for knowledge mobilization as a practice that challenges the models of knowledge transfer that often reign in academic environments and can manifest through a hierarchical transmission of knowledge from the top down. This hierarchical structure is challenged by giving voice to typically marginalized groups (mostly those outside of academia) through establishing productive channels of communication (Anderson and McLachlan 2015). Other approaches implement fairly novel methods, such as network analysis, in order to measure knowledge mobilization in community-based organizations—a technique that enables organizations to serve as a reliable voice for the various groups they represent (Gainforth et al. 2014). Notably, most knowledge mobilization strategies unfold in interdisciplinary realms where collaborative practices between different groups are the founding element of successful practices (Cooper and Levin 2010). Landry, Amara, and Lamri (2001) conduct research on how faculty members in Canadian universities promote the utilization of their research. Present theories on knowledge utilization generally fall into three categories: instrumental use (knowledge used for decision making and problem solving), conceptual use (knowledge that provides new ideas, theories, or hypotheses), and symbolic use (knowledge used for legitimizing views); however, the authors argue that these categories fail to take into account all the complexities of knowledge utilization, and therefore call for new theories for measuring this process. Authors in this category highlight the value of implementing knowledge mobilization strategies, and delve into possibilities, challenges, and solutions based on concrete examples that employ both new and old theoretical frameworks.

## A. Annotations

Anderson, Colin R., and Stéphane M. McLachlan. 2015. "Transformative Research as Knowledge Mobilization: Transmedia, Bridges, and Layers." *Action Research* 14(3): 295–317. DOI: https://doi.org/10.1177/ 1476750315616684.

Anderson and McLachlan attempt to create a transformative research paradigm that champions knowledge mobilization over the institutional knowledge transfer model, in which the scientific community occupies the elite central stage and transmits knowledge from the top down. Primarily, this mobilization is done by disrupting power relations and including typically marginalized agents, such as farmers and other community-based researchers, within the scientific conversation. The authors conduct a case study on the Participatory *Action Research* (PAR) program in the Canadian Prairies in order to highlight the processes involved. They suggest that shifting to knowledge mobilization is a messy but necessary step in order to achieve inclusive, useful, and reflective scholarship and practice. The authors employ three major strategies in order to bring the academic and nonacademic actors involved in the project closer together. The first is layering, which involves determining the right language and the level of detail and complexity in a way that would be accessible to all parties involved instead of adhering to alienating jargon. The second communications strategy—building bridges—works to overcome the boundaries that separate knowledge mobilizers in terms of their 'epistemological, discursive, and disciplinary divides' (307). This can be as simple as meeting in an informal, friendly setting where all parties are encouraged to voice their opinions in a respectful environment. The final knowledge mobilization strategy, transmedia, allows actors to present their ideas through different media formats in order to communicate them more effectively and to a wider audience. Although this study succeeds at bringing academic and community-based researchers into communication with each other, the institutional hierarchy that still operates according to a knowledge transfer model (versus a knowledge mobilization model) often undermines these efforts.

Cooper, Amanda, and Ben Levin. 2010. "Some Canadian Contributions to Understanding Knowledge Mobilisation." *Evidence & Policy: A Journal of Research, Debate and Practice* 6(3): 351–69. DOI: https://doi.org/10.1332/174426410X524839.

Cooper and Levin describe the challenges associated with knowledge mobilization and suggest various methods to overcome them. They define knowledge mobilization as an emerging field dedicated to strengthening the links between research, policy, and practice across various disciplines and sectors. The authors assert that gaps between research, policy, and practice are the result of two major factors: the absence of research impact evidence, and the fact that knowledge mobilization is often interdisciplinary, and therefore lacks a formalized system. Cooper and Levin point out that the Canada Institutes of Health Research (CIHR) and the Canadian Health Services Research Foundation (CHSRF) have supported the majority of contributions to knowledge mobilization. They assert that collaborative practices are vital to knowledge mobilization, since overall improvement depends on different groups working together. The authors also present the Research Supporting Practice in Education (RSPE) program, which is dedicated to empirical studies in various educational settings. They conclude by providing a list of quick, attainable practices that can improve knowledge mobilization in various environments.

Gainforth, Heather L., Amy E. Latimer-Cheung, Spencer Moore, Peter Athanasopoulos, and Kathleen A. Martin Ginis. 2014. "Using Network Analysis to Understand Knowledge Mobilization in a Community-based Organization." *International Journal of Behavioral Medicine* 22(3): 292–300. DOI: https://www.doi.org/10.1007/s12529-014-9430-6.

Gainforth et al. present a method for measuring the feasibility of utilizing network analysis to trace the flow of knowledge mobilization within a community-based organization. They address the challenges that arise in conducting network analysis in community-based organizations and research environments and provide practical and ethical solutions. Based on a case study conducted on a specific group operating within the organization, the authors demonstrate that network analsyis is able to generate a rich description of the processes of a community-based organization that practises knowledge mobilization. The major limitations of the study include the lack of a comparison group in relation to which they can test the efficiency of their method, the fact that network analysis is only able to provide information about a specific moment within a study rather than an ongoing process, and the fact that the researchers were unable to retest their findings with the network analysis instrument and had to take the results at face value. Despite these limitations, the authors assert that network analysis is a rich knowledge mobilization method, useful for helping community-based organizations attain their goal of being a reliable voice for the various communities they work with.

Graham, Ian D., Jacqueline Tetroe, and KT Theories Research Group. 2007. "Some Theoretical Underpinnings of Knowledge Translation." *Academic Emergency Medicine* 14(11): 936–41. https://onlinelibrary. wiley.com/doi/full/10.1111/j.1553-2712.2007.tb02369.x.

Graham and Tetroe determine the primary planned action theories within the science implementation field. The motivation for this study stems from a desire to remediate the gap found in implementing research into practice, and from recognizing that implementation practices themselves are more successful when situated within a conceptual framework. The study was carried out in the fields of education, health sciences, management, and social sciences, where 31 planned action theories were identified and analyzed for their origin, meaning, logical consistency, generalizability and parsimony, testability, and usefulness. The authors assert that the selection of a model should be based on a review of how its elements relate to the action categories that were derived from their theory analyses, and that the specific needs of end users should be an integral part of the planning and evaluation process. Graham and Tetroe point out that many models have not yet been tested, and urge those who use them to record and share their experiences in order to enrich research in the field.

Keen, Peter, and Margaret Tan. 2009. "Knowledge Fusion: A Framework for Extending the Rigor and Relevance of Knowledge Management." In *Selected Readings on Information Technology Management: Contemporary Issues*, edited by George Kelley, 358–74. Hershey, PA: IGI Global. DOI: https://www.doi.org/10.4018/978-1-60566-092-9. ch020.

Keen and Tan propose a knowledge fusion framework for leveraging their work in order for it to serve as a vehicle for knowledge mobilization in the knowledge management field. They point out major gaps in existing knowledge, and assert that a clear distinction between knowledge management and knowledge mobilization ought to be maintained in order to produce a meaningful discourse instead of perpetuating the blurry definitions of the past. The authors argue that knowledge management itself is axiomatic rather than definitional. Partitioning these multiple domains is necessary to link them to the existing body of knowledge and to identify their theories and practices. The four main partitions of knowledge fusion are knowledge management, knowledge mobilization, knowledge embodiments, and knowledge regimes. These partitions are aimed at making links to the existing body of knowledge and practice related to knowledge management. The authors claim that this framework is an attempt to contextualize and shape knowledge management rather than to homogenize it or to serve as a model or theory.

**Landry, Réjean, Nabil Amara, and Moktar Lamari. 2001. "Utilization of Social Science Research Knowledge in Canada."** *Research Policy* **30(2): 333–49. DOI: https://doi.org/10.1016/S0048-7333(00)00081-0.**
Landry, Amara, and Lamari explore the extent to which social science research is used in Canada, how it is distributed across disciplines within the field, and what determines the utilization of this research. Instead of basing their studies on tracing how policymakers employ this knowledge, the authors focus on how individual researchers promote the usage of their research. The authors provide an overview of existing theoretical models of knowledge utilization, including the science push model, the demand pull model, the dissemination model, and the interaction model. They conduct a survey of 3,252 faculty members from 55 Canadian universities, who were asked about the extent of the utilization of their research. The authors also study whether there is a difference in this utilization across social science disciplines; the results show that research carried out in professional social sciences, such as social work and industrial relations, is more frequently used than in disciplinary social sciences, such as anthropology, economics, political science, and sociology. They conclude that knowledge utilization primarily depends on the behaviour of researchers and the users' context rather than the research product itself. Their findings also show that existing theories are inefficient in measuring the utilization of research since the process is far more complex than these theories propose.

**Lavis, John N. 2006. "Research, Public Policymaking, and Knowledge-Translation Processes: Canadian Efforts to Build Bridges."** *Journal of Continuing Education in the Health Professions* **26(1): 37–45. DOI: https://doi.org/10.1002/chp.49.**
Lavis addresses the processes involved in public policymaking when carrying out institutional arrangements, and the need for timely knowledge translation in these cases. The author conducts research in the health sciences field, and observes that public policymakers are sometimes asked to make fairly quick decisions with a lack of relevant high-quality research at hand. He argues that knowledge translation can make meaningful connections between research and public policymaking in a number of ways: through systematic reviews that address the questions asked by public policymakers; through 'push' efforts by researchers of interested parties that present research about a certain issue to the policymakers; through the 'user pull' method by

these same groups that can help policymakers identify the relevant research in relation to a topic they are working with; and through the 'friendly front ends' method that stands for systematic reviews having a graded-entry format. Lavis strongly advocates bridging the gap between research and policymaking by improving knowledge translation processes.

**Orlikowski, Wanda J. 2002. "Knowing in Practice: Enacting a Collective Capability in Distributed Organizing."** *Organization Science* **13(3): 249–73. DOI: https://doi.org/10.1287/orsc.13.3.249.2776.**
Orlikowski presents a knowledge-in-practice perspective on successful work in complex organizational environments, with a focus on the process involved in the effective distribution of organization in global product development settings. Her main argument is that effective work is the result of properly distributed organizational knowledge carried out in everyday practices. She conducts a case study on Kappa, a large software company headquartered in the Netherlands with branches in other countries. Apart from certain variables involved in success, such as creativity, leadership, and strategic positioning, the author argues that overall success is primarily grounded in the way in which employees go about everyday practices related to 'temporal, geographic, political, cultural, technical, and social boundaries they routinely encounter in their work' (256). Specifically, success is decided by the ways that employees navigate and negotiate between these boundaries. According to Orlikowski, the social aspect plays a vital role in successfully managing projects, and frequent communication ensures that participants are aware and up to date regarding their work and work distribution. She concludes that Kappa owes much of its success to knowing how to efficiently distribute product development and organize knowledge in a continuous and stable manner.

**Phipps, David. 2012. "A Report Detailing the Development of a University-Based Knowledge Mobilization Unit that Enhances Research Outreach and Engagement."** *Scholarly and Research Communication* **2(2): n.p. DOI: https://doi.org/10.22230/src.2011v2n2a31.**
Phipps shares his perspective on knowledge mobilization as a practitioner who has been delivering various knowledge mobilization services in a university-based setting for more than five years. He defines knowledge mobilization as 'a suite of services, actions, and activities that work together to support research outreach and engagement' (2), one that connects researchers and decision-makers. Phipps describes six services developed by the knowledge mobilization unit that fall under four general methods: producer

push, user pull, knowledge exchange, and co-production. He argues that a successful knowledge mobilization strategy may be achieved when researchers and decision-makers communicate effectively, and are supported by trained brokers who can utilize the appropriate knowledge mobilization services in order to meet decision-makers' needs. Phipps provides general recommendations that may help in a knowledge mobilization action plan, including finding appropriate leaders, collecting data that may serve as a basis for evaluation over time, finding grants for seed funding, and hiring the right knowledge brokers.

**Ward, Vicky, Allan House, and Susan Hamer. 2009. "Developing a Framework for Transferring Knowledge into Action: A Thematic Analysis of the Literature."** *Journal of Health Services Research & Policy* **14(3): 156–64. DOI: https://doi.org/10.1258/jhsrp.2009.008120.**
Ward, House, and Hamer attempt to categorize the scholarship on knowledge transfer into an organized conceptual framework. This is done by identifying 28 modes of knowledge transfer literature and subjecting them to thematic analysis that would help identify the processes involved in transferring knowledge into action. According to the authors, the five main components involved in knowledge transfer are problem identification and communication, knowledge/research development and selection, context analysis, knowledge transfer activities or interventions, and knowledge/research utilization. These five components are generally categorized into three knowledge transfer processes, which can be linear, cyclical, or dynamic multidirectional processes. The authors state that the importance and applicability of these components within the conceptual framework is unknown, which is why their study utilizes this framework as a basis for drawing research from various case studies. Ideally, they hope to create a model that can serve as an infrastructure for planning and evaluating the processes involved in knowledge transfer.

### B. Reference List

Anderson, Colin R., and Stéphane M. McLachlan. 2015. "Transformative Research as Knowledge Mobilization: Transmedia, Bridges, and Layers." *Action Research* 14(3): 295–317. DOI: https://doi.org/10.1177/1476750315616684.

Cooper, Amanda, and Ben Levin. 2010. "Some Canadian Contributions to Understanding Knowledge Mobilisation." *Evidence & Policy: A Journal of Research, Debate and Practice* 6(3): 351–69. DOI: https://doi.org/10.1332/174426410X524839.

Gainforth, Heather L., Amy E. Latimer-Cheung, Spencer Moore, Peter Athanasopoulos, and Kathleen A. Martin Ginis. 2014. "Using Network Analysis to Understand Knowledge Mobilization in a Community-based Organization." *International Journal of Behavioral Medicine* 22(3): 292–300. DOI: https://www.doi.org/10.1007/s12529-014-9430-6.

Graham, Ian D., Jacqueline Tetroe, and KT Theories Research Group. 2007. "Some Theoretical Underpinnings of Knowledge Translation." *Academic Emergency Medicine* 14(11): 936–41. https://onlinelibrary.wiley.com/doi/full/10.1111/j.1553-2712.2007.tb02369.x.

Keen, Peter, and Margaret Tan. 2009. "Knowledge Fusion: A Framework for Extending the Rigor and Relevance of Knowledge Management." In *Selected Readings on Information Technology Management: Contemporary Issues*, edited by George Kelley, 358–74. Hershey, PA: IGI Global. DOI: https://www.doi.org/10.4018/978-1-60566-092-9.ch020.

Landry, Réjean, Nabil Amara, and Moktar Lamari. 2001. "Utilization of Social Science Research Knowledge in Canada." *Research Policy* 30(2): 333–49. DOI: https://doi.org/10.1016/S0048-7333(00)00081-0.

Lavis, John N. 2006. "Research, Public Policymaking, and Knowledge-Translation Processes: Canadian Efforts to Build Bridges." *Journal of Continuing Education in the Health Professions* 26(1): 37–45. DOI: https://doi.org/10.1002/chp.49.

Orlikowski, Wanda J. 2002. "Knowing in Practice: Enacting a Collective Capability in Distributed Organizing." *Organization Science* 13(3): 249–73. DOI: https://doi.org/10.1287/orsc.13.3.249.2776.

Phipps, David. 2012. "A Report Detailing the Development of a University-Based Knowledge Mobilization Unit that Enhances Research Outreach and Engagement." *Scholarly and Research Communication* 2(2): n.p. DOI: https://doi.org/10.22230/src.2011v2n2a31.

Ward, Vicky, Allan House, and Susan Hamer. 2009. "Developing a Framework for Transferring Knowledge into Action: A Thematic Analysis of the Literature." *Journal of Health Services Research & Policy* 14(3): 156–64. DOI: https://doi.org/10.1258/jhsrp.2009.008120.

## 2. Data Management

Data management concerns effective methods for organizing data and documents through the application of a systematic mechanism. The works included here address metadata, database management, and data visualization (Fear 2011; Hedges, Hasan, and Blanke 2007). Some articles investigate ethical uses of data obtained from research, as well as accountability mechanisms and guidelines to ensure that collected data is properly managed, stored, and preserved (Krier and Strasser 2014; Lewis 2010; Romary 2012; Surkis and Read 2015; Wilson et al. 2011). The resources in this category address what can be done with data collected from research projects and how research can be conducted more efficiently, with specific attention paid to data preservation and curation strategies (Krier and Strasser 2014; Yakel 2007). Overall, the resources address the life cycle of data management and the necessary infrastructural mechanisms for effective governance of digital information.

### A. Annotations

**Akers, Katherine G., and Jennifer Doty. 2013. "Disciplinary Differences in Faculty Research Data Management Practices and Perspectives." *International Journal of Digital Curation* 8(2): 5–26. http://ijdc.net/index.php/ijdc/article/view/263.**
Akers and Doty conduct a survey on disciplinary differences in faculty research data management practices and perspectives. The authors divide faculty members into four broad research domains: arts and humanities, social sciences, medical sciences, and basic sciences. The percentages of faculty per area are considered, as well as attitudes toward open access data and familiarity with basic terms of data management. The survey also seeks to understand faculty attitudes toward digital documentation and preservation. Both authors worked to create Shibboleth authentication access for Emory University researchers to the DMPTool that walks researchers through the creation of data management plans for grant proposals. The authors also point out that OpenEmory, the current institutional repository, does not warrant further research data development and that more effort could be focused on facilitating the deposit of data in disciplinary repositories or setting up instances of the Dataverse Network. Serious consideration of both similarities and dissimilarities among disciplines can guide academic librarians in the development of a range of data management related services.

Corrall, Sheila, Mary Anne Kennan, and Wasseem Afzal. 2013. "Bibliometrics and Research Data Management Services: Emerging Trends in Library Support for Research." *Library Trends* 61(3): 636–74. DOI: http://www.doi.org/10.1353/lib.2013.0005.

Corrall, Kennan, and Afzal analyze current trends in library support for research. Funding bodies are increasingly viewing libraries as 'bottomless pits' rather than self-evident positive support for researchers, especially as the Web becomes more accessible and user friendly (637).[5] According to the authors, e-research should provide libraries with the impetus to extend their services beyond the material archive. Libraries in the U.S., such as those at MIT, are quicker to adapt to digital services; in 2009, the Association of Research Libraries found 21 libraries that already provide infrastructure or support for e-science and another 23 that intend to do so. The authors conducted a questionnaire that asked respondents about their organizations, bibliometrics, research data management, and future plans. Corrall, Kennan, and Afzal suggest that academic librarians involved in research support need to understand governmental and institutional research agendas so that they can support strategy and policy development and implementation.

**Crompton, Constance, Cole Mash, and Raymond G. Siemens. 2015. "Playing Well with Others: The Social Edition and Computational Collaboration." *Scholarly and Research Communication* 6(3). n.p. DOI: https://doi.org/10.22230/src.2015v6n3a111.

Crompton, Mash, and Siemens study the use of microdata formats as a means of including larger groups of researchers and editors working on a digital social edition. They also provide readily parsable data about the content of *A Social Edition of the Devonshire Manuscript*, the main object of their study. The authors argue that adopting linked data standards allows for an interconnection between texts and virtual collaboration across projects and scholars. Crompton, Mash, and Siemens explain how Resource Descriptions Framework in Attributes (RDFa) is well suited for academic projects, and elaborate on the idea of encoding for the Semantic Web. They discuss technical decisions that would shift the focus of the encoder on data entry instead of the technical details of encoding. In their conclusion, the authors suggest that with the RDFa enhancement, *A Social Edition of the Devonshire Manuscript* will provoke new research questions about the culture and contexts of the Tudor court.

---

[5] Corrall, Kennan, and Afzal are quoting from *Beyond Survival: Managing Academic Libraries in Transition* (2007), edited by Elizabeth J. Wood, Rush Miller, and Amy Knapp (Westport, CT: Libraries Unlimited), 3.

**Fear, Kathleen. 2011. "'You Made It, You Take Care of It': Data Management as Personal Information Management."** *International Journal of Digital Curation* 6(2): 53–77. DOI: https://doi.org/10.2218/ijdc.v6i2.190.

Fear's article explores data management at the University of Michigan, investigates the factors that have shaped the practices of researchers, and seeks to understand the motives for extending or inhibiting changes in data management practices. She argues that institutions should have an interest in protecting the data of their researchers. For Fear, improving infrastructure for data sharing and accessibility is one way of improving data management standards. She conducts a survey with questions such as whether the researcher believes data to be personal information, how researchers manage their data over the short term, what kind of data management plans are provided when researchers apply for funding, what the methods for preserving data are over the long term, and the extent of their general familiarity with the basics of data management. The study concludes with the observation that data management is part of a continuum of processes that tend to blur together as researchers move from document to document. According to Fear, researchers regard separating data management from other research activities as confusing and counterproductive.

**Harth, Andreas, Katja Hose, and Ralf Schenkel, eds. 2014.** *Linked Data Management.* **Boca Raton, FL: CRC Press.**

Harth, Hose, and Schenkel edit an anthology that covers the concept of linked data management. The anthology begins by describing how modern computers still struggle with the idiosyncratic structure and semantics of natural language due to ambiguity. The authors outline many of the key concepts in emerging linked data management systems, including RDF vocabularies and foundational terms such as the Semantic Web. A list of SPARQL and OWL queries are given, and the authors state that the novel Web of Data requires new techniques and ways of thinking about databases, distributed computing, and information retrieval. Topics range from the digital architecture of linked data applications, to the Bigdata RDF Graph database, to different methods of query processing.

**Hedges, Mark, Adil Hasan, and Tobias Blanke. 2007. "Management and Preservation of Research Data with iRODS."** In *Proceedings of the ACM First Workshop on CyberInfrastructure: Information Management in eScience* **(CIMS '07), 17–22. New York: ACM. http://dl.acm.org/citation.cfm?id=1317358.**

Hedges, Hasan, and Blanke provide recommendations for the management and preservation of research data using the integrated Rule-Oriented Data

System (iRODS)—a recently developed automated, scalable digital preservation tool, equipped with Rule Engine, that allows the system to actively react to events. The Rule Engine enables iRODS data grids to exceed previous limitations through a flexible mechanism for implementing application-specific processing. The article provides information on driver requirements for managing large amounts of data, curation and preservation, automation, and transparency, as well as a list of rules used to implement preservation and data management. iRODS is capable of executing rules conditionally and can define multiple rules to implement alternative means toward the same goal simultaneously. The authors conclude that they will continue with an analysis of different preservation strategies and procedures currently followed by the Arts and Humanities Data Service archive in order to increase the automation and reliability of the preservation process.

Henty, Margaret, Belinda Weaver, Stephanie J. Bradbury, and Simon Porter. 2008. "Investigating Data Management Practices in Australian Universities." Australian Partnership for Sustainable Repositories (APSR). http://eprints.qut.edu.au/14549/1/14549.pdf.
Henty, Weaver, Bradbury, and Porter conduct a survey on changing expectations for the provision of data management infrastructure at Australian universities. Most of the respondents are academic staff, with significant postgraduate student participation and a low response rate from emeritus or adjunct professors. The questions asked of respondents are oriented toward researcher awareness of digital data, the types of digital data collected, the sizes of the data selections, the software used for analysis and manipulation of digital assets, and research data management plans. The questions also concern institutional responsibility and structure for data management, such as whether researchers outside the team are allowed to access shared research data, and how the data is accessed and used. Henty et al. compile data from the Queensland University of Technology, the University of Melbourne, and the University of Queensland.

Jackson, Michael J., Mario Antonioletti, Bartosz Dobrzelecki, and Neil Chue Hong. 2011. "Distributed Data Management with OGSA–DAI." In *Grid and Cloud Database Management*, edited by Sandro Fiore and Giovanni Aloisio, 63–86. Berlin and Heidelberg: Springer. DOI: https://doi.org/10.1007/978-3-642-20045-8_4.
Jackson, Antonioletti, Dobrzelecki, and Hong outline the OGSA-DAI framework for sharing and managing distributed data. The system can manage and share relational data, XML files, and RDF triples. The chapter provides basic definitions of workflows and how they are executed, list markers and how

they are used to group outputs, concurrent execution, and client requests, and discusses how to access the OGSA-DAI framework. Several graphs and taxonomies are provided to illustrate workflows and workflow execution. The authors suggest that data delivery is slower through web services than direct methods such as FTP and GridFTP, and outline OGSA-DAI's approach to security, distributed query processing, relational views, interoperability, performance requirements, and a list of related programs. Complete data abstraction is not possible with the program; however, it can be used to build higher-level capabilities and enhance distributed data management.

Jackson, Mike, Mario Antonioletti, Alastair Hume, Tobias Blanke, Gabriel Bodard, Mark Hedges, and Shrija Rajbhandari. 2009. "Building Bridges Between Islands of Data—An Investigation into Distributed Data Management in the Humanities." In *Proceedings of the 2009 Fifth IEEE International Conference on e-Science*, 33–39. Los Alamitos, CA: IEEE Computer Society. DOI: https://www.doi. org/10.1109/ e-Science.2009.13.

Jackson, Antonioletti, Hume, Blanke, Bodard, Hedges, and Rajbhandrari contribute their research to conference proceedings on digital data management of ancient and classical materials. The 'islands of data' they refer to are resources that are separate from larger repositories and often largely inaccessible. The authors discuss the LaQuAT project: an initiative that attempts to link and query ancient texts through cooperation of a group of diverse experts from different institutions. The article describes the databases constructed under the LaQuAT initiative, including Project Volterra, a database of Roman legal texts and associated metadata, and the HGV, a database of papyrological metadata in relational and TEI XML formats. Problems shared by initiatives such as these are the contamination of data by control characters, which can invalidate XML documents. Database drivers and lack of funds can also pose considerable roadblocks.

Johnston, Lisa, Meghan Lafferty, and Beth Petsan. 2012. "Training Researchers on Data Management: A Scalable, Cross-Disciplinary Approach." *Journal of eScience Librarianship* 1(2): 79–87. DOI: http:// dx.doi.org/10.7191/jeslib.2012.1012.

Johnston, Lafferty, and Petsan offer advice on how to train researchers in data management through a scalable, cross-disciplinary approach. They describe the curriculum, implementation, and results of research data management training offered by the University of Minnesota Libraries. The authors provide a description of Minnesota's 'Creating a Data Management Plan' workshop, which trains university faculty and researchers in the basics of file management, metadata standards, and data accessibility. The research team conducts a survey to understand workshop attendee roles, college affiliations, and the most useful parts of the workshop. The workshop leaders introduced a team-teaching approach that has had an overwhelmingly positive impact on the libraries' ability to respond to research data management needs.

**Jones, Sarah, Alexander Ball, and Çuna Ekmekcioglu. 2008. "The Data Audit Framework: A First Step in the Data Management Challenge."** *International Journal of Digital Curation* **3(2): 112–20. DOI: https:// doi.org/ 10.2218/ijdc.v3i2.62.**

Jones, Ball, and Ekmekcioglu provide a summary of their tool, the Data Audit Framework, which provides organizations with the means to identify, locate, and assess the current management of their research assets. The framework was designed to be applied without dedicated or specialist staff, making librarians suitable auditors for the program. Common issues plaguing data management at the institutional level are storage metadata, lack of awareness of data policy, and a lack of long-term legacy data mechanisms. The authors argue that institutional data policies with guidance on best practices in data creation, management, and long-term preservation would greatly assist departments in maintaining digital assets. They then provide a list of organizations from which departments can receive advice on best practices and services that can equip postgraduates and department members with the support needed to produce sound data management plans. The Data Audit Framework identifies main data issues, including areas in which data is at risk, and helps to develop solutions.

**Krier, Laura, and Carly A. Strasser. 2014.** *Data Management for Libraries: A LITA Guide.* **Chicago: ALA TechSource.**

Krier and Strasser's guide is intended for libraries in the early stages of initializing data management programs at their institutions. The opening chapters provide definitions of data management, different types of research data, curation, and life cycle. The guide contains advice on how to start a new service, and point-form questions to help the reader decide what kind of plan works best for their institution. The authors suggest identifying researchers who are receptive to working with the library and requesting assistance with data management plans or curation services. An overview of descriptive, administrative, and structural metadata is provided, along with an explanation of its role in data management. The differences between storage, preservation, and archiving are discussed, along with definitions of domains and institutional repositories. The authors then briefly describe the preservation process. The final chapters loosely cover access and data governance issues that have caused problems with data management in the past.

**Lewis, M. J. 2010. "Libraries and the Management of Research Data." In *Envisioning Future Academic Library Services*, edited by Sue McKnight, 145–68. London: Facet Publishing.**
Lewis begins his chapter by asking the rhetorical question of whether managing data is a job for university libraries. He argues that it is part of the role of the university library to help manage data as part of the global research knowledge base; however, the scale of the challenge requires concerted action by a range of stakeholders who are not all necessarily employees of the library. Lewis advises that institutions develop several policies for research data management that include developing library workforce data confidence, providing research data advice, developing research data awareness, teaching data literacy to postgraduate students, bringing data into undergraduate research-based learning, developing local data curation capacities, identifying required data skills with LIS schools, leading local data policy development, and influencing national data policy. Non-trivial research funding is needed for these initiatives and should be funneled through a primary 'pathfinder' phase of two years from major research councils. Lewis concludes with the observation that in order to develop such expertise, award-bearing programs (master's level training for data managers and career data scientists looking to pursue career track positions in data centres), short course accredited provision, and training for data librarians are needed.

**Research Data Canada. 2013. "Research Data Canada Response to *Capitalizing on Big Data: Towards a Policy Framework for Advancing Digital Scholarship in Canada*." http://www.rdc-drc.ca/wp-content/uploads/Research-Data-Canada-Response-to-the-Tri-Council-Consultation-on-Digital-Scholarship.pdf.**
This document is a response by Research Data Canada (RDC) to the release of the paper *Capitalizing on Big Data: Towards a Policy Framework for Advancing Digital Scholarship in Canada*. The RDC Steering Committee notes that the paper addresses three foundational elements crucial to digital scholarship in Canada: stewardship, coordination of stakeholder engagement, and development of capacity and future funding parameters. The document emphasizes the importance of coordination, and the need for clear coordination guidelines and policies, in order to achieve exemplary digital scholarship in

Canada. The authors suggest that the paper would be strengthened by addressing the four following areas: long-term data curation, development of data professionals, data generated by both government-based research and private research, and engagement with the international data community. The authors conclude by committing to full engagement in the ongoing discussion on behalf of Research Data Canada.

**Romary, Laurent. 2012. "Data Management in the Humanities."** *ERCIM News* **89, April 3. https://ercim-news.ercim.eu/en89/special/ data-management-in-the-humanities.**
Romary describes several data management tools in the humanities, beginning with HAL, a multidisciplinary open access archive for the deposition and circulation of scientific research documents, regardless of publication status. The author then shifts focus to the Digital Research Infrastructure for the Arts and Humanities (DARIAH) project, which aims to create a solid infrastructure to ensure the long-term stability of digital assets and the development of wide ranging services for the original tools. DARIAH depends on the notion of digital surrogates, which can be metadata records, scanned images, digital photographs, or any kind of extract or transformation of existing data. A unified data landscape for humanities research would stabilize the experience of researchers in circulating their data. Romary suggests that an adequate licensing policy must be defined to assert the legal conditions under which data assets can be disseminated; researchers involved with projects such as DARIAH need to converse with data providers on how to create a seamless data landscape.

**Sakr, Sherif, and Eric Pardede. 2012.** *Graph Data Management: Techniques and Applications.* **Hershey, PA: IGI Global.**
Sakr and Pardede's anthology of essays on techniques and applications of graph data management covers the use of graphs in the Semantic Web, social networks, biological networks, protein networks, chemical compounds, and business process models. The mechanisms for the main types of graph queries are prioritized throughout the collection, and both algorithmic and applied perspectives are considered. The book covers data storage, labelling schemes, data mining, matrix decomposition, and clustering vertices in weighted graphs. The editors claim that the anthology provides a comprehensive perspective on how graph databases can be effectively utilized in different situations.

Schmidt, Albrecht, Florian Waas, Martin Kersten, Michael J. Carey, Ioana Manolescu, and Ralph Busse. 2002. "XMark: A Benchmark for XML Data Management." In *Proceedings of the 28th International Conference on Very Large Data Bases* (VLDB '02), 974–85. https://dl.acm.org/citation.cfm?id=1287455.

Schmidt, Waas, Kersten, Carey, Manolescu, and Busse discuss emerging XMark technology and its role in XML data management. The authors argue that XML is currently in great need of new benchmarks to provide coverage for XML processing. The XMark benchmark features a toolkit for evaluating the retrieval performance of XML stores and query processors. It contains a workload specification, a scalable benchmark document, and a comprehensive set of queries designed to feature natural and intuitive semantics. The authors then provide an outline of XML query processing and related work, database description, hierarchical element structure in XML, as well as benchmark queries. Schmidt et al. conduct an experiment that uses six different systems to measure size/bulk load time ratios operating with XMark. The experiment concludes with an analysis of the essential primitives of XML processing in data management systems. The authors suggest that a W3C standard still needs to be defined, and that specifications should be updated.

Surkis, Alisa, and Kevin Read. 2015. "Research Data Management." *Journal of the Medical Library Association* 103(3): 154–56. DOI: https://www.doi.org/10.3163/1536-5050.103.3.011.

Surkis and Read provide an introductory resource for librarians who have had little or no experience with research data management. Basic concepts are defined, such as the fluidity of data in process and analysis as well as the data life cycle. The authors suggest that the line between publications and data is blurry, and that data management is essential in making data and publications discoverable. This, they argue, is a central task of the librarian. The authors then recommend the online course, MANTRA: Research Data Management Training, to introduce librarians and researchers to the topic.

Venugopal, Srikumar, Rajkumar Buyya, and Kotagiri Ramamohanarao. 2006. "A Taxonomy of Data Grids for Distributed Data Sharing, Management, and Processing." *ACM Computing Surveys* 38(1): 1–53. DOI: https://www.doi.org/10.1145/1132952.1132955.

Venugopal, Buyya, and Ramamohanarao provide a taxonomy of data grids for distributed data sharing, management, and processing. The authors propose that grid computing is a paradigm that proposes aggregating geographically distributed storage and network resources for unified, secure, and pervasive access to their combined capabilities. The study contains a comprehensive discussion on data replication, resource allocation, and scheduling. The authors focus on the architecture of data grids, as well as the fundamental requirements of data transport mechanisms, data replication systems, and resource allocation and job scheduling.

Ward, Catharine, Lesley Freiman, Sarah Jones, Laura Molloy, and Kellie Snow. 2011. "Making Sense: Talking Data Management with Researchers." *International Journal of Digital Curation* 6(2): 265–73. http://www.ijdc.net/article/view/197/262.

Ward, Freiman, Jones, Malloy, and Snow cover the goals and methods of Incremental, a program that identifies institutional requirements for digital research data management and pilots relevant infrastructure projects. The majority of projects piloted are those of soft infrastructure designed to break down the barriers that information professionals have unintentionally built with the use of specialist terminology. The authors note that researchers organize their data in *ad hoc* fashion, and that a lack of clear file naming practices and version control leads to later difficulties when legacy data needs to be retrieved. Language barriers and late starts to digital preservation are both substantial barriers in accessing legacy works and new research. Researchers indicated that they desire diverse, web-based modes of training (online tutorials, videos, and interactive learning resources). The authors argue that collating and repurposing existing guidance, training, and support will be effective in the long run.

Wilson, James A.J., Luis Martinez-Uribe, Michael A. Fraser, and Paul Jeffreys. 2011. "An Institutional Approach to Developing Research Data Management Infrastructure." *International Journal of Digital Curation* 6(2): 274–87. DOI: https://doi.org/10.2218/ijdc.v6i2.203.

Wilson, Martinez-Uribe, Fraser, and Jeffreys suggest that the University of Oxford needs to develop a centralized institutional platform for managing data through all stages of its life cycle that mirrors the framework of the institution in its highly federated structure. The Bodleian Libraries are currently developing a data repository system (Databank) that promises metadata management and resource discovery services. Researchers are given the role of guiding and validating each strand of data development as projects progress. Institutional data management is favoured over the establishment of national repositories. The authors conclude with the suggestion that data management may be better placed in, or integrated with, cloud-based services that are implemented in institutions but do not belong to them.

**Yakel, Elizabeth. 2007. "Digital Curation."** *OCLC Systems and Services: International Digital Library Perspectives* **23(4): 335–40. DOI: https:// doi.org/10.1108/10650750710831466.**
Yakel's article on digital curation provides an overview of the basic aspects necessary to ensure that digital objects will be maintained, preserved, and available for future use. Yakel remarks that digital curation is becoming an umbrella concept that includes digital preservation, data curation, records management, and digital asset management. She briefly traces the history of the term 'digital curation' from its first use in the National Science Foundation's 2003 report to a later report by Liz Lyon.[6] The Digital Curation Centre in the UK defines digital curation as the maintenance and adding of value to a trusted body of digital information for current and future use. Yakel provides many official definitions of the term for various official organizations. The article concludes by suggesting that the range of diverse definitions of digital curation has brought the scientific, educational, and professional communities together with governmental and private sector organizations.

### B. Reference List

Akers, Katherine G., and Jennifer Doty. 2013. "Disciplinary Differences in Faculty Research Data Management Practices and Perspectives." *International Journal of Digital Curation* 8(2): 5–26. http://ijdc.net/index. php/ijdc/article/view/263.

Corrall, Sheila, Mary Anne Kennan, and Wasseem Afzal. 2013. "Bibliometrics and Research Data Management Services: Emerging Trends in Library Support for Research." *Library Trends* 61(3): 636–74. DOI: http://www. doi.org/10.1353/lib.2013.0005.

Crompton, Constance, Cole Mash, and Raymond G. Siemens. 2015. "Playing Well with Others: The Social Edition and Computational Collaboration." *Scholarly and Research Communication* 6(3). n.p. DOI: https://doi. org/10.22230/src.2015v6n3a111.

Fear, Kathleen. 2011. "'You Made It, You Take Care of It': Data Management as Personal Information Management." *International Journal of Digital Curation* 6(2): 53–77. DOI: https://doi.org/10.2218/ijdc.v6i2.190.

---

[6] Liz Lyon, "Dealing with Data: Roles, Rights, Responsibilities and Relationships" (2007), Consultancy Report, https://purehost.bath.ac.uk/ws/portalfiles/por-tal/419529/dealing_with_data_report-final.pdf.

Harth, Andreas, Katja Hose, and Ralf Schenkel, eds. 2014. *Linked Data Management*. Boca Raton, FL: CRC Press.

Hedges, Mark, Adil Hasan, and Tobias Blanke. 2007. "Management and Preservation of Research Data with iRODS." In *Proceedings of the ACM First Workshop on CyberInfrastructure: Information Management in eScience (CIMS '07)*, 17–22. New York: ACM. http://dl.acm.org/citation.cfm?id=1317358.

Henty, Margaret, Belinda Weaver, Stephanie J. Bradbury, and Simon Porter. 2008. "Investigating Data Management Practices in Australian Universities." Australian Partnership for Sustainable Repositories (APSR). http://eprints.qut.edu.au/14549/1/14549.pdf.

Jackson, Michael J., Mario Antonioletti, Bartosz Dobrzelecki, and Neil Chue Hong. 2011. "Distributed Data Management with OGSA-DAI." In *Grid and Cloud Database Management*, edited by Sandro Fiore and Giovanni Aloisio, 63–86. Berlin and Heidelberg: Springer. DOI: https://doi.org/10.1007/978-3-642-20045-8_4.

Jackson, Mike, Mario Antonioletti, Alastair Hume, Tobias Blanke, Gabriel Bodard, Mark Hedges, and Shrija Rajbhandari. 2009. "Building Bridges between Islands of Data—An Investigation into Distributed Data Management in the Humanities." In *Proceedings of the 2009 Fifth IEEE International Conference on e-Science*, 33–39. Los Alamitos, CA: IEEE Computer Society. DOI: https://www.doi.org/10.1109/e-Science.2009.13.

Johnston, Lisa, Meghan Lafferty, and Beth Petsan. 2012. "Training Researchers on Data Management: A Scalable, Cross-Disciplinary Approach." *Journal of eScience Librarianship* 1(2): 79–87. DOI: http://dx.doi.org/10.7191/jeslib.2012.1012.

Jones, Sarah, Alexander Ball, and Çuna Ekmekcioglu. 2008. "The Data Audit Framework: A First Step in the Data Management Challenge." *International Journal of Digital Curation* 3(2): 112–20. DOI: https://doi.org/10.2218/ijdc.v3i2.62.

Krier, Laura, and Carly A. Strasser. 2014. *Data Management for Libraries: A LITA Guide*. Chicago: ALA TechSource.

Lewis, M. J. 2010. "Libraries and the Management of Research Data." In *Envisioning Future Academic Library Services*, edited by Sue McKnight, 145–68. London: Facet Publishing.

Research Data Canada. 2013. "Research Data Canada Response to *Capitalizing on Big Data: Towards a Policy Framework for Advancing Digital Scholarship in Canada*." http://www.rdc-drc.ca/wp-content/uploads/Research-Data-Canada-Response-to-the-Tri-Council-Consultation-on-Digital-Scholarship.pdf.

Romary, Laurent. 2012. "Data Management in the Humanities." *ERCIM News* 89, April 3. https://ercim-news.ercim.eu/en89/special/data-management-in-the-humanities.

Sakr, Sherif, and Eric Pardede. 2012. *Graph Data Management: Techniques and Applications*. Hershey, PA: IGI Global.

Schmidt, Albrecht, Florian Waas, Martin Kersten, Michael J. Carey, Ioana Manolescu, and Ralph Busse. 2002. "XMark: A Benchmark for XML Data Management." In *Proceedings of the 28th International Conference on Very Large Data Bases* (*VLDB '02*), 974–85. https://dl.acm.org/citation.cfm?id=1287455.

Surkis, Alisa, and Kevin Read. 2015. "Research Data Management." *Journal of the Medical Library Association* 103(3): 154–56. DOI: https://www.doi.org/10.3163/1536-5050.103.3.011.

Venugopal, Srikumar, Rajkumar Buyya, and Kotagiri Ramamohanarao. 2006. "A Taxonomy of Data Grids for Distributed Data Sharing, Management, and Processing." *ACM Computing Surveys* 38(1): 1–53. DOI: https://www.doi.org/10.1145/1132952.1132955.

Ward, Catharine, Lesley Freiman, Sarah Jones, Laura Molloy, and Kellie Snow. 2011. "Making Sense: Talking Data Management with Researchers." *International Journal of Digital Curation* 6(2): 265–73. http://www.ijdc.net/article/view/197/262.

Wilson, James A.J., Luis Martinez-Uribe, Michael A. Fraser, and Paul Jeffreys. 2011. "An Institutional Approach to Developing Research Data Management Infrastructure." *International Journal of Digital Curation* 6(2): 274–87. DOI: https://doi.org/10.2218/ijdc.v6i2.203.

Yakel, Elizabeth. 2007. "Digital Curation." *OCLC Systems and Services: International Digital Library Perspectives* 23(4): 335–40. DOI: https://doi.org/10.1108/10650750710831466.

## 3. Prototyping

Prototyping, or the modelling of digital objects, has proliferated within and outside of scholarly environments for the last two decades. The resources in this category generally fall under experimental and product-based prototyping (Ruecker 2015). Experimental prototyping is often carried out in academic contexts by approaching the prototyping process itself as a research endeavour that aims to manifest a thought process, explore a concept, or answer a question. Product-based prototyping is aimed at generating a robust product that is published and used. These two can overlap: in experimental prototyping, the digital object often moves through stages of development and is eventually disseminated for use by others; product-oriented prototypes often maintain an element of experimentation in order to deliver refined objects to their users. The research prototypes in this category experiment with conventional forms of scholarly communication by offering alternative modes of production and dissemination that are supported by the digital medium (Belojevic 2015; Saklofske 2014; Saklofske, with INKE Research Group 2016; Siemens et al. 2009). The more product-oriented prototypes explore alternative design methods to ensure usability and access for their users (Given et al. 2007; Ruecker et al. 2007; Ruecker, Radzikowska, and Sinclair 2011). Despite the end goal, all prototypes in this category carry an experimental quality and seek to innovate particular aspects of their respective fields.

### A. Annotations

**Belojevic, Nina. 2015. "Developing an Open, Networked Peer Review System."** *Scholarly and Research Communication* 6(2): n.p. DOI: https://doi.org/10.22230/src.2015v6n2a205.
Belojevic presents the Personas for Open, Networked Peer Review wireframe prototype: an open, networked peer review model initiated by Belojevic and Jentery Sayers in 2013 that was further developed by the Electronic Textual Cultures Laboratory (ETCL) in partnership with University of Victoria Libraries, the Humanities Computing and Media Centre, and the Public Knowledge Project. In this environment, articles undergo open peer review and can be commented on by a specific group of reviewers or the public. The prototyping process followed an approach similar to the one described in Katie Salen and Eric Zimmerman's *Rules of Play: Game Design Fundamentals* (2003), which outlines common game design principles. Belojevic describes how the project moved from iterative prototyping to agile development, an approach that permits researchers to break down the project into smaller chunks.

This approach allows stakeholders to ensure that their goals are being met at every stage, and allows scholars and researchers to maintain the quality of the project. Further research will focus on determining the aspects of agile development adaptable by the project in order to facilitate a balance between project development and deliverables, while being flexible enough to pursue and integrate novel insights that may appear during the prototyping process.

Given, Lisa M., Stan Ruecker, Heather Simpson, Elizabeth Sadler, and Andrea Ruskin. 2007. "Inclusive Interface Design for Seniors: Image-Browsing for a Health Information Context." *Journal of the American Society for Information Science and Technology* 58(11): 1610–17. DOI: https://doi.org/10.1002/asi.20645.

Given, Ruecker, Simpson, Sadler, and Ruskin demonstrate a prototype of a web-based resource for identifying and providing information on medications for senior citizens with an image-based retrieval system interface. This prototype stems from a lack of research on the usefulness of existing web-based resources and an understanding of the complexities that arise in accommodating the various needs of seniors. The authors conduct a case study on twelve people, six men and six women aged between 65 and 80, who are comfortable using computers; they are asked to search for, identify, and find information on a number of medications using two different resources: a more common commercial consumer-driven database (www.drugs.com) and the prototype used in this case study. In the former, participants were unable to identify the proper medication, and generally found the platform to be crowded and confusing, with a lack of images to disambiguate between the forms and colours of medications. Given et al.'s prototype, by contrast, was built with usability theory in mind—an approach that sets users' needs at the forefront of the design process and is meant to accommodate users with various impairments and abilities in a straightforward, simple, and effective manner. Most of the participants were able to find information on the medications using the prototype, and reported it being easier and more straightforward to use. However, certain drawbacks still exist, such as the general overflow of information and the ambiguity in relation to the exact physical attributes of the medication, such as the colour and shape. Further studies will work on ensuring that the prototype goes further in aiding the needs of its potential users.

Ruecker, Stan. 2015. "A Brief Taxonomy of Prototypes for the Digital
Humanities." *Scholarly Research and Communication* 6(2): n.p. DOI:
https://doi.org/10.22230/src.2015v6n2a222.
Ruecker's paper intervenes at the intersection of digital humanities and
design as he presents a taxonomy for project prototyping. He begins by acknowledging the wide variety of prototype taxonomies that have been previously proposed before turning to his own. Ruecker suggests that prototypes
should be categorized based on the kind of project they are supporting: pro-
duction-driven, experimental, and provotypes (provocative prototypes). He
recognizes that prototyping is defined and understood differently depending on the community and uses various examples, such as Xinyue Zhou's na-
tionalist baby bottles and Juan Salamanca's crosswalk, to illustrate different
types of prototypes and to trace their evolution. Ruecker argues that any of
these categories of prototypes can be used effectively for pedagogy. In conclusion, Ruecker argues that clearly distinguishing the purposes of different
prototypes can help manage and encourage their use.

Ruecker, Stan, Lisa M. Given, Elizabeth Sadler, Andrea Ruskin, and
Heather Simpson. 2007. "Design of a Rich-Prospect Browsing
Interface for Seniors: A Qualitative Study of Image Similarity
Clustering." *Visible Language* 41(1): 4–21.
Ruecker, Given, Sadler, Ruskin, and Simpson apply inclusive design delivery by designing an interface for access to health care resources for seniors.
Their goal is to test whether an alternative visual browsing interface would
be helpful to seniors in pill identification. They detail inclusive design principles and pose research questions that address the effect of interface design
on usability of online drug databases. The authors discuss their results by
comparing interfaces, looking at search task results from www.drugs.com
and the prototype produced, and reading into implications for design. They
also highlight their future research plan, which includes an expansion of
search features for drug databases and the development of interfaces that
adhere to inclusive design theory.

Ruecker, Stan, Milena Radzikowska, and Stéfan Sinclair. 2011. *Visual
Interface Design for Digital Cultural Heritage: A Guide to Rich-Prospect
Browsing.* Farnham, UK, and Burlington, VT: Ashgate.
Ruecker, Radzikowska, and Sinclair apply a rich-prospect browsing approach
to the design of cultural heritage collections—a methodology that involves
the investigation of an entire collection rather than focusing on search-
oriented interfaces that have been used in the past. The authors dedicate

the book to explaining the various affordances of rich-prospect browsing by laying out the theoretical framework for such an approach and balancing it with various prototypes and examples. They also address some central principles of rich-prospect browsing, such as the importance of meaningful representation of each item in the collection and what the most beneficial affordances for various audiences are. The book includes a total of nine prototypes that test rich-prospect browsing by balancing theory and practice; together, these are meant to serve as a guide for those who may want to implement this approach in their projects. They specifically address how to determine the type of affordances to include and how to steer them toward the potential audiences for their cultural heritage artefacts collection.

**\*\*Saklofske, Jon. 2014. "Exploding, Centralizing and Reimagining: Critical Scholarship Refracted Through the NewRadial Prototype." *Scholarly and Research Communication* 5(2): n.p. DOI: https://doi. org/10.22230/src.2014v5n2a151.**

In light of the focus of the Implementing New Knowledge Environments (INKE) research team on the ways in which digital environments affect the production, dissemination, and use of established venues for academic research, the NewRadial prototype has been extended for further investigation of this research direction. NewRadial is a data visualization environment that was originally designed as an alternative way to encounter and annotate image-based databases. It allows users to engage with humanities data outside of scholarly paradigms and the linear nature of the printed book, and encourages user contributions through collective commentary rather than isolated annotation. This prototype investigates a number of questions, such as whether the aforementioned venues can coexist in their present form, the ways in which scholarship can be visualized through time and space, how critical ideas are born and evolve, and whether the collaborative elements of alternate reality games (ARGs) and massively multiplayer online role-playing games (MMORPGs) can be adopted into the peer review process and secondary scholarship. This prototype is a response to the established view of a finished work existing in a print-based format and is, rather, a way of experimenting in an interactive and dynamic digital environment that invites dialogue and collaborative curation—as well as numerous alternative narrative opportunities.

**\*\*Saklofske, Jon, with the INKE Research Team. 2016. "Digital *Theoria*, *Poiesis*, and *Praxis*: Activating Humanities Research and Communication through Open Social Scholarship Platform Design." *Scholarly and Research Communication* 7(2/3): n.p. DOI: https://doi.org/10.22230/src. 2016v7n2/3a252.**
Saklofske states that although research has drastically changed in the last two decades, scholarly communication has remained relatively stable, adhering to standard scholarly forms of publication as a result of materialist economies. He argues for the necessity of innovating digital means of scholarly communication with *theoria*, *poiesis*, and *praxis* in mind. Saklofske offers a number of case studies that experiment with unconventional ways of carrying out research that utilize these concepts, among which is the NewRadial prototype: an online environment that brings in secondary scholarship and debate, in which outside information can be added to and visualized with the primary data without affecting the original databases. NewRadial is taken as a model for other spaces that facilitate such dynamic organization and centralized spacing as an alternative solution to typical, isolated forms of monographs and linear narrativization. Saklofske, a proponent of open social scholarship, argues that this type of scholarship is an essential part of the transformation of scholarly research and communication in a way that would take advantage of the digital medium, rather than propagate conventional forms of knowledge creation into this environment. This type of research platform is also more inclusive and public-facing.

**\*\*Siemens, Raymond G., Claire Warwick, Richard Cunningham, Teresa Dobson, Alan Galey, Stan Ruecker, Susan Schreibman, and the INKE Research Group. 2009. "*Codex* Ultor: Toward a Conceptual and Theoretical Foundation for New Research on Books and Knowledge Environments." *Digital Studies / Le champ numérique* 1(2): n.p. DOI: http://doi.org/10.16995/dscn.270.**
Siemens, Warwick, Cunningham, Dobson, Galey, Ruecker, Schreibman, and the INKE Research Group investigate the 'conceptual and theoretical foundations for work undertaken by the Implementing New Knowledge Environments research group' (n.p). They address the need for designing new knowledge environments, taking into consideration the evolution of reading and writing technologies, the mechanics and pragmatics of written forms of knowledge, and the corresponding strategies of reading—as well as the computational possibilities of written forms due to emerging technology. The authors highlight the importance of prototyping as a research activity, and outline corresponding research questions that target the experiences of

reading, using, and accessing information, as well as issues of design. They discuss their research methods, which include digital textual scholarship, user experience evaluation, interface design prototyping, and information management. Siemens et al. conclude that the various reading interface prototypes produced by INKE allow a transformation of engagement methods with reading materials.

**Stafford, Amy, Ali Shiri, Stan Ruecker, Matthew Bouchard, Paras Mehta, Karl Anvik, and Ximena Rossello. 2008. "Searchling: User-Centered Evaluation of a Visual Thesaurus-Enhanced Interface for Bilingual Digital Libraries." In *Research and Advanced Technology for Digital Libraries*, edited by Birte Christensen-Dalsgaard, Donatella Castelli, Bolette Ammitzbøll Jurik, and Joan Lippincott, 117–21. Berlin and Heidelberg: Springer.**

Stafford, Shiri, Ruecker, Bouchard, Mehta, Anvik, and Rossello conduct a user-centred evaluation using Searchling, an experimental visual interface that combines a thesaurus, query, and document space, and is based on rich-prospect and metadata-enhanced visual interfaces for an improved search experience. The study is carried out with fifteen participants, most of whom are researchers at the University of Alberta studying the usefulness of understanding different types of information clustering and the relationships between them. The assigned task asks participants to select as many possible features on the interface without paying particular attention to the content. The study is based on both qualitative feedback and a user rank of items using a 5-point Likert scale. Results show that among the numerous positive impacts, the most useful feature of the interface is that it solves the problem of formulating queries, which is considered the greatest problem with other search tools. According to the participants, the most prominent limitation is that Searchling fails to isolate keyword search terms on a specific topic.

### B. Reference List

Belojevic, Nina. 2015. "Developing an Open, Networked Peer Review System." *Scholarly and Research Communication* 6(2): n.p. DOI: https://doi.org/10.22230/src.2015v6n2a205.

Given, Lisa M., Stan Ruecker, Heather Simpson, Elizabeth Sadler, and Andrea Ruskin. 2007. "Inclusive Interface Design for Seniors: Image-Browsing for a Health Information Context." *Journal of the American Society for Information Science and Technology* 58(11): 1610–17. DOI: https://doi.org/10.1002/asi.20645.

Ruecker, Stan. 2015. "A Brief Taxonomy of Prototypes for the Digital Humanities." *Scholarly Research and Communication* 6(2): n.p. DOI: https://doi.org/10.22230/src.2015v6n2a222.

Ruecker, Stan, Lisa M. Given, Elizabeth Sadler, Andrea Ruskin, and Heather Simpson. 2007. "Design of a Rich-Prospect Browsing Interface for Seniors: A Qualitative Study of Image Similarity Clustering." *Visible Language* 41(1): 4–21.

Ruecker, Stan, Milena Radzikowska, and Stéfan Sinclair. 2011. *Visual Interface Design for Digital Cultural Heritage: A Guide to Rich-Prospect Browsing.* Farnham, UK, and Burlington, VT: Ashgate.

Saklofske, Jon. 2014. "Exploding, Centralizing and Reimagining: Critical Scholarship Refracted Through the NewRadial Prototype." *Scholarly and Research Communication* 5(2): n.p. DOI: https://doi.org/10.22230/src.2014v5n2a151.

Saklofske, Jon, with the INKE Research Team. 2016. "Digital *Theoria, Poiesis,* and *Praxis*: Activating Humanities Research and Communication through Open Social Scholarship Platform Design." *Scholarly and Research Communication* 7(2/3): n.p. DOI: https://doi.org/10.22230/src.2016v7n2/3a252.

Siemens, Raymond G., Claire Warwick, Richard Cunningham, Teresa Dobson, Alan Galey, Stan Ruecker, Susan Schreibman, and The INKE Research Group. 2009. "Codex Ultor: Toward a Conceptual and Theoretical Foundation for New Research on Books and Knowledge Environments." *Digital Studies / Le champ numérique* 1(2): n.p. DOI: http://doi.org/10.16995/dscn.270.

Stafford, Amy, Ali Shiri, Stan Ruecker, Matthew Bouchard, Paras Mehta, Karl Anvik, and Ximena Rossello. 2008. "Searchling: User-Centered Evaluation of a Visual Thesaurus-Enhanced Interface for Bilingual Digital Libraries." In *Research and Advanced Technology for Digital Libraries,* edited by Birte Christensen-Dalsgaard, Donatella Castelli, Bolette Ammitzbøll Jurik, and Joan Lippincott, 117–21. Berlin and Heidelberg: Springer.

## 4. Social Justice and Open Knowledge Facilitated by Technology

The advent of the digital age has drastically affected the means by which social justice operates. Authors in this category study how open knowledge is a tool for social justice, and how it can enhance fields such as medicine and the humanities, as well as society more generally. The articles vary between those that study the relationship between open knowledge and social justice and those that argue for open knowledge as a means for social justice. Various case studies are addressed, such as the Bringing Europe's eLectronic Infrastructures to Expanding Frontiers (BELIEF) Project Digital Library, which investigates how social justice activists have worked toward shaping Internet technologies in a way that serves their needs (Castelli, Taylor, and Zoppi 2010). Resources also explain how Internet technologies are used in rural areas and the Global South (Paliwala 2007). This category addresses issues pertaining to open access and open source, such as Chopra and Dexter's consideration of Freedom Zero, the freedom to use software in any way or for any purpose (2009). Overall, this category addresses the various technologies and approaches that enable the development of open knowledge and social justice.

### A. Annotations

Castelli, Donatella, Simon J.E. Taylor, and Franco Zoppi. 2010. "Open Knowledge on E-Infrastructures: The BELIEF Project Digital Library." *IST-Africa, 2010*, 1–15. Dublin: IIMC International Information Management Corporation. https://ieeexplore.ieee.org/document/5753044.

Castelli, Taylor, and Zoppi discuss the Bringing Europe's eLectronic Infrastructures to Expanding Frontiers (BELIEF) Project, which aims to ensure the development and adoption of e-infrastructures on a worldwide scale. They focus on providing users with documentation that matches their search criteria based on their professional profiles. The authors outline the objectives of the project, introduce the methodology, provide a technology description, and discuss system developments. In the results section, Castelli, Taylor, and Zoppi analyze the impact of the Digital Library on the target audience and explain that there was a remarkable growth of the community due to the successful outcomes of the organized events. They study statistical data on user provenance, top sites, top operations, and yearly trend. On business benefits and sustainability, the authors summarize their views by explaining that the implementation and operation costs of a Digital Library include training Content Providers' Correspondents, maintaining the network of liaisons necessary to promote the community leveraged by the Digital Library, and delegating the performance of harvesting operations to OpenDLib Administrators. They conclude that the effective implementation of the Digital Library was achieved, especially in terms of harmonization of metadata from the various information sources.

**Chopra, Samir, and Scott Dexter. 2009. "The Freedoms of Software and Its Ethical Uses."** *Ethics and Information Technology* 11(4): 287–97. DOI: https://doi.org/10.1007/s10676-009-9191-0.

Chopra and Dexter explain that the difference between free and proprietary software is that the latter restricts user actions through end user licence agreements, while the former eliminates restrictions on users. The authors explain the concept of free software, discussing software freedom, the Freedom Zero problem, the ethical use of scientific knowledge, and scientific knowledge and property rights. They then discuss community discourse and Freedom Zero (the freedom to use software in any way or for any purpose), explaining that Freedom Zero supports deliberative discourse within development and user communities. When exploring the ethical uses of software, Chopra and Dexter answer the question of whether Freedom Zero is inaccurate, and whether a free software licensor could be liable for granting Freedom Zero. The authors conclude that Freedom Zero facilitates a broader debate about software's larger social significance.

**Christians, Clifford G. 2015. "Social Justice and Internet Technology."** *New Media & Society* 18(11): 2760–73. DOI: https://doi.org/10.1177/1461444815604130.

Christians looks at Internet technology from a social/cultural point of view. He claims that relativism is a crisis in ethics, proposing an intellectual flow as coherent articulation of social justice with Internet technology. This flow consists of ontological realism, justice as intrinsic worthiness, and a human-centred philosophy of technology. Christians discusses relativism as a watershed for ethics, talking about media ethics in particular, and listing a few problems, including the Gamergate controversy, Wikileaks.org, privacy in Facebook networks, red envelopes in China, and online hate speech. He then moves to naturalism, explaining that moral anti-realism denies the validity of an intellectual apparatus for ethics, and that philosophical realism is needed for a credible concept of social justice. The author proposes that justice in the moral realist term is grounded in the inherent dignity of the human species. Christians denies the epistemology of the neutral view on Internet technology, and proposes that instead of looking for technical improvements in instruments, one needs to reconceive the technology itself. The author then poses the issue of common good, emphasizing the importance of community.

He concludes that through social justice, individuals can do great things to help with the development of today's world.

**Dunlop, Judith M., and Graham Fawcett. 2008. "Technology-Based Approaches to Social Work and Social Justice." *Journal of Policy Practice* 7(2–3): 140–54. DOI: https://doi.org/10.1080/15588740801937961.**
Dunlop and Fawcett investigate the need for integration of conventional and electronic advocacy models in the field of social work. They investigate whether social workers are able to assist organizations enter the information age by using technology-based approaches to help disadvantaged populations, and by implementing electronic advocacy practices to promote social justice in local communities. The authors offer a historical background on social work advocacy by examining conventional and electronic advocacy practices. They continue by exploring types of social or free software that could be used by nonprofit organizations, and investigate the application of social software to social work advocacy practices in the age of technology. Dunlop and Fawcett conclude that there is a need for technologically competent social workers to organize virtual communities and provide leadership in the electronic advocacy practice.

**Edwards, Heather R., and Richard Hoefer. 2010. "Are Social Work Advocacy Groups Using Web 2.0 Effectively?" *Journal of Policy Practice* 9(3–4): 220–39. DOI: https://doi.org/10.1080/15588742.2010.489037.**
Edwards and Hoefer address social work advocacy efforts and explore the potential of Web 2.0 technology in the field. The authors explain that there are various approaches allowing social workers to succeed in their advocacy efforts, including communicating with decision-makers, resource management, and information sharing. They also investigate Web 2.0 and how it allows decentralized knowledge building by going through examples of social media such as blogs, RSS feeds, wikis, podcasting, video sharing, social networking, and social bookmarking. When discussing Web advocacy, Edwards and Hoefer talk about the ways in which social work advocates using Web 2.0. The article continues with a presentation of previous research, and an explanation of the methods employed, such as sampling and data collection. The results include two sections: the use of various Internet components, and differences between general social work organizations and state chapters of the National Association of Social Workers. The authors then discuss the results and explain that social work organizations do not often use Web 2.0 or previous Web technologies for advocacy. They conclude that Web 2.0 technologies enhance inclusion in political discourse, accessibility of information, and the formation of relationships that strengthen the advocacy effort.

Farrington, John, and Conor Farrington. 2005. "Rural Accessibility, Social Inclusion and Justice: Towards Conceptualisation." *Journal of Transport Geography* 13(1): 1–12. DOI: https://doi.org/10.1016/j.jtrangeo.2004.10.002.

Farrington and Farrington explain the concept of accessibility in the rural context and discuss its central placement in social inclusion and social justice policy agenda. The authors discuss accessibility and the welfare concept in human geography, accessibility as normative and relative, and accessibility from the perspective of social inclusion and social justice. They also elaborate on accessibility and policy, noting that accessibility and social justice are two characteristics of policy adjustment. They list four dimensions that add value and accessibility to a construct of social justice and its application: space and location, sustainability, integration within the structural view of the causes of social exclusion, and empowerment of citizens through participation. Farrington and Farrington conclude that the accessibility of life opportunities is a necessary condition for social inclusion and justice.

Goldkind, Lauri. 2014. "E-Advocacy in Human Services: The Impact of Organizational Conditions and Characteristics on Electronic Advocacy Activities among Nonprofits." *Journal of Policy Practice* 13(4): 300–15. DOI: https://doi.org/10.1080/15588742.2014.929073.

Goldkind explores the organizational characteristics related to the use of electronic advocacy strategies and conducts a survey on nonprofit executives. She starts with a literature review on policy advocacy and electronic, Internet-based interactive tools in the fields of electronic advocacy and nonprofit organizations. Goldkind then studies the barriers to advocacy practice, draws the conceptual framework, and provides her hypotheses, in which she claims that organizations use electronic technologies because their organizational cultures are conducive to them. The author uses two demographic characteristics (organizational age and budget size) in her study. She concludes that organizational success depends on the capacities of organizations to invest in social media tools while being attentive to policy advocacy.

Kline, Jesse. 2013. "Why Canada has 'Third World Access to the Internet.'" *National Post*, September 24. http://news.nationalpost.com/full-comment/jesse-kline-why-canada-has-third-world-access-to-the-internet. Archived at https://perma.cc/BH8L-K33K.

Kline addresses the Internet problem that Canada is facing: namely, that it pays some of the highest rates for Internet access among countries in the developed world. The author argues that this is a result of the lack of competition in the Canadian marketplace. Existing companies have created a monopoly, and Canada has a relatively small population that is widely dispersed across the country, making investment costly. Kline argues that in order to remediate this problem, the Canadian government should allow new competitors easier entry by cancelling the foreign ownership restrictions currently placed on Internet Service Providers (ISPs) and wireless carriers in order to create a more profitable opportunity to invest in Canada. Another solution Kline proposes is to have municipalities support building network infrastructure by removing current bureaucratic impediments to place cable in new houses, as well as banishing restrictions on where wireless towers can be built. The author concludes that this problem requires immediate attention.

Langman, Lauren. 2005. "From Virtual Public Spheres to Global Justice: A Critical Theory of Internetworked Social Movements." *Sociological Theory* 23(1): 42–74. DOI: https://doi.org/10.1111/j.0735-2751.2005.00242.x.

Langman claims that new types of Internet-based social movements and cyberactivism require new kinds of theorizations. She explains various perspectives on social movements, including resource mobilization, framing and meaning construction, political process, new social movements, and the Frankfurt School. Langman also explores domination and ideology, as well as the adverse consequences of globalization, and moves toward a critical theory of internetworked social movements (ISMs). The author studies electronic media and 'Virtual Public Spheres,' collective identities and social movements, internetworked social movements, alternative media (blogs, global civil societies, alternative professional networks, and radical geeks), global justice, global forums, anti-war movements (global justice, the World Social Forum movement, anti-war mobilization), and the move from virtual networks to cyberactivism. She concludes that the legacy of critical theory offers a comprehensive framework to chart new forms of social mobilization and to inspire participation in the struggle for global justice.

Milberry, Kate. 2006. "Reconstructing the Internet: How Social Justice Activists Contest Technical Design in Cyberspace." *M/C Journal* 9(1): n.p. http://journal.media-culture.org.au/0603/10-milberry.php.

Milberry explores how activists have shaped the Internet to fit technical needs and movement goals. She begins by exploring 'geeks and global justice'—namely, how tech activism joins the free software ethos and concerns for social justice. As she explains, the novelty of tech activism is the incorporation of democratic goals of the global justice movement (GJM) into the technology itself. Milberry elaborates on the concept of politicizing technology, arguing that tech activists in global justice return to computer technology development for their political action. She addresses constructs such as Indymedia (the Independent Media Center; https://www.indymedia.org/), free software, and wiki software (what she calls 'Wild Wild Wikis: The Latest Frontier'). The author concludes that since the Internet is socially constructed, users are able to contribute to its development by shaping its future direction, allowing it to bridge the gap between 'geek' and activist communities, and supporting a digital infrastructure for progressive world-wide activism.

**Paliwala, Abdul. 2007. "Free Culture, Global Commons and Social Justice in Information Technology Diffusion."** *Law, Social Justice and Global Development Journal* **1: n.p. https://warwick.ac.uk/fac/soc/law/elj/lgd/2007_1/paliwala/.**
Paliwala explores the role of digital intellectual property rights in the realm of the digital divide between developing countries of the Global South. He starts by exploring the discussion of intellectual property rights in information technology at the World Summit on Information Society (WSIS) and the World Intellectual Property Organization (WIPO). The author also studies the nature of change in production relations in the Age of Information, and the importance of Free and Open Source Software and Content (FOSS-C) movements. Paliwala then investigates the potential for digital social justice with regard to the application of arguments based on changed production and property relations in the Global South, the way digital divides are affected by property and piracy issues, and the reformist arguments based on the *Right to Development*. He concludes that millennial ideologies of new modes of production are to be cautiously treated, as they form hidden modes of domination.

### B. Reference List

Castelli, Donatella, Simon J.E. Taylor, and Franco Zoppi. 2010. "Open Knowledge on E-Infrastructures: The BELIEF Project Digital Library." *IST-Africa, 2010*, 1–15. Dublin: IIMC International Information Management Corporation. https://ieeexplore.ieee.org/document/5753044.

Chopra, Samir, and Scott Dexter. 2009. "The Freedoms of Software and Its Ethical Uses." *Ethics and Information Technology* 11(4): 287–97. DOI: https://doi.org/10.1007/s10676-009-9191-0.

Christians, Clifford G. 2015. "Social Justice and Internet Technology." *New Media & Society* 18(11): 2760–73. DOI: https://doi.org/10.1177/1461444815604130.

Dunlop, Judith M., and Graham Fawcett. 2008. "Technology-Based Approaches to Social Work and Social Justice." *Journal of Policy Practice* 7(2–3): 140–54. DOI: https://doi.org/10.1080/15588740801937961.

Edwards, Heather R., and Richard Hoefer. 2010. "Are Social Work Advocacy Groups Using Web 2.0 Effectively?" *Journal of Policy Practice* 9(3–4): 220–39. DOI: https://doi.org/10.1080/15588742.2010.489037.

Farrington, John, and Conor Farrington. 2005. "Rural Accessibility, Social Inclusion and Justice: Towards Conceptualisation." *Journal of Transport Geography* 13(1): 1–12. DOI: https://doi.org/10.1016/j.jtrangeo.2004.10.002.

Goldkind, Lauri. 2014. "E-Advocacy in Human Services: The Impact of Organizational Conditions and Characteristics on Electronic Advocacy Activities among Nonprofits." *Journal of Policy Practice* 13(4): 300–15. DOI: https://doi.org/10.1080/15588742.2014.929073.

Kline, Jesse. 2013. "Why Canada has 'Third World Access to the Internet.'" *National Post*, September 24. http://news.nationalpost.com/full-comment/jesse-kline-why-canada-has-third-world-access-to-the-internet. Archived at https://perma.cc/BH8L-K33K.

Langman, Lauren. 2005. "From Virtual Public Spheres to Global Justice: A Critical Theory of Internetworked Social Movements." *Sociological Theory* 23(1): 42–74. DOI: https://doi.org/10.1111/j.0735-2751.2005.00242.x.

Milberry, Kate. 2006. "Reconstructing the Internet: How Social Justice Activists Contest Technical Design in Cyberspace." *M/C Journal* 9(1): n.p. http://journal.media-culture.org.au/0603/10-milberry.php.

Paliwala, Abdul. 2007. "Free Culture, Global Commons and Social Justice in Information Technology Diffusion." *Law, Social Justice and Global Development Journal* 1: n.p. https://warwick.ac.uk/fac/soc/law/elj/lgd/2007_1/paliwala/.

## 5. Action and Activism

Most often, activism involves campaign-based practices calling for social or political action. In recent years, there has been an increase of activism in the digital medium due to the wider scope of outreach and visibility available online. This category offers resources on how the Internet and social media help enhance social activism. It contains articles on 'hacktivism' (i.e., hacking computer systems for political and social purposes) (Losh 2012), activist blogging (Merry 2013), and social networks such as Twitter (Boyraz et al. 2011; Merry 2013; Sandoval-Almazan and Gil-Garcia 2014). Certain authors approach online activism critically (Bennett 2004), and others study the growth of activism by looking at how specific websites allow for greater potential in political and social work. Various case studies are referenced in this category to highlight the potential of online tools in specific revolutionary movements, including the Dutch campaign 'Wij vertrouwen stemcomputers niet,' which translates to 'We do not trust voting computers' (a campaign against electronic voting discussed in Oostveen 2010), and 'Stop the War Coalition' (a British anti-war organization discussed in Pickerill 2009). Also included in this category are contemporary examples of how activism has been carried out through various online platforms, and an examination of the effectiveness of such practices.

### A. Annotations

**Bennett, W. Lance. 2004. "Communicating Global Activism: Strengths and Vulnerabilities of Networked Politics." In *Cyberprotest: New Media, Citizens and Social Movements*, edited by Wim van de Donk, Brian D. Loader, Paul G. Nixon, and Dieter Rucht, 123–46. London and New York: Routledge.**
Bennett explores how digital communication affects political movements in favour of individuals and communities with limited resources. The author's observations suggest that digital communication practices affect the growth and forms of global activism. He claims that there is a relationship between communication practices and the evolution of democracy, suggesting that personal digital networks are channelling the movement known as media democracy. In his article, Bennett conducts an analysis that studies the strengths and vulnerabilities of communication practices that allow transnational activism. The various sections address the social contexts of Internet activism, identity in distributed social networks, politics in distributed communication networks, and the organization of protest networks. Bennett studies communication as a political strategy and organizational resource

by analyzing online protest activities. The author also addresses permanent campaigns and political organization and suggests that network structures shape the coherence of communication content. He concludes that the distributed electronic public sphere has the potential of becoming the exemplar of public information in various aspects of politics.

Bennett, W. Lance, and Alexandra Segerberg. 2011. "Digital Media and the Personalization of Collective Action." *Information, Communication & Society* 14(6): 770–99. DOI: https://doi.org/10.1080/1369118X.2011. 579141.

Bennett and Segerberg investigate the 2009 G20 London Summit during the global financial crisis and analyze how protest networks used digital media to mobilize engaged individuals. They study different forms of personalization and personalized politics, including degrees of flexibility in affiliation, issue definition, and expression. The authors address digital communication in the organization of protest and focus on the political capacity of collective action networks as well as the mobilization of individualized publics. Bennett and Segerberg explore individualized technology and organization of protest networks, asking questions about conventional political capacities and organizational communication. They also address protests against the economic crisis, as well as protest coalitions and personalized communication, in order to analyze methods used during the mobilization process. Bennett and Segerberg investigate personalized communication and protest capacity, including engagement strength, agenda strength, and network strength. The authors conclude that the coalition adopting more personalized communication strategies maintained the strongest network, and that organization networks can benefit from digital media applications for more coherent, collective work.

Boyraz, Maggie, Aparna Krishnan, and Danielle Catona. 2011. "Who is Retweeted in Times of Political Protest? An Analysis of Characteristics of Top Tweeters and Top Retweeted Users During the 2011 Egyptian Revolution." *Atlantic Journal of Communication* 23(2): 99–119. DOI: https://doi.org/10.1080/15456870.2015.1013103.

Boyraz, Krishnan, and Catona study factors that affected retweets on Twitter during the Egyptian revolution of 2011. They present an overview of Twitter and briefly contextualize the revolution. The authors focus on factors such as source and content that increase how viral a message on Twitter becomes in times of crisis. They also address top tweeters versus top retweeted users by studying what characteristics might differentiate the former from the latter, and stress the importance of content during a political protest. The authors discuss source characteristics—credibility, sociability, connectivity, and content choices (the latter considers language intensity, information sharing, and social action)—to assess persuasiveness according to the number of retweets. The data set was obtained from the archive TwapperKeeper, which contains 150,000 tweets from 45,000 users posted between January 25 and February 11, 2011, using the #Jan25 hashtag. The findings show that users closer to the action, with more media affiliation, longer account duration, and more followers, are more likely to be retweeted. The authors also found that sharing information did not affect the number of retweets, and that there was an absence of social action features. They conclude that microblogging should be further explored by communication scholars, since tools such as Twitter can be utilized in various ways and are outlets that allow immediate sharing of information when other channels are blocked.

**Deibert, Ronald J. 2000. "International Plug 'n Play? Citizen Activism, the Internet, and Global Public Policy."** *International Studies Perspectives* **1(3): 255–72. DOI: https://doi.org/10.1111/1528-3577.00026.**
Deibert examines the use of the Internet and the World Wide Web by citizen users lobbying against the Multilateral Agreement on Investment (MAI). The author highlights various reasons why this case is instructive, emphasizing that press accounts, academic studies, and state and civil society participation in this campaign suggested a strong connection between the anti-MAI movement and the Internet. He suggests that the Internet helped groups to pressure politicians and publicize anti-MAI views. Deibert explores the inclusion of the nonstate actor in international policy processes, the legitimacy of nongovernmental organizations, and the Internet configuration for a viable public sphere. He claims that a rethinking of the architecture of global politics is necessary for the inclusion of citizen networks in the world operating system. He also studies the role of the Internet in the success of the citizen networks and the alternative results of the campaign without the Internet. Deibert continues to look at the global public policy implications, elaborating on issues regarding domestic and international forum actors, the multiplicity and diversity of citizen networks and their issues of classification, inclusion of citizen networks, and Internet governance public policy. He concludes that the MAI exemplifies how the Internet is responsible for boosting the reach of citizen networks, and refutes arguments suggesting that the Internet is an unsustainable platform, thereby legitimizing civil society networks in world politics.

**Filipacchi, Amanda. 2013. "Wikipedia's Sexism Toward Female Novelists."**
*New York Times,* April 24. http://www.nytimes.com/2013/04/28/
opinion/sunday/wikipedias-sexism-toward-female-novelists.html.
Archived at https://perma.cc/X526-R7NJ.

Filipacchi addresses an important gender-related activity on Wikipedia that
she noticed in April 2013: female authors listed on the 'American Novelists'
Wikipedia page were being moved to the category 'American Women Novelists,' whereas male authors listed on the same page remained. Wikipedia
editors justified this migration by stating that there were too many entries
under the 'American Novelists' category. What Filipacchi found most troubling, however, was that the original page was not renamed 'American Male
Novelists,' implying that American novelists are de facto male. The entries
were moved by alphabetical order, and after some investigation, the author
also noticed that the same was true for Haitian novelists. Filipacchi notified
the Word of Mouth (WOM) published female writer listserv about this problem, which responded with outrage and immediate action to remediate the
issue. She concludes by highlighting the need for Wikipedia editors and users
to acknowledge the weight of such decisions.

**Ghobadi, Shahla, and Stewart Clegg. 2015. "'These Days Will Never**
**Be Forgotten ...': A Critical Mass Approach to Online Activism."**
*Information and Organization* 25(1): 52–71. DOI: https://doi.
org/10.1016/j.infoandorg.2014.12.002.

Ghobadi and Clegg explore the phenomenon of social activism by studying its
dynamics in a Web environment. They present an overview of the literature
available on online activism, the theoretical perspectives of political systems, and their vulnerability to change. Their research methodology consists
of three complementary cases, including data collection and data analysis.
The results of their longitudinal study demonstrate that online activism
helped organize social movements. For their cross-case analysis, they examined three key elements—initial conditions, interventions, and subsequent
conditions—in order to better understand the formative factors of collective
action. Ghobadi and Clegg conclude that their study shows how two opposing
forces of encouraging and inhibiting interventions are initiated, and what
societal outcomes their interplay would create.

**Häyhtiö, Tapio, and Jarmo Rinne. 2007. "Hard Rock Hallelujah! Empowering**
**Reflexive Political Action on the Internet."** *Journal for Cultural Research*
11(4): 337–58. DOI: https://doi.org/10.1080/14797580802038702.

Häyhtiö and Rinne study individualized online political participation and
activity by looking into a Finnish Internet protest campaign against gossip

journalism that occurred in May 2006. They claim that this study provides insight into the dynamics, patterns of change, and variety of political activity on the Internet. The authors set the case study in the context of reflexive politics, referring to the politicization of private worries and issue-specific questions, and also focus on the motivations of the protest from the perspective of political consumerism. Häyhtiö and Rinne explore how the repertoire and forms of citizen-oriented politics are transformed into individualized politics through a complex multi-spatial environment. The authors discuss the phenomenon of reflexive politics, explaining that reflexivity proposes active interaction between the individual and the surrounding world, and claiming that politicized issues are enhanced by personal interests and aims. As an example, they discuss the 2006 Eurovision Song Contest, at which a Finnish hard rock band, Lordi, performed in monster masks and costumes and won the competition. Häyhtiö and Rinne examine the political aftermath of the Lordi incident, including the backlash against newspapers and magazines that published 'unmasked photographs of the band members' against their wishes (341). They go on to discuss de-medialisation (the circulation of unfiltered and unedited communication) and self-made publicness as an arena of politics (347). The authors conclude that access to the Internet makes it possible for all individuals to participate in public discussions and to shape their agendas online.

**Hill, Benjamin Mako, and Aaron Shaw. 2013. "The Wikipedia Gender Gap Revisited: Characterizing Survey Response Bias with Propensity Score Estimation."** *PLOS One* **8(6): n.p. DOI: https://doi.org/10.1371/journal.pone.0065782.**

Hill and Shaw demonstrate a novel approach to calculating the demographics of Wikipedia contributors. They design their calculation as a response to a 2008 survey by the Wikimedia Foundation and the United Nations University at Maastricht (WMF/UNU-Merit), which sought to calculate Wikipedia contributor demographics and flagged a gender imbalance: less than 13 per cent of contributors were female. The Wikimedia Foundation then launched an initiative to raise the number of female Wikipedia contributors to 25 per cent. According to the authors, the WMF/UNU-Merit estimate was inaccurate, since it failed to take into account the numerous complexities involved in calculating the number of contributors. This resulted in a discrepancy in the actual number of women contributors to Wikipedia, which, according to Hill and Shaw's calculations, was 26.8 per cent higher than the WMF/UNU-Merit estimate, with a total of 16.1 per cent instead of 12.7 per cent. The authors also found that married people and parents were underestimated, and that students' and immigrants' contributions to Wikipedia had been overestimated. Although they acknowledge that there is no ultimate formula to calculate the exact ratio, the authors claim that the study described in this article has a sounder approach than the one in the original WMF/UNU-Merit study.

Howard, Philip N., Sheetal D. Agarwal, and Muzammil M. Hussain. 2011. "When Do States Disconnect Their Digital Networks? Regime Responses to the Political Uses of Social Media." *The Communication Review* 14(3) 216–32. DOI: https://doi.org/10.1080/10714421.2011. 597254.

Howard, Agarwal, and Hussain study various cases during which governments have censored and interfered in Internet networks. They claim that democratization movements preceded technologies such as the mobile phone and the Internet, but that these technologies have allowed individuals to build networks, create social capital, and organize political action. The authors suggest that digital media and online social networking applications have affected the organization of dissent around the world. They explain that before the age of digital media, authoritarian regimes were able to control broadcasts easily during political crises. The new media has complicated the task, and occasionally forces regimes to disable their national information infrastructures. Howard, Agarwal, and Hussain claim that by collecting known incidents during which the state intervenes in information networks, one can map out contours of crisis situations, political risks, and civic innovations for the purpose of understanding the relationship between state power and civil society. They conduct a comparative case analysis of instances in which regimes disconnected portions of their national digital infrastructures. In doing so, Howard, Agarwal, and Hussain can define the range of situations in which states have hindered substantial segments of their national information infrastructure. They reveal that democracies— not just authoritarian regimes—also disconnect their communication networks. The authors claim that the Internet is an information infrastructure independent of the state for the most part, making it an incubator for social movements. Howard, Agarwal, and Hussain discuss states' tactics, explaining that two themes govern the states' interference: the first theme includes protecting political leaders and state institutions, while the second theme is about preserving the public good. They conclude that information infrastructure is in itself politics, as its disconnection creates stop-gap measures that reinforce public expectations for global connectivity.

Lam, Shyong K., Anuradha Uduwage, Zhenhua Dong, Shilad Sen, David R. Musicant, Loren Terveen, and John Riedl. 2011. "WP: Clubhouse? An Exploration of Wikipedia's Gender Imbalance." Paper presented at 7th Annual International Symposium on Wikis and Open Collaboration (WikiSym 2011). http://files.grouplens.org/papers/wp-gender-wikisym2011.pdf.

Lam, Uduwage, Dong, Sen, Musicant, Terveen, and Riedl recognize the role of Wikipedia as a central public venue of knowledge in contemporary scholarship populated by thousands of volunteer editors. However, an important imbalance in the structure of Wikipedia is that the number of male editors vastly outweighs that of female editors. Lam et al. explore possible explanations for such a radical imbalance, and whether this affects the types of topics that are covered more thoroughly in the online encyclopedia. The authors apply quantitative statistical analysis to the English data available on Wikipedia. The results show that the gender gap is substantial, and that it does indeed skew the coverage quality of certain topics, adversely affecting its goal of being a high quality, comprehensive, open encyclopedia. Results also show that female editors are more likely to leave Wikipedia sooner than males; that the gender gap has not been closing over time; that articles with a high female editor involvement are often more highly disputed; that female editors face more reversion than males; and that female editors have a higher chance of being indefinitely blocked. All of these findings point to a Wikipedia culture that is resistant to female participation. Lam et al. conclude that more research needs to be done, and concrete steps taken to address this gender imbalance and its underlying reasons.

+Losh, Elisabeth. 2012. "Hacktivism and the Humanities: Programming Protest in the Era of the Digital University." In *Debates in the Digital Humanities*, edited by Matthew K. Gold, 161–86. Minneapolis: University of Minnesota Press. http://dhdebates.gc.cuny.edu/debates/text/32.

Losh argues that examining theories of hacking and hacktivism (hacking computer systems for political and social purposes), as well as the nonviolent political investment in digital tools, is becoming of greater importance. She supports this claim by pointing to the relationship with political protests in educational institutions and in the realms of coding and programming. Starting with the issue of digital dissent, Losh explains that not everyone using software for political dissent thinks that hacktivism and research go together naturally. The author uses the example of *HyperCities* (Presner, Shepard, and Kawano 2014, annotated below) to show how GIS-based digital humanities practices have adopted digital mapping technologies originally used in the human rights work of NGOs. She argues that this potentially positions digital humanities scholars as agents of change. Losh continues to discuss electronic civil disobedience, describing it as a form of political resistance in the field of digital humanities—one that is becoming more prominent in professional associations. She also addresses critical information studies, tackling digital ephemera, political coding, and performative hacking. When talking about hacking the academy, the author suggests that change in the university is necessary, and partnerships between social actors and political interests are encouraged. Losh asks whether or not hacktivism is relevant to the field, and claims that the answer depends on the context. She concludes that systems may need to be broken in order to understand how the relationship between symbolic representation humanists and political representation activists is formed.

McDonald, Kevin. 2015. "From Indymedia to Anonymous: Rethinking Action and Identity in Digital Cultures." *Information, Communication & Society* 18(8): 968–82. DOI: https://doi.org/10.1080/1369118X.2015. 1039561.

McDonald explores Anonymous, an international collaboration of hacktivists and activists, particularly its emergence and role in the campaign against Scientology (2008) and in the Occupy Wall Street movement (2011). According to McDonald, Anonymous emphasizes dimensions of digital culture, including the ephemeral, the grotesque, and memes. He argues that the analysis of contemporary conflicts and political mobilizations (such as the Arab Spring, Occupy Wall Street, and the Indignados anti-austerity movement in Spain) need to encompass new forms of communication in the digital realm. McDonald looks beyond collective identity and networks to focus on movements, information, and communication. The author also addresses the legacy of Indymedia and its networking practices. In addition, he addresses the use of masking as a social practice, stating that it is done primarily to symbolize the transformation from one state to another, or to access a form of power, rather than merely as a means of concealing an identity. He explains that microblogs such as *We Are the 99 Percent* and the Anonymous movement cannot be classified as networking practices, as they construct singularity through the relationship between what is visible and what is not. He concludes that his article is the beginning of an exploration of practices framed around masking, the ephemeral, contingency, creativity, temporality, and refusal of a fixed identity in the realm of collective action, power, and conflict in online spaces.

Merry, Melissa K. 2011. **"Interest Group Activism on the Web: The Case of Environmental Organization."** *Journal of Information Technology & Politics* 8(1): 110–28. DOI: https://doi.org/10.1080/19331681.201 0.508003.

Merry analyzes the content of 200 environmental group websites in order to answer two questions: 'to what extent has the Internet disrupted patterns of resource accumulation and voice among interest groups?' and 'how do groups use the Internet to connect citizens to government, and to what extent do group characteristics explain those uses?' (110). Merry attempts to assess the effects of the Internet on interest groups by reviewing the nature of interest group politics before the Internet, suggesting that the internet disrupts the uneven distribution of resources and political influence. She explains that the Internet allows groups to have stronger links between citizens and government by enhancing political participation. The author argues that popularity of groups' websites is tied to their financial resources. Merry explains that there are two criteria for the inclusion of groups: that these groups work on national or regional level environmental issues, and that they have websites. According to the study, political participation is encouraged by campaigns that include action alerts and requests for donations. She concludes that the Internet has helped smaller and lesser-known organizations, and suggests that groups use their websites for purposes of information dissemination and political participation.

Merry, Melissa K. 2013. **"Tweeting for a Cause: Microblogging and Environmental Advocacy."** *Policy and Internet* 5(3): 304–27. DOI: https://doi.org/10.1002/1944-2866.POI335.

Merry discusses the implications of social media in public policy and government issues. She approaches Twitter as a microblogging site and evaluates how environmental interest groups use it for purposes of public outreach. She focuses on features of Twitter and how they shape interest group advocacy, exploring the implications of the activities of Twitter groups and the role they play in defining the problems, specifically those related to the government. Her content analysis of the communications about the oil spill in the Gulf of Mexico (2010), she claims, shows that Twitter was a quicker and more sustainable medium for interest groups during the disaster. In a section on cyberactivism and the policy process, the author explains that the Internet is integral to advocacy strategies, as it is a low-cost medium for activists and a platform that supports information dissemination. She also addresses Twitter's unique features and implications for advocacy, highlighting its transformative potential for interest groups. Merry follows the event-centred approach to conduct the study at hand, focusing on environmental groups and their responses to the disaster. The results of the study consider the speed of communication, patterns of issue attention over time, policy-relevant content, hyperlinks, and hashtags. She concludes that the medium used by interest groups plays a role in framing events and speeding up dissemination.

Mihailidis, Paul. 2014. "The Civic-Social Media Disconnect: Exploring Perceptions of Social Media for Engagement in the Daily Life of College Students." *Information, Communication & Society* 17(9): 1059–71. DOI: https://doi.org/10.1080/1369118X.2013.877054.

Mihailidis studies the perception of young adults in terms of social media habits and dispositions. He explores how young people's perception of social media influences the ways they use these tools to engage in daily social and civic life. He also studies how they use social networks to engage in conversations around public issues. Mihailidis asks, 'how do college students use social media for daily information and communication needs?' and 'how do college students perceive social media's role in daily life?' (1061). He conducts a study of 873 college students from nine universities by asking them to complete a 57-question survey. From these, the author selected a sample of 71 participants. The study results in findings that the author discusses according to the following separate sections: peer-content as driving news consumption and political expression, extending relationships through public networks, social learning, and leisure. Several findings emerged, including the resistance to using popular social networks in professional settings, which suggests that the tools in question are not the best tools for serious matters. Furthermore, the article suggests that the tools are social amplifiers that lack real context for concrete civic uses. The third implication is that the tools integrate various forms of content, disrupt the typical information flow, and facilitate peer-to-peer communication. Mihailidis concludes that social media enhances expression, sharing, creation, consumption, and collaboration, and that a full recognition of the opportunities provided by social media is essential in order to preserve the value of social media tools in daily civic life.

**Milberry, Kate. 2006. "Reconstructing the Internet: How Social Justice Activists Contest Technical Design in Cyberspace." *M/C Journal* 9(1): n.p. http://journal.media-culture.org.au/0603/10-milberry.php.

Milberry explores how activists have shaped the Internet to fit technical needs and movement goals. She begins by exploring 'geeks and global justice'—namely, how tech activism joins the free software ethos and concerns for social justice. As she explains, the novelty of tech activism is the incorporation of democratic goals of the global justice movement (GJM) into the technology itself. Milberry elaborates on the concept of politicizing technology, arguing that tech activists in global justice return to computer technology development for their political action. She addresses constructs such as Indymedia (the Independent Media Center; https://www.indymedia.org/), free software, and wiki software (what she calls 'Wild Wild Wikis: The Latest Frontier'). The author concludes that since the Internet is socially constructed, users are able to contribute to its development by shaping its future direction, allowing it to bridge the gap between 'geek' and activist communities, and supporting a digital infrastructure for progressive worldwide activism.

**Oostveen, Anne-Marie. 2010. "Citizens and Activists: Analysing the Reasons, Impact, and Benefits of Civic Emails Directed at a Grassroots Campaign."** *Information, Communication & Society* **13(6): 793–819. DOI: https://doi.org/10.1080/13691180903277637.**
Oostveen studies the exchange of emails between citizens and campaigners, specifically how such interactions can inform campaign tactics. She refers to Ennis and Schreuers's (1987) notion of weak supporters who claim to be neglected in the social movement literature.[7] The author studies whether individuals are engaged in political writing in the Internet age by reviewing emails sent by citizens to the general email addresses of a campaign. She also investigates reasons for which citizens used emails as their means of communication with activists, particularly whether or not these emails influenced the tactics of the activists and contributed to the outcomes of the campaign. She introduces the Dutch campaign she is working with, 'Wij vertrouwen stemcomputers niet,' which translates to 'We do not trust voting computers.' The content of the emails studied varied between the following categories: proponents vs. opponents, complaints, off-topic messages, information provision, volunteering, discussion and alternative solutions, and strategic input. She concludes that those emailing received personal replies and that getting serious feedback is a positive experience that increases the sense of political efficacy and commitment for citizens, in addition to making the activists more aware of their own strategies.

---

[7] James G. Ennis and Richard Schreuer (1987), "Mobilizing Weak Support for Social Movements: The Role of Grievance, Efficacy, and Cost," *Social Forces* 66(2): 390–409.

Pickerill, Jenny. 2009. "Symbolic Production, Representation, and Contested Identities: Anti-War Activism Online." *Information, Communication & Society* 12(7): 969–93. DOI: https://doi.org/10.1080/13691180802524469.

Pickerill explores the value of the symbolic dimension of collective action. She conducts three cumulative forms of analysis, which aim to explain how the symbolic domain is used. The author explains the strategic choices behind this use and links these representational choices to the subjective experience of the individual and to their processes of political identity construction. This is done through five case studies of British anti-war and peace organizations: the Stop the War Coalition, Faslane 365, the Society of Friends, Justice Not Vengeance, and Campaign for Nuclear Disarmament. She starts by studying online representations and collective identities, and claims that considering collective action as cognitive praxis is essential for an understanding of the operations and achievements of social movements. Pickerill continues to unpack how groups represent themselves, focusing on multiple online interventions, the use of iconic and confirmatory material, and the use of representation as projection. She also explains representational strategies that include organizational principles and ideological frameworks, diversity and frame bridging, and information and communication technologies (ICTs), as well as the enduring importance of face-to-face communication. The last section investigates the change of the politics of identity through the case of Muslim anti-war activists. The author concludes that groups have used ICT in three common ways: in multifarious formats and interventions, in confirmatory ways, and as means of symbolizing power and alliance with other groups.

Presner, Todd, David Shepard, and Yoh Kawano. 2014. *HyperCities: Thick Mapping in the Digital Humanities.* Cambridge, MA: Harvard University Press. https://escholarship.org/uc/item/3mh5t455.

In this monograph, Presner, Shepard, and Kawano explore digital humanities mapping. They begin by emphasizing the multiplicity implied by the prefix 'hyper,' and draw on the multiple spaces, media, records, and participants in hypertexts and HyperCities. They describe HyperCities as a series of evolving maps of real cities overlaid with thick information documenting the place's past, present, and future. The authors first introduce their audience to the theories and ideas of HyperCities, thick mapping, and digital humanities before turning to the specifics of the HyperCities project. Presner, Shepard, and Kawano highlight the collaborative authorship of the book and use different fonts to signal each of their authorial voices. They argue that by including multiple voices (theirs and those of other project leaders) they are able to open up 'windows' into the HyperCities project as well as showcase the texture and variety of digital mapping projects more generally. Overall, the authors make clear how digital mapping initiatives endeavour to recreate representations of place by bringing together the methods, content, and values of humanities research.

**Ritzer, George, and Nathan Jurgenson. 2010. "Production, Consumption, Prosumption: The Nature of Capitalism in the Age of the Digital 'Prosumer.'"** *Journal of Consumer Culture* **10(1): 13–36. DOI: https://doi.org/10.1177/1469540509354673.**
Ritzer and Jurgenson discuss the rise of prosumer capitalism. They define 'prosumer' as the dual focus on production and consumption, rather than privileging one over the other. The authors present an overview of production, consumption, and presumption, investigating prosumer society and capitalism in the age of the prosumer. Ritzer and Jurgenson address 'the inability of capitalists to control contemporary prosumers and their greater resistance to the incursions of capitalism' (22). They explain that one 'cannot ignore the gains for individuals as reasons for the rise of prosumption' (25). The authors explore the possibility of the emergence of a new economic form through Web 2.0, and investigate elements of abundance and effectiveness. They conclude with the notion that prosumer capitalist companies stand back from prosumers rather than attempting to control them.

**Sandoval-Almazan, Rodrigo, and J. Ramon Gil-Garcia. 2014. "Towards Cyberactivism 2.0? Understanding the Use of Social Media and Other Information Technologies for Political Activism and Social Movements."** *Government Information Quarterly* **31(3): 365–78. DOI: http://doi.org/10.1016/j.giq.2013.10.016.**
Sandoval-Almazan and Gil-Garcia present a model for analyzing the use of social media tools in social and political activism and apply this model to three protests in Mexico. They also investigate the effects of these tools on political activism. The authors aim to understand the process and the various stages of the development of the new form of activism known as Cyberactivism 2.0. Dividing their article into five different sections, Sandoval-Almazan and Gil-Garcia present a literature review on social movements, cyberactivism, and Internet technologies, and propose a stage-based model of cyberactivism and social media. They delineate their research design and methods, emphasizing the idea that their work aims to analyze the evolution of activism using technology, and to combine standard and online forms of data collection. The authors also read into the evolution of cyberactivism

by studying three cases in Mexico that include Cyberactivism 1.0, Twitter activism, and Cyberactivism 2.0. When discussing the results and implications, Sandoval-Almazan and Gil-Garcia identify differences and similarities across the three cases. They conclude that the use of online tools in social protest has had significant impact on promoting political activism, mobilizing certain portions of the society, and enhancing dissemination potentials for activist causes.

Tambini, Damian. 1999. "New Media and Democracy: The Civic Networking Movement." *New Media & Society* 1(3): 305–29. DOI: https://doi.org/ 10.1177/14614449922225609.

Tambini examines the use of computer-mediated communication (CMC) by civic networks, and how it encourages democratic citizenship, by studying the general implications of new media and democratic communication. He argues that CMC has implications for the formation and organization of political identity, and that the realization of CMC's democratic potential requires that access to digital media be non-redistricted. Tambini explores the civic networking movement, and how it became a trend due to the interplay of different strategies in political contexts; the author also explores various network designs. He explains that new civic networking occurs 'when many of the institutions of democratic communication … come into question because of migration and multiculturalism' (308). Tambini also claims that mass access and user-friendliness are new phenomena and constitute a turning point in public spheres. The author aims to understand the problem of regulating media in relation to the broader realm of social, political, and technological change. The author also discusses computer-mediated communication and democracy and investigates ways of using CMC to rejuvenate active citizenship, including information provision/access to information, preference measurement (referenda, polls, and representation), deliberation, and will formation/organization. On issues in network design, he lists bias, regulation, and access. Tambini concludes that civic networking is still in its early stages, and emphasizes the value of the future of civic networking.

Van Aelst, Peter, and Stefaan Walgrave. 2002. "New Media, New Movements? The Role of the Internet in Shaping the 'Anti-Globalization' Movement." *Information, Communication & Society* 5(4): 465–93. DOI: https://doi.org/10.1080/13691180208538801.

Van Aelst and Walgrave discuss the impact of the growth of the Internet on political processes. They argue that information and communication technologies facilitate participation in politics, which is thus made easier, faster, and more universal. The authors focus on anti-globalization protests and the formation of new social movements affected by these new media. Van Aelst and Walgrave study three conditions that establish movement formation, which are a shared definition of the problem as a basis for collective identity, actual mobilization of participants, and a network of different organizations. They provide an overview of transnational protest actions against globalization, and investigate the limitations and opportunities of the Internet. They select 17 websites for their data, choosing sites of organizations mentioned in news reports on major anti-globalization protests. The websites are divided into three different groups: sites devoted to single events, social organizations or action groups fully or partly engaged in anti-globalization, and supportive organizations. The study aims to discover whether the mentioned sites define anti-globalization in a similar manner, what mobilization function they fulfill, and the links between the organizations. They conclude that globalization is framed as an economic problem that has negative consequences on human beings and the environment, that politically there is lack of democratic legitimacy, and that the websites analyzed are hyperlinked to each other, which creates a network of related organizations.

Van Laer, Jeroen, and Peter Van Aelst. 2010. "Internet and Social Movement Action Repertoires: Opportunities and Limitations." *Information, Communication & Society* 13(8): 1146–71. DOI: https://doi.org/10.1080/13691181003628307.

Van Laer and Van Aelst explain how the Internet contributes to the shaping of the collective action repertoire of social movements involved in social and political change. They explain that the Internet allows new forms of online protest activities and enhances offline forms of social movements. The authors define social movements as networks of informal interaction engaged in causes based on shared collective identity, and their action repertoire as a means available for collective use to make claims on individuals and groups. They particularly focus on unorthodox and unconventional political behaviour. Discussing a typology of new digitalized action repertoire, Van Laer and Van Aelst study the actual possibilities the Internet provides. They present four quadrants of the digital action repertoire: Internet-supported action with low threshold, Internet-supported action with high threshold, Internet-based action with low threshold, and Internet-based action with high threshold. The authors explore the limitations of the internet and the action repertoire of social movements, arguing that digital media are fundamentally unable to create stable ties between activists to help maintain collective action. They conclude that the Internet has changed the action repertoire of social movements by allowing existing action forms to reach more people in faster and easier ways, and by creating new tools for activism.

**B. Reference List**

Bennett, W. Lance. 2004. "Communicating Global Activism: Strengths and Vulnerabilities of Networked Politics." In *Cyberprotest: New Media, Citizens and Social Movements*, edited by Wim van de Donk, Brian D. Loader, Paul G. Nixon, and Dieter Rucht, 123–46. London and New York: Routledge.

Bennett, W. Lance, and Alexandra Segerberg. 2011. "Digital Media and the Personalization of Collective Action." *Information, Communication & Society* 14(6): 770–99. DOI: https://doi.org/10.1080/1369118X.2011.579141.

Boyraz, Maggie, Aparna Krishnan, and Danielle Catona. 2011. "Who is Retweeted in Times of Political Protest? An Analysis of Characteristics of Top Tweeters and Top Retweeted Users During the 2011 Egyptian Revolution." *Atlantic Journal of Communication* 23(2): 99–119. DOI: https://doi.org/10.1080/15456870.2015.1013103.

Deibert, Ronald J. 2000. "International Plug 'n Play? Citizen Activism, the Internet, and Global Public Policy." *International Studies Perspectives* 1(3): 255–72. DOI: https://doi.org/10.1111/1528-3577.00026.

Filipacchi, Amanda. 2013. "Wikipedia's Sexism Toward Female Novelists." *New York Times*, April 24. http://www.nytimes.com/2013/04/28/opinion/sunday/wikipedias-sexism-toward-female-novelists.html. Archived at https://perma.cc/X526-R7NJ.

Ghobadi, Shahla, and Stewart Clegg. 2015. "'These Days Will Never Be Forgotten ...': A Critical Mass Approach to Online Activism." *Information and Organization* 25(1): 52–71. DOI: https://doi.org/10.1016/j.infoandorg.2014.12.002.

Häyhtiö, Tapio, and Jarmo Rinne. 2007. "Hard Rock Hallelujah! Empowering Reflexive Political Action on the Internet." *Journal for Cultural Research* 11(4): 337–58. DOI: https://doi.org/10.1080/14797580802038702.

Hill, Benjamin Mako, and Aaron Shaw. 2013. "The Wikipedia Gender Gap Revisited: Characterizing Survey Response Bias with Propensity Score

Estimation." *PLOS One* 8(6): n.p. DOI: https://doi.org/10.1371/journal.pone.0065782.

Howard, Philip N., Sheetal D. Agarwal, and Muzammil M. Hussain. 2011. "When Do States Disconnect Their Digital Networks? Regime Responses to the Political Uses of Social Media." *The Communication Review* 14(3) 216–32. DOI: https://doi.org/10.1080/10714421.2011.597254.

Lam, Shyong K., Anuradha Uduwage, Zhenhua Dong, Shilad Sen, David R. Musicant, Loren Terveen, and John Riedl. 2011. "WP: Clubhouse? An Exploration of Wikipedia's Gender Imbalance." Paper presented at 7th Annual International Symposium on Wikis and Open Collaboration (WikiSym 2011). http://files.grouplens.org/papers/wp-gender-wiki-sym2011.pdf.

Losh, Elisabeth. 2012. "Hacktivism and the Humanities: Programming Protest in the Era of the Digital University." In *Debates in the Digital Humanities*, edited by Matthew K. Gold, 161–86. Minneapolis: University of Minnesota Press. http://dhdebates.gc.cuny.edu/debates/text/32.

McDonald, Kevin. 2015. "From Indymedia to Anonymous: Rethinking Action and Identity in Digital Cultures." *Information, Communication & Society* 18(8): 968–82. DOI: https://doi.org/10.1080/1369118X.2015.1039561.

Merry, Melissa K. 2011. "Interest Group Activism on the Web: The Case of Environmental Organization." *Journal of Information Technology & Politics* 8(1): 110–28. DOI: https://doi.org/10.1080/19331681.2010.508003.

———. 2013. "Tweeting for a Cause: Microblogging and Environmental Advocacy." *Policy and Internet* 5(3): 304–27. DOI: https://doi.org/10.1002/1944-2866.POI335.

Mihailidis, Paul. 2014. "The Civic-Social Media Disconnect: Exploring Perceptions of Social Media for Engagement in the Daily Life of College Students." *Information, Communication & Society* 17(9): 1059–71. DOI: https://doi.org/10.1080/1369118X.2013.877054.

Milberry, Kate. 2006. "Reconstructing the Internet: How Social Justice Activists Contest Technical Design in Cyberspace." *M/C Journal* 9(1): n.p. http://journal.media-culture.org.au/0603/10-milberry.php.

Oostveen, Anne-Marie. 2010. "Citizens and Activists: Analysing the Reasons, Impact, and Benefits of Civic Emails Directed at a Grassroots Campaign."

*Information, Communication & Society* 13(6): 793–819. DOI: https://doi.org/10.1080/13691180903277637.

Pickerill, Jenny. 2009. "Symbolic Production, Representation, and Contested Identities: Anti-War Activism Online." *Information, Communication & Society* 12(7): 969–93. DOI: https://doi.org/10.1080/13691180802524469.

Presner, Todd, David Shepard, and Yoh Kawano. 2014. *HyperCities: Thick Mapping in the Digital Humanities.* Cambridge, MA: Harvard University Press. https://escholarship.org/uc/item/3mh5t455.

Ritzer, George, and Nathan Jurgenson. 2010. "Production, Consumption, Prosumption: The Nature of Capitalism in the Age of the Digital 'Prosumer.'" *Journal of Consumer Culture* 10(1): 13–36. DOI: https://doi.org/10.1177/1469540509354673.

Sandoval-Almazan, Rodrigo, and J. Ramon Gil-Garcia. 2014. "Towards Cyberactivism 2.0? Understanding the Use of Social Media and Other Information Technologies for Political Activism and Social Movements." *Government Information Quarterly* 31(3): 365–78. DOI: http://doi.org/10.1016/j.giq.2013.10.016.

Tambini, Damian. 1999. "New Media and Democracy: The Civic Networking Movement." *New Media & Society* 1(3): 305–29. DOI: https://doi.org/10.1177/14614449922225609.

Van Aelst, Peter, and Stefaan Walgrave. 2002. "New Media, New Movements? The Role of the Internet in Shaping the 'Anti-Globalization' Movement." *Information, Communication & Society* 5(4): 465–93. DOI: https://doi.org/10.1080/13691180208538801.

Van Laer, Jeroen, and Peter Van Aelst. 2010. "Internet and Social Movement Action Repertoires: Opportunities and Limitations." *Information, Communication & Society* 13(8): 1146–71. DOI: https://doi.org/10.1080/13691181003628307.

# Complete Reference List

Access2Research. 2019. "Access2Research." https://en.wikipedia.org/wiki/Access2Research.

Adema, Janneke. 2010. "Overview of Open Access Models for eBooks in the Humanities and Social Sciences." OAPEN Project Report. http://project.oapen.org/images/documents/openaccessmodels.pdf.

African Copyright and Access to Knowledge Project. 2019. "African Copyright and Access to Knowledge Project (ACA2K)." https://www.idrc.ca/en/project/african-copyright-and-access-knowledge-network-aca2k.

Akada Network. 2014. "Akada Network." https://www.facebook.com/akadanetwork/.

Akers, Katherine G., and Jennifer Doty. 2013. "Disciplinary Differences in Faculty Research Data Management Practices and Perspectives." *International Journal of Digital Curation* 8(2): 5–26. http://ijdc.net/index.php/ijdc/article/view/263.

Alliance for Taxpayer Access. 2019. "Alliance for Taxpayer Access." http://www.taxpayeraccess.org.

American Academic & Scholarly Research Center. 2019. "American Academic & Scholarly Research Center." http://aasrc.org.

Andersen, Christian Ulrik, and Søren Bro Pold. 2014. "Post-digital Books and Disruptive Literary Machines." *Formules: Revue des créations formelles* 18: 164–83.

Anderson, Charles. 1998. "Universal Access—Free and Open Access—It Depends ..." *Reference & User Services Quarterly* 38(1): 25–27.

Anderson, Colin R., and Stéphane M. McLachlan. 2015. "Transformative Research as Knowledge Mobilization: Transmedia, Bridges, and Layers." *Action Research* 14(3): 295–317. DOI: https://doi.org/10.1177/1476750315616684.

Anokwa, Yaw, Carl Hartung, Waylon Brunette, Gaetano Boriello, and Adam Lerer. 2009. "Open Source Data Collection in the Developing World."

*Computer* 42(10): 97–99. http://ieeexplore.ieee.org/xpl/articleDetails. jsp?arnumber=5280663&tag=1.

Arbuckle, Alyssa, Nina Belojevic, Tracey El Hajj, Randa El Khatib, Lindsey Seatter, and Raymond G. Siemens, with Alex Christie, Matthew Hiebert, Jon Saklofske, Jentery Sayers, Derek Siemens, Shaun Wong, and the INKE and ETCL Research Groups. 2017. "An Annotated Bibliography of Social Knowledge Creation." In *Social Knowledge Creation in the Humanities*, edited by Alyssa Arbuckle, Aaron Mauro, and Daniel Powell, 29–264. Toronto: Iter Press; Tempe: Arizona Center for Medieval and Renaissance Studies.

Arbuckle, Alyssa, Nina Belojevic, Matthew Hiebert, and Ray Siemens, with Shaun Wong, Derek Siemens, Alex Christie, Jon Saklofske, Jentery Sayers, and the INKE and ETCL Research Groups. 2014. "Social Knowledge Creation: Three Annotated Bibliographies." *Scholarly and Research Communication* 5(2): n.p. DOI: https://doi.org/10.22230/ src.2014v5n2a150.

Arbuckle, Alyssa, and Alex Christie, with the ETCL Research Group, INKE Research Group, and MVP Research Group. 2015. "Intersections Between Social Knowledge Creation and Critical Making." *Scholarly and Research Communication* 6(3): n.p. DOI: https://doi.org/10.22230/ src.2015v6n3a200.

Arbuckle, Alyssa, Alex Christie, Lynne Siemens, Aaron Mauro, and the INKE Research Group, eds. 2016. Special issue. *Scholarly and Research Communication* 7(2/3): n.p. http://src-online.ca/index.php/src/issue/ view/24.

Arbuckle, Alyssa, Constance Crompton, and Aaron Mauro. 2014. Introduction: "Building Partnerships to Transform Scholarly Publishing." *Scholarly and Research Communication* 5(4): n.p. http://src-online.ca/index.php/ src/issue/view/18.

Asmah, Josephine. 2014. "International Policy and Practice on Open Access for Monographs." Federation for the Humanities and Social Sciences. http://www.ideas-idees.ca/sites/default/files/aspp-oa-appendix.pdf.

Association for Computers and the Humanities. 2019. "Association for Computers and the Humanities." http://ach.org.

Association of Universities and Colleges of Canada–Canadian Association of Research Libraries Task Force on Academic Libraries and Scholarly Communication. 1997. "The Changing World of Scholarly Communication: Challenges and Choices for Canada—Final Report of the AUCC–CARL/ABRC Task Force." *Canadian Journal of Communication* 22(3): n.p.

Auer, Soren, Christian Bizer, Georgi Kobilarov, Jens Lehmann, Richard Cyganiak, and Zachary Ives. 2007. "DBpedia: A Nucleus for a Web of Open Data." In *The Semantic Web*, edited by Karl Aberer, Key-Sun Choi, Natasha Noy, Dean Allemang, Kyung-Il Lee, Lyndon Nixon, Jennifer Golbeck, et al., 722–35. Berlin and Heidelberg: Springer. http://link.springer.com/chapter/10.1007/978-3-540-76298-0_52.

Australasian Open Access Strategy Group. 2019. "Australasian Open Access Strategy Group." https://aoasg.org.au.

Authors Alliance. 2019. "Authors Alliance." https://www.authorsalliance.org.

Ayris, Paul, Erica McLaren, Martin Moyle, Catherine Sharp, and Lara Speicher. 2014. "Open Access in UCL: A New Paradigm for London's Global University in Research Support." *Australian Academic & Research Libraries* 45(4): 282–95.

Bailey, Charles W., Jr. 2007. "Open Access and Libraries." *Collection Management* 32(3–4): 351–83.

Barnes, Jessica V., Emily L. Altimare, Patricia A. Farrell, Robert E. Brown, C. Richard Burnett III, LaDonna Gamble, and James Davis. 2009. "Creating and Sustaining Authentic Partnerships with Community in a Systemic Model." *Journal of Higher Education Outreach and Engagement* 13(4): 15–29. https://files.eric.ed.gov/fulltext/EJ905410.pdf.

Bastian, Mathieu, Sebastien Heymann, and Mathieu Jacomy. 2009. "Gephi: An Open Source Software for Exploring and Manipulating Networks." In *Proceedings of the Third International AAAI Conference on Weblogs and Social Media*, 361–62. Palo Alto, CA: Association for the Advancement of Artificial Intelligence (AAAI). https://www.aaai.org/ocs/index.php/ICWSM/09/paper/view/154/1009.

Bath, Jon, Scott Schofield, and the INKE Research Group. 2015. "The Digital Book." In *The Cambridge Companion to the History of the Book*, edited by Leslie Howsam, 181–95. Cambridge: Cambridge University Press.

Bauer, Florian, and Martin Kaltenböck. 2012. *Linked Open Data: The Essentials.* Vienna: edition mono/monochrom. https://www.reeep.org/sites/default/files/LOD-the-Essentials_0.pdf.

Belojevic, Nina. 2015. "Developing an Open, Networked Peer Review System." *Scholarly and Research Communication* 6(2): n.p. DOI: https://doi.org/10.22230/src.2015v6n2a205.

Bennett, W. Lance. 2004. "Communicating Global Activism: Strengths and Vulnerabilities of Networked Politics." In *Cyberprotest: New Media, Citizens and Social Movements*, edited by Wim van de Donk, Brian D. Loader, Paul G. Nixon, and Dieter Rucht, 123–46. London: Routledge.

———, ed. 2008. *Civic Life Online: Learning How Digital Media Can Engage Youth.* Cambridge, MA: MIT Press.

Bennett, W. Lance, and Alexandra Segerberg. 2011. "Digital Media and the Personalization of Collective Action." *Information, Communication & Society* 14(6): 770–99. DOI: https://doi.org/10.1080/1369118X.2011.579141.

Berkman Klein Center for Internet & Society at Harvard University. 2018. "Harvard Open Access Project." https://cyber.law.harvard.edu/research/hoap.

Besser, Howard. 2004. "The Past, Present, and Future of Digital Libraries." In *A Companion to Digital Humanities*, edited by Susan Schreibman, Ray Siemens, and John Unsworth, 557–75. Oxford: Blackwell.

Bioline International. 2019. "Bioline International." http://www.bioline.org.br.

Björk, Bo-Christer. 2004. "Open Access to Scientific Publications—An Analysis of the Barriers to Change?" *Information Research* 9(2): n.p. http://informationr.net/ir/9-2/paper170.html.

Bohannon, John. 2013. "Who's Afraid of Peer Review?" *Science* 342: 60–65. DOI: www.doi.org/10.1126/science.342.6154.60.

Bonaccorsi, Andrea, and Cristina Rossi. 2003. "Why Open Source Software Can Succeed." *Research Policy* 32(7): 1243–58. DOI: https://doi.org/10.1016/S0048-7333(03)00051-9.

Bonney, Rick, Caren B. Cooper, Janis Dickinson, Steve Kelling, Tina Phillips, Kenneth V. Rosenberg, and Jennifer Shirk. 2009. "Citizen Science:

A Developing Tool for Expanding Science Knowledge and Scientific Literacy." *BioScience* 59(11): 977–84. DOI: http://dx.doi.org/10.1525/bio.2009.59.11.9.

Borgman, Christine L. 2007. *Scholarship in the Digital Age: Information, Infrastructure, and the Internet.* Cambridge, MA: MIT Press.

Bowdon, Melody A., and Russell G. Carpenter, eds. 2011. *Higher Education, Emerging Technologies, and Community Partnerships: Concepts, Models and Practices.* Hershey, PA: IGI Global.

Bowen, William R., Constance Crompton, and Matthew Hiebert. 2014. "Iter Community: Prototyping an Environment for Social Knowledge Creation and Communication." *Scholarly and Research Communication* 5(4): n.p. DOI: https://doi.org/10.22230/src.2014v5n4a193.

Boyraz, Maggie, Aparna Krishnan, and Danielle Catona. 2011. "Who is Retweeted in Times of Political Protest? An Analysis of Characteristics of Top Tweeters and Top Retweeted Users During the 2011 Egyptian Revolution." *Atlantic Journal of Communication* 23(2): 99–119. DOI: https://doi.org/10.1080/15456870.2015.1013103.

Bradley, Jean-Claude, Robert J. Lancashire, Andrew S.I.D. Lang, and Antony J. Williams. 2009. "The Spectral Game: Leveraging Open Data and Crowdsourcing for Education." *Journal of Cheminformatics* 1(9): 1–10. DOI: https://doi.org/10.1186/1758-2946-1-9.

Brown, Susan. 2016. "Towards Best Practices in Collaborative Online Knowledge Production." In *Doing Digital Humanities: Practice, Training, Research*, edited by Constance Crompton, Richard J. Lane, and Ray Siemens, 47–64. London and New York: Routledge.

Brown, Susan, and John Simpson. 2014. "The Changing Culture of Humanities Scholarship: Iteration, Recursion, and Versions in Scholarly Collaboration Environments." *Scholarly and Research Communication* 5(4): n.p. DOI: https://doi.org/10.22230/src.2014v5n4a191.

———. 2015. "An Entity By Any Other Name: Linked Open Data as a Basis for a Decentered, Dynamic Scholarly Publishing Ecology." *Scholarly and Research Communication* 6(2): n.p. DOI: https://doi.org/10.22230/src.2015v6n2a212.

Bruns, Axel. 2008. *Blogs, Wikipedia, Second Life, and Beyond: From Production to Produsage*. New York: Peter Lang.

Burke, Peter. 2000. *A Social History of Knowledge: From Gutenberg to Diderot*. Cambridge: Polity Press.

Butin, Dan W. 2010. *Service-Learning in Theory and Practice: The Future of Community Engagement in Higher Education*. New York: Palgrave Macmillan.

———. 2012a. "Rethinking the 'Apprenticeship of Liberty': The Case for Academic Programs in Community Engagement in Higher Education." *Journal of College and Character* 13(1): 1–8. DOI: https://doi.org/10.1515/jcc-2012-1859.

———. 2012b. "When Engagement is Not Enough: Building the Next Generation of the Engaged Campus." In *The Engaged Campus: Certificates, Minors, and Majors as the New Community Engagement*, edited by Dan Butin and Scott Seider, 1–11. New York: Palgrave Macmillan.

Butin, Dan W., and Scott Seider, eds. 2012. *The Engaged Campus: Certificates, Minors, and Majors as the New Community Engagement*. New York: Palgrave Macmillan.

Canadian Association of Research Libraries. n.d. "Canadian Association of Research Libraries." http://www.carl-abrc.ca.

———. n.d. "Open Access." Canadian Association of Research Libraries. http://www.carl-abrc.ca/advancing-research/scholarly-communication/open-access/.

Cantor, Nancy, and Steven D. Lavine. 2006. "Taking Public Scholarship Seriously." *The Chronicle of Higher Education* 52(40): B20. https://www.chronicle.com/article/Taking-Public-Scholarship/22684.

Caplan, Scott E., Elizabeth M. Perse, and Janice E. Gennaria. 2007. "Computer-Mediated Technology and Social Interaction." In *Communication Technology and Social Change: Theory and Implications*, edited by Carolyn A. Lin and David J. Atkin, 39–57. Mahwah, NJ: Lawrence Erlbaum Associates.

Carletti, Laura, Derek McAuley, Dominic Price, Gabriella Giannachi, and Steve Benford. 2013. "Digital Humanities and Crowdsourcing: An Exploration."

*Museums and the Web 2013 Conference* (*MW2013*). Silver Spring, MD: Museums and the Web LLC. http://mw2013.museumsandtheweb.com/ paper/digital-humanities-and-crowdsourcing-an-exploration-4/.

Castelli, Donatella, Simon J.E. Taylor, and Franco Zoppi. 2010. "Open Knowledge on E-Infrastructures: The BELIEF Project Digital Library." *IST-Africa, 2010*, 1–15. Dublin: IIMC International Information Management Corporation. https://ieeexplore.ieee.org/document/5753044.

Causer, Tim, and Melissa Terras. 2014. "Crowdsourcing Bentham: Beyond the Traditional Boundaries of Academic History." *International Journal of Humanities and Arts Computing* 8(1): 46–64. DOI: http://dx.doi. org/10.3366/ijhac.2014.0119.

Causer, Tim, Justin Tonra, and Valerie Wallace. 2012. "Transcription Maximized; Expense Minimized? Crowdsourcing and Editing *The Collected Works of Jeremy Bentham*." *Digital Scholarship in the Humanities* (formerly *Literary and Linguistic Computing*) 27(2): 119–37. DOI: http:// dx.doi.org/10.1093/llc/fqs004.

Center for Open Science. 2019. "Center for Open Science." https://cos.io.

Center for the Study of the Public Domain. 2019. "Center for the Study of the Public Domain." Duke University School of Law. https://law.duke.edu/ cspd/.

Chan, Leslie. 2004. "Supporting and Enhancing Scholarship in the Digital Age: The Role of Open-Access Institutional Repositories." *Canadian Journal of Communication* 29(3): 277–300. https://www.cjc-online.ca/index.php/ journal/article/view/1455/1579.

Chang, Yu-Wei. 2015. "Librarians' Contribution to Open Access Journal Publishing in Library and Information Science From the Perspective of Authorship." *Journal of Academic Librarianship* 41(5): 660–68. DOI: https://doi.org/10.1016/j.acalib.2015.06.006.

Childs, Merilyn, and Regine Wagner. 2015. "Open Sourced Personal, Networked Learning and Higher Education Credentials." In *Open Learning and Formal Credentialing in Higher Education*, edited by Shirley Reushie, Amy Antonio, and Mike Keppell, 223–44. Hershey, PA: IGI Global.

Chopra, Samir, and Scott Dexter. 2009. "The Freedoms of Software and Its Ethical Uses." *Ethics and Information Technology* 11(4): 287–97. DOI: https://doi.org/10.1007/s10676-009-9191-0.

Christians, Clifford G. 2015. "Social Justice and Internet Technology." *New Media & Society* 18(11): 2760–73. DOI: https://doi.org/10.1177/1461444815604130.

Coalition for Open Access Policy Institutions. 2018. "Coalition for Open Access Policy Institutions." https://sparcopen.org/coapi/.

Cohen, Daniel J. 2010. "Open Access Publishing and Scholarly Values." Personal blog post, May 27. https://dancohen.org/2010/05/27/open-access-publishing-and-scholarly-values/. Archived at https://perma.cc/78MH-PK43.

Compute Canada. 2014. "Sustainable Planning for Advanced Research Computing (SPARC)." News release, June 23. https://www.compute-canada.ca/news/compute-canada-announces-sustainable-planning-for-advanced-research-computing-sparc/.

Confederation of Open Access Repositories. 2019. "Confederation of Open Access Repositories." https://www.coar-repositories.org.

Coonin, Bryna, and Leigh Younce. 2009. "Publishing in Open Access Journals in The Social Sciences and Humanities: Who's Doing It and Why." Paper presented at the *ACRL Fourteenth National Conference*. http://www.ala.org/acrl/sites/ala.org.acrl/files/content/conferences/confsandpreconfs/national/seattle/papers/85.pdf.

Cooper, Amanda, and Ben Levin. 2010. "Some Canadian Contributions to Understanding Knowledge Mobilisation." *Evidence & Policy: A Journal of Research, Debate and Practice* 6(3): 351–69. DOI: https://doi.org/10.1332/174426410X524839.

Cooper, Caren B., Janis Dickinson, Tina Phillips, and Rick Bonney. 2007. "Citizen Science as a Tool for Conservation in Residential Ecosystems." *Ecology and Society* 12(2): Article 11. http://www.ecologyandsociety.org/vol12/iss2/art11/.

Corrall, Sheila, Mary Anne Kennan, and Wasseem Afzal. 2013. "Bibliometrics and Research Data Management Services: Emerging Trends in Library Support for Research." *Library Trends* 61(3): 636–74. DOI: http://www.doi.org/10.1353/lib.2013.0005.

Crompton, Constance, Alyssa Arbuckle, and Raymond G. Siemens, with the Devonshire Manuscript Editorial Group. 2013. "Understanding the Social Edition Through Iterative Implementation: The Case of the *Devonshire MS* (BL Add MS 17492)." *Scholarly and Research Communication* 4(3): n.p. DOI: https://doi.org/10.22230/src.2013v4n3a118.

Crompton, Constance, Cole Mash, and Raymond G. Siemens. 2015. "Playing Well with Others: The Social Edition and Computational Collaboration." *Scholarly and Research Communication* 6(3): n.p. DOI: https://doi.org/10.22230/src.2015v6n3a111.

Crompton, Constance, Raymond G. Siemens, and Alyssa Arbuckle, with the INKE Research Group. 2015. "Enlisting 'Vertues Noble & Excelent': Behaviour, Credit, and Knowledge Organization in the Social Edition." *Digital Humanities Quarterly* 9(2): n.p. http://www.digitalhumanities.org/dhq/vol/9/2/000202/000202.html.

Dahlander, Linus, and Mats G. Magnusson. 2005. "Relationships between Open Source Software Companies and Communities: Observations from Nordic Firms." *Research Policy* 34(4): 481–93. DOI: https://doi.org/10.1016/j.respol.2005.02.003.

Davies, Tim. 2010. "Open Data, Democracy and Public Sector Reform. A Look at Open Government Data Use from Data.gov.uk." *Open Data Impacts.* http://www.opendataimpacts.net/report/.

Deibert, Ronald J. 2000. "International Plug 'n Play? Citizen Activism, the Internet, and Global Public Policy." *International Studies Perspectives* 1(3): 255–72. DOI: https://doi.org/10.1111/1528-3577.00026.

Deuze, Mark, Axel Bruns, and Christopher Neuberger. 2007. "Preparing for an Age of Participatory News." *Journalism Practice* 1(3): 322–38. DOI: https://doi.org/10.1080/17512780701504864.

Di Noia, Tommaso, Roberto Mirizzi, Vito Claudio Ostuni, Davide Romito, and Markus Zanker. 2012. "Linked Open Data to Support Content-Based Recommender Systems." In *Proceedings of the 8th International Conference on Semantic Systems (I-SEMANTICS '12)*, 1–8. New York: ACM. DOI: http://dl.acm.org/citation.cfm?id=2362501.

Dumova, Tatyana. 2012. "Social Interaction Technologies and the Future of Blogging." In *Blogging in the Global Society: Cultural, Political and*

*Geographical Aspects,* edited by Tatyana Dumova and Richard Fiordo, 249–74. Hershey, PA: IGI Global.

Dunlop, Judith M., and Graham Fawcett. 2008. "Technology-Based Approaches to Social Work and Social Justice." *Journal of Policy Practice* 7(2–3): 140–54. DOI: https://doi.org/10.1080/15588740801937961.

Edwards, Heather R., and Richard Hoefer. 2010. "Are Social Work Advocacy Groups Using Web 2.0 Effectively?" *Journal of Policy Practice* 9(3–4): 220–39. DOI: https://doi.org/10.1080/15588742.2010.489037.

Eisenstein, Elizabeth L. 1979. *The Printing Press as an Agent of Social Change.* 2 vols. Cambridge: Cambridge University Press.

Estellés-Arolas, Enrique, and Fernando González-Ladrón-de-Guevara. 2012. "Towards an Integrated Crowdsourcing Definition." *Journal of Information Science* 38(2): 189–200. DOI: http://dx.doi.org/10.1177/0165551512437638.

European University Association. 2019. "European University Association: The Voice of Europe's Universities." http://www.eua.be.

Eve, Martin Paul. 2015. "Open Access Publishing and Scholarly Communication in Non-Scientific Disciplines." *Online Information Review* 39(5): 717–32. DOI: https://doi.org/10.1108/OIR-04-2015-0103.

Farrington, John, and Conor Farrington. 2005. "Rural Accessibility, Social Inclusion and Justice: Towards Conceptualisation." *Journal of Transport Geography* 13(1): 1–12. DOI: https://doi.org/10.1016/j.jtrangeo.2004.10.002.

Fear, Kathleen. 2011. "'You Made It, You Take Care of It': Data Management as Personal Information Management." *International Journal of Digital Curation* 6(2): 53–77. DOI: https://doi.org/10.2218/ijdc.v6i2.190.

Federation for the Humanities and Social Sciences. 2019a. "Issues." Federation for the Humanities and Social Sciences / Fédération des sciences humaines. http://www.ideas-idees.ca/issues/open-access-aspp.

———. 2019b. "Our Members." Federation for the Humanities and Social Sciences / Fédération des sciences humaines. http://www.ideas-idees.ca/about/members.

Feller, Joseph, and Brian Fitzgerald. 2002. *Understanding Open Source Software Development.* Boston: Addison-Wesley Longman.

Filipacchi, Amanda. 2013. "Wikipedia's Sexism Toward Female Novelists." *New York Times,* April 24. http://www.nytimes.com/2013/04/28/opinion/sunday/wikipedias-sexism-toward-female-novelists.html. Archived at https://perma.cc/X526-R7NJ.

FinnOA. 2008. "Finnish Open Access Working Group (FinnOA)." http://www.openaccess.fi/info/english.html.

Fitzgerald, Brian. 2006. "The Transformation of Open Source Software." *MIS Quarterly* 30(3): 587–98. DOI: https://www.doi.org/10.2307/25148740.

Fitzpatrick, Kathleen. 2007. "CommentPress: New (Social) Structures for New (Networked) Texts." *Journal of Electronic Publishing* 10(3): n.p. DOI: http://dx.doi.org/10.3998/3336451.0010.305.

———. 2011. *Planned Obsolescence: Publishing, Technology, and the Future of the Academy.* New York: New York University Press.

Fjällbrant, Nancy. 1997. "Scholarly Communication—Historical Development and New Possibilities." In *Proceedings of the IATUL Conferences.* West Lafayette, IN: Purdue University Libraries. http://docs.lib.purdue.edu/iatul/1997/papers/5/.

FORCE11. 2019. "FORCE11." https://www.force11.org.

Foundation for Open Access Statistics. 2013. "Foundation for Open Access Statistics." http://www.foastat.org.

Franklin, Michael J., Donald Kossman, Tim Kraska, Sukriti Ramesh, and Reynold Xin. 2011. "CrowdDB: Answering Queries with Crowdsourcing." In *Proceedings of the 2011 ACM SIGMOD International Conference on Management of Data (SIGMOD '11),* 61–72. New York: ACM.

Free Knowledge Institute. 2015. "Free Knowledge Institute." http://freeknowledge.eu.

Fund, Sven. 2015. "Will Open Access Change the Game? Hypotheses on the Future Cooperation of Libraries, Researchers, and Publishers." *Bibliothek Forschung und Praxis* 39(2): 206–9. DOI: https://doi.org/10.1515/bfp-2015-0025.

Gahran, Amy. 2012. "SeeClickFix: Crowdsourced Local Problem Reporting as Community News." *Knight Digital Media Center*, September 19. http://www.knightdigitalmediacenter.org/blogs/agahran/2012/09/seeclick-fix-crowdsourced-local-problem-reporting-community-news.html. Archived at https://perma.cc/T6NF-EGZX.

Gaines, Annie M. 2015. "From Concerned to Cautiously Optimistic: Assessing Faculty Perception and Knowledge of Open Access in a Campus-Wide Study." *Journal of Librarianship & Scholarly Communication* 3(1): 1–40. DOI: https://doi.org/10.7710/2162-3309.1212.

Gainforth, Heather L., Amy E. Latimer-Cheung, Spencer Moore, Peter Athanasopoulos, and Kathleen A. Martin Ginis. 2014. "Using Network Analysis to Understand Knowledge Mobilization in a Community-based Organization." *International Journal of Behavioral Medicine* 22(3): 292–300. DOI: https://www.doi.org/10.1007/s12529-014-9430-6.

Gallo, Travis, and Damon Waitt. 2011. "Creating a Successful Citizen Science Model to Detect and Report Invasive Species." *BioScience* 61(6): 459–65. DOI: https://doi.org/10.1525/bio.2011.61.6.8.

Gargouri, Yassine, Chawki Hajjem, Vincent Larivière, Yves Gringas, Les Carr, Tim Brody, and Stevan Harnad. 2010. "Self-Selected or Mandated, Open Access Increases Citation Impact for Higher Quality Research." *PLOS One* 5(10): n.p. DOI: https://doi.org/10.1371/journal.pone.0013636.

Geiger, Christian P., and Jörn von Lucke. 2012. "Open Government and (Linked) (Open) (Government) (Data)." *eJournal of eDemocracy and Open Government* 4(2): 265–78. DOI: https://doaj.org/article/0bc5e4c6a0e84ee3a74c4aa4190c8126.

German Research Foundation. 2019. "Alliance of Science Organisations in Germany." http://www.dfg.de/en/dfg_profile/alliance/.

Ghobadi, Shahla, and Stewart Clegg. 2015. "'These Days Will Never Be Forgotten …': A Critical Mass Approach to Online Activism." *Information and Organization* 25(1): 52–71. DOI: https://doi.org/10.1016/j.infoandorg.2014.12.002.

Ghosh, Arpita, Satyen Kale, and Preston McAfee. 2011. "Who Moderates the Moderators? Crowdsourcing Abuse Detection in User-Generated Content." In *Proceedings of the 12th ACM Conference on Electronic*

*Commerce (EC '11)*, 167–76. New York: ACM. DOI: https://doi.org/ 10.1145/1993574.1993599.

Given, Lisa M., Stan Ruecker, Heather Simpson, Elizabeth Sadler, and Andrea Ruskin. 2007. "Inclusive Interface Design for Seniors: Image-Browsing for a Health Information Context." *Journal of the American Society for Information Science and Technology* 58(11): 1610–17. DOI: https://doi.org/10.1002/asi.20645.

Godfrey, Michael W., and Qiang Tu. 2000. "Evolution in Open Source Software: A Case Study." In *Proceedings of the International Conference on Software Maintenance (ICSM '00)*, 131–42. Washington, DC: IEEE Computer Society. http://svn-plg.uwaterloo.ca/~migod/papers/2000/icsm00.pdf.

Goldkind, Lauri. 2014. "E-Advocacy in Human Services: The Impact of Organizational Conditions and Characteristics on Electronic Advocacy Activities among Nonprofits." *Journal of Policy Practice* 13(4): 300–15. DOI: https://doi.org/10.1080/15588742.2014.929073.

Görlitz, Olaf, and Steffen Staab. 2011. "Federated Data Management and Query Optimization for Linked Open Data." In *New Directions in Web Data Management 1*, edited by Athena Vakali and Lakhmi C. Jain, 109–37. Berlin: Springer. DOI: https://doi.org/10.1007/978-3-642-17551-0_5.

Government of Canada. 2015a. "Digital Canada 150 2.0." Industry Canada. http://www.digitaleconomy.gc.ca/eic/site/028.nsf/eng/home.

———. 2015b. "Tri-Agency Open Access Policy on Publications." Science and Technology for Canadians. http://www.science.gc.ca/default. asp?lang=En&n=F6765465-1.

Graham, Ian D., Jacqueline Tetroe, and KT Theories Research Group. 2007. "Some Theoretical Underpinnings of Knowledge Translation." *Academic Emergency Medicine* 14(11): 936–41. https://onlinelibrary.wiley.com/ doi/full/10.1111/j.1553-2712.2007.tb02369.x.

Gray, Jonathan. 2015. "Five Ways Open Data Can Boost Democracy around the World." *The Guardian*, February 20. https://www.theguardian.com/ public-leaders-network/2015/feb/20/open-data-day-fairer-taxes. Archived at https://perma.cc/2P4P-4V3A.

Grumbach, Elizabeth, and Laura Mandell. 2014. "Meeting Scholars Where They Are: The Advanced Research Consortium (ARC) and a Social

Humanities Infrastructure." *Scholarly and Research Communication* 5(4): n.p. DOI: https://doi.org/10.22230/src.2014v5n4a189.

Gurstein, Michael B. 2011. "Open Data: Empowering the Empowered or Effective Data Use for Everyone?" *First Monday* 16(2): n.p. https://first-monday.org/article/view/3316/2764.

Hall, Peter V., and Ian MacPherson, eds. 2011. *Community-University Research Partnerships: Reflections on the Canadian Social Economy Experience.* Victoria: University of Victoria. https://ccednet-rcdec.ca/sites/cced-net-rcdec.ca/files/Comm_Univ_Res_Partnerships_SE.pdf.

Hamlyn, Hilda M. 1946. "Eighteenth-Century Circulating Libraries in England." *The Library* 5(3–4): 197–222. DOI: https://doi.org/10.1093/library/s5-I.3-4.197.

Hampson, Crystal. 2014. "The Adoption of Open Access Funds Among Canadian Academic Research Libraries, 2008–2012." *The Canadian Journal of Library & Information Practice & Research* 9(2): 1–14. DOI: https://doi.org/10.21083/partnership.v9i2.3115.

Harris, Michael H. 1999. *History of Libraries in the Western World.* 4th ed. Lanham, MD: Scarecrow Press.

Hars, Alexander, and Shaosong Ou. 2001. "Working for Free?—Motivations of Participating in Open Source Projects." In *Proceedings of the 34th Annual Hawaii International Conference on System Sciences (HICSS '01)*, 7014. Washington, DC: IEEE Computer Society.

Hart, Angie, and Simon Northmore. 2011. "Auditing and Evaluating University-Community Engagement: Lessons from a UK Case Study." *Higher Education Quarterly* 65(1): 34–58. DOI: https://doi.org/10.1111/j.1468-2273.2010.00466.x.

Hart, Angie, and David Wolff. 2006. "Developing Local 'Communities of Practice' through Local Community-University Partnerships." *Planning Practice and Research* 21(1): 121–38. DOI: https://doi.org/10.1080/02697450600901616.

Harth, Andreas, Katja Hose, and Ralf Schenkel, eds. 2014. *Linked Data Management.* Boca Raton, FL: CRC Press.

Hartung, Carl, Adam Lerer, Yaw Anokwa, Clint Tseng, Waylon Brunette, and Gaetano Borriello. 2010. "Open Data Kit: Tools to Build Information

Services for Developing Regions." In *Proceedings of the 4th ACM/IEEE International Conference on Information and Communication Technologies and Development (ICTD '10)*, Article 18. New York: ACM. DOI: https://doi.org/10.1145/2369220.2369236.

Hausenblas, Michael, and Marcel Karnstedt. 2010. "Understanding Linked Open Data as a Web-Scale Database." In *Proceedings of the Second International Conference on Advances in Databases, Knowledge, and Data Applications (DBKDA 2010)*, 56–61. Los Alamitos, CA: IEEE Computer Society. DOI: https://doi.org/10.1109/DBKDA.2010.23.

Häyhtiö, Tapio, and Jarmo Rinne. 2007. "Hard Rock Hallelujah! Empowering Reflexive Political Action on the Internet." *Journal for Cultural Research* 11(4): 337–58. DOI: https://doi.org/10.1080/14797580802038702.

Heath, Malcolm, Michael Jubb, and David Robey. 2008. "E-Publication and Open Access in the Arts and Humanities in the UK." *Ariadne* 54: n.p. http://www.ariadne.ac.uk/issue/54/heath-et-al/. Archived at https://perma.cc/NKM4-E3T5.

Hedges, Mark, Adil Hasan, and Tobias Blanke. 2007. "Management and Preservation of Research Data with iRODS." In *Proceedings of the ACM First Workshop on CyberInfrastructure: Information Management in eScience (CIMS '07)*, 17–22. New York: ACM. http://dl.acm.org/citation.cfm?id=1317358.

Henty, Margaret, Belinda Weaver, Stephanie J. Bradbury, and Simon Porter. 2008. "Investigating Data Management Practices in Australian Universities." Australian Partnership for Sustainable Repositories (APSR). http://eprints.qut.edu.au/14549/1/14549.pdf.

Hiebert, Matthew, Raymond Siemens, William R. Bowen, the ETCL and Iter Advisory Groups, and the INKE Research Group. 2015. "Implementing a Social Knowledge Creation Environment." *Scholarly and Research Communication* 6(3): n.p. DOI: https://doi.org/10.22230/src.2015v6n3a223.

Hill, Benjamin Mako, and Aaron Shaw. 2013. "The Wikipedia Gender Gap Revisited: Characterizing Survey Response Bias with Propensity Score Estimation." *PLOS One* 8(6): n.p. DOI: https://doi.org/10.1371/journal.pone.0065782.

Holland, Barbara, and Judith A. Ramaley. 2008. "Creating a Supportive Environment for Community-University Engagement: Conceptual Frameworks." In *Engaging Communities, Proceedings of the 31st HERDSA Annual Conference, Rotorua, 1–4 July 2008*, 11–25. http://www.herdsa.org.au/system/files/Holland%20%26%20Ramaley.pdf.

Holley, Rose. 2010. "Crowdsourcing: How and Why Should Libraries Do It?" *D-Lib Magazine* 16(3/4): n.p. DOI: https://www.doi.org/10.1045/march2010-holley.

Howard, Philip N., Sheetal D. Agarwal, and Muzammil M. Hussain. 2011. "When Do States Disconnect Their Digital Networks? Regime Responses to the Political Uses of Social Media." *The Communication Review* 14(3) 216–32. DOI: https://doi.org/10.1080/10714421.2011.597254.

Hoy, Ariane, and Matthew Johnson, eds. 2013. *Deepening Community Engagement in Higher Education: Forging New Pathways*. New York: Palgrave Macmillan.

International Community for Open Research and Education. n.d. "Welcome to ICORE, the International Community for Open Research and Open Education." http://www.icore-online.org.

International Federation of Library Associations and Institutions. 2011. "IFLA Open Access Taskforce Established." News release, October 11. https://www.ifla.org/news/ifla-open-access-taskforce-established.

Jackson, Michael J., Mario Antonioletti, Bartosz Dobrzelecki, and Neil Chue Hong. 2011. "Distributed Data Management with OGSA-DAI." In *Grid and Cloud Database Management*, edited by Sandro Fiore and Giovanni Aloisio, 63–86. Berlin and Heidelberg: Springer. DOI: https://doi.org/10.1007/978-3-642-20045-8_4.

Jackson, Mike, Mario Antonioletti, Alastair Hume, Tobias Blanke, Gabriel Bodard, Mark Hedges, and Shrija Rajbhandari. 2009. "Building Bridges Between Islands of Data—An Investigation into Distributed Data Management in the Humanities." In *Proceedings of the 2009 Fifth IEEE International Conference on e-Science*, 33–39. Los Alamitos, CA: IEEE Computer Society. DOI: https://www.doi.org/10.1109/e-Science.2009.13.

Jain, Prateek, Pascal Hitzler, Amit P. Seth, Kunal Verma, and Peter Z. Yeh. 2010. "Ontology Alignment for Linked Open Data." In *The*

*Semantic Web - ISCW 2010*, edited by Peter F. Patel-Schneider et al., 402–17. Berlin and Heidelberg: Springer. DOI: https://doi.org/10.1007/978-3-642-17746-0_26.

Janssen, Katleen. 2012. "Open Government Data and the Right to Information: Opportunities and Obstacles." *The Journal of Community Informatics* 8(2): n.p. http://www.ci-journal.net/index.php/ciej/article/view/952.

Janssen, Marijn, Yannis Charalabidis, and Anneke Zuiderwijk. 2012. "Benefits, Adoption Barriers and Myths of Open Data and Open Government." *Information Systems Management* 29(4): 258–68. DOI: https://doi.org/10.1080/10580530.2012.716740.

Jenkins, Henry, and Mark Deuze. 2008. "Convergence Culture." *Convergence: The International Journal of Research into New Media Technologies* 14(1): 5–12. DOI: https://www.doi.org/10.1177/1354856507084415.

Jensen, Klaus Bruhn, and Rasmus Helles. 2011. "The Internet as a Cultural Forum: Implications for Research." *New Media & Society* 13(4): 517–33. DOI: https://doi.org/10.1177/1461444810373531.

Johns, Adrian. 1998. *The Nature of the Book: Print and Knowledge in the Making.* Chicago: University of Chicago Press.

Johnson, Jeffrey Alan. 2014. "From Open Data to Information Justice." *Ethics and Information Technology* 16(4): 263–74. DOI: https://doi.org/10.1007/s10676-014-9351-8.

Johnston, Lisa, Meghan Lafferty, and Beth Petsan. 2012. "Training Researchers on Data Management: A Scalable, Cross-Disciplinary Approach." *Journal of eScience Librarianship* 1(2): 79–87. DOI: http://dx.doi.org/10.7191/jeslib.2012.1012.

Jones, Sarah, Alexander Ball, and Çuna Ekmekcioglu. 2008. "The Data Audit Framework: A First Step in the Data Management Challenge." *International Journal of Digital Curation* 3(2): 112–20. DOI: https://doi.org/10.2218/ijdc.v3i2.62.

Jones, Steven E. 2014. "Publications." In *The Emergence of the Digital Humanities*, 147–77. New York and London: Routledge.

Jordan, Mary Wilkins. 2015. "Public Library History on the Lewis and Clark Trail." *Public Library Quarterly* 34(2): 162–77. DOI: https://doi.org/10.1080/01616846.2015.1036709.

Jordan, Rebecca C., Heidi L. Ballard, and Tina B. Phillips. 2012. "Key Issues and New Approaches for Evaluating Citizen-Science Learning Outcomes." *Frontiers in Ecology and the Environment* 10(6): 307–9. DOI: https://doi.org/10.1890/110280.

Kalampokis, Evangelos, Efthimios Tambouris, and Konstantinos Tarabanis. 2011. "Open Government Data: A Stage Model." In *Proceedings of the 10th IFIP WG 8.5 International Conference* (*EGOV 2011*), edited by Marijn Janssen et al., 235–46. Heidelberg: Springer. DOI: https://doi.org/10.1007/978-3-642-22878-0_20.

Keen, Peter, and Margaret Tan. 2009. "Knowledge Fusion: A Framework for Extending the Rigor and Relevance of Knowledge Management." In *Selected Readings on Information Technology Management: Contemporary Issues*, edited by George Kelley, 358–74. Hershey, PA: IGI Global. DOI: https://www.doi.org/10.4018/978-1-60566-092-9.ch020.

Kelly, Thomas. 1966. *Early Public Libraries: A History of Public Libraries in Great Britain Before 1850.* London: Library Association.

———. 1973. *A History of Public Libraries in Great Britain, 1845–1965.* London: Library Association.

Kelty, Christopher M. 2008. *Two Bits: The Cultural Significance of Free Software.* Durham, NC: Duke University Press.

Kingsley, Danny. 2013. "Build It and They Will Come? Support for Open Access in Australia." *Scholarly and Research Communication* 4(1): n.p. DOI: https://doi.org/10.22230/src.2013v4n1a39.

Kitchin, Rob, Sandra Collins, and Dermot Frost. 2015. "Funding Models for Open Access Digital Data Repositories." *Online Information Review* 39(5): 664–81. DOI: https://www.doi.org/10.1108/OIR-01-2015-0031.

Kline, Jesse. 2013. "Why Canada has 'Third World Access to the Internet.'" *National Post*, September 24. http://news.nationalpost.com/full-comment/jesse-kline-why-canada-has-third-world-access-to-the-internet. Archived at https://perma.cc/BH8L-K33K.

Knowledge Exchange. n.d. "KE: Knowledge Exchange." http://www.knowledge-exchange.info.

Koehn, Philipp, Hieu Hoang, Alexandra Birch, Chris Callison-Burch, Marcello Federico, Nicola Bertoldi, Brooke Cowan, et al. 2007. "Moses: Open

Source Toolkit for Statistical Machine Translation." In *Proceedings of the 45th Annual Meeting of the ACL on Interactive Poster and Demonstration Sessions*, 177–80. https://www.aclweb.org/anthology/P07-2045.

Kogut, Bruce, and Anca Metiu. 2001. "Open Source Software Development and Distributed Innovation." *Oxford Review of Economic Policy* 17(2): 248–64. https://www.jstor.org/stable/23606809.

Kondratova, Irina, and Ilia Goldfarb. 2004. "Virtual Communities of Practice: Design for Collaboration and Knowledge Creation." *Proceedings of the European Conference on Products and Processes Modelling* (*ECPPM 2004*). NRC Publications Archive. https://nrc-publications.canada.ca/eng/view/accepted/?id=9a521a4b-bd4b-43c6-88bf-28288de1b1ff.

Krier, Laura, and Carly A. Strasser. 2014. *Data Management for Libraries: A LITA Guide*. Chicago: ALA TechSource.

Laakso, Mikael, and Bo-Christer Björk. 2012. "Anatomy of Open Access Publishing: A Study of Longitudinal Development and Internal Structure." *BMC Medicine* 10(124): n.p. DOI: https://doi.org/10.1186/1741-7015-10-124.

Lakhani, Karim R., and Eric von Hippel. 2003. "How Open Source Software Works: 'Free' User-to-User Assistance." *Research Policy* 32(6): 923–43. DOI: https://doi.org/10.1016/S0048-7333(02)00095-1.

Lam, Shyong K., Anuradha Uduwage, Zhenhua Dong, Shilad Sen, David R. Musicant, Loren Terveen, and John Riedl. 2011. "WP: Clubhouse? An Exploration of Wikipedia's Gender Imbalance." Paper presented at 7th Annual International Symposium on Wikis and Open Collaboration (WikiSym 2011). http://files.grouplens.org/papers/wp-gender-wikisym2011.pdf.

Lampe, Cliff, Robert LaRose, Charles Steinfield, and Kurt DeMaagd. 2011. "Inherent Barriers to the Use of Social Media for Public Policy Informatics." *The Innovation Journal* 16(1): Article 6.

Landry, Réjean, Nabil Amara, and Moktar Lamari. 2001. "Utilization of Social Science Research Knowledge in Canada." *Research Policy* 30(2): 333–49. DOI: https://doi.org/10.1016/S0048-7333(00)00081-0.

Lane, Richard J. 2014. "Innovation through Tradition: New Scholarly Publishing Applications Modelled on Faith-Based Electronic Publishing and Learning Environments." *Scholarly and Research Communication* 5(4): n.p. DOI: https://doi.org/10.22230/src.2014v5n4a188.

Langman, Lauren. 2005. "From Virtual Public Spheres to Global Justice: A Critical Theory of Internetworked Social Movements." *Sociological Theory* 23(1): 42–74. DOI: https://doi.org/10.1111/j.0735-2751.2005.00242.x.

Lavis, John N. 2006. "Research, Public Policymaking, and Knowledge-Translation Processes: Canadian Efforts to Build Bridges." *Journal of Continuing Education in the Health Professions* 26(1): 37–45. DOI: https://doi.org/10.1002/chp.49.

Leadership Council for Digital Research Infrastructure. 2014. "'Think Piece' on a DI Roadmap." http://digitalleadership.ca/wp-content/uploads/2014/01/DI-Roadmap-Think-Piece-Jan-2014.pdf.

Lerner, Josh, and Jean Tirole. 2001. "The Open Source Movement: Key Research Questions." *European Economic Review* 45(4–6): 819–26. DOI: https://doi.org/10.1016/S0014-2921(01)00124-6.

———. 2002. "Some Simple Economics of Open Source." *The Journal of Industrial Economics* 50(2): 197–234. DOI: https://doi.org/10.1111/1467-6451.00174.

Lewis, M. J. 2010. "Libraries and the Management of Research Data." In *Envisioning Future Academic Library Services*, edited by Sue McKnight, 145–68. London: Facet Publishing.

Lewis, Vivian, Lisa Spiro, Xuemao Wang, and Jon E. Cawthorne. 2015. *Building Expertise to Support Digital Scholarship: A Global Perspective*. Arlington, VA: Council on Library and Information Resources. https://www.clir.org/pubs/reports/pub168/pub168.

Lin, Carolyn A., and David J. Atkin, eds. 2007. *Communication Technology and Social Change: Theory and Implications*. Mahwah, NJ: Lawrence Erlbaum Associates.

Lithuanian Research Library Consortium. 2019. "Lithuanian Research Library Consortium." http://www.lmba.lt/en.

Liu, Alan. 2007. "Imagining the New Media Encounter." *In A Companion to Digital Literary Studies*, edited by Ray Siemens and Susan Schreibman, 3–25. Oxford: Blackwell.

Lorimer, Rowland. 2013. "Libraries, Scholars, and Publishers in Digital Journal and Monograph Publishing." *Scholarly and Research Communication* 4(1): n.p. DOI: https://doi.org/10.22230/src.2013v4n1a43.

———. 2014. "A Good Idea, a Difficult Reality: Toward a Publisher/Library Open Access Partnership." *Scholarly and Research Communication* 5(4): n.p. DOI: https://doi.org/10.22230/src.2014v5n4a180.

Losh, Elisabeth. 2012. "Hacktivism and the Humanities: Programming Protest in the Era of the Digital University." In *Debates in the Digital Humanities*, edited by Matthew K. Gold, 161–86. Minneapolis: University of Minnesota Press. http://dhdebates.gc.cuny.edu/debates/text/32.

Lowe, Megan W. 2014. "In Defense of Open Access: Or, Why I Stopped Worrying and Started an OA Journal." *Codex* 2(4): 1–11.

Manzo, Christina, Geoff Kaufman, Sukdith Punjasthitkul, and Mary Flanagan. 2015. "'By the People, For the People': Assessing the Value of Crowdsourced, User-Generated Metadata." *Digital Humanities Quarterly* 9(1): n.p. http://www.digitalhumanities.org/dhq/vol/9/1/000204/000204.html.

Max Planck Society. 2019a. "Berlin Declaration on Open Access to Knowledge in the Sciences and Humanities." http://openaccess.mpg.de/Berlin-Declaration.

———. 2019b. "Max Planck Society." https://openaccess.mpg.de.

Maxwell, John W. 2014. "Publishing Education in the 21st Century and the Role of the University." *Journal of Electronic Publishing* 17(2): n.p. DOI: http://dx.doi.org/10.3998/3336451.0017.205.

———. 2015. "Beyond Open Access to Open Publication and Open Scholarship." *Scholarly and Research Communication* 6(3): n.p. DOI: https://doi.org/10.22230/src.2015v6n3a202.

Mayer, Amy. 2010. "Phenology and Citizen Science." *BioScience* 60(3): 172–75. DOI: https://www.jstor.org/stable/10.1525/bio.2010.60.3.3.

McDonald, Kevin. 2015. "From Indymedia to Anonymous: Rethinking Action and Identity in Digital Cultures." *Information, Communication & Society* 18(8): 968–82. DOI: https://doi.org/10.1080/1369118X. 2015.1039561.

McGregor, Heidi, and Kevin Guthrie. 2015. "Delivering Impact of Scholarly Information: Is Access Enough?" *Journal of Electronic Publishing* 18(3): n.p. DOI: http://dx.doi.org/10.3998/3336451.0018.302.

McKinley, Donelle. 2012. "Practical Management Strategies for Crowdsourcing in Libraries, Archives and Museums." Report for the School of Information Management, Faculty of Commerce and Administration, Victoria University of Wellington (NZ), 1–13. http://nonprofitcrowd.org/wp-content/uploads/2014/11/McKinley-2012-Crowdsourcing-management-strategies.pdf.

McLuhan, Marshall. 1962. *The Gutenberg Galaxy: The Making of Typographic Man.* Toronto: University of Toronto Press.

McNall, Miles, Celeste Sturdevant Reed, Robert Brown, and Angela Allen. 2009. "Brokering Community-University Engagement." *Innovative Higher Education* 33(5): 317–31. DOI: https://doi.org/10.1007/s10755-008-9086-8.

Meadows, Alice. 2015. "Beyond Open: Expanding Access to Scholarly Content." *Journal of Electronic Publishing* 18(3): n.p. DOI: http://dx.doi.org/10.3998/3336451.0018.301.

Mediterranean Open Access Network. n.d. "MEDOANET 2012: Mediterranean Open Access Network." http://www.medoanet.eu.

Merry, Melissa K. 2011. "Interest Group Activism on the Web: The Case of Environmental Organization." *Journal of Information Technology & Politics* 8(1): 110–28. DOI: https://doi.org/10.1080/19331681.2010.508003.

———. 2013. "Tweeting for a Cause: Microblogging and Environmental Advocacy." *Policy and Internet* 5(3): 304–27. DOI: https://doi.org/10.1002/1944-2866.POI335.

Mihailidis, Paul. 2014. "The Civic-Social Media Disconnect: Exploring Perceptions of Social Media for Engagement in the Daily Life of College Students." *Information, Communication & Society* 17(9): 1059–71. DOI: https://doi.org/10.1080/1369118X.2013.877054.

Milakovich, Michael E. 2012. *Digital Governance: New Technologies for Improving Public Service and Participation.* New York: Routledge.

Milberry, Kate. 2006. "Reconstructing the Internet: How Social Justice Activists Contest Technical Design in Cyberspace." *M/C Journal* 9(1): n.p. http://journal.media-culture.org.au/0603/10-milberry.php.

Mockus, Audris, Roy T. Fielding, and James D. Herbsleb. 2002. "Two Case Studies of Open Source Software Development: Apache and Mozilla." *ACM Transactions on Software Engineering and Methodology* 11(3): 309–46. DOI: https://www.doi.org/10.1145/567793.567795.

Molloy, Jennifer. 2011. "The Open Knowledge Foundation: Open Data Means Better Science." *PLOS Biology* 9(12): 1–4. http://journals.plos.org/plos-biology/article?id=10.1371/journal.pbio.1001195.

Mortensen, Mette. 2015. "Connective Witnessing: Reconfiguring the Relationship Between the Individual and the Collective." *Information, Communication & Society* 18(11): 1393–1406. https://www.tandfonline.com/doi/abs/10.1080/1369118X.2015.1061574.

Murray-Rust, Peter. 2008. "Open Data in Science." *Serials Review* 34(1): 52–64. http://www.tandfonline.com/doi/abs/10.1080/00987913.2008.10765152.

Newman, Greg, Andrea Wiggins, Alycia Crall, Eric Graham, Sarah Newman, and Kevin Crowston. 2012. "The Future of Citizen Science: Emerging Technologies and Shifting Paradigms." *Frontiers in Ecology and the Environment* 10(6): 298–304. DOI: https://doi.org/10.1890/110294.

Ober, Josiah, Walter Scheidel, Brent D. Shaw, and Donna Sanclemente. 2007. "Toward Open Access in Ancient Studies: The Princeton-Stanford Working Papers in Classics." *Hesperia* 76(1): 229–42. https://www.jstor.org/stable/25068017.

Oberhauser, Karen, and Gretchen LeBuhn. 2012. "Insects and Plants: Engaging Undergraduates in Authentic Research through Citizen Science." *Frontiers in Ecology and the Environment* 10(6): 318–20. DOI: https://doi.org/10.1890/110274.

O'Donnell, Daniel, Heather Hobma, Sandra Cowan, Gillian Ayers, Jessica Bay, Marinus Swanepoel, Wendy Merkley, Kelaine Devine, Emma Dering, and Inge Genee. 2015. "Aligning Open Access Publication with the Research and Teaching Missions of the Public University: The Case of the Lethbridge Journal Incubator (If 'if's and 'and's were pots and pans)." *Journal of Electronic Publishing* 18(3): n.p. DOI: http://dx.doi.org/10.3998/3336451.0018.309.

O'Meara, Kerry Ann, Lorilee R. Sandmann, John Saltmarsh, and Dwight E. Giles, Jr. 2011. "Studying the Professional Lives and Work of Faculty

Involved in Community Engagement." *Innovative Higher Education* 36(2): 83–96. DOI: https://doi.org/10.1007/s10755-010-9159-3.

Oostveen, Anne-Marie. 2010. "Citizens and Activists: Analysing the Reasons, Impact, and Benefits of Civic Emails Directed at a Grassroots Campaign." *Information, Communication & Society* 13(6): 793–819. DOI: https://doi.org/10.1080/13691180903277637.

Open Access India. 2019. "Open Access India." http://openaccessindia.org.

Open-Access.net. 2019. "Open Access: Free Access to Scientific Information." https://www.open-access.net/startseite/.

Open Access Network. 2019. "Open Access Network." http://openaccessnetwork.org.

Open Access Scholarly Publishers Association. 2019. "Open Access Scholarly Publishers Association." http://oaspa.org.

Open Access Working Group. n.d. "Open Access Working Group." http://access.okfn.org.

OpenAIRE. 2019. "OpenAIRE." https://www.openaire.eu.

Open Humanities Alliance. n.d. "Open Humanities Alliance." http://openhumanitiesalliance.org.

Open Knowledge International. n.d. "Open Knowledge International." https://okfn.org.

Open Scholarship Initiative. 2019. "Open Scholarship Initiative." http://osiglobal.org/.

Organisation for Economic Cooperation and Development (OECD). 2015. "Making Open Science a Reality." *OECD Science, Technology and Industry Policy Papers* 25. Paris: OECD Publishing.

Orlikowski, Wanda J. 2002. "Knowing in Practice: Enacting a Collective Capability in Distributed Organizing." *Organization Science* 13(3): 249–73. DOI: https://doi.org/10.1287/orsc.13.3.249.2776.

Paliwala, Abdul. 2007. "Free Culture, Global Commons and Social Justice in Information Technology Diffusion." *Law, Social Justice and Global Development Journal* 1: n.p. https://warwick.ac.uk/fac/soc/law/elj/lgd/2007_1/paliwala/.

Pasque, Penny A., Ryan E. Smerek, Brighid Dwyer, Nick Bowman, and Bruce L. Mallory, eds. 2005. *Higher Education Collaboratives for Community Engagement and Improvement.* Ann Arbor, MI: National Forum on Higher Education for the Public Good. https://files.eric.ed.gov/fulltext/ ED515231.pdf.

Peekhaus, Wilhelm, and Nicholas Proferes. 2015. "How Library and Information Science Faculty Perceive and Engage with Open Access." *Journal of Information Science* 41(5): 640–61. DOI: https://doi. org/10.1177/0165551515587855.

Phipps, David. 2012. "A Report Detailing the Development of a University-Based Knowledge Mobilization Unit that Enhances Research Outreach and Engagement." *Scholarly and Research Communication* 2(2): n.p. DOI: https://doi.org/10.22230/src.2011v2n2a31.

Pickerill, Jenny. 2009. "Symbolic Production, Representation, and Contested Identities: Anti-War Activism Online." *Information, Communication & Society* 12(7): 969–93. DOI: https://doi.org/10.1080/13691180802524469.

Pinfield, Stephen. 2015. "Making Open Access Work: The 'State-of-the-Art' in Providing Open Access to Scholarly Literature." *Online Information Review* 39(5): 604–36. DOI: https://doi.org/10.1108/OIR-05-2015-0167.

Piwowar, Heather A., and Todd J. Vision. 2013. "Data Reuse and the Open Data Citation Advantage." *PeerJ* 1:e175. DOI: https://doi.org/10.7717/ peerj.175.

Powell, Daniel, Raymond Siemens, Matthew Hiebert, Lindsey Seatter, and William R. Bowen. 2015. "Transformation through Integration: The Renaissance Knowledge Network (ReKN) and a Next Wave of Scholarly Publication." *Scholarly and Research Communication* 6(2): n.p. DOI: https://doi.org/10.22230/src.2015v6n2a199.

Powell, Daniel, Ray Siemens, and the INKE Research Group. 2014. "Building Alternative Scholarly Publishing Capacity: The Renaissance Knowledge Network (ReKN) as Digital Production Hub." *Scholarly and Research Communication* 5(4): n.p. DOI: https://doi.org/10.22230/ src.2014v5n4a183.

Prelinger, Rick. 2007. "Archives and Access in the 21st Century." *Cinema Journal* 46(3): 114–18. DOI: https://www.doi.org/10.1353/cj.2007.0027.

Presner, Todd, David Shepard, and Yoh Kawano. 2014. *HyperCities: Thick Mapping in the Digital Humanities*. Cambridge, MA: Harvard University Press. https://escholarship.org/uc/item/3mh5t455.

Prestopnik, Nathan R., and Kevin Crowston. 2011. "Gaming for (Citizen) Science: Exploring Motivation and Data Quality in the Context of Crowdsourced Science through the Design and Evaluation of a Social-Computational System." In *Proceedings of the 2011 IEEE Seventh International Conference on e-Science Workshops (ESCIENCEW '11)*, 28–33. Washington, DC: IEEE Computer Society. DOI: http://doi.org/10.1109/eScienceW.2011.14.

Price, Kenneth M., and Raymond G. Siemens, eds. 2013. *Literary Studies in the Digital Age*. New York: Modern Language Association.

Public Knowledge Project. 2019. "Public Knowledge Project." Simon Fraser University Library. https://pkp.sfu.ca.

Purdam, Kingsley. 2014. "Citizen Social Science and Citizen Data? Methodological and Ethical Challenges for Social Research." *Current Sociology* 62(3): 374–92. DOI: https://doi.org/10.1177/0011392114527997.

Rath, Prabhash Narayana. 2015. "Study of Open Access Publishing in Social Sciences and its Implications for Libraries." *DESIDOC Journal of Library & Information Technology* 35(3): 117–83. DOI: https://www.doi.org/10.14429/djlit.35.3.8720.

Raymond, Eric S. 2001. *The Cathedral and the Bazaar: Musings on Linux and Open Source by an Accidental Revolutionary*. Rev. ed. Sebastopol, CA: O'Reilly.

RECODE Project Consortium. 2014. "Policy Recommendations for Open Access to Research Data." https://zenodo.org/record/50863/files/recode_guideline_en_web_version_full_FINAL.pdf.

Research Data Canada. 2013. "Research Data Canada Response to *Capitalizing on Big Data: Towards a Policy Framework for Advancing Digital Scholarship in Canada*." http://www.rdc-drc.ca/wp-content/uploads/Research-Data-Canada-Response-to-the-Tri-Council-Consultation-on-Digital-Scholarship.pdf.

Ridge, Mia. 2013. "From Tagging to Theorizing: Deepening Engagement with Cultural Heritage through Crowdsourcing." *Curator* 56(4): 435–50. DOI: http://dx.doi.org/10.1111/cura.12046.

Ridley, Michael, Clare Appavoo, and Sabina Pagotto. 2014. "Seeing the Forest and the Trees: The Integrated Digital Scholarship Ecosystem (IDSE) Project of the Canadian Research Knowledge Network (CRKN)." Chicago: Association of College & Research Libraries (ACRL). http://www.ala.org/acrl/sites/ala.org.acrl/files/content/conferences/confsandpreconfs/2015/Ridley_Appavoo_Pagotto.pdf.

Right to Research Coalition. 2017. "Right to Research Coalition." http://www.righttoresearch.org.

Ritzer, George, and Nathan Jurgenson. 2010. "Production, Consumption, Prosumption: The Nature of Capitalism in the Age of the Digital 'Prosumer.'" *Journal of Consumer Culture* 10(1): 13–36. DOI: https://doi.org/10.1177/1469540509354673.

Roberts, Jeffrey A., Il-Horn Hann, and Sandra A. Slaughter. 2006. "Understanding the Motivations, Participation, and Performance of Open Source Software Developers: A Longitudinal Study of the Apache Projects." *Management Science* 52(7): 984–99. DOI: https://doi.org/10.1287/mnsc.1060.0554.

Rockwell, Geoffrey. 2012. "Crowdsourcing the Humanities: Social Research and Collaboration." In *Collaborative Research in the Digital Humanities*, edited by Marilyn Deegan and Willard McCarty, 135–54. Farnham, UK, and Burlington, VT: Ashgate.

Rodriguez, Julia. 2014. "Awareness and Attitudes about Open Access Publishing: A Glance at Generational Differences." *Journal of Academic Librarianship* 40(6): 604–10. DOI: https://doi.org/10.1016/j.acalib.2014.07.013.

Romary, Laurent. 2012. "Data Management in the Humanities." *ERCIM News* 89, April 3. https://ercim-news.ercim.eu/en89/special/data-management-in-the-humanities.

Rosen, Lawrence E. 2004. *Open Source Licensing: Software Freedom and Intellectual Property Law.* Upper Saddle River, NJ: Prentice Hall PTR.

Rosenzweig, Roy. 2006. "Can History Be Open Source? *Wikipedia* and the Future of the Past." *Journal of American History* 93(1): 117–46. DOI: https://www.doi.org/10.2307/4486062.

Ross, Stephen, Alex Christie, and Jentery Sayers. 2014. "Expert/Crowd-Sourcing for the Linked Modernisms Project." *Scholarly and Research Communication* 5(4): n.p. DOI: https://doi.org/10.22230/src.2014v5n4a186.

Rotman, Dana, Jenny Preece, Jen Hammock, Kezee Procita, Derek Hansen, Cynthia Parr, Darcy Lewis, and David Jacobs. 2012. "Dynamic Changes in Motivation in Collaborative Citizen-Science Projects." In *Proceedings of the ACM 2012 Conference on Computer Supported Cooperative Work* (*CSCW '12*), 217–26. New York: ACM. DOI: https://doi.org/10.1145/2145204.2145238.

Ruecker, Stan. 2015. "A Brief Taxonomy of Prototypes for the Digital Humanities." *Scholarly Research and Communication* 6(2): n.p. DOI: https://doi.org/10.22230/src.2015v6n2a222.

Ruecker, Stan, Lisa M. Given, Elizabeth Sadler, Andrea Ruskin, and Heather Simpson. 2007. "Design of a Rich-Prospect Browsing Interface for Seniors: A Qualitative Study of Image Similarity Clustering." *Visible Language* 41(1): 4–21.

Ruecker, Stan, Milena Radzikowska, and Stéfan Sinclair. 2011. *Visual Interface Design for Digital Cultural Heritage: A Guide to Rich-Prospect Browsing.* Farnham, UK, and Burlington, VT: Ashgate.

Saklofske, Jon. 2014. "Exploding, Centralizing and Reimagining: Critical Scholarship Refracted Through the NewRadial Prototype." *Scholarly and Research Communication* 5(2): n.p. DOI: https://doi.org/10.22230/src.2014v5n2a151.

Saklofske, Jon, with the INKE Research Team. 2016. "Digital *Theoria, Poiesis,* and *Praxis*: Activating Humanities Research and Communication through Open Social Scholarship Platform Design." *Scholarly and Research Communication* 7(2/3): n.p. DOI: https://doi.org/10.22230/src.2016v7n2/3a252.

Saklofske, Jon, and Jake Bruce. 2013. "Beyond Browsing and Reading: The Open Work of Digital Scholarly Editions." *Scholarly and Research Communication* 4(3): n.p. DOI: https://doi.org/10.22230/src.2013v4n3a119.

Sakr, Sherif, and Eric Pardede. 2012. *Graph Data Management: Techniques and Applications.* Hershey, PA: IGI Global.

Sandoval-Almazan, Rodrigo, and J. Ramon Gil-Garcia. 2014. "Towards Cyberactivism 2.0? Understanding the Use of Social Media and Other Information Technologies for Political Activism and Social Movements." *Government Information Quarterly* 31(3): 365–78. DOI: http://doi.org/10.1016/j.giq.2013.10.016.

San Martin, Patricia Silvana, Paola Carolina Bongiovani, Ana Casali, and Claudia Deco. 2015. "Study on Perspectives Regarding Deposit on Open Access Repositories in Context of Public Universities in the Central-Eastern Region of Argentina." *Scholarly and Research Communication* 6(1): n.p. DOI: https://doi.org/10.22230/src.2015v6n1a145.

Schloss, Patrick D., Sarah L. Westcott, Thomas Ryabin, Justine R. Hall, Martin Hartmann, Emily B. Hollister, Ryan A. Lesniewski, et al. 2009. "Introducing mothur: Open-Source, Platform-Independent, Community-Supported Software for Describing and Comparing Microbial Communities." *Applied and Environmental Microbiology* 75(23): 7537–41. DOI: https://www.doi.org/10.1128/AEM.01541-09.

Schmidt, Albrecht, Florian Waas, Martin Kersten, Michael J. Carey, Ioana Manolescu, and Ralph Busse. 2002. "XMark: A Benchmark for XML Data Management." In *Proceedings of the 28th International Conference on Very Large Data Bases* (*VLDB '02*), 974–85. https://dl.acm.org/citation.cfm?id=1287455.

Scholarly Publishing and Academic Resources Coalition. 2019. "SPARC: The Scholarly Publishing and Academic Resources Coalition." http://sparcopen.org.

Schreibman, Susan, Ray Siemens, and John Unsworth, eds. 2004. *A Companion to Digital Humanities*. Oxford: Blackwell.

Science International. 2015. *Open Data in a Big Data World*. Paris: International Council for Science (ICSU), International Social Science Council (ISSC), The World Academy of Sciences (TWAS), and InterAcademy Partnership (IAP). https://council.science/cms/2017/04/open-data-in-big-data-world_long.pdf.

Shadbolt, Nigel, Kieron O'Hara, Tim Berners-Lee, Nicholas Gibbins, Hugh Glaser, Wendy Hall, and M.C. Schraefel. 2012. "Linked Open Government Data: Lessons from Data.gov.uk." *IEEE Intelligent Systems* 27(3): 16–24. http://eprints.soton.ac.uk/340564/.

Shearer, Kathleen, and Bill Birdsall. 2002. "The Transition of Scholarly Communications in Canada." http://www.moyak.com/papers/scholarly-communications-canada.pdf.

Siemens, Lynne. 2009. "It's a Team if You Use 'Reply All': An Exploration of Research Teams in Digital Humanities Environments." *Digital Scholarship in the Humanities* (formerly *Literary and Linguistic Computing*) 24(2): 225–33.

———. 2012a. "Understanding Long-Term Collaboration: Reflections on Year 1 and Before." *Scholarly and Research Communication* 3(1): n.p. DOI: https://doi.org/10.22230/src.2012v3n1a48.

———. 2012b. "Firing on All Cylinders: Progress and Transition in INKE's Year 2." *Scholarly and Research Communication* 3(4): n.p. DOI: https://doi.org/10.22230/src.2012v3n4a72.

———. 2013. "Responding to Change and Transition in INKE's Year Three." *Scholarly and Research Communication* 4(3): n.p. DOI: https://doi.org/10.22230/src.2013v4n3a115.

———. 2014. "Research Collaboration as 'Layers of Engagement': INKE in Year Four." *Scholarly and Research Communication* 5(4): n.p. DOI: https://doi.org/10.22230/src.2014v5n4a181.

———. 2015. "'INKE-cubating' Research Networks, Projects, and Partnerships: Reflections on INKE's Fifth Year." *Scholarly and Research Communication* 6(4): n.p. DOI: https://doi.org/10.22230/src.2015v6n4a198.

———. 2016. "'Faster Alone, Further Together': Reflections on INKE's Year Six." *Scholarly and Research Communication* 7(2/3): n.p. DOI: https://doi.org/10.22230/src.2016v7n2/3a250.

Siemens, Lynne, Ray Siemens, Richard Cunningham, Teresa Dobson, Alan Galey, Stan Ruecker, and Claire Warwick. 2012. "INKE Administrative Structure: Omnibus Document." *Scholarly and Research Communication* 3(1): n.p. DOI: https://doi.org/10.22230/src.2012v3n1a50.

Siemens, Raymond G. 2002. "Scholarly Publishing at its Source, and at Present." In *The Credibility of Electronic Publishing: A Report to the Humanities and Social Sciences Federation of Canada*, compiled by Raymond G. Siemens, Michael Best, Elizabeth Grove-White, Alan Burk, James Kerr, Andy Pope, Jean-Claude Guédon, Geoffrey Rockwell, and

Lynne Siemens. *TEXT Technology* 11(1): 1–128. https://web.archive.org/web/20151012065051/https://web.viu.ca/hssfc/Final/Overview.htm.

Siemens, Raymond G., Teresa Dobson, Stan Ruecker, Richard Cunningham, Alan Galey, Claire Warwick, and Lynne Siemens. 2011. "HCI-Book? Perspectives on E-Book Research, 2006–2008 (Foundational to Implementing New Knowledge Environments)." *Papers of the Bibliographical Society of Canada / Cahiers de la Société bibliographique du Canada* 49(1): 35–89. http://web.uvic.ca/~siemens/pub/2011-HCI-Book.pdf.

Siemens, Raymond G., and David Moorman, eds. 2006. *Mind Technologies: Humanities Computing and the Canadian Academic Community.* Calgary: University of Calgary Press.

Siemens, Raymond G., Claire Warwick, Richard Cunningham, Teresa Dobson, Alan Galey, Stan Ruecker, Susan Schreibman, and the INKE Research Group. 2009. "*Codex* Ultor: Toward a Conceptual and Theoretical Foundation for New Research on Books and Knowledge Environments." *Digital Studies / Le champ numerique* 1(2): n.p. DOI: http://doi.org/10.16995/dscn.270.

Silka, Linda, G. Dean Cleghorn, Milago Grullon, and Trinidad Tellez. 2008. "Creating Community-Based Participatory Research in a Diverse Community: A Case Study." *Journal of Empirical Research on Human Research Ethics* 3(2): 5–16. DOI: https://doi.org/10.1525/jer.2008.3.2.5.

Silka, Linda, and Paulette Renault-Caragianes. 2007. "Community-University Research Partnerships: Devising a Model for Ethical Engagement." *Journal of Higher Education Outreach and Engagement* 11(2): 171–83.

Silka, Linda, and Robin Toof, guest eds. 2011. "International Perspectives on Community-University Partnerships" issue. *Metropolitan Universities* 22(2). Towson, MD: Coalition of Urban and Metropolitan Universities.

Silvertown, Jonathan. 2009. "A New Dawn for Citizen Science." *Trends in Ecology & Evolution* 24(9): 467–71. DOI: https://doi.org/10.1016/j.tree.2009.03.017.

Snijder, Ronald. 2015. "Better Sharing Through Licenses? Measuring the Influence of Creative Commons Licenses on the Usage of Open Access Monographs." *Journal of Librarianship & Scholarly Communication* 3(1): 1–21. DOI: https://doi.org/10.7710/2162-3309.1187.

Social Sciences and Humanities Research Council. 2019. *"Dialogue*, SSHRC's Newsletter." http://www.sshrc-crsh.gc.ca/about-au_sujet/publications/dialogue-eng.aspx.

Stadler, Claus, Jens Lehmann, Konrad Höffner, and Soren Auer. 2012. "LinkedGeoData: A Core for a Web of Spatial Open Data." *Semantic Web* 3(4): 333–54. DOI: https://doi.org/10.3233/SW-2011-0052.

Stafford, Amy, Ali Shiri, Stan Ruecker, Matthew Bouchard, Paras Mehta, Karl Anvik, and Ximena Rossello. 2008. "Searchling: User-Centered Evaluation of a Visual Thesaurus-Enhanced Interface for Bilingual Digital Libraries." In *Research and Advanced Technology for Digital Libraries*, edited by Birte Christensen-Dalsgaard, Donatella Castelli, Bolette Ammitzbøll Jurik, and Joan Lippincott, 117–21. Berlin and Heidelberg: Springer.

Stein, Bob. 2015. "Back to the Future." *Journal of Electronic Publishing* 18(2): n.p. DOI: http://dx.doi.org/10.3998/3336451.0018.204.

Stranack, Kevin. 2008. *Starting A New Scholarly Journal in Africa*. Public Knowledge Project. https://pkp.sfu.ca/files/AfricaNewJournal.pdf.

Sturm, Susan, Timothy Eatman, John Saltmarsh, and Adam Bush. 2011. *Full Participation: Building the Architecture for Diversity and Public Engagement in Higher Education.* Catalyst paper, Imagining America: Artists and Scholars in Public Life. http://imaginingamerica.org/wp-content/uploads/2015/09/fullparticipation.pdf.

Suber, Peter. 2004. "Open Access Overview." Last modified December 5, 2015. https://legacy.earlham.edu/~peters/fos/overview.htm.

———. 2005. "Promoting Open Access in the Humanities." *Syllecta Classica* 16: 231–46. DOI: https://www.doi.org/10.1353/syl.2005.0001.

Surkis, Alisa, and Kevin Read. 2015. "Research Data Management." *Journal of the Medical Library Association* 103(3): 154–56. DOI: https://www.doi.org/10.3163/1536-5050.103.3.011.

Tambini, Damian. 1999. "New Media and Democracy: The Civic Networking Movement." *New Media & Society* 1(3): 305–29. DOI: https://doi.org/10.1177/14614449922225609.

Tananbaum, Greg. 2014. "North American Campus-Based Open Access Funds: A Five-Year Progress Report." Scholarly Publishing and Academic

Resources Coalition (SPARC). https://sparcopen.org/wp-content/uploads/2016/01/OA-Fund-5-Year-Review.pdf.

Truscello, Michael. 2003. "The Architecture of Information: Open Source Software and Tactical Poststructuralist Anarchism." *Postmodern Culture* 13(3): n.p. http://pmc.iath.virginia.edu/issue.503/13.3truscello.html.

University of Cambridge. n.d. "Open Access at the University of Cambridge." https://www.cam.ac.uk/research/research-at-cambridge/open-access.

Van Aelst, Peter, and Stefaan Walgrave. 2002. "New Media, New Movements? The Role of the Internet in Shaping the 'Anti-Globalization' Movement." *Information, Communication & Society* 5(4): 465–93. DOI: https://doi.org/10.1080/13691180208538801.

Vandegrift, Micah, and Josh Bolick. 2014. "'Free to All': Library Publishing and the Challenge of Open Access." *Journal of Librarianship & Scholarly Communication* 2(4): 107–16. DOI: https://doi.org/10.7710/2162-3309.1181.

Vandendorpe, Christian. 2012. "Wikisource and the Scholarly Book." *Scholarly and Research Communication* 3(4): n.p. DOI: https://doi.org/10.22230/src.2012v3n4a58.

Van de Sompel, Herbert, Sandy Payette, John Erickson, Carl Lagoze, and Simeon Warner. 2004. "Rethinking Scholarly Communication: Building the System that Scholars Deserve." *D-Lib Magazine* 10(9): n.p. DOI: http://dx.doi.org/10.1045/september2004-vandesompel.

Van Laer, Jeroen, and Peter Van Aelst. 2010. "Internet and Social Movement Action Repertoires: Opportunities and Limitations." *Information, Communication & Society* 13(8): 1146–71. DOI: https://doi.org/10.1080/13691181003628307.

Veletsianos, George. 2015. "A Case Study of Scholars' Open and Sharing Practices." *Open Praxis* 7(3): 199–209. DOI: https://doi.org/10.5944/openpraxis.7.3.206.

Venugopal, Srikumar, Rajkumar Buyya, and Kotagiri Ramamohanarao. 2006. "A Taxonomy of Data Grids for Distributed Data Sharing, Management, and Processing." *ACM Computing Surveys* 38(1): 1–53. DOI: https://www.doi.org/10.1145/1132952.1132955.

Vision, Todd J. 2010. "Open Data and the Social Contract of Scientific Publishing." *BioScience* 60(5): 330–31. DOI: https://doi.org/10.1525/bio.2010.60.5.2.

Von Hippel, Eric, and Georg von Krogh. 2003. "Open Source Software and the 'Private-Collective' Innovation Model: Issues for *Organization Science*." *Organization Science* 14(2): 209–23. DOI: https://doi.org/10.1287/orsc.14.2.209.14992.

Von Krogh, Georg, and Eric von Hippel. 2006. "The Promise of Research on Open Source Software." *Management Science* 52(7): 975–83. DOI: https://www.doi.org/10.1287/mnsc.1060.0560.

Von Krogh, Georg, Sebastian Spaeth, and Karim R. Lakhani. 2003. "Community, Joining, and Specialization in Open Source Software Innovation: A Case Study." *Research Policy* 32(7): 1217–41. DOI: https://doi.org/10.1016/S0048-7333(03)00050-7.

Walsh, Brandon, Claire Maiers, Gwen Nally, Jeremy Boggs, and Praxis Program Team. 2014. "Crowdsourcing Individual Interpretations: Between Microtasking and Macrotasking." *Digital Scholarship in the Humanities* (formerly *Literary and Linguistic Computing*) 29(3): 379–86. DOI: http://dx.doi.org/10.1093/llc/fqu030.

Ward, Catharine, Lesley Freiman, Sarah Jones, Laura Molloy, and Kellie Snow. 2011. "Making Sense: Talking Data Management with Researchers." *International Journal of Digital Curation* 6(2): 265–73. http://www.ijdc.net/article/view/197/262.

Ward, Vicky, Allan House, and Susan Hamer. 2009. "Developing a Framework for Transferring Knowledge into Action: A Thematic Analysis of the Literature." *Journal of Health Services Research & Policy* 14(3): 156–64. DOI: https://doi.org/10.1258/jhsrp.2009.008120.

Waters, Donald J., and Joseph S. Meisel. 2007. "Scholarly Publishing Initiatives." In *The Andrew W. Mellon Foundation: 2007 Annual Report*, 31–45. New York: Andrew W. Mellon Foundation. https://mellon.org/media/filer_public/42/76/4276ef43-d0b2-42e5-8747-e63db6a7bd68/2007.pdf.

Weber, Steven. 2004. *The Success of Open Source*. Cambridge, MA: Harvard University Press.

West, Joel. 2003. "How Open is Open Enough? Melding Proprietary and Open Source Platform Strategies." *Research Policy* 32(7) 1259–85. DOI: https://doi.org/10.1016/S0048-7333(03)00052-0.

West, Joel, and Scott Gallagher. 2006. "Challenges of Open Innovation: The Paradox of Firm Investment in Open Source Software." *R&D Management* 36(3): 319–31. DOI: https://www.doi.org/10.1111/j.1467-9310.2006.00436.x.

Whitmer, Ali, Laura Ogden, John Lawton, Pam Sturner, Peter M. Groffman, Laura Schneider, David Hart, et al. 2010. "The Engaged University: Providing a Platform for Research that Transforms Society." *Frontiers in Ecology and the Environment* 8(6): 314–21. DOI: https://doi.org/10.1890/090241.

Wiggins, Andrea, and Kevin Crowston. 2011. "From Conservation to Crowdsourcing: A Typology of Citizen Science." In *Proceedings of the 2011 44th Hawaii International Conference on System Sciences (HICSS '11)*, 1–10. DOI: https://doi.org/10.1109/HICSS.2011.207.

Wikimedia Foundation. 2019. "Wikipedia: About." https://en.wikipedia.org/wiki/Wikipedia:About.

Willinsky, John. 2003. "The Nine Flavours of Open Access Scholarly Publishing." *Journal of Postgraduate Medicine* 49(3): 263–67.

———. 2006a. *The Access Principle: The Case for Open Access to Research and Scholarship.* Cambridge, MA: MIT Press.

———. 2006b. "History." In *The Access Principle: The Case for Open Access to Research and Scholarship*, 189–207. Cambridge, MA: MIT Press.

———. 2007. "What Open Access Research Can Do for Wikipedia." *First Monday* 12(3): n.p. https://firstmonday.org/ojs/index.php/fm/article/viewArticle/1624/1539.

Wilson, James A.J., Luis Martinez-Uribe, Michael A. Fraser, and Paul Jeffreys. 2011. "An Institutional Approach to Developing Research Data Management Infrastructure." *International Journal of Digital Curation* 6(2): 274–87. DOI: https://doi.org/10.2218/ijdc.v6i2.203.

Xu, Guan-Hua. 2007. "Open Access to Scientific Data: Promoting Science and Innovation." *Data Science Journal* 6: 21–25. DOI: https://doi.org/10.2481/dsj.6.OD21.

Yakel, Elizabeth. 2007. "Digital Curation." *OCLC Systems and Services: International Digital Library Perspectives* 23(4): 335–40. DOI: https://doi.org/10.1108/10650750710831466.

Yang, Zheng Ye (Lan), and Yu Li. 2015. "University Faculty Awareness and Attitudes towards Open Access Publishing and the Institutional Repository: A Case Study." *Journal of Librarianship & Scholarly Communication* 3(1): 1–29. DOI: https://doi.org/10.7710/2162-3309.1210.

# Contributors

**Alyssa Arbuckle** is associate director of the Electronic Textual Cultures Lab at the University of Victoria, where she is operational lead for the Implementing New Knowledge Environments Partnership and a co-facilitator of its Connection cluster, as well as a co-director of the Digital Humanities Summer Institute with her colleagues Ray Siemens and Randa El Khatib. Alyssa holds an Interdisciplinary PhD from the University of Victoria; her dissertation focused on open social scholarship and its implementation. Alyssa's work has appeared in *Digital Studies*, *Digital Humanities Quarterly*, *KULA: Knowledge Creation, Dissemination, and Preservation Studies*, and *Scholarly and Research Communication*, among other venues, and she has co-edited print and online book collections titled *Social Knowledge Creation in the Humanities* and *Feminist War Games?: Mechanisms of War, Feminist Values, and Interventional Games.*

**John F. Barber** convenes with the Creative Media and Digital Culture program at Washington State University Vancouver. His scholarship, teaching, and creative endeavors arise from the collision (collusion?) of art, humanities, and technology. He has published in *Digital Humanities Quarterly*, *Digital Studies*, *Electronic Book Review (ebr)*, *Hyperrhiz: New Media Cultures*, *Leonardo*, *MATLIT (Materialities of Literature)*, *Scholarly Research and Communication*, and other journals. His radio+sound art is exhibited and broadcast internationally. Barber developed, and curates, *American Dust* (www.brautigan.net), an online, interactive information structure known as the preeminent resource for the life and writing of American author Richard Brautigan. *Richard Brautigan: An Annotated Bibliography* (McFarland, 1990) and *Richard Brautigan: Essays on the Writings and Life* (McFarland, 2007) are offshoots of this work.

**Lee Skallerup Bessette** is assistant director for digital learning at the Center for New Designs in Learning and Scholarship (CNDLS), Georgetown University. At the University of Mary Washington, she focused on strategies to include digital fluency in the university's general education curriculum. Her current research includes affective labor in alternative academic (alt-ac) roles, as well as effective storytelling in educational technology (ed-tech) innovation spaces. She is also an affiliate faculty member in the master's program in Learning, Design, and Technology at Georgetown University.

**Martha Burtis** is associate director and learning developer in the Open Learning and Teaching Collaborative (Open CoLab) at Plymouth State

ISBN 978-1-64959-008-4 (paper) ISBN 978-1-64959-009-1 (pdf) ISBN 978-1-64959-084-8 (epub)
*New Technologies in Medieval and Renaissance Studies 8 (2022) 511–518*

University. Prior to leaving the University of Mary Washington, she was the founding director of the Digital Knowledge Center, where her work centered on fostering student agency around digital work. In her current role, she is engaged in building open, collaborative, and sustainable communities for teaching and learning.

**Alex Christie** is associate professor of digital prototyping at Brock University's Centre for Digital Humanities. He has published internationally in a number of journals and collections, including *Digital Humanities Quarterly*, *Social Knowledge Creation in the Humanities*, and *Reading Modernism with Machines*, among others. In addition to creating warped 3D maps of literary spaces (z axis research) and an online platform for sharing humanities open educational resources (pedagogy toolkit), he is currently completing a monograph on modern manuscripts and humanities computing.

**Sarah Connell** is associate director of the Women Writers Project and the NULab for Texts, Maps, and Networks at Northeastern University. Her research focuses on text encoding and text analysis, medieval and early modern historiography, and pedagogies of digital scholarship. Her current projects include *Making Room in History*, a text encoding project on early modern narratives of national identity; Word Vectors for the Thoughtful Humanist, an NEH-funded seminar series on research and teaching with word embedding models; and "Representing Racial Identity in Early Women's Writing," a project examining discourses around race in the Women Writers Online collection.

**Ben Daigle** is associate professor and director of Information Systems and Digital Access at the University of Dayton, providing leadership and strategic thinking to library leaders and staff in the areas of library technology and digital scholarship. He was formerly the principal investigator of an Andrew W. Mellon Foundation grant, titled Digital Collections: From Projects to Pedagogy and Scholarship, and the founding director of the Collaborative for Digital Engagement and Experience (CODEX) at the Five Colleges of Ohio. A strong collaborator, Ben works to foster partnerships between library staff, technologists, and faculty to advance strategic digital initiatives such as digital scholarship, digital preservation, and emerging library technology innovations.

**Tracey El Hajj** is a PhD candidate in the Department of English at the University of Victoria (UVic) in the field of science and technology studies. Her research focuses on the "algorhythmics" of networked communications. She was a 2019–20 President's Fellow in Research-Enriched Teaching at UVic, where she taught an advanced course on Artificial Intelligence and Everyday Life. She is also a programmer with the *Map of Early Modern London* and Linked Early Modern Drama Online, as well as a research fellow in residence at the Praxis Studio for Comparative Media Studies, where she investigates the relationships between artificial intelligence, creativity, health, and justice.

**Randa El Khatib** is a postdoctoral fellow in the Department of Arts, Culture and Media at the University of Toronto Scarborough. She is also co-director of the Digital Humanities Summer Institute and editor of *Early Modern Digital Review*. El Khatib's dissertation "Building Literary Geographies: Modelling and Prototyping as Modes of Inquiry" (University of Victoria 2021) focuses on prototyping web mapping tools for geolocating and visualizing cultural materials. Her work appears in *Digital Scholarship in the Humanities*, *Digital Humanities Quarterly*, *Digital Studies/Le champ numérique*, and other scholarly venues.

**Julia Flanders** is professor of the practice in the Department of English, Northeastern University, director of the Digital Scholarship Group at the university's library, and a member of the core faculty of the NULab for Texts, Maps, and Networks. She also directs the Women Writers Project and serves as editor-in-chief of *Digital Humanities Quarterly*. Her research interests focus on data modeling, textual scholarship, and humanities data curation. She is the co-editor, with Neil Fraistat, of the *Cambridge Companion to Textual Scholarship* (Cambridge UP, 2013), and the co-editor, with Fotis Jannidis, of *The Shape of Data in Digital Humanities: Modeling Texts and Text-based Resources* (Routledge, 2019).

**Richard Furuta** is a faculty member at Texas A&M University, where he is professor in the Department of Computer Science, and director of the Center for the Study of Digital Libraries. Dr. Furuta received his BA from Reed College in 1974, MS in computer science from the University of Oregon in 1978, and PhD in computer science from the University of Washington in 1986. Dr. Furuta's areas of research include digital libraries, digital humanities, and hypermedia systems and models. He serves as an editor-in-chief of the *International Journal of Digital Libraries*, on the steering committee for the ACM–IEEE Joint Conference on Digital Libraries, and as a member of a number of other editorial boards and conference program committees.

**Erin Rose Glass** has a decade of experience working at the intersection of technology and education and currently leads the Developer Education team at DigitalOcean. Previously, she served as the digital scholarship librarian at UC San Diego, where she founded KNIT (an open-source digital commons for students), co-founded Ethical Edtech (an online community promoting open and ethical forms of edtech), and co-directed the Cultured Data Symposium. She has a Ph.D. in English from The CUNY Graduate Center and has published on digital humanities, edtech, digital pedagogy, and technical education and infrastructure in libraries and universities. Her dissertation research focused on liberatory and humanistic approaches to software adoption and development in higher education.

**Nigel Haarstad** is an instructor in the Department of Communication at the University of Missouri. He teaches several courses, including Quantitative Research Methods and Organizational Advocacy. Nigel's previous research has investigated the utility of instructional communication in risk and crisis situations, contributing to grant-funded initiatives for the United States Geological Survey and the National Center for Food Protection and Defense. His current research investigates the organizing behaviors of extremist and fringe communities that utilize social media. His research aims to understand the communication processes and characteristics that lead to these groups' growth, stability, and impact on the identification of individual members.

**Jacob Heil** is assistant director of digital learning in Davidson College's E.H. Little Library, where he partners with library colleagues, students, faculty, and staff to explore digital technologies and resources for teaching and research. Previously, he was the College of Wooster's digital scholarship librarian and director of its Collaborative Research Environment (CoRE). In addition to his work at Davidson and Wooster, Jacob has developed expertise in shaping large-scale, interinstitutional collaborations through his work as a project manager on Texas A&M University's Early Modern OCR Project (eMOP), as the Ohio Five's Mellon Digital Scholar, and as an organizational driver of the Institute for Liberal Arts Digital Scholarship (ILiADS).

**Caroline Klibanoff** is the program manager at the Smithsonian National Museum of American History for *Made By Us*, a cross-institutional collaboration that will engage the public with history and civic participation in the years leading up to the nation's 250th anniversary. Previously, Caroline project-managed exhibitions at the MIT Museum, and developed digital strategies and the American Civic Collaboration Awards for the Bridge Alliance. She began her career in communications and video at the Pew Research Center and the FrameWorks Institute. She received an MA in public history and certificate in digital humanities from Northeastern University in 2018, and holds a BA in American studies and film/media studies from Georgetown University.

**John R. Ladd** is assistant professor in Computing and Information Studies at Washington and Jefferson College, where his teaching and research focuses on the use of data across a wide variety of domains, especially in cultural and humanities contexts. Previously, he was a Postdoctoral Fellow in Digital Humanities at Northwestern University, where he worked on EarlyPrint, and in 2017 he worked as a research fellow for *Six Degrees of Francis Bacon* at Carnegie Mellon University. His current book project, *Network Poetics*, traces the history of early modern literary collaboration using social network analysis and argues that shifts in the networks of print production allowed for the emergence of new literary forms.

**Conrad Leibel** (he/him) is a poet, performer, essayist, and musician. He graduated from the University of Victoria's MA in English literature program with a concentration in medieval and early modern studies, and holds a BA in English and film studies from the University of Alberta.

**Juliette Levy** is associate professor of history at the University of California, Riverside, and an affiliated faculty member at Centro de Investigación y Docencia Económicas (CIDE) in Mexico, where she co-directs MX.digital, a data digitization project of historical Mexican statistics. Her research explores informal and pre-banking forms of finance and credit in Latin America. Her book *The Making of a Market: Credit, Henequen, and Notaries in Yucatán, 1850-1900* was published by Penn State University Press in 2012. She has created online courses for the University of California, and her latest digital collaborative project is a mixed reality learning module that generates critical thinking and intellectual engagement for application in large-scale lecture courses.

**Hector Lopez** earned a BA with honours in English literature from the University of Puerto Rico, Mayagüez Campus. He is currently a general English MA candidate at the University of Victoria. His research interests are in the dialectical exchange of labour between the player and the video game. His other interests are experimental media, film, music, and literature.

**Aaron Mauro** is assistant professor of digital media at Brock University's Centre for Digital Humanities. He teaches on topics relating to digital culture, natural language processing, and app development. He has published articles on US literature and culture that have appeared in *Modern Fiction Studies*, *Mosaic*, and *Symploke*, among others. He has also published on issues relating to digital humanities in *Scholarly and Research Communication*, *Digital Studies*, and *Digital Humanities Quarterly*. He is the author of *Hacking in the Humanities: Cybersecurity, Speculative Fiction, and Navigating a Digital Future* (Bloomsbury 2022).

**Luis Meneses** is an instructor in the Department of Computer Science at Vancouver Island University. He is a Fulbright scholar, and a Mitacs Elevate Postdoctoral Fellow. He has served on the board of the TEI Consortium and on the IEEE Technical Committee on Digital Libraries. His research interests include digital humanities, digital libraries, information retrieval, and human-computer interaction. His research focuses on the development of tools that facilitate and preserve open multidisciplinary scholarship.

**Cara Marta Messina** is assistant professor of English at Jacksonville State University. Her research interests include digital rhetoric, fan studies, game studies, and feminist digital humanities. She received the 2019 Kairos Teaching Award, honorable mention for the 2021 *Computers and Composition* Hugh Burns Distinguished Dissertation Award, and the Northeastern University Outstanding Graduate Student Award in Humanics in 2021. Her work has appeared in the *Journal of Writing Analytics, Digital Humanities Quarterly*, and several edited collections.

**Belaid Moa** is an adjunct faculty member in the electrical and computer engineering (ECE) department at the University of Victoria, as well as an advanced research computing specialist working with Compute Canada, West-Grid, and University of Victoria Systems. He holds a PhD in computer science from the University of Victoria, a master's in electronics and signal processing from the École nationale supérieure d'électrotechnique, d'électronique, d'informatique, d'hydraulique et des télécommunications (ENSEEIHT) in Toulouse, France, and a BSc in electrical engineering from the École Hassania des travaux publics in Morocco. With more than fifteen years of experience in interdisciplinary research areas, he is currently collaborating with, guiding, mentoring, teaching, and supporting many researchers across Canada so that they can take full advantage of the advanced research computing systems, technologies, and tools available; these include machine learning, bioinformatics, big data, dockers, and high performance computing.

**Sean Michael Morris** is senior instructor in the School of Education and Human Development at the University of Colorado Denver. He is also the co-founder and director of the Digital Pedagogy Lab, an international professional development event focused on the intersections of pedagogy and classroom practice, digital technology, and social justice. His current research focuses on the role imagination plays in cultural, social, and educational change, and on critical instructional design, an approach to course design grounded in critical pedagogy.

**Sarah Payne** is instructional designer and formerly a postdoctoral fellow in the digital liberal arts at Middlebury College. She received her PhD in English literature from Northeastern University, where she was involved with the Digital Scholarship Group and NULab for Text, Maps, and Networks. Her research interests include digital pedagogy, the social dimensions of technology, feminist theory, and twentieth-century literature.

**Jessica Reingold** is a web project manager in the Web Services group at Georgetown University and has an MS in user-centered design from Brandeis University. Her previous area of focus, as the Domain of One's Own program manager at the University of Mary Washington, was digital identity, content strategy, and collaboration. Today she focuses on developing and organizing project plans, leading website migrations, and identifying users' needs.

**Lindsey Seatter** is a faculty member in the Department of English at Kwantlen Polytechnic University and a doctoral candidate in the Department of English at the University of Victoria. Her research focuses on the British Romantic period and digital humanities, with a special interest in women writers, the evolution of the novel, reader engagement, and online communities of practice.

**Kris Shaffer** is a data scientist and web intelligence analyst. He has consulted for multiple US government agencies, non-profits, and universities on matters related to digital disinformation, data ethics, and digital pedagogy. Kris is the author of *Data versus Democracy: How Big Data Algorithms Shape Opinions and Alter the Course of History* (Apress, 2019), and co-authored a report commissioned by the US Senate on Russian social media influence operations. He has taught courses in music theory and cognition, computer science, and digital studies at Yale University, the University of Colorado Boulder, the University of Mary Washington, and Charleston Southern University. He holds a PhD from Yale University.

**Ray Siemens** (http://web.uvic.ca/~siemens/) is Distinguished Professor in the Faculty of Humanities at the University of Victoria, in English and computer science, and past Canada Research Chair in Humanities Computing (2004–15); in 2019, he was also Leverhulme Visiting Professor at Loughborough University and Global Innovation Chair in Digital Humanities at the University of Newcastle (2019–22). He is founding editor of the electronic scholarly journal *Early Modern Literary Studies*; his publications include, among others, *A Companion to Digital Humanities* (Blackwell, 2004, 2015, with Schreibman and Unsworth); *A Companion to Digital Literary Studies* (Blackwell, 2007, with Schreibman); *A Social Edition of the Devonshire Manuscript* (MRTS/

Iter and Wikibooks, 2012, 2015, with Crompton et al.); *Literary Studies in the Digital Age* (MLA, 2014, with Price); *Doing Digital Humanities* (Routledge, 2016, with Crompton and Lane); and *The Lyrics of the* Henry VIII Manuscript (ACMRS, 2018). He directs the Implementing New Knowledge Environments (INKE) project, the Digital Humanities Summer Institute, and the Electronic Textual Cultures Lab (ETCL), and recently served as a member of the governing council for the Social Sciences and Humanities Research Council (SSHRC) of Canada, as vice-president/director of the Canadian Federation for the Humanities and Social Sciences (for research dissemination), chair of the MLA Committee on Scholarly Editions, and chair of the international Alliance of Digital Humanities Organizations (ADHO).

**Jesse Stommel** is a faculty member in the Writing Program at University of Denver. He is also co-founder of *Hybrid Pedagogy: The Journal of Critical Digital Pedagogy* and Digital Pedagogy Lab. He has a PhD from University of Colorado Boulder. He is co-author of *An Urgency of Teachers: The Work of Critical Digital Pedagogy.* Jesse is a documentary filmmaker and teaches courses about pedagogy, film, and new media. He experiments relentlessly with learning interfaces, both digital and analog, and his research focuses on higher education pedagogy, critical digital pedagogy, and assessment.

**Christian Vandendorpe** is professor emeritus in the Department of French at the University of Ottawa. With an interest in semiotics (especially cognitive semiotics) and rhetoric, he specializes in theories of reading. He has also worked on the didactic function of the written word, the links between digital technology and knowledge (its production, dissemination, reception, and absorption, in the form of both text and hypertext), and dream-narratives.